130° E
RUSSIA
Vladivostok
140° E
40° N
Sea of Japan
38° N
KOREA
JAPAN
Tokyo
TSUSHIMA
ISLAND
Kure
Iwakuni
Sasebo
KYUSHU
30° N
Pacific
Ocean
OKINAWA
Tropic of Cancer
130° E
140° E
20° N

THE BRITISH PART IN THE KOREAN WAR

VOLUME II

The author of this, as of the official histories of the Second World War, has been given free access to official documents. He alone is responsible for the statements made and the views expressed.

OFFICIAL HISTORY

The British Part in the KOREAN WAR

Volume II

AN HONOURABLE DISCHARGE

Anthony Farrar-Hockley

LONDON : HMSO

ISBN 0 11 630 958 X

Published by HMSO and available from:

HMSO Publications Centre
(Mail, fax and telephone orders only)
PO Box 276, London SW8 5DT
Telephone orders 0171 873 9090
General enquiries 0171 873 0011
(Queuing system in operation for both numbers)
Fax orders 0171 873 8200

HMSO Bookshops
49 High Holborn, London WC1V 6HB 0171 873 0011 Fax 0171 831 1326
(Counter service only)
68-69 Bull Street, Birmingham B4 6AD 0121 236 9696 Fax 0121 236 9699
33 Wine Street, Bristol BS1 2BQ 0117 9264306 Fax 0117 9294515
9-21 Princess Street, Manchester M60 8AS 0161 834 7201 Fax 0161 833 0634
16 Arthur Street, Belfast BT1 4GD 01232 238451 Fax 01232 235401
71 Lothian Road, Edinburgh EH3 9AZ 0131 228 4181 Fax 0131 229 2734

HMSO's Accredited Agents
(see Yellow Pages)

and through good booksellers

Printed in the United Kingdom for HMSO
Dd 298174 3/95 C20 3396 10170

CONTENTS

PREFACE

This second, and concluding, volume covers the period 1951 to 1953 and the immediate consequences of the armistice, which came into force on 27th July of the latter year. It encompasses the reversal of Chinese military superiority in Korea in a series of major actions on the battlefield which persuaded the Soviet Union, China, and North Korea, to enter negotiations to end the fighting, and the political activity related directly and indirectly to these events.

In writing this volume, I have had the advantage of authoritative evidence, disclosed since the publication of the first, concerning the responsibility of the Soviet Union for the war, and the Chinese conduct of operations. In the first case, documents discovered by Kathryn Weathersby, a research scholar working in the Moscow archives, and others revealed by Colonel-General Dmitri Volkogonov, Director of the Russian Military History Institute, are sufficient of themselves to confirm earlier indications that Stalin permitted the invasion of South Korea by Kim Il-sung's Army. Truth will out. Further details are emerging. It is now apparent that the Chinese decided to conclude an armistice immediately after Stalin's death.

The People's Republic of China has released selected documents concerning the war from its archives. In part, this is due to Mao's wish to expose personal grievances: for example, his sense of betrayal when Stalin reneged on his promise to provide air cover for the launching of the Chinese armies into North Korea, his rising outrage at the extent to which China was expected by Stalin to maintain the burden of costs in men and material as the war continued. These have tended to be manifested in official biographies or collections of speeches and documents. More generally, appreciations, orders and reports relating to the higher direction of the war in Peking and P'eng Te-huai's command in the field have been circulated, often by obscure publishing houses with limited print runs. Still, I have been fortunate in obtaining numerous individual titles illuminating strategic decisions or the tactical environment. Relative to the latter, the interrogation reports of both Chinese and North Korean prisoners of war and defectors have continued to be a valuable source of collateral evidence.

As so many of the base documents in Chinese, including, for example, those of the armistice agreement, employ the Wade-Giles system as distinct from the current pinyin, I have continued to use it. The McCune-Reichschauer system for romanisation has been maintained for Korean names but, as previously, with limited accentuation. I have also persisted in avoiding the use of foreign titles relative to China and Korea, for example, 'Formosa' for what is properly 'Taiwan', 'Manchuria' for 'North East China'. Unavoidably, some of the documents quoted use Japanese forms, notably in naval usage of names from charts based on the surveys made by Japan during her long occupation of Korea.

Between my own two volumes, Series II of 'Documents on British Policy Overseas, Volume IV', by Heather Yasamee and K A Hamilton, has been published (1991). This comprehends the war from June 1950 to April 1951. It is invaluable to an understanding of British politico-military policy during the period and I have drawn on it extensively. Across the whole term, I have referred the reader to the placement of certain Foreign Office documents in the Chiefs of Staff files where this relates them to a range of sources. Extensive use has again been made of the United States' records and, where expedient, I have quoted the State or Defense Department record of Anglo-American consultations to convey the American outlook.

As in the first six months of fighting in Korea, the political policies of the United Kingdom and United States during 1951–1953 were periodically modified or changed by the influence of the other in remarkably frequent and frank communications. In those years, at any rate, the Anglo-American relationship was flourishing. At the same time, the British authorities came to recognise that the concept of imperial defence was defunct. As both volumes indicate, the governments of Mr Attlee and Mr Churchill were successful in developing a strategic understanding with Australia, Canada and New Zealand during the Korean War, and to no mean extent because of it, on the basis of common interest and goodwill.

Between January and July 1951, the British Commonwealth elements in Korea made a notable contribution to operations, a contribution of crucial importance on the Imjin river and at Kap'yong in breaking the Chinese offensive in April of that year.

Thereafter, the independent brigades were brought under common command in the Commonwealth Division as the line of battle became static for the remainder of the war. I am very conscious that in recounting the fortunes of the division, itself a highly successful cooperative body, many units will be disappointed that I have failed to mention their part in contributing to that reputation. This omission does not in any way disparage their service. I am acutely aware, for example, of the spirit, skills, and bodily effort involved in a patrol or raid, but except where any one of these contributed to the higher tactical picture, narration must be looked for in regimental or corps annals.

The same principle must apply to air operations and, above all, operations at sea. Simply patrolling the treacherous waters of the west coast in winter, for example, made extraordinary demands on ships' companies. I have described the greater part of naval operations in a single chapter to avoid fragmentary reference to the varied services performed by the British Commonwealth Task Force, with its attachments from other nations, and have sought to show by selected actions a representative picture of their accomplishments.

The war in Korea also imposed a novel challenge to those made prisoners of war—novel in the sense that, for the first time, British sailors, soldiers and airmen were subjected to a course of political subversion. For many, this followed or ran concurrently with, physical privation, during which a number of their comrades died. As a prisoner myself from 1951–53, I have drawn primarily on original documents smuggled out of the camps by returning prisoners, and experiences in many camps, to avoid reliance on personal impressions. As a further mean of judging the nature of that captivity, I have described the circumstances of the North Korean and Chinese prisoners of war held by the United States and Republic of Korea, into which British troops were briefly drawn.

It will be evident that I have criticised a number of the American flag and general officers and their command system. The United States bore a huge military burden at that time; commitments to NATO were adding to them. It would be surprising if their selection system had proved to be faultless. Britain has rarely conducted a major campaign without discovering that a proportion of its senior officers lacked the talents for the unrelenting demands of war.

I have also been obliged to mention the failings of the Army of the Republic of Korea but recognise the extraordinary difficulties of a force then almost wholly without seasoned leaders and lacking for much of the time a proper complement of artillery. What is remarkable is that regiments and divisions of the ROK Army held together on many testing occasions while these problems were being remedied.

All this is clear to us now. With hindsight, too, the British people may reflect that the nation, impoverished by war, burdened with major military commitments nearer home, was able to send over the years 100,000 members of her armed forces to engage in a distant conflict as a matter of principle, and won considerable international respect as a consequence.

ANTHONY FARRAR-HOCKLEY

AUTHORS ACKNOWLEDGEMENTS

As in the first volume of this history, I have been assisted in the production of the second by numerous individuals and institutions. Mentioned or otherwise, I thank them for the time and interest they have offered. In addition to those named among the source notes or in the provision of material, a select number have given me help to an extent which obliges me to identify them.

To begin, I thank the Heads and staffs of the Historical Sections of the Royal Navy, the Army, and The Royal Air Force. Captain J D Brown RN drew my attention to a number of errors of detail in respect of the naval entries. Alex Ward and John Harding provided me with material, searched records and made valuable suggestions relating to the British Army entries. Group-Captain Ian Madelin RAF made a similar contribution in production of records and advice on Service relationships. John Andrews was Chief of the Ministry of Defence Library during the greater part of the compilation of both volumes and with his staff gave me a great deal of support in the identification and loan of books, and access to translation facilities. In the latter aspect, I must also thank Jack Thorington for his expertise in the translation of long texts and his initiative in providing valuable comments upon them; and Jean Heng, of the Chinese University in Hong Kong, for the discovery of a series of publications and extensive research in the columns of newspapers from the People's Republic of China.

The Director and staff of the Public Record office at Kew have been helpful and forbearing throughout the preparation of both volumes, and no less the Heads and staffs of the Royal Marine Archives, and the libraries at the Foreign and Commonwealth Office, the Staff College, Camberley, the Royal Military Academy, Sandhurst, the Prince Consort's Library, Aldershot, and the London Library in prolonged use of their documents and books.

Among those who have given me personal help, I owe thanks to Majors-General A.E. Younger and Peter Downward, the late Brigadier Boris Eastwood, Colonels Denis Harding, Reggie Jeffes, and Paddy Victory, Majors R H Cooke and John de Quidt. As previously, Tony Eagles, and Sam Mercer, the late Alan Moody and Peter Farrar, have contributed from their own experiences and sought out members of the British Korean Veterans Association to provide similar assistance. To their names, I must add Majors S W Cooper and Antony Wilson, who compiled a precise record of those who were killed or otherwise lost their lives due to service in the Korean War. Both died, alas, before the completion of this volume but with their invaluable work completed. Brigadier Anthony Millen continued to search out and marshal the photographs for this as for the first volume, a task involving a great deal of his time, for which I am in his debt.

I have continued to enjoy the unstinted help of the staff of the National Archives and Record Service of the United States in Washington DC and at Suitland, Maryland, the Australian National Archives in Canberra, and the Canadian National Archives in Ottawa. The Minister of Defence in the Republic of Korea and the several institutions who maintain the national Korean war records arranged for me to receive translations of various documents. I thank them all.

Successive Chiefs of Naval and Military History in the United States, and a number of their historians, have long aided my research into the Korean war period, led as previously by Billy Mossman. From first to last, I have benefitted from the friendship and advice of Major-General Jack Houston in the participation of the United States Air Force during his incumbency as Chief of United States Air Force History and, later, as a professor at the Naval Academy, Annapolis. Similarly, I must express my thanks to Professor Robert O'Neill, Dr Jeffrey Grey, and Ian McGibbon, for the trails they have blazed in the Commonwealth aspects of the Korean War. It was my good fortune that Heather Yasamee and her colleagues were working on their Korean volume of DBPO at the same time as myself and thank her and them for their unreserved cooperation.

The Head of the Cabinet Office Historical and Records Section, Pat Andrews, has been a patient friend and expert coordinator of those involved in the production departments of the Office and Her Majesty's Stationery Office. I owe special thanks to her and to Richard Ponman, senior member of the historical staff. In the extensive preliminaries to publication, Bob Cavanagh, Head of Cabinet Office Graphics and Publications, and his team have accepted readily and with great good humour the piecemeal presentation of the text, maps and photographs, and overcome the problems of matching diverse computer systems.

My late wife, Pat, extended her long support for my work into this book; her searches gathered in many documents relating to KOPA. Linda Wood, now my wife, has been involved in seeking and finding people and documents connected with the war, safeguarding and checking, for more than a decade. I owe thanks to both of them for their high generosity in my endeavours.

ACKNOWLEDGEMENTS FOR THE USE OF PHOTOGRAPHS

Thanks are due to those who have kindly permitted their original photographs to be shown in this book at various points in the text. Their titles are shown in each case.

Special thanks are also due to the Master Gunner and the Royal Artillery for their kind permission to reproduce their painting by Terence Cuneo of the 45th Field Regiment in close action on the Imjin River as a frontispiece on the jacket of this volume.

MAPS

PHOTOGRAPHS

17. The Rev S J Davies conducting a service of Holy Communion immediately before the opening of the Fifth Phase Offensive in the GLOSTERS' Battalion Headquarters area. Of those shown, eight were killed in the battle and a number wounded and taken prisoner. The battalion's command vehicle (operations centre) is seen in the background. (Royal Army Chaplains' Department)

18. Major John Shaw, commanding the detachment of 1 RUR on the Route 11 saddle south of the Imjin, seen at Battalion Headquarters just prior to his return to that position. He was killed twenty minutes after the picture was taken. (Brigadier M N S McCord)

19. Mortar positions of A Troop, 170 Light Battery, 1 RNF and 1 RUR, just prior to withdrawal from the Imjin area, 24th April 1951. The litter of empty ammunition boxes illustrates the high consumption of bombs during the battle. (Brigadier M N S McCord)

20. The track running north west from Chuktun-ni in the Kap'yong river valley, April 1951. (Major B Reed)

21. Chinese soldier in fighting order killed in the Kapy'ong battle, April 1951. By this date, the 'Volunteers' had discarded their padded winter uniforms for the light cotton jacket and trousers. The soldier is wearing rubber-soled canvas 'basket ball' boots. Individual equipment included a leather belt, small arms bandolier, two cotton haversacks, one for domestic possessions, the other for grenades and magazines for the machine carbine or light mortar bombs, and an entrenching tool, a small spade partially seen here on the ground just above the soldier's head. (Major B Reed)

22. Major-General A J H Cassels, Commander, 1st British Commonwealth Division, with Brigadier T Brodie, Commander, 29th Infantry Brigade, August 1951. (Imperial War Museum)

23. Centurion tank of the 8th Hussars moving across captured enemy positions to support the advance of 3 RAR during Operation Commando, October 1951. (Imperial War Museum)

24. Crawl trench on Point 210 captured by 1 KSLI during Operation Commando, October 1951. (This picture, showing the view to the west, was taken in December). (Major P Duckworth)

25. 25-pounder detachment, having just crossed to the north side of the Imjin river, supporting Operation Commando, October 1951. (Imperial War Museum)

26. Kowang-san, Point 355. (King's Own Scottish Borderers)

27. Maryang-san, Point 317. (King's Own Scottish Borderers)

28. The permanent bridge built by 28th Field Engineer Regiment at 'Teal', formerly 'Gloster Crossing'. The pontoon bridge is seen in use. The water level is at its lowest point. (5th Royal Inniskilling Dragoon Guards)

29. The Imjin in spate. (Major-General P Downward)

30. Teal bridge roadway is threatened by floods and remnants from Pintail, summer 1951. (Royal School of Military Engineering)

31. The bridge at 'Pintail'. (Major-General A E Younger)

32. Bayton-Evans bridge. (Major-General A E Younger)

33. Combat Engineer of 28th Field Engineer Regiment clearing mines following Operation Commando. (Imperial War Museum)

34. A late sortie by an aircraft of 17th Carrier Air Group, HMS *Theseus*, striking junks moving south with NKPA troops on the west coast, April 1951. (D House)

35. Lieutenant Leonard RN returns to *Theseus* after being shot down into the sea, 1951. (D House)

36. The United States Navy H03S-1 helicopter aboard *Theseus*, piloted by Chief Petty Officer Fridley USN. These aircraft were generously loaned to the British Commonwealth Naval Force by the United States until the Westland Dragonfly was brought into service. (D House)

37. Royal Naval and Royal Marine raiding party assembles to land at Choppeki Point, May 1951. (K Cox)

38. The party moves inshore—just prior to the opening of the action, May 1951. (K Cox)

39. Royal Naval landing party from HMS *Morecombe Bay* recovers a ROK raiding force from islands in the mouth of the Taedong, March 1952. (P D G Turk)

40. As above, the withdrawal. (P D G Turk)

41. *Ocean* (upper works seen top left) and *Bataan* refuelling at sea, June 1952, as Sub-Lieutenant Clapp RN is transferred to the oiler (tanker) by jackstay. Thirteen Royal Fleet Auxiliary tankers were employed in operational waters from 1950–53, together with five store and victualling ships, earning numerous official commendations for their devoted service. (G C David)

42. HMS *Crane* (frigate) negotiating ice between Cho-do and Sok-to, January 1953. (T W Cooper)

43. The anchorage at Cho-do in summer, 1952. (Lieutenant Colonel T Kitcat)

44. The same in winter. (Lieutenant-Colonel T Kitcat)

45. Beached fishing boat used for guerrilla raids and clandestine activities on Paengyong-do, Colonel Davenport's base for TE 95.15. (Lieutenant-Colonel T Kitcat)

46. Assault landing craft of 41 Royal Marine Commando during a raid in the Songjin area, north east Korea, 10th April 1951. (Royal Marines Museum)

47. The same—laying charges to cut the coastal railway. (Royal Marines Museum)

48. The same—the line is severed. (Royal Marines Museum)

49. The Samich'on river, summer, 1952. (Major J A Foulis, RAPC)

50. The reverse slope of Point 159, an advanced infantry and tank outpost south west of Kowang-san. (5th Royal Iniskilling Dragoon Guards)

51. Bunker built by the Royal Engineers to protect the Centurion tank of 5DG on Point 187, August 1952. (5th Royal Iniskilling Dragoon Guards)

52. Tank entering the bunker. (5th Royal Iniskilling Dragoon Guards)

53. The same, taken from the front of the bunker. On 5th September, by a million to one chance, an HE shell entered the turret when the tank had drawn back essentially for maintenance, killing the crew, Sergeant Wykes, Lance Corporal Metcalfe, Troopers Cahill and McFadyen, *Change and Challenge* History of 5th Royal Iniskilling Dragoon Guards 1928–1978 by General Sir Cecil Blacker and Major General H G Woods, p 110 (Colchester, 1978).

54. 14th Field Regiment, Royal Artillery positions in the Commonwealth area, summer 1952. (Imperial War Museum)

55. 'The Hook' position: the feature is top right, 'Green Finger' is in the left foreground, with 'Warsaw' behind. The 'Ronson' standing patrol 'Knob' site is right centre. (Imperial War Museum)

56. Repairing defences on the reverse slope of the Hook area, summer 1952. (Imperial War Museum)

57. 5DG tanks in harbour, summer 1952. (Major F W Garnett)

CALENDAR—1951

	JANUARY	FEBRUARY	MARCH	APRIL
Sun	7 14 21 28	4 11 18 25	4 11 18 25	1 8 15 22 29
Mon	1 8 15 22 29	5 12 19 26	5 12 19 26	2 9 16 23 30
Tue	2 9 16 23 30	6 13 20 27	6 13 20 27	3 10 17 24
Wed	3 10 17 24 31	7 14 21 28	7 14 21 28	4 11 18 25
Thu	4 11 18 25	1 8 15 22	1 8 15 22 29	5 12 19 26
Fri	5 12 19 26	2 9 16 23	2 9 16 23 30	6 13 20 27
Sat	6 13 20 27	3 10 17 24	3 10 17 24 31	7 14 21 28

	MAY	JUNE	JULY	AUGUST
Sun	6 13 20 27	3 10 17 24	1 8 15 22 29	5 12 19 26
Mon	7 14 21 28	4 11 18 25	2 9 16 23 30	6 12 20 27
Tue	1 8 12 22 29	5 12 19 26	3 10 17 24 31	7 14 21 28
Wed	2 9 16 23 30	6 13 20 27	4 11 18 25	1 8 15 22 29
Thu	3 10 17 24 31	7 14 21 28	5 12 19 26	2 9 16 23 30
Fri	4 11 18 25	1 8 15 22 29	6 13 20 27	3 10 17 24 31
Sat	5 12 19 26	2 9 16 23 30	7 14 21 28	4 11 18 25

	SEPTEMBER	OCTOBER	NOVEMBER	DECEMBER
Sun	30 2 9 16 23	7 14 21 28	4 11 18 25	30 2 9 16 23
Mon	3 10 17 24	1 8 15 22 29	5 12 19 26	31 3 10 17 24
Tue	4 11 18 25	2 9 16 23 30	6 13 20 27	4 11 18 25
Wed	5 12 19 26	3 10 17 24 31	7 14 21 28	5 12 19 26
Thu	6 13 20 27	4 11 18 25	1 8 15 22 29	6 13 20 27
Fri	7 14 21 28	5 12 19 26	2 9 16 23 30	7 14 21 28
Sat	1 8 15 22 29	6 13 20 27	3 10 17 24	1 8 15 22 29

CALENDAR—1952

	JANUARY	FEBRUARY	MARCH	APRIL
Sun	6 13 20 27	3 10 17 24	30 2 9 16 23	6 13 20 27
Mon	7 14 21 28	4 11 18 25	31 3 10 17 24	7 14 21 28
Tue	1 8 15 22 29	5 12 19 26	4 11 18 25	1 8 15 22 29
Wed	2 9 16 23 30	6 13 20 27	5 12 19 26	2 9 16 23 30
Thu	3 10 17 24 31	7 14 21 28	6 13 20 27	3 10 17 24
Fri	4 11 18 25	1 8 15 22 29	7 14 21 28	4 11 18 25
Sat	5 12 19 26	2 9 16 23	8 15 22 29	5 12 19 26

	MAY	JUNE	JULY	AUGUST
Sun	4 11 18 25	1 8 15 22 29	6 13 20 27	31 3 10 17 24
Mon	5 12 19 26	2 9 16 23 30	7 14 21 28	4 11 18 25
Tue	6 13 20 27	3 10 17 24	1 8 15 22 29	5 12 19 26
Wed	7 14 21 28	4 11 18 25	2 9 16 23 30	6 13 20 27
Thu	1 8 15 22 29	5 12 19 26	3 10 17 24 31	7 14 21 28
Fri	2 9 16 23 30	6 13 20 27	4 11 18 25	1 8 15 22 29
Sat	3 10 17 24 31	7 14 21 28	5 12 19 26	2 9 16 23 30

	SEPTEMBER	OCTOBER	NOVEMBER	DECEMBER
Sun	7 14 21 28	5 12 19 26	30 2 9 16 23	7 14 21 28
Mon	1 8 15 22 29	6 13 20 27	3 10 17 24	1 8 15 22 29
Tue	2 9 16 23 30	7 14 21 28	4 11 18 25	2 9 16 23 30
Wed	3 10 17 24	1 8 15 22 29	5 12 19 26	3 10 17 24 31
Thu	4 11 18 25	2 9 16 23 30	6 13 20 27	4 11 18 25
Fri	5 12 19 26	3 10 17 24 31	7 14 21 28	5 12 19 26
Sat	6 13 20 27	4 11 18 25	1 8 15 22 29	6 13 20 27

CALENDAR—1953

	JANUARY	FEBRUARY	MARCH	APRIL
Sun	4 11 18 25	1 8 15 22	1 8 15 22 29	5 12 19 26
Mon	5 12 19 26	2 9 16 23	2 9 16 23 30	6 13 20 27
Tue	6 13 20 27	3 10 17 24	3 10 17 24 31	7 14 21 28
Wed	7 14 21 28	4 11 18 15	4 11 18 25	1 8 15 22 29
Thu	1 8 15 22 29	5 12 19 26	5 12 19 26	2 9 16 23 30
Fri	2 9 16 23 30	6 13 20 27	6 13 20 27	3 10 17 24
Sat	3 10 17 24 31	7 14 21 28	7 14 21 28	4 11 18 25

	MAY	JUNE	JULY	AUGUST
Sun	31 3 10 17 24	7 14 21 28	5 12 19 26	30 2 9 16 23
Mon	4 11 18 25	1 8 15 22 29	6 13 20 27	31 3 10 17 24
Tue	5 12 19 26	2 9 16 23 30	7 14 21 28	4 11 18 25
Wed	6 13 20 27	3 10 17 24	1 8 15 22 29	5 12 19 26
Thu	7 14 21 28	4 11 18 25	2 9 16 23 30	6 13 20 27
Fri	1 8 15 22 29	5 12 19 26	3 10 17 24 31	7 14 21 28
Sat	2 9 16 23 30	6 13 20 27	4 11 18 25	1 8 15 22 29

	SEPTEMBER	OCTOBER	NOVEMBER	DECEMBER
Sun	6 13 20 27	4 11 18 25	1 8 15 22 29	6 13 20 27
Mon	7 14 21 28	5 12 19 26	2 9 16 23 30	7 14 21 28
Tue	1 8 15 22 29	6 13 20 27	3 10 17 24	1 8 15 22 29
Wed	2 9 16 23 30	7 14 21 28	4 11 18 25	2 9 16 23 30
Thu	3 10 17 24	1 8 15 22 29	5 12 19 26	3 10 17 24 31
Fri	4 11 18 25	2 9 16 23 30	6 13 20 27	4 11 18 25
Sat	5 12 19 26	3 10 17 24 31	7 14 21828	5 12 19 26

INTRODUCTION: 1950

Six months: four men; three strategies

The Korean War began under summer rain clouds in the early morning of 25th June 1950. The Koreans in the north attacked those in the south, apparently the opening move in a civil war. From the first hour, however, it was an event of international importance: the northern state was the protégée of the Soviet Union; the southern a state declared sovereign by majority vote of the United Nations including the United States. Within a few days, the struggle to preserve that sovereignty drew in international forces, including those of the United States, the British Commonwealth, other members of the United Nations*, and eventually the People's Republic of China. By the beginning of January 1951, operations had run through three successive strategies. None were decisive. The four men responsible for them had by then discovered that victory in war is an elusive prize.

First came Kim Il-sung†, master of the Communist state of North Korea, misleadingly styled the Democratic People's Republic of Korea. Kim had been put into power by Stalin, but whilst he relied upon the Soviet Union for political support, economic aid, and military supply, and was thus its client, he was not Stalin's puppet. His prime aim was to bring the state of South Korea—created by the United Nations as the Republic of Korea‡—under his authority. Initially he sought to achieve this by subversion and guerrilla operations during 1946–49. When these failed, he decided on invasion. But he lacked the means to sustain an offensive by the NKPA—the North Korean People's Army. Reserves of tanks, artillery, ammunition, spare parts, and oil were among a range of their requirements to ensure outright victory. In March 1949, therefore, he asked Stalin to provide them.

The request was in some measure satisfied as part of a greater package of agreements between the two states[1], but at this time Stalin

---

* Namely combat contingents from Australia, Belgium, Canada, Colombia, Ethiopia, France, Greece, Luxembourg, the Netherlands, New Zealand, the Philippines, South Africa, Thailand, Turkey, the United Kingdom, the United States; and medical contingents from Denmark, India, Italy, Norway, and Sweden.

† For details of principal personalities, see Volume I.

‡ For the circumstances leading to the division of Korea and the enmity between the two states, see Volume I.

was by no means ready to agree to the annexation of South Korea by force of arms. The division of the peninsula suited his regional aims[2]. By fitting out NKPA divisions, he buttressed the security of the Democratic People's Republic of Korea—and to the benefit of the Soviet economy; for, as ever in his capacity as an arms salesman, he expected full payment for all items supplied and interest on any associated loans.

Curiously, Stalin appears to have overlooked the fact that, just as the American development of a lightly armed border defence force inclined the South Korean President Syngman Rhee to propose invasion of the North, his own supply of armour, artillery and aircraft encouraged Kim Il-sung to seize the territory of the south. Some indication of this became apparent on 19th January 1950 when a telegram was received in Moscow from General T F Shtykov, Soviet ambassador in P'yongyang, the North Korean capital.

> ... A reception was held in the evening at the Chinese Embassy in honour of the ambassador's departure. During it, Kim Il-sung spoke to me as follows: "Now that the liberation of China is complete, the next question concerns the liberation of Korea. It cannot be decided by guerrillas. I am unable to sleep at night for thinking about reunification. Mao has said that there is no need to invade the south. Though if Syngman Rhee should attack we would have to launch a counter-attack. But Syngman Rhee is not attacking... He, Kim Il-sung, needs to visit Stalin and request permission to attack in order to liberate South Korea. Mao has promised to help and he, Kim Il-sung, will be meeting him". Kim Il-sung insists on making a personal request to Stalin for permission to attack the South from the North.
>
> Kim Il-sung was somewhat the worse for wear and he conducted the conversation in an excited state[3].

Mao Tse-tung was in Moscow when the telegram reached Stalin, negotiating, among other things, a mutual defence treaty with the Soviet Union. Kim's claims to the Chinese leader's support for his project were authenticated. On 30th January, Stalin informed Shtykov that he agreed in principle to an enforced unification of Korea and indicated that the Red Army would oversee the preparatory arrangements. The price of this support would include supply of 25,000 tons of lead per annum.

In a series of telegrams, Kim asked for acceleration of the original armament programme, further materials and credits. He requested approval—so it was expressed—for the expansion of the NKPA from seven to ten divisions. On 9th February all these requests were approved.

In accepting the proposals, Stalin drew upon himself responsibility for opening the Korean war. Without his material support, Kim's forces would have been impotent. As evidence of his decisions emerges from the Russian archives, it is said that he was placed in a difficult position with Kim having, for example, paid lip service on several occasions to unification of the peninsula under his leadership and was thus under a moral obligation to assist him materially to this end. Such views ignore all that is known of Stalin's character and the immense power he commanded within the Soviet Union and its satellites. He had previously refused Kim's requests to invade South Korea. Since moral obligations would not have persuaded him to change his mind, what factors caused him to do so at the beginning of 1950?

One theory suggests that Stalin expected that the loss of South Korea would harden American determination to support Chiang Kai-shek's forces in occupation of Taiwan and thus close all doors to any settlement between Peking and Washington. As a consequence, Communist China would become wholly reliant on the Soviet Union for political support and to a great extent on the Soviet *bloc* for trade.

This may be true. If so, Stalin was unaware that Mao was most anxious to convince him of his devotion to Marxism-Leninism by demonstrations of loyalty to the Soviet camp. But the wider context of Stalin's circumstances should not be overlooked. By the beginning of 1950, it suited Stalin to mount a limited war, using a surrogate, in this corner of East Asia. In Europe, his efforts to expand Soviet power beyond the Red Army's occupation zone by subversion and threats of force had largely failed in Denmark, Austria, France, and over Berlin. These tactics had persuaded the United Kingdom to propose counter measures. The Atlantic Alliance formed in 1949 on the initiative of the British Foreign Secretary, Ernest Bevin, engaged the United States and Canada in the collective security of western Europe. While Stalin developed a major propaganda exercise to inhibit the formation of the North Atlantic Treaty Organisation, the Korean option offered a means of distracting his enemies and articulating his power: an extension of his presence on the horizons of Japan; the slighting of the United States, sponsor of the Republic of Korea; a reminder to small and non-aligned nations that he was not to be trifled with; and a similar warning to the United Nations.

These considerations were not negligible provided that the risks were low. Pre-eminently, Stalin had to be convinced that in backing a civil war in Korea he would not be drawn into a confrontation of any sort with the United States, let alone one which might lead to war. The preparatory arrangements were designed *inter alia* to satisfy this requirement. The North Korean People's Army had been developed by his officers; many remained in staff and training functions within it, and a special group had been formed to draft the plan of operations. This would be approved in Moscow. Thereafter, it would be translated into Korean prior to distribution from the Ministry of Defence. The NKPA had more and better equipped divisions to put into the field than those evolving with American support in South Korea. Their ranks had been filled out with veterans who had returned from operational service in the People's Liberation Army of Communist China. The prospect of success was high.

Whatever the outcome, Soviet political independence and security would not be compromised; Stalin made it clear that Soviet military forces would be witheld from the battlefield. When General Shtykov represented Kim's wish to restore Soviet advisers to operational units as the war opened, the response from Moscow on 28th June 1950 was sharp.

> It appears that you are acting improperly, as you have promised the Koreans to supply advisers without asking us.
>
> You should bear in mind that you are representing the USSR and not Korea.
>
> I desire that our advisers should go to the frontline HQ and to the Army Groups in civilian dress as correspondents of *Pravda* in the numbers required.
>
> You will be personally responsible to the Soviet Government for ensuring that they are not captured[4].

Stalin's appreciation of the risks was for the most part sound but reckoned without Kim's personality. The war opened successfully by surprise. The poorly trained, lightly equipped Army of the Republic of Korea fought bravely at the outset but was rapidly broken. The rump retreated in disorder. When a division of United States troops was committed early in July to counter the offensive, against Stalin's and Kim's expectations, the robust North Korean advanced guards captured its general and drove it back towards the southern port of Pusan.

In the third week of that month, as the United States sought to reinforce South Korea sufficiently to stabilise a defensive perimeter round Pusan, Kim had the means to take this essential entry port and eliminate the American and residual South Korean troops in the peninsula. Fortunately for the American command, Kim's obsessive wish to garner the territories of the south misled him. Political temptation overcame military prudence. He sent his 6th Division in a wide diversion into the south west provinces though he knew from his numerous agents there that they were empty of enemy troops. If this force had instead reinforced a shallow manoeuvre on Pusan through Chinju and Masan in the middle weeks of July, the NKPA would assuredly have triumphed. As it was, when he brought the 6th into the battle at the end of the month, substantial United States reinforcements had arrived, and American aircraft had established supremacy over the greater part of Korea, including his lengthening road and rail communications. From the beginning of August, then, the prospects for Kim's strategy progressively diminished.

By this date, a seasoned American general, Douglas MacArthur, had been appointed to command the United Nations' forces in the theatre of war. He was then in his 71st year. Outstandingly successful in the Pacific during the Second World War, General MacArthur was already stationed in Tokyo as Supreme Commander of the Allied Powers' occupation forces in Japan, principally elements of the United States Navy, Army, and Air Force, of which he was also the national Commander-in-Chief. He quickly saw that committal of all his reinforcements to the Pusan bridgehead, with the aim of ultimately breaking out of it in a counter-offensive, would be costly in time and lives. In any case, though such an operation would drive back the North Korean People's Army, it would not necessarily destroy it. Controlling the surrounding seas and air, his strategy was therefore to hold the bridgehead with forces just sufficient to ensure its integrity, drawing the NKPA on to that line, while launching an amphibious force far behind the enemy to cut his supply lines to and routes of withdrawal from the south. Throughout the operation, his air forces would support the troops in the bridgehead, attack the North Korean lines of communication, and cover the amphibious landings. His maritime supremacy gave him the option of landing at any point on the coastline.

Despite numerous crises in the bridgehead as the summer advanced, General MacArthur held to his plan, gathering meantime an independent corps in Japan. In mid-September, this body, led by the United States 1st Marine Division, landed three hundred miles behind the battle line at Inch'on on the west coast of Korea.

A huge tidefall and narrow access channels through random shoals multiplied the risks; but MacArthur believed that these factors enhanced surprise. He was right. The landings on 15th and 16th September were wholly successful. The American Eighth Army covering Pusan, which comprehended the Republic of Korea's Army—the ROK Army—broke out from its perimeter defences to join the amphibious X Corps advancing inland from Inch'on. Decimated by air and ground fire, weakened further by desertion, the NKPA was squeezed to pieces between the two United Nations components. Remnants, notably officers and non-commissioned officers, withdrew northwards through the mountains or elsewhere joined local Communist guerrillas. By the end of the first week in October, North Korean military power in the south was destroyed apart from guerrilla bands, themselves widely separated. The United Nations command spilled in local actions across the 38th parallel of latitude, which marked the border between North and South Korea. On 7th October, the United Nations General Assembly passed a resolution which effectively gave General MacArthur formal permission to cross into the Democratic Republic of Korea.

This decision shifted the original strategic aim of the Security Council from restoring South Korean territory to the unification of Korea as a whole. Unification had long been the policy of a majority of the United Nations, an aim frustrated by Soviet and North Korean intransigence. General MacArthur's instructions now required him to 'ensure conditions of stability throughout Korea'[5]. That meant that that he must eliminate whatever remained of the NKPA, thereby removing the power of Kim and his government to resist the entry and operation of the United Nations Electoral Commission. Otherwise, it was believed, given safe haven behind the 38th Parallel, Kim would raise new armed forces and, at leisure, invade South Korea again.

An advance to the extremities of the north, however, would carry United Nations troops to the limited Russo-Korean border and, more extensively, the Korean border with China. In common with their partners in the United Nations, the United States and Britain had agreed, from the outset of hostilities, that they must not in any circumstances provoke a war with the Soviet Union in the course of intervention. Britain, aiming to detach the People's Republic of China from an exclusive alliance with the Soviet Union, and sensitive to the vulnerability of Hong Kong, was also anxious not to isolate, still less to provoke war with China. This attitude was shared with qualifications by the United States. Both recognised that, in crossing the 38th parallel, they risked Chinese intervention; Chou En-lai, the Prime Minister in Peking, indicated the likelihood to the Indian Ambassador in a dramatic interview early in the morning of 3rd October 1950. If he had spoken more directly, they might have heeded the warning. As it was, the risks of allowing Kim Il-sung to rearm in safety outweighed the threat; some indeed thought it was a bluff.

Still, bluff or not, the United States and Britain recognised that the contiguity of foreign, especially American, troops would be objectionable to the Communist Chinese regime. Orders were therefore given to General MacArthur that all but South Korean forces should hold back from the border provinces as the advance continued. When it was plain that this this order was being disregarded, no action was taken by President Truman, his Defense, or State Departments to bring him to order. American governmental tradition was cited by these authorities to excuse their passivity: American commanders-in-chief in the field were left on the loosest of reins to pursue their objectives. It was manifest, however, that the American Chiefs of Staff stood so much in awe of General MacArthur that they shrank from tightening them. The further north he went, the more strategic policy and practice were left wholly in his hands. He had, moreover, from 9th October, an important discretionary power. If Chinese troops should be encountered, '...you should continue if, in your judgement, action by forces now under your control offers a reasonable chance of success'[6].

He chose to advance his main force on the western front, while projecting the independent X Corps into north east Korea by an unnecessary and, as it transpired, belated landing. It was his firm intention to penetrate to the very banks of the Yalu river separating China and Korea. Convinced that he knew the 'oriental mind' which respected strength, he judged that the Chinese would not oppose him in arms.

The fourth principal in the trials of strategy was Mao Tse-tung—'Chairman Mao' of the Communist People's Republic established in Peking in October 1949, following the expulsion of Chiang Kai-shek's Nationalists from the mainland of China by the People's Liberation Army. On 14th February 1950, Mao completed a Treaty of Friendship, Alliance, and Mutual Assistance with the Soviet Union, and returned to Peking from Moscow to grapple with the huge problem of economic recovery from years of international and civil war. In the following months, the prime focus of his military deployment was the recovery of the island province of Taiwan from the Nationalists and the occupation of Tibet.

After the opening of the offensive into the Republic of Korea on 25th June, the government in Peking appeared to confine itself until October to propaganda support for a North Korean victory. Yet Mao and his associates, watching the battle keenly, took precautionary measures in mid-July to reinforce their frontier defences along the Yalu[7], despite the triumphant claims issuing from P'yongyang, the North Korean capital. The Frontier Defence Army of four corps with supporting formations began to concentrate close to the Yalu river under 13 Army Group headquarters[8]. By the end of August, the Central Military Commission in Peking judged that the NKPA might be defeated in South Korea. A warning order was sent to the Fourth Field Army in North East China to prepare to intervene. Three army groups were to make ready[9]. After the Inch'on landing in mid-September, apprehensions grew that American forces would shortly be moving towards the Yalu river. On 4th October, Mao appointed P'eng Te-huai, one of his most experienced generals, to take command of the intervention force. To preserve China's status as a non-belligerent, its membership would be described as 'volunteers'—the 'Chinese People's Volunteers'—once they crossed into Korea.

Mao's directives at this time indicate that, *faute de mieux*, his aim was to check the United Nations forces, obliging them to discontinue their advance. Initially, he expected that his armies would establish bases over a period of weeks in the mountain mass north of the P'yongyang-

Wonsan railway, from which they would make sorties, somewhat as the Chinese Communist forces had operated within their own territory against the Japanese and Nationalist forces for a decade and more. But it soon became apparent that the United Nations divisions, mounted in vehicles, might enter these highlands ahead of his soldiers marching on foot. Other factors necessitated a review by the Central Military Commission, notably the news that Stalin would not honour an agreement to provide air cover for the Volunteers[10]. The run of events and the immense fire potential, ground and air, of the enemy suggested to many of Mao's colleagues and military subordinates that intervention should be delayed for some months to permit training and armament with Soviet equipment. However, despite Stalin's perfidy which shook him emotionally, he had strong personal and political reasons for maintaining his original decision including, by some accounts, his determination to demonstrate solidarity with the Soviet Union[11]. On 15th October, orders were issued to launch the first echelon of the CPV into Korea. Marching by night out of sight of American aircraft, P'eng's troops crossed the Yalu river into Korea between the 17th and 25th October to halt General MacArthur's Eighth Army.

The Eighth Army then included contingents from nine nations, principally from the United States and Republic of Korea together with a Turkish brigade and the 27th British Commonwealth Brigade. Its mood was triumphant. Though frequently delayed by small North Korean rearguards in skirmishes, and sometimes in danger of outrunning supplies, it advanced north steadily on a wide front. Led by tanks, and infantry mounted in trucks, the advanced guards received close support from more than one hundred artillery batteries and the American 5th Tactical Air Force.

As originally conceived, P'eng's strategy was to select strong defensive positions among the mountains and foothills on to which the United Nations command would run. Given the numbers available to him and the concealment skills of his soldiers, P'eng believed that they would be able to hold their foes, if not indefinitely, for some considerable time, though he and Mao had discussed the possibility that they might have to withdraw ultimately across the Yalu. But on 21st October, Mao sent new instructions. The CPV armies in Korea should not engage in static defence but, as a body, take the offensive, attacking the United Nations' columns in darkness, when they customarily halted for rest and replenishment. Now altogether lacking in air support, P'eng doubted whether this was practicable; he feared that the enemy would sit out these night attacks and strike his soldiers in the open after daybreak with their immense firepower. He proposed the establishment of a widespread defence followed by local night actions on a selective basis to force the enemy back to P'yongyang. Mao insisted on an immediate strategic offensive. The orders issued by P'eng reflect some compromise, but comprehended major ambushes or offensive action by five of the six armies he had in hand. The precise opening date was uncertain; they would wait for the leading United Nations divisions to close up to them. Evidence on the ground suggests that time was short for arrangements. Some CPV divisions were still marching towards assembly areas when forward detachments, members of reconnaissance and liaison parties, were taken prisoner by ROK Army forces between 25th and 28th October.

Before this intelligence was assimilated at Eighth Army headquarters, night attacks began across the whole front. The most damaging tore open the flank between the United Nations westernmost corps—the US I Corps—and its right hand neighbour, the ROK II Corps. The divisions of the latter broke in disorder. Other ROK and American formations began to crumble as they were attacked from the rear, isolated when relief columns were themselves ambushed. Reliant on transport for all their movement, the Americans were soon confused as the hardy, lightly armed Chinese marched across mountain ridges and crests to block the greater part of the network of roads behind their battle lines. The United Nations army, corps, and divisional commanders began to lose control of the battle.

For quite different reasons, control was also slipping from P'eng and his subordinate commanders. Like the People's Liberation Army in the homeland, the Chinese People's Volunteers lacked comprehensive radio communications and soon lost touch with their regiments, battalions, and companies. Many of these, growing bolder in their triumph, continued to press in upon the fragmented United Nations divisions in daylight. The Fifth Air Force fell upon them. Although P'eng was later to state that he broke off the battle to lure General MacArthur into further advances[12], the confusion of his units and the growing tally of casualties manifest other reasons. To the astonished relief of the United Nations Command, it became apparent from the morning of 6th November that the Chinese had drawn back out of contact.

Even so, this profound and damaging check caused political as well as military consternation among the United Nations alliance. The prime cause was the fact that the Chinese had intervened. Apprehensions that a third world war was about to begin arose briefly. But although these receded when Peking and Moscow declared that the Chinese soldiers in Korea were volunteers supporting North Korea, somewhat on the lines of the International Brigades in the Spanish civil war in the 1930s, the fact remained that the huge pool of military manpower in China was now on tap for Korea[13].

Numerous appreciations and consequential policy options were then propounded within the alliance and among those on the periphery. Military options for United Nations strategy were restricted, however, to three. The first was to renew the offensive as quickly as possible to overthrow the intervention forces. The second to establish a strong defensive line across the narrow neck of North Korea, roughly from Sinanju eastwards across the peninsula, to consolidate gains, to free the process of political revision or innovation from the pressures of the battlefield, and to provide a base for a renewal of offensive action if this should be decided upon. The third was to withdraw to the line of the 38th Parallel and fortify it to ensure the security of the Republic of Korea.

This last course was not regarded seriously by the United States or British governments. The British Chiefs of Staff, however, urged the second: preparation of a defensive line on the narrow neck, as rapidly as possible, because they had grave doubts concerning the balance of political advantage or the military practicability of advancing to the Sino-Korean frontier in the circumstances of Chinese intervention. Mr Bevin was among a number who favoured negotiation of a demilitarised or buffer zone between the United Nations line and North East China. Mr Acheson and the State Department toyed with the idea. But General MacArthur and the American Chiefs of Staff took the view that to abandon offensive action after a brief if sharp reverse was foolhardy. Forewarned of Chinese intervention, the United Nations Command was forearmed. '...it would be fatal to weaken the longstanding policy of the United Nations to destroy all resisting armed forces in Korea and bring that country into a united and free nation'[14]. The American force structure in Korea was being run down on the assumption that victory was imminent. Let that be reversed, let the engagement rules prohibiting air attack upon the Yalu bridges and hot pursuit of Chinese and North Korean aircraft into Chinese air space be rescinded, and the United States Eighth Army, X Corps, and their supporting air forces would clear Korea of Communist power.

Those politicians and officials who sought to dismiss this latter proposal as lacking in political insight or subtlety were reminded that the initiative did not rest alone with the United Nations. China and North Korea were not members of that body*. The Soviet Union was their supporter and spokesman within it and had never been a party to United

* The Communist People's Republic of China asserted its right to China's seat in the United Nations in place of the Nationalists expelled to Taiwan. This change had been resisted, chiefly by the United States.

Nations intervention on behalf of the Republic of Korea*. Proposals for a buffer zone might simply be rejected by the Communist side. Kim was certainly not going to abdicate power by agreeing to a buffer zone administered by a United Nations commission. Withdrawal to a defensive line at any point would almost certainly result in the intervening Korean territory being occupied by Chinese and North Korean forces.

On this basis, the argument in favour of resuming the offensive was adopted, a decision in which the United States, as the majority shareholder, led the remainder. The manning and supply lines were reloaded for Korea. Within the peninsula, intensive engineering activity improved the road and rail lines. Airfields and supply bases were advanced. Air search and attack increased though, due to British intervention, operations were not permitted into North East China or against the Yalu bridges† [15]. On the west coast and in central Korea, the Eighth Army made plans to advance again but with greater emphasis on ground reconnaissance and local security between corps. In October, the Army had moved in pursuit. Now it would advance to feel out a fully manned enemy defence line; what General MacArthur would describe later in common military parlance as 'a reconnaissance in force'. It would maintain flank contacts so far as this was possible in the mountainous terrain. On the east coast sector, X Corps was now ready to join the offensive, aiming to reach the Yalu by thrusting the United States 1st Marine and 7th Infantry Divisions through the formidable mountains on either side of the Changjin reservoirs, while the ROK I Corps advanced towards the Soviet frontier in the extremities of the north east. Operations were to begin the day after Thanksgiving, 24th November 1950.

A month had elapsed since the first Chinese offensive. Mao and P'eng claim that they knew precisely what the United Nations side would do and had prepared accordingly[16]. This is unlikely. There was considerable international discussion before the decision to resume the advance was made. Though United Nations political security was poor throughout this process, the planners in Peking had to provide several options for the event of withdrawal of the United Nations force into a winter defence line. Reinforcement of P'eng's command by a second army

---

* Ostensibly on this issue of Communist China's admission to the United Nations, the Soviet delegate absented himself from the Security Council from April 1950 but returned in August as it became apparent that the North Korean offensive was waning.

† When General MacArthur decided arbitrarily to bomb the Yalu bridges on 6th November, the Joint Chiefs of Staff ordered him to cancel the operation. '... One factor is the present commitment not to take action affecting Manchuria [North East China] without consulting the British...' This led MacArthur to accuse the British of indulging in appeasement. Agreement to attack the bridges was given on 8th November but air operations into North East China, even in hot pursuit of enemy raiders, remained forbidden.

group, which continued throughout November, was a requirement to meet any of the contingencies.

Yet if the United Nations commanders considered themselves better informed as to enemy tactics following the clashes in late October and early November, the Chinese People's Volunteers were the greater beneficiaries of this experience. Political officers at every level reminded the soldiers that they had taken on the best equipped army in the world and thrown it into disorganisation and panic. The American air forces had been incapable of attacking them except for the occasions when enthusiasm or mishap had exposed Chinese forces in daylight. They would take greater care in the forthcoming 'Second Phase Offensive'.

For all the notions of local sorties from mountain strongholds had been abandoned absolutely by this date within the Chinese high command. If some still doubted the wisdom of intervention at this stage, they did not advocate restraint in the Politburo or Central Military Commission. Mao and P'eng were of one mind. As soon as the United Nations columns, bound to the roads, were fully into the mountains and thus separated, the 13th Army Group in the west and centre, the 9th Army Group in the east, would fall upon them in darkness: five of the six armies in the 13th, all three armies in the 9th; in all, 300,000 men in fighting formations*. Local attacks would hold the United Nations advanced guards while whole armies marched across country to cut into and behind the main bodies of the Eighth Army and X Corps, their artillery lines, supply and transport columns, and headquarters. They would run them all the way back to P'yongyang, and 'if the enemy in P'yongyang retreated, then to strike down to the 38th Parallel'[17].

General MacArthur launched his reconnaissance in force in the last week of November, remarking that his advance was the only means of discovering the Chinese strength and dispositions. But he also characterised the renewed offensive as 'a massive compression envelopment'[18]; an envelopment of enemy forces his staff estimated to number 167,000, including 70,000 Chinese. Thus operations began in the expectation of finding an enemy in moderate strength in static defences.

Optimism flourished in MacArthur's headquarters. As soon as the Yalu bridges had been cut by air attack it was thought that the Chinese and North Korean elements south of the river would be isolated from

* Broadly, a Chinese 'army group' corresponded to an army on the Western model, an 'army' to a corps. An army usually had under command three divisions, each about 10,000 men strong, little more than half the strength of its United States counterpart. However, its ratio of fighting to supporting and administrative elements was high, and thus the numbers engaged in combat were close to the fighting element of an American division. The figure of 300,000 for the 9th and 13th Army Groups includes three artillery divisions but not a railway division and other logistic bodies subordinate to P'eng's headquarters. Overall, the CPV in Korea at this time totalled 450,000.

their supplies. Yet air reconnaissance had not found a single target of importance when the offensive opened, and it was soon apparent that, though the main bridges had lost spans, pontoons connected the banks by night. The river ice was, in any case, capable of bearing foot traffic in many places.

Closed up, embracing their artillery, the leading ground formations of Eighth Army and X Corps began to move forward. They were not hustled by their senior commanders. Rather, advanced and main guards were exhorted to maintain a deliberate pace except where, in the north east, several small flying columns, travelling on country tracks, reached the Yalu river. On the western front, resistance was negligible; the leading elements did not reach the Chinese outpost line until the end of the second day. But the advance of the ROK II Corps in the depths of the mountain range of central Korea was stubbornly resisted from the outset. Progressively, through the 24th and 25th November, the 5th Tactical Air Force began to pick up targets, principally troops dispersing from assembly areas for tactical positions. Major clashes were thus expected by the Eighth Army on 26th November.

This assumed a monopoly of the initiative which they did not possess. On the night of the 25th, P'eng Te-huai opened his own offensive. The ROK II Corps was the closest target. While its foremost regiments were attacked before midnight, a strong force of Chinese encircled its open eastern flank. Within twelve hours the corps had been routed. This opened the right flank of the American IX Corps. Problems multiplied. The latter was also fighting across its own front. In attempting to draw back, one of its divisions was severely mauled. Impulsive decisions by the corps commander brought his force to the edge of disaster and endangered the US I Corps to the west. Thus the battle ran against Eighth Army through the 26th and 27th. Unable to regain control while in contact, the army commander wisely broke away on the 28th. Once more the Chinese penetrated his battle lines and threatened his withdrawal routes. Contact was broken again. By the beginning of December, the Eighth Army began rolling back behind British and Commonwealth rearguards. By then it had outrun the marching Chinese, but no attempt was made to form a new line on the Taedong river. The mass of United Nations vehicles, carrying among them their infantry, sped south.

On the X Corps front, the US 7th Division suffered serious loss north east of the Changjin reservoir. West of this feature, the 1st Marine Division, which included 41 Royal Marine Commando, began an epic withdrawal, maintaining cohesion and spirit though greatly outnumbered. Fighting by night, moving by day with close maritime air support, they returned to the coast carrying all that remained serviceable of their weapons and equipment. On 24th December, X Corps evacuated the last of its units by sea from north east Korea.

By this time, the Eighth Army was already below the 38th Parallel, holding a line which in the west covered the Republic of Korea's capital, Seoul, but without any certainty as to how long it could be maintained. Since breaking away on 30th November, the Army had retired 300 miles without pausing long enough to check the following Chinese and North Koreans. General MacArthur's strategy, launched so brilliantly at Inch'on three months previously, had failed. In and beyond Korea, it seemed possible that the United Nations force would be ejected from the peninsula.

President Truman confirmed that use of the atom bomb had been considered as a means of countering the numerous and persistent enemy. He failed to make it clear that he had rejected its use, an omission which prompted a visit from the British Prime Minister, Mr Attlee. The heads of the two governments then considered policy options and agreed that the best of these was dismal. But they agreed to persist together in Korea, even though they had differing views as what should or, rather, what could be done if they were forced out.

It was now the Chinese who seemed invincible to their foes, as to many onlookers. Actually, they were were far from that. Mao's strategy was exhausting the strength of his soldiers and the capacity of their supply lines. He had pressed them south from P'yongyang to completion of the Second Phase Offensive, which would end just short of the 38th Parallel. Political considerations persuaded him to engage, with scarcely a halt, in a 'Third Phase'. As early as 4th December, he picked out as a weapon of opportunity a perceived desire among the United Nations to negotiate peace in Korea. He directed that,

> The cease fire negotiations could be held only after UN imperialism agrees to withdraw troops from Korea or at least first to the south of the 38th Parallel. It would be best for us to capture not only P'yongyang but also Seoul... which would more forcefully impel US imperialism to withdraw[19].

The 38th Parallel, which he and his associates had regarded as the sacrosanct frontier of North Korea in October, was valued indifferently in December as the frontier of the Republic of Korea.

Although a general in the People's Liberation Army was expected to consider pre-eminently the political objective of any operation*, P'eng was more concerned just then with the practicality of crossing the Parallel and the capture of Seoul. Whilst the pursuit from P'yongyang had been

* P'eng Te-huai was specifically the appointed military and political commander of the Chinese People's Volunteers.

uncontested, it had been made on foot, largely across country at night, when temperatures dropped frequently below 30 degrees Celsius. His soldiers were approaching exhaustion. A substantial number were still in their summer uniforms supplemented by blankets; the incidence of frostbite among them was rising[20]. Weapons often became unserviceable as moving parts froze in their housings. They needed time to bring forward their supplies, principally ammunition, clothing, food, and communications equipment. If the enemy withdrew again there was a danger that a weak CPV force would be drawn down towards the old Pusan perimeter with its line of communications further attenuated. Discussing the position with his army group and army commanders, P'eng proposed a pause just north of the Parallel until February or early March. Some members of the Central Military Commission supported him[21].

Their representations persuaded Mao to modify his ideas simply to crossing the Parallel as a demonstration, to deny the enemy its recovery, and desirably but not essentially to capture Seoul. If necessary, they could make a limited withdrawal after attacking. But on timing Mao insisted on the Third Phase Offensive opening in early January. On 26th December, he told P'eng to 'strengthen political activism among the soldiers...they should be determined not to return home until the enemies in Korea are all destroyed'[22].

So the Third Phase Offensive began on New Year's Eve. Its brief run seemed to justify Mao's confidence in the residual strength of the Communist forces. In the eastern sector, the United Nations line collapsed at once under pressure from the North Koreans. The centre withdrew precipitately before P'eng's Sixty Sixth Army. To the west, sharp local fighting which involved the British 29th Brigade carried the Thirty Eighth, Thirty Ninth, and Fortieth Armies down to the northern bank of the Han river and possession of Seoul.

There was then a pause, fortunately for the United Nations cause, as the North Koreans made their way through the eastern mountains, and the Chinese People's Volunteers sought to recover their physical strength. They retained, however, their massive moral superiority. The majority of their foes dreaded their approach. For once, General MacArthur lacked strategic inspiration. He apprehended defeat. However, the death in a road accident of the Eighth Army commander late in December brought a fresh mind to the struggle. Lieutenant-General Matthew B Ridgway was his successor. The fortunes of the United Nations depended on his ability to devise a new strategy and, no less, to persuade his soldiers that they had the ability to carry it through.

SOURCE NOTES: Introduction

1 See *Pravda*, 21st March 1949, pp 48–49, and p 268.

2 Weathersby, Kathryn, *Soviet Aims in Korea and the origins of the Korean war, 1945–50*: new evidence from Russian Archives, Working Paper No. 8, Cold War International History Project Woodrow Wilson International Center for Scholars, November 1993 (hereafter Weathersby WP No 8). See for example, p 18.

3 Volkogonov, General D, *Is this anything to be afraid of?* Behind the scenes of the Korean War, article in *Ogonyek* No 25, June 1993 pp 28–29.

4 *Ibid.*

5 United Nations General Assembly Resolution 376(V) of 7th October 1950. For full text, see Volume I, Appendix M.

6 United Nations Joint Chiefs of Staff (JCS) un-numbered signal to CINCFE of 9th October 1950 (United States National Archives and Records Service (USNARS), Suitland).

7 Tsiang Hui, *The rivalry of the strategic decisions between China and America* in *Party History Corpus*, (Peking) June, 1988.

8 Hsü, Yen *The first trial of strength: historical review and analysis of the war of Resist American and Aid Korea (RAAK)* Peking, 1990, Publishing House of Chinese Radio and Television Department), p 18.

9 *Ibid*, p19.

10 Chai Cheng-wen and Chao Yong-tian, *A record of the actual events of the War to resist America and Aid Korea*, (Peking 1987), pp 113–116.

11 See, for example, Ye' Yumeng' *Black snow: the first account of the CPV's fighting in Korea* (Peking, 1989, Writers' Press), p 52.

12 P'eng Te-huai, *Autobiographical notes of P'eng Te-huai*, (Peking 1988), p 341; and Hsü Yen, *op cit*, p 50.

13 Hu Kuan-cheng, *A wise decision and a great achievement,* Party Historical Research, (Peking January 1983).

14 Signal CINCFE to Army Department for Joint Chiefs of Staff, C68572 of 9th November 1950 (USNARS, Suitland).

15 Signal JCS (Personal) for MacArthur JCS 95878 of 6th November 1950 (USNARS, Suitland).

16 See 4, above.

17 Mao Tse-tung, *Mao Tse-tung's manuscripts from the establishment of the People's Republic of China, vol 1*, (Peking 1987), p 680. For details of the force, see Hsü Yen, *op cit*, Appendix.

18 GHQ United Nations Command Communique No 12, issued 24th November 1950.

19 *History of the War of Resist-America-Aid Korea*, Military History Research Section, Military Science Academy, (Peking 1988), p 76.

20 Hsü, *op cit*, p 162.

21 See, for example, Tu P'ing, *In the Headquarters of the CPV* (Peking, 1988) pp 14–141; and Nieh Jung-chen, *Memoirs*, Vol 2, (Peking, 1984) pp 740–741.

22 Mao Tse-tung, *op cit*, pp 719–720.

CHAPTER 1

The condemnation of China

The Chinese recovery of North Korea in just over three weeks shocked the governments participating in or supporting the United Nations Command. In judging their reactions, it is important to remember that some individuals among them—politicians, officials, and senior service officers—believed that the world was once more on the brink of general war. Stalin had maintained huge military forces to back his expansionism in Europe since 1945. Surely, so ran the conclusion, the Soviet Union was equally engaged in a dynamic strategy for revolution throughout Asia in which China was to take a leading role. Any attempt to counter this by force might lead to intervention by Russian arms. The Australian and Indian Prime Ministers shared this apprehension. Some British authorities were of a similar mind. Malcolm MacDonald, Commissioner-General for South East Asia, suggested in an appreciation on 5th January 1951 that '... Although we must hope that it will not materialise, we have to reckon with war...with China; but with China covertly supported by Russia; i.e. a war conducted (possibly as a prelude to global war but possibly as a distinct end in itself) in the Far East alone, while a state of nominal peace continues in the West'[1].

Mr Bevin and the Foreign Office staff did not believe that Russia was about to go to war in the Far East, or that Stalin was pursuing a short term policy towards the domination of Asia. Even so, he remarked to the Commonwealth Prime Ministers meeting in London in January 1951,

> The main outline of the joint strategy of the two Powers [Russia and China] seemed clear enough—in the Far East to use Chinese manpower to contain large numbers of the troops of the democracies; and in Europe to neutralise Germany and thus to frustrate the plans of the democracies for the defence of Western Europe, which could not be satisfactorily defended without fighting on German soil[2].

It was Britain's policy to separate China from the Soviet Union, to encourage Mao Tse-tung to emulate Tito*, and incidentally but more

---

* Marshal (Josip Broz) Tito, President of Yugoslavia, broke away from Stalin's control in 1948. Stalin sometimes spoke of Mao as a 'potential Tito'.

immediately to preserve the integrity of Hong Kong. In furtherance of that policy, a British mission was in Peking to negotiate full diplomatic relations with Mao's government. Persistent American refusals to admit Communist China to the United Nations in place of Nationalist China, and resolve to defend Taiwan, the island fortress of the Nationalists, seemed to the British Foreign Office likely to persuade the Communist Chinese Government that the Soviet Union was the only available ally of substance. However, despite this difference of view, Britain agreed with the United States that the Chinese should not secure any political advantages as an inducement to withdraw from Korea. Their objective continued to be the survival of the Republic of Korea until and unless the two Korean states were united by democratic process.

These differences of perception caused the British Government to oppose the United States wish to name China formally as an aggressor in the General Assembly of the United Nations in December 1950. But in the matter of opposing the Chinese intervention forces, they were of a common mind. 'We're with you in this,' Mr Attlee had assured President Truman when the two men met in Washington at the beginning of December, 'and we stand together'*. This included a clear understanding that they would not accept any proposal that withdrawal of Chinese troops would necessarily be matched by a similar withdrawal of United States forces in time and numbers.

At the end of that meeeting, there was general agreement that their forces within the United Nations Command would go on fighting as long as practicable in Korea. Voluntary withdrawal was unacceptable to the two leaders not only because it would suggest that the democratic powers were unable to hold back Communist encroachments but also because it would abandon the citizens of the Republic to widespread reprisals, if not by the Chinese most certainly by Kim Il-sung and his agents. It was therefore disturbing to the British authorities to receive from a variety of sources indications that General MacArthur, perhaps even the Joint Chiefs of Staff, were retaining the option of a staged voluntary evacuation.

For example, Marguerite Higgins, Far East correspondent of the New York Herald Tribune, wrote from Tokyo on 4th January 1951 that '... Under present military handicaps it is very likely that we must pull out of Korea completely.' Whilst this was not attributed to the Commander-in-Chief, it smacked of a briefing off the record by his staff. His request for reinforcements having been refused, General MacArthur had signalled four proposals to Washington on 30th December for the recovery of ascendancy in the theatre. Three of these involved carrying operations into mainland China, using United States naval and air forces in combination with landings by Chiang Kai-shek's Nationalist forces

---

* See Volume I, p 362.

from Taiwan. The fourth proposed acceptance of Nationalist Chinese forces for the United Nations Command[3]. Without substantial reinforcement, or the opening of war against China, General MacArthur doubted his ability to retain a foothold in Korea. The opening of the Chinese 'Third Phase Offensive' as the new year began, and the consequent abandonment of Seoul and the Han river line, sharpened the discussions between Tokyo and Washington, and the anxieties in London.

'Eyes only Lord Tedder*,' the British Chiefs signalled to Washington on 5th January, 'Please pass the following to General Bradley' [Chairman of the JCS].

> *Begins* We are becoming increasingly concerned at our almost complete lack of what General MacArthur's plans are for future operations in Korea, or of any appreciation by the U.S. Joint Chiefs of Staff as to the probable course of events, and in particular the ability of the U.N. Forces to hold any sort of line or bridgehead in Korea. While everyone realises that the U.S. have by far the largest forces engaged, there are two brigades of British troops involved for whom H.M.G. is responsible to Parliament, and there is increasing disquiet in this country as to the conduct of the campaign. This feeling is bound to find expression in Parliament and any government would be placed in an impossible position if it transpired that (as in fact is the case) they had virtually no idea of the United Nations Commander's strategic intentions or of how the situation might be expected to develop.
>
> 2. We take it for granted that there has been no change in the military intentions of the United States Government, as affirmed in the P[rime] M[inister]/President conversations [in December 1950], to resist and fight it out in Korea. We feel that to stabilise some sort of a position on the Peninsula is essential if there is to be any chance of a settlement by negotiation, which we understand is desired by the United States Government as much as by ourselves. The effect of being kicked out of Korea would be calamitous, not only to the prestige and interests of the Western Powers throughout Asia, but also to the morale of European nations just at a time when General Eisenhower is taking over his command†... And finally it could hardly fail to encourage the Communist Powers to further adventures with little fear of effective resistance. In fact our relative security could—at least for some years—rest solely on the somewhat uncertain foundations of the atom bomb.
>
> 3. Frankly we find it difficult to believe that, with the backing of overwhelming air and sea power, the United Nations forces could not maintain a substantial hold on the Korean peninsula. In this connection we feel that the essential cause of Anglo-American solidarity would not be

---

* Marshal of the Royal Air Force, Lord Tedder was Head of the British Joint Services Mission to the United States. As such he was the representative of the British Chiefs of Staff to the United States Joint Chiefs. This was a continuation of the Combined Chiefs of Staff organisation established in the Second World War.

† Supreme Allied Commander, Europe (SACEUR) in the newly created North Atlantic Treaty Organisation.

served by lack of frankness, and must convey to you first our impression that General MacArthur's intelligence is not serving him and the United Nations well. We have no evidence that the Chinese forces in Korea are in fact anything like as strong as his repeated communiques make out—which frankly we find it difficult to believe. ...it cannot be sound to alarm the troops by constant harping on the overwhelming strength of their enemies, or by the issue of the script of a broadcast such as that handed to [the British Commonwealth] DADPR*...which stated flatly, "A frantic atmosphere prevails. Everybody is scared. We are losing and everybody knows it. Nobody likes it". All we hear from our own people in the battle shows they at least are convinced that they are not up against anything like the numbers stated, and that they by no means regard themselves as beaten.

4. Secondly, we feel that you are entitled to know that reports, reaching not only us but Ministers and the public from such a wide variety of sources that they must be taken seriously, cast grave doubts on the morale and determination of some American units in Korea. We could not say this to you but for our acute sense of the importance of Anglo-American friendship and mutual confidence. Some of the reasons for a drop in their morale are obvious, such as a sudden grave reverse after being so near to victory and the factor referred to in 3 above. There have been many instances in the history of war when good troops including our own have failed in determination. But we feel that this is a question of leadership and inspiration from the top, and in this connection we welcome the assumption of command by General Ridgway...

5. We have not in the past pressed you or MacArthur for any share in the determination of events, though you are well aware of the grave doubts we felt, for instance, about the advance to the Manchurian [North East China] frontier. We feel now however that the time has come when we as your major ally must be taken into your confidence and, indeed, consultation, in a situation in which not only the fate of some thousands of British troops is at stake, but still more which contains such enormously far-reaching implications for us in Asia and the West.

6. The situation now has many features in common with that with which we were faced in Burma in 1943. We then found that the only effective military course was to select the main defensive position on which we intended to stand, and then disengage and fall back on it, instead of remaining at the mercy of events and continuing piece-meal withdrawals under pressure, which is not only dangerous and costly, but is bound to further lower the morale of the troops engaged. Once back on our main defence line we must resist with the utmost determination, and our defence should be characterised by seizing every opportunity to counter-attack and kill Chinese, as well as by the utmost exploitation of air and sea power.

7. We understand the U.S. policy remains to localise the conflict in Korea and avoid any form of hostilities with China. Our views on this point have already been conveyed to you by Lord Tedder.

---

* Deputy Assistant Director of Public Relations—the British Commonwealth public relations staff officer in Japan.

8. We regard this situation as so critical and so fraught with dangerous possibilities that we suggest that one of us should come immediately to Washington or one of you should come here...as it would enable whoever came to discuss this question not only with us but also our Ministers, and to obtain some idea of the climate of opinion on this matter in this country. *Ends*[4].

There was an error of fact in this signal—the numbers of Chinese then in Korea were indeed 450,000, though General MacArthur's estimate was purely a guess; and he had little idea of where they were located. It may also have erred in tact, as Field-Marshal Lord Slim was later to recognise, in referring to his own profound experience of turning defeat into victory in Burma. 'Teaching a grandmother to suck eggs always invites a sharp reponse, but we were intensely frustrated'[5]. Still, while they showed no resentment or dissent on receipt of this signal* [6], the American Joint Chiefs were not so sensitive to British public opinion that they wished to send a representative to London to study it closely. It was agreed that Sir John Slessor, Chief of the Air Staff, should travel to Washington on 13th January for a discussion with the Joint Chiefs of Staff.

On the day the British Chiefs sent their signal to Washington, 5th January 1951, Mr Acheson, the American Secretary of State despatched a message to Mr Bevin seeking to clarify the United States proposal to name China as an aggressor[7]. Omission of any reference to fighting for Korea raised the anxieties of the Foreign Office. The defence departments were disturbed to learn from Lord Tedder on the 6th January that General Bradley and his colleagues did not feel it right to put any additional forces into Korea '...sooner or later we shall have to come out'[8]. The Prime Minister sent a personal message to President Truman on 8th January† to discover if there had been any change of policy on his part.

Dear Mr President,
I am greatly disturbed by present developments in the Far East, and feel that I should open my mind to you in order that there may be no possibility of misunderstanding between our two Governments.

My colleagues and I have been basing our policy on the assumption that we should fight it out in Korea and try to localise the conflict. This was my understanding of the common position which we reached together in Washington in December. It is on these assumptions, and on the assumption that if we could hold a line and build up a position of strength

---

* Lord Tedder omitted paragraph 4 but gave General Bradley 'the gist of it verbally'.

† On this same day, General Ridgeway advised General MacArthur that the ROK Army was coming to believe that it was to be abandoned, to the point that it might disintegrate. He suggested that the Commander-in-Chief should publish a reassurance that the United Nations intended to continue to fight for Korea. MacArthur passed this message to the Joint Chiefs of Staff with the comment that he could not give reassurance 'unless and until the basis for such a statement is established by policy determination at government level'.

in Korea the Chinese might then be in a mood to respond to a suggestion for a negotiated settlement, that His Majesty's Government have been pressing that the possibility for a negotiation with China should be kept open. ... It now appears from the information we are receiving that the intention of the United Nations Command is to evacuate rather than fight it out. I feel compelled to ask you to give me an authoritative indication of the intentions of the United States Government in this respect. I am left with the impression, particularly from Secretary Acheson's message to Mr Bevin of 5th January, that the United States Government may wish to substitute for a policy of localising the conflict in Korea, a policy aimed at developing limited action against China.

It may be that it is militarily impossible to hold on in Korea. This possibility was recognised between us in Washington last month. Moreover, we are not blind to the possibility that China may intend to spread hostilities in the Far East. But looking at the world situation as a whole, and bearing in mind that the Soviet Union is the principal enemy, we think it unwise to provoke China unnecessarily to further aggression. The wiser course, it seems to us, is to harbour our forces and build them up in order to meet Communist attacks wherever they may come. It is true that, in his message of 5th January, Mr Acheson states that the United States intends to do everything they can to prevent hostilities spreading from Korea to wider areas in the Far East. But the kind of action against China for which the United States appear to be pressing at the United Nations will, in our view, almost certainly provoke China to extend hostilities. There can be little doubt that, for example, a campaign of subversion or guerrilla warfare against China involving the use of Chiang Kai-shek's forces would certainly have that effect. I do not know whether such a project is intended by the United States Government, and I should like to know whether they would intend to recommend such action by the United Nations after China had been declared an aggressor.

It was for all these reasons, which I have felt bound to explain to you frankly, that we have been opposing the introduction at this stage of a resolution in the United Nations condemning China as an aggressor and calling on the Collective Measures Committee* to consider what measures should be taken.

In any case we consider it desirable, in order to consolidate opinion in the United Nations which is at present disarrayed, and ensure the greatest measure of support on the part of the free world, that an immediate step should be taken at the United Nations which, while recognising the facts of the situation in Korea, would show that all concerned were prepared to go to the utmost limit in giving the Chinese a chance to reach a peaceful settlement. Such an immediate step might take the form of a resolution based perhaps on the latest set of principles drawn up by the Cease Fire Committee. This might include a clause condemning Chinese intervention in Korea and might lay more stress on the 5th point of the principles. There was a good deal of support among our Commonwealth friends here for the notion that the Big Powers have a special responsibility in this crisis.

---

* Established to report on means to maintain and strengthen international peace and security.

> It would be of the greatest assistance to me if you could possibly let me have a reply in time for tomorrow's meeting [of Commonwealth Prime Ministers]. With all good wishes,
>
> C. R. ATTLEE[9].

President Truman responded at once with full assurances that the understandings he had reached with Mr Attlee as to their policy concerning Korea were unchanged, though he made a shrewd point in remarking that, 'Should the Chinese Communists extend hostilities as, for example, by an attack on Hong Kong or Indo-China or Japan or by massive air attacks from Chinese territories on UN forces, I should assume that you would agree that our desire and intention [not to attack Chinese territory] might be impossible of fulfilment'[10]. Conceding that they should attempt peace negotiations, he added,

> By all means let us keep all doors open for peaceful settlement. That is our duty under the Charter of the United Nations. But, if the truth be that aggression has occurred, let us not shrink from stating that truth, because of the fact that the power which launches it is formidable. If we take that attitude the great common problems which you and we have are insoluble.

Negotiation for a cease fire was proposed formally to the People's Republic of China on 13th January, originating with the 'Cease Fire Committee' of the General Assembly*, and embodying ideas for a general settlement agreed among the Commonwealth Prime Ministers at their immediately preceding meeting in London[11]. It embraced the 'Five Principles':

> 1. An immediate cease fire with arrangements to ensure that this event was not used as a screen to mounting a new offensive.
>
> 2. Pursuit of further steps to secure permanent peace in Korea.
>
> 3. All non-Koreans to withdraw from Korea on a staged basis to permit the emergence of a unified, independent, democratic state with a government based on free popular elections, as envisaged in the General Assembly's resolution.
>
> 4. Pending this process, interim arrangements in accordance with United Nations' principles to be established for the administration of Korea and the maintenance of peace and security there.
>
> 5. Given agreement on a cease fire, an appropriate body determined by the General Assembly, including the Governments of the United Kingdom, the United States of America, the Union of Soviet Socialist Republics, and

---

* Formed on 14th December 1950 by majority vote of the General Assembly to determine the basis for a satisfactory cease fire in Korea. It comprised: Nasrollah Entezam, Iranian ambassador to the United States and the Iranian delegation to the General Assembly (he was then also President of the 5th Session of the General Assembly); Rt Hon Lester Pearson (Canada); and Sir Benegal Rama Rau (India).

the People's Republic of China, should meet to achieve a settlement of far eastern problems including those relating to Taiwan [Formosa] and the representation of China in the United Nations in conformity with international obligations and the United Nations Charter[12].

These proposals were answered from Peking by Chou En-lai on 17th January. He remarked that he had already informed Mr Entezam on 22nd December* that

the Central People's Government has always maintained and still maintains that a rapid termination of the hostilities in Korea should be sought by negotiations among the various countries concerned...on the basis of the withdrawal of all foreign troops from Korea and the settlement of Korean domestic affairs by the Koreans themselves; that United States armed forces must be withdrawn from Taiwan; and that the representatives of the People's Republic of China must assume their rightful place in the United Nations...

He noted that the First Committee of the General Assembly had adopted principles on 13th January without the participation of his government. The purpose of a cease fire was 'to give the United States a breathing space'† and that it 'would only help the United States to maintain and extend its aggression...' In order to find a genuine and and peaceful solution, his government proposed:

(a) Negotiations...on the basis of the withdrawal of all foreign troops from Korea and the settlement of Korean domestic affairs by the Korean people themselves...

(b) The subject matter of the negotiations must include the withdrawal of United States armed forces from Taiwan and the Taiwan Straits and the Far Eastern related problems.

(c) The countries to participate in the negotiations should be the following seven countries: the People's Republic of China, the Soviet Union, the United Kingdom, the United States of America, France, India, and Egypt, and the rightful place of the Central People's Government of the People's Republic of China in the United Nations should be established as from the beginning of the seven-nation conference.

(d) The seven-nation conference should be held in China, at a place to be selected[13].

The reaction to this response varied between the principal powers awaiting it. The United States considered it 'an outright rejection' of the United Nations proposal[14]. Pandit Nehru believed it to offer the basis

---

* In response to an initial proposal by the Cease Fire Committee.

† This same accusation was made by Mr J Malik, head of the USSR mission to the United Nations in a speech to the First Committee of the General Assembly on 13th December 1950.

for a settlement, a view which Mr Attlee described as 'a very charitable interpretation...'[15]. The British, nonetheless, wished to clarify the terms for a cease fire, and asked the United States to delay action at least until this had been accomplished.

To this point British moderation had served the United Nations well in the war. During the latter part of January, however, it was overplayed, for two reasons at least. The first was that Mr Bevin was absent from Cabinet during a crucial period; he entered hospital with pneumonia following the Cabinet meeting on the morning of 22nd January and did not return until 1st March*. The second was that some members of the government were, at heart, anti-American†. As a consequence, Sir Gladwyn Jebb at the United Nations headquarters was instructed to temporise and tinker while the resolution on aggression and its consequences was put to the First Committee of the General Assembly.

The United States wished to name China as an aggressor; the British Foreign Secretary, his senior officials, the Chiefs of Staff, the British Ambassadors in Washington and at the United Nations all agreed that China was an aggressor in Korea. Yet a Cabinet majority was against a statement to this effect by the General Assembly. There was indeed a case for censuring China more widely in this respect; the People's Liberation Army was then in process of occupying Tibet but this matter was disregarded at the time by the United Nations as a matter of expediency.

The stipulations in the Chinese reply of 17th January ran counter to everything Mr Attlee had agreed with President Truman: tribute was demanded for peace in Korea. They were reiterated in the 'clarification' offered by the Vice-Minister for Foreign Affairs in Peking to Sir John Hutchison, Head of the British Mission, and the Indian Ambassador: the People's Republic of China was to be admitted to the United Nations in place of Nationalist China without further demur; and the subsequent settlement would require the withdrawal of United States military forces from Taiwan and the Taiwan Strait[16]. Whatever the merits of these issues, merits which the British Government accepted in principle, Mr Attlee and Mr Truman had agreed that they were not to be conceded as a consequence of aggression in Korea.

Mr Bevin had argued against formal condemnation of China as an aggressor because he believed that the United States would on that basis press for 'consequences', namely, political and economic sanctions against

---

* However, due to his frail health, his tenure as Foreign Secretary ended on 12th March, though he retained a Cabinet seat as Lord Privy Seal. He died on 14th April.

† Members of the Labour Party resented the abrupt ending of dollar credits to the United Kingdom in 1945; and further resented American pressure on the British Government to rearm substantially to meet NATO commitments at the expense of domestic expenditure.

China, possibly even peripheral military action against the Chinese mainland. But by the middle of January, he knew that President Truman had rejected any wider military enterprise; the President's letter to Mr Attlee made that clear. In any case, the State Department recognised that such proposals would not command majority support in the General Assembly: the Asian and Middle Eastern nations would oppose such ideas, and so would the European democracies. On that account, Mr Acheson had conceded referral of 'consequences' to the Collective Measures Committee[17].

Finally, the British Government failed to see that the support it had itself commanded for moderation in condemnation of China was falling away[18]. France, for example, needed American support in Indo-China, Australia wished to engage the the United States in a Pacific security pact with herself and New Zealand[19].

The danger of a serious division between the United States and United Kingdom was apparent to an important minority in the Cabinet. Hugh Gaitskell, Chancellor of the Exchequer, noted in his diary that,

> ...there has been a far more serious split developing on foreign policy. This came out clearly over the United Nations resolution on China. Until Ernie [Bevin] became ill our line was to try and restrain the Americans in every way; to try and delay the resolution going before U.N.O., but in the last resource to accept it. But last Thursday evening [25th January]...during the final meeting of the Cabinet* to approve the defence programme, we were told that we had to decide on our attitude; that it was unlikely that the Americans would agree to any amendments that would have met us, and that we must assume that the resolution would be put in an unpalatable form. Kenneth Younger [Minister of State, deputising for Mr Bevin] was there without any Foreign Office officials, and rather to my surprise...made it plain that he was actually in favour of voting against it. There was a short and rather emotional discussion in the course of which the majority of the Cabinet agreed with him, especially of course the Minister of Labour [Aneurin Bevan]. Hector McNeil† alone had the courage to say that he was in favour of voting 'for'. I then suggested, since it was obvious that we would be defeated on that, that at least we ought to abstain. I think the P.M. agreed with that...Kenneth [Younger] saying that in his opinion there was no difference between voting against or abstaining[20].

It is difficult to understand why Mr Attlee, who had taken on the oversight of foreign affairs in Mr Bevin's absence, made no effort to call for the advice of senior Foreign Office officials and the Chiefs of Staff

---

* The Cabinet had discussed the matter during its morning meeting. The second meeting had been called in the House of Commons to discuss finally the increase in the defence budget and had not expected to discuss the Korean war vote in the General Assembly.

† McNeil, Rt Hon Hector, (1907–55), Secretary of State for Scotland, was Kenneth Younger's immediate predecessor as Minister of State in the Foreign Office.

to be given to the Cabinet on a matter of such importance. As it was, he did not comment on the majority opinion that,

> The Government believed that the resolution as a whole represented a mistaken approach...if, notwithstanding this, they now voted in favour of the United States resolution, it would be equally plain that they had voted, against their convictions, for the sole purpose of supporting the United States Government. Thereby, they would forfeit their independence and their self respect; and they would deprive themselves of any power to influence the United States Government on any future occasion...[21]

Mr Gaitskell was determined to bring about a change of policy. Overnight, he used his own senior officials to contact their colleagues in the Foreign Office to discover their opinion, and lobbied those members of Cabinet who might agree to change their view. In a private meeting with the Prime Minister and Kenneth Younger, to which Sir William Strang, the Permanent Under-Secretary to the Foreign Office, had been called, he asked the latter to give his advice and his own understanding of Mr Bevin's position. Sir William reminded them that Mr Bevin had accepted, when the bargaining was done, that Britain should support the United States resolution[22]. Finally, by fortunate chance during this activity, news came from America of further concessions on terminology and procedure—what Sir William described as 're-entry cards'.

At the Cabinet meeting on 26th January, Mr Gaitskell noted,

> the P.M. explained the new situation, but this did not prevent some of them, four in number—Dalton, Bevan, Chuter Ede and Jim Griffiths—from arguing for a time against any change. The P.M. however was now quite firm and very good with them... It was left that if the Americans would agree amendments on these lines we could vote 'for'. If they did not the decision would be left to the P.M.'[23]

In Washington, Sir Oliver Franks, in New York at the United Nations, Sir Gladwyn Jebb, continued to explore the possibilities of securing an agreement by changing single words or phrases, or of deletions, in the United States resolution standing in the First Committee. Though under considerable national political pressure to stand firm, Mr Acheson sought to meet these. Australia, Canada and New Zealand intervened with advantage. Disagreement concerning the use of the word 'aggressor' fell away; Britain accepted it. The United States moderated the terms describing China's rejection of the cease fire proposal, and accepted that a Good Offices Committee* should explore further options for a cease fire before any collective measures against China were considered. At

---

* This was not formed until mid-February due to reluctance of a number of states, notably India, to serve. The committee then comprised Mexico and Sweden under the chairmanship of Iran.

the end of January, the British Government shed the obstinacy and prejudice which were leading it to the impotence of a bystander. It voted in favour of the American resolution, and for Resolution 498 (V) submitted to the plenary meeting of the General Assembly on 1st February 1951.

China was thus identified as an aggressor in Korea; the ruse to describe its troops in the peninsula as 'volunteers', acting independently of their government, was rejected. The United Nations called upon China to cease hostilities and withdraw its troops; meantime the struggle against them would continue. All states and authorities were enjoined not to assist China or North Korea. The Collective Measures Committee—so ran the final wording agreed between Washington and London—was requested 'to consider additional measures to be employed to meet this aggression and to report thereon to the General Assembly, it being understood that the Committee is authorised to defer its report if the Good Offices Committee...reports satisfactory progress in its efforts...'*.

This outcome was thus a compromise between the original British and American positions; with hindsight, a beneficial compromise to the United Nations proceedings. A striking feature of this period of intense political negotiation over some four weeks is the extent to which Mr Acheson was prepared to shift or change his position to seek British agreement, even after the British Government had isolated itself[24]. British abstention from the motion of condemnation and attendant consequences would have been regrettable, a vote against it would have been serious but not fatal. There was no question that such a vote would have signified British withdrawal from the Korean engagement, or for that matter from the commitment to NATO. If anything, isolation would have reacted to the detriment of British standing as a world power by illustrating that her cooperation was not critical to security in Asia.

Yet Mr Acheson persisted. Those who deride the notion of a special relationship between the United States and United Kingdom, at this time at any rate, neglect the evidence of these and other negotiation records, official and otherwise.

Among those who dissociated themselves from the compromise motion, there remained a conviction that an opportunity for an early peace settlement had been lost. They were in error, despite Chou En-lai's remark to the Indian Ambassador that 'the Americans do not realise the seriousness of what they have done'[25]. It is now apparent that Mao had no intention of agreeing to suspend operations. Throughout December and January, against the advice of P'eng and others, he ordered the continuance of offensive operations. As late as 28th January 1951, he was

---

* For the full text of this resolution, see Appendix A.

advising P'eng that he would not enter the proposed peace negotiations until completion of the Fourth Offensive just opening, 'when conditions would be more advantageous for the Chinese/North Korean command[26]'. Mao was not only anxious to demonstrate his reliability to Stalin—who was at last in process of delivering arms and equipment for the CPV—but was no less seized of the view that a complete victory could be accomplished in Korea. It is notable that the propaganda line adopted in Peking at that time proclaimed that the Americans were going to be 'run into the sea'. P'eng was coming unhappily to realise that he would be urged to mount one final offensive after another until that objective was accomplished.

SOURCE NOTES: Chapter 1

1 Telegram from Mr. MacDonald, Commissioner-General for South-East Asia to Mr Bevin No 20 of 5 Jan 51, FZ 1193/1 (FO 371 93075). See also Documents on British Policy Overseas, Series II, Volume IV, Korea, 1950–51, ed H J Yasamee and K A Hamilton (London, 1991), hereafter, DBPO).

2 Minutes of the Third Meeting of the Commonwealth Prime Ministers, 5 Jan 51. CAB 133/90. See also DBPO, cit, Nos 104 and 108.

3 Signal from CinCFE to Army Department for JCS C-52391 of 30 Dec 50. (Foreign Relations of the United States, 1950, Volume vii, Korea, p 1630–1633, hereafter FRUS).

4 MOD DEF 420 to BJSM, Washington, of 5 Jan 51 (DEFE 11/206 f 1723).

5 Conversation, author with FM Lord Slim.

6 DEFE 11/206, f 1727.

7 FRUS 1951, *cit*, p 27.

8 DEFE 11/206, f 1727. See also f 1766, and DEFE 11/204, f 1776.

9 FK 1071/47 (FO 371 92766) and FK 1071/59 (FO 371 92767). For the United States context, see FRUS, 1951, *cit*, pp 37 40, also pp 72–73, and connect with F 10345/6 (FO 371 92067). See also DBPO *cit*, No 106, note 8.

10 Telegram 795.00/1–351 of 9th January 1951. For text see also FRUS, 1951, *cit*, pp 38–39.

11 CAB 133/90 and CAB 21/1780. For a more detailed view of the cease fire discussions, see DBPO *cit*, Nos 99, 100, 102–104, 109, and 113.

12 For the official text, see United Nations documents A/6.1/645 and A/C1\651.

13 For the full text, see United Nations document A/C.1/653.

14 For the text, see FRUS, 1951, *cit* pp 92–93.

15 FK 1071/134–5 (FO 371 92769).

16 FK 1071/53 (FO 371 92767).

17 FK 1071/136 (FO 371 92769) and FK 1071/170 (FO 371 92770).

18 For example, see FK 1071/215 (FO 371 92771).

19 For a Commonwealth view, see O'Neill, Professor Robert, *Australia in the Korean War* (Canberra, 1981), volume i, pp 179–184.

20 *The Diary of Hugh Gaitskell, 1945–1956*, ed Philip M Williams (London, 1983), pp 23–232. See also CAB 128/19 CM (51) 8. See also DBPO, *cit*, Nos 116–118 and footnotes thereto.

21 CAB 128/19, CM (51) 8.

22 See DBPO, *cit*, No 116, fn 4.

23 Gaitskell, *op cit*, p 232. See also CAB 128/19, CM (51) 9.

24 For example, see FK 1071/221 (FO 371 92771).

25 FK 1071/304 and 306 (FO 371 92775).

26 Hsü Yen, *op cit*, p 85.

CHAPTER 2

Changing fortunes

A defeated army is a dismal sight. Its confidence, essential to fighting capacity, is impaired. In January 1951, most of the senior commanders and staff officers, many of the regimental officers and soldiers, in the Eighth Army in Korea had lost belief in their capacity to outmatch, even to hold, the enemy in a major engagement of arms. They doubted their fighting skill and, within themselves, their fortitude. The marks of this condition were manifest in the general atmosphere of exhaustion in the winter season despite adequate rest, ample food and clothing; in a readiness to believe any rumour, however wild, which suggested the imminent presence of the enemy; in an eagerness to continue the process of withdrawal.

This want of spirit was confined almost wholly to the United States and Korean element of the Army, though it was not universal. The 1st Marine Division, for example, had not been cowed by its experiences in the north*, quite the contrary. Several ROK Army commanders, such as General Paik Sun-yup, and a few notable ROK regiments were confident of their ability to hold the advancing Chinese or North Koreans. Still, these exceptions illustrated the otherwise wretched generality.

Among the other overseas contingents who had been in action, the Australians, British, and Turks maintained a high morale and cohesion. They were nonplussed by the scurry south. They looked for robust leadership from the high command and thus warmed to their new chief, General Ridgway, as he travelled among them and made his policies known.

'I want you all to know that I am not going to fight for a particular piece of Korean real estate. If they attack us before we are ready, we shall roll with the punches. But then we shall attack them when they are extended. They may have the numbers but we have the firepower.' He spoke thus to a small group of Royal Artillerymen and tank crews of the 8th Hussars, a detachment of the British 29th Brigade, clustered round him as he stopped his jeep to talk to them some miles south of Suwon one clear, chill morning in the last week of January 1951. It was just the message they wanted to hear. Both the 27th Commonwealth and the 29th Brigade Group† had received formal notice of this philosophy

---

* For details of this formation and its fighting capacity, see Volume I, Chapter 14.

† For details of these formations at this time, see Appendix B.

to read to their membership, but soldiers prefer to see their generals so that they can make some personal judgement of their character. A war correspondent had put it about that General Ridgway was 'given to strutting'[1]. This was not how he seemed to the British and Commonwealth soldiers he encountered on his travels. He met them eye to eye. They found him straightforward and judged him to be reliable. Although he was becoming known among them as 'old tin tits', this was due to his practice of wearing two fragmentation grenades on his chest. It was a term of acceptance, not of derision.

Having failed to bring the Army to a halt at the end of December, in the first few days as its commander, Ridgway had come to realise that he had to demonstrate to his command that they were capable of defeating the enemy. If he could do that, he remarked in a letter to General Collins in Washington, they would 'achieve more, far more, than our people think possible—and perhaps inflict a bloody defeat on the Chinese which even China will long remember'[2].

He wrote those words on 3rd January 1951 as the Eighth Army was withdrawing south of the Han river, accustomed to the idea that as soon as the enemy caught up with them again they would refuse the challenge and withdraw out of contact. He needed a pause, time to permit the establishment of a defensible line on which to break the enemy strength, a first step in regaining confidence, from which he could take a second step by launching a limited offensive. He had selected a line on which to make such a stand. Identified as Line D, it ran from the village of P'yongt'aek in the west, through Wonju in central Korea, to a point just north of Chumunjin on the east coast. They would move back to that, imposing casualties on the enemy as they withdrew, gaining time by forcing the enemy to mass to attack, then further deplete the advancing Chinese and North Korean forces, bringing them to a halt again on Line D.

Yet within a matter of a few days, this scheme was in jeopardy. It became apparent that the two western corps, Major-General Frank W Milburn's I Corps, and Major-General John B Coulter's IX, had not complied with his orders. 'Reports so far reaching me,' he signalled to Generals Milburn and Coulter on 7th January,

> indicate your forces withdrew to 'D' line without evidence of having inflicted any substantial losses on enemy and without material delay. In fact, some major units are reported as having broken contact. I desire prompt confirming reports and if substantially correct, the reasons for non-compliance with my basic directives...[3]

Receipt of such a message obliges an errant subordinate commander to refocus his ideas promptly. It is no coincidence that instructions were shortly issued from both corps headquarters to patrol extensively to the north.

Major-General Edward M Almond's X Corps—the central corps in the army line—to the east of IX, was not open to the same reproach. Having disembarked from its operations in north east Korea at the end of December, the headquarters and leading division came straight up to Line D, and almost at once was pressed by a large body of the North Korean People's Army, which also threatened the ROK III Corps to the east. Members of the Army headquarters staff apprehended an urgent need to site new defence lines to the south of Line D.

In this central region, two North Korean corps, II and V*, were moving south ahead of the Chinese. V Corps, with five divisions, was attacking Wonju directly from the north and outflanking it to the east, aiming to rout X Corps. East again, the four divisions of II Corps were attempting to infiltrate through the heights of the Taebaek mountains to capture Andong, 50 miles to the south, an area containing several large Communist guerrilla bands. X Corps was to be finally crushed between these forces. So much was partially known to, partially assumed by, General Ridgway and his staff from prisoners-of-war taken in initial engagements.

At the outset of the ensuing battles in the centre, the run of operations seemed to be following a familiar course. ROK troops gave way prematurely; an American division withdrew several miles further south than ordered. Corps and divisional commanders left little scope to the judgement and initiative of their subordinates, detailing, for example, precise strengths, types and numbers of units to be deployed for a task by subordinates two down in the chain of command. Staff officers rarely left their headquarters to visit battle locations or indeed any forward areas and thus their own contribution to the command and control process was confined to map study. But General Ridgway's instructions that formations and units were to fight to the limit of their capability had begun to take effect in X and the ROK III Corps.

Their fortitude was rewarded. The North Koreans were by no means as strong as formation titles suggested—V Corps had only some 30,000 men, and was short of artillery. Many of its attacks were conducted in daylight; and although weather conditions hampered American air support, the American and ROK artillery steadily reduced General Pang's strength. Both sides suffered in the biting cold—numbers of men fighting

---

* II Corps was commanded by Lieutenant-General Ch'oe Hyon, then aged 44, a longstanding associate of Kim Il-sung as a minor guerrilla commander in North East China against the Japanese. Like Kim, he also had close ties with the Soviet Union and returned to Korea with the Soviet Forces in 1945. V Corps commander was Pang Ho-son (also -sang), who had commanded the 6th Division during the invasion of the south in June, 1950. See Volume I, p 132 fn.

on hillsides became frostbitten—but the North Koreans were also suffering from typhus. Their ranks contained many young and inexperienced soldiers. After ten days, these factors, combined with a serious lack of ammunition, obliged Pang to withdraw.

Ch'oe's corps continued its march south. By this time, however, General Almond and General Yu Jai-heung, commanding the ROK III Corps, had drawn in forces from areas unassailed, and had been reinforced by General Ridgway. The American 1st Marine Division was advanced to long stop positions below Andong. Day and night, strong patrols quartered the area. In clearing weather, American aircraft struck heavily at columns moving across country. The North Korean II Corps faltered, halted, and was defeated, the remnant of its 10th Division escaping into the mountains. The ruined town of Wonju was reoccupied by the United States 2nd Division on 23rd January and the line on either side restored.

During a difficult fortnight, there had been no expectation in X Corps or the ROK III Corps of permission to abandon Line D; the character of General Ridgway's orders and his presence in visits had excluded any such consideration. But news that a series of defence lines had been selected in Army headquarters to the very outskirts of Pusan, and provisional instructions for occupation of Line E drafted, had become known widely. For some days, there was gossip in I and IX Corps that a move south was imminent. In the ROK Army as a whole, anxiety increased that, after all, they might be abandoned to Kim Il-sung.

Ridgway urged General MacArthur and his contacts in Washington* to make it clear that if they had to withdraw from Korea at some stage the ROK Army would be evacuated with all United Nations troops, an assurance that was given by President Truman to General MacArthur on 15th January†. Apprehensions in I and IX Corps of impending withdrawal were gradually dispelled by movement of forces to the north.

Anxious to avoid any engagement which would sap further the confidence of his soldiers, General Ridgway might well have left the two western corps in their positions until the outcome of the North Korean offensive in the centre was decided. That would have been a safe course but it would also have surrendered all initiative to the enemy. Local patrolling in the west following his admonition of the two corps commanders on 7th January, convinced the army commander that the enemy had halted after crossing the Han river. He did not know why;

---

* Immediately prior to his appointment to command Eighth Army, General Ridgeway had been a deputy chief of the United States Army Staff in Washington.

† The British supported the principle but doubted the capability of moving and resettling such huge numbers. See, for example, *Documents on British Policy Overseas, Series II, Volume IV, Korea, 1950–51*, No 124 and notes.

his intelligence staff had no hard evidence as to enemy strengths and locations, let alone intentions. Ridgway decided to find out for himself.

General Milburn was ordered to send forward a regimental group—three battalions of infantry with tanks, artillery and engineer support—through Osan to Suwon to reconnoitre in force. They were not to become engaged in a major battle if they met the enemy in strength; they were not to exploit beyond Suwon unless personally authorised by General Ridgway. The right flank of the advance was to be secured by modest, temporary advances by units to the east. General Milburn named the operation 'Wolfhound', the nickname of the 27th Infantry ordered to make this reconnaissance. Their start line was P'yongt'aek, held by the British 29th Brigade.

A glance at the brigade's activities and outlook at this mid-point of January 1951 illustrates several abiding problems of command and control in war. The first is the difficulty high commanders have in imparting their policy not only down the chain to the battalion or equivalent on the ground but even to all sections of their own headquarters. General Ridgway was at that moment sending a force northwards. But the British, and indeed forces of all nations engaged, had just received detailed operation orders providing for a withdrawal to Line E. Notwithstanding General Ridgway's instructions, the staff at Eighth Army headquarters continued with contingency planning, apparently overlooking the fact that such a disclosure undermined their commander's policy. Then, at divisional level, orders had been issued that all forces along the line would be in their defences day and night, with half of each unit awake throughout each night. The 29 Brigade positions were on the coastal plain, in rice paddy. Trenches were thus half filled with water. The sub-zero night temperatures did not rise to freezing point until an hour or two after dawn. Breech mechanisms of small arms and machine-guns were frozen solid after nightfall unless they were coated with paraffin just prior to the practice of standing to arms at dusk.

Apart from the impracticability of keeping men fit to fight in these conditions, a considerable number of men were required day and night to maintain some sort of control over the huge refugee columns still passing through unit defences, principally on the roads. At night, exhausted refugees liked to rest among the soldiers to obtain their protection, and often had to be pushed physically out of company positions, whose defensibility they inhibited. By day, close observation had to be maintained over the columns to ensure that North Korean soldiers were not moving among them disguised as civilians. As great a problem as either of these was the moral compulsion to give such aid as possible to those in particular need, the sick and wounded among the large numbers of old and very young. Regimental medical officers and staffs were engaged in this work almost continuously. They were unable to cope with more than a fragment of those in dire need.

Thus the movement north of the American 27th Infantry was merely a passing event on 15th January. By then, Brigadier Brodie who, with members of his staff, frequently visited units, had arbitrarily decided to reduce the level of night manning and long spells in trenches. Defence was maintained by greater use of standing patrols forward in darkness and observation posts by day. Otherwise, companies concentrated in such shelter as was to hand with weapons and ammunition ready to man fighting positions at immediate notice.

Ten more days were to pass before it became apparent in the west that the character of operations was changing. It became known that Operation Wolfhound had found no enemy in strength below Suwon. I Corps began to close up northward. IX Corps stirred. Selected units were ordered to advance on a broad front, combing out the ground between roads. The Army was wary but not anxious as it began this work; General Ridgway's declaration, made to many soldiers personally, that they would roll with the punches and attack when conditions were right had impressed them.

The British units got out of their positions to make ready for this role, which would entail the movement of the infantry away from their vehicles, carrying their fighting requirements on their backs. To assist them, a company of Korean porters was allotted to each battalion*. At the end of the month, 29 Brigade moved forward to the area of Osan and Suwon, on call to reinforce any part of the I Corps sector. 45 Field Regiment, the brigade's principal artillery, was detached to support 1st ROK Division, advancing up the main road towards Seoul.

Less than a month had passed since the United Nations forces abandoned Seoul. Operation Thunderbolt, less tentative than Wolfhound, had carried the I and IX Corps line north of Suwon on the coastal plain, north of Ich'on† and Yoju on the lateral road, Route 20, to the central region. To the east of Yoju, X Corps was beginning its own advance from Wonju through the road junctions at Chip'yong-ni and Hoengsong. General Almond had selected Hongch'on, fifteen miles to the north, as the final objective of this thrust. All these movements involved combing out the hills between roads, arduous work for the infantry and their accompanying artillery observation parties, constraining the pace of daily movement. So much so, among the high jagged peaks in the X Corps sector, that General Almond bypassed them, leaving the search to his

---

* Part of the Civil Transport Corps comprising 82 porter companies recruited mainly through the ROK Army National Guard.

† Not to be confused with Inch'on, the port of Seoul.

T-6 Mosquitoes* and armed reconnaissance aircraft. On the ground and from the air many blackened Chinese bodies were discovered, killed by the cold.

From prisoners—many of them stragglers—ROK agents, air observation and other sources, General Ridgway's intelligence staff were able to provide him on 10th February with information for which he had pressed them: a detailed and, as it transpired, largely accurate picture of enemy movements and capabilities[4].

This showed, *inter alia*, that four of the six Chinese armies in the forward area were in or moving into the central region; in order the Forty Second, the Thirty Ninth, Fortieth, and Sixty Sixth Armies, comprising twelve divisions. All belonged to Li T'ien-yu's 13 Army Group. Their strength was believed to total 110,000. From the run of communications, two axes of advance suggested themselves: through Chip'yong-ni–Yoju–Changhowon–Ch'ongju; and Hoengsong–Wonju–Ch'ungju. It was expected that the offensive would open as soon as 9 Army Group under Sung Shih-lun reached the forward area to provide exploitation forces, some time after 15th February.

General Ridgway considered his best course of action over the night of 10th/11th February. I Corps had reached the Han river opposite Seoul and was completing occupation of Inch'on and the Kimpo peninsula. Their opponents across the river were North Koreans and Chinese. He had already decided that General Milburn's corps should hold fast on the southern bank until options for enveloping Seoul to the east developed. General Moore's IX Corps† was held back by a substantial and stubborn Chinese bridgehead on the southern bank of the Han upstream from Seoul stretching towards Chip'yong-ni, probably to protect the right flank of the impending offensive. He decided to continue pressure on this area. But X, and to an extent the ROK III Corps to its east, lay in the path of the Chinese concentration. On the 11th, General Ridgway instructed Almond to halt his advance towards Hongch'on, restricting activity to patrolling. Moreover, he was uneasy about the increasingly convoluted command chain on X Corps front. Using ROK forces for the principal manoeuvre, Almond had reinforced these with mixed detachments of American artillery, armour, and infantry, controlled by representatives at corps headquarters. He had also posted several American battalions at what he assessed to be key points, but at a distance from their parent formations. Still, it is difficult for an army commander to interfere with

* This aircraft was not the second world war de Havilland fighter bomber of the same name, but a light single engined high-wing monoplane, intended for pilot training but taken into use to direct air-to-ground strikes and for artillery spotting.

† Major-General Bryant E Moore assumed command of IX Corps on 31st January 1951 in place of General Coulter.

a corps commander's arrangements without eroding confidence. A passing word of warning by the one to the other is probably the only means of correction unless the fault is gross. Thus the X Corps organisation remained in operation as night fell on 11th February.

That night, P'eng Te-huai opened his 'Fourth Phase Offensive'. It was hastily mounted, an operation for which he was far from ready. His troops were not fully rested; sick and wounded who had remained in their army areas were not yet fit for action. The lengthened supply line from China was frequently disrupted by enemy air attacks and thus the forward dumping programme for the spring offensive in course of preparation was incomplete. Shortage of supply was the principal reason why the movement south of a second army group had been delayed*. But the United Nations advance alarmed Mao, and Kim Il-sung needed no persuading to reactivate the advance. His own enterprise by II and V NKPA Corps in January had been launched without consulting his ally, and he had concealed its failure from them.

Mao instructed P'eng on 28th January to destroy twenty to thirty thousand Americans and South Koreans while advancing to occupy the region immediately north of the line Taejon—Andong. Thus the Forty Second, Thirty Ninth, Fortieth, and Sixty Sixth were ordered to make ready. On their eastern flank, the North Korean V Corps, reinforced but reduced to three divisions was to cooperate. The III Corps in rear was ordered to come into the line. These formations totalled 160,000 in all[5].

Between 8.30 and 9 pm on the evening of the 11th February, three Chinese divisions struck the regiments of the 8th ROK Division occupying a rough semicircle about seven miles west and north of Hoengsong. The assaults were well coordinated in time and direction—they had been cunningly reconnoitred two days previously—a remarkable achievement considering that the assailants were from three different armies. The ROK forces were taken by surprise, the majority of their positions overwhelmed in the course of an hour and a half. Those members of the 8th ROK who could do so escaped down the mountain sides towards Hoensong, leaving all their heavy weapons, ammunition, and equipment in place†.

The Chinese swept on in parallel to the road systems. Some began to attack the ROK and American artillery positions in rear. The weakness of General Almond's eccentric chain of command was now exposed. The American support forces—artillery protected by infantry—and teams—principally armoured detachments—all subordinated, as noted, to corps

---

* Another reason was the huge reinforcement needed. Shung's army group lost over 45,000 men in their brief struggle against X Corps round the reservoirs in north east Korea during November and December, 1950.

† The 8th ROK, effectively destroyed in this action, lost 9,844 officers and men.

headquarters did not receive the timely direction which would have been available to them from the local commander at Hoengsong. They were held forward too long. When brought under fire, some elements broke away at once. But the majority bound together, fighting their way out on the 12th under determined leaders to reach Hoengsong.

For a period of hours during that day, General Almond rationalised the chain of command, recovered the 3rd ROK Division on his eastern flank under heavy pressure from Chinese to the north and the NKPA V Corps, and boldly drew in forces to close up his defences. During the night of the 12th February, those withdrawing from Hoensong were moving back to the Wonju area, protected by the Netherlands battalion who had fought steadfastly throughout this period*. The approaches to Wonju were strengthened but west and east to the boundaries of the flanking corps there were considerable gaps in an inverted line stretched over 40 miles. With a view to shortening it, Almond decided to pull back from Chip'yong-ni to the upper reaches of the Han river close to Yoju.

This did not suit General Ridgway. He was not prepared to abandon Chip'yong-ni, an important road junction; its possession would open development options to the Chinese command. But the maintenance of this outpost required a blocking force in rear, preferably east of Yoju. Since Chip'yong-ni would not be held with less than a reinforced regimental group, Almond had nothing to offer. However, IX Corps had located the 27th British Commonwealth Brigade in the Yoju area and had the 6th ROK Division to hand. Both formations and the town of Yoju were passed to X Corps command.

Following withdrawal south of the Han River early in January, the 27th Brigade had come to a halt on Line D about 12 miles south of the town of Ich'on. They remained under command of the United States 24th Division and were allotted the left forward portion, some 8,000 yards, of the divisional line. The 6th ROK were immediately to the west, 'under strength and ill equipped, and due to lack of transport...a tired division having had to undertake many long marches...'[6]. The Brigade knew well what it was like to be short of transport; they had no second line vehicles† of their own. They were seriously also under strength, lacking their own artillery and engineer support, ordnance stores and workshops. But they had a fine spirit, as all visitors agreed; and like good soldiers immediately

---

* At one time, the Chinese penetrated to their command post but were ejected in close fighting led by their commanding officer, Lieutenant-Colonel M P A den Ouden, who was subsequently killed.

† First line vehicles are those established within units. Infantry battalions have none to move their principal fighting elements, the rifle companies. Second line vehicles are required by a formation such as a brigade to lift these troops, to collect and deliver supplies including petrol, oil lubricants and ammunition. Throughout the campaign, 27 Brigade had to rely on temporary allocations of United States transport for these purposes. See also Volume I, p 128.

began to patrol vigorously as soon as they had settled in, so much so that the 24th Division asked them why they were so active[7].

Even so, they began to take precautions for, and expected, further withdrawal when a reconnaissance party was ordered to Line E on 7th January. The only route to the south exclusively within the brigade sector was a mud track. A temporary thaw on the 7th revealed that it was impassable to all but an occasional jeep or light tracked vehicle. Most unit transport required forward—the F echelon*—was therefore ordered to concentrate behind the right flank positions, held by the Argylls†, on a single track metalled road shared with their 24th Division neighbours. On this account, and because they had an American tank company in support, this was likely to be crowded if they were obliged to withdraw in contact with the enemy. Thus the A echelon settled with brigade headquarters about five miles behind the Argylls.

Like 29 Brigade, the battalions were also heavily committed in policing and assisting the long, packed columns of Korean civilians moving south. The persistence of these refugees suggested an advance by the enemy; indeed, a few Koreans speaking English warned that the Chinese were close behind them. But the 27 Brigade patrols, reconnoitring up to two miles beyond their positions, saw no enemy movement and were sceptical of alarmist reports from their neighbours, which included sightings of '200–300 enemy with camels at CS 8118 also dogs!...'[8].

As in I Corps, so in IX, General Ridgway's rebuke to the corps commanders on 7th January, led to deeper patrolling. On the right flank of 24th Division, Yoju was a focus of interest, on the left, Ich'on. 27 Brigade was ordered to patrol to this small town alternately with 5th Regimental Combat Team, their right hand neighbour in the divisional line. The task was passed to 3 RAR.

A reconnaissance patrol normally consists of two or three men, the smaller the better when the enemy is close. But Ich'on lay 13 miles north of the Australian positions. Over such a distance, a patrol required transport for mobility and sufficient fire power to fight its way out of an ambush. Colonel Ferguson, commanding officer of 3 RAR, began by sending out a rifle platoon, the first of which was struck mistakenly but

---

* Battalion transport was divided into echelons to minimise the risk of loss by enemy action. F echelon, mainly, but not exclusively, jeeps and light tracked carriers, comprised principally transport required for command, control, and liaison including radio vehicles. A echelon comprising transport for immediate operational and administrative support included 15-cwt trucks. B Echelon, mostly 3-ton trucks, carried the principal administrative resources, ammunition, rations, petrol, oil and lubricants, vehicle recovery, spare parts, stores and company baggage.

† The three batallions of the brigade were:
1st Battalion, The Middlesex Regiment (1 MX);
1st Battalion, The Argyll & Sutherland Highlanders (1 A&SH);
3rd Battalion, The Royal Australian Regiment (3 RAR).

without incurring casualties by a Royal Navy flight launched from *Theseus* on 14th January. The second laid an ambush on the northwestern outskirts of Ich'on on the night 16th/17th and caught a Chinese group moving in darkness. In the brief encounter, 15–20 of the enemy were killed or wounded. Remote from his battalion, the platoon commander, Lieutenant J M Church, wisely decided to withdraw as soon as the Chinese drew off. Just as well: as they scrambled into their transport nearby, a comprehensive attack was launched on the trenches they had vacated.

The news that X Corps had been attacked by, and had held, the two North Korean corps, taken with a series of minor contacts across their own front encouraged IX Corps to believe that the Chinese were scouting for an imminent offensive. As indicated, this was premature; P'eng did not receive his instructions from Mao until 28th January. The enemy with which 27 Brigade and other IX Corps patrols were skirmishing was a screen put out by 13 Army Group to cover its main line. When threatened at any point, the screen was reinforced.

By the third week in January, the western sector advance was being planned. Seeking more information, Colonel Ferguson established a patrol base on either side of the Seoul road north west out of Ich'on on 20th January with A Company Group*, including mortar support. At 6pm, a reconnaissance patrol under Lieutenant Angus McDonald was sent in the evening darkness to discover whether Magyo-ri, the next village along the road, was occupied by the enemy. It was not. But the patrol discovered, creeping up to and then into the village silently, found numerous empty trenches.

The reason why these were empty was that the occupants had departed with others, making several hundred in all, to attack A Company, observed taking up their positions in the late afternoon on the 20th. At 0100 in the bitingly cold morning air of the 21st January, the Chinese attacked. They failed to break in and drew off. The company commander, Captain B S O'Dowd, had orders to withdraw if engaged and gave instructions to move back to their vehicle harbour about 2 miles south of Ich'on. Before the company could do so, a second Chinese attack was launched. Covered in part by mortar fire, A Company managed to break contact, and to stay out of contact during the five mile march to the harbour area.

The main body reached this about 0300. Figures were seen to be closing from the north west. It was thought that they might be Lieutenant Church's platoon, the company rearguard, but soon others were reported closing from the west. They were all Chinese. A fire fight began. Closing,

---

* A rifle company of three platoons, equipped with light weapons, numbered at full strength 132. On occasion, it was reinforced with supporting detachments, for example, tanks, medium machine-guns, or mortars, when it became, in British military terminology, a 'company group'.

Church's numbers joined in, catching some of the enemy in the flank and rear, which caused them to draw back, some carrying off dead or wounded. Quickly assembled, the company group drove off taking their own casualties, one killed and two wounded. Five were missing: Lieutenant McDonald and his reconnaissance patrol[9].

As a result of this action, the divisional commander decided to patrol the Ich'on area with an American battalion group. The three battalions of 27 Brigade continued to patrol extensively across country. Those in the night defences suffered from a further run of very low temperatures, below 30 degrees Celsius on several nights. Different means of keeping warm while also secure were used by units. The Argylls installed small, screened fires in the sides of their trenches. The Middlesex, in reserve, were able to maintain several sheltered sites in each company area to which men were brought periodically from exposed posts.

In the last week of January, there were important operational changes for 27 Brigade. First, they celebrated the arrival of the 16th Field Artillery Regiment from New Zealand* under Lieutenant-Colonel J W Moodie RNZA on 21st January. It was to be a permanent member of their order of battle, a unit which they had long awaited. Second, it became apparent that the 2nd Battalion, Princess Patricia's Canadian Light Infantry—2 PPCLI—had been posted to the brigade, which they would join later in the month†. Of more immediate importance, the apprehension of withdrawal could finally be dismissed: IX Corps was moving forward in partnership with I Corps. The reconnaissance parties on Line E, 25 miles to the south, were recalled.

On 1st February, the brigade became a part of IX corps reserve, returning to the tiresome job of guarding corps headquarters, while also patrolling daily down the upper reaches of the Han river, the eastern boundary with X Corps. Occasionally they journeyed into X Corps territory to make contact with 23rd Regimental Combat Team and the French battalion at Chip'yong-ni. Yoju, long thought by 24th Division to be a Chinese stronghold, was discovered almost inadvertently by 3 RAR to be empty. Their headquarters moved into the town.

When General Ridgway passed 27 Brigade to X Corps command, on 13th February, therefore, the ground on which they were to operate was familiar. Units were, in any case, concentrating in the area to consolidate the inter-corps flank under the instructions of IX Corps

---

* By agreement among the Commonwealth participants, New Zealand had raised a field (originally conceived as a medium) artillery regiment, equipped with the British 25-pounder field gun in three batteries as its land force contribution to the United Nations Command. It was supported by a transport platoon of the Royal New Zealand Army Service Corps.

† This battalion had been posted originally to 29 Brigade but the low strength of 27 Brigade in January 1951 prompted its direction to the latter. See Chapter 3.

commander: the Argylls established a defensive position north east of Yoju and the Han from first light on 13th February, covered by patrols of the Middlesex and 3 RAR.

Reports from their own patrols during the first half of February, coupled with information that reports of a battle at Koksu-ri by American forces had been exaggerated, led the brigade commander and staff to conclude as the 13th passed that the Chinese attack into X Corps was being comfortably held. Directions from corps headquarters that evening to pass to X Corps command did not indicate that the corps line contained wide gaps. They were to operate under the 2nd United States Division whose representative would bring orders to Yoju at 0600 on the morning of the 14th. At midnight, however, there was a warning that Chip'yong-ni was under heavy attack.

The O Group* met under Lieutenant Colonel Man† at 0600 at 3 RAR headquarters in Yoju, 18 miles south of Chip'yong-ni. No one arrived from the 2nd Division until 0730, when, as the War Diary observed, 'it was the commanding officer of a neighbouring battalion and not a staff officer [from divisional headquarters] and no representative of 6th ROK Division [with whom they were expected to cooperate]'.

Misleading information was given that they were to move north to the crossroads at Chuam-ni to permit the withdrawal of 23 RCT and the French from Chip'yong-ni. No timings were available, and no transport was offered.

Colonel Man went off to make contact with the divisional staff by telephone. He learned that there was no question of a withdrawal from Chip'yong-ni. He was to move up the road indicated to open it for reinforcement and supply to the garrison as soon as possible. But in so far as his own movement was concerned, the division had only sufficient trucks available to lift one of his battalions. Ahead of him, an American detachment had been positioned to hold the cross roads at Chuam-ni, seven miles distant, roughly half way to Chip'yong-ni. The 6th ROK Division would come up on 27 Brigade's right to prevent any infiltration across country in that sector. The left flank remained open.

Colonel Man returned to the O Group, which he had directed to reassemble at the Argylls headquarters at Tangu-ri, astride Route 24. Three hours had passed since their first meeting. As they drew together, about a dozen American soldiers drove into the Argyll's positions, some wounded. They were the survivors of the detachment at Chuam-ni,

---

* In British military usage, the O Group consists of those who assemble to receive orders for an operation, usually the immediately subordinate commanders, those providing one or another form of support, and essential members of staff, where applicable.

† Commanding Officer of the Middlesex who was acting as brigade commander in the temporary absence of Brigadier Coad. Major R A Gwyn was in command of the Middlesex for this operation.

overwhelmed by Chinese forces in regimental strength earlier that morning*. Some part of the enemy was now in position on or south of these cross roads, a factor which caused the abandonment of plans for a motorised advance. Route 24 was narrow and followed a stream between heights to Chuam-ni. The lower hill slopes offered no ground for the attached company of American tanks to manoeuvre; an advance on a one tank front would make them vulnerable to close ambush by Chinese with light anti-tank weapons—mines, rocket launchers and satchel charges thrown from ditches on to engine louvres. The infantry must therefore lead and, since their transport was unarmoured, vulnerable to small arms fire, they would lead on foot, supported by direct fire from the tanks. The Middlesex would be brought forward to the Argylls' position, from which they would begin the advance to the crossroads. The transport would return to bring 3 RAR up behind them. The Argylls would remain in their positions. The New Zealand guns, and the attached company of American heavy mortars were deployed to cover the support the movement.

These orders were completed by 10 am. By sending advanced warning of the transport arrangements and bringing forward his own O Group to Tangu-ri, Major Gwyn had the Middlesex on the move at 1145. By 1 pm they had integrated with the American tank company and advanced a mile up Route 24. This was a fair pace as they were clearing the hills on foot as they advanced. Not long afterwards they observed figures active on a long hill, Point 112, to the right of the road. They were Chinese and not very attentive; some did not get under cover until fired upon.

Point 112 was a long, narrow hill running north to south. The Middlesex quickly secured a foothold aided by concentrations of shells and mortar bombs. Thereafter, along the high ridge the movement was confined on a narrow front which restricted the volume of covering fire for assault parties advancing in brief rushes. Two hours passed between first encounter to final possession of the hill. Evening approached. Major Gwyn was ordered to consolidate the battalion on 112 against probable night counter-attack.

During the struggle, Colonel Man had advanced 3 RAR to secure a height just to the rear of the Middlesex, to the west of Route 24. Guns and mortars, and the Vickers medium machine-guns registered defensive fire tasks in the two forward battalions. Captain John Shipster in the Middlesex position noted that 'the next few hours were spent in furious digging, distributing ammunition, and laying telephone cables. Except where the sun had melted the southern sides of the spurs, everything

* The 2nd Division Reconnaissance Company reinforced by a rifle company of the American 9 RCT. From attacks overnight, and in running the gauntlet during withdrawal on 14th February, this force lost 212, including 114 killed.

was still covered by snow. The moon was up and visibility was good'[10]. Throughout the night, the New Zealanders fired intermittently on roads and tracks leading into the brigade area to inhibit their use by an approaching enemy.

The moon set at 0400, when all units stood to arms. At 0510, the Middlesex came under mortar and machine-gun fire. They heard trumpets. Out of the darkness, waves of Chinese broke over their positions. 'The main attacks...fell on A and D Companies, who were at the northern end [of the hill]. The right flank platoon of the former was overrun after they had run out of ammunition—one section was temporarily taken prisoner while the remaining two sections managed to pull back into higher ground...there were many cases of hand to hand fighting....The [American] 4.2-inch mortar Forward Observation Officer's [radio] set had a grenade through it very early on, and the only means of communication we had with [A] Company was via the New Zealand FOO, Lieutenant Roxburgh, who put up a wonderful show throughout—shooting with one hand and working his set with the other[11].'

A and D Companies had been attacked, as the interrogation of prisoners later revealed, by a battalion of the Chinese 119th Division. While one regiment of this formation was engaged at Chip'yong-ni, another had marched down Route 24 to dispose of the American detachment at Chuam-ni. The assault on the Middlesex had cost it 65 dead and 14 prisoners-of-war. Chinese wounded had been removed by their comrades as they withdrew. The question for 27 Brigade was, where was the remainder of the enemy regiment?

The commander of 2nd Infantry Division, Major-General Clarke L Ruffner, had visited 27 Brigade headquarters in the latter part of 14th February to confirm that the object of his operations was to relieve, not to withdraw, the Chip'yong-ni garrison. He was disappointed that they had not reached Chuam-ni, having been informed by his staff that the British Commonwealth force had started at 0600 that morning. The causes of delay were made known to him. He confirmed that 27 Brigade's task was to clear Route 24 thoroughly to the positions of 23 RCT, then to take up defensive positions to the east, filling the gap in the line. The 6th ROK Division, which had not yet come forward, would extend the line to the east, as previously ordered.

Meantime, the most urgent requirement was to resupply Chip'yong-ni. General Ruffner had been given a task force to open—and to keep open—Route 24A, to the west of Route 24, behind which trucks and ambulances were being assembled. Task Force Crombez* comprised the 5th Cavalry Regiment—three infantry battalions—reinforced by two companies of

---

* Under Colonel Marcel G Crombez, commanding 5th Cavalry.

tanks, two battalions of artillery, and a platoon of field engineers. They expected to reach Chip'yong-ni on 15th February[12].

This advance was delayed almost immediately for some hours by a bridge demolition a few miles north of Yoju. About 0700 on 15th February the column was able to move on until, about 2 miles below Koksu-ri, it was held up by Chinese on either side of the road, principally on the higher ground to the east. The infantry began to clear these positions, an operation that extended to 1300. Apprehending that the enemy held the line of the road all the way to Chip'yong-ni, Colonel Crombez realised that steady clearance by infantry supported by armour, artillery, and air attack might take several days. He decided to force a passage with his tanks and, to support them against Chinese ambushes through the hill passes and villages, he mounted a rifle company on the tanks.

A brave but costly drive followed. The infantry dismounted several times to overcome Chinese road blocks. Sometimes the tanks thrust on without waiting for the infantry to remount. The tank column was also swept intermittently by small arms fire, killing and wounding the exposed infantrymen. Several tanks were lost to satchel charges and rocket launchers. But at 1715, Task Force Crombez entered Chip'yong-ni. It had lost 78 casualties, 71 of whom were infantry. Its appearance, however, sufficiently alarmed the Chinese to cause their withdrawal from the area by the morning of 16th February[13].

Meantime, 27 Brigade continued with its painstaking clearance of Route 24, overcoming height by height the remainder of the regiment opposing them, each battalion taking the lead in turn. In Chuam-ni, they found bodies of the American detachment killed in the onslaught there, some lying still in sleeping bags in which they had been surprised. A number of American and ROK prisoners, released by the Chinese who had abruptly pulled back out of contact, came into the brigade lines. On and around the hills, abandoned weapons and equipment were collected.

As P'eng Te-huai's Fourth Phase Offensive was opening, 29 Brigade was ordered forward as Army Reserve to Kumnyangjang-ni, between General Milburn's I Corps and General Moore's IX. But within a matter of hours, General Milburn had persuaded the army commander to release it to his command.

The brigade thus joined the drive against the enemy forces in an enclave to the east of Seoul held by P'eng Te-huai's Thirty Eighth Army, and part of the North Korean I Corps*. The ground was well chosen for defence: it rose steeply to long jagged ridges on either side of Routes 13

---

* As a part of the redeployment for the Fourth Phase Offensive, the North Korean I Corps progressively replaced the Chinese Fiftieth Army in the line in the western sector. The NKPA 8th Division, which had lost the better part of a regiment in an ill-judged counter-attack at Kwangju on 14th February, was in line opposing the United States 3rd Infantry Division and 1 RUR.

and 7, the principal roads leading north. On these heights, and on the spurs covering the roads, a division of the Thirty Eighth was dug in, well supplied with ammunition, and ordered to hold the United Nations forces while the Fourth Phase Offensive developed through Chip'yong-ni and Hoensong. Its weakness was a lack of supporting weapons, which were confined to mortars.

When the change of orders arrived to move into the line, the brigade was beginning its move to Kumnyangjang-ni. The vehicle columns thus passed on through this ruined town, still burning after an earlier battle. In the blackened cells of the police station, the charred body of a prisoner clung still to the bars through which he had vainly sought to escape. Fifteen miles to the north, after a slow journey in dense traffic moving up and back, units reached the positions of the 5th Cavalry, moving towards its commitment at Chip'yong-ni, and completed their relief by noon on 12th February.

They found themselves holding an awkward angle of the line. On the left, the Royal Ulster Rifles were in touch with the United States 3rd Infantry Division. Two thousand yards distant, south south-east, the Royal Northumberland Fusiliers held the centre. Almost 2,000 yards again to the south east, the Glosters on the right flank were in touch with the United States 1st Cavalry Division. The line was thus stretched to breaking point. An advance by 29 Bde had to wait upon the movement forward of 1st Cavalry. Meantime, the three battalions, the armour, artillery, and engineers engaged in local enterprises.

Preparations for living away from vehicles in the mountain were now rewarded. The Ulster Rifles were the most remote, occupying a huge feature marked by two high points, 401 and 415, 4,000 yards from the nearest motorable track. They could only be supplied across country by porters, a burden which required all their Koreans and B Company, held back for this task. Major G P Rickord, the battalion second-in-command*, and headquarters company commander, Captain K Neely, casting about for some means of improving the system, found a footpath over the intervening hill mass.

> By dint of much spade work through the night...the new route was opened to traffic about midday on the 14th. The first loaded jeeps...set off up the track to try it out. The climb up from the south was relatively easy, as the hairpin bends and steep rough, gradients were free from snow. At the top, on a level saddle about 20 yards long, they were stopped by Captain Neely, who had established a control point with wireless... From this point, the track fell steeply into the Oyaso valley, winding dizzily down the mountainside with a gradient in places of about one in three. Although the Sappers† had

* Successor to Major C A H B Blake, killed while commanding the battalion in the previous month. See Volume I, Chapter 16.

† Field engineers of 55 Squadron, Royal Engineers.

> scattered pine branches on the snow, the surface was packed hard and almost as slippery as solid ice. At the steepest point, a dozen porters under Colour-Sergeant Sturgeon stood by.
> ...going down was simple but terrifying. The jeep was started in four wheel drive and in bottom gear, and eased gently on to the slope—both passenger and driver ready to 'bale out' in a flash if necessary; as speed increased, the use of brakes was impossible, but on the steepest part of the gradient, the porter party flung themselves at the sliding jeep, dug in their heels, and braked it safely down the slope[14].

It was better than humping. The rifle companies on 401 and 415, together with Lieutenant-Colonel Carson's tactical headquarters in their midst, were more confident that they would not run out of ammunition if, as expected, the enemy attacked. For although the Chinese had withdrawn beyond the range of the Rifles' initial reconnaissance—a mile or so forward—they were patrolling around their positions by night, perhaps seeking to draw fire to identify company locations or, aware of some change among the United Nations troops in this locality, to capture a prisoner for identification. The Rifles responded to these incursions with their own mortars and the shells of 45 Field Regiment, reserving their small arms.

There were occasional minor clashes by day. Sergeant Kennedy took three men of C Company down the hillside to investigate a little feature—nicknamed Slag Heap Hill—just to the east of Route 13. Closing, the sergeant dropped off Rifleman Lyons to watch their backs and, a little further on, posted Rifleman Smith with a signal pistol. This was to be fired if Sergeant Kennedy and the fourth man, Rifleman Platts, met the enemy. A signal flare fired would bring machine-gun and artillery fire down immediately; the weapons were laid on the targets in readiness.

While still on the move, Sergeant Kennedy was surprised to hear the signal flare shoot up. Looking back, he discovered the explanation: about a dozen armed men in Korean civilian clothing had surrounded Lyons. Friendly fire now began to fall on Slag Heap Hill, isolating Kennedy and Platts. They were obliged to move north to take shelter in the river bed. Both were delighted to be identified by a Mosquito spotter aircraft, but as this disappeared they were surrounded by six North Korean soldiers.

Sergeant Kennedy expected to be shot; the United Nations Command had ample evidence since their first encounters during the previous summer that this was common practice in the North Korean People's Army*. But the two captives were identified as British soldiers, as distinct from Americans, the foremost objects of hatred propagated by the political officers of the NKPA, and this seemed to weigh in their favour.

---

* But see Volume I, p 345

After a short pause, while aircraft attacked the hills above them, the North Koreans moved away, signifying that Kennedy and Platts were free. Next day, Koreans brought in news that Rifleman Smith, wounded, was nearby. A stretcher party brought him in* [15].

The Rifles' Battle Patrol† had an encounter with a small group of North Koreans on the same day, 15th February, who had come down into a Korean village demanding breakfast. They killed two NKPA officers and four soldiers, and captured a medical officer, but lost their commander, Captain G W H Cocksedge, who was seriously wounded[16].

Meanwhile the Northumberland Fusiliers and the Glosters, having extended their positions, awaited the movement forward of 1st Cavalry Division. Chinese patrols entered their localities from the night of 12th February onwards. A Company of the Glosters had a sharp minor battle that night, holding their fire until the enemy were within sight at a few yards range, killing 11 and capturing 2. These enemy parties had come from the eastern side of Route 13; for neither the Fusiliers nor the Glosters patrols found any positions within a mile of their own. Lieutenant-Colonel Carne, commanding officer of the Glosters, decided to encroach a mile or so north east to cover the road and stream junction below his anticipated objective, Hill 327. He cleared this with his own C Company and C Squadron of the 8th Hussars‡ on the 13th and at once moved the greater part of the battalion forward[17].

The Glosters were now ready to attack Hill 327 on 14th February, but the enemy decided otherwise. During the night 13th/14th, the Chinese attacked the left flank of 1st Cavalry Division, running in almost to the edge of the Glosters headquarters, which lost several men from mortar fire. The foremost Cavalry flank positions were driven out. This late setback brought I Corps commander to the site next morning. Fighting was continuing and, satisfying himself that the Glosters were holding firm, General Milburn moved along Route 13 on foot, collecting several groups of stragglers personally, and sending them back to their positions[18]. By this time, defensive fire was swelling. The hill mass immediately topped by Point 350, immediately to the right of 29 Brigade's eastern boundary, was wholly recovered, but the event retarded reliefs

---

* Less fortunate, Rifleman Lyons was retained as a prisoner, and did not return home until 1953.

† The anti-tank platoon of 1 RUR had been converted to a quick reaction force under this title. Using various sources of manpower, some infantry battalion commanders favoured such an organisation as an immediate reserve during the second world war.

‡ The 8th Hussars—8H—was the armoured regiment in the brigade. It was equipped with the excellent Centurion tank which some believed was too cumbersome for use in the narrow Korean valleys and too heavy for the bridges. On appointment to command, Lieutenant-Colonel Sir William Lowther insisted that his force would operate wherever the brigade was required, a promise he kept to the full. The British term 'regiment' in this connexion signified a unit of battalion size.

and rearrangements—the United States 25th Division was relieving 1st Cavalry Division. The capture of Hill 327 was finally fixed for 16th February.

Point 327 was the southernmost height on a mountain running due north for about a mile and a half with several high points along the ridge and spurs projecting on either side. Behind it lay two more mountains, topped respectively by Points 454, 596, and 535. Brigadier Brodie's orders were to clear these, together with the high ground to the west of Route 13, to complete the advance to the Han river in the sector.

The Glosters were to capture the whole feature topped by Hill 327, with abundant fire support from the following sources:

three batteries, 45 Field Regiment*	— 24 x 25 pounders
three troops, 170 Battery	— 18 x 4.2-inch mortars
mortar platoons, 1 Glosters *and* 1 Northumberland Fusiliers	— 12 x 3-inch mortars

and by the direct fire of 18 Centurion tanks of C Squadron, 8th Hussars. The observation posts of all three battalions had identified positions on the entire feature, but some were thought to be unoccupied, possibly dummy positions. When the attack began, the Royal Ulster Rifles were to block the road in the area of Slag Heap Hill[19].

Colonel Carne chose to capture Point 327 at the outset, launching C Company almost directly at it, with D Company from due west. The slopes were steep and scrub covered. The assault parties reached the 200 metre contour line after an hour, pausing there to coordinate the final ascent. Conscious that he had strayed to the north on a flank march through deep scrub, Major W A Wood closed D Company towards C, though the latter were out of sight. Warned by the fire controllers with both companies that they were moving on, guns and mortars lifted their fire and the infantry scrambled up the final slope, in places approaching the vertical.

However weighty and excellent the supporting fire, infantry in attack come at some point to the exacting work of closing with the enemy to fight through his defences. If the Glosters needed a reminder of this, grenades came bouncing down the the slopes upon them.

Major C E B Walwyn's C Company had been so directed as to approach Point 327 from the south west and thus immediately behind

---

* The regiment was the organic artillery unit of the brigade. Its commanding officer was also the coordinator of artillery support for the brigade commander, comprehending that of 170 Independent Light Battery, and external support from US artillery.
As with 8H, the British designation 'regiment' signified here a unit of battalion size.

the height. The hillside screened them from the southern and eastern defences but about a dozen groups entrenched to the rear began firing directly at them. Major Walwyn was wounded as the leading platoons closed, and the command fell temporarily to Second-Lieutenant Peter Ware. Adjusting his inner flank to C Company, Major Wood closed forcefully with the Chinese positions behind the high point. By 1300, both companies were on and around 327.

Colonel Carne followed his leading companies closely. With him came Captain R S Mardell, the second-in-command of C Company, hotfoot from the company base. Anxious to enter the battle, he was armed only with a pistol and carried in his hand a millboard and papers relating to company supply, a task he had in hand when the news of Major Walwyn's incapacitation was received. Soon those watching in battalion headquarters saw him among the leading assault parties, directing them with waves of his millboard as they wheeled to clear the eastern end of Point 327. Major Wood, meantime, having evacuated D Company's wounded turned north to capture the next feature on the mountain.

No fire was opened as they approached. The positions were deserted, and similarly those to the north above Slag Heap Hill. They were occupied by B and D Companies during the afternoon.

'Well done, Fred!' Brigadier Brodie commented to the Glosters' commanding officer on the battalion radio net, abandoning, as he was apt to do, the normal discipline of signalling phraseology[20]. The operation had ended satisfactorily, with the important secondary advantage of opening a less adventurous route to the forward companies of the Royal Ulster Rifles. Fifty-seven Chinese had been killed, 2 wounded and captured. Other wounded had been carried off by the remainder of the Chinese defence, a weak battalion, which withdrew 6,000 yards to the north. The Glosters' losses were 1 officer and 9 other ranks killed, 1 and 28 wounded*. The latter were patched up in the regimental aid post and carried off by ambulance to the advanced dressing station of 26 Field Ambulance. As night fell, 55 Squadron engineers were bridging a crater in Route 13, and sweeping the road and verges ahead for mines[21].

The advance to the Han was resumed on 17th February. It was now the turn of the Northumberland Fusiliers to abandon their vehicles as they cleared the mountains east of Route 13, relieving the United States 3rd Division in this sector as they did so. For three days, they moved forward across the snow which, melting by day, freezing again at night, made movement difficult. Each evening they dug defences, patrolled, and watched for the porters bringing the evening meal and breakfast rations. But for all their diligence, and despite prompting occasional bursts of

* In addition, the forward observation parties of 70 Battery lost 1 killed and 3 wounded. These were immediately replaced in the middle of the action.

enemy mortar and machine gun fire, they found no enemy, though there were many traces in abandoned positions as they moved from height to height. A few prisoners were taken, mostly stragglers left behind in error, hungry and unhappy men. Below them, a mobile patrol of the 8th Hussars, pushing through the valley, successfully intercepted a group of soldiers from the North Korean 15th Division on the southern bank of the Han.

As the western heights of Route 13 were cleared, the Royal Ulster Rifles cleared the slopes on either side of the valley in through which it ran. To the east, the United States 24th Regiment was cooperating along the ridge line through the massive feature topped by Point 630. Observation and, subsequently, fire confirmed that the rear slopes and spurs of the mountain were heavily occupied.

The Royal Ulster Rifles closing to attack these localities on 20th February came under heavy machine-gun and mortar fire, to which a substantial part of the brigade's weapons responded:

Two troops of 8H Centurions with their 8 x 20-pounder guns.

Four troops of C Squadron, 7 R Tks Churchills with 16 x 17-pounder guns.

Two troops of the 11th (Sphinx) Light Anti-Aircraft with 16 x Bofors.

Medium machine-gun platoon, 6 Vickers, 1 RUR.

3-inch mortar platoon, 6 x 3-inch mortars, 1 RUR.

Twelve 4.2-inch mortars, 170 Light Battery.

All but the last two were firing directly at the targets. The mortars were able to fire effectively due to their high trajectory but the lie of the mountain ridges and spurs sheltered the Chinese positions from the fire of 45 Field Regiment. Perched on the hillside as three companies of the battalion ascended, it was difficult to coordinate these sources, and a fire control centre was established on the valley floor by Major Rickord, to whom the adjutant, Captain Hugh Hamill, sent instructions by radio[22]. To the north, at the valley exit, a diversionary force—a detachment of the 8th Hussars and the Rifles' Battle Patrol—were firing on their own observation.

Despite the accuracy—and preponderance in weight—of the fire returned, the determined and resourceful Chinese continued to resist, greatly aided by the broken ground, much of it scrub covered, much of it steep; some few positions even concealed in cliff faces. The enemy fire held back the advance to the ascent. Colonel Carson stood off his three companies until the Americans, somewhat to the rear, captured Point 630.

By the afternoon of the 21st, the Royal Ulster Rifles had reached the top of the main spur, where they formed a close perimeter for the night. With darkness, the air temperature fell abruptly. The American and British soldiers spent an uncomfortable night on the mountain. Porters, which included those of the Northumberland Fusiliers, did not reach the Rifles until 0300 on the 22nd. When they advanced again at 0700, the enemy had withdrawn. Heavy rain began to fall.

Route 13 was now open to the southern bank of the Han. Having completed their task, the brigade was thankful to be ordered to move back to Suwan, concentrated once more as I Corps reserve.

Preoccupied with operations, the Eighth Army had scarcely realised the change in its character. Under General Ridgway's careful leadership, it had held the enemy and then obliged Chinese and North Koreans to fall back across the entire front. Those who had not doubted their ability to meet and match the Communist forces, such as the two British and Commonwealth brigades, the Turkish Brigade, the French battalion at Chip'yong-ni, the Netherlands Battalion at Hoengsong, took the change as a matter of course. Many others who had doubted their ability to hold had risen admirably to the test of confrontation. A remnant was now shamed into accepting that the enemy was indeed vulnerable.

Settled in the Suwan area, 29 Brigade made themselves comfortable, aware that they could be returned to a place in the forward area at short notice. However, a Chinese pamphlet, picked up by 45 Field Regiment, made them wonder whether a new enemy had to be faced. Translated, it read,

> We are the girls of the Chinese Superior Race. We must endeavour to develop our civilisation and military technique. We must learn the art of fencing and early morning exercise. Do not hesitate to question whenever feeling in doubt. China is always hoping for the peace of the world despite Anglo-American invasion of Korea[23].

SOURCE NOTES: Chapter 2

1 AIR 20/8879—from report attached to First Sea Lord's Minute 347 of 20th February 1951.
2 Letter to General Lawton J Collins, Chief of Staff, United States Army, 3rd January 1951. Ridgway Papers, Fort Carlisle, Pennsylvania.
3 Radio GX-1-526 KGOO of 7 Jan 51. Eighth Army G3 file, January 1951, (USNARS, Suitland).
4 Eighth Army G-2 Estimate of Enemy Situation, 10 Feb 51 (USNARS, Suitland). See also Mossman, Billy C, *Ebb and Flow, November 1950-July 1951*, (second volume in the series, The United States Army in the Korean War (Washington,DC 1990) pp 264–65.
5 Hsü Yen, among others such as P'eng himself, provides an account of this, *op cit*, Chapter 2, Part 4, *Switching from rest and reorganisation to mobile defence, and exchanging space for time—the Fourth Campaign*.
6 27 Brigade War Diary, 7th January 1951.
7 *Ibid*, entry for 9th January 1951.
8 *Ibid*, 10th January 1951.
9 See Patrol Report attached to 3 RAR War Diary, 23rd January 1951. 27 Brigade War Diary for 21st and 22nd January 1951. Also O'Neill, *op cit*, pp 99–100, and p 542, which tells the story of their subsequent survival.
10 Colonel J N Shipster, *The Diehards in Korea* (Middlesex Regiment, 1979), p 55.
11 *Ibid.*
12 29 Brigade War Diary, 14th February 1951. Conversation, author with Colonel A M Man. Mossman, *op cit*, p 291.
13 See monograph by Martin Blumenson, *Task Force Crombez* held by the Office of the Chief of Military History, Washington, DC. Also Mossman, *op cit*, pp 291 and 296–300. For a Chinese account of the battle, see Hsü Yen, *op cit*, Chapter 2.
14 *The Royal Ulster Rifles in Korea*, (Belfast, 1953), pp 42–43.
15 See 29 Brigade War Diary, February 1951, and attached copy of 1 RUR patrol report.
16 1 RUR War Diary, 15th February 1951. Also *The Royal Ulster Rifles in Korea*, *cit*, p 44.
17 War Diaries, 1 NF and 1 GLOSTERS, 12th–15th February 1951.
18 The author witnessed this event.
19 29 Brigade Operation Order No 19, attached to War Diary, February 1951.
20 The author was with Brigadier Brodie at the time.
21 1 GLOSTERS and 29 Brigade War Diaries, 16th February 1951.
22 *The Royal Ulster Rifles in Korea*, *cit*, p 48.
23 29 Brigade Operations/Intelligence Summary No 31, enclosed with War Diary, February 1951.

CHAPTER 3

Mutatis mutandis

General Ridgway's corrrespondence with General Collins, the United States Chief of the Army Staff, and others in the Pentagon*, combined with reports of the successful reconnaissance in force in the third week of January passed back by General MacArthur, raised hopes in the capitals of the United Nations allies that the tide of misfortune had turned in Korea. Indeed, as the I and IX Corps line shifted forward in the following fortnight, and the ROK division on the east coast made a minor sortie across the 38th Parallel, an optimist in the State Department drafted a 'Tentative Plan for obtaining a Cease-Fire' based on the United Nations 'continuing its irresistible advance...'[1]. Though few were ready to believe that the Communist forces in Korea were about to be thrown back, there was sufficient confidence to consider a range of options which included negotiations for peace on equal political and military terms. Dean Rusk, Assistant Secretary of State for Far Eastern Affairs, offered the following to the Secretary of State in a memorandum on 11th February:

A. *To reinforce U.S. and U.N. forces sufficiently to unify all of Korea by force*—he concluded that this was not a viable option.

B. *To withdraw promptly, either with or without a pretext*—he rejected this on the grounds of political penalties.

C. *To resolve the Korean affair by bringing down the Peiping [Peking] regime through action against China*—there was no assurance that this could be accomplished.

D. *To maintain indefinitely a military stalemate in Korea*—a course to be avoided on the balance of political and military penalties.

E. *To accept a cease-fire along the lines of the December 1950 proposals and a modus vivendi in Korea providing for a phased withdrawal of all foreign troops from Korea*—the course best suited to the U.S. and U.N. interest under present circumstances[2].

Mr Rusk then considered policy to follow such a cease fire: the denial of reinforcements to either side; acceptance of the *status quo ante* 25th June 1950; assistance to the Republic of Korea. Discussion of other Far

---

* Location of the American Department of Defense.

Eastern questions with the People's Republic of China would be unavoidable. In any case, the United Nations Command should aim to recover the territory of the Republic of Korea, and establish sufficiently robust ROK forces to retain it, permitting the withdrawal of allied contingents. On reaching the 38th Parallel, they should pause *inter alia* to make a fresh strategic appreciation and diplomatic effort for peace; but the Parallel should not be sacrosanct for political or military purposes. The Good Offices Committee of the General Assembly should continue to seek agreement on terms for a cease fire.

At about the same time, Mr R H Scott, representative of the Foreign Office on the Chiefs of Staff Committee, an assistant under-secretary of state with extensive service in China, was presenting his own view of Chinese circumstances and intentions. Among several conclusions, he remarked that,

> ... The Chinese do not want war and discount the risk of it. But they are preparing in case they have made a miscalculation. The 'triumphant mood' to which you refer is an important element making for miscalculation; there is no doubt that they suffer from megalomania and overweening self-confidence. Their record—already somewhat glamorised—seems to them to show that nothing is impossible, nothing out of their reach. They have already prepared maps of East Asia showing for example Korea and Indo-China as satellite communist states in alliance with China...
>
> ... The American analysis of what is happening in China is wrong. They are not mere satellites of Moscow, the Chinese Government is firmly entrenched, the opposition is inconsiderable, and the Nationalists have no prospects. American tactics in dealings with the new China have likewise been wrong. They have strengthened the extremists and the pro-Russian element in China. They have given colour to the anti-western slogans and helped to whip up support for its programmes. They have frightened the small countries of South East Asia and helped the isolationists there. By ignoring the views of Asian nations the Americans are bringing about the downfall of the United Nations, an umbrella whose cover they have stretched to breaking point. The obvious reluctance of many western European countries to be dragged into Far Eastern commitments springs, not so much from sympathy for China, as from doubts about the quality of American leadership and political judgement...
>
> Yet the basic American strategy is probably right. The new China is a menace to the peace of Asia and a formidable ally of Russia in a bid for world domination, and it would be very unwise of us to allow our irritation at the stupidity of American tactics to blind us to this. Our analysis and our tactics have been right, but there is a risk that in pursuit of these tactics we may lose sight of the real nature of Chinese long-term intentions. The proper course, to my mind, is to pursue our policy of negotiation whilst recognising that even negotiation from strength, coupled with firmness and patience, may not stop the Chinese and that we face the alternatives of big sacrifices or stopping China by force. ...[3]

These two appreciations, overlapping but not coinciding in their objectives, revived discussion in Washington and London respectively concerning strategy. The opinions expressed in them reflected shifts in outlook which were the effects of the crisis—a crisis of impending defeat with very disagreeable consequences—through which the responsible ministers and officials had passed. For the first time an American policy was developing which took account of the realities of Communist China's power and glimpsed the possibility that the People's Republic was not a satellite of the Soviet Union. Robert Scott's paper—composed to address an inter-departmental matter—was widely read in the Foreign Office, in the defence ministries*, and by the Prime Minister. It exposed the arrogance of the view that the British were entirely right, the Americans wholly wrong in their respective China policies. It was not that Mr Rusk or Mr Scott induced a sudden revelation among superiors or colleagues; rather that each expressed what others had gradually been coming to recognise but had resisted due to longstanding pride or prejudice. All difficulties in negotiating a common position were not swept away as a consequence—the governments in Washington and London had, after all, matters of essential self interest to pursue, and initially there were British suspicions of American moderation[4]—but agreements on objectives and methods of attaining these were facilitated.

For example, the British were relieved to know that the United States, abandoning the extreme pessimism favouring withdrawal from Korea, would not be passing to the other extreme of an advance to the Yalu. Anxieties that the State Department, perhaps due to Republican pressure or indeed the majority of the Congress, might revert to immediate sanctions against China were dispelled†. The United States was reassured that Britain was not going to pursue peace with China at the expense of agreements made personally between Mr Truman and Mr Attlee. They obliged the Americans to look progressively at the significance of the 38th Parallel; and persuaded the British to draw back from declarations on this subject which would offer the Chinese valuable strategic intelligence.

At the outset of this process, unaware of ideas developing in Washington, the British Chiefs of Staff sent the following to Lord Tedder on 6th February:

---

* At that time, the British Ministry of Defence coordinated but conceded considerable autonomy to the three separate Service ministries: the Admiralty; the War Office; and the Air Ministry.

† The United states Chief of Naval Staff gave his view to the Joint Chiefs of Staff that a naval blockade of China's coastline, desirably with the support of the Royal Navy, would effectively reduce China's war potential including the ability to invade Taiwan, but it was agreed that this would apply only if the United Nations Command was forced out of Korea. (See Serial 000124P30 enclosure to JCS 2118/16 of 16 February 1951).

> ... 3. We conclude that in the present situation our policy should be based on:
>
> (a) If we are to achieve the object for which the United Nations forces went to Korea, it is essential to hold a position covering as great an area of the country as possible up to the 38th Parallel.
>
> (b) There is no military reason in view of latest developments why this should not be possible.
>
> (c) The best military line to hold is one of the 'southern waist' of Korea covering Seoul and Inch'on and thence following roughly the 38th Parallel. If this is accepted no question of a major crossing of the Parallel by our land forces arises.
>
> (d) If there is to be a cease fire involving the establishment of a demilitarised zone its southern boundary should run along the 'southern waist' line. ...
>
> 4. The extreme importance of ensuring that this time our policy is co-ordinated with that of the Americans before the question of a recrossing becomes actual, will be obvious to you. We are strongly opposed to crossing the 38th Parallel because we consider that if we do so the possibility of negotiating with the Chinese will be seriously prejudiced and at the same time they will lead to a repetition of the events that followed the original crossing...[5].

The Chiefs of Staff were arguing against crossing on both military and political grounds, as they had done in September, 1950[6]. Their political reasoning was flawed; China, as noted, would only come to the negotiating table when it was expedient, as indeed was the case for the United Nations allies. However, their military argument was sound; the more the Chinese were pushed back on their lines of communication, the stronger they would be. In the matter of the Parallel, they were preaching to the converted. Already, at the National Security Council Meeting on 30th January, General Collins had remarked that, even if a military opportunity offered itself for a return to North Korean territory, there seemed to be no advantage in going back there, a view supported by the State Department representatives.

Lord Tedder confirmed this in a response on 8th February,

> ... Bradley said they are expecting a major attack in the centre [the Fourth Phase Offensive] in the next few days. Once that had been disposed of, the intention was to establish a firm line, using the Han river (which after the thaw would help to establish a strong position). This line would not be related to the actual 38th Parallel but would in fact approximate to the latitude ... Once stabilised they propose to withdraw the South Korean divisions for re-equipment and intensive training with a view to their subsequently

> relieving U.N. forces. In the meantime forces from other U.N. nations who have voted and talked without fighting would be very acceptable...* [7]

The United States Government had by this time formally decided that, having regard to its NATO commitments, it could not send any further troops to Korea, other than replacements for casualties, together with certain support units, principally artillery. If more were required, they must be found by other nations[8]. Canada would be asked to send the brigade it had offered in 1950. Australia and New Zealand might be persuaded to add to their numbers in Korea†. Inadvertently, these requests were to lead to the formation of a Commonwealth division in Korea.

In the desperate days of July 1950, when it was anticipated that Australia, Britain, and New Zealand would be sending land as well as other forces to Korea, the United States Defense Secretary‡ suggested to Mr Menzies, the Australian Prime Minister, that 'the United Kingdom, Australian, and New Zealand contingents might ultimately form a British Commonwealth light division'[9], a view endorsed by Mr Menzies during a speech to the Congress on 1st August. By this date, Canada had agreed to send a land force in addition to her three destroyers and an air transport squadron already committed to the United Nations Command.

Even so, the problems of proceeding immediately to form a division were twofold. The first and most difficult was that a formation of this size demanded resources greater than most, if not all, the contributors believed they could spare, particularly in manpower. The regular forces in Australia, Canada, and New Zealand were small. Britain retained large forces manned principally by conscription but had many imperial commitments, with a rising requirement for NATO, and apprehended correctly that the greater share of the fighting, support and administrative elements would have to be found from the British Army. The second difficulty during the first weeks of the war was that Canada preferred the idea of a mixed division—the '1st United Nations Division' was a a title suggested in Ottawa—comprehending all the small contingents of brigade or battalion size promised by a dozen states in and outside the Commonwealth. Neither the Americans nor the other Commonwealth participants cared for this. In any case, all the other foreign units, except for the Belgians¶, used United States weapons and

---

* Dean Rusk confirmed his Government's position on 16th February at a regular briefing of ambassadors from those states with armed forces in Korea.

† Anxious not to impair plans for the defence of Europe, the State and Defense Departments decided not to ask any of their NATO allies for additional forces.

‡ Then Louis A Johnson.

¶ The Belgian Army retained the British arms and equipment it had received during the Second World War. The Belgian (and Luxembourg) battalion entered Korean operations on 31st January 1951.

equipment. Supply of mixed British and American items would have been complicated; maintaining the range of essential administrative support even more so.

Under pressure of events, the strong 29 Infantry Brigade Group had been despatched from the United Kingdom but preceded by the weak 27th Brigade from Hong Kong. As noted, it was convenient to reinforce the latter with the Australian contingent, 3rd Battalion, The Royal Australian Regiment, and later the Indian 60th Parachute Field Ambulance. The New Zealand 16th Field Regiment was a welcome and valuable increment. The 2nd Battalion, Princess Patricia's Canadian Light Infantry, embarked for Korea, the advanced element of the Canadian brigade group. In both Japan and Korea, the British Commonwealth Korean Base was developing under command of an Australian commander-in-chief, Lieutenant-General Sir Horace Robertson[10].

The gathering of some of these forces was subjected to stop and restart; as the United Nations Command advanced to the Yalu, expecting final victory in Korea before Christmas 1950, the whole process of reinforcing the United Nations command by forces in course of preparation, such as the balance of the Canadian brigade, was halted. Even so, on 15th November, General Robertson informed London, Melbourne, and Wellington,

> ... The Americans are so used to us managing our own affairs that they cannot understand our present piecemeal organisations and from the top down I get the feeling that they hope we will take over all our own affairs and organise British Commonwealth forces as one body. They already have so many small and odd units from various other nations that they are embarrassed in fixing a chain of command in the field...[11]

It is quite possible that this idea was raised by General Robertson with the American command on his own initiative; he had earlier remarked to Brigadier Brodie, commander of 29 Brigade, on the untidy and wasteful organisation imposed upon them[12]. Energetic, insistent on professional high standards, he was irked by these circumstances. He was also a showman, ever restless to demonstrate his presence and importance. Whatever the origin of the representation, there were several strong reasons for the formation of a Commonwealth division in Korea.

The first was operational control. The two brigades tended to be committed to tasks at short notice and with inadequate orders. This was particularly true for 27 Brigade which was kept too long in the line and badly served by indifferent American staff work[13] of the sort criticised by General Ridgway at the time*. Within a Commonwealth parent division

---

* See p 88

it would have been rested at regular intervals by rotation of forces. Repeated staff errors would have been corrected by complaint to the divisional commander or his principal staff officer, a remedy more readily adopted in the Commonwealth system than that of the United States Army.

Another reason was that resources were not being used economically. As earlier remarked, for the greater part of its service in Korea, 27 Brigade was dependent on American troop carrying transport for its operational moves, and rarely satisfied. For many months, its supply chain was ad hoc. 29 Brigade had a full range of supporting and administrative units and much more. Because it was so distant from a main base, it had been necessary to send with it a slice of the services—reinforcement agencies, medical, storeholding, recovery and repair—found customarily within a division, corps, and army in the field. Moreover, because these service units were themselves isolated, many carried additional numbers to provide for their domestic needs. A division of three brigades would have been operating with twice, not thrice their total.

Still, the British War Office, anxious to avoid additional commitments of any kind, did not favour the formation of a division. Following General Robertson's representation, the Director of Military Operations sent a memorandum on 20th November to his colleague, the Director of Staff Duties, which included the following observations,

> ... It had always been intended that 27 Infantry Brigade less the Australian battalion would leave Korea as soon as 29 Brigade Group arrived. In view of the Chinese intervention, we have put 27 Brigade at the disposal of General MacArthur until he can spare it. He knows that we want them back [in Hong Kong] as soon as possible.
>
> Commander-in-Chief, British Commonwealth Occupation Force* has now suggested that a Commonwealth Division is formed. The argument...is based on the assumption that 27 Brigade remain in Korea. The necessity for a Divisional Headquarters is, therefore, examined under two headings:
>
> (a) If 27 Infantry Brigade is withdrawn shortly from Korea.
>
> (b) If 27 Infantry Brigade remains in Korea.
>
> On the assumption that 27 Infantry Brigade is shortly withdrawn, the Commonwealth troops [remaining] in Korea would consist of three United Kingdom infantry battalions, one Australian and one Canadian infantry battalion, a United Kingdom armoured regiment, one United Kingdom and one New Zealand field regiment, an Indian field ambulance and other ancillary arms. This force would have its own supporting arms and be self-

* The Force was the Australian residuum of British Commonwealth troops contributing to the allied occupation of Japan post 1945. On this nucleus, the British Commonwealth Base for Korea was to develop. See Volume I, p 322.

> contained administratively. It is for consideration whether a single Brigade Headquarters is capable of commanding a force of this size or whether a second Brigade Headquarters is necessary—the whole force being grouped under a Major-General with a modified Divisional Headquarters.
>
> If a Commonwealth divisional organisation should be formed, it will be even more difficult to withdraw 27 Infantry Brigade than it is now. Furthermore, the conception of a Commonwealth Division, if accepted, will most likely lead to requests for additional supporting arms and administrative overheads which it would be most difficult to provide.
>
> ... If 27 Infantry Brigade is to remain for more than a short time in Korea, there are operational reasons and those of prestige, as well as administrative convenience, for grouping the two British Brigades under one headquarters.
>
> ... meantime, an examination should be made in the War Office to determine the minimum size of the headquarters required for this purpose, and what would be the 'bill' for additional supporting arms and services[14].

This proposal was shelved during the crises of December and the first part of January, which further delayed 27 Brigade's departure. By the beginning of 1951, casualties, and the need to give its officers and men leave on the same basis as all others in the theatre, reduced the numbers available for operations.

Under the British system, a soldier evacuated with wounds or sickness remained on his unit's strength for 21 days, normally a sensible economy; a number of these casualties would be treated within the Army area and returned within that time. Although a twenty second day of absence triggered the despatch of a replacement, the process of issuing orders, selection, and travel forward meant that four or five weeks would have passed before the newcomer arrived to fill the vacancy. 29 Brigade, on full war establishment*, could bear this deficit. In any case, it had a pool of replacements in Japan. 27 Brigade could not call upon its base, Hong Kong, where infantry were acutely short, or elsewhere in the Far East due to the claims of counter-guerrilla operations in Malaya, to make good further losses. To ease the immediate difficulties, Brigadier Brodie agreed that the 29 Brigade pool should also be drawn upon by the Middlesex and Argylls. But this arrangement could not compensate for the numbers due for leave, 90† at a time which, with an inevitable overlap for movement, involved an absence of 180, almost a company in each

---

* The infantry battalions of 29 Brigade were each established at 38 officers and 945 other ranks. Those of 27 Brigade (1MX and 1 A&SH) were on a special establishment of 27 officers and 618 other ranks. A draft from Germany and the United Kingdom in September 1950 raised their numbers by about 150 each. See Volume I, p 128 and footnote, and p 180.

† Of this total, 40 leave vacancies were given to married officers and soldiers with families in Hong Kong every 14 days, 50 to others for leave in Japan. Leave began in November 1950. These vacancies were sufficient to permit only half the brigade to take leave during the following four months.

British battalion. The War Office drafted 264 officers and soldiers by air to 27 Brigade from the United Kingdom to ensure that the leave scheme continued and expanded* [15].

The draft, together with those from the 29 Brigade pool, substantially overposted 27 Brigade as it resumed operations with IX Corps on the central front in the latter part of January. Brigadier Coad was therefore surprised when General Robertson proposed a radical reorganisation of his force during the fourth week in January. The Australians and the Canadian battalion, 2 PPCLI, then coming to the end of battle training in Korea, each numbered about 1,000 all ranks. He planned to post the latter to 27 Brigade, and to form one strong British batttalion within it by combining the Middlesex and Argylls. Those in excess of the requirement would be posted to Taegu to rest and protect the British administrative base elements in that location[16].

Brigadier Coad knew that formation of a composite unit would strike hard at the strong regimental spirit in each battalion. Such an amalgamation had taken place for short periods in past wars following extraordinary losses, but this did not obtain in Korea in January 1951, and as there was no sign of 27 Brigade's relief it might continue for weeks if not months. The idea was similarly unacceptable in London. Field Marshal Slim, Chief of the Imperial General Staff, sent a personal response on 31st January. Concerning the posting of 2 PPCLI to 27 rather than 29 Brigade, the Chiefs of Staff believed this was a matter for General Robertson's judgement and within his powers. As regards the formation of a composite battalion, however,

> We are not happy about the proposal to loan one company of the Argylls to the Middlesex and vice-versa, except for a specific operation and as a temporary expedient. Its adoption permanently would result in the Argylls and Middlesex never being together as battalions in 27 Brigade again, and this would not only be most unfortunate in view of the great reputation that they have established together but would seem to present administrative difficulties to the commanding officers concerned.
>
> ... In short, while we are delighted at the prospect of Commonwealth forces serving in either of the United Kingdom brigades as you direct, we hope that you may be able to avoid juggling with companies of the Argylls and Middlesex. We cannot on any account agree to any measure which suggests the amalgamation of A & SH and Mx into one unit[17].

It is difficult to know why General Robertson pressed his plan. Air Vice-Marshal Bouchier, representative of the British Chiefs of Staff to General MacArthur, believed he had it in mind to reduce the British

---

* The draft was flown to Singapore by RAF Transport Command, and then transported to Korea in HMS *Unicorn*, the aircraft maintenance carrier.

element in 27 Brigade with a view to bringing in an Australian brigade commander when Brigadier Coad's term expired[18], but this was supposition. It is more likely that, frustrated in his wish to see a Commonwealth division in the field, he hoped to force the British hand by building up a second largely Commonwealth brigade which would reduce pressure to return it to Hong Kong. Whatever his motives, the two battalions retained their identity, the Taegu Commonwealth base defences were not reinforced—without the least consequence—and 27 Brigade acquired a fourth battalion, 2 PPCLI. But within the package of reorganisation discussed in late January, General Robertson succeeded in changing War Office policy in one not unimportant particular. On 5th January, the Director of Staff Duties announced that all five British battalions in Korea would be maintained at a common level of 780, a figure which would have detracted significantly from the operational capability of 29 Brigade, committed to a long tour in Korea, without helping the overposted battalions of 27 Brigade surely approaching the end of their term. The CIGS accepted General Robertson's representation to cancel this scheme[19]. He also adopted the recommendation that a tour in Korea should not exceed one year—'one winter was quite enough' in Field Marshal Slim's view[20].

By chance, as these matters were settled, the Canadian Government announced on 21st February that it would be sending the 25th Infantry Brigade Group to Korea to join 2 PPCLI[21]. By then, largely due to Australian intervention in Ottawa, the Canadian objections to serving within a Commonwealth force had been overcome. This news fired the enthusiasm of the Commonwealth Relations Office. One of its under-secretaries, Mr J J S Garner*, wrote on 2nd March to the Vice-Chief of the Imperial General Staff,

> ... An integrated division comprising Canadian, Australian, New Zealand and possibly Indian units, besides those from the United Kingdom, would most powerfully demonstrate to world opinion the capacity of the Commonwealth to act in concert in time of need. ...[22]

With this, the Foreign Office agreed. The War Office was not dismissive, foreseeing the opportunity to form a two brigade division and thus recover 27 Brigade[23]. By this time, however, the CIGS believed that withdrawal of 27 Brigade without replacement, just as the United Nations Command needed every assistance to develop its counter-offensive, would set a poor example in the alliance[24]. Unless General MacArthur was prepared to release it, therefore, without qualification, the War Office would have to provide a relief. On 12th March, he signalled General

* Garner, (John Joseph) Saville (later, Baron, of Chiddingly) (1908–1983)

Robertson to discover General MacArthur's views[25]. They were expressed in these words:

> ... I comprehend entirely the critical pressure which exists to reconstitute a [British] strategic reserve and I basically feel that each nation completely controls the privilege of withdrawal of its forces from the United Nations Command when it deems necessary and appropriate. I would be recreant to realities however if I did not say that the command in Korea is woefully outnumbered and fighting under the severest handicaps and hazards. Its needs and necessity is for reinforcement and steps to the contrary would not fail to increase its difficulties and jeopardy...[26]

'Although he leaves the door open to their immediate withdrawal I suggest [General MacArthur's] views are expressed in such a manner as to make it impossible for us to do this,' the Director of Military Operations wrote to the CIGS on 19th March.

> We are therefore faced with two possible alternatives:
>
> (a) To postpone a decision for a further two months as suggested by General Robertson...[27]
>
> (b) To take immediate action to relieve 27 Bde by other units.
>
> I consider that any further delay in reaching a decision on 27 Bde is unsatisfactory. We have been continuously postponing it for so long... Plans for [relief] are already under examination.
>
> You will note that General MacArthur strongly supports the formation of a Commonwealth division. If we are to have two British brigades remaining for any length of time the need for a division is all the greater. The implications are now being examined in some detail. A relative statement of requirements for a two-brigade and a three-brigade division is at Encl. A. A meeting has been held with Commonwealth representatives who, with the exception of New Zealand*, hold out *no* hope of any assistance being given towards these requirements. ... The indefinite retention of a second British brigade in Korea and the formation of a Commonwealth division will therefore have grave repercussions on our plans for a strategic reserve...[28]

The CIGS wrote on the base of the minute,

> Yes, we must resign ourselves to two brigades in Korea for some time, I fear. Proceed at once with arrangements to relieve units of 27 Brigade, which should go back to Hong Kong. Later if possible we will bring them, or two other battalions, home.

The plans 'under examination' provided for relief by 28 Brigade headquarters and two battalions in Hong Kong, 1st Battalion, The King's

* New Zealand agreed to send a general transport company of the Royal New Zealand Army Service Corps as a contribution to divisional troops.

Shropshire Light Infantry, and 1st Battalion, the King's Own Scottish Borderers*. This force was to take the field within six weeks.

From the third week in March then, the War Office, the Colonial Office, the Commonwealth Relations Office, and to a minor extent the Foreign Office, developed arrangements for the formation of a Commonwealth Division of three brigades. The War Office was obliged to find men and equipment for the additional units to be formed—a divisional headquarters, for example—and drafted, and consulting its Commonwealth partners for agreement in principle to formation of the division[29]. Arrangements had to be made with the Commander-in-Chief, Far East Land Forces, concerning the temporary reduction in the strength of the Hong Kong garrison; 28 Brigade would have to move to Korea before 27 Brigade returned. General Robertson had to be informed of developments—he made an immediate representation that 27 Brigade should not be replaced by a new formation, and the reasons for change had to be explained[30]. A proposal for the formation of the division had to be drafted for the Defence Committee of the Cabinet[31]. The Commonwealth Relations and Colonial Offices carried forward formal proposals to the Commonwealth governments, including South Africa, India, and Pakistan; and to the Hong Kong Government, which protested at the exchange arrangements. This work continued into April. The aim was to form the division in July.

Meantime, the Directors of Staff Duties and Manpower Planning had to begin work on another, connected, task: the replacement of 29 Brigade by the end of 1951. Although, in March, this was a comparatively distant requirement, a single factor militated for early resolution: about half the men in the brigade—more than half the infantry—were recalled reservists or regular soldiers retained after their engagement had expired†.

Whilst the enforced service had been accepted with goodwill by those concerned, they were becoming anxious to know, after six months service, the term of their retention. The chaplain of 1 Glosters, Padre S J Davies‡, who spent many hours talking to individual soldiers during the waiting period on Line D, remarked to the adjutant that this question was asked of him with increasing frequency. It was a matter put also to regimental officers throughout the brigade and represented by them from time to

* For the details of this meeting, see Appendix C.

† For details of the recall of reservists and retention of regulars, see Volume I, pp 103–122

‡ 'Padre' is the longstanding though unnofficial title of chaplains in the British armed forces. In the Army, the members of the Royal Army Chaplains Department wore officers' badges according to classification (ie, Chaplains Class IV upwards), but did not use the corresponding rank titles. A pool of four chaplains served with 29 Brigade, (two Church of England, one Roman Catholic and one Free Church). By custom, three of these were attached to, and identified themselves with, the three infantry battalions, but also worked among other units.

time. But it was not a subject pressed by the soldiers concerned with their regimental officers because those concerned had no wish to give the impression that they were looking for an excuse to leave their comrades in the midst of operations in a hard climate. Their relationship with the chaplain was different; in such a matter he was better informed as to their state of mind.

From this prompting the matter was referred through ascending headquarters to the War Office[32]. It landed on the desk of the Director of Personal Services, passed upwards to the Adjutant-General, then across branch boundaries to the General Staff*.

The Adjutant-General had not forgotten the regulars retained or the reservists recalled. He was in any case reminded of their circumstances from time to time by letters from families of the latter, addressed to Members of Parliament or directly to him, for the early return of respective fathers, husbands, or sons. Similar requests were received in the Admiralty concerning members of the Royal Navy in the same situation. The problem for both Service ministries was the same: too many commitments for the numbers of men available. The Army's problem was the greatest because it was the largest element among the three armed forces with the greatest number of calls on its manpower.

However, it was felt that until the General Staff could review its commitments in Malaya, the Middle East, NATO, and lesser though essential garrisons such as Hong Kong, and devise a means with the Adjutant-General's staff for meeting these, it was not possible to say definitely when reservists and retained regulars would be released. Padre Davies' initiative reminded those concerned in Whitehall that a decision was long overdue. Mr Shinwell, Minister of Defence, called on the Admiralty and War Office to agree a policy. On 29th January, the Prime Minister announced to the House of Commons that all those concerned would be required to serve for between twelve and eighteen months.

Thus it was clear to those planning organisational and manpower requirements that replacements would have to be found for retained regulars and recalled reservists by the late summer or early autumn of 1951[33]. The officers and men themselves concluded that they would be home for Christmas, and were comforted by the prospect. For some of their number, however, the run of battle was to dictate otherwise.

---

* The General Staff was responsible *inter alia* for operational commitments and organisation; the Adjutant-General and his staff *inter alia* for manning and drafting, and for the personal administration of officers and soldiers.

SOURCE NOTES: Chapter 3

1 FRUS, 1951, *cit*, pp 163-164.

2 *Ibid*, pp 165-168. These courses had been put to a meeting of the National Security Council on 6th February on the initiative of Mr Rusk.

3 FC 1015/41 (FO 371 92193), memorandum of 1st February 1951. For the full text and several important notes, see also DBPO, *cit*, pp 346-352.

4 American Views on Possible Developments in Korea, FK 1093/34, (FO 371 92809).

5 COS (W) 951 to BJSM, Washington of 6 Feb 51 (DEFE 11/208, f 1872). See also DBPO *cit*, No 125.

6 See Volume I, pp 204-205.

7 DEFE 11/208, f 1882.

8 For British ideas on this matter see FK 1201/3/G (FO 371 92835).

9 Australian Commonwealth Records Service (CRS) A5954, Box 1661, file 2.

10 For details, see Volume I, Chapters 4 and 5. Also Grey, Dr Jeffrey, *The Commonwealth Armies and the Korean War*, Chapter 6; O'Neill, *op cit*, vol i, pp 224-227; Wood, Lieutenant Colonel Henry Fairlie, *Strange Battleground*, Chapter II.

11 CRS A5799, 50/182. Connect with War Office MO1 Collection, unnumbered folio: MO2/240/50 of 17th November 1950 (DMO to VCIGS).

12 Conversation, Major-General T Brodie with author.

13 See, for example, Brigadier B A Coad's Report (WO 308/45, Part IV, p 9).

14 WO 216/341, 'Formation of Commonwealth Division for Korea,' f 76A (not in sequence).

15 This draft was badly prepared administratively for the journey. For details, see WO 316/342, ff 4A and 5A.

16 DEFE 11/207, f 1829B.

17 DEFE 11/207, f 1847A. See also f 1864B.

18 DEFE 11/207, f 1829B, para 8. The proposal was first mentioned in a signal to the British Commonwealth Base in Korea on 26th December 1950, (CRS A2107, K2.05), but General Robertson already knew that the draft of s.n. 26 below was being gathered in the United Kingdom (WO 216/342, f 1A).

19 WO 216/346, ff 3A and 6A.

20 Conversation, author with Field Marshal Lord Slim.. This limitation was signalled to General Robertson on 30th March 1951, WO 216/342, f 7A.

21 Canadian *House of Commons Debates*, 1951, I, 563.

22 WO 216/341, 'Formation of Commonwealth Division for Korea', un-numbered folio. See also DBPO *cit*, No 129.

23 War Office MO1 Collection, unnumbered folio: Loose Minute to 0185/737(SD2), DSD to DMO of 9th March 1950.

24 Conversation, the author with FM Lord Slim.

25 CIGS to General Robertson of 12 Mar 51 (MO/54/51 MO 1 Collection f 2461; also DEFE 11/209, f 1987A).

26 *Ibid.*, (and DEFE 11/209 f 2009).

27 Robertson Z8113 to CIGS, 16 Mar 51 (DEFE 11/209, f 2009).

28 Memo: (Deputy) DMO to CIGS of 19 Mar 51 (MO 1 Collection, f 2461 (not in sequence)). For the background to defence manpower difficulties, see CAB 129/44, CP (51) 16, 18, 20, 22, 23, 25 and 26.

29 See, for example, FK 1201/10/G (FO 371 92834).

30 WO 216/342, f 7A.

31 War Office MO Collection, f 2460 (not in sequence).

32 Special Routine Order No 103 of 15th February 1951, enclosed with War Diary, 29 Brigade, February 1951.

33 See WO 32/14307, in particular Minute of Adjutant-General to the Secretary of State (AG/BM/C/14 of 12th February 1951.

CHAPTER 4

Return to the Parallel

However successful in the field, a military commander is reminded from time to time that politicians and the public at home do not want to be advised of the precise nature of his work. In looking for a name for his operation to advance the Eighth Army northward in February, General Ridgway had chosen the word 'Killer'. It was consistent with his view—much welcomed by his soldiers—that, against such superior numbers, they should not fight for a particular plot of Korean territory but 'roll with the punches' when attacked, and attack themselves when the enemy was exhausted and broken by their fire power. In attacking, he meant to demonstrate to the Chinese and North Korean commanders that they did not possess a monopoly of the initiative, and were vulnerable to local defeat at least when he seized it. As an experienced soldier he knew that action on the battlefield involved a deadly price; but he was still finding his way as an army commander with regard to military politics. General Collins sought to educate him by a 'quick but courteous protest', as soon as the press picked up the word 'Killer', that it 'struck an unpleasant note as far as public relations was concerned'[1].

General Collins, Chief of the Army Staff, was influenced by the comments of the State Department in Washington, itself in discussion informally with the British Embassy on the subject. The acting head of the United Kingdom Liaison Mission in Japan, George Clutton*, added his own views on 6th March.

> ... For the last month, the Armed Forces Radio and the *Stars and Stripes*† have been calling the present military campaign 'Operation Killer' and this has merely re-echoed General Ridgway's own pronouncements in Korea...
>
> ... MacArthur, of course, at one time tried the cry 'You are fighting to free Asia' and was immediately rapped on the knuckles for his indiscretion. In default of anything else the only cry likely to appeal to the American G.I. is that of killing communists, which is a militarily feasible operation and is stimulated by American fear and hatred of communism in all its aspects.

---

* The Mission provided diplomatic representation among the Occupying Powers (see Volume I, p 49, fn). Mr Clutton, Counsellor, was in charge following the departure of Sir Alvary Gascoigne at the end of January, pending the arrival of Sir Esler Dening.

† The American Army newspaper, complementing the Armed Forces Radio.

> As far as the Japanese are concerned, I do not think that this propaganda line seems strange or that it will have any harmful effects. On the other hand to a European it strikes me as being somewhat repellent, though I do not know, of course, if, and how far, it is likely to do harm to our cause in Europe...[2]

John Shattock, Head of the China and Korea Department in the Foreign Office, responded on 18th April 1951,

> 2. ...we consider this particular line of propaganda ill-advised. His Majesty's Embassy at Washington had previously asked us for our views about a statement, which the State Department were suggesting might be issued by those members of the United Nations with troops fighting in Korea, saying how much they regretted the loss of Chinese lives in the campaign. We replied that nothing would be gained by such a statement and that short of abandoning the policy of killing as many Chinese as possible, which would be out of the question, the only course is to keep quiet about it. Merely to say that it makes us all very sad would be quite useless and, besides laying us open to the charge of hypocrisy, would probably be very bad for the troops who have to do the killing.
>
> 3. We added that any such statement, even if subscribed to by Asian Governments, would only tend to publicise the very idea which we wish to avoid, and which the Chinese are trying to put over, namely that this is a war by the imperialist Western Powers against Asians...[3]

Operation Killer closed effectively at the end of February. Perhaps with tongue in cheek, General Ridgway titled its successor 'Ripper'. By the beginning of March, the United Nations line—Line Arizona—was roughly abreast of the southern outskirts of Seoul, though, by deliberate choice, the lower reaches of the Han river had yet to be crossed to gain acces to the capital.

Whilst the United Nations allies now anticipated the approach of the Eighth Army to the 38th Parallel, General Ridgway's eyes were fixed on more limited objectives. Although he was determined to continue his counter-offensive, and spent much time fostering an offensive spirit among his commanders* and, necessarily, among his staff†, he had no illusions that the weaknesses of the early winter months had been wholly eliminated. For example, he had deliberately limited the process of 'dumping forward'—creating second line stocks of ammunition, fuels, and rations immediately behind the advancing troops, a common practice during an advance—because he recognised the risk of losing these by

---

* By this date, six general officers had been relieved in their appointments, some due to ineptitude, some to teach the lessons of the conflict to the Army at home.

† As late as 18th February, the plans section recommended, without prior rejection by the Chief of Staff, that the Army should hold its current line until the spring and then retire to the Pusan bridgehead.

a sudden reverse, a reversion to panic, such indeed as he had observed in central Korea in mid-February during P'eng's Fourth Phase Offensive.

The resumption of the advance during March was thus to be a deliberate process, aiming to destroy enemy troops and equipment, thereby spoiling attempts to open a new offensive against the United Nations. They would advance to Line Idaho. In the west, General Milburn's I Corps was to protect the port of Inch'on, still under repair[*] but now admitting over 500 tons of supplies daily, to isolate Seoul by outflanking it, west and east, and to hold the confluence of the Han and Pukhan rivers, anchoring the right flank of IX Corps. IX, under Major-General William M Hoge[†], was to seize the road junction at Kap'yong and, more importantly, in succession Hongch'on and Ch'unch'on, believed to be an enemy supply centre. These tasks, clearing Routes 17 and 29 in the process, involved an advance of about 30 miles. In the central east sectors, General Almond's X Corps and General Yu Jai-heung's ROK III Corps were to capture the lateral road between P'ungam-ni–Soksa-ri, from which III Corps had been thrown back, and Hajinbu-ri. The ROK I Corps, under General Kim Paik-il, was re-established on the east coast, where the line had already reached Chumunjin.

Anxious to preserve surprise, General Ridgway sought help in deception measures. The most important of these involved Admiral Joy, commander of the United Nations naval forces, whose warships simulated landing preparations on the west and east coasts. Believing that the Chinese derived considerable intelligence from the broadcasts of the Armed Forces Radio and publications of the *Stars and Stripes* in Tokyo, he took correspondents into his confidence, asking them to hold their reports to maintain security, an appeal which succeeded. And knowing that General MacArthur was in the habit of visiting Korea on the eve of offensives, when he made unrestricted statements to the press to assert his responsibility for their inception, he tactfully suggested to the Commander-in-Chief that he should not visit Korea until the battle was under way.

Choosing an opening date was difficult because road and rail demolitions during the withdrawal, and the onset of late winter rain, inhibited forward dumping. But the consequent delay gave him the opportunity to scrutinise enemy deployment and, as far as he was able, to ensure that he was not himself about to be attacked once more by the enemy. Reasonably assured that this was not the case, and with

---

* The Inch'on port facilities had been demolished by the Eighth Army engineers during the withdrawal in late December-early January, an operation later regretted by General Ridgway.

† General Moore died of a heart attack on 24th February 1951, following a helicopter accident. His place as corps commander was held by General Smith of the United States Marine Corps until the appointment of General Hoge.

essential engineer work on his supply routes completed, General Ridgway opened Operation Ripper on 6th March.

During the next ten days, the entire line advanced steadily. I Corps outflanked Seoul on the east, then by default on the west. ROK forces reoccupied the capital thereafter, finding it empty apart from a handful of anxious North Korean deserters. IX, X, and III Corps moved forward day by day. Hongch'on was taken, Soksa-ri recovered. The major effort in the eastern sector was confined to running down the rump of the NKPA 10th Division which had taken refuge in the mountains during the first fortnight of February* and was now seeking to move back with some 2,000 soldiers into North Korea. In division, corps, and army headquarters, staff officers redrew at intervals the forward edge of the battle on the situation maps, inching ever northwards.

These advances were won by persistent effort in wretched conditions, as the experiences of 27 Brigade illustrate. The four battalions had remained in operations through the second half of February, 2 PPCLI rapidly earning its place by a series of attacks across a series of high features. The infantry were moving across steep slopes, checked frequently by small arms and mortar fire. Between attacks, they cut through scrub or snow on exposed hillsides to excavate slit trenches in the stony earth. In these they found some shelter from the wind but little from the sleet. They boiled water on their Tommy cookers for tea and coffee, for shaving and washing hands, faces and feet. Few men reported sick but, besides wounds there were casualties from accidents, notably heavy falls on the slippery hillsides. Digging latrines was impossible. Men evacuated their bowels squatting over holes scraped within their defences; and, as ever in war, some were occasionally caught in this act by mortar fire or the bursting grenades of Chinese night raiders.

The bridge at Yoju was washed away, likewise portions of the rough roads used daily by the quartermasters to motor forward ammunition and rations each evening. The Korean porters were never more valuable. The New Zealanders ran short of 25-pounder ammunition until they were resupplied by a parachute drop at Chuam-ni.

Still, they pressed the Chinese defences, keeping in close touch with their neighbours to the west, the 7th Cavalry†, pulling up those to the east, 6th ROK Division. Sometimes held off the heights ahead, they patrolled with vigour and enterprise. When Operation Killer came to an end, they were abreast of Hoengsong.

A glance at the war diaries indicates that daily advances were made by hundreds rather than thousands of yards. Beyond each immediately dominating height gained, as often as not the enemy held the next in

---

* See p 34

† The 7th had relieved the 5th Cavalry on the right flank of 1st Cavalry Division.

sight. Attacks were not pressed across ground covered by heavy defensive fire; time was taken to seek flanking routes forward. Both sides patrolled actively by night, scouting, raiding and counter-raiding. By day, the steep approaches to the Chinese defensive positions often restricted access to single companies. On several occasions, a day of pressure persuaded the enemy to abandon positions during the following night.

The pace was also limited by days of thaw and of rainstorms alternating with snowfall. Track beds were swept away in places, delaying the advance of the New Zealand batteries and supply trucks. It is remarkable that 27 Brigade, at the forefront of operations through much of the autumn and winter of 1950, continuously active in contact or reserve since the turn of the year, and engaged in arduous offensive operations from 14th February until 13th March, remained morally and physically effective. Still, none affected reluctance when at last, due to Brigadier Coad's* representations, they were relieved by 5th Cavalry. After visiting the brigade on 4th March, General Ridgway ordered IX Corps to withdraw the brigade for a complete rest.

From 29 Brigade, in army reserve, two elements were soon returned to operations: the field artillery, and the engineers. The guns were required forward to complement the immense fire potential of the Eighth Army; the engineers to ensure, during this offensive phase, access to all part of the battlefield.

55 Field Engineer Squadron did not have to travel far from their base in the brigade area to join the immense labour of road mending, bridge and culvert repair, chiefly along the lateral road from Suwon eastward to Ich'on. Roadstone, gravel, cement, all the materials required for this work, were provided by the Corps engineer organisation. The squadron's trucks and plant were soon in action. There were also frequent calls for assistance in mine and bomb clearance; occasional Russian 'Krapper' mines overlooked on the verges of main roads and, more numerous, on sections of side roads. 57 Company, the Royal Army Service Corps transport unit of 29 Brigade, needed help when it discovered an unexploded American aircraft bomb in its forward base.

With his force thus committed, Major A E Younger and his intelligence officer ranged freely over the road and track network within the I Corps area, discovering their state, and gathering information concerning the range of mining and demolition operations by the Chinese and North Koreans as they withdrew. The brigade had lost a number of men and vehicles on this account since the tide of battle had turned, the first being Lieutenant Eric Sargeant of 45 Field Regiment, who had lost his driver and signaller killed when their jeep struck a Chinese mine

* Brigadier Coad completed his extended tour of command on 23rd March. He was succeeded by Brigadier B A Burke DSO, formerly deputy commander of 29 Brigade.

in early February. On these travels, Major Younger received a sudden request to assist in the preparation of battery positions for 45 Field Regiment.

From 23rd February, the three batteries of 45 Field were supporting once more General Paik Sun-yup's 1st ROK Division, now on the southern bank of the Han. The divisional artillery was a single battalion of 105-mm guns and thus unable to cover more than, at most, half the divisional front. For the remainder, General Paik was reliant on external fire support. The Regiment with its total of twenty four British 25-pounders was thus assured of a welcome, but was particularly valued on two counts. First, the British artillery organisation differed from the American in devolution of authority. In an American battalion, the senior officers were located in rear—the battery commander, for example, was in the gun position. Fire tasks were sent by junior officers manning the forward observation posts, and these required approval by those behind. The British batteries, commanded by majors, were sited with the battalion commander receiving support, the troop commanders—captains—were located with the company commanders. The troop or battery commander gave fire orders which were responded to immediately. The British artillery regimental command post was run by a captain. The regimental commanding officer was only drawn in if extraordinary circumstances arose or all the regimental guns were asked to fire by a battery commander forward. General Paik preferred this system; aside from other aspects, it provided his inexperienced subordinate commanders with experienced artillery advisers[4]. His own artillery battalion liked it because the British drew any local ROK battery into their gun lines, in which they were less vulnerable to sudden thrusts or raids by the enemy.

Supporting the ROK Division in January, the British discovered a fundamental problem. At company level, no one spoke English.

> The ROK officers were surprisingly good map readers…their method of asking for artillery support was to put a pencil on the map and say 'Boom, boom'. Their only word of English was 'O.K.'. The rest was up to the O[bservation] P[ost] officer and his wits.
>
> These unorthodox methods seemed to work…[5]

The American 64th Field Artillery Battalion had supported the 15th Regiment [brigade] of 1st ROK Division up to the Han but were now required elsewhere, hence the commital of 45 Field. But the British reconnaissance party found that rain had reduced the American gun position to a field of mud; new sites had to be found on higher ground. But the sites selected were boulder strewn and access routes had not been fully cleared of mines, hence the request for engineer assistance.

While this work was in hand, the gunner observation posts were deployed along the flood embankments of the Han river opposite Seoul. In these positions, they spent a quiet week, firing occasionally when small numbers of the enemy moved carelessly in view by day.

Those observed were North Koreans. During the last week of February, they were thinning out prior to abandonment of the capital. It was at this time that General Ridgway prepared to cross the Han, and 45 Field Regiment was switched during the first week in March to support the United States 25th Division crossing to the east of Seoul. Driving east, they turned up to Hill 327, then north along Route 17, cleared by 29 Brigade a fortnight earlier.

During the night 6th/7th March, they harrassed the enemy in slow time. The tempo changed just before dawn when the divisional artillery, augmented by the British regiment, fired a bombardment.

> For the next 20 minutes we fired at a very high rate engaging no fewer that 84 different targets. Each of the six troops* was allotted 14. This meant crystal-clear orders in writing down to the guns and some very quick work by layers and loaders.
>
> At 0615 hours, when a bare glimmer of light touched the river, the assault crossing started. This was supported by another detailed artillery programme. In this the Regiment took its full share but it was a holiday compared with those first furious 20 minutes, when we fired over 1300 shells.
>
> In this battle we were mere mercenaries shooting where we were bid. We had no O.P.s out and were not intimately involved in the operation... The Americans advanced fast through positions where the enemy were either dead or dazed[6].

The advancing troops, the 25th and 3rd Divisions, soon began to outstrip 45 Field Regiment's range. After several shifts of gun position, they were ordered forward by Major-General Robert H Soule, commander of the 3rd Division, but forbidden to use the one bridge constructed across the river. It was in almost continuous use by armour, infantry, and supplies required to maintain the momentum. A divisional staff officer was posted on the approaches with a traffic control team to restrict the crossing to specifically nominated units.

45 Field was not among them. 3rd Division orders required it to make a circuitous journey of 120 miles via a ford upstream across indifferent roads. Lieutenant-Colonel MT Young, the commanding officer, had other ideas.

Lining his regimental column up on a road close to the bridge, he went forward to the traffic control post. The American staff officer in charge agreed that there would be a gap in the traffic shortly and if the

* Each battery comprised two troops, each of four 25-pounders.

British were on hand at the appropriate moment he would pass them over. This news was passed by radio to the regimental column. It moved to the bridge at precisely the right moment and soon the vehicles and guns were crossing. But as the last battery approached, a jeep bearing two stars appeared. It was General Soule, who pulled over to discover why the British unit was using the bridge and subsequently to express his wrath. Fortunately, this took some time; sufficient time for the third battery to cross. That evening, the regiment 'dropped into action' in the gardens of the Republic of Korea's legislature.

The successful crossing of the River Han on either side of Seoul, the capture of Ch'unch'on in the centre, and the parallel advance of the line to the east by the middle of March brought congratulations to General Ridgway's headquarters from divers sources, not least from President Syngman Rhee and the Government of the Republic of Korea. Yet, while he recognised the political accomplishment, the Eighth Army commander was far from satisfied with the military result of Operation Ripper so far as it had run. He had aimed to 'seize or destroy enemy personnel and equipment' so as to cripple or diminish the enemy's capability to attack his own forces. The army had killed or wounded some 30,000 Chinese and North Koreans, and captured 4,000 prisoners*, but these losses were not going to limit P'eng Te-huai's capabilities. Captured material consisted principally of small arms, mortars, and a few light guns. The enemy was fighting successfully a dogged withdrawal action, helped by the broken, mountainous nature of the country and the bad weather which restricted ground and air operations. The capture of Ch'unch'on and the withdrawal locally of the enemy from contact reduced immediate prospects for encirclement of enemy formations in the centre. In the west, however, the advance of I Corps seemed to offer a means of cutting out a sizeable enemy force, the North Korean I Corps, before it drew back across the Imjin river.

General Ridgway had 187 Airborne Regimental Combat Team in reserve and, as a former parachute commander, had confidence in their ability to operate ahead of his ground forces, given assurance of an early junction with the latter†. He had considered its use at Ch'unch'on, but the unexpected abandonment of the town made this pointless. A second option was already in his mind to drop the airborne force on the approaches to the Imjin river at Munsan-ni, blocking thereby the North Korean withdrawal along Route 1. To close all avenues of escape, and to ensure the security of the parachutists, I Corps would advance as rapidly as

---

* Known enemy dead on 15th March totalled 7,151 rising to 7,409 by the end of the month. Prisoners rose to 4,800.

† 187 Airborne RCT had been used similarly in the previous autumn in North Korea. See Volume I, pp 248—252.

possible after their landing. General Milburn, the corps commander, formed an armoured column, Task Force Growdon*, to thrust directly to Munsan-ni. Two bridge-laying Churchill tanks were detached from 29 Brigade to join the column. 45 Field Regiment supported 1st ROK Division as it occupied the Task Force start line on 22nd March.

On 23rd March 1951, Good Friday, in clear weather, 187 Airborne RCT† was dropped by United States air transports immediately south and north east of Munsan-ni at 0900. Due to an error by the air force, the whole force was put down on the northern dropping zone‡, but this made little difference; there was almost no opposition. General Ridgway, given to landing in forward areas in his light aircraft, came to see the airborne force shortly after the landing. He informed them that Task Force Growdon was on its way. What he did not know was that, having started at 0700, Task Force Growdon was crawling along, delayed by demolitions and mines, real and dummy.

These mishaps did not wreck General Ridgway's plan. As it happened, the greater part of the North Korean corps had already crossed the Imjin river by the night 22nd/23rd March. The focal point of his own I Corps' operations shifted eastward to Route 33, the main road running due north from Uijongbu. Just beyond this town, elements of the Chinese Twenty Sixth Army were holding stubbornly to the heights commanding the road. A plan was hatched in Eighth Army headquarters to thrust 187 Airborne and Task Force Growdon behind the Chinese defences, cutting off their means of withdrawal.

It was worth trying, but the mountainous country immediately south of the Imjin river, concentrations of mines, and blockage of road passes by North Korean and Chinese field engineers delayed the movement eastward. With all vehicles obstructed the pace became that of the infantryman on foot. By the time they arrived, many of the Chinese had fallen back. Sufficient remained to offer a stiff battle to the parachutists and their supporters before this rearguard melted away.

By 31st March, the United Nations Command had advanced to the line of the Imjin in the west, across Route 33 fifteen miles north of Uijongbu, onwards north of Kap'yong, covering Ch'unch'on, then rising gradually to Chosan-ni on the east coast. The greater part of this line was just below, the final extension just above, the 38th Parallel.

---

* Named after the commanding officer of the 6th Medium Tank Battalion, Lieutenant-Colonel John S Growdon.

† In this operation, named 'Courageous' a detachment of 60th Indian Parachute Field Ambulance, detached from 27 Brigade, accompanied 187 Airborne RCT.

‡ The leading aircraft of the stream for the southern DZ had to return to Taegu with engine trouble. The second aircraft captain joined the northern stream. When the unserviceable aircraft returned, it dropped its load on to the empty southern DZ.

SOURCE NOTES: Chapter 4

1 General Matthew B Ridgway, *The Korean War* (London, 1968), p 110. See also, for example, FRUS, 1951, *cit*, pp 228–229.

2 G Clutton PA.5/5/51 of 6th March 1951 (FK 1093/32, FO 371 92809). See also DBPO, *cit*, No 130.

3 *Ibid.*

4 Conversation, author with General Paik.

5 WO 308/44, p 42.

6 *Ibid.* See also 45 Field Regiment War Diary, March 1951.

CHAPTER 5

Tail wags dog.

As noted, the greater General Ridgway's success in Korea, the greater apprehensions grew among the governments supporting him as to where he, and more particularly, his Commander-in-Chief, General MacArthur, intended to advance the ground forces of the United Nations Command. General Ridgway's occasional statements concerning strategy tended to be reassuring. Pressed by correspondents on 12th March on aims and achievements, he remarked that the recovery of the ground south of the 38th Parallel would be a 'tremendous victory'. General MacArthur's comments, following recovery of the initiative, made them anxious. After visiting Korea at the launch of Operation Ripper, he told a press conference that unless he received 'major additions' of troops, 'the battle lines in the end will reach a point of theoretical stalemate', on which there would be 'savage slaughter' when the enemy sought to break in. To avoid such a pointless struggle decisions on 'the highest international level' must be taken[1]. On 15th March, he informed Hugh Baillie, President of United Press,

> As I have on several occasions pointed out, the conditions under which we are conducting military operations in Korea do not favour engaging in positional warfare on any line across the peninsula. Specifically with reference to the 38th Parallel, there are no natural defense features anywhere near its immediate proximity. The terrain is such that to establish a conventional defense system in reasonable depth would require such a sizable force that if we had it, and could logistically maintain it, we would be able to drive the Chinese Communists back across the Yalu, hold that river as our future main line of defense, and proceed to the accomplishment of our mission in the unification of Korea. Under the realities existing, however, we can and will, unless the situation is radically altered, continue our campaign of maneuver as the best means to neutralize the military disadvantage under which we fight and keep the enemy engaged where it best serves our own military purposes. Such a point of engagement will of necessity be a fluctuating variable, depending on the shifting relative strengths of the forces committed and will constantly move up or down. The problem involved requires much more fundamental decisions than are within my authority or responsibility to make as the military commander—decisions which must not ignore the heavy cost in Allied blood which a protracted and decisive campaign would entail[2].

As an indirect yet manifest criticism of the political authorities, and a means of putting pressure upon them to change their policy of restraint, the statement was a brilliant composition. As a prospectus which covered him against almost any military contingency, it was a model. President Truman—who had not then seen the full text of the statement—turned enquiries by press correspondents on 15th March as to his reactions by remarking that a decision to cross the Parallel was a matter for the commander in the field, which occasioned anxiety in the Departments of State and Defense, though needlessly. What the President was saying was what they had all agreed: the land forces should not be limited precisely to the line of the Parallel but to the ground giving tactical advantage in its vicinity.

Next day, Mr Rusk, Assistant Secretary of State for Far Eastern Affairs, reassured the allied ambassadors that there was no change in United States policy concerning policy or plans. A decision concerning the limitation or otherwise of movement across the Parallel—that is, into any substantial encroachment on to North Korean territory—continued to be studied, and any developments would be discussed fully with their governments[3].

This was not a soothing of feathers ruffled by the Commander-in-Chief. It was true. Mr Rusk's and Mr Scott's memoranda in recent weeks and all that flowed from them was directed to bringing hostilities to an end. General Ridgway's successful advance to the 38th Parallel was an important, probably the principal, means of influencing the enemy to agree to a cease fire. While the Eighth and ROK Armies successes had temporarily hardened the attitude of the Joint Chiefs of Staff to the terms for such an outcome[4], they gave no support to the few wild men in government service, and the greater numbers in the United States Congress, who continued to argue for reinforcement of Korea, the occupation of the north, and the dictation of peace terms to the Chinese and North Koreans. The United States and British Governments, individually and collectively, were working towards an early peace negotiated on the basis of a military balance on the battlefield.

An immediate difficulty was to decide on who should be approached, which government or governments of the opposite side, would be most likely to respond favourably. Trygve Lie, Secretary-General of the United Nations, wondered whether the Communist camp wished all negotiations to be made directly with the North Koreans, but decided that on balance they should try the Soviet Union[5]. He suggested that when the Four Power representatives met in Paris for periodic talks on Germany, the British representative, Mr E Davies*, might suggest privately, over a drink

---

* Then Parliamentary Under-Secretary of State, Foreign Office.

perhaps, to his Russian colleague, Mr A A Gromyko, the idea of mediation by his Government. Consulted, Mr Davies decided that this idea was 'undesirable'. It was dropped. Mr Rusk suggested a statement of actions and intentions by all those contributing to or supporting the United Nations Command[6]. Sir Gladwyn Jebb proposed a public reminder of their pacific intentions by Britain, France, and the United States as permament members of the Security Council. Mr Shattock in the Foreign Office, suggested,

> 4 ... Our view is that if an initiative of this kind is to be undertaken, it should be a more positive one. We have for some time been considering whether any assistance could be afforded to the Good Offices Committee in its efforts to pave the way to a negotiated settlement with the Chinese, and what further steps might be taken to achieve this end if the Committee failed in its efforts. So far they have made no progress in gaining contact with the Chinese. Indeed, their unaided efforts may not be sufficient to end the present stalemate. A declaration, however, issued by the Governments providing forces in Korea...would serve the three-fold purpose of:
>
> (i) Strengthening United Nations morale and rallying world opinion.
>
> (ii) Clarifying the position at a time when United Nations forces are near the 38th Parallel, and
>
> (iii) Offering the Central People's Government of China the opportunity of making some favourable response either by way of the Good Offices...Committee or through diplomatic channels with...the Governments concerned[7].

Mr Morrison*, Mr Bevin's successor as Foreign Secretary, responded to this memorandum,

> I have a hunch that at this moment in the military moves we have a chance to propose with USA to USSR &/or China that without loss of face to anybody a peace about Korea should be arranged. Our own & world opinion would like it. If the move failed, well we should be on the side of peace & the angels. If we succeeded it wd be good. But if things drag on without an effort for peace, they may drag on to confusion. Shld like to raise by a minute to PM at once & then Cab. [on] Thurs [22nd March]. (I assume we are round about 38th par). H.M. 19/3[8].

At the Thursday cabinet, then, Mr Morrison aired his ideas,

> ... One possible course might be to issue a fresh declaration of United Nations aims in Korea, and to seek to open direct negotiations for a settlement between, on the one hand, the United Kingdom and the United States in association, perhaps, with France and India and, on the other, the Peking Government and possibly the Soviet Government. Unless some fresh political

* See Volume I, p 114, fn.

initiative were taken, there seemed to be some risk that the United Nations Commander in Korea [General MacArthur] might again advance north of the 38th Parallel and seek to justify that course on military grounds.

In discussion the Cabinet reaffirmed their view that, on both military and political grounds, it would be most inexpedient for the United Nations forces to advance north of the 38th Parallel. They also agreed that the United States Government should be left in no doubt of the strength of the views held by the United Kingdom Government on this question... Some Ministers thought it best that the United Nations forces should hold a stabilised line south of the 38th Parallel and, by making no attempt to preserve contact with the Chinese and North Korean forces, should allow the hostilities to die away. Meanwhile the search for a political settlement could be left to the Good Offices Committee appointed by the United Nations[9].

When it was pointed out that the Good Offices Committee had been unable to obtain any answer from Peking to their communications, Ministers agreed to leave the form of initiative to the Foreign Secretary, but advised him to take the Indian Government 'fully into our confidence at every stage'[10].

Mr Morrison seems to have been unaware that the Indian Government had had no response from Peking to its proposals to reconsider a cease-fire, a point made to the British High Commissioner in mid-March, as also by the United States Ambassador in New Delhi[*] [11]. But he was in any case planning to develop consultation with Mr Acheson before sounding out others. Before he could do so, General MacArthur intruded once more.

It was evident to the Commander-in-Chief from signals passing to and from himself and his political adviser that new proposals towards cease-fire negotiations were advancing in Washington. This was confirmed by a signal on 20th March.

JCS 86276. [Department of] State planning Presidential announcement shortly that, with clearing of bulk of South Korea of aggressors, United Nations now prepared to discuss conditions of settlement in Korea. Strong UN feeling persists that further diplomatic effort towards settlement should be made before any advance with major forces north of 38th Parallel. Time will be required to determine diplomatic reactions and permit new negotiations that may develop. Recognising that parallel has no military significance, State has asked JCS what authority you should have to permit sufficient freedom of action for next few weeks to provide security for UN forces and maintain contact with enemy. Your recommendations desired.

General MacArthur replied next day,

---

* However, Mr S Radhakrishnan, Indian ambassador to the Soviet Union, had reported that on a visit to London in the first week in March the Soviet Ambassador had told him it was time for a cease-fire and a seven-power conference on Korea.

> C-58203 ... Recommend that no further military restrictions be imposed upon the United Nations Command in Korea.... The military disadvantages arising from restrictions upon the scope of our Air and Naval operations coupled with the disparity between the size of our command and the enemy ground potential renders it completely impracticable to attempt to clear North Korea or to make any appreciable effort to that end...[12]

On 23rd March, Good Friday, President Truman received from Mr Acheson the draft of a statement which the latter proposed should be made in the following week, once consultation had been completed with the allied governments. Its wording was moderate. It proposed peace.

> ... There is a basis for restoring peace and security in the area which should be acceptable to all nations which sincerely desire peace.
>
> The Unified Command is prepared to enter into arrangements which would conclude the fighting and ensure against its resumption. Such arrangements would open the way for a broader settlement for Korea, including the withdrawal of all foreign forces from Korea...[13]

Precisely what possessed General MacArthur during the three days between his reply to the Joint Chiefs and 24th March will probably never be known*. But the corruption of his character by power over many years, his innate vanity, the overweening confidence in his judgement, were at work within him. On 24th March—23rd March in Washington—he issued a long written statement which extolled the brilliant exploits of the United Nations forces in Korea and the inherent weakness of the Chinese.

> ... Even under inhibitions which now restrict activity of the United Nations forces and the corresponding military advantages which accrue to Red China, it has been shown its complete inability to accomplish by force of arms the conquest of Korea.
>
> The enemy therefore must by now be painfully aware that a decision by the United Nations to depart from its tolerant effort to contain the war to the area of Korea through expansion of our military operations to his coastal areas and interior bases would doom Red China to the risk of imminent collapse.
>
> These basic facts being established, there should be no insuperable difficulty arriving at decisions on the Korean problem if the issues are resolved on their own merits without being burdened by extraneous matters not directly related to Korea, such as Formosa [Taiwan] and China's seat in the United Nations.
>
> ... Within the area of my authority as military commander, however, it should be needless to say I stand ready at any time to confer in the field with the

---

* He was to tell a gathering of the American Legion in the following October that, in the final months of his command, he had uncovered a plot to subvert American interests in the Far East. (See *New York Times* of 18th October 1951).

> Communist Commander-in-Chief of the enemy forces in an earnest effort to find any military means whereby the realization of the political objectives of the United Nations in Korea, to which no nation may take exceptions, might be accomplished without further bloodshed[14].

This pronouncement, raising publicly the notion of operations directly against China and suggesting that the Chinese armies in Korea were incapable of enterprise, effectively pre-empted the President's statement on behalf of the allied governments. As soon as he saw it, Mr Acheson called an emergency meeting at his house in Georgetown at 11 pm on the night of the 23rd March, at which exasperation was expressed commonly with the assertion that MacArthur must be relieved of his command. The general was out of control, Acheson surmised, quoting Euripides to his associates, 'Whom the gods destroy, they first make mad [sic]'. After some discussion, he decided that they should not contact the President immediately but let him rest. Actually, Mr Truman was wide awake, reading the statement, 'deeply shocked' at 'a challenge to the authority of the President under the Constitution. It also flouted the policy of the United Nations'[15].

At noon next day, the President discussed with close foreign and military advisers the action to be taken to protect policy and limit the damage done to allied cooperation; and how to correct the extraordinary indiscipline of General MacArthur. Immediately, these matters were to be dealt with on a restrained basis. A press release pointed out that the political points raised by the Commander-in-Chief were beyond his authority, and correspondents were informed, off the record, that the Tokyo statement had not been cleared with Washington. General MacArthur was reminded of his duty to clear comment on political policy before publication. Plans were set in hand to reassure the ambassadors of the thirteen nations engaged in the United Nations Command at their next periodic briefing on 27th March[16].

A fuller and more immediate explanation was, however, available to the British. At 8 pm on the 24th, after a long and difficult day ending with the release of the statement to the press, Dean Rusk saw Christopher Steel*, *chargé d'affaires* in the absence of Sir Oliver Franks. The latter reported later,

> ... Before I could raise the question of MacArthur's statement in detail, Rusk said that he would like to speak first. He did so on the President's instructions but his communication was for His Majesty's Government and not for publication. He then made a clean breast of the whole incident. ...the statement was unknown to any one in Washington and all the more unauthorised. The President wished you to know that action had been taken at the highest...level to ensure that this did not happen again. Rusk then

* Mr (later, Sir Christopher) Steel was Minister in the British Embassy.

said that the problem now was how to pick up the pieces. The Government were faced with a bitter dilemma. On the one hand MacArthur had made a statement entirely at variance with their policy. On the other the political situation at home was such that, were they explicitly to disown him, the whole of their foreign policy might be jeopardised including troops for Europe. Rusk said that in his personal opinion the state of Congress had never been more deplorable and difficult. They had accordingly decided to 'try and roll with the situation' and hope that the Easter holidays and other preoccupations would help them to keep control of it. I asked him what in fact rolling with it would involve and he then read us the statement which had just been made...

5. After this there was not much point in rubbing in still further the enormity of the General's latest exploit but I took occasion to say that, however much the situation might be accepted eventually in Europe, the effect on the Chinese could only be to extinguish any possibility of their being willing to treat. Rusk did not dissent though he said he did not consider they were as yet willing to do so. In more casual conversation afterwards he made no secret of the acute consternation in the State Department and indeed in the Government. He criticised the inconsistencies in MacArthur's statement and finally suggested the moral for us all was to speed the conclusion of the Japanese Peace Treaty.

6. I do not think the stupidest Western reader of the State Department's release quoted above can do other than realise that General MacArthur has been repudiated but as we pointed out to Rusk this does not include the Chinese and Communists generally. Nevertheless to this extent the [United States] Government have gone a fair way to meet our reproaches. I fear moreover that Rusk's allusions to the state of Congress are only too well founded. The President's prestige has been greatly weakened by the recent spate of scandals in and around the Administration and this has coincided with with one of the usual troughs in the shifting ocean of opinions. Fear is no longer imposing unity and the public is therefore swinging badly in default of other leadership. In short, the United States Government is as fully aware as we are of the deplorable character of this business and while they expect reproaches I do not think that ours will be any more severe than those which will descend on their heads from their own people[17].

Reading his copy of this telegram, the British representative at the United Nations, Sir Gladwyn Jebb, commented to the Foreign Office on 26th March,

This is all very well, but my personal view is unless we can use this incident to force a show down of some kind over this mad satrap, we may well be pushed into a full scale war in the Far East involving (*inter alia*) the disruption of the United Nations. It is indeed a classic instance of the tail wagging the dog[18].

A show down was certainly coming, but not of governmental contrivance. General MacArthur was now past restraint, as was shortly to become apparent.

SOURCE NOTES: Chapter 5

1 See the *New York Times*, 8th March 1951.

2 Published in the *New York Times*, 16th March 1951.

3 FRUS, 1951, *cit* p 235–238. See also record of Secretary of State's news conference on 21st March 1951.

4 State Policy & Planning Staff: Lot File 64D563, notably, meeting of 15th March 1951. See also Memo, Exec. Scy. NSC to NSC Senior Staff, 'United States National Objectives and Policy in Asia', 15th March 1951; and NSC 48/2 (1949) (as amended) and NSC48/5, both in series RG407, (USNARS, Washington, DC).

5 See, for example, his draft letter published in FRUS, 1951, *cit*, pp 224–226.

6 See DBPO *cit*, No 132, notes 4 and 1, respectively.

7 FK 1071/445. (FO 371 92781). For the full text of this memorandum, see DBPO, *cit*, No 132.

8 *Ibid*; for context see also DBPO, *cit*, No 132, note 6.

9 CAB 128/19, CM (51) 22.

10 *Ibid*.

11 FRUS, 1951, *cit*, p 227.

12 These signals are contained in the FEC/UNC file (USNARS, Suitland), and are also set out in FRUS, 1951, *cit*, pp 251 and 255–256.

13 795.00/3-2351 (USNARS, Washington, DC). For the text, see also FRUS, 1951, *cit*, pp 261–262.

14 For the text, see FRUS, 1951, *cit* p 265–6.

15 Acheson, *op cit*, p 518, and Truman, *op cit*, p 469.

16 A summary of action proposed and taken is in FRUS, 1951, *cit* pp 266–268; and p 272.

17 Washington 874 to FO of 24th March 1951, FK 1096/9 (FO 371 92813). See DBPO, *cit*, No 134 for context and cross reference.

18 New York 368 to FO of 26th March 1951, F 1017/10 (FO 371 92061). See also DBPO, *cit*, No 134, note 3.

CHAPTER 6

To Line Kansas

The political excitement between Tokyo and Washington over Easter did not impinge upon General Ridgway. Rightly so, he was then conducting the late stages of Operation Ripper north of Seoul and Ch'unch'on. He was also turning over in his mind aims and objectives for April within the limitations of the general area of the 38th Parallel. General MacArthur warned him on 22nd March that he anticipated further restrictions on movement and hastened to encourage the advance with a broad remit in a signal on 22nd March.

> C. 58292. ... My present intention is to continue current type of action north of the parallel, but not to proceed further than your logistics would support a major operation...[then] to pass from the present tactics which you have so ably conducted to ranger-type probing by battalions or companies from divisional fronts... If you have any suggestions, let me have them[1].

Two assumptions underlay this interim directive. The first was that the United Nations would continue to hold the initiative; the second that there should be no shift of major logistic bases northward.

The Eighth Army command—army and corps commanders—sensed no immediate threat to their offensive capability. When he received the Commander-in-Chief's signal, General Ridgway was still hoping to outmanoeuvre the North Korean I Corps before it withdrew across the Yesong on the road to P'yongyang. To this end, I Corps would continue its pursuit towards the river and Sibyon'ni, while IX Corps secured Ch'orwon to the east.

Soon, air and ground reports made it plain that the North Koreans had withdrawn behind the River Yesong to cover Namch'onjom. There were also signs of a major reinforcement approaching Sibyon'ni. Ridgway shifted his attention to a second option, the roads joining Ch'orwon—P'yonggang*—Kumhwa. Possession of this triangular network would give him control of communications including the railway in Central Korea. But as before, gaining ground was secondary to reducing enemy strength, spoiling P'eng Te-huai's opportunities to reopen an offensive. For once

* Not to be confused with the capital of North Korea, P'yongyang.

his own forces came to a halt, as sooner rather than later Ridgway recognised they must, an enemy offensive would follow. Against this contingency, he planned to gain and prepare a defensible line[2]. He named this Line 'Kansas'.

There was no question of advancing logistic bases north of the parallel. Those forces he moved towards Ch'orwon and Kumwha—part of I and all of IX Corps—would, if severely pressed, withdraw into or behind Kansas.

In the interview he gave to United Press on 15th March, General MacArthur had remarked, 'Specifically, with reference to the 38th Parallel, there are no natural defense features anywhere near its immediate proximity'[*]. This was nonsense. The line of the Imjin river along its lower reaches extending eastward through Hwach'on to the east coast offered a continuous run of commanding positions. Even more defensible, and on a shorter run, was the ground from the lower Imjin through Ch'orwon and Kumwha to the coast, but it rose some 25 miles into North Korea. It may be that General Ridgway hoped to establish this if later operational circumstances permitted. Kansas was 10 miles below the parallel in the west, 10 above in the east.

On 27th March, all the corps commanders[†] came to Eighth Army headquarters at Yoju for a review of Operation Ripper and a preview of the next phase of events. As to Ripper, General Ridgway criticised the persistently poor staff work, notably in the accuracy of battle and location reports,

> ...slipshod reporting, indicative of complacency, or inadequate supervision, or insufficient staff visits to front line units as unforgivable in my book. If I was to maintain proper control of this army, reports to my headquarters were to be complete, truthful, and specific, with no glossing over of unpleasant facts... I wanted no more units reported 'out of communications' for any extended period. We had liaison aircraft, with personnel specifically trained to pick up and drop messages. ...[3]

Looking ahead, he advised them of his plans to advance from an established defence line without a pause. Intelligence reports from prisoners and aerial observation indicated a spring offensive and he wished to give the enemy no respite. They must thrust actively but be prepared to close ranks rapidly in defence.

Operation Rugged succeeded Ripper to put the Eighth and ROK Armies on Line Kansas. Immediately thereafter, Operation Dauntless would carry forward the centre and right of General Milburn's I and the

---

* See p 79.

† On the return journey to his headquarters from this meeting, Major-General Kim Paik-il, Commander I ROK Corps, was killed when his light aircraft crashed. He was replaced by Major-General Paik Sun-yup, Commander of 1st ROK Division.

whole of General Hoge's IX Corps, first to the intermediate Line Utah, finally to Wyoming, on the threshold of Ch'orwon and Kumhwa. This general advance began as April opened*.

To discharge his tasks in the western sector, General Milburn was obliged to reorganise the wings of I Corps on a piecemeal basis. Spread across a front of 50 miles, he was to advance the eastern wing towards Ch'orwon and the approaches to Kumhwa. He calculated that this would require two divisions†. But he had also to develop defences along his portion of Line Kansas. He therefore chose to attack with three divisions, each of which would leave its reserve regiment on Kansas, digging, wiring, and mining. The western wing, from the mouth of the Imjin to its junction upstream with the Hant'an river, was to remain static, similarly preparing defences.

The 1st ROK Division was engaged in this work at the end of March, but on its right was the 65th Infantry which had to be disengaged and tucked in behind its parent, the United States 3rd Division. The British 29th Brigade was to relieve the 65th. Thus Brigadier Brodie came forward on 29th March to reconnoitre the Imjin river line.

In a straight line, his frontage was about 12 miles, but the river banks, the heights overlooking them, and the approaches to both, do not run straight. The actual frontage was almost 20 miles. Even with the sturdy, seasoned, Belgians under command, giving him a fourth battalion, the span was far too great for 29 Brigade to cover. When this was put to General Milburn he agreed to extend the frontage of 1st ROK Division as soon as practicable.

At the end of March, 1st ROK Division was in process of reorganisation. Next to them, upstream, the 65th was still clearing the mountain mass of Kamak-san, and on their right the 7th Infantry Regiment was still fighting to capture parallel heights topped by Mau-san‡, to bring the 3rd Division on to Line Kansas. Crossing the River Han, passing through the largely deserted streets of Seoul, the 29 Brigade transport columns took the road to Uijongbu early in the morning of 31st March, beyond which the infantry battalions dispersed along separate routes. None came under fire as they entered the battle zone. As ordered, the relief of the 65th Infantry Regiment was completed by 1600 hours¶ [4]. At the same time, the brigade itself came under the command of 3rd Division.

---

* Between the 2nd and the 4th. Formations started on different days and at different hours because those out of contact were ordered to push ahead, those engaged were obliged first to clear their front.

† In order to keep the thrust to Line Utah under one command, the 24th Division was passed to I from IX Corps.

‡ Shown now on maps as Macho-san.

¶ The Philippines Battalion, attached to the 65th Regiment, remained in the line under 29 Brigade command until it was relieved on 4th April.

During the next ten days, the British and their Belgian comrades closed up and settled into the Imjin river line. The Glosters, having completed digging and wiring a position 6 miles south of the Imjin, a contribution to developing the defences of Line Kansas, moved up to cover the river on the brigade's left flank. The Fifth Fusiliers sidestepped to the centre; the Royal Ulster Rifles concentrated on the right. The Belgian Battalion moved into reserve positions on the road leading south behind the latter two. As promised, the 1st ROK Division extended eastwards to connect with the Glosters on the brigade left flank. Brigadier Brodie's frontage was reduced to some 14 miles, but in the meantime his right flank battalion, the Royal Ulster Rifles, was required to seize hinge positions on Line Utah.

Left forward, the Glosters held 6,500 yards, close to four miles, with three rifle companies on hill tops over a wide arc covering the approaches from the river, from which a rough track ran southwards. One company was posted 2,000 yards behind these where the track ran into a gorge below the western slopes of Kamak-san. With such a frontage, Colonel Carne was obliged to accept wide gaps between the Glosters' forward companies, with the result that none could give small arms support to the others. But this weakness was remedied in part by the siting of the battalion's 3-inch mortars to reach to the river bank and hence all company localities, and the six Vickers medium machine-guns, whose arcs covered the slopes of the forward localities and the areas between them. The 4.2-inch mortars of C Troop, 170 Battery, were placed close to the mouth of the gorge from which they could reach out to the far bank of the river and the extremities of the battalion's flanks.

On 8th April, the Northumberland Fusiliers moved into the positions on the right of the Glosters. Colonel Foster's front also ran for almost four miles. As he was required to cover the impending advance of the Royal Ulster Rifles, his companies were drawn eastwards, so that there was a gap of 3,000 yards between his left hand company, Major R M Pratt's X Company, and Major Denis Harding's B Company, holding the Gloster's eastern or right flank. Y Company overlooked the loop of the river in this sector, W and Z occupied the high ground in rear. These necessarily widespread localities were covered by the potential of heavy and medium mortars, and Vickers machine-guns.

In the absence of 45 Field Regiment, still supporting 1st ROK Division, the guns of the American 39th Field Artillery Battalion provided close support across the brigade front. Behind them, the field and medium artillery of the 3rd Division were on call and, on the basis of priorities, the corps and army artillery within range. Armoured support was limited to a single squadron of the 8th Hussars—B Squadron under Major W

G O Butler. The remainder of the regiment was held south of the Han river in I Corps reserve.

To tell the truth, 29 Brigade was glad to be back in operations. They had been held in army or corps reserve since the end of February, had briefly been poised to hasten forward to reinforce the parachute landing at Munsan-ni, had reconnoitred numerous other commitments without being required to execute any, and were beginning to wonder why. There had been benefits. They had trained with recent battle lessons in their mind. They had slept through many nights under the watch of a handful of close sentries, had time to wash their clothes, scrub under the hot showers of the Royal Army Ordnance Corps bath section, and had been able to select at leisure their NAAFI* ration. Numbers had been to Japan on leave, whetting on their return the appetites of those awaiting vacancies. They knew the discomforts of the battle line, no less the dangers it held; yet they were drawn to experience them again.

Looking across the river, there was considerable uncertainty as to where the enemy was located—if indeed there was any enemy there at all. By day, each forward rifle company maintained a number of observation posts, some in cooperation with the artillery observation parties, and the mortar fire controllers in their midst. By night standing patrols were sent forward to listen and watch. Reconnaissance and fighting patrols were active.

On the right and left flanks respectively, Major Rickord of the Royal Ulster Rifles, and the adjutant of the Glosters, took representatives of the 8th Hussars and Royal Engineers into the Imjin at selected crossing sites. The former group, wading into the water in daylight, were sniped at as they found a sweeping current and pools too deep to wade even with tanks; but a second reconnaissance found a route across the Hant'an leading to another over the Imjin The latter, working at night in the Glosters sector, discovered that the river bed widened and the current diminished as it turned to loop in front of A and D Companies. At the deepest point the water rose chest high. Here an age old track ran through a deep cutting on the southern bank to an 'underwater bridge', probably developed by the North Koreans earlier in the campaign†, sufficient to carry a tank across.

The Royal Ulster Rifles needed their crossings almost immediately. Their advance to seize the 'hinge' of Line Utah, a group of hill features across the Imjin, was due to begin on 10th April, an operation geared to the thrust of the 3rd Division towards Ch'orwon[5]. Working throughout

---

* The Navy, Army, and Air Force Institutes service, provided by Expeditionary Force Institutes and the Royal Army Service Corps, supplied canteen goods and circulated, whenever possible, a tea and buns wagon.

† See Volume I, p 133, fn.

the night 9th/10th April in the very cold water, two troops of 55 Field Squadron attempted to build footbridges but were hindered by the current. One bridge was swept away in the darkness, the other was only partially built as dawn approached. Colonel Carson decided that he must improvise, accepting the risk of Chinese fire at the crossing. At 0630, two troops of Major Butler's tanks waded across the Hant'an and Imjin just above the rivers junction followed by the remainder carrying two companies of infantry and the Battle Patrol crammed upon the hulls. The third and fourth companies used the incomplete footbridge, in the centre of which the engineers waited with arms linked to carry them on their shoulders over the gap of ten feet. The 39th Field Artillery Battalion with A and B Troops, 170 Mortar Battery, pounded the target area. By 1315, the main and distant height, Point 194, was captured without meeting an enemy soldier. To the north, the 3rd Division was engaged in a break-in battle. As the engineers returned to bridge building, aiming to instal a jeep crossing, the remaining elements of the battalion with their Korean porters manhandled loads into their tracked Oxford carriers to wade with them to the far bank[6].

Across the British front, attempts were intensified to discover the whereabouts of the enemy. Each battalion patrolled extensively, but most of the positions discovered were empty. Exceptionally, a platoon of the Northumberland Fusiliers commanded by Lieutenant M D Young seized a Chinese position during a daylight raid two miles north of the river on 13th April. Documents were captured from enemy bodies. The villagers nearby reported that the area had been strongly held to the 11th, when the main body had departed northwards[7]. But clearly there were other groups active in the vicinity; D Company of the Royal Ulster Rifles was attacked early in the morning of 14th April. From time to time, enemy mortar fire fell at one point or another across the brigade front, though with little effect.

During the following week, there were six major sweeps across the river by combined infantry and tank forces*. Colonel Carne of the Glosters led one by night, another by day. His second-in-command, Major D B A Grist, followed with a third throughout the hours of daylight. A fourth, involving his B and C Squadrons of the 8th Hussars was undertaken by Lieutenant-Colonel Sir Guy Lowther, the commanding officer. Colonel Foster conducted the deepest sweep. In all, a few enemy prisoners were taken, poorly clad, half starved men who had no knowledge of the whereabouts of their units, having been told to watch and wait for their comrades to return at the opening of a new offensive[8]. British casualties were light, two dead and five wounded in the course of all contacts on

---

* In all these, the bulk of the infantry were carried in the trucks of 57 Company, RASC.

and beyond their main positions, principally from exploding mines. Several Centurions and wheeled vehicles had also been damaged by mines, all of which were promptly recovered by regimental and REME crews.

By the end of the third week of April, 29 Brigade had come to know well its operational area on either side of the Imjin. But neither the brigade commander nor his commanding officers were complacent. The fact that their foes had broken contact decisively supported all the intelligence gathered across the army front that P'eng would shortly mount a counter-offensive. All were aware of the gaps in their extended positions.

Meantime, to the east, IX Corps had joined I in pushing forward. Still short of Line Kansas on 1st April, the advance was made by 27 Brigade, 6th ROK Division and the United States 1st Cavalry reinforced by a regiment of the United States Marines. Kansas was reached on 6th April and, without pausing, all three formations moved on towards Lines Utah* and Wyoming.

Detached from the 24th Division when the latter was passed to I Corps, 27 Brigade was operating directly under the corps commander's orders. Its task in Operations Rugged and Dauntless was to clear the road along the River Kap'yong, a tributary of the Pukhan. Running almost due north, the dwindling stream winds between heights which draw close on the upper reaches, and was crossed and recrossed by a single track road until it passed beyond the headwaters, flanking a mountain mass *en route* to Ch'orwon.

This route was ideal country for a delaying action. Brigadier Burke first seized two mountain tops, Points 1055 and 750, ascents which were fortunately not opposed as the Middlesex and 3 RAR scrambled up the steep slopes. But they were closing on the enemy rearguard: the Argylls had several sharp encounters on 4th and 5th April, losing 3 dead and 11 wounded; the Chinese were not playing 'tip and run' but required deliberate attacks with gun and mortar fire to drive them out of their positions. Thereafter, every advance was contested. 3 RAR reached the 38th Parallel on the 4th and during the next few days, with the Argylls, had to clear routes through an anti-personnel minefield laid several years previously as part of the original defences of South Korea. There were also delays in opening the valley track, parts of which had been washed away by rain. Even so, 27 Brigade reached Line Kansas on 8th April, where it was ordered to pause and link flanks with its neighbours. In the process,

> ...6 ROK Div reported intercepting an enemy wireless message which said, 'We know of a gap between ROK troops and the British.' There was no cause

---

* Only a fraction of Line Utah lay within IX Corps' boundaries. The greater part of it was on 27 Brigade's front.

> for worry in the brigade sector, for if the enemy exploited this gap, the Brigade holds the commanding ground and is disposed in depth[9].

Dauntless—the advance to Line Utah—began on 11th April. As before, they moved from height to height, mostly across narrow connecting ridges, sometimes on footpaths, often across country, through scrub and occasional thin woodlands, a battalion on either side of the valley. Below, the New Zealand batteries leapfrogged forward, seeking to keep the infantry inside their range. Within the greater limitations of their weapons, the American 4.2-inch mortar company and the battalion 3-inch mortar platoons emulated them. The brigade's vehicles, command, support, and administrative, followed as a snake, wriggling slowly up the track. But this was now so broken and confined that it was impassable to anything but jeeps and light tracks. An engineer company sent forward by corps headquarters* to assist had protested on arrival that it was trained for bridge building, but nonetheless set to work. Their enthusiasm waxed as the tasks mounted. While they laboured with plant, pick and shovel, the units forward relied once more on their Korean porters, humping ammunition, rations and water, radio batteries and spare parts, up the slopes day and night.

During the pause between 8th and 11th April, it is probable that the Chinese reinforced their rearguards; for when the Middlesex† and PPCLI‡ resumed the advance the resistance was manifestly greater. On the left of the road, the Middlesex moved on the 11th through low clouds and occasional flurrys of sleet to capture four hills, 'Sole', 'Kipper', 'Dab', and 'Cod', the last two of which defied capture for two days. Early on 13th April, a patrol found Dab deserted, its deep defences protected by earth and timber. Cod fell shortly thereafter, but that night the Chinese counter-attacked, pressing into Major D C L Nolda's D Company. They were ejected by a spirited assault from the reserve platoon under 2nd Lieutenant Ralph Brown, which killed 18 of the enemy.

Next day, the struggle continued. The Middlesex fought for Sardine, 1,000 yards north of Cod, but were driven back. Second Lieutenant E W Martin stormed it with his platoon on the morning of 15th April but was mortally wounded on the summit by misplaced American shellfire. On that same morning, on the other side of the road, 2 PPCLI, confined by the ground to a company front, became engaged in a battle for Hill 826 which continued to the morning of the 16th. 3 RAR succeeded the

---

* From the 74th Engineer Battalion.

† Lieutenant-Colonel Man completed his tour of command at this time and was succeeded by Lieutenant-Colonel C M Nicholson, MC, Royal Warwickshire Regiment.

‡ Lieutenant-Colonel Stone was evacuated with smallpox as the advance began. Major H D P Tighe assumed command in his absence.

Middlesex and with the Canadians seized the remaining heights including Salmon and Turbot, whose possession brought them on to Line Utah[10]. On the afternoon and evening of 17th April, 27 Brigade was relieved by a regiment from 6th ROK Division and passed into IX Corps reserve. As the British infantry marched down the road to their transport, spirits were particularly high. They expected to be relieved within ten days by 28 Brigade. Advanced parties had already departed for Hong Kong.

Next day, however, enjoying what was called 'a period of administration and rest', another topic captured the interest of all ranks and all members, Australian, British, Canadian, and New Zealand. General MacArthur had been replaced by General Ridgway. A new army commander had been appointed in Korea, Lieutenant-General James Van Fleet III*.

* Van Fleet, Lieutenant-General, (later, General) James Alward III (1892–1993)

SOURCE NOTES: Chapter 6

1 Signal, C 58292 of 22nd March 1951, Personal for Ridgway from MacArthur, CG's and G-3 files, (USNARS, Suitland).

2 Army Commander's signal GX-3-5384 of 29th March 1951 to corps commanders, (G3 file, USNARS, Suitland). For a clear description of the development of the Rugged plan, see Mossman, *op cit*, pp 347–350.

3 Ridgway, *op cit*, pp 118–119.

4 Details of the commitment of 29 Brigade are to be found in the war diaries of its units. Copies of some signals missing from the brigade headquarters diaries are included in unit covers for the period. 1 NF has an almost comprehensive collection.

5 For details, see 29 Brigade Operation Order No 3 in the War Diary for April 1951.

6 See entries in the War Diaries of 1 RUR, 170 Mortar Battery, and 55 Field Squadron, 9th and 10th April 1951. Also *The Royal Ulster Rifles in Korea, cit,* pp 56–59.

7 For an account of this raid, see 1 NF War Diary, April 1951.

8 For a Chinese description of the state of the defensive screen force at this time, see Hsü Yen, *op cit,* Chapter 2.

9 27 Brigade War Diary, 8th April 1951.

10 See 27 Brigade, 1 Middlesex, 1 A&SH, 2 PPCLI, 3 RAR, 16 New Zealand Field Regiment War Diaries, 3rd–16th April 1951. Also O'Neill, *op cit*, pp 125–128, Wood, *op cit,* pp 70– 72, and Shipster, *op cit,* pp 62–64. Conversations, author with Mr JR Macaulay (A&SH), and Major G G Norton (Mx).

CHAPTER 7

A cure for MacArthuritus

Although General MacArthur's frustration of the peace initiative in March vexed the governments in Washington and London commonly, it unsettled the relations between them. Senior members of the State Department, sensing criticism by their principal ally of the licence apparently enjoyed by the 'mad satrap', found fault with British conduct of Far Eastern policy. They complained to Mr Acheson that London seemed bent on obstruction of the United States in such matters as the Japanese Peace Treaty and the Pacific Pact planned with Australia and New Zealand. Had the British, Mr Acheson asked Sir Oliver Franks on 3rd April, new ideas about the Far East which were not being disclosed to the Americans?[1]

Sir Oliver, recognising the causes of this unease, reassured the Secretary of State[2]. But he had also to contend with what he termed a fresh outbreak of 'MacArthuritis' in Whitehall. A telegram of 2nd April from the Foreign Office objected to prospective 'coat trailing' by the American 7th Fleet off the Chinese coast opposite Taiwan, and proposed a new and more explicit directive for General MacArthur as part of reconstructing a peace initiative in Korea[3]. Sir Oliver decided to discuss this with Mr Rusk informally to clear away any misunderstanding, believing he was one of those stung to the point of complaining of British obstructions.

> Rusk replied that the firm presence of United Nations forces at or around the 38th Parallel gave, in the American view, a possible basis for negotiations. The Americans were completely clear and convinced about this, no matter what might be said by anybody in the press.
>
> 3. But at the present time State Department and Pentagon were in full agreement that United Nations forces in Korea faced the prospect of an all out major, carefully mounted, offensive designed to drive them into the sea. ...and they believed further, with some evidence to support the belief, that the Russians and Chinese were in full agreement on this policy. The Americans were in fact worried whether the extent of the agreement between the Russians and the Chinese did not cover the extensive supply of arms and air support to the Chinese.
>
> 4. Rusk said because of these views the Americans felt strongly that the Chinese would not negotiate for the present. It might be different if their

> offensive were made and failed. It was for this reason that the troop dispositions made by General Ridgway and the points taken up in the vicinity of the 38th Parallel were essentially designed to make good our defence against the offensive. In a broad sense the nature of all General Ridgway's operations in Korea had been defensive. They had gone better than could have been hoped last December when the expectation was that we should have to hold a series of lines retreating South. Actually General Ridgway had been able to conduct his defensive with greater success and had occupied a series of lines advancing North. He now faced the probability of a very heavy test[4].

Mr Rusk himself recorded that he told Sir Oliver,

> ... I thought there was one difference of emphasis between London and Washington that it might be helpful to recognise. It was my impression that London considered that after reaching a suitable line in Korea, a position would be held on a more or less static basis in the hope that negotiations would open up. I told him that we were prepared to move toward a period of negotiation but that we saw no hope of it on the other side. ...[5]

Sir Oliver reported that the President and Secretary of State were preparing to make new public statements to assist the peace process.

> ... Rusk said the Americans would wish to show us and agree with us both the [presidential] statement and the [Secretary of State's] speech.
>
> 6. Rusk further said the State Department were interested in the possibility of approaching Peking and possibly Moscow in some way after our position had been stated. ... They inclined to the view that whatever precise means were adopted we should not sound Peking or Moscow for their proposals on the Korean situation. That would be too dangerous and offer too easy an opportunity to divide friends. It would be better to put something up to the Chinese and Russians.
>
> 7. ... I suggest that the way in which we now press our own views on the Americans must take full account of their preoccupations, whether we agree with their assessment of the military situation or not. ...[6]

This was good advice, but the onset of 'MacArthuritis' in Whitehall militated against acceptance. Similarly, Air Marshal Bouchier's reports of rising enemy strength[7] were discounted. The British Chiefs of Staff preferred the advice of Brigadier Ferguson, military adviser to the United Kingdom Liaison Mission in Tokyo, that MacArthur's headquarters was 'once again building up "vast hordes" [of enemy numbers] who can be held responsible for any reverse UN forces may suffer'[8]. This was more in tune with their notion that a foundation was again being laid for an extension of the war into North Korea and the bombing of Chinese territory, perhaps even bombardment or landings on the coast of China. They did not believe that the Chinese possessed the 'massive' air strength reported from Tokyo* [9]. Still, they were persuaded by Sir John Slessor, Chief of the Air Staff, that if enemy air intervention exceeded 'a few light raids across the frontier,' and became 'really serious...we should have no reasonable alternative but to counter-attack, although such counter-attacks should be confined to the enemy air bases'[10]. In such case, as they signalled to Lord Tedder on 6th April,

> 7. ...we agree that it would be a good thing to have a carefully prepared announcement to be issued in the appropriate manner if and when the necessity arose, to the effect that, while most anxious to localize hostilities, we cannot accept without appropriate action the extension of the area of conflict that would be represented by strong enemy air attacks from bases outside Korea. We agree that such a warning must come from Washington and not be left to MacArthur. ...[11]

They concluded by pressing acceptance of the new directive for the UN Commander-in-Chief, with all of which the Foreign Office concurred[12].

When Sir Oliver and Lord Tedder attended a 'friendly and reasonable' meeting with the Pentagon and State Department on this subject, it became apparent that they were all of one mind, apart from the matter of a further directive. As to numbers of enemy aircraft constituting a major attack, General Bradley stated that they were thinking of 'an attack by say 50, 100 or 200 aircraft but not of an attack by say 6 aircraft'. They considered three options for retaliation: immediately following an attack; or following an unheeded warning to desist; or an advanced warning that if an attack was made from air bases outside North Korea there would be retaliation. General Bradley and Mr Rusk thought that the latter course

> would also give some opportunity for consulting other governments in advance, though it was clear that provided they got our agreement they would not wish to waste much time consulting others.
>
> 6. ...[Sir Oliver] thought it might be difficult if this train of circumstances took place, for Ministers of His Majesty's Government to say publicly that the responsibility for the decision was entirely with the United States Chiefs of Staff. Mr Rusk pointed out that if we agreed to give warning now in advance that would be a political decision in which we would have fully shared.

The problem of Russian air intervention was considered; all hoped that it might even so be possible to continue to localise the conflict. The Americans asked whether British carrier aircraft and the Australian and

---

* Their mistrust was increased by details of an interview given by General MacArthur to the Defence Correspondent of the *Daily Telegraph* published in the newspaper on 5th April 1951. *Inter alia*, he claimed that if the political constraints were removed, 'the UN forces could easily defeat opposing Communist forces'.

South African air squadrons would join in retaliatory strikes in North East China to manifest a United Nations response, an option which would require prior consideration. They agreed to meet again 'as soon as we had each considered the points raised'[13].

Before they could meet, however, President Truman was also beset by a further severe attack of 'MacArthuritis'. On 5th April, a prominent Republican in the House of Representatives, Joseph W Martin, read out a letter he had received from General MacArthur in response to one of his own[*] [14]. The reply, written on 20th March but not previously made public, included the following,

> ... It seems strangely difficult for some to realize that here in Asia is where the Communist conspirators have elected to make their play for global conquest, and that we have joined the issue thus raised on the battlefield; that here we fight Europe's war with arms while the diplomatic [sic] there fight it with words; that if we lose this war to Communism in Asia the fall of Europe is inevitable, win it and Europe most probably would avoid war and yet preserve freedom. As you point out we must win. There is no substitute for victory[15].

When he read the report of this on the evening of Thursday, 5th April, President Truman was incensed. He decided to dismiss General MacArthur. Yet, as a shrewd politician, he moved a step at a time, first calling together Mr Acheson and Mr Harriman, Generals Marshall and Bradley, on the Friday morning before a prearranged cabinet meeting. They met again immediately after it. They gathered also on the Saturday, when Mr Truman continued to invite the opinions and reflections of his advisers. All recognised the political implications of dismissal. By Monday morning, following much discussion of the issue in the national press, in which commentators inevitably divided on party lines, and a good deal of hostile commentary in the British press, the opinions were unanimous including those of the individual Chiefs of Staff. General MacArthur must be removed. The President told them then that this was the decision he had already reached[16]. General Ridgway would succeed as Commander-in-Chief. Lieutenant-General Van Fleet would assume command of the Eighth Army in his place. These arrangements were to commence as a continuous process from 11th April, Washington time.

Tokyo was already filled with rumours, however, probably based on press guesses; political secrets are rarely secured for long. President Truman did not wish to give General MacArthur an opportunity to pre-

---

* This covered the text of an enclosed speech, delivered in New York on 21st February, charging President Truman with failing to open a second front in Asia, and concluding with 'If we are not in Korea to win, then this Truman administration should be indicted for the murder of thousands of American boys'.

1. Changhowon-ni, site of Battalion Headquarters, 1 MX, January 1951. The battalion defensive positions were on the immediately surrounding hills. (Major B Reed)

2. Yoju town is seen on the distant (north) bank of the River Han. Pack ice has collected on the United States Army Engineers' pontoon bridge, January 1951. (Lieutenant Colonel H R Jeffes)

3. Sergeant Joe Ryan's detachment of 16th New Zealand Field Regiment is seen supporting the advance of 1 A&SH in 27 British Commonwealth Brigade northwards on Route 24 towards Chuam-ni, February 1951. (New Zealand Archives)

4. Members of 1 MX observing Route 24 in the valley just south of Chuam-ni, February 1951. (Major B Reed)

5. A soldier of 1 MX in fighting order on the advance to Chuam-ni. As a trial, he is wearing rubber boots over plimsolls, but this footwear was found insufficiently robust for the rough terrain, February 1951. (Major B Reed)

6. Centurion tanks of the 8th Hussars supporting 1 GLOSTERS' attack on Hill 327 (the principal height on the left), February 1951. (Imperial War Museum)

7. Napalm and bursting shells on Hill 327 precede the GLOSTERS' assault, February 1951. (Major-General A E Younger)

8. Members of 1 RUR advancing to the River Han close to Route 24 with Centurion tanks of the 8th Hussars, February 1951. (Imperial War Museum)

9. A 4.2-inch mortar detachment of 170 Light Battery in action supporting the advance of 1 RUR, February 1951. (Imperial War Museum)

10. Korean porters with 1 MX escorts moving up to supply the battalion during operations to advance to Line Kansas, March 1951. (Major B Reed)

11. An American helicopter collects casualties from the Regimental Aid Post of 1 MX, March 1951. (Major B Reed)

12. The light bridge under construction by 55 Field Engineer Squadron across the River Hant'an from the southern bank (left), early April 1951. (Major-General A E Younger)

13. 1 RUR crossing the bridge while it is still in process of repair and construction, early April 1951. (Major-General A E Younger)

14. Korean labourers assisting 55 Field Engineer Squadron to clear a track forward to positions of 1 NF on the Imjin, early April 1951. (Major-General A E Younger)

15. 1 GLOSTERS returning across the Imjin ford at 'GLOSTER Crossing' after a deep reconnaissance sortie, mid-April 1951. The left shoulder of the cutting (in picture) and that on the right (out of view) were used by the battalion's ambush parties to check the Chinese immediately prior to the opening of the Fifth Phase Offensive. (Major W A Wood)

16. Lieutenant-Colonel J P Carne, commanding officer of the GLOSTERS, seen in his Battalion Headquarters area, mid-April 1951. (Major R S Mardell)

17. The Rev S J Davies conducting a service of Holy Communion immediately before the opening of the Fifth Phase Offensive in the GLOSTERS' Battalion Headquarters area. Of those shown, eight were killed in the battle and a number wounded and taken prisoner. The battalion's command vehicle (operations centre) is seen in the background.
(Royal Army Chaplains' Department)

18. Major John Shaw, commanding the detachment of 1 RUR on the Route 11 saddle south of the Imjin, seen at Battalion Headquarters just prior to his return to that position. He was killed twenty minutes after the picture was taken. (Brigadier M N S McCord)

19. Mortar positions of A Troop, 170 Light Battery, 1 RNF and 1 RUR, just prior to withdrawal from the Imjin area, 24th April 1951. The litter of empty ammunition boxes illustrates the high consumption of bombs during the battle. (Brigadier M N S McCord)

20. The track running north west from Chuktun-ni in the Kap'yong river valley, April 1951. (Major B Reed)

21. Chinese soldier in fighting order killed in the Kapy'ong battle, April 1951. By this date, the 'Volunteers' had discarded their padded winter uniforms for the light cotton jacket and trousers. The soldier is wearing rubber-soled canvas 'basket ball' boots. Individual equipment included a leather belt, small arms bandolier, two cotton haversacks, one for domestic possessions, the other for grenades and magazines for the machine carbine or light mortar bombs, and an entrenching tool, a small spade partially seen here on the ground just above the soldier's head. (Major B Reed)

empt dismissal by resignation. The arrangements were modified and accelerated. A signal bore the news to the Commander-in-Chief on the afternoon of the 11th in Tokyo just as the radio began to report it to the world.

In Korea, Operation Dauntless was proceeding. General Ridgway was authorised to remain in command of the Eighth Army if he thought it necessary. He decided to hand over at once to General Van Fleet. 'It's up to him, now.' General Ridgway remarked lightly in answer to a question as to the run of operations, called to him as he passed a newspaper correspondent. Of course, this was by no means true. It was no less a matter for General P'eng Te-huai.

SOURCE NOTES: Chapter 7

1 Washington 987 to FO of 3rd April 1951, F 10345/14, (FO 371 92067). See also DBPO, *cit*, No 138.
2 Conversation, author with Lord Franks.
3 FO to Washington of 2nd April 1951, FK 1071/395, (FO 371 92779). See also as DEFE 11/209, f 2054A.
4 Washington 1024 to Foreign Office of 6th April 1951 (FK 1071/402, FO 371 92779). See also DBPO, *cit*, No 139.
5 FRUS, 1951, *cit*, p 297.
6 As note 4, above.
7 AVM Bouchier in Tokyo CAB 237 to MOD of 28 Mar 51, (DEFE 11/209, f 2048).
8 Defence Liaison Mission in Tokyo MA/137/30/03 of 30 Mar 51, (DEFE 11/210, f 2061A).
9 BJSM Washington AWT 130 to MOD of 5 Apr 51, (DEFE 11/210, f 2066. See also f 2073A).
10 COS(51) 59th meeting (DEFE 4/41), see also DEFE 11/210, f 2071.
11 Chiefs of Staff (W) MOD 997 to BJSM, Washington of 6 Apr 51, (DEFE 11/210, f 2072).
12 FO 1347 to Washington of 6th April 1951, (DEFE 11/210, f 2072A).
13 Washington 1034 to FO of 6th April 1951, FK 1022/37, (FO371 92757) but see DBPO, *cit*, No 140 for complete context. FRUS, 1951, *cit*, pp 307–309 provides a summary from the United States point of view but is omissive—for example, it makes no mention of Mr Rusk's presence or contribution, though his office record shows that he attended.
14 For a copy, see FRUS, 1951, *cit*, pp 298–299.
15 *Ibid.*
16 See Truman, *op cit*, pp 474–477, and for example the *Washington Post* and London *Times* of 7th April, and *Observer* of 8th April 1951.

CHAPTER 8

'Prepare for a long war; strive for a short war.'*

Understanding the mind of the enemy may not be essential to victory in war but it saves a good deal of effort in the process of winning.

As observed, some members of the British Government believed in the early months of 1951 that the abandonment of offensive action by the United Nations forces would lead to hostilities withering to an end in the peninsula. The view was reiterated by several Ministers in Cabinet on 22nd March that stabilising a line 'to the south of the 38th Parallel and, by making no attempt to preserve contact with the Chinese and North Korean forces, should allow the hostilities to die away'[1]. A greater number, together with the Chiefs of Staff, recognised that this was wishful thinking, yet themselves clung to the view that they would mitigate the hostility of China, and perhaps even that of the Soviet Union, if operations were conducted solely on a defensive basis precisely on the line of the 38th Parallel.

Neither opinion was valid; the first was ingenuous. Reverses notwithstanding, China and North Korea continued to look for victory in arms, to 'drive the imperialist aggressors into the sea'[2]. Only a fraction of China's military manpower had been engaged. There was no pressure of public opinion on either government to show dividends for effort expended, no electorate threatening to throw them out of office for delay or failure. In any case, a Chinese Government's tolerance of time spent in war was greater than that of the Americans and the British Commonwealth.

The Americans, brought up to enter contests with the sole aim of winning rather than simply enjoying the competition, had a clearer perception of the enemy. Mr Scott in the Foreign Office had recognised the realities more clearly than many British colleagues and superiors in his memorandum of 1st February:

> ...the basic American strategy is probably right. The new China is a menace to the peace of Asia and a formidable ally of Russia in a bid for world domination... The proper course, to my mind, is to pursue our policy of

---

* Mao Tse-tung, personal instructions to P'eng Te-huai, in an interview at the end of February 1951. See P'eng Te-huai—a personal memoir, (People's Publishing Company, 1981), p 261.

> negotiation whilst recognising that even negotiation from strength, coupled with firmness and patience, may not stop the Chinese and that we face the alternatives of big sacrifices or stopping China by force[3].

This conclusion remained true for the remainder of the war, though it was obscured by the apprehensions of many members of the United Nations that China was a surrogate of the Soviet Union. In pursuing a common determination to localise the conflict—to withold any challenge to Moscow in the theatre—the governments in Washington and London, at least, were mistaken in believing that Stalin was looking for a *casus belli* in Korea. As noted, he was determined to stay out of the war[4], though content to encourage Chinese and North Korean aggression to the limit as long as it was at low, preferably no, cost to Russian resources.

Mao Tse-tung and a majority among his principal associates in party and government were of one mind in the necessity of holding the Americans back from the Chinese-Korean frontier[5]; and most were sufficiently fired by the early successes of the 'Volunteers' to support attempts to defeat outright the 'Anglo-American'* forces in Korea. The high command, political and military, in Peking was thus prepared as General Ridgway nurtured his defeated forces, to return as often as necessary to the offensive until a complete victory was gained[6].

Yet the Chinese hierarchy, misled by Marxist preconceptions, some peculiar to itself, was equally unable to understand the mind of its enemies. Proposals from Washington and London for peace in Korea were judged crudely: if the United Nations was losing, they were made to save further loss, a fair assumption; if winning, the offers were false, a perverse conclusion. Then, as the fount of propaganda, the Central Committee was also the victim of the ideas propounded. For example, several members of the hierarchy at least believed that General MacArthur pursued the conflict because he had commercial interests in South Korea[7]. None was capable of seeing members of the United States or British Governments as rational men; all dismissed the influence of their electorates as negligible.

Still, Mao was more realistic about the outcome of the battlefield. The fizzling out of the Third and Fourth Phase Offensives had disappointed him but he appears to have accepted that it was due to not so much to a want of 'revolutionary spirit' as a lack of men, weapons, and supplies in the face of the United Nations' strength and flexibility in firepower. P'eng's reports were overwhelmingly endorsed in this respect by many senior officers in Korea and in the Logistics Headquarters of the North East China Military Region, the base of the Chinese People's Volunteers. The Central Military Commission was therefore ordered at

---

* British participation was frequently coupled with that of the United States in Chinese propaganda.

the beginning of March to hasten and augment the reinforcement of the Volunteers.

Much had already been done. Two army groups, 9 and 19, were in or close to the line. 3 Army Group was moving forward to join them*. Given their strength and the additional artillery and engineer forces in their company, P'eng believed that, when concentration was complete, he would have the means to break open the front, inflict severe damage on the United Nations Command, and make a major advance into South Korea.

Yet even with forty assault divisions in hand, he foresaw two threats to his strategy. The first was that, from the moment of crossing the 38th Parallel, his own supply and transport chain would be insufficient to sustain an advance of 300 li—about 100 miles—the depth of penetration he judged essential to the success of his offensive. The second was his vulnerability to an amphibious landing by the enemy behind his own lines. The Chinese and North Koreans alike had been impressed by the United Nations amphibious operations at Inch'on and Wonsan, and the lesser airborne assaults by 187 Regimental Combat Team in 1950 and 1951. They believed erroneously that additional American forces were arriving in Japan, and that the whole of the 11th Airborne Division—the parent of 187 RCT—was available to General MacArthur† [8], all of which would supply the numbers for landings in North Korea. Longstanding apprehensions in Peking that Nationalist Chinese forces were to be used on the Korean battlefield had led to the mistaken identification by the beginning of April of 30,000 of their number on the South Korean island of Cheju. Such was the dividend of General MacArthur's flirtation with Generalissimo Chiang Kai-shek.

In so far as the first problem was concerned, P'eng was dealing with a matter of which he had first hand knowledge. Stocks for 20 days were to be brought forward into army areas.

> ... When this campaign is launched, every unit will itself carry field rations for 5 days, and the various logistics detachments must also be ready with another 5 days of field rations to advance along with the troops. At the same time, every effort must be made to overcome the difficulty of the 300 li

---

* 13 Army Group, which had marched south from the Ch'ongch'on in December 1950, progressively disengaged from the main defensive front during March. Its headquarters moved to the eastern edge of the zone chosen for the offensive, where its depleted formations were replaced. For the Communist forces order of battle at this time, see Appendix D.

† Although United States plans had been drawn up in Washington at the end of 1950 to send additional formations to Korea, including the remainder of the 11th Airborne Division, none were despatched. However, because Chinese broadcasts referred specifically to the deployment of additional airborne troops during the early months of 1951, General Ridgway proposed that the individual soldiers arriving to replace men due for relief should, as a deception, wear the shoulder patches of the 82nd Airborne Division, but this was not implemented.

> foodless zone when we advance southwards to ensure that the troops are able to get uninterrupted supplies of food and ammunition.
>
> In order to make up for our difficulties relating to means of transport, when in action, each unit must pay conscientious attention to salvaging captured motor vehicles. On every occasion, before going into action, it should should organise a batch of drivers in advance, and at the same time make use of prisoners-of-war for salvage operations; if each company could salvage one vehicle this would be of very great benefit for the transport operations of our forces. ...inside our country the maximum possible effort has already been made to satisfy our needs, and there is no way any more can be transferred to us...
>
> In order that our transport operations can be speeded up, from now in each army group and each army within the area in which it is stationed must carry out repairs on the relevant sections of the road; if they come across any damage, they must repair it right away—they cannot simply rely on the engineers troops and sit idly by watching them. They must also teach the troops to help in the unloading and concealment of motor transport vehicles, while such disgraceful behaviour as wantonly damaging vehicles and attacking their drivers, and also not giving way to vehicles on the road must absolutely be prohibited.
>
> Engineer headquarters must immediately send troops to carry out more repairs to the road which runs from Huich'on via ...Meng-shan* to Yangdok; we must make this road into an extremely important transport supply line.
>
> Medical departments must be ready to take in 40 or 50,000 injured personnel. The casualty receiving station of each detachment should be as close as possible to the front line units, and the necessary medical orderlies and stretcher bearing parties should be organised in advance. Injured personnel must be put in suitable places of concealment. To this end, each army group and army should immediately start planning digging and construction operations in the regions where they are assembled. ...[9]

These injunctions by P'eng to an assembly of senior political officers—including those who were concurrently military and political commanders—on 6th April at Sanyang-ni, 12 miles behind the front line on the Kumhwa front, say as much about the low professional standards of commanders and staffs of the Chinese Peoples' Volunteers—and hence the People's Liberation Army—as about his difficulties in mustering and providing for the contingencies of a great offensive. They are also a reflection of the lessons learned from looting and damaging captured enemy supplies in the First and Second Phases of the campaign†. P'eng was determined that the political staffs should bring their considerable

---

* Maeng-san in Korean. This is a simple transliteration between the two languages. Many Chinese names for towns and villages were less easy to connect with their Korean names.

† High level conferences had been held in North Korea and in Shenyang in late January to consider logistics lessons of the first three campaigns. See, for example, Hung Hsüeh-chih, *Memoirs of the War to Resist the United States of America and Aid Korea* (Peking, 1990), p 115.

influence from army group down to company level* to ensure that military policies and orders were fully implemented, a task interlinked with 'really good pep-talks' to the soldiers in which 'the requirements for victory in this campaign should be explained to them'[10].

Another activity which the political 'cadres' were to influence was training, specifically, the proper organisation and use of time in training during halts on the march and once the troops had arrived in their assembly areas. The immediate requirement was familiarisation with the Russian weapons which had been arriving in quantities since January, from assault rifles and machine carbines through mortars, anti-tank and anti-aircraft equipments to artillery. None of these were new. Some items, notably the T-34 tanks, were in a poor state of repair[11]. Range practice with the new weapons was extremely limited by the standards of the United Nations Command due to the need to conserve ammunition; rifle practices were restricted to 10 rounds per weapon. Still, the new range increased target cover and permitted a greater measure of standardisation. The old Japanese rifles, many manufactured before 1914, were passed back to the militia in China. For tactical training, instructors were attached to the new armies from those experienced in the first four campaigns.

Attachments of experienced officers and men, including a few from seasoned North Korean corps, were also arranged to each of the new army groups to assist in the formation and operation of deep reconnaissance units, numbering between 200–300 apiece. Each army formed one, some two. Carrying,

> ...cash, field rations, explosives, automatic weapons, walkie-talkies and so on, they should have Korean and English interpreters, and they should be prepared to destroy roads, overturn enemy vehicles, wreck enemy depots, capture prisoners, investigate the enemy situation and terrain, and actively coordinate operations with those of the front line units[12].

The notion that 'walkie-talkies', captured light American radios, would suffice to maintain communication between the reconnaissance units and parent armies was absurd, if only because the equipment lacked the necessary power. Moreover, the fact that this was the only mention of communications equipment throughout this entire conference, or indeed the subject of intercommunication as a whole, shows that P'eng

* Each formation and unit had a political staff appropriate to size. At company level there was one officer. He was instructed and reported through a chain of authority discrete from the military. The political officers had the right to participate in the development of military policy and plans, and if the senior at any level felt that these were misguided or contrary to higher directions would represent this through the political chain. The system of 'concurrent' political and military command at high levels ensured that overall military requirements or considerations were not overborne by political theory. At lower levels, political opinions sometimes obliged military commanders to change their decisions.

had not grasped that of all his weaknesses, this was the greatest, as it had been since the Volunteers entered Korea six months before. In contradistinction to the North Koreans, his limited radio capability and high dependency on telephones connected by cable meant that communications ceased to be effective below divisional level, often between division and army, once mobile operations began. This omission is the more surprising because all levels of command down to division maintained stations listening to the United Nations open networks, from which they obtained low level intelligence of value occasionally, but which demonstrated the extensive capability of the United Nations units to communicate by radio to troop and platoon level on the move as well as in static positions.

As April passed, P'eng found himself pressed for time. Over half a million soldiers had to be deployed or redeployed for the offensive. Eleven armies were being brought into assembly areas for the offensive. Four others together with armour were to be disposed with North Korean forces to resist landings in the rear areas*. He proposed to delay the opening date to the first ten days of May, but was anxious that the advancing Eighth Army might break into the open country round Ch'orwon where it would make devastating use of its armour. He was later to say also that he expected imminently a landing in the rear area by the United Nations 'Sixteenth Army'†. For one or both of these reasons, 22nd April was chosen to open the Fifth Phase Offensive[13].

By 18th April, it had also become apparent that the attacking armies would again be without air support. During the withdrawal in the previous winter, the United States Fifth Air Force had destroyed its forward strips, thereby conceding air control as far south as the Ch'ongch'on river to the air command of the People's Liberation Army. In February, a delivery of Ilyushin-10 ground attack aircraft from the Soviet Union raised the total in Chinese hands to fifty. The air commander, Liu Ya-lou, had already set in hand repair of the airfields at Sinuiju, Uiju, and Sinanju, bases within the cover of his Mig-15s, the majority of which were crewed by Russians[14]. At risk, he then began to rebuild as a joint Chinese and North Korean venture selected airfields south of the Ch'ongch'on, round Wonsan and P'yongyang. Once these were operational, the United Nations ground forces would be within range of the Il-10s.

---

* The Thirty Eighth, Forty Second, Forty Seventh, and Fiftieth Armies. Two of these were at low strength but the whole was reinforced by the bulk of the armoured increment. The Forty Seventh was employed on airfield repair. The Sixty Sixth Army, long in battle, returned to China in early April.

† Hung Hsüeh-chih suggests in his *Memoirs of the War to Resist America and Aid Korea* (Peking, 1990) pp 136–138, that the expectation of a landing was used as an excuse by P'eng to controvert the proposal of some CPV Party Committee members to draw the United Nations Command further north. Still, although the UN Command did not possess a 'Sixteenth Army', the Communist high command was convinced of its existence and menace.

Despite attempts to conceal the recovery of these southernmost airfields, reconnaissance aircraft of the Far East Air Force observed the work during February and March*. Accepting that the enemy had considerable labour resources to repair damage, General Briggs†, commanding the bomber force, decided simply to neutralise the operational facilities rather than attempting to destroy them[15]. The sorties he launched from 17th April did just that. Immense efforts made by the Eighth Army engineers restored sufficient forward airfields to the Fifth Air Force to extend their range to the extremities of North Korea and to provide close air support in the expected offensive.

Yet P'eng was hopeful of success; he was a robust commander. Above all, he felt that he and his senior subordinates had drawn the correct lessons from their experience of fighting the United Nations Command. They would continue to strike to as great an extent as possible by night. They would not try to break in across too wide a front—what Mao called 'opening our mouths too wide'—but aim in the 'first impulse' to destroy a limited number of formations sufficient to make an opening for the second.

On 18th April, he issued confirmatory orders.

> For our Spring Offensive, we have decided to make our objective the wiping out of three divisions (less one regiment) of the American Army, three brigades of British and Turkish troops, and two divisions of the Puppet [Republic of Korea] Army to the west of the northern Han River. First of all, we will mass our forces to wipe out the 6th Division of the Puppet Army, the British 27th Brigade, the American 3rd Division (less one regiment), the Turkish Brigade, the British 29th Brigade and the 1st Division of the Puppet Army, and after this we can wipe out the American 24th Division and 25th Division. ...[16]

Four days remained. The main bodies of troops made ready, sending forward reconnaissance parties and guide detachments for the approach march of 15 to 20 miles. The deep reconnaissance units began covert infiltration from 20th April. The Fifth Phase Offensive was in motion.

---

* This information, taken with other intelligence concerning the delivery of additional Il-10s to North East China, prompted the anxiety of the United States Chiefs of Staff that they might be vulnerable to substantial air attack. (See pp 98–99, above)

† Brigadier-General James E Briggs succeeded Major-General Emmet O'Donnell jr, in January, 1951.

SOURCE NOTES: Chapter 8

1 CAB 128/19, CM (51) 22. See also DBPO, *cit*, No 132, note 6.

2 This slogan, first developed in an editorial in *Jen Min Ji Pao* of 5th January 1951, was used many times in one form or another over the following year.

3 FC 1015/41, (FO 371 92193) (Mr Scott's memorandum) from p 89, above. See also DBPO, *cit*, No 123.

4 See Weathersby, *op cit*.

5 See, for example, Hsü Yen, *op cit*, p 19.

6 See Mao, *op cit*, (1987) pp 152, 603, 678, and 726. Also Ch'i Te-hsueh, *Military History* periodical, (June 1989), 'The "Reportage" fails to report events faithfully'.

7 For example, see Nieh Jung-chen, *Memoirs*, (Peking, 1984), volume 2.

8 See 'A speech given at the Fifth Enlarged Session of the Chinese People's Volunteers Party Committee, 6th April 1951' in *A selection of P'eng Te-huai's Military Writings*, (Central Documentary Publishing Company, September, 1988).

9 *Ibid.*

10 *Ibid.*

11 See, for example, Hsü Yen, *op cit*, Chapter IV.

12 *Selected writings on Chinese military affairs of P'eng Te-Huai* (Peking, 1988) (see here often as *P'eng's Te-Huai's Military Writings*). Speech to the CPV Party Committee, 6th April 1951.

13 Among references to this erroneous intelligence, see Hsü Yen, *op cit*, Chapter 2, Part 5.

14 See, for example, article by Smorchkov, Aleksandr, 'Speak Korean in Battle, *Komsomolskaya Pravda*, 9th June 1990.

15 *Far East Air Force Report on the Korean War*, Volume I, p 76; also *The United States Air Force in Korea, 1950–1953*, Robert Frank Futrell (New York, 1961), pp 275–276.

16 *P'eng Te-huai's Military writings, cit*, signal sent on 18th April at 2100 hours to each Army and copied to the Central Military Commission and the Eastern Department.

CHAPTER 9

'A mighty clash of arms'
I : The Battle on the Imjin River

The valleys of the Imjin and Hant'an rivers lay quiet on Saturday, 21st April 1951. A hard winter was clearly over. Though nights remained cold, the air no longer carried its penetrating chill. Yet there were few signs of spring: the scrubby bush and trees on the hillsides remained sere; decaying stubble lined the rice paddy below. In the Korean villages there were no young men; they were away in the armed forces or serving as porters to the foreign soldiers. But even in the front line, villages were occupied by elders getting basic implements ready for tilling and sowing, women fetching water, washing clothes, watching children. In the late afternoons, smoke would appear from the mud chimneys as fires were lit for the single hot meal of the day. The villagers did not stray far from their houses.

Doors were bolted at nightfall. Gossip from village to village, unfamiliar sights and sounds in the night, an instinct, perhaps, told them that there would soon be fighting outside their walls.

In the 29 Brigade sector, expectancy of a battle was based on the growing number of indicators: an enemy which had deliberately broken contact; the reports of prisoners-of-war; aircraft reports of anti-tank ditches being filled in at road centres such as Namch'onjom and Sibyon-ni; and smoke clouds to mask daytime movement twenty and thirty miles behind the enemy line. Patrolling apart, however, there was nothing Brigadier Brodie and his forces could do to increase readiness. The only change in deployment was the relief of the Royal Ulster Rifles after ten days in the isolated 'hinge' position. The Belgian Battalion, under Lieutenant-Colonel Albert Crahay, replaced them on Friday, 20th April.

The Royal Ulster Rifles enjoyed some hours of rest on the Saturday after throughly cleaning their weapons, equipment and vehicles. Colonel Carson with a group of officers and men departed for a few days leave in Japan. NAAFI rations were waiting. 'The Regimental Pipes came up to A Echelon and played 'Retreat'*, a mobile cinema was borrowed† [1]...'

* Beating 'Retreat' with pipes or bugles, and drums, is a longstanding custom in the British Army, following the old practice of warning those outside fortified townships to withdraw into the protection of the walls before darkness. It continued as a bugle call in barracks and camp at dusk into the second half of the 20th century, and has persisted as a means of providing, on occasion, a simple programme of music for entertainment.
† Provided by a uniformed detachment of the Services Kinema Corporation.

The battalion had redeployed into brigade reserve five miles down the track running due south from the Imjin, known as Route 11. Their presence, on and behind a pass between two mountains, gave depth to the right hand sector in which the greater part of the brigade was disposed. From front to rear, units were in place as follows:

The Belgian Battalion and B Troop, 170 Mortar Battery.

(*The Imjin River*)

W and Z Companies, and Battalion Headquarters,
Royal Northumberland Fusiliers

70 Battery) 116 Battery) 176 Battery)	with Regimental Headquarters, 45 Field Regiment	C Squadron, 8th Hussars

Brigade Headquarters, 55 Field Engineer Squadron,
and Headquarters, 170 Mortar Battery

Royal Ulster Rifles.
26 Field Ambulance.

The central area was held by X and Y Companies of the Northumberland Fusiliers, with A Troop of 170 Mortar Battery. On the left were the Glosters with C Troop, and R Troop of 45 Field Regiment*.

On the Saturday night, numerous listening posts were established along the river bank. One of these was manned by Corporal Cook, Privates Eagles and Hunter, drummers and buglers† from the Glosters. After dark, they sat upon the low cliffs overlooking 'Gloster Crossing'. They had a telephone to battalion headquarters. The night was clear and moonlit.

About 2200, the three saw figures moving along the far beach. Corporal Cook reported this to the adjutant and flares were fired by 70 Battery. Fourteen Chinese soldiers were illuminated. When the flares faded, these men entered the water.

The river level had dropped during the past week. The leader was soon in midstream, waist high. Corporal Cook received orders to open fire. Although outnumbered almost five to one, his 'quiet manner and matter-of-fact confidence had a steadying effect on the other two'[2]. Armed only with rifles, they fired steadily on the approaching enemy. Those in

---

* R Troop, under Captain C S R Dain, comprised two radar equipments, nicknamed 'Rancid' and 'Ringworm'. They were under trial as a means of picking up tracks of enemy mortar bombs in flight and computing the location of the mortar base plate which had fired them.

† The operational task of a battalion's drummers and buglers or pipers was to protect battalion headquarters. They took their turn in minor patrolling tasks.

front were all hit. Some floated away, some were recovered by those behind as they hurriedly returned to cover on the far bank. The 'listening post' had repelled a reconnaissance party of the Chinese Sixty Third Army.

Next day, Sunday, 22nd April, from dawn to dusk, sightings and contacts were numerous across the front—groups of men from tens to hundreds, batteries of guns, some horse drawn, some towed by trucks[3]. The fighters and fighter-bombers of the United States Fifth Air Force attacked them throughout the day. Army air observers in Mosquitos directed shellfire on numerous targets on the fronts of the 24th and 25th Divisions. The 3rd Division found that it had a prisoner from 3 Army Group, hitherto unidentified. The Turkish Brigade snapped up six members of the Chinese 2nd Motorised Artillery Division, a survey party which had lost its way. They reported that the offensive was to open that night[4].

During the Sunday morning and afternoon, Padre Davies of the Glosters, Padre Kelly of the RUR, and Padre Bell of 45 Field Field held church services for the Protestants, Padre Ryan for the Catholics. As ever, the expectation of battle swelled congregations.

At brigade headquarters, Captain R H Sinclair, acting as brigade major*, expected orders from I Corps and 3rd Division to adjust the frontage to Line Kansas†, principally in withdrawing the Belgians to the south of the Imjin. Drafting instructions through the evening, he included these remarks from the intelligence section:

> ... Though the attack pattern has not developed sufficiently to reveal the enemy plan at this time, it seems likely that following the attacking probes on the bulge [of the Imjin] the usual flanking attacks and encircling movement will be attempted.
>
> The appearance of artillery in quantity suggests that the pattern of the enemy attack will conform to a Main Supply Route axis of advance more closely than in previous engagements...on the lines of the January [1951] attack with crossings at fords not only on the brigade front but also in 1 ROK Div sector[5].

He set out Brigadier Brodie's plan. On receipt of codeword 'Foxhound', the Belgians would move back to the areas held by X and Y Companies, and these two would concentrate with W and Z. The Royal Ulster Rifles would remain in reserve. The only element of the brigade then located—just—north of Line Kansas thereafter would be A

* Then the title of a brigade's chief of staff.

† As originally conceived by General Ridgway, all formations were to fall back on to Line Kansas when the offensive opened, occupying positions sited and to an extent prepared beforehand. Authority to order this withdrawal was delegated to corps commanders. Overall, this move shortened the frontage. See pp 88–89.

Company of the Glosters, retained on Castle Hill above the village of Choksong because this feature offered exceptional observation over the approaches from the river bank.

Contemplating the enemy offensive, there was a common assumption among commanders and staffs in I Corps at least that the first night would involve probing attacks, and infiltration. Sightings during daylight on the 22nd strengthened this notion in 3rd Division, 29 Brigade and 1st ROK Division. Moreover, the distance of enemy main bodies from the defences on the lower Imjin river, fifteen to twenty miles, suggested a full night's march to bring them to the northern bank. Massed attacks were therefore expected on the night of the 23rd.

What they did not know was that P'eng's reconnaissance forces had already completed a thorough process of identification. His 'deep reconnaissance units' had already put detachments on heights such as the summit of Kamak-san separating the Glosters from the remainder of 29 Brigade. Others had returned to brief division and army headquarters of their findings. What they had failed to do was to penetrate in numbers behind the United Nations lines: some had lost their way; one party had been captured by the Korean military police; others in concealment were swept into the storm of battle and scattered.

The detailed information gathered permitted P'eng to run his armies directly at their targets in column of divisions. Short of maps as ever, he had been able to establish guide posts *en route* to the Imjin. He had no doubt that his soldiers could march 20 miles and move into attack without a pause. This confidence was not misplaced.

Like a swollen wave curling from its foremost edge to break upon a shore, the Chinese People's Volunteers drew in upon the United Nations line, falling first in the east, extending rapidly across the IX and I Corps fronts, where the two sides were closest, and then upon the Imjin positions.

Captain Sinclair learned about 1930 that the 24th Division reported the approach of 'huge forces'. Brigadier Brodie ordered the Royal Ulster Rifles to place a rifle company group*, and their Battle Patrol at 30 minutes notice to move. The remainder of the battalion was to be at 2 hours notice. This permitted time to load essential items on to fighting vehicles. The Northumberland Fusiliers were instructed to prepare a company group for a reconnaissance in force of the north bank of the Imjin next morning.

Otherwise, the brigade commander left the level of readiness to his commanding officers. With a major battle impending, as many as possible should be resting. Even so, at the very least, two sentries were on watch in each infantry section; an officer or sergeant was awake in each platoon position. In the foremost companies, half were standing to

---

* A rifle company—about 130 strong—with additional elements; in this case two 3-inch mortars and two medium machine-guns.

arms. When at rest—not firing—the guns and mortars were trained on Defensive Fire SOS tasks, targets critical to the infantry defence, with sufficient crews to fire on demand. In company, battery, and squadron headquarters, battalion, regimental and brigade headquarters, officers, warrant officers, assistants and signallers in appropriate numbers, maintained watches at their stations.

One of several important command centres was the Regimental Headquarters of 45 Field Regiment. Lieutenant-Colonel Maris Young had decided that all radios in his unit should be on the same frequency. On a single net, all stations were able to keep abreast of events simultaneously. The system worked because the gunners' speech discipline was exceptionally high. When it occasionally dropped, the commanding officer was there to restore it.

'Wait 3', a signaller replied in signals parlance to a comrade asking a question from another station. '3 what?', came back; the operator was inclined to be querulous. 'Minutes, twit, out', said the colonel from a third station. Net discipline soared as chatter subsided.

A similar system was used by Major Fischer-Hoch, commanding the widely distributed troops of 170 Mortar Battery. As a consequence, he was often able to supplement the flow of information to brigade headquarters with news from his observation posts[6].

As was his habit, Lieutenant-Colonel Carne, commanding officer of the Glosters, spent the evening hours of 22nd April with those on watch in his command vehicle, a reinforced 3-ton office truck. Inside there was light and warmth, with all the communications forward to his companies, the radio rear link to brigade headquarters. At 2220, the heavy mortar net reported that one of the Belgian companies was under attack. A few minutes later, the telephone at Gloster Crossing reported a large number of enemy on the ford.

Colonel Carne had an ambush at this site. After dark, fifteen men under Second-Lieutenant G F B Temple had occupied a number of former ROK positions on the cliffs on either side of the track cutting down to the water's edge. Half their number were on watch, half rested. At 2230, as if they had learned nothing from Corporal Cook's sharpshooting the previous night, Chinese soldiers suddenly crowded the far bank and began crossing. As the column leaders reached the southern shallows, Second-Lieutenant Temple gave the order to open fire. In the following hour, the ambuscade became a denial action[7].

As the sound of firing at Gloster Crossing rose, a listening post returned to report to Major Pratt, commanding X Company, left hand position of the Northumberland Fusiliers. Its members had seen 20 Chinese crossing the river, 800 yards to the north. While this news was being digested, an enemy party came up to the nearest platoon, possibly off their intended line. At all events, there was a clash. The enemy appeared to draw off, but within 30 minutes, all three platoons were under attack. Major Pratt called A Troop to fire its heavy mortars on the forward approach to his hilltop position—his Defensive Fire SOS—which was delivered immediately. Shortly, enemy mortars began ranging for A Troop's position, but the bombs fell harmlessly to the south.

Towards midnight on the 22nd, then, there were reports of Chinese in the brigade area. No position was critically engaged. Events seemed to confirm expectations of a probing operation a day in advance of the main offensive. Still, Brigadier Brodie decided to secure 'Ulster Crossing', the Imjin bridges to the Belgians. With a detachment of 14 field engineers, the Battle Patrol set off in Oxford carriers from 1 RUR at midnight. Major Rickord instructed Lieutenant Hedley Craig, the commander, to withdraw, if pressed, either back to the battalion or to the Belgians[8].

Far from probing at midnight, the Chinese were crossing by thousands into the 29 Brigade sector, a principal target in this opening phase of the offensive. Here Yang Te-chih had committed his Sixty Third Army to two thrusts across the Imjin: on the west to destroy the Glosters and open the road they held; on the east to overwhelm X and Y Companies and to eliminate the Belgian 'hinge' position as a means of working round and behind the units supporting them. The 187th Division led the 188th and 189th. These would 'wipe out' the British force in accordance with P'eng's orders[9].

Thus Second-Lieutenant Temple's action at Gloster Crossing gave early and valuable information of their approach, and for a time checked movement of a battalion over the Gloster Crossing towards D Company*. But downstream, others were crossing to attack A Company on Castle Hill. Similarly, X Company and the Belgians were able to indicate a degree of movement in their areas but were unaware of the numbers passing around them.

The RUR Battle Patrol passed over the bridges but was halted by intense small arms fire from two sides. Grenades followed, setting two of the carriers on fire. Carrying 10 wounded, the Patrol managed to scramble back across the bridges into positions on the southern bank. In view of his orders, Lieutenant Craig instructed the greater number with him to withdraw, while he and a covering party, including some of the engineers, maintained fire. Those sent off reassembled within the Northumberland Fusiliers' defences. Craig and his party were captured†.

---

* A battalion of 559 Regiment, 187th Division.

† Following an air strike next day, their captors began to shoot the prisoners. Lieutenant Craig and a rifleman escaped but the remainder, including Lieutenant Keith Eastgate of the Royal Engineers, were killed.

A little later, in one of those astonishing chances of war, two members of the Brigade Royal Signals Squadron, on their rounds in a jeep to deliver written orders, passed a number of Chinese streaming away from the bridges, who ignored them as they sharply reversed. Nearby, a Royal Signals line party, working alone and similarly unaware of developments, encountered some of the Battle Patrol withdrawing, who wondered whether they had been fired on in error by a Belgian detachment at the bridges.

As midnight passed, the size of the enemy incursion became progressively apparent. Pressure on the Belgians grew; at times, its whole perimeter was fighting simultaneously[10]. Strong forces began to attack A Company of the Glosters. When the ambush party was withdrawn from Gloster Crossing, its ammunition almost exhausted, those members of 187th Division waiting to cross surged over through the shellfire of 70 Battery to attack D Company. X Company, was attacked by fresh forces from the north west. Brigadier Brodie gave authority to withdraw it into the main body if necessary. Enemy parties assailed Z Company, breaking into one of its positions. Colonel Foster's headquarters came under fire and withdrew to the overnight perimeter held by C Squadron*, 8th Hussars. The Royal Ulster Rifles, preparing to send a company to the bridges at first light to find the missing members of the Battle Patrol, were ordered to move forward as a whole to secure hill feature 398, two miles behind the Northumberland Fusiliers' position, and to be prepared to clear the ground to Ulster Crossing after first light.

When daylight dispelled the leaping uncertainties of darkness, the situation disclosed was grim. The Chinese held the abandoned centre of the brigade position. The Belgian battalion remained under mortar and small arms fire, its approaches for a time enveloped in the smoke of burning scrub. Immediately south of Ulster Crossing, many of the heights were occupied by Chinese. In the Glosters' sector, fresh attacks were being mounted on A and D Companies by about 1,000 enemy—an estimate confirmed soon after 0715 by an air observer. Colonel Carne wished to withdraw these two elements but did not want to uncover 1st ROK Division's right flank, or any redeployment of the Northumberland Fusiliers on his right.

In considering a plan to stabilise his defence, Brigadier Brodie took comfort in three circumstances. The 65th Infantry on his right flank had generally held firm against the night attacks. With daylight, the Fifth Air Force would add weight to his fire support; and C Squadron, 8th Hussars, would be able to operate to assist the infantry.

---

* B Squadron had been relieved by C, temporarily under Captain P C Ormerod on 22nd April. The squadron commander, Major Henry Huth, reassumed command on 23rd April.

The immediate requirement was to sustain the Belgian position until 3rd Division, falling back on Line Kansas, was abreast of the 'hinge'; if that should be lost the enemy would be able to cut the division's main line of withdrawal. The longer the Belgians remained, however, the greater the danger of their isolation and loss. To ensure the security of the withdrawal route across the bridges, he needed to expand westward again, to restore to as great an extent as possible his centre position, and to keep open his own line of communication, Route 11, the track running due south behind his headquarters. And he needed to reinforce the Glosters, now more than ever separated from the remainder of the brigade, and accessible from the rear only by a track, Route 5Y, winding down through a gorge. These requirements exceeded his resources.

He spoke to General Soule at 0725, and at once received help. A rifle company and two platoons of tanks were to be sent along the bank of the Hant'an to reinforce the Belgians. The 1st Battalion, 7th Infantry, would move shortly to occupy the brigade centre. Assurances were given that the British sector would receive a full share of air support. Helicopters were made available to lift out the seriously wounded collecting in unit regimental aid posts including that of the Glosters[11].

Strikes by the F-80s, bold sorties by the Centurion tanks, and the devoted support of the artillery, including an American medium battery, inhibited the movement of the Chinese round and below Ulster Crossing. The Royal Ulster Rifles occupied Hill 398, a commanding feature topped by a broken castle. This secured the northern entrance to Route 11. A second and smaller group from the battalion, under Major John Shaw, occupied the pass across the saddle 5,000 yards to the south. For a time, he was obliged to dispose also a reserve for the Glosters but this was fortunately cancelled; engaged also in clearing small parties of enemy from various sites, the battalion was already stretched beyond its limits.

Mid-morning, the guns came under fire from an adjacent hilltop. 55 Field Squadron entered the battle. Supported by the Bofors light anti-aircraft troop on the position*, 3 and 2 Troops of field engineers under Captains Bayton-Evans and John Page scrambled up the hill in succession to rout 40 Chinese on the heights. This incident persuaded Colonel Young that he should move his guns back. Local dangers apart, the shift in positions now made it increasingly difficult to provide support throughout the brigade sector. Still, he was sensitive to the effect that the departure of the guns might have on those fighting and arranged to move southward piecemeal, ensuring that there were never less than two batteries in position and operational at any time[12].

---

* A Troop of 11 Sphinx Light Anti-Aircraft Battery. The remainder of the battery was covering the lower Han bridges and the environs of the Seoul fighter air strip.

Intermittently, through the morning, the Northumberland Fusiliers was pressed from its positions. The 23rd was St George's Day, their regimental day. They had hoped to celebrate it modestly; but all they could do by way of commemoration was to wear some of the roses, ordered from Tokyo, in their caps. Y Company ran a gauntlet of fire in withdrawal from its isolated locality, all three platoon commanders were among the wounded. Z Company was driven off Hill 257, which commanded the bridges, and was unable to regain it in a counter-attack. For the Chinese, reinforced by arrivals from the 188th Division, continued to attack unrelentingly on either side of the river long after daylight. W Company was drawn back to relieve the Royal Engineers on their hilltop opposite the RUR's feature 398. Passage to the bridges was now closed to 29 Brigade.

In mid-morning, orders had been issued from I Corps to revert to Line Kansas. The 65th Infantry Regiment began to move back promptly at 13.30. The Chinese in this sector, elements of both the Fifteenth and the Twelfth Armies had been subjected to widespread air attack through the morning and made no attempt to follow. By mid-afternoon, as the main body of the 3rd Division passed to the south of the Hant'an, the 'hinge' position became redundant. This was the circumstance signified by the codeword 'Foxhound', but the brigade no longer had the freedom of manoeuvre to respond to it.

General Soule placed a strong infantry battalion group* on the main road and river crossing to safeguard the ground to the east of Colonel Crahay's Belgian force while he contrived with Brigadier Brodie how they should be evacuated.

The two commanders discussed this on the telephone. The brigadier proposed that the Belgian Battalion and those grouped with them should destroy their unarmoured vehicles and withdraw east along the Hant'an bank to the 3rd Division's ground. General Soule preferred a plan of his own. The 1st Battalion, 7th Infantry, attempting to recapture 29 Brigade's central position should attack Hill 287—Z Company's original location—and hold it while Colonel Crahay withdrew his force over the bridges. Meantime, the 10th Philippine Battalion Combat Team†—10 BCT—would be sent to provide a reserve for 29 Brigade.

Lieutenant-Colonel Fred C Weyand, commanding the 1st/7th, already in the brigade sector *en route* to the former X Company area, turned his battalion round and marched back to a point below Z

---

* 3rd Battalion, 65th Infantry, the 64th Tank Battalion, and a reconnaissance company.

† The Philippines Expeditionary Force to Korea (PEFTOK) was the 10th Battalion Combat Team, 64 officers and 1,303 other ranks. Its fighting element included three strong rifle companies, a company of medium tanks, a reconnaissance company of light tanks and armoured cars and a battery of self-propelled artillery.

Company's Hill 287. This took about 3 hours. Much to the admiration of the British tank and artillery elements cooperating with him, the colonel integrated them swiftly and neatly into his plan and launched the whole at 1800 hours. But in two hours of fighting, neither the initial assault forces, nor the reserve launched through them, reached the top of the first spur. The Chinese had doubled their numbers on 287. In the gathering dusk, small parties of Chinese with grenades and pole charges stalked the tanks firing in support of the American infantry.

Yet the attempted attack was not wholly a failure. As it began, the Chinese on 287 were drawn to resist Colonel Weyand's advance. The Belgians drew away under the cover of artillery fire. A few mortars engaged the marching Belgian infantry until, wading across the Imjin, they passed beyond range. Their vehicles, escorted by the American tanks sent earlier in the day, raced across the bridges to turn east along the Hant'an bank. Raked by machine guns while crossing, four only were disabled or destroyed, despite their proximity to the mass of enemy lying in cover close by. The end of the column drew away without pursuit as Colonel Weyand's companies continued to press the opposite face of Hill 287.

On the evening of 23rd April, the Royal Ulster Rifles had three companies on 398, the Northumberland Fusiliers held the high ground to the west. Route 11 was thereby contained. Major Shaw's RUR detachment held firm on the pass. A mile and a half south again, brigade headquarters and 55 Field Squadron were resited close to 26 Field Ambulance. The new gun line of 45 Field Regiment lay at Sangbi-ri, 2,000 yards to the east. Into this position at 2000 hours came the Philippine 10 BCT.

Though preoccupied during much of the day with maintaining the 'hinge' and recovering the Belgians, Brigadier Brodie had not forgotten the Glosters. Twice he had disposed reserves in case of a crisis in their location, and twice had been relieved that no call came. That evening, after the withdrawal of the former, he reviewed their position.

The Glosters' two foremost companies stood to arms when Second-Lieutenant Temple's ambush on the Imjin was sprung at 2230 on 22nd April. Even at that time, some 500 Chinese were crossing downstream to attack A Company. This Chinese battalion group mistakenly believed that Major Angier's company had outlying or night patrol positions close to their crossing and delayed their advance searching for them. They did not therefore reach his position until 0200. The company was waiting, finally alerted to their approach by the rattling of tin cans on the thin line of their barbed wire*. Silence was preserved as the enemy closed. Then as the latter sprang forward, they encountered a storm of small arms fire, a hail of grenades. The 3-inch mortars firing from positions behind battalion headquarters, dropped bombs on to the lower slopes. There were many Chinese casualties. In confusion, the assault parties dropped back.

About this time, the enemy held back by the ambush on Gloster Crossing finally reached D Company, where the pattern of repulse was similar. Shortly, both Chinese battalions attacked again. Indeed, they had no other option; the removal of these foremost companies was essential to use of the Imjin crossings by their own artillery and supply vehicles. By 0430, the two Glosters' positions had been attacked four times. Well supported by artillery and mortars, and by the Vickers machine-guns firing on mutual arcs, they had lost no ground and their casualties were light.

It had been expected that, after sunrise with the appearance of United Nations aircraft, the attacks would abate, but they did not: if anything, enemy mortar fire and assaults were pressed more strongly between 0600 and 0700 on 23rd April, when the summit of Castle Hill was lost to A Company. It was then that Brigadier Brodie received information from a Mosquito aircraft that several thousand Chinese—a regiment—were moving on and round the front of the Glosters position, with 1,000 swarming round A and D Companies. A platoon of the latter was driven back but counter-attacked successfully. Informing Colonel Carne about the withdrawal of X Company and the battle on the Belgian front, the Brigadier said that the withdrawal of Major Angier's and Captain Harvey's companies would not endanger either flank†; the east was now wholly exposed. He could only offer, with difficulty, a rifle company from the RUR to assist any counter-attack necessary to withdraw those forward, and it would take three or four hours to get them to the Glosters' battalion headquarters.

Colonel Carne decided that he would be unable to wait that long. Even so, his two companies would have to hold on as he devised a means of extraction from those surrounding them. They were intermittently in close action. There were wounded to be recovered. In A Company, the loss of the Castle hilltop made a clean break unlikely; the success of a

---

* Barbed wire was short along Line Kansas due to demand. A and D Companies had been given the greater share of the allocation to the Glosters but it was sufficient only for a single coil round each platoon position.

† Crossing the Imjin on the morning of 23rd April to attack the 1st ROK Division, the Chinese 192nd Division had been heavily attacked from the air in complement to artillery fire. Weakened and much confused, those south of the river offered only tentative thrusts at the ROK regiment adjoining the Glosters.

local counter-attack being mounted would be crucial to recovery of any sort. Two optional fire plans were being made: one for a deliberate withdrawal if the attack was successful; the other to cover a running fight. Meantime, Colonel Carne told Major Angier, 'You will stay [in position] at all costs until further notice'[13].

On the top of Castle Hill, the Chinese had established a machine-gun. Behind mud walls*, this weapon was able to sweep two platoon positions and the forward company headquarters. The first attempt to take this by Lieutenant Philip Curtis's platoon was driven back with some loss. Curtis was himself wounded. Ordering those with him to remain in cover, he ran forward alone, a pistol in one hand, a grenade in the other. Missed by the first riposte of fire from the enemy position, Lieutenant Curtis paused to throw the grenade, but while it looped towards its target he was killed by a second. The grenade in flight dropped into the Chinese post, destroying it†.

By this time, the morning struggles and, in particular, fire from the hilltop had substantially reduced the company's strength. Major Angier was dead, together with Second-Lieutenant J M Maycock and 8 others. The remaining platoon commander, Second-Lieutenant T E Waters was wounded among 16. On the high ground, Company Sergeant-Major Gallagher took command, and when the order came to abandon the position he brought it out, the platoons commanded by sergeants.

The first artillery plan was fired. Shells from forty eight field and twelve medium guns‡ fell simultaneously round A and D Companies, destroying or driving back the Chinese pressing in upon them. C Troop, 170 Heavy Mortar Battery, fired salvoes between their engagements. A pair of F-80s struck the forward slopes of Castle Hill and the D Company feature with napalm and rockets just after 1000[14]. Captain Harvey, who had lost his artillery observation officer, Lieutenant A B S Hudson, among his own tally of killed and wounded, drew D Company back at about the same time as A. Oxford carriers manned by Support Company made a sortie to collect the wounded and some of the dead, together with the Vickers machine gun crews.

Meantime, B Company, located on the hillocks known as the 'Pimples', on the right and somewhat to the rear of D, had received random fire through the first part of the night; and had become aware that Chinese were passing to and fro below them, occasionally setting off the company's warning flares. Major Harding had brought 4.2- and 3-inch mortar fire down on these. Then,

---

* The machine-gun was sited in a sheltered stand constructed some weeks before as an observation post for General Ridgway.

† Lieutenant Curtis was awarded the Victoria Cross posthumously for this action.

‡ The guns of 45 Field Regiment were supplemented by 3rd Division and I Corps artillery units.

> ... At about 0015 hours 4 and 6 Platoons were attacked. Enemy were heard climbing the path...and approached to within 10 yards of Corporal Juggins' section. Private Robson on the Bren [light machine-gun] withheld his fire until the enemy were virtually on top of him. As a result, 13 Chinese were killed and the enemy were not too keen to make a second approach...[15]

Those attacking had earlier passed over the Imjin near X Company. They appeared to be uncertain of B Company's location at first but gradually discovered its lineaments during minor clashes, without loss to the defence. Major Harding continued to call periodically for artillery fire, which further disrupted enemy action. The sun rose soon after 0440, when large numbers of Chinese were seen moving south through the hills in the central sector of the brigade*, and these were shelled by Captain M Newcombe, the forward observation officer, as artillery was available. The company patrolled extensively round the hill features, re-laying some of the warning flares, and driving off small enemy parties. They found many Chinese bodies. Colonel Carne had already made up his mind to form a close perimeter round the battalion headquarters and mortar lines. Major Harding's reports, and those of his artillery observer, persuaded him that with so many Chinese on and round his right flank, he must bring B Company into the close perimeter without delay. At 0815 he ordered the company back to feature 314, eight hundred yards east of C. In triumphant spirits, though heavily laden, the company withdrew south for a mile unchallenged until they approached their objective. From this, in a brief assault, they swept a small party of enemy before settling in to develop defences round the rocky height.

While the struggle continued to bring the Belgian battalion back from the 'hinge', the Glosters consolidated their positions. A and D Companies climbed to Hill 235, on the heights immediately to the west of and immediately above battalion headquarters, somewhat to the relief of the Assault Pioneer Platoon under Captain HJ Pike, conscious of its slender numbers on this spacious hill top. The Korean porters continued to labour extensively, ascending and reascending many times this height with battle requirements. A complete replacement of ammunition was drawn by all companies, and C Troop was resupplied with 4.2-inch mortar bombs. With the expectation of a close night battle ahead, the adjutant sent out the majority of the F Echelon transport in the late morning, and Captain Dain sent the lumbering Rancid and Ringworm with these vehicles. Of his own volition, he remained to replace Lieutenant Hudson as a forward observation officer. Last to leave the area that afternoon was the battalion second-in-command, Major D B A Grist. He and his

* Some of these were in civilian clothes, and Sgt P V Petherick of the Glosters, following capture, was among several armed units in Korean civilian dress. These may have been deep reconnaissance parties but, if so, they were latecomers.

driver, Private George Bainbridge, drove off and had barely covered two miles up the gorge before they found themselves running a gauntlet of fire. The enemy were gathering in strength behind the battalion and these two travellers were fortunate to escape with minor wounds.

Mulling over his arrangements for the night and next day, Brigadier Brodie decided against deploying 10 BCT behind the Glosters that night, but to hold them in reserve in their debussing area. They certainly would not have made a passage through the Chinese cordon on the gorge in the approaching darkness. His chief anxiety was the extent to which the enemy was passing round his flanks, and what use was to be made of the considerable enemy force on the great height of Kamak-san. However, his orders were clear: General Soule had reiterated that 3rd Division, including 29 Brigade, would hold Line Kansas.

Indeed, General Van Fleet, the new army commander had confirmed that the line would be held. He believed that, with his immense fire potential, he could hold the enemy. Visiting his corps and divisions during the day, he had made this policy clear, though several of his commanders were of a different mind[16]. He did not order any of them to hold ground indefinitely regardless of loss but insisted that localities should be held in close perimeters by night, from which devastating fire would be directed by day. As reserves were committed, new ones must be disposed. Withdrawal to the shorter Line Kansas had not permitted him to establish a forward line on which every unit's flanks brushed those of its neighbours, but the reduced frontage promoted the size of reserves.

These were the principles on which General Ridgway had operated as army commander, but the emphasis was different; divisions were not going to roll with the punches but to accept body blows before they drew back. This change was no doubt due to the the nature of General Van Fleet's character, but he was also influenced by the apprehension that a series of premature withdrawals would draw down the confidence General Ridgway had fostered since January. He seems to have overlooked, or at any rate been unwilling to recognise, that his predecessor had drawn up a limited withdrawal plan in the face of an enemy spring offensive precisely to preserve his army's confidence.

It must be said that, on the evening of 23rd April, his line remained intact with the exception of a gap on the front of 6th ROK Division on the left flank of IX Corps. But all the evidence suggested that it was tattered and stretched after the first full day of operations. P'eng's 'first impulse' was waxing. General Milburn for one guessed that to preserve the fighting power of his corps he would have to break away from the Chinese numbers which had penetrated the flanks of his formations in the west, and these included 1st ROK Division and 3rd Division with 29 Brigade.

That night, 23rd/24th April, the Sixty Third Army brought the remainder of its divisional columns across the Imjin. The remainder of the 188th Division joined the greater part of the 187th in the centre and eastern half of the brigade sector. The 189th was directed on to and round the Glosters.

About midnight, a company of the 189th established itself between C and B Companies. It ranged with machine guns on B Company from about 600 yards and, a little later, supported by mortar fire attempted, but failed, to break into the company locality. From this same site, others developed a strong attack on C Company about 0330 on the 24th, driving it off its position, securing ground which, in daylight, would command the Glosters' battalion headquarters and mortar lines. As soon as this was reported, Colonel Carne gave orders to evacuate the area, carrying all essentials up to Hill 235 held by A, D, and elements of Support Company. In this move, part of C Company, including the company commander, became separated, and the Royal Signals rear link detachment under Lance Corporal Jennings temporarily lost radio contact with brigade headquarters. The adjutant relayed details of the situation over the 45 Field net at 0530, including the news that a large column of enemy was moving south along Route 5Y.

With C Company's departure, attacks continued against B throughout the remainder of the night. With light machine guns, rifles and grenades, and greatly aided by frequent artillery fire, the company held the majority of its ground. Just after dawn, Lieutenant Geoffrey Costello counter-attacked with his platoon to recover an adjacent position. Some of those with him, already wounded, were hit a second time, yet remained in action.

After dawn, Colonel Carne was able to offer some limited assistance to B Company, at best to help it to break away to join the remainder of the battalion, at worst to give them some respite. Sergeant Sykes' medium machine-gun section opened fire on enemy moving upwards to join those pressing in on the dwindling company. Captain Dain directed artillery fire on to targets out of Captain Newcombe's view.

> ... By now the situation was very serious. Ammunition was virtually expended and many wounded were lying in the company area with little or no cover to protect them. After withdrawing for reorganisation, a short pause ensued and the seventh and final attack was launched at 08.10 hours. Hordes of Chinese rushed up to the summit of the hill and charged through 4 Platoon's area. Sheer weight of numbers forced the platoon over the rear face of the hill...[17]

In such circumstances, against such odds, a company disintegrates. Fifteen officers and men under Major Harding came into the view of those watching on Hill 235 as they withdrew across the rocky slopes towards some trees. Efforts to give them covering fire were intensified, to the point that a rifle section commander among those watching, Corporal Walker, made a sortie of his own volition, firing a Bren gun from the hip to drive back one of the pursuing groups. Scrambling down, obliged by an almost sheer drop to make a detour, the remnant of B Company reached the valley floor amidst shot and shell from both sides. Forty minutes after coming into view, Major Harding's party reached the comparative safety of Hill 235. B and C formed a composite company to defend a segment of the battalion position.

These exchanges had the secondary effect of persuading the enemy to draw back from the crests immediately overlooking the former battalion headquarters and mortar sites. Regimental Sergeant-Major Hobbs was given the task of organising a strong party of Glosters, gunners, cooks, and Korean porters to make a sortie down the hill to carry off small arms ammunition, grenades, bazooka rockets, radio batteries, water and food. Captain Wisbey's heavy mortarmen had already carried away their mortar barrels, sights, and radios, but now needed small arms ammunition for their role on 235 as infantry. Supplies were required by Captain R P Hickey, the medical officer from the regimental aid post. All the casualties incurred since Route 5Y was cut on 23rd April had accumulated in his care.

Covering fire was opened. Smoke shells from 45 Field cloaked the recovery party from view; the Vickers machine guns swept the eastern slopes of Kamak-san. The sortie was made successfully. Those on Hill 235, some 400 unwounded, had the means to sustain the defence for a further term, say, for another night. What then?

Brigadier Brodie had launched 10 BCT to clear Route 5Y from the south to the Glosters' position. They were reinforced by half of C Squadron, 8th Hussars, to hasten their passage to the mouth of the gorge. Starting at 0800, the aim was to reach Hill 235 in time to complete the return of both Glosters and Philippine groups in daylight. But while any relief attempt was welcome, Colonel Carne personally doubted that 10 BCT was strong enough to reach his battalion. The numbers of Chinese which had passed round his positions during the previous twelve hours exceeded regimental strength, and considerable enemy had been swarming on Kamak-san prior to this. Two miles separated the Filipino concentration area from the southern entrance to the gorge. Hill 235 lay a further two and a half through the gorge itself. He had proposed fighting back at 0700 but had been told to remain in position[18]—General Soule's decision.

At 0900, permission was granted to withdraw, but by this time the Philippines group was reported to be making progress. Colonel Carne decided to wait; if he fought his way back, the wounded would have to be left behind. At 1240, Major Huth reported an advance of a mile, at 1415 of a second mile against gathering opposition. They were in sight of the gorge mouth, and under small arms fire from the hills enclosing it. At that point, the leading Filipino light tank hit a mine, and the column stopped behind it. As no one else was helping, two of the Centurions squeezed past the other light tanks and, under their covering fire, the disabled crew were able to join the main body. The 10 BCT commanding officer proposed to Major Huth that his Centurions should assume the leading role, an offer wisely declined. The Centurions were too heavy and too wide for the track through the gorge, but even if, in this emergency, they attempted to move down it, the sides were so steep that they would be unable to apply fire effectively. If a Centurion hit a mine *en route*, it would block the track until an armoured recovery vehicle came to pull it out. At this point, the relief operation on 24th April came effectively to an end[19].

Later, when the course of the battle was analysed, undue attention was paid to why the Philippines Group withdrew with C Squadron, ordered back at that time, and whether Brigadier Brodie or his staff should have stopped their movement. In so far as relief of the Glosters is concerned, it is immaterial. The force had no prospect of clearing either the gorge or a route through hills parallel to it: a battalion of 187th Division confronted them on one side of Route 5Y, at least a battalion on the other*. A reinforced brigade or regimental combat team was the minimum force required to effect a relief.

This became apparent to General Soule as he reviewed the progress of the Philippines BCT. Shortly after 3 o'clock that afternoon, he informed Brigadier Brodie that he was moving a task force comprised of two battalions of the 65th Infantry, the majority of the 64th Tank Battalion, and the 10th Field Artillery Battalion, to effect the relief early on 25th April by an advance acrss the hills west of Route 5Y. 'How are the Glosters doing?' he asked the brigadier. 'A bit sticky; things are pretty sticky down there,' was the reply. British officers were expected to report in a low key; but Brigadier Brodie was not communicating to a British commander. 'Pretty sticky' was taken by General Soule to mean unpleasant but sustainable. Thus, when Generals Ridgway, Van Fleet, and Milburn, visiting his headquarters that afternoon, asked why the stronger relief force was not being launched immediately, he responded that the task force would not complete their concentration behind 29 Brigade until 1730 hours. He had ordered the Glosters to hold fast. They were meantime

* Nine Glosters under Sergeant Wateridge, captured at the A Echelon location on 23rd April, were taken to the upper slopes of Kamak-san, from which they escaped during an early morning air strike on 24th April. Reaching brigade headquarters, they reported 1,000 Chinese on this feature.

acting as a useful break on the enemy advance. To help stabilise the area, he had returned the Belgian Battalion to the brigade to hold a blocking position to the west of the junctions of Routes 5Y and 11[20].

When this information was passed to Colonel Carne at 1510, he replied,

> I understand the position quite clearly. What I must make clear to you is that my command is no longer an effective fighting force. If it is required that we shall stay here, in spite of this, we shall continue to hold. But I wish to make known the nature of my position[21].

Arrangements were notified to the battalion for resupply by light aircraft that evening of radio batteries, light machine guns and ammunition. Requests for helicopters to remove the most critically wounded had to be refused because Hill 235 was within small arms range of the enemy.

The daylight hours had not been easy for the remainder of the brigade. The Northumberland Fusiliers were forced back by continual pressure along the west side of Route 11, their movement assisted by the other half of C Squadron firing from the paddy fields on either side of the track. The three companies of the Royal Ulster Rifles on Hill 398, particularly A Company under Major Sir Christopher Nixon on the northern slopes, were attacked more than a dozen times. Mortar and shellfire helped to break them up. Artillery and air strikes were employed to staunch the enemy groups moving south round the flanks. Gradually, this resistance, causing immense casualties to the Chinese 188th Division, brought an easement in the late morning. Even when the scrub, ignited by white phosphorus smoke, took fire round A Company, forcing it temporarily from cover, the enemy made no attempt to exploit the confusion. Casualties were taken down to the regimental aid posts to be evacuated by helicopter, or down Route 11 to the advanced dressing station of 26 Field Ambulance[22]. Captain Patchett, regimental medical officer of the 8th Hussars, assisted in this process. After visiting C Squadron, he had decided to remain forward, and ferried casualties back in his half track* through the day.

Although the route south remained open, those travelling along it in the late afternoon came under occasional sniper fire. Anxious to ensure that those forward were fully supplied for 25th April, Major Eastwood, the DAA&QMG†, dumped forward stocks in 57 Company transport to bolster unit supply echelons. Additional REME recovery detachments were also brought forward at this time.

* A half track was propelled on rear tracks but steered by front wheels. The vehicle used was an American White scout car, retained in British service from the Second World War.

† DAA & QMG, principal administrative staff officer at brigade headquarters. See Volume I, p 163, fn.

When night fell, a C-47 transport dropped flares along the Imjin river. Selected batteries fired volleys to mark targets for bombers. These measures caught random targets among the 190th Division joining the 192nd of Sixty Fourth Army pressing a resolute 1st ROK Division. A stick of bombs fell also on an artillery battery of the Sixty Third Army just below Gloster Crossing. The 189th Division, completing its move into the former A and D Company areas, seem otherwise to have escaped the attacks. The 188th, seeking to 'wipe out' the 29 Brigade forces on Route 11, was generally too far south of the bomb line to be endangered, though one of the B-26s, dropping short, straddled the Northumberland Fusiliers without causing damage.

On the right of I Corps' line, after a quiet day, Wang Chin-shan's Fifteenth and Sixtieth Armies opened a series of massed attacks, beginning at dusk on the 25th Division, right hand neighbour to the 3rd. On the other flank, it was evident that I NKPA Corps was crossing the Imjin at Munsan-ni to join the offensive against 1st ROK Division. The gaps in the 29 Brigade line and, later, on the remaining frontage of 3rd Division, threatened the piecemeal destruction of these formations.

General Milburn decided that he must withdraw from Line Kansas to Line Delta, 4 miles behind 1st ROK, 12 miles behind the 24th Division, a contingency for which he had previously prepared a plan*. Confirmatory orders to move back were issued at 0500 hours on the morning of Wednesday, 25th April[23].

On the previous day, he had committed his one reserve formation, the 15th Infantry Regiment, to blocking positions behind 1st ROK and clearance of the road connecting Routes 1 and 3 at Uijongbu, a prescient move; Chinese groups were already on or threatening to occupy these. But he did not intend to abandon the Glosters. General Soule was specifically instructed to relieve them, if necessary by mounting a counter-attack[24].

To this end, the 65th Infantry's task force had been disposed to attack at 0630, clearing a route across Kamak-san to Hill 235. But earlier in the morning, General Soule had become apprehensive that the Chinese groups passing through the gaps in the 29 Brigade line over three days were moving to cut his withdrawal route—Route 33—towards Uijongbu. He therefore cancelled the relief operation, sending two battalions of the 65th, with 10 BCT, and his divisional reconnaissance company to counter this movement, leaving one battalion with 29 Brigade to keep open the withdrawal route of the Northumberland Fusiliers and the Royal Ulster Rifles from Route 11 to Route 3.

He could not ignore his clear instructions from General Milburn, however, to effect the Glosters' relief. But in making these dispositions,

* I Corps Plan 'Golden', 17th April 1951.

all he had left was a battalion of medium and a company of light tanks. He instructed Colonel Harris, commander of the 65th Infantry, to devise a relief plan using these forces in cooperation with Brigadier Brodie. Colonel Harris expressed the view that a sortie by the light tanks down the gorge would be adequate and, after some delay, a tank platoon—indeed, a tank platoon less one of its complement—set off at 0900 without artillery observers or indeed contact with Colonel Harris's headquarters. The run of these events lay along that narrow line between tragedy and farce.

From the moment that General Soule cancelled the 65th Infantry relief operation, the prospect of relieving the Glosters expired. At 0610, Brigadier Brodie spoke to Colonel Carne, telling him what had happened, giving him permission to break out. He said he would hold in his area as long as he could but the nearest point of friendly forces was 1st ROK Division to the south west of Hill 235. American tanks were supporting a sortie by General Kang's 12th Regiment. 45 Field would stay in action as long as possible. He did not mention the light tank antics under discussion. Colonel Carne said he could not move immediately; the position was surrounded, but he would break away when sufficient numbers of the enemy had been destroyed or driven back.

The Glosters had been fighting on and off throughout the night. Attacks had been launched from three directions from 2200 and, these having failed, various permutations as to line and main thrust were used to take Hill 235. Lacking radios, the Chinese used trumpets to direct their battalions. As a countermeasure, Drum-Major P E Buss was instructed to sound a range of British calls to confuse the enemy. His excellent performance silenced the Chinese for a time. After dawn, 45 Field and 5th Air Force gave frequent support, striking the dense columns climbing the hillsides with shellfire and napalm. None struggling to hold their positions debated the ethics of using the latter.

On several occasions, the leading Chinese cohorts thrust into parts of the defensive line. There were grenade exchanges. Between the bursting of these lethal little bombs, and the spread of their fragmented steel cases, officers and men bobbed up and down at ranges of ten or a dozen yards, firing small arms as they saw a target. When the weight of numbers threatened to overwhelm the obduracy of the defence, local commanders among the latter called supporting fire on to their own positions[25]. The Glosters and artillery observers concerned, fighting from the rudimentary shelter of trenches and sangars* accepted the risk of being hit by their own fire. The enemy, lacking cover, was exposed to the full force of it.

---

* Where stony ground denies excavation of trenches in defensive positions, defensive walls—sangars—are raised of stone and rocks.

In making a plan to fight back to the main body of 29 Brigade, Colonel Carne relied almost wholly on intensive air and ground fire support. Attempts to drop replacement weapons, ammunition and radio batteries to him that morning had rightly been abandoned; the crest of Hill 235 was too narrow to offer a dropping zone. But what remained on the hill after the intense fighting of the night and early morning was insufficient to sustain an infantry battle. A Company, for example, had 3 rounds per rifle, with a magazine and a half for its light machine-guns, half a magazine for the machine carbines. Among the forty in action, there were 7 high explosive and 4 white phosphorus smoke grenades.

The battalion with its comrades of C Troop, 170 Battery, the 70 Battery observation posts, and the Royal Signals rear link detachment, made ready to move at 1000, accompanied by the walking wounded. Those unable to walk were to be left in the area of the regimental aid post, marked plainly by a Red Cross flag.

A little before 10, Major Grist managed to make contact on the fading radio link—the last surviving link—with 45 Field. The remainder of 29 Brigade were falling back; the guns might have to move shortly out of range. Any attempt to fight back to their area was hopeless. The final order he passed from the brigade commander was that the battalion should split up: 'every man is to make his own way back'*.

Colonel Carne held a final brief conference. He pointed out to his company and detachment commanders two saddles over the hills to the south of 235, illuminated by bright sunlight. Across the left of these lay the route recommended by brigade headquarters to carry them into the advancing elements of 1st ROK Division. Everyone should be informed of that route. Thereafter, in a matter of minutes, Hill 235 was to be generally abandoned.

Generally, but not wholly; the regimental medical officer, Captain Hickey, had decided that he must stay with the wounded, renouncing all hope of personal escape. Padre Davies and Sergeant Brisland, the medical sergeant, joined him in this selfless act†. Their presence was reassuring to those left in a hollow by the Red Cross flag, and as the enemy were expected at any moment, Sergeant Brisland began to wave the flag vigorously. Drum-Major Buss was passing at that moment and, unaware of the situation, began to remonstrate with Sergeant Brisland, believing that he was engaged in surrendering a defensive position. There

---

* This message was picked up by Chinese radio monitors. (Statement by Song Jun-u, Thames Television Series, Korea, The Unknown War, 1987).

† After the battle, it was erroneously reported that Colonel Carne also stayed with the wounded. If he had done so, he would have been liable to trial by court martial. All soldiers—and notably commanding officers—have a duty to evade capture in a close action. If it appears that they have failed to do so to the best of their ability, disciplinary action is taken when they are repatriated. As it was, Colonel Carne was awarded the Victoria Cross for his conduct in this battle.

were hasty explanations by the medical officer and padre with urgent advice to the drum-major to hasten on[26]. He was just able to catch up the remainder, racing away in a broad sweep down the hillside.

None lingered. Some of those on the left drew away below the ridge line. A few succesfully negotiated a gulley on a parallel route to the saddle. The broad mass moving south east through the valley immediately below Hill 235 were halted by Chinese fire[27]. The great majority of these were captured at once, others were taken over the next few days. But on the right, Captain Harvey with D Company, and a smaller group under Lieutenant R J Martin, took the line of the right hand saddle, passing by good fortune, to the south of a Chinese regiment of the 192nd Division halted to reorganise on the lateral road parallel with the Imjin.

Initially unimpeded, these parties, drawing together, sped on. Their progress was observed by a Mosquito pilot, originally following the abortive light tank sorties launched by Colonel Harris. He flew low, waggling his wings to show recognition to and encourage those on the ground. What he could not do was to tell them that they were on course to a point where a battalion of 1st ROK Division and two platoons of American heavy tanks* were fighting a battle. The Glosters groups now found themselves moving between entrenched Chinese—a battalion of the 192nd Division—which increasingly opened fire from two sides. Yet, losing some of their number, they pressed on, made furiously energetic by the sight of American tanks in action to the south. Closing, hatless and mudstained from ditches along which they had crawled, they were taken for Chinese by several of the tank crews, who opened fire, hitting six.

Further disaster was avoided by the Mosquito pilot. He dropped a note prompting a sortie by the nearest tanks, which gathered the survivors, Captain Harvey and 39 others, into the United Nations lines.

Meantime, the remainder of 29 Brigade was fighting its way out of Line Kansas. Withdrawal to Line Delta had been stood over temporarily during the first part of the morning while there were late hopes of relieving the Glosters. From about 0700, however, it was essential to issue firm orders in order to prevent the entrapment of the Northumberland Fusiliers and Royal Ulster Rifles.

Both battalions had been attacked intermittently from 0130 onwards, the heaviest assaults falling on Hill 398. In the absence of his company holding the pass, Major Rickord had no reserve in hand but, given unfailing support by the artillery and mortars, peripheral losses were recovered. To the west of Route 11, the Northumberland Fusiliers

---

* 2nd Battalion, 12 ROK Regiment, and part of C Company, 73rd Heavy Tank Battalion had been ordered forward by General Kang Moon-bong to recapture a feature on the divisional right flank and to make contact with the Glosters.

came increasingly under small arms fire from the spurs and outcrops of Kamak-san. Major John Wynn reported just before dawn that he had 25 seriously wounded men in Z Company, obliging him to contract his position. Colonel Foster prepared to reinforce the area in daylight to enable the wounded to be brought down. He hoped that some of Major Huth's Centurions would be available to support this operation.

At dawn, Route 11 was hidden in mist, but a troop of C Squadron began to make its way forward. Its progress was hampered by a combination of poor visibility and small groups of Chinese infiltrated from the west during the night The greater part of the enemy regiment on Kamak-san was now following to block Route 11 on the pass, and immediately to the north of it, while others worked south to close the exits.

The tank advance destroyed or drove into cover the advanced elements from Kamak-san. In the belief that the route had been opened, Brigadier Brodie arranged that the two forward battalions should withdraw under covering fire from their positions and march south along Route 11, led by the Northumberland Fusiliers. Colonel Foster was appointed to command the combined force until it broke out of the hills. By 1100, however, the tens of Chinese in place at dawn had grown to hundreds. A further thousand were moving towards Mau-san and its southern spurs.

Assembled on Route 11, the Northumberland Fusiliers began their march. Astride the pass, they encountered machine-gun fire, soon augmented by sniper fire from the hill slopes on either side. Companies scattered, some groups pressing south, others sought a route over the hills to the east. The Centurions did what they could to suppress the enemy but they were fighting on narrow ground.

By extraordinary devotion, a number of wounded were recovered during this phase, mostly in small groups carried at high speed in jeeps rattling over ruts and potholes. The armoured half track of Captain Patchett, medical officer of the 8th Hussars, was better protected and larger if slower. It became a principal means of evacuation as the enemy grew closer to the road. His task was not easy as he was driving himself—his driver had just had a mouthful of teeth extracted and was far from fit. Returning from a run south to the advanced dressing station, he encountered Colonel Foster's jeep on the pass. The colonel, his driver, and orderly lay dead within.

Major John Shaw's position on the saddle—at the centre of the pass—had become increasingly pressed from about 0915. A battle developed for possession of this vital link with the south which successfully destroyed the Chinese immediately involved. North of the pass, two Centurions were put out of action, one ditched, the other ablaze after attack by Chinese pole charges. Captain Patchett's half track also became ditched in the confusion. With the casualties inside and others close to the ambulance, he was shortly made prisoner.

The leading element of the Royal Ulster Rifles, some way behind the Fusiliers, broke contact successfully and began their march. As they approached the pass the rattle of small arms and the boom of the tank guns swelled. Although they could not prevent fire from falling on the area, the men of B and Support Companies continued to deny occupation by the enemy. C Squadron tanks were still in action there, enabling the approach of the Royal Ulster Rifles' C Company with part of Major Rickord's headquarters. To the rear, a force of Chinese began to fire into the column. As it broke into open order, Lieutenant John Mole dismounted his 3-inch mortars into emergency action as a counter-measure.

Along Route 11, a stony track, numerous vehicles were by this time on fire or disabled southward through the pass. C Company, hemmed in by the enemy, rode south on the back of the Centurions.

> But the road for a mile and a half south of [the pass] was seething with Chinese; every bank, ditch, and house was filled with them and though many were actually crushed under the tracks of the Centurions, the unprotected infantry riding on the outside came under a continuous hail of small arms fire, grenades and mortar bombs. Many were killed on the tanks and many wounded lost their grip on the wildly pitching hulls and fell to the ground. Two tanks were knocked out by pole charges but the remainder, with their load of dead and living, broke through to the comparative safety of the brigade headquarters valley[28].

It was clear to Major Rickord that he must get his force out of the valley floor and over the high ground to the east. With one other tank, Major Huth gave covering fire before they, too, drew back down the pass.

By mid-afternoon, brigade headquarters, the heavy engineer vehicles and equipment, and 26 Field ambulance had moved south to Uijongbu. 45 Field and 170 Mortar Battery were leapfrogging back, keeping always guns or mortars in action. From 1500, the F-80s returned to the brigade sector, falling upon the enemy moving across the hills on either side of Route 11.

Throughout the morning, the southern end of the withdrawal route had been held by Captain Desmond Holmes' Field Engineer Troop, and retained after several attempts to drive it off. Through their position the greater number of the Northumberland Fusiliers and some of the Royal Ulster Rifles passed. The last troops fighting as infantry to withdraw from this battle were, therefore, Royal Engineers. But they were not quite the last overall. The final task for Major Huth, who had lost six tanks*, was

---

* Five Centurions and one Cromwell tank RA observation post.

to cooperate with the Belgian Battalion. Blocking the approaches from the west, Colonel Crahay's force was involved in a rearguard action with those approaching from the Glosters' gorge. Given a combination of air strikes and shellfire from the corps artillery, he broke away, but not before part of the battalion had been scattered into the hills.

Withdrawn from the line, almost every unit of the brigade gathered in men who had been captured and escaped or, more numerous, those who had been separated and found empty routes back. The casualties from the three days of fighting were heavy, 1,091, involving every Regiment and Corps drawn in. About half of these belonged to the Glosters.

> Dear Van, [General Ridgway wrote to General Van Fleet on 7th May]... there is another matter which we discussed, which I want again to emphasise, and that relates to the sacrifice of any unit, particularly that of another nationality. The case of the Gloucester Battalion is, of course, uppermost in my mind.
> While I have not yet received the factual report you are preparing, I cannot but feel a certain disquiet that down through the channel of command, the full responsibility for realising the danger to which this unit was exposed, then for extricating it when that danger became grave, was not recognised nor implemented. ...[29]

> Dear Matt, [General Van Fleet replied on 11th May]...
> In reviewing the action in the light of available information it appears that the Gloucester Battalion Commander did not indicate the seriousness of his position and the need for either additional help or withdrawal. Fortunately it was his decision to hold. I say fortunately because had he not held and inflicted terrific casualties on the 63rd CCF Army, I believe it would have been a proper decision for higher commanders to order him to hold. It was a case of holding on that Northwest sector sufficiently long to permit the withdrawal of troops further north as well as the bulk of the British and Corps Artillery which was threatened by the power drive which overran the Gloucester Battalion. I feel that this Battalion was not lost in vain—that this is one of those great occasions in combat which call for a determined stand, and the loss of 622 officers and men saved many times that number. ...[30]

This criticism was scarcely fair to Colonel Carne: he was damned for not asking permission to withdraw; and should have been ordered to hold fast if he had done so. But this was all part of a general embarrassment and, it must be said, a search for scapegoats. Moreover, the lesson of General Soule's inept judgement and handling had not been lost on General Van Fleet. On the day before he responded to General Ridgway, he remarked to X Corps commander, 'Give when you are pressed hard. I don't want units cut off and I want you to handle UN units [that is, allied units] very carefully to avoid their being cut off. I don't want a repetition of the Gloucester loss—622 men lost. Only forty got back. Our men are too valuable. No last ditch stands. ...'[31]

After further enquiry, the main blame was attributed by General Van Fleet to Brigadier Brodie—he should have known Colonel Carne better, and should have seen what was happening. He also blamed General Soule. None stated what lay at the root of the matter: the many reminders by General Ridgway that positions should be held as long as was feasible. Directives of this kind are entirely justified but implementation requires a nice judgement. The battalion commander is not the man to be seeking withdrawal orders. Perhaps Brigadier Brodie should have brought the Glosters out on the afternoon of the 23rd, but that would have required a withdrawal by 1st ROK Division's right flank. On the 24th, relief might have been possible given a sortie by a regimental combat team during the morning. If the Glosters had been kept in position deliberately because they were destroying and delaying a substantial portion of the Chinese 63rd Army, their loss might have been justified. Actually, they were lost by oversight.

Such matters were for the divisional commander to judge; he should have been watching his subordinate elements two levels down, and he did not watch them well.

After his orders to the battalion to break out, Brigadier Brodie entered in the Brigade operations log in a moment of high emotion, 'No one but the Glosters could have done it'. This was flattering but not true. The other members of the brigade fought no less well. Neither they nor the Glosters sought to be heroes; only to acquit themselves honourably and competently, one among another.

That is the best of the soldier's calling.

SOURCE NOTES: Chapter 9

1 *The Royal Ulster Rifles in Korea, cit,* p 61.

2 Mr A Eagles, private memoir.

3 For an incomplete but useful summary, see 29 Brigade War Diary, Operation Order, April 1951, No 33.

4 See Eighth Army Periodic Intelligence Report for 22nd April 1951, G-2 Sect, (USNARS, Suitland).

5 29 Brigade Operation Order No 33 (see note 3, above).

6 For an example of the timely general information the artillery nets provided, see, for example, the 29 Brigade operations log for 22nd–23rd April 1951 (in War Diary).

7 *The Edge of the Sword,* Anthony Farrar-Hockley, (London, 1954), p 19. This book was written just after the end of the Korean War and the battle descriptions were based on discussion with many of the participants.

8 For the outline of main events, see the headquarters and unit war diaries of 29 Brigade for the period, also *The Royal Ulster Rifles in Korea, cit.*

9 Regimental and divisional tasks within the Sixty Third Army are drawn principally from the prisoner-of-war interrogation reports and documents captured during the period. The majority of these are held with Eighth Army G-3 section monthly reports by USNARS, Suitland.

10 Details of the Belgian action at this time and later are contained in the battalion's journal, and in *Les Belges En Corée, 1951–55,* Albert Crahay (Brussels, 1967).

11 29 Brigade headquarters War Diary. See also 3rd Division G3-Journal, 23rd April 1951, (USNARS, Suitland).

12 War Diaries, 29 Brigade headquarters, 8H, 1 RUR, 45 Field Regiment, 170 Mortar Battery, 55 Field Squadron.

13 I am grateful to Colonel J P Carne, and Major G T Ward, commanding 70 Field Battery at this time, for their recollections in conjunction with my own, of these events. See also *The Edge of the Sword, cit,* pp 29–31.

14 In *The Edge of the Sword, cit,* I recorded erroneously that the battalion received no air support on 23rd April, 1951. 29 Brigade log (in War Diary) correctly shows the one sortie by a pair notified at 1000 hours.

15 Major E D Harding's B Company Battle Report, 22nd–25th April 1951. Copy held at Regimental Headquarters, The Gloucestershire Regiment

16 See, for example, Mossman, *op cit,* pp 397 and 430.

17 Major Harding's Report, *cit.*

18 29 Brigade War Diary, 24th April 1951.

19 Conversation, author with Major H Huth, 8H.

20 For a valuable summary of these events, see Mossman, *op cit,* p 413.

21 *Edge of the Sword, cit,* p 49. The author was present during this conversation.

22 War diaries of the units concerned. *The RUR in Korea, cit,* pp 66–67.

23 I Corps signal CX4329 of 250500 *inter alia* to all subordinate divisions. G-3 diary (USNARS, Suitland)

24 3rd Division G-3 Journal, 25th April 1951 (USNARS, Suitland). See also Mossman, *op cit,* pp 416–419.

25 See *The Edge of the Sword, cit,* Chapter 4.

26 Recounted to the author by the Rev S J Davies.

27 *The Edge of the Sword, op cit,* pp 66–67. See also *The Imjin Roll,* Colonel E D Harding, Regimental Records, The Gloucestershire Regiment (1976).

28 *The Royal Ulster Rifles in Korea, cit,* pp 70–71.

29 Personal file of CINCUNC (USNARS, Suitland). A copy is also held in General Ridgway's private papers at Fort Carlisle.

30 Personal correspondence of CG, Eighth Army (EUSAK), (USNARS, Suitland).

31 CG's Journal, 10 May 1951, (USNARS, Suitland).

CHAPTER 10

'A mighty clash of arms'
II : The Battle on the Kap'yong River

> The main task of the Fortieth Army [attached to 9 Army Group] will be to wipe out the 6th Puppet [ROK] Division and open up a critical breach so as to sever the links between the American forces on the eastern and western fronts; once they have succeeded in doing this, the main force will penetrate directly to Mu-dong-li [Yu-dong-ni] and Kap'yong and cut the Ch'unch'on road...
> The three armies of 9 Army Group will first concentrate an absolute superiority of troop strength and fire power, and quickly wipe out the British 27th Brigade, while using part of their strength to pin down the American 24th Division, and sever the links between the British 27th Brigade and the American 24th Division; once they have succeeded in doing this, they will penetrate directly to [the area of P'och'on] where, attacking from the south east to the north west, they can wipe out the American 24th and 25th Divisions*.

As the British 29th Brigade was the first obstacle to be removed in the west by 19 Army Group, so the 27th British Commonwealth Brigade was to be removed first on the eastern front of the offensive by 9 Army Group. In each case, the destruction of a brigade would open a means of cutting in behind American forces on its flank: the 3rd Division became vulnerable with the elimination of the 29th Brigade, the 24th Division with removal of the 27th. The break up of the 3rd and 24th Divisions would lead to the loss of the 25th Division and the Turkish Brigade. By this means, P'eng sought to tear a huge breach in the United Nations' line and overcome a hundred thousand of its fighting men.

In this central sector of the front, Sung Shi-lun† had disposed his Twentieth Army to attack astride the United States I and IX Corps boundary, engaging the 24th Division with one division, while crushing the 27th Brigade with another. To the east, his Fortieth Army would mask the United States Marine Division while destroying the 6th ROK Division. What Sung did not know as his army group moved to attack was that the identification of 27th Brigade in the line was out of date. It had been relieved by 6th ROK and returned to a reserve position at Kap'yong‡.

---

* Operational Directive of 18th April from P'eng Te-huai to army group commanders (signal of 2100, 18th April 1951 from Headquarters, Chinese People's Volunteers).

† Commander, 9 Army Group, from the outset of the Chinese intervention.

‡ See p 95.

On the afternoon of 22nd April, 6th ROK was advancing north towards Line Wyoming with its 19th Regiment on the left, its 2nd on the right. Motorised patrols, ranging ahead of them at a distance of about 3 miles, had made no contact. But IX Corps artillery observation aircraft suddenly picked up very large bodies of enemy moving south and flashed a warning of their approach, news which alerted the entire Eighth Army front.

Brigadier-General Chang Do-yong, commanding 6th ROK Division, halted his two leading regiments at 1600 hours and ordered them to take up defensive positions on adjoining mountains, a tidy position which closed the gap between the inner flanks of the two formations. He brought his 7th Regiment up behind the 2nd. The division thus had the potential to develop in daylight defences over a depth of 5 miles. In support, he had his own ROK field artillery battalion, the 16th New Zealand Field Regiment, and a company of American 4.2-inch mortars[1]. Further support was available from a battalion of 155-mm howitzers and four batteries of 105-mm guns of IX Corps artillery.

At dusk, then, the 6th ROK Division appeared from its locations marked on the maps in divisional and corps headquarters to be well sited. But if General Chang or any senior member of his staff had visited the regimental areas, which unfortunately they did not, they would have found a very different situation. Redeployment into defensive positions had been slow, the location of fire positions muddled. Groups of junior officers, non-commissioned officers and men were hanging about, inactive, though many essential items for a night defensive battle remained to be carried up to the heights from the tracks below. This was in part due to a want of training, but no less to anxiety among units at the imminence of a Chinese offensive. Leadership among the officers, many arbitrarily selected and poorly trained, was inadequate to cope with these problems[2].

In such circumstances, they had good reason to be apprehensive. After an hour of darkness, without any preliminary fire or other warning, the leading regiment of the Chinese 60th Division engulfed the left foward battalion of the ROK 2nd Regiment. While all was confusion there, a second Chinese regiment moved through it upon the reserve battalion. Resistance was limited to random small arms fire. The 19th Regiment, enquiring about this fire, learned of the 2nd Regiment's difficulties.

Within the hour, the greater number surviving in the 2nd Regiment and the whole of the 19th began to desert their posts, some running off into the darkness without arms or equipment, others more deliberately, carrying weapons and ammunition and radios. Even so, much fighting material was abandoned. Members of the 2nd Regiment alarmed the 7th in reserve as they hastened through its lines between 2200 and 2230. Soon, this formation was also breaking away.

The American and New Zealand batteries had not deployed observation posts with the ROK division; targets for their fire were relayed through the ROK fire support centre. As the ROK forward artillery observers were moving among the scattering infantry, there were no calls for supporting fire. The ROK battery positions were shortly abandoned in the general flight.

At about 2230, a KMAG* adviser warned the New Zealand command post that the foremost two ROK regiments had withdrawn 5 kilometres under attack. Half an hour later, the divisional staff admitted that it had lost all communication with its regiments. By this time, small groups of ROK soldiers were moving past the New Zealand guns, disappearing down the track running alongside the Kap'yong river. By 0100 on the 23rd, continuous lines of retreating men filled this track.

Fortunately, they had outpaced their foe. In the darkness, the 60th Division was searching out the abandoned positions, its reserve regiment still waiting to pass through. Perhaps they were surprised to find all the evidence of ROK occupancy where they had thought to find British Commonwealth troops. To the west, the Chinese 59th Division had cut into the centre of the American 24th. To the east, the United States 1st Marine Division sought to occupy the flank positions vacated by 6th ROK. A battalion advancing to this end during the night was hindered by ROK soldiers streaming south. But on this flank also, the Chinese Fortieth Army was unaware of the limits of the gap opened. Much of the night was spent in searching the vacated ground and attacking the marines on the corner of an empty corridor.

The 6th ROK Division commander and staff spent the early hours of the 23rd attempting to halt the flow southward. Forward, a few dozen devoted officers gathered men from all regiments to form a temporary blocking position astride the track. When a staff officer brought a message to the New Zealanders asking them to provide fire support, Lieutenant-Colonel Moodie agreed subject to the re-establishment of a fire control centre. Meantime, he ordered his batteries to be ready to withdraw at immediate notice. At 0400, he still had no means of obtaining targets, but the flash and sound of small arms fire directly to the north was moving towards him. On this advice, 27th Brigade headquarters drew the regiment back to back to their area through the dawn.

With extraordinary energy and persistence, General Chang and elements of his own and the various regimental headquarters, engineers, and military police, gathered about 2,500 of the division during the night and an assortment of weapons and equipment. Some hundreds of

---

* Each ROK formation had a detachment from the United States Korean Military Advisory Group—KMAG—with its headquarters.

stragglers were added to the number during the late morning of the 23rd. This force, assembling in the upper Kap'yong valley, was ordered to take up a position roughly on Line Kansas. Regimental headquarters and two batteries of 16th Field Regiment were sent back to provide it with fire support. The Middlesex accompanied them: 'Just to make sure we can get you back if there is an emergency' Brigadier Burke told Colonel Moodie.

The prospect of an emergency in that sector was also in the mind of General Hoge, IX Corps commander. Under pressure, the 24th Division had withdrawn to Line Kansas to the west, the Marine Division—its near flank bent sharply back—to the east. That morning, he ordered 27th Brigade to reconnoitre a blocking position above Kap'yong. Confirming the requirement during the afternoon, he came to brigade headquarters just north of the town and found Brigadier Burke wearing a rose in his cap for St George's Day*.

The brigadier reminded him that he was in process of handing over the sector to the 28th Brigade before departing to Hong Kong. He had only two battalions for deployment. The Argylls were transferring their entire battle equipment to 1st Battalion the King's Own Scottish Borderers—1 KOSB—though one or the other would be available as a reserve in emergency. The Middlesex were forward with the New Zealanders. Immediately, he planned to occupy two principal features to block the junction of tracks leading to the north west—and 6th ROK—north, and north east to the Marines' sector. 2 PPCLI would hold Hill 677 on the left, 3 RAR Hill 504 on the right. He intended to place 1 Middlesex on its return below the PPCLI and behind the New Zealand gun positions[3].

General Hoge attached two companies of American 4.2-inch mortars† to 27th Brigade, the greater part of A Company, 72nd Tank Battalion and, having no further infantry in hand, two companies of engineers to act in that role. He also promised to send forward a field artillery battalion to reinforce the fire support of 6th ROK[4].

While the corps and brigade commanders consulted, 16th New Zealand Field Regiment reported that 6th ROK were not moving to Line Kansas but seemed to be 'firmly set' in their assembly area. In case of a second retreat by this force, Brigadier Burke was ordered to place a stop line on the track passing between his blocking positions. The task was given to 3 RAR and Lieutenant-Colonel Ferguson was not pleased to be the recipient. It required a rifle company but he decided against bringing one down; he was already thinly spread on the approaches to

* Brought by his staff as a surprise gift from Tokyo.

† Each of 12 mortars. These were part of 2nd Chemical Mortar Battalion, a unit of IX Corps artillery.

and top of Hill 506. Instead, he posted battalion headquarters, reinforced by elements of Headquarters and Support Companies, including a section of Vickers machine-guns, adjoining the road. Five Shermans* of the American tank company, which had arrived promptly, would be in his vicinity. It was just as well, the Australian headquarters were committed to a position in the foremost line.

About 5 pm that afternoon, in drizzling rain, a number of ROK vehicles came down the track to the north west and occupied an area by Chuktun village, a point on the valley floor directly between the two battalions and just below the track junction. Sergeant C McGregor, intelligence sergeant of 3 RAR, was sent to make contact. He encountered Brigadier Chang with what remained of 6th ROK divisional headquarters.

> ... There were two telephones, which seemed to be in constant operation and as I watched the map staff continually moved the positions of friendly troops further south and replaced them with red arrows showing the Chinese Communist Force advance. Even at that time, the position in the valley seemed to be chaotic. ... My last glimpse of the situation map showed that the two brigades [regiments] were approximately 6 miles north of the battalion position. The ROK division HQ did not remain in position very long[5].

For a time, Colonel Ferguson maintained the check post he had established in their vicinity, but from 2000 it was unable to operate. ROK vehicles and troops were streaming south. Stopping them in the darkness proved impossible; those impeded simply disengaged and marched or drove across country. The New Zealanders reported that the remaining element of 6th ROK was under attack, 'and it looked as if another retrograde movement had started as many ROK soldiers were pouring through the gun areas...'[6]. The regiment and Middlesex were ordered to return at once to the brigade. They arrived in company with 213rd Field Artillery Battalion sent by IX Corps to reinforce them. There had been no contact with the enemy during their journey and the only loss was a runaway American howitzer, ditched in a traffic accident. The New Zealanders rejoined their third battery a mile behind Colonel Ferguson's battalion headquarters; the Middlesex were sited a short distance behind the gun lines.

The night was cold. On the high ground above the valley, snow still lay along north facing slopes. The rain had stopped and the sky had cleared. From 2115, the moon illuminated the Kap'yong valley and its surrounding heights. The Canadians and Australians in the topmost positions, though warmed by a hot meal, felt somewhat isolated from events. Lights were

---

* This medium tank (the Sherman M4A3E80) was armed with a 76mm gun, a coaxial .300 machine-gun, a second hull mounted machine-gun and an independently mounted .5-inch cannon.

flashing along the valley—actually, headlights of ROK vehicles. Now and then racing vehicle engines and shouts were heard. Fragments of news came to them from their own and the artillery nets concerning the flight of 6th ROK Division and the arrival of the New Zealand guns but much of this did not reach the rifle sections in their slit trenches and sangars. Two of the three companies of 3 RAR—B, and D on Point 504 itself—soon had difficulty in communicating with Colonel Ferguson's command post as passing vehicles broke the telephone cables. The run of ground screened their radio signals. Many messages to battalion headquarters had to be relayed through A and C Companies[7].

Colonel Ferguson's immediate anxiety was that Chinese forces would infiltrate past him among the ROKs, and indeed an impression that they did so has persisted. But it is unlikely. Even if many of the British Commonwealth complement found it difficult to differentiate between the Koreans and the Chinese, the Koreans had no difficulty in identifying a Chinese presence. Detection among the columns would have prompted them to abandon the tracks, and of this there was no report. Still, the Chinese were following at a steady pace.

The 60th Division was not among their number. Elements of the three subordinate formations of Twentieth Army, 58th, 59th, and 60th Divisions were thrusting at 24th Division while simultaneously others were sliding south west along its right flank, seeking to cut round behind it.

Between 2130 and 2200, the advanced guard of a virtually fresh force from Fortieth Army, the 118th Division, encountered the foremost of the two tank platoons covering B Company, 3 RAR, whose position blocked their approach down the track from the north. Tank machine-gun and cannon fire drove this Chinese party back. The whole of 3 RAR stood to arms before a second assault was launched on the tanks at 2230. Keen to see their targets more clearly in the moonlight, the tank commanders were sitting up in their turrets, heads exposed. Two were hit within a few minutes. Mortally wounded himself, the platoon commander instructed the platoon to draw back towards the Kap'yong river ford.

This was probably a wise decision, and one followed despite attempts to hold them in position. Lacking infantry in close support, with two of five commanders out of action and other wounded among the crews, the platoon needed to reorganise out of contact. But the ardent Chinese followed at a run. Accelerating away across the two shallow fords, the tanks were drawn in by the company commander, First-Lieutenant Kenneth W Koch, on the road below Colonel Ferguson's command post.

Under fire as soon as he dismounted, he reconstituted two crews of unwounded men and sent the remainder back to his leaguer in rear. Koch's group swelled to eight tanks.

At the northern ford, the pursuing Chinese went to ground, uncertain of what lay on the far side. Meantime, those immediately behind them were already reconnoitring the ridge held by B Company and the spur occupied by A below Point 504; for none had any idea where the 27th Brigade defences were sited. Their work was not made easier as the two Australian company commanders directed mortar and artillery fire round and between their positions; but those listening and probing persisted among the Australian defences. About midnight, they guided two battalions of the Chinese 354th Regiment*, waiting in the shadowed valley to the north, to sites identified. Very early on 24th April these units began a series of attacks on B and A Companies, sometimes supported by mortar fire, sometimes without.

Captain D P Laughlin clung fast with B Company and a platoon of Shermans to the ridge above Somak-tong village, recovering part of his defences by a dogged counter-attack towards dawn. Above him, Major B S O'Dowd's A Company resisted all attempts to move them from the spur leading to Point 504. 1 Platoon, covering the ascent from the lower ground, was attacked repeatedly from two sides. All were mortared frequently. Grenades rained upon them. Before 1 am, 17 of the 30 men in the platoon were casualties. Major O'Dowd withdrew them during a lull, reorganising on his remaining two platoons. After a vain rush on the vacated defences, Chinese trumpets sounded to redirect the assailants.

As dawn broke, it became apparent that a small but well armed group of Chinese had infiltrated between 2 Platoon, highest on the spur, and the remainder of the company. Outcrops prevented the former from firing down on to the intruding enemy. In full daylight two Chinese light machine guns began to sweep with fire Major O'Dowd's headquarters, 1, and 3 Platoons, forcing them to crouch in their slit trenches. The headquarters in particular was in danger of piecemeal destruction.

At 0600, a patrol under Corporal C J Eveleigh was sent out from 2 Platoon to stalk the enemy group. Picking a way down through the outcrops of the spur, this party came suddenly upon the Chinese infiltrators and, reacting swiftly, the Australians killed or captured them with minor loss to themselves.

As the sun rose on Hill 504, the four companies of 3 RAR were able to take advantage of their commanding ground. B Company broke up a final attack on their hill at 0445, when it was ordered to move up

* The other two regiments of the 118th Division were the 352nd and 353rd.

to the Hill 504 positions. The advanced party under Company Sergeant-Major Eric Bradley captured 40 prisoners as they ascended. C and D Companies, engaged during the night only by random enemy patrols, were able to observe Chinese movement around them and bring them under direct fire. A late attack on D Company was broken up by artillery fire at 0700. About this time, A Company recovered 1 Platoon's position by counter-attack. Artillery and mortar fire were directed on to groups of Chinese in between positions, some of which, unwisely lodging near C Company, were killed or captured by snipers and skirmishing parties. As the enemy, exposed and fragmented, was destroyed or expelled, it became clear that a considerable battle was just drawing to a conclusion in the Kap'yong river valley below.

The third battalion of 354th Regiment had looped westwards from the approach march, directed on the village of Chegur'yong, some 2,000 yards upstream from the fords. Crossing the paddy fields, they passed through the Kap'yong waters, bypassing Colonel Ferguson's headquarters positions and First-Lieutenant Koch's tank group to establish a blocking position on the road behind them. From this site, attacks were developed north against Colonel Ferguson's headquarters, while reconnaissance patrols moved south along the road to Kap'yong town.

Although they did not discover the presence of B Company, 2nd Chemical Heavy Mortar Battalion 500 yards to the west, the latter was alarmed by the onset of the battle with 3 RAR headquarters. Abandoning 4.2-inch mortars, vehicles, and equipment, the entire company made off eastwards along a narrow track through the hills.

A mile behind them, the outposts defending 16th Field Regiment's gun positions became aware of Chinese surveillance about midnight. With the run of the battle, Colonel Moodie was already concerned that his batteries might be drawn into a small arms battle and he now despatched a reconnaissance and survey party four miles to the rear. There, close to brigade headquarters and the bivouacs of 1 KOSB, he planned to find a site from which his batteries could continue unimpeded their supporting fire.

Meantime, the brigade headquarters staff were trying to contact 3 RAR, whose rear link radio vehicle had temporarily been put out of action. At 0130, during a lull in the battle, Colonel Ferguson made his way back through his Headquarters Company position immediately in rear, to the Middlesex. Speaking on their rear link at 0140, he gave a resume of events in his area, though he could only say that his forward companies were holding for the time being as his radio contacts with them were limited. This confirmed what the artillery forward observation parties with three of his companies had reported on their net. He was, however, able to report his own tenuous hold below the river fords, the disappearance of the American mortar company, and the likelihood of attacks upon the New Zealanders and Middlesex.

Brigadier Burke instructed 16th Field to move at once, and warned the Middlesex to be ready to occupy the low hills 2,000 yards to the south west through which the road ran back to Kap'yong. He was minded to move the Middlesex at once but, on balance, decided that they were more immediately needed as a haven for Colonel Ferguson's headquarters' group[8].

The Chinese involved in this battle drew off to reorganise between 0100 and about 0330, at the same time removing their wounded. The medical officer of 3 RAR, Captain D D Beard, was also able to send back over a dozen casualties collected in his regimental aid post during the night battles. After 0330, the road came under heavy fire again as attacks were launched under mortar fire from the features immediately north west, assisted by considerable machine-gun fire from Chuktun-ni.

For the next two hours, some or all of the Australian command post, Support and Headquarters Companies elements, and First-Lieutenant Koch's tank crews, were engaged either in small arms exchanges at a distance of several hundred yards or a close quarters battle. With his own rear link restored, Colonel Ferguson told brigade headquarters at 0400 that, due to growing numbers of casualties, his situation was becoming critical. The Middlesex were ordered to send a company to reinforce him.

Major Nolda brought D Company to within 200 yards of 3 RAR headquarters, meeting Colonel Ferguson, 'who was calm and unruffled as ever...most of his HQ had been overrun...[9]' He directed Major Nolda to a ridge overlooking his position from the north west. If the Chinese held this, they would be able to encircle his location rapidly.

Tracer fire was passing close overhead as D Company moved in open order towards the ridge. It soon became clear that this fire was supporting a Chinese advance directly towards them, an advance observed by the leading Middlesex platoon as they reached their objective. The enemy had reached the next ridge, 75 yards distant and a little higher. D Company sought to check them.

Meantime, Colonel Ferguson's position was closely threatened. His perimeter had been driven back on to lower ground. Some relief had been obtained by tank fire into Chuktun-ni—one 76mm round hit a house at the southern end of the village packed with enemy, when fire from the buildings diminished. But the Australian numbers were fast dwindling. The colonel ordered a withdrawal back to the area of 1 Middlesex, now astride the pass *en route* to Kap'yong. In small groups in jeeps or on foot, they pulled back, preceded by the regimental aid post.

Captain Jack Gerke with the Headquarters Company detachment did not receive the orders and was thus the last to withdraw under covering fire from the New Zealanders.

Major Nolda's company was also withdrawing. The Chinese had brought up a captured American anti-tank gun to add to their mortar and small arms fire. He was relieved to make radio contact with Lieutenant-Colonel Nicholson, his commanding officer, who instructed him to break away. Finding that the road back was blocked, D Company followed the route into the eastern hills taken the night before by the fleeing American heavy mortar company.

In mid-morning, a fresh Chinese regiment entered the struggle, pressing the Australian companies. Although these assaults were driven back by artillery fire and air support—which unwittingly set the scrub on fire—it was clear that bringing in their many wounded, and resupplying them would be difficult. They would become increasingly isolated after dark. Brigadier Burke ordered them back. Colonel Ferguson, his command post re-established within the Middlesex defences, began a deliberate withdrawal from 1730, in which First-Lieutenant Koch's company played an abiding part*. A Sherman carried the colonel forward to give orders to his companies. The whole tank force covered the battalion out, adding their own direct fire to the salvoes of artillery fire. Completing its withdrawal in darkness, pursued in the latter stages from the heights to the valley floor, 3 RAR was recovered with all its vehicles, wounded, and prisoners to the area of brigade headquarters[10]. The tanks also assisted the returning American heavy mortar company to bring out its abandoned equipment†.

Expressing his satisfaction that the Kap'yong valley defence had been maintained, General Hoge was nonetheless anxious that it should remain secure. Security of an important section of the lateral road to Ch'unch'on depended on it. He sent 5th Cavalry to reinforce Brigadier Burke's command. The regiment took up positions a little to the north of brigade headquarters.

Having threatened 27th Brigade sufficiently to bring about the withdrawal of 3 RAR from Hill 504, it might be said that the 118th Division had possession of foot tracks to convey them to the Ch'unch'on road. But this was not P'eng's scheme of things. His aim was to destroy the brigade and thus permit a free run for a greater force through the area, including its artillery and supply vehicles. Though his soldiers' requirements were simple, they had to be met, particularly in the 'foodless

---

* In addition to United States decorations awarded to members of A Company, 72nd Medium Tank Battalion, the British Commonwealth Military Cross was awarded to First-Lieutenant Koch for his exceptional conduct in the battle.

† The two companies of United States field engineers under brigade command assisted in this task.

zone' they had entered. Some might have picked up abandoned United Nations supplies but he could not rely upon it. As it happened, little had been lost outside the 6th ROK area.

The battle on the Kapy'ong river thus had to be continued until the enemy was destroyed or driven out. The 118th Division planned on the night of 24th to move along the eastern flank from Hill 504, to explore what lay above Kap'yong town, while putting its main weight against 2 PPCLI, some of whose positions had been observed during the daylight hours of 24th April.

Lieutenant-Colonel Stone, recovered from his smallpox and once again in command of 2 PPCLI, had himself observed the Chinese during the 24th from his command post about a mile north of and well above the first New Zealand gun position. Some of those outflanking the Australians' headquarters approached his own, persuading him to bring his own B Company close to hand, occupying a spur overlooking Naech'on village*.

B Company's move was also seen by numerous enemy parties, and was also nearest to their positions. Thus identified, they were the first to be attacked. At 2215, after suppressive machine-gun fire including tracer streams judged to be direction indicators, a Chinese assault began on 6 Platoon's position. Defensive fire from the battalion's 81-mm mortars and medium machine-guns† broke this up[11].

A second assault at 2300 entered B Company's position but was ejected by a local counter-attack. Several wounded men insisted in taking part in this, one of whom, Private W R Mitchell, had been hit in the chest in the first assault. During these operations, a Chinese company ascended the re-entrant leading to Colonel Stone's headquarters and the mortar line. Major Lilley, commanding B Company, noted that,

> ...[the] company was powerless to stop it as it came in through our back door. It was a heartening sight to see the battalion 81-mm mortars firing at their shortest range [200 metres] together with their 50-calibre machine-guns which literally blew the Chinese back down the ravine[12].

Some minutes after 0100, a Chinese battalion attacked D Company, occupying the top of Point 677. The first thrust was against its 10 Platoon and medium machine-gun post. When this was thrown back, the assault was directed upon 12 Platoon, breaking in, as Captain J G W Mills remarked,

---

* During this redeployment, the American tanks engaged in a running battle near the road, mistook B Company for Chinese and opened fire, without serious effect.

† The Canadian battalion was equipped with the American 81-mm medium mortar as distinct from the British 3-inch. The bombs of the former were superior. The American .5-inch was used as the medium machine-gun. Despite its greater weight of impact, the control system was less reliable than that of the Vickers .303-inch in British and Australian service.

> ...by sheer weight of numbers. The [medium] machine-gun continued firing until the position was completely overrun. Four men...protecting the MMG post were able to disengage and make their way over to 10 Platoon position where they carried on the fire fight. ...also two Koreans who comprised part of the MMG section [as porters] were able to make their way to 10 Platoon positions[13].

At this point, Captain Mills decided to bring artillery fire on top of his position. The New Zealanders obliged, whilst the supporting United States artillery* fired on the surrounding approaches. This cleared the company position and discouraged the Chinese for some time.

After dawn, however, it became apparent that the Canadian position was cut off from the remainder of the brigade by blocks on roads and tracks. Uncertain of how long he would be required to hold his dominating heights, Colonel Stone asked for resupply by air, a request which was promptly rewarded. Six hours after making the request, four C119 transport aircraft appeared and dropped all but 4 per cent of its load into the Canadian perimeter. Helicopters followed to carry out those most seriously wounded.

This was completed shortly after 1030. By this time, the intrepid First-Lieutenant Koch had made a sortie with his tanks to fire upon the remnant of the Chinese on the northern slopes of 2 PPCLI's feature. The track to Chuktun-ni was was swept as 5th Cavalry moved forward to recapture the former 3 RAR position, a return resisted by the Chinese. About 1600, as reoccupation continued under artillery and air support, the enemy withdrew.

Locally, the battle was over. So, too, was 27 Brigade's operational tour in Korea. Next day, Brigadier Burke passed command to Brigadier G Taylor, and the force became 28th British Commonwealth Brigade. The Argylls had sailed for Hong Kong on the USS *Montrose*. Their replacement, 1 KOSB, were active in operations. The Middlesex and 11th Infantry Workshops, though retained in Korea until mid-May, were relieved to know that their advanced parties had returned to Hong Kong with the Argylls. 27th Brigade headquarters and its Royal Signals component withdrew in phases as their successors progressively assumed responsibility[14].

3 RAR remained with the new formation. Just before he drove away to Seoul, Brigadier Burke presented the brigade flag to Lieutenant-Colonel Ferguson.

'This is a token, a very small token of what your British friends think of your battalion. We shall never forget our days together in Korea'. It was not a grand valediction. The comradeship between the Australians and British units concerned made a speech superfluous.

---

* 213th and 61st Field Artillery Battalions, and an 8-inch howitzer battery.

SOURCE NOTES: Chapter 10

1 See Mossman, *op cit,* pp 382–382. Also War Diary, April 1951, 16th New Zealand Field Regiment.

2 For details of the performance of the 6th ROK Division during this period, see Eighth Army Adjutant-General's files, 1951, '6th ROK Division', (USNARS, Suitland). I must also thank the Chief of Army Staff, Republic of Korea, for permitting me to talk to former members of the division during April–May, 1991.

3 War Diary, 27th British Commonwealth Brigade, 23rd April 1951. Conversations, the author with Brigadier B A Burke and Colonel H R Jeffes.

4 War Diary, 27th Brigade; Mossman, *op cit,* pp 390–391. Conversation, author with Colonel H R Jeffes. See also O'Neill, *op cit,* pp 134–138, and Wood, *op cit,* pp 72–73. IX Corps Journal, 23rd April 1951 (USNARS, Suitland).

5 Norman Bartlett, *With the Australians in Korea,* (Canberra, 1954), pp 92–93.

6 War Diary, 27th British Commonwealth Brigade, 23rd April 1951.

7 O'Neill, *op cit,* p 143. See also War Diary, 3 RAR, 23rd April 1951.

8 Conversation, author with Brigadier B A Burke.

9 Shipster, *op cit,* p 66.

10 War Diaries, 27th British Commonwealth Brigade and 3 RAR, 24th April 1951, including a summary of the battle's course. See also, Bartlett, *op cit,* pp 101–106, and O'Neill, *op cit,* pp 147–159.

11 2 PPCLI War Diary, 24th and 25th April 1951. See also Stone, *op cit,* pp 76–79.

12 Quoted, Stone, *op cit,* p 77.

13 Quoted, Stone, *op cit,* pp 77–78.

14 For a brief statement concerning the exchange of command, see DEFE 11/211, f 2238A, Appx I.

CHAPTER 11

'There can be no rapid victory in the Korean War, and we must adopt a policy of protracted fighting'*

By the evening of 25th April it was becoming apparent to P'eng Te-huai that the offensive was faltering. The opposition of 1 Glosters on the left and the remainder of 29th Brigade on the right on the Imjin had held up the movement of his Sixty Fourth and Sixty Fifth Armies respectively.

> ... The result was that five divisions, totalling about 50,000 men or more, were squeezed into a confined space of about 20 square kilometres on the south bank of the Imjin river for as long as two days, during which time they were subjected to concentrated enemy air and artillery bombardment and suffered severe losses... After this, although the troops managed to continue their advance, the main strength of the enemy forces to the north of Seoul had already made a complete withdrawal. By 29th April, the 19 Army Group had reached the northern outskirts of Seoul, while the eastern front troops of the 3 and 9 Army Groups and the [North Korean] People's Army had advanced to the south of the 38th Parallel along the entire front... By this time, the food and ammunition which the men of the Volunteer Army had been carrying for themselves had basically been used up, and since the situation for attacking a strongly defended city was clearly unfavourable, P'eng Te-huai resolutely decided to halt the attack, and the troops were switched to rest and reorganisation[1].

Reorganisation was the first requirement. As on previous occasions, sustained fighting entailed widespread deployment of the Chinese formations, when control of regiments was lost due to poor communications and lack of adequate maps. Drawn away from their march axes, units waited for instructions or moved blindly across country. The artillery, moving by night to avoid air attack, often received orders late so that the motorised batteries were rarely able to move more than 10 miles before entering hides at first light, the horsed artillery less. The infantry thus lacked close support in many of their actions[2].

Then, the substantial casualties and damage to equipment incurred during the four days of fighting in late April necessitated the reinforcement or merging of units. Swathes of men had been cut from columns by napalm attacks or intense shellfire. The adjutant of the Glosters, walking back across the Imjin battlefield during a temporary

---

* P'eng Te-huai addressing the Party Committee of the Chinese People's Volunteers at an extended conference on 25th June 1951.

escape, saw evidence of this—areas strewn with bodies, dead mules among shattered field guns and limbers, equipment scattered and torn by shellfire.

On the other side of the line, General Van Fleet was encouraged that, while his defensive front had in places been penetrated, it was nowhere breached. On this basis, he was confident that with the artillery he was now able to mass around and within Seoul, he could hold the city. Still, Chinese infiltrators behind his forward divisions, and pressure of numbers at random points, persuaded him to accept General Milburn's orderly withdrawals towards Line Golden, prepared in early April as a contingency against the Chinese spring offensive. Measures had also to be taken against a westerly outflanking movement across the lower reaches of the Han river on to the Kimpo peninsula. Some 2,000 North Koreans were seen on 28th April concentrating on the northern bank. The 29th Brigade was sent to deny them access.

That night artillery and the gunfire of the USS *Toledo** broke a massed attack by the elements of the Chinese Sixty Fifth Army and the North Korean 8th Division on Seoul. More than 900 of their dead were found next morning by patrols of 1st ROK Division. From the area of Uijongbu, the Chinese Sixtieth Army attempted to force open the United States 25th Division line during the afternoon and evening of the 29th, and were similarly broken by artillery and naval gunfire.

These measures, in combination with a successful struggle by the United Nations infantry to hold their positions, halted P'eng's assault forces just to the north of Golden. I and IX Corps restored and developed the defences of substantial outposts†. To the rear, reserves were reorganised, ammunition and other supplies dumped against a renewed battle. Few in the United Nations Command believed that the enemy had been brought to a standstill. By 1st May there was ample intelligence that, high casualties notwithstanding‡, P'eng had considerable numbers of soldiers in hand for a renewal of the offensive, probably 300,000. I Corps reported that the enemy was regrouping for a new onslaught[3]. In fact, this movement was the initial phase of deployment away from the western front.

Determined that the Chinese should not have a clear run across an unoccupied No Man's Land in a renewed offensive[4], General Van Fleet instructed all corps to advance wherever possible, while continuing to

---

* Heavy cruiser stationed off Inch'on.

† General Van Fleet declined to give this a name, but for ease of reference the Army staff called it 'No Name Line'.

‡ Chinese and North Korean losses identified from 22nd–29th April were 13,349 killed, with 246 prisoners of war. Estimates of total losses, including those dying of wounds, totalled 24,000. The United Nations losses were 547 killed, 2,024 wounded in action, 2,170 captured.

develop the defences on Lines Golden and No Name and their extensions to the east. Everywhere, the United Nations line advanced, a few miles a day in the west against rearguards, at a greater pace in the centre where opposition was scant, rapidly in the east. General Milburn set I Corps yet again along the road to Munsan-ni and Uijongbu. General Hoge's advanced guards reopened the road along the Pukhan valley towards Kapy'ong, abandoned in the general withdrawal at the end of April. X Corps moved from the Hongch'on river towards the upper waters of the Soyang, recovering its former line on Route 24 across the rising peaks of the Taebaek spine. Eastwards III ROK Corps moved on Inje; and on the east coast a flying column of ROK I Corps entered Kansong, 20 miles above the 38th Parallel.

On this basis in the second week of May, General Van Fleet aspired briefly to the early recovery of Line Kansas. As an intermediate step, he planned to recover Munsan-ni, Chunch'on, and Inje—linking points on Line Topeka. But as orders were being drafted the intelligence picture became more detailed. Five Chinese armies were concentrating behind screening forces between Chunch'on and Inje. Eighth Army was instructed to halt and brace itself against the massing *puissant* foe.

P'eng's report to Mao Tse-tung on 26th April discloses a somewhat different perspective of the battlefield, influenced still by the false notion of the high command that a seaborne landing by the United Nations Command was imminent.

> ...after three days and nights of operations, the plan...has not been achieved. It looks as if the limited results of the battle will not quash the landing attempt... The next campaign should prepare to fight against the enemy landing troops... Thus in this campaign, the Chinese People's Volunteers' main force should be deployed in areas favourable to manoeuvreability along and above the 38th Parallel to prepare to annihilate the landing troops of the enemy...[5]

The Central Military Commission assented to this concept but suggested that the withdrawal forced on the United Nations forces by the April operations might well delay their amphibious landing, now expected at Wonsan. They proposed that attempts to breach the enemy line should therefore continue for the time being[6].

Surveying prospects at the beginning of May, P'eng decided against a renewal of operations on the western front—the Chinese term for the sectors of the American I and IX Corps. Therein lay the greatest strength of the United Nations' ground forces both in professional skill and firepower. But towards and along the Taebaek mountains the eastern front was held predominantly by ROK troops. The steep slopes and soaring crests in that country afforded better opportunities for surprise in attack than that in the west and reduced the advantages of his enemy's mobility. The morale of the South Korean soldiers was volatile, their military proficiency and support was inferior to that of the Americans and British and the other foreign allies. He decided to feint in the west and attack in the east.

> For the second stage of the Fifth Campaign [he signalled to army groups on 6th May*], our principal objective is first of all to concentrate our forces to wipe out the puppet [ROK] 3rd Division, 5th Division, and the 9th Division in the Hyon-ni region; after this, in the light of the circumstances, we may go on to wipe out the Puppet Capitol Division and the 11th Division...[7]

Once more, the orders betray the imperfections of P'eng's battlefield intelligence. The 5th ROK Division was separated from the 9th and 3rd by the 7th ROK, whose presence was discounted. The locations of the United States 2nd and 7th Divisions, to the west of 5th ROK were inaccurately recorded and, most surprisingly, the presence of the United States 1st Marine Corps Division appears to have been overlooked in P'eng's headquarters†. Moreover, his operational liaison with the NKPA was inadequate. P'eng expected the North Korean III Corps to attack, though it was relegated wholly to a screening role. The II Corps, lying back, was to join V in the offensive. Perhaps Kim Il-sung was asserting his right to decide on the formations employed within P'eng's overall plan.

The essence of the plan was to drive the ROK formations south east, encircling and destroying them in the process. They would be separated from the adjacent United States formations by a simultaneous attack on the 7th and 2nd Divisions. The 9 Army Group, assisted by the two Korean corps, was made responsible for the first of these tasks, 3 Army Group the second‡. To the west, 19 Army Group and the North Korean I Corps were required 'to pin down the main force of the American Army and hold them on the western front'. This was to be accomplished by seeking out two or three targets of battalion size across their front for destruction by massed numbers, a ploy to draw in local United Nations reserves. All involved,

> ...carrying enough food and ammunition for 9 or 10 days, will set out by night for their prepared positions for the offensive (each army group will carry out its own selection of positions); the time limit is that assembly must have been completed before dawn on the 14th, and the offensive is set to begin at dusk on the 15th or 16th[8].

---

* These orders were signed jointly by his military and political deputy, Teng Hua.

† However, the location of the Marine Division was known to Thirty Ninth Army headquarters. See also Mossman, *op cit*, p 443 fn 14.

‡ 3 Army Group comprised: Fifteenth Army, Sixtieth Army, Two divisions, (from Thirty Ninth Army, 13 Army Gp), and 9 Army Group comprised: Twentieth Army, Twenty Seventh Army, Twelfth Army, (from 3 Army Gp)

From 11th May, when he cancelled the advance to Line Topeka, to the 14th, General Van Fleet received a series of reports which confirmed his expectation of an offensive on his central front—in the IX and X Corps sectors—of which the most conclusive were reports from prisoners-of-war and deserters. But the siting of very large numbers along the Soyang river above Ch'unch'on and the lie of the land led him to believe that the principal thrust would seek to open up a corridor south south west along the valley of the Pukhan. With many of his subordinates, he continued to assume that the remote and precipitous Taebak spine would not be suitable for a major turning movement against him.

Accordingly, he instructed General Hoge to cover the Pukhan corridor with the greater part of his artillery. 'I want to stop the Chinese here and hurt him', he told General Hoge. 'I welcome his attack and want to be strong enough in position and fire power to defeat him'[9]. Corps stocks of ammunition were to be built up to permit expenditure at five times the normal daily rate for each of seven days* [10]. From 11th May, the United States 3rd Division was progressively withdrawn from I Corps into army reserve.

On Monday, 14th May, the weather broke. Low cloud and frequent rain covered the continuing movement of P'eng's forces eastwards from air observation. By the 16th, roads, particularly the side tracks brought into service as divisional or regimental supply routes, began to break up. The engineers moved in haste from one site to another effecting emergency repairs. On either side of the line the fighting soldiers marched or squatted uncomfortably under waterproof sheets.

At dusk on the 16th, the Chinese Twenty Seventh Army thrust its 81st Division straight down the boundary between the ROK 5th and 7th Divisions—on the right of X Corps—breaking up both formations. Without deviating to pursue those routed, the 81st continued across country to the road junction at Sangam-ni, blocking the pass immediately to the north, a movement involving a march of about 20 miles along footpaths winding through the hills, a route secretly reconnoitred and faultlessly followed through the remaining hours of darkness into the morning mists and rain of the 17th. When the ROK III Corps, easterly neighbours of 7th ROK, began to pull back through Sangam-ni, its columns were similarly checked.

From this opening thrust, P'eng won several important advantages. The ROK III Corps was caught between the advancing North Korean V Corps and the Chinese 81 Division. It disintegrated. The right flank of General Almond's X Corps was opened wide, both from this cause

---

* What became known as the 'Van Fleet Day of Fire' rate was: 300 rounds per 105-mm howitzer; 250 rounds per 155-mm howitzer; 200 rounds per 155-mm gun; 200 rounds per 8-in howitzer; 250 rounds per 175-mm howitzer.

and the routing of 5th and 7th ROK Divisions. The United States 2nd Division was assailed by the Chinese Twelfth Army and part of the Fifteenth, and in danger of being enveloped by both. General Van Fleet shifted the IX Corps boundary eastwards, reducing X Corps sector, sent General Almond the 3rd Division less two regimental combat teams, and called northward the ROK 8th Division from anti-guerrilla duties.

No less importantly, he passed a battery of 155-mm guns and a battery of 8-inch howitzers to reinforce the corps artillery[11]. The Van Fleet daily rates were authorised for all artillery batteries within X Corps. The Fifth Air Force and Marine Corps aircraft flew ground attack sorties intensively by day against enemy infantry and artillery, though weather conditions reduced their observation. By night, Far East Air Force medium bombers, diverted from interdiction, directed by radar, attacked enemy massing for assault, sometimes within a few hundred yards of their own ground forces[12].

This combination of fire, associated with a dogged defence by the infantry as they withdrew short distances day by day, reduced the pressure on the greater part of X Corps front. The ROK III Corps was removed from the battle, its sector falling under General Almond's command. The remainder of the United States 3rd Division reinforced X Corps. On the east coast, General Paik Sun-yup held the two divisions of I ROK Corps firmly under his control, though Chinese and North Korean forces continued to march south through his extended lines and the open right flank of X Corps.

At this point, on 18th May, General Ridgway intervened. He pointed out to General Van Fleet the enemy's weakness in the west and centre—the limited attacks by the NKPA I Corps and Yang Te-chih's 19 Army Group had driven in outposts but had failed to disrupt the defensive lines of Generals Milburn and Hoge. An attack by the Eighth Army towards the enemy road and rail centre at Ch'orwon would at least oblige P'eng to halt his own offensive[13]. Next day, he met Van Fleet, Hoge, and Almond at the latter's headquarters, when the offensive concept was enlarged to include IX Corps and the Marines on X Corps' left flank. These central corps were directed on to the more limited objective of the road junctions round Ch'unch'on. The aim overall was no longer simply to cause P'eng to draw back in the east but to trap his forces in the process of withdrawal. The drive north would begin on the 20th[14].

Some members of the army intelligence staff doubted that the advancing United Nations forces could make their presence felt before P'eng's divisions broke out south west towards the United Nations road and rail junction at Chech'on. Air reconnaissance discovered four new divisions on the axis of Route 2 and flanking the east coast Route 20 on the late afternoon of 20th May. Given the night marching capability of the Chinese People's Volunteers and the absence of forces in this area, they could reach the road and rail centre of Chech'on in two days. Its loss would have required, at the least, considerable redeployment of United Nations' forces.

General Paik's I ROK Corps came under pressure from North Korean forces late on 21st May. Part of X Corps' neighbouring flank remained open and various Chinese elements were passing through it but unaware of their opportunity. Several, notably a part of the 31st Division, had lost direction and were out of touch with their headquarters. But these circumstances were not known at Eighth Army headquarters. The reports of their advance from aircraft during the afternoon caused grave concern.

In fact, the United Nations had won the battle. P'eng had already signalled his army groups to draw back. His decision was not due to the advance against him—his instructions had been drafted while General Milburn's corps was still closing up on 21st May[15]—but to his losses of men and equipment*. Supply through the heights of the Taebaek mountains had been difficult but the evacuation of wounded on the return route doubly so; on 22nd May, 8000 casualties were still in the immediate battle area[16]. P'eng made the best of it.

> In the Fifth Campaign, by means of two attacks on the western front and the eastern front, we have achieved a major victory in wiping out nearly 40,000 of the effective strength of the American and Puppet armies and causing the enemy to use up large quantities of material and equipment; we have smashed the enemy's secret plan of trying to occupy the Ch'orwon –Pyonggang–Dochon line to coordinate with landings at Wonsan and attack our forces; at the same time, we have steeled those of our troop units newly arrived in Korea, gained experience in operations against the American imperialists, and won preparation time.
>
> At present, because of our shortage of means of transport, supplies of food and ammunition cannot be kept up, while the American forces from the western front are also now going eastward with reinforcements; this means that it is becoming increasingly difficult for us to extend our offensive, and thus the Fifth Campaign is about to come to an end for the time being.
>
> In order to assemble our main force for rest and reorganisation, sum up our operational experience, and create favourable battle opportunities in the future, so that we shall be able to wipe out the enemy in even greater numbers, we have decided to move the main strength of the various army groups to the north of the line Haech'ang-ni–Yonch'on–Sach'ang-ni–

* The Chinese casualties, principally among the assault echelons, were 17,000 dead, 36,000 wounded, of whom some remained with their units. These round figures are calculated from Eighth Army returns set against the numbers required by the CPV headquarters to bring divisions back to strength. The total is extraordinarily high—over 20% of those engaged, probably over 25% of those in the Twelfth and Fifteenth Armies.

> Yanggu–Wont'ong-ni. Each army group will leave a force of between one division and an army which, starting from its present position, will adopt measures of mobile defence and repeated blocking actions to inflict casualties on the enemy and wear them down, and to gain time...[17]

As the general withdrawal of the Communist forces became apparent beyond doubt, the three American corps commanders sought to secure road junctions essential to the evacuation of Chinese vehicles and artillery, some in use also by marching men who had abandoned mountain tracks in their haste to disengage. Three communications centres were selected: in the I Corps sector, the junction of Routes 3 and 3A with the lateral on the line of the 38th Parallel; for IX Corps the junctions of Routes 17 and 29 west of the Hwach'on reservoir; and for X, the roads meeting round Yanggu and Inje at the eastern end of the reservoir.

Following his original orders to advance on the 20th, General Milburn pushed forward rapidly, delayed only by mined roads and demolished bridges—hindrances partly of his own making in late April and early May. The ROK 1st Division entered Munsan-ni on the morning of 21st May, and the corps advanced to Line Topeka on the afternoon of the 23rd. Road blocks were established on 25th May at the sites chosen. But the birds had flown. Yang Te-chih had withdrawn his widespread army group north of the Imjin and Yangp'yong rivers on the nights of the 22nd and 23rd.

General Hoge's advance began slowly. His vehicles were restricted to a single road initially, and from the morning of the 23rd he was required to adjust his boundaries eastwards to permit the concentration of the Marines in X Corps. Kap'yong was recaptured, threatening Ch'unch'on from the west, while the 7th Division moved on it from the south. Next day, a series of adventures obliged 7th Division's commander to hide among boulders from Chinese rear parties, while Captain Charles E Hazell, outstripping them, undertook a daring sortie into Ch'unch'on with eleven armoured vehicles, so alarming the Chinese that they accelerated their withdrawal in daylight, secured in part against air attack by continuing clouds and rain. Even so, IX Corps' bag of prisoners between Ch'unch'on and Chiam-ni, north of Kapy'ong swelled by thousands*.

The slow pace on the left front of X Corps drove General Almond to frenzied activity. He accepted—just—General Thomas's* contention that the steep and trackless slopes which his men had to traverse limited movement. The United States 2nd Division, right hand neighbours of the Marines, were among the first to experience the corps commander's predisposition for centralised command in critical circumstances. It was

---

* Amongst these was the greater part of the 180th Division, a former Kuomintang formation.

true that X Corps responded cautiously to the change from defence to advance, but all its formations had been engaged in a struggle simply to hold the line. X Corps would have been better served if a single warning order had been issued while divisional and regimental commanders were briefed on philosophy and plan, whereafter the normal chain of command would have operated effectively. As it was, instructions rained upon subordinates much as they had done in the March battles. Once again, the corps commander decided on the precise nature of task forces, down to platoon level, the chain of command was broken, and more haste made for less speed.

By 27th May General Van Fleet realised that his opportunity to deny the enemy's withdrawal *en masse* along the line of the 38th Parallel had passed. Orders were issued for a new operation, Piledriver, which required I and IX Corps to secure Ch'orwon and Kumwha, the base of the 'Iron Triangle', to block the roads running south east towards the Hwach'on reservoir. The United States 3rd and ROK 9th Divisions passed to I Corps, charged with the capture of the base line. IX Corps was to block the road. X Corps was to extend Line Kansas northward to cover the coastal town of Kansong, carrying the line halfway to the 39th Parallel[18]. Though the army commander did not disclose it, his intention was to advance a Marine detachment by sea early in June to the edge of the parallel[19].

General Ridgway judged that this was reaching too far. He gave his approval to the deliberate approach to Line Kansas, its extension eastward, and an advance to Wyoming to the base of the 'Iron Triangle', but no further: the territory to be gained did not justify the risks involved in its seizure. The Eighth Army was to consolidate on Wyoming and Kansas. The army commander was to prepare an appreciation of his situation and operational prospects over the next two months. On these terms, as the victor, General Ridgway brought the Fifth Phase Campaign to an end.

---

* Major-General Gerald C Thomas assumed command of the 1st Marine Division in April 1951.

SOURCE NOTES: Chapter 11

1 Hsü Yen, *op cit,* Chapter 2, Part 5.
2 *Ibid.*
3 Signal CICCG4-24 of 30th April 1951, G3-Journal, (USNARS, Suitland).
4 Conversation, author with General Van Fleet.
5 The Military History Research Section, Military Science Academy of China, *History of the War of Resist America, Aid Korea* (1987), pp 135–136.
6 *Ibid.*
7 *P'eng Te-huai's Military Writings, cit,* second of three telegrams relating to the Fifth Campaign.
8 *Ibid.*
9 Mossman, *op cit,* p 441.
10 *Ibid* p 442, fn.
11 Signal Eighth Army GX-5-2972 to IX and X Corps, 17 May 51, G-3 Journal, (USNARS, Suitland).
12 See Futrell, Robert F, *The United States Air Forces in Korea, 1950–53* (New York, 1961), pp 338–40.
13 Signal CINCFE C 62789 of 18 May 51 to CG Eighth Army, G-3 Journal, (USNARS, Suitland).
14 Ridgway, *op cit,* p 178. See also Mossman, *op cit,* pp 464–465.
15 *P'eng Te-huai's Military Writings, cit,* three telegrams: third telegram sent at 1600 hours on 21 May 51.
16 Hsü Yen, *op cit,* Chapter 2, Part 5.
17 *P'eng Te-huai's Military Writings, cit,* three telegrams.
18 Mossman, *op cit,* pp 485–487.
19 Conversation, author with General Van Fleet. Signal, CG Eighth Army GX-5-5099 KGOP to CINCFE, 28 May 51, G-3 Diary, (USNARS, Suitland). See also Schnabel, *op cit,* p 397.

CHAPTER 12

The hunt for peace talks

When the political excitement of General MacArthur's dismissal had abated, the United States and Britain resumed their associated pursuit of a settlement in Korea[1]. Reviewing prospects and options in a telegram to Sir Oliver Franks on 11th April, Mr Morrison favoured hoisting bright, clear signal flags for their opponents to read. This should be done without regard to the battlefield, though he accepted that

> ...we must take full account of increased American preoccupation with future developments in the military situation. Please let State Department know that I have their worries fully in mind. Despite this I believe that in order to rally world opinion the present is the psychological moment for making a broad declaration re-affirming our objectives in Korea with specific proposals for a settlement. There is a feeling everywhere that the political issues are being allowed to drift.
>
> 3. A statement by the President on behalf of the Unified Command will not by itself be sufficient. What is needed is a broad declaration of policy by all the governments contributing forces.
>
> 4. Though the Chinese might well be more amenable to negotiations after any offensive of theirs has been halted we cannot afford to wait for this. It may, indeed, be some long time before the military situation again presents so favourable an opportunity for such an initiative.
>
> 5. I would therefore like you to press the State Department to give further urgent consideration to the programme which I have suggested [on 30th March[2]]. If they should be able to agree to my suggested declaration I would welcome in addition a message to the Secretary-General of the United Nations from the President in the name of the Unified Command setting forth the objectives of the United Nations forces in Korea... Please convey to the State Department my appreciation of their offer to show and agree with us both the [President's] Statement and the [accompanying] speech...[3]

The text of Mr Morrison's proposed 'declaration of policy', had already been passed to the State Department. Its preamble gave assurances of the good intentions of the United Nations alliance, and was worded to avoid any implication of aggression by the North Koreans or Chinese. Specific proposals followed, essentially based on a conference between the United States, United Kingdom, France, the People's

Republic of China, the Soviet Union, and India, which should appoint a cease fire committee under the President of the General Assembly and, hostilities having ceased, negotiate a 'unified, independent and democratic Korea'[4].

The State Department took no exception to the general thrust of this draft. However, Mr U Alexis Johnson of the North East Asian Office commented to Dean Rusk on 10th April,

> ... With respect to the proposal itself for Korea I believe the following should be noted:
>
> 1. The fate of Korea would be decided by the 'Big 6' without any Korean participation whatever. The proposal entirely ignores the legitimate status and presence of the Republic of Korea. Its exclusion would undoubtedly present us with very serious problems in Korea itself.
>
> 2. The proposal entirely ignores the UN vs Communist China aspect of the Korean situation and treats Communist China on the basis of entire equality with the countries which have at tremendous sacrifice been opposing its criminal acts...[5]

Discussion of the respective viewpoints continued over some days, Mr Morrison believing, quite falsely as it transpired, that the Peking government might be interested in a cease fire following the removal of General MacArthur, and more amenable to an approach by those participating in the 'Unified Command' in Korea as distinct from the United Nations as an institution. The American response, an Australian intervention[6], Foreign Office reservations[7], and cooler counsels within the Cabinet[8], checked a drift towards appeasement by the Foreign Secretary. On 16th April, the ideas he sent to Sir Oliver Franks were more robust.

> We must avoid giving the impresssion of weakness and at the same time we must if possible avoid the risk of a direct rebuff from the Chinese. I think therefore that we might regard this operation as in two stages, first a declaration of aims and secondly an approach to the Chinese[9].

The Foreign Office also recognised that the Republican Party, aroused by MacArthur's dismissal, was ready to campaign against any softening of United States' policy towards 'Red China'. The Democrat administration was under greater and more closely focussed domestic pressure from the right—including some members on its own right wing—in its conduct of the Korean war than the Labour government in Britain was either from the Conservative opposition or from its own left-wing, though just at that moment a split was developing within the British Government in part due to the high level of its military expenditure*. Hence Mr Morrison's references to being under 'strong pressure in the House to make a statement'[10].

Intermingled with the consideration of peace negotiations were discussions and differences concerning future military operations between the United States and United Kingdom. There were two points of dissension. Both related to the enemy's capacity in a renewed offensive: the ground forces available to the Chinese and North Koreans; and the enemy capacity to launch cooperative air attacks.

As remarked†, the British Chiefs of Staff discounted the very large enemy numbers which General MacArthur's intelligence staff had claimed to be massing in Korea. Their incredulity was heightened by a signal from Brigadier Fitzgerald in Washington to the Director of Military Intelligence in the War Office on 13th April. In this he pointed out that,

> ...we and G2 here [the intelligence section of the United States General Staff] roughly equate a CCF army or NK corps as equivalent in fighting power to a US division[11].

This analysis overlooked the fact that 95% of a Chinese division took part in combat against 65% of an American division; and whilst the latter had far greater armour and artillery support, the former brought more infantry weapons to bear. The broad comparison was thus pointless.

Brigadier Fitzgerald discounted both the numbers and the readiness ascribed to them by his American associates. Due to land, sea, and air action, he judged, 'Fourth Field Army formations are in no shape for large scale action and may be on way out for refitting... G2 intelligence is based almost entirely on Far East Command and there is practically no independent check...'[12]

It is surprising that the British Chiefs of Staff allowed their scepticism, a hangover from MacArthuritis, to be fed by such patently subjective judgements. Like their colleagues in Washington, they too relied on the Commander-in-Chief's headquarters for information about the battlefield. For all the British Chiefs' allusions to 'our own sources', they had none in the sense of regular, reliable collateral information. Any claim to a national and, by implication, a better informed view of operations depended, therefore, on the extent to which British analysis

---

* Aneurin Bevan, Minister of Labour from 17th January, was moving with a small group of other Government members towards resignation on the issue of Health Service charges, introduced among many savings to ease a budget swollen by military expenditure—14% of GDP. The greater part of this was for NATO, but the left wing of the Party propagated the view that the Korean war was no less an intolerable financial burden on the British economy.

† See p 98.

of American information was superior to that of the supplier. Sometimes it was, sometimes it was not.

With the arrival of General Ridgway in Tokyo, there were expectations that the manipulation of battlefield reports to support the personal inclinations of the Commander-in-Chief would be abandoned. This was indeed the outcome. However, the benefit of this change did not at once accrue to the British Chiefs. It took Air Vice-Marshal Bouchier some weeks to develop a personal relationship with General Ridgway, during which he lacked access to the run of the Commander-in-Chief's ideas and intentions at first hand. No less importantly, as a foreign liaison officer in an American headquarters, however senior, the lack of any special mark of interest by the incumbent Commander-in-Chief diminished the range and depth of his contacts among the senior members of the staff[13]. As a consequence, battlefield information in Whitehall during April continued to be late and, often, disjointed. These circumstances contributed to the misjudgements in the four defence ministries concerning the impending enemy offensive which was to engulf their own soldiers in 27 and 29 Brigades in the fourth week of the month.

The scepticism of the British Chiefs and Joint Intelligence Staff were nearer the mark in the matter of the air threat. They began with a foundation of knowledge acquired jointly and agreed with the United States agencies before the outbreak of war. Recognising that it would be unwise to discount altogether the Chinese and North Korean air capability*, they were right in concluding that the Soviet air force would not intervene. But while the two senior Royal Air Force officers involved, Sir John Slessor in London and Lord Tedder in Washington, were in no doubt that if the Chinese mounted air attacks out of bases in China these bases must be destroyed, they were at one with the other two Chiefs of Staff and the Foreign Office in insisting that, even if such counter-attacks were confined to United States aircraft, they should only be mounted after consultation between Washington and London, and if possible with all those nations fielding forces in Korea. Their reservations were due in great measure to the fact that General MacArthur was in command when air retaliation was first discussed, but persisted as a matter of principle after his removal[14].

However, Lord Tedder became more sympathetic to American anxieties when he was briefed in detail on the high density of aircraft on the limited number of United Nations air bases in Korea†. These

---

* See p 99.

† Five only were serviceable, including those occupied by the five fighter squadrons of the United States Marine Corps. These were supplemented by interceptors embarked on the carriers of Task Forces 75 and 77 and the Royal Navy, on call. Construction would provide two more bases in June, 1951. (See Futrell, op cit, pp 334–337, and Field, op cit, pp 346–347.)

circumstances might, after all, encourage an exceptional enemy air incursion. Doubts were expressed to him in Washington as to the ability of Brigadier-General Briggs' bombers to incapacitate the enemy airfields being renovated in North Korea*.

Discussions on the principle of consultation continued over some days, as much between the Americans themselves as with their British associates† [15]. At a national meeting on 18th April, the Joint Chiefs with colleagues from the State Department and National Security Council attempted to relate the option of a Chinese air offensive against the United Nations command with options for peace and the progress of land operations in Korea. Attitudes of their allies in the war, particularly the British, were frankly discussed, during which General Vandenberg, Chief of the Air Force Staff, continued to manifest an extraordinary ignorance of the British maritime and land contribution to operations.

> **MR RUSK** : There is, as you know, a considerable sentiment abroad that the dismissal of General MacArthur has opened the way for a peaceful settlement. We have told our friends abroad to be careful in their analysis of this problem... However, the change in command is stimulating new approaches to the Chinese Communists. The Good Offices Committee [of the United Nations General Assembly] is now trying to see whether it can't get an answer from Peiping [Peking] to the approach it made some weeks ago. Others are in touch with the Soviet Union to see whether the Soviets have anything to say.
>
> We do not yet know how to evaluate the North Korean statement‡... There was an interesting editorial in *Pravda* this morning. It is the first official indication of the Soviet line on the dismissal of General MacArthur. The line seems to be that we set out to attack China and that when we found that this was an impossible venture we relieved General MacArthur to cover ourselves. The interesting thing about the editorial is that it says, in effect, that we are not going to attack China.
> ... We should remember, however, that it was a little remark by Stalin which opened the way to the settlement of the Berlin blockade. The ambassadors of the nations participating in the Korean war have been fairly quiet lately. However, if the situation gets more complicated—if, for example—the Chinese Communists continue to withdraw and if we continue to move north—we are likely to have political problems once again.

---

* See p 108–109.

† In this process, the Foreign Office learned that the Netherlands government had been asked whether they would consider warning the Chinese that any air attack in Korea from bases in North East China might invite retaliatory attacks. The Netherlands declined, suggesting that India might convey such a message.

‡ The North Korean Foreign Minister, Pak Hön Yöng, wrote to the President of the Security Council on 15th April 1951 recommending the settlement of the Korean war on the basis of the World Peace Council conference in East Berlin in February. As the Council was organised and financed sub rosa by the Soviet Union, its recommendations and the abusive language used in presenting it suggested that it was a propaganda exercise. (For the text, see UN Document S/2092/Corr. 1.)

... We will have no trouble with the ambassadors if the Chinese do undertake a big offensive. We will not have a political problem if our forces build a defensive line. We may, however, have a large political problem if the Chinese Communists realize that they cannot obtain their political price for a settlement [and let the fighting peter out]...
... In summary, there is nothing of significance to report on the negotiating situation. We have made contacts of various kinds, but there have been no responses to date. Secondly, if the Chinese pull back, what course of action do we follow and what do we say about it to other governments? Thirdly, if the Chinese Communists make a big attack including air, what can we do to give the other governments advance information and what reaction do we make to the attack?

GENERAL BRADLEY : We have been considering here in the JCS whether we should give a complete[ly] new directive to General Ridgway... He is now operating under a directive to kill all the Chinese he can while taking prudent measures to protect the safety of his troops. If there is any chance of this thing petering out, it will require us to let them withdraw... If we kept after them they could not let the fighting come to an end. Of course, they could withdraw all the way to the Yalu. We could not follow them that far in any event because it would lengthen our line of communications too much. If the thing is to peter out, we have got to stop at some point.

GENERAL COLLINS : ...how far north is it satisfactory for us to go? Are we going to stabilize and hold elections and create a government of Korea except for the part of Korea we do not hold?...

GENERAL VANDENBERG : ...I would like to address my remarks for a moment to Mr Rusk's point about lining up our allies. In my view, it will not help to talk with the Australian representatives here. Their air force general in Korea attends all our briefing sessions and must be in touch with his government*. The problem we have here in Washington is to persuade these governments that we believe that the air build-up is being made with serious intentions. The U.K. is ready to sacrifice the brigade [sic] it has in Korea if that is necessary to save the British Isles from attack. However, we cannot sacrifice nine divisions† for that purpose. We have got to insist that those governments look at the problem from our point of view... As long as they continue to build airfields and to employ Chinese Communist forces, the enemy poses a serious threat. There is talk now about a volunteer air force. That could be a Russian air force. The Russians have 4,000 aircraft in the area. They could use half of that if they thought it could do the job. They could mount an offensive which could seriously upset us. We need earnest efforts to persuade our allies that an air offensive could be serious. We cannot handle this thing on a wait-and-see basis as the U.K. desires...

* There was no Royal Australian Air Force officer of this seniority in Korea. The most senior officer in the theatre, a group-captain (colonel) based in Kure, was. not admitted to daily briefing on air operations.

† Actually, seven divisions in Korea plus 187 Airborne RCT. The two National Guard divisions sent to Japan were an essential part of the occupation force there.

GENERAL BRADLEY: The British will not give you the answer you want. They are going to wait and see what develops.

GENERAL VANDENBERG: But we have got to push them to give us an answer.

GENERAL COLLINS: I agree, but I don't know how we can push them unless we are sure that they are adequately briefed. The British and the Australians are briefed but I am not sure that the others are.

GENERAL VANDENBERG: The British are the main obstacle.

GENERAL BRADLEY: The U.K. is now asking us for our order of battle* in order to discuss the problem in the Cabinet. This request scares us on security grounds. Our present decision is that we should not provide this information. However, the British say that they cannot make up their minds without all the facts which bear on the situation.

MR NITZE: I have had a further conversation with Sir Oliver Franks. He is disturbed about how to report to his government. In our first conversation, we indicated that we had not yet decided to react in the event of an air attack; and in our second conversation, we indicated that we had decided to react. I told him that the U.S. is responsible for the unified command and that the lack of a decision is tantamount to a decision that we would not react promptly. I also told him that because of our responsibility we had to be in a position to decide what reaction to make. He then said that he thought he could present our point of view to his government, but he was disturbed that a decision had been taken in advance of the receipt of British views...

GENERAL BRADLEY: Should we extend our briefing to governments other than the Australian and British governments? Would this involve a sacrifice of security?...

MR NITZE: I think that the whole thing will fall into place if we get the British in.

GENERAL VANDENBERG: I think we should concentrate on trying to get the British to understand our problem...

GENERAL COLLINS: We have to maintain our position that we can take whatever decision is necessary. We cannot be in the position that we have to consult with our allies for [or] Congress would 'blow its top'.

MR NITZE: We all agree that we have to maintain our right to decide. We should try to get an understanding with them [the British] of the conditions under which we would have to react even though they will still want to consider the problem in reacting in light of the specific situation.

GENERAL BRADLEY: If this happens, we ought to be able to get in touch with them in 20 minutes, and Sir Oliver should be able to get us an answer in an hour's time if the attack comes at the right time of day. We should consult

---

* This meant the Chinese order of battle and that of the Soviet forces in the Far East, obtained in part from sources the United States reserved to itself.

with them if we can. If we can get ahold of every one we should do that. What we now have is authority to act in an emergency. If the President is in the White House and if the Secretary of State is in his office, we will, of course, check again with them. We can assure the British that we will consult with them if it is at all possible, but we must make it clear to them that we cannot wait 24 hours.

GENERAL COLLINS : Another problem is that even if their answer is in the negative, we are still going to have to react.

MR NITZE : That is right. But, of course, we will have to recognise the consequences. If we decide and act unilaterally, we are going to have to face the consequences of unilateral decision and action.

GENERAL COLLINS : Those consequences aren't too bad. In the event of war, we are going to have to carry the load out there in any event.

MR NITZE : But it does affect the use of U.K. bases in the event of general war.

GENERAL COLLINS : If general war comes, the U.K. will come into it.

GENERAL BRADLEY : We might just have a Pacific war.

MR NITZE : Sir Oliver has expressed his personal view that an attack on Japan would mean a general war.

GENERAL BRADLEY : I suggest the Joint Chiefs of Staff consider the problem of a new directive to General Ridgway... He is not going to run way up north and leave his flank exposed, but I think he is going to need a new directive soon[16].

Progress towards peace negotiations and retaliatory air attacks north of the Yalu were thrust aside by the opening of the Fifth Phase Offensive. 'We held our breath,' Field-Marshal Slim recalled, 'as the battle started. Much depended on the outcome'[17]. With that, the United States Chiefs and Government would have agreed. As Sir Oliver Franks had observed on 15th April,

> ... The chief political risk the President runs in having removed MacArthur does not rise from anything that might happen in the United States. It arises from the possibility of a successful enemy attack in Korea which might seem to vindicate MacArthur. This will tend to make the Americans very sensitive in the next few weeks to what the enemy in Korea does by land and air[18].

If P'eng had indeed triumphed, it might also have been similarly awkward for the British Government. The State Department reminded its ambassador in London on 17th April that the British were believed

---

* The Foreign Relations and Armed Forces Committees of the Senate in joint session began a formal enquiry into the circumstances of General MacArthur's dismissal on 3rd May 1951.

by Republican standard bearers to have been influential in securing General MacArthur's dismissal as part and parcel of a tendency towards appeasement on Korean issues[19], a grievance that might be publicised when the Congress enquired into the matter*. The British Chiefs of Staff had already foreseen the possibility that they might be obliged to defend their progressive lack of confidence in the United Nations Commander-in-Chief and prepared their defences accordingly[20].

The outcome of the fighting between 22nd and 25th April was thus doubly welcome to the Governments in Washington and London. But while it eased, it did not solve their differences. Mr Acheson reviewed these in a telegram to Mr Morrison on 31st April.

> ... We each ought to understand the other's position what we think; why we think it. We start from the common ground of desiring peace and security in the Pacific and the earliest conclusion of the Korean conflict. We are doing everything possible to limit the fighting in Korea.
>
> This country, which fronts on two oceans, has heavy responsibilities in the Pacific, as well as in the Atlantic...
>
> Short of a change in the aggressive Communist purpose, I do not see how hostilities can cease. So long as this purpose persists there will be fighting in Korea. So far there has been no indication of a change in purpose. In fact, a new and massive offensive is under way.
>
> Under these circumstances, we must fight. And our economic and political measures and attitudes should back up our military ones. We must convince the enemy that a cessation in hostilities is in his interest.
>
> ... There are many indications that a major air attack may be launched at any time against the United Nations forces from bases on Chinese territory. If this occurs, we must assume that a decision has been made to attempt to drive the United Nations forces from Korea whatever the cost or consequences. Under these circumstances, it may be imperative to attack the bases from which the attack upon our forces comes.
>
> Should the air blow be launched against us, the safety of the forces, land, sea, and air, will be gravely imperilled. Time will be a factor of the most vital importance in launching a counter blow against the bases from which the attack comes.
>
> We realise fully that the Governments which have forces in Korea are deeply concerned in this decision, and for this reason we have been holding consultations to reach the widest possible agreement on the procedure to be followed... As a practical matter, consultation after the event between Washington and London—to say nothing of additional consultations with the other Governments—would require a passage of hours, even days, during a time of grave peril to our forces.
>
> For these reasons, we believe that this Government, as the Unified Command[21], must retain the latitude to determine whether an attack requires immediate counter-action...

Another question which has been much discussed between our Governments is the use of economic means to aid the military ones.

...on April 27th you voiced objection to the Additional Measures Committee rushing ahead and submitting a report at once to the Political Committee of the General Assembly. I do not believe that the issue is really one between precipitate action and considered and deliberate action.

The proposal for economic measures has been under discussion since last January, and the Resolution to the General Assembly providing for a committee to consider it was taken on February 1. At that time it was understood that the [Additional Measures] Committee might defer its report if the Good Offices Committee reported satisfactory progress... For almost three months now the Good Offices Committee has been at work, and yet it cannot even report progress.

... In the past some members of the United Nations have believed that the development of economic measures would further alienate the Chinese Communists and increase their hostility. I do not see how their hostility can be increased. I do not see any possibility of any basic realignment of the Chinese Communists towards the free world unless and until they end their attack... So it seems to me that the addition of economic measures to the military ones we are already taking will move the Chinese in the direction of this decision and that failure to take it moves them away from it.

... The United States...has ended all commercial and financial relations with Communist China. We would welcome similar actions by all United Nations members. But we recognise the great importance of unity in action; and, therefore, in the effort to get general agreement, suggest something considerably less than what we have done.

So far as the United Kingdom is concerned, what we have proposed means little more than proclaiming publicly what is already being done.

... In the political field our Governments have differed in the past regarding the wisdom and advisability of admitting the Chinese Communists to the United Nations. Whatever may have been the merits of this debate, can we not now agree to a moratorium upon it? At a time when the Chinese Communists are defying the United Nations, fighting its forces on a major scale, and denying the validity of every provision of the Charter, the discussion of their possible admission to the United Nations seems to me to have the most divisive possible effect between us and to give them the greatest encouragement in continuing their present course. ...admitting the enemy to the organisation which they are fighting seems to me to be so utterly confusing to the average man as to imperil the whole United Nations operation in Korea.

I am still giving careful thought to the possibility which we suggested last month, and which you have also developed on somewhat different lines, of having a new declaration of aims, which will reemphasise our desire for peaceful settlement upon conclusion of the aggression... I am sure, however, that you are already aware of the serious objections which we have to certain elements in your counter-proposal. These objections can be developed during the forthcoming talks.

In any event it is my immediate suggestion that the present moment is not an opportune one for a public statement. The military issue in Korea is still being fought out. General Ridgway believes that he can meet and repulse the attack. It is clearly a great one and is not yet fully developed. In this situation any statement by us looking toward a peaceful settlement is, in my judgement, sure to be rejected with contempt as a cry for peace from nations which are sorely pressed. So I think we would retard rather than help the chances of a peaceful settlement by a statement now[22].

Reading this message, Mr Scott in the Foreign Office became concerned that a decision in the matter of retaliatory air attacks should not be allowed to drift through the approaching Whitsun holiday. He drafted a memorandum which he proposed Mr Morrison should submit to the Prime Minister, noting that President Truman had already agreed, *ad interim*, to strike back at air bases in China from which bombers were launched against Korea.

6 ...the onus will be on China and Russia without whose assistance large scale air attacks would be impossible. On the merits of the case I see no alternative but to meet this new threat by the most effective military means at our disposal, i.e., by bombing the bases from which the attacks have been launched. If China takes the grave decision to extend the war she must accept the consequences, and I believe that it would be a profound mistake for us to flinch from taking the decision, unpalatable as it is.

7. This general conclusion, which I have reached with great reluctance but which is in my view inescapable if we are not to surrender all along the line, is strengthened by my anxiety about the results if we take a contrary decision or even if we delay taking this decision. If we hesitated for even a few days, after the Americans had unilaterally authorised retaliation, the domestic and international consequences for us might be very serious. There would be a crisis in this country, in our relations with the United States and with other countries, and at the United Nations, and our best prospect of controlling the situation would be to announce at once where we stood and seek to influence others in the same direction.

8. I do not doubt that in the long run we would find ourselves participating in action against China if she were to provoke this by air attacks on United Nations forces in Korea, and I believe that the people of this country would understand and endorse that course however much they shared the government's lack of enthusiasm for it[23].

This advice was accepted by the Prime Minister and Cabinet, on 3rd May. They agreed in principle to retaliatory strikes on Chinese bases used for major bombing raids in Korea*. The United States was to be

* They reserved the right to full consultation before retaliation if air attacks were to be launched from bases in the Soviet Union, which the United States readily conceded.

informed that the British Government would expect consultation prior to action but that views would be communicated with the minimum of delay. The Prime Minister, Foreign Secretary, and Minister of Defence were authorised to act for the Cabinet in responding to United States' proposals in this matter* [24].

Actually, it was much ado about nothing. No doubt a matter of principle was involved, but the actual air threat at the beginning of May was no greater than it had been at any other time in the war. The Chinese and North Korean air forces had certainly been reinforced from Russian sources and benefitted by the training of air crew in the latter part of 1950 and the early months of 1951, but the United Nations air forces, in particular those of the United States, had added considerably to their power in the theatre during the same period. Given the continuous disablement of the North Korean air bases, what the United States feared was a series of missions launched from behind the Yalu or from the Shantung peninsula with limited expectations of recovery. Perhaps they were haunted by the ghosts of Pearl Harbour. None among the Chinese, North Korean, or Russian hierarchy contemplated such desperate operations. The first two were anxious to build up their forces to as high a level as possible for defence as much as cooperation in ground offensives. The Russians were as determined not to offer the slightest provocation to the United States in the air as at sea and on land in the Korean theatre.

Mr Morrison replied to Mr Acheson comprehensively on 10th May. His comments on the extension of economic sanctions showed that the British view had scarcely shifted from earlier discussions of the subject, and with good reason; the United States continued to conjure with theories despite evidence that these were flawed. State and Defense Departments wanted a host of nations to impose a general embargo on trade with China, or at as great a level as could be agreed. Unity in this matter would daunt China. But unity had proved a pipe dream; many smaller nations in Europe and Asia could not afford or would otherwise not agree to cut trade which made no contribution to military operations. Britain was carrying out its promises to deny China goods in that category, including any produced in or passing through Hong Kong. The Government was ready to support a resolution from the Additional Measures Committee recommending 'a selective embargo on the supply of war materials to China'† but continued to oppose imposition of a general embargo because, far from showing China international unity in the matter, a vote would disclose disunity. It was thought tactful not to

---

* The British Government also expressed a wish to keep Australia, Canada, New Zealand, and South Africa informed about the arrangements involved.

† The United Nations resolution to embargo strategically important goods to China and North Korea was passed on 18th May 1951. Its effect was minimal.

reiterate the longstanding British view that, by excluding China from all commerce with the western world, her only source of trade would be the Soviet *bloc*.

As regards Communist China's seat in the United Nations, Mr Morrison did not agree with Mr Acheson, making the point that the issue of proposing entry did not lie with America or Britain but Russia. However, he alarmed the State Department by hawking a conscience in the matter.

> The legal arguments for seating them are in our view conclusive, though I should certainly not wish to display any enthusiasm in championing the claims of the Central People's Government of China...as long as they are set on their present course. On the other hand, I could not act in such a way as might imply support for the fiction that Chiang Kai-shek's representative in the United Nations speaks for China[25].

The Foreign Secretary conceded that the run of operations in Korea militated against an immediate public statement of United Nations aims but urged that one should be manifested as soon as possible.

> The opportunity may occur if the United Nations forces succeed in blunting the Chinese offensive. Perhaps the Chinese may then be in a more chastened mood and less unwilling to negotiate, but whether they are so or not I believe we owe it to our peoples and to our troops to define our policy. I therefore welcome your suggestion that further talks should be held with Sir Oliver Franks about the form which this declaration should take.

> Mr Gifford [the United States Ambassador to the United Kingdom] said to me that he thought our differences on foreign policy in the Far East had been narrowing in recent months. I think that is true, and I am glad. He went on to say however that he thought we might now be at a crossroads and our paths might begin to diverge again. I hope this is not so; at any rate, if the risk exists, the best way to guard against it is for us to exchange occasional messages. That is why I especially valued the candour and friendliness of your message, and I have tried to reply in the same spirit[26].

Mr Gifford might well have been right; the new Foreign Secretary was inconstant in matters of policy, inclined to be swayed by instincts which lacked maturity in diplomacy.

> ... I would describe the feeling here as restive, rather than pessimistic [he wrote to Sir Gladwyn Jebb on 17th May 1951]: people are worried by the lack of Chinese response, by the apparent lack of clarity of policy, and by the fear that we are drifting into war. This is rather guesswork for there is little active manifestation of public opinion...[27]

Mr Attlee, a lone figure of authority in a government losing public confidence*, felt the loss of Mr Bevin keenly, and was already rueing the

---

* In May, polls indicated 57% public support for Mr Attlee as Prime Minister, but only 40% for the Government.

appointment of Herbert Morrison as his successor in the Foreign Office[28]. He missed Bevin's enterprise in the partnership with the United States and sensed that it was declining due to Morrison's inability to master the political complexities of the war in Korea. These reflections were not invalidated by the surprising news on 24th June that a Russian initiative appeared to open the prospect of an armistice there.

From the beginning of May, rumours of 'peace feelers' had circulated among the diplomatic community and the press at the United Nations headquarters in New York—indeed they may have originated in either or both of these bodies. Sir Gladwyn Jebb reported several to London, remarking on 24th May—'a further spate of rumours here in the last day or two... I am satisfied there is nothing in this[29]'. On the 25th, Sir Oliver Franks noted that rumours in Washington '...have been kept alive here to some extent by speculation on the significance of the publication in full by Pravda of the text of Senator [Edwin] Johnson's resolution calling for an armistice in Korea[*] [30]'. The rumours persisted, and were notable in as much as they were the first to suggest that the Communist side might be ready to negotiate a cease fire since the war began. The news from the battlefield encouraged them; the United Nations Command was just then affirming that it had not only checked the Fifth Phase Campaign but was driving the enemy out of all the ground it had recently gained.

On the other side of the hill, the reversal of the Chinese People's Volunteers in April and May at first suggested to Mao that it might well be advantageous to draw the United Nations army northward.

> As for the place of annihilation of the enemy, the more northerly the better for us if only the enemy will press on, provided that the P'yongyang–Wonsan line is not crossed[31].

However, P'eng's reports towards the end of May made it clear that he would not be be in a position to remount an offensive for some considerable time; supply and equipment shortages apart, he had much work to do rebuilding the confidence of forces in which he had again lost many of his best young leaders including political officers. When the Central Committee of the Communist Party met to consider the position, Nieh Jung-chen, acting chief of staff of the People's Liberation Army[†] observed,

> ... The majority of those attending maintained that our troops should stop in the area of the 38th Parallel, fighting while negotiating, aiming then to settle the Korean issue through negotiations. I was one of this point of view.

---

* Editorial comment in Pravda remarked that the resolution reflected a recognition by the 'imperialists' that they had failed and were seeking peace.

† This term embraced all the defence forces, land, sea, and air, of the People's Republic of China.

> My opinion was, our political objective of driving the enemy away from the northern part of Korea had been achieved; to halt around the 38th Parallel consolidated the original frontier, a situation likely to be accepted by all sides. If the war continued, that would not dismay us, and we would grow stronger in combat. However, there were difficulties. Guided by Comrade Mao Tse-tung, the meeting finally adopted this course...[32]

As this meeting did not take place until the end of May, the earlier rumours did not, therefore, spring from Peking. It is unlikely that any came from P'yongyang; Kim was not acquainted with the change of policy until 3rd June. Of course, he might have had indications from Moscow that Stalin was coming to the view that prosecution of the war was pointless, for on some day in May Stalin evidently inclined to it—as the account of immediately following events will manifest. But it is unlikely that he would have discussed the matter with Kim without doing so previously or simultaneously with Mao. And if rumours emanated from the Kremlin, the likelihood is that they would have been deliberately inspired and directed towards the western powers[33].

The earliest rumours almost certainly originated in attempts by the State Department to find some means of developing peace negotiations under their own arrangements. 'We cast about,' as Mr Acheson later recorded, 'like a pack of hounds searching for a scent'[34]. On 3rd May, two American foreign service officers, members of their national mission to the United Nations, travelled into Manhattan from Flushing Meadows with Mr Malik and his associate S K Tsarapkin after a Security Council Meeting. Conversation flowed freely and informally, embracing a wide range of topics including settlement of the Korean war. In this matter, Mr Malik twice observed that any Korean settlement must contain honourable terms for all interested parties[35].

This seemed to offer some faint scent of success, but a report of prospective negotiations in the *New York Times* immediately thereafter, from one source or another, apparently discouraged further discussion by the Russians. With President Truman's agreement, Mr Acheson tried again.

George Kennan, a former minister in the United States embassy in Moscow*, widely respected as an expert in Soviet affairs, was on leave of absence at Princeton University. On 18th May, he was asked to approach Mr Malik informally and representing no one but himself to discover Russian views if any about a possible cease-fire in Korea The two men met 'in a sort of pagoda' in Mr Malik's residence on 31st May. 'Overcoming an initial embarrassment when Malik upset a tray of fruit and wine, they circuitously approached the question, which, predictably, Malik was unable to answer'[36].

* See Volume I, p 10.

When Mr Kennan

> ... pressed him to say whether he thought that it would or would not be useful for us to meet again, he was evasive but not negative, saying that he thought it was a good thing in general for people to talk things over and that he would always be happy to receive me and to pass the time of day. I had the feeling that his reluctance to say anything more definite on this point stemmed from an unwillingness to indicate that he would ask for further instructions from his Government. I therefore said that I would like to give further thought to what he said and would come back on another occasion at his convenience. ...[37]

The two met again on 5th June. Mr Kennan led the opening conversation by putting some specific questions.

> ... I could understand, I said, why the Soviet Government might not care to express itself...on the questions I had introduced. But there was, as I hoped he would recognise, good reason on our part for making the enquiry. If we were to approach with a view to arriving at a cease fire the regimes whose forces were opposing ours in Korea, a number of questions would certainly arise in which the Soviet Government would surely take an interest and in which it would be useful for us to know their views. Who should be invited to participate in conversations looking to a cease fire? What should be the status of the discussions? If a control commission should be established to supervise the execution of a cease fire, what countries should furnish it with its members and personnel? In the absence of any knowledge of the views of the Soviet Government on these matters we would have no choice but to work them out as best we could with whoever would talk to us. But in these circumstances we could certainly give no assurance that the arrangements arrived at would be agreeable to the Soviet Union. ... I pointed out, as an example, the dilemma we would be in if the Chinese Communist forces just disappeared again from the Korean scene. Who would give us any assurance, in this case, that they would not reassemble their forces and intervene in Korea again at some future date?
>
> My host then stated that he was in a position to say the following to me:
>
> The Soviet Government wanted peace and wanted a peaceful solution of the Korean question—and at the earliest possible moment. However, since its forces were not participating in the hostilities in Korea, it did not feel that it could take part in any discussion of the question of a cease fire.
>
> He did not know whether I wanted his personal advice, but if I did, it would be that the United States Government should get in touch with the North Koreans and Chinese in this matter...[38]

This second meeting led Mr Acheson and his staff to believe that the Soviet Union was ready to pull the necessary strings to bring about a cease fire, but they were unsure how to proceed. Discussions followed within the very narrow circle of those privy to Mr Kennan's meetings with Mr Malik—a handful of officers in the State Department and the diplomatic mission at the United Nations, and two members of the President's staff beside Mr Truman himself. Was it to be through Moscow? Mr Malik had reiterated that the Soviet Government did not feel that they had any connection with negotiations. Should they approach Peking? The British, or neutral nations such as India or Sweden, had the means to undertake enquiries; but the Chinese also tended to disclaim any reponsibility for the activities of the 'Volunteers' in Korea. The North Korean authorities would be even more difficult to contact; the only diplomatic missions accredited to them belonged to the Communist *bloc*. A further question arose: to what extent would enquiries at these locations be limited if they continued to restrict the knowledge to American nationals only?

As if to encourage perseverance, Mr Malik included the following remarks on the evening of 23rd June* in a talk sponsored by the United Nations radio.

> ... The peoples of the Soviet Union believe that it is possible to defend the cause of peace.
>
> The Soviet peoples further believe that the most acute problem of the present day—the problem of the armed conflict in Korea—could also be settled.
>
> This would require the readiness of the parties to enter on the path of a peaceful settlement of the Korean question. The Soviet peoples believe that as a first step discussions should be started between the belligerents for a cease-fire and an armistice providing for the mutual withdrawal of forces from the 38th Parallel.
>
> Can such a step be taken?
>
> I think it can, provided there is a sincere desire to put an end to the bloody fighting in Korea. ...

These remarks gave Mr Acheson the collateral to resume discussions on peace negotiations on an international basis, immediately with the British. The Foreign Office was eager to 'lose no opportunity to test the genuineness of this move' and proposed informal joint American and British consultation with Mr Malik[39]. This put Mr Acheson into a difficulty. Would Mr Malik refer to his talks with Mr Kennan in meeting the representatives? If so, the British might become aware that they had been excluded from an important initiative. A decision on a joint approach was held over for this and other reasons, of which one was due to cooling feet in the State Department; perhaps, after all, they were being deceived by the Russians. Mr Rusk showed Mr Steel—acting on behalf of Sir Oliver Franks on leave—five comments raised by his associates after studying the text of the Russian broadcast.

---

* Released in London on 24th June 1951.

(a) 95 per cent of the speech was an able and succinct summary of the Soviet propaganda line. The references to Korea could conceivably have been designed to call attention to the rest of the speech.

(b) the fact that Malik did not mention impossible political conditions did not preclude the possibility that he had them in mind.

(c) the reference to discussions 'between the belligerents' was ambiguous. From the Soviet and Chinese points of view the only belligerents on the enemy side were the North Koreans.

(d) Malik's statement may possibly have been designed to induce a wait-and-see attitude in the United Nations forces from which the enemy could derive advantage.

(e) there was no indication whatever of the attitude of Peking[40].

Next day, Monday, 25th June, Messrs Rusk and Hickerson* gave Mr Steel a list of the questions they proposed should be put to Mr Malik for the purposes of clarification as distinct from negotiation.

1. Mr Malik used the expression 'the Soviet peoples believe'. Are we entitled to believe that this is also the view of the Soviet Government? If so, is the Soviet Government prepared to lend its support to the taking of steps towards a peaceful settlement?

2. Is there any special significance in the phrase 'a cease fire and an armistice'? What does Mr Malik have in mind in appearing to draw a distinction between the two? Does this refer to a development of peaceful arrangements by stages? Does it contemplate provisions for assurance against the resumption of hostilities, as for example by supervision of any cease-fire or armistice arrangement?

3. What is the significance of the expression 'to enter on the path of a peaceful settlement of the Korean question'? Does the Soviet Government have any specific steps in mind? If so, what precise arrangements do they envisage?

4. Does the Soviet Government know whether Mr Malik's statement represents the view of the authorities in Peking? If *not* how does the Soviet Government suggest views of Peking be ascertained?

5. Should one understand Mr Malik's statement to mean that the Soviet Government is prepared to support a meeting of representatives of the opposing commands in the field to discuss arrangements for a cease fire and an armistice which would contain adequate assurances against renewal of hostilities?[41].

By this time, Mr Acheson had agreed to a joint approach to Mr Malik, Mr Gross representing the United States, Sir Gladwyn Jebb the

* John D Hickerson, Assistant Secretary of State for United Nations Affairs.

British—those in the close circle reasoning that if the Kennan talks were by chance uncovered to the latter, they were neither shameful nor injurious to their British ally. The list of questions was also being sent to Moscow to enable Admiral Kirk* to seek clarification from Mr Vyshinsky, Commissar for External Affairs†.

The hunt for a path to a cease-fire intensified among the United Nations allies. Discussions and telegrams flowed, many to no purpose. Sir Gladwyn became worried that the French would be offended if they were not included in the meeting with Malik; but they were not, though insistent like others in the alliance that they should be kept informed of developments. Mr Lamb‡ whetted appetites by reporting from the British diplomatic mission in Peking that the 'People's Daily', commenting approvingly on Mr Malik's broadcast, noted that the peace offer would give America a way out of her military and economic difficulties[42]. Attempts to meet Mr Malik in New York and Mr Vyshinsky in Moscow failed, and, similarly, American attempts to make contact with the Chinese.

It is highly probable that this searching out process was exasperating to Generalissimo Stalin and his immediate subordinates in the foreign policy field. In his talks with George Kennan, Mr Malik had made it clear that the Soviet Government was not going to become involved overtly in peace negotiations in Korea. He advised getting in touch with the Chinese and North Koreans. But this did not point to contact with the respective governments. The foreign affairs departments in Washington, London, Paris, Canberra, Ottawa, and Wellington, and equally all the Asian nations interested, knew that China declined to accept any implication of involvement in the Korean war, and that the North Koreans were inaccessible.

As the Americans failed to move to the next conclusion, Mr Malik dropped another clue on 23rd June, 'as a first step discussions should be started between the belligerents', a phrase meant to be taken literally; discussions between those fighting in Korea, the Commanders-in-Chief in the field. A further clue was given to James Reston of the *New York Times* on 25th June during enquiries at the Soviet Embassy in Washington. What did the Russians mean by 'belligerents'? The explanation was everybody fighting on each side and this included the 'Chinese People's Volunteers'. The editorial in the *Peking People's Daily* signalled a readiness to receive approaches to the 'Volunteers'.

---

* United States Ambassador to the Soviet Union. See Volume I, p 89.

† See Volume I, p 221.

‡ Lamb (later, Sir) Lionel Henry (1900–1992) succeeded Sir John Hutchison as Head of Mission in Peking on 6th March 1951. (See also Volume I, p 51 and fn.)

The trail was laid but the hunters could not see it. Instead they continued poking about for other clues, hanging about the Chinese embassy in Moscow, pursuing Mr Vyshinsky. On 27th June, Admiral Kirk was given an appointment to see Mr Gromyko, Deputy External Affairs Commissar* at which the idea of a meeting of the principal commanders on the battlefield was spelled out[43].

At last the State Department saw the trail that led to the objective[44], though its promise was not immediately acceptable to General Vandenberg, Chief of the United States Air Force Staff[45]. In London, even at this point, Mr Morrison failed to comprehend that the trail was crooked because Stalin and Mao insisted on the neutral status of their countries. 'A little preparation of the ground in Peking, now or later, may perhaps contribute to the success of the negotiations,' he advised Mr Steel on 29th June, 'though I think that we can safely fall in line with the present American proposal for immediate action by General Ridgway'[46].

On the other side of the world, this message was broadcast from Tokyo at 8 am on 30th June to 'The Commander-in-Chief, Communist Forces in Korea'.

> As Commander-in-Chief of the United Nations Command I have been instructed to communicate to you the following:
>
> I am informed that you may wish a meeting to discuss an armistice providing for the cessation of hostilities and all acts of armed forces in Korea, with adequate guarantees for the maintenance of such armistice.
>
> Upon the receipt of word from you that such a meeting is desired I shall be prepared to name my representative. I would also at that time suggest a date at which he could meet with your representative. I propose that such a meeting could take place aboard a Danish hospital ship in Wonsan harbour.
>
> (Signed) M.B. Ridgway, General, United States Army,
> Commander-in-Chief, United Nations Command.

Next day, Radio P'yongyang responded†.

> General Ridgway, Commander-in-Chief of the United Nations Forces: Your statement of June 30th this year concerning peace talks has been received.
>
> We are authorised to inform you that we agree to meet your representatives to conduct talks concerning cessation of military action and establishment of peace. We propose that the place of meeting be in the area of Kaesong

* See Volume I, p 17.

† Radio Peking broadcast this message as a special news item.

on the 38th Parallel. If you agree, our representatives are prepared to meet your representative between July 10th and 15th, 1951.

(Signed) Kim Il-sung,
Supreme Commander of the Korean People's Army.

P'eng Te-huai,
Commander of the Chinese People's Volunteers.

1st July, 1951.

General Ridgway accepted the site but proposed that they should hasten arrangements. After further exchanges, it was agreed that liaison teams should meet on 8th July to enable the armistice representatives to open talks on the 10th.

Thus, a year and fifteen days after the North Korean People's Army opened its offensive across the 38th Parallel, some nine months after the Chinese People's Volunteers crossed the Yalu to rescue them, the two sides sat down to bring hostilities to an end.

SOURCE NOTES: Chapter 12

1 See DBPO No 139.
2 FO 1214 to Washington of 30th March 1951 FK 1071/385, (FO 371 92778). For text and associated documents, see DBPO No 136.
3 FO 1437 to Washington of 11th April 1951 (DEFE 11/210 f 2097C), and DBPO Nos 136 and 139, note 5.
4 CRO Y204 to UK High Commissioners of 9th April 1951 (DEFE 11/210, f 2083C; also DBPO No 136, note 3, and FRUS 1951, *cit*, p 328).
5 FRUS *cit,* above, pp 329–330.
6 See O'Neill, *op cit*, volume i, pp 214–219, and DEFE 11/210, f 2083A. See also FRUS *cit,* pp 346–347.
7 See, for example, Sir Pierson Dixon's minute under FK 1093/51 (FO 371 92809) of 9th April 1951 and DBPO No 142.
8 See Korean item in CAB 128/19, Cabinet CM (51) 27th Meeting, 12th April 1951.
9 FO 1523 to Washington of 16 th April 1951 (DEFE 11/210, f 2125A).
10 *Ibid.*
11 Signal BJSM(AS) Washington GI 1873 to War Office of 13 Apr 51 (DEFE 11/210, f 2115A. Connect also with f 2098A).
12 *Ibid.*
13 See signal Bouchier TRAIN 20 of 191350Z (Apr 51) to Ministry of Defence (DEFE 11/210, f 2147 and forward through ff 2179 and 2180. Also FJ 1203/4 (FO 371 92656).
14 CAB 131/10, Defence Committee DO (51), 8th Meeting, 9th April 1951; also FO 1548 to Washington of 17th April 1951 to Washington and DEFE 10/210, f 2133A.
15 See, for example, FRUS, *cit,* pp 338–342 and 343–344, also FO 726 to Peking of 13th April 1951, and Peking 614 to Foreign Office of 15th April 1951, (DEFE 11/210, ff 2098 and 2116, respectively).
16 FRUS, *cit,* pp 353–362. See also BJSM, Washington AWT 14 of 18th April 1951, DEFE 11/210, f 2143A.
17 Conversation, author with FM Lord Slim.
18 Washington 1150 to Foreign Office of 15th April 1951 (DEFE 11/210, f 2121).
19 FRUS, *cit,* p 353.
20 DEFE 4/11, COS (51) 68th Meeting, 18th April 1951, (Confidential Annex). See also DEFE 11/210, f 2159.
21 The State Department's concept of American responsibilities as the executive power in the Unified Command are set out in two drafts of 21st and 27th April 1951, see 795B.00/4-2051, (USNARS, Washington DC).
22 United States Secretary of State 4969 of 3019.00 April 1951 to the British Foreign Secretary through the US Embassy in the United Kingdom, FRUS *cit*, pp 390–392.
23 Memorandum, Secretary of State, Foreign Office to Prime Minister (undated), and letter Foreign Office, to Secretary to Chiefs of Staff, 2nd May 1951, (DEFE 11/211, ff 2215 and 2215A, respectively).
24 CAB 128/19, CM (51) 33rd Meeting, 3rd May 1951. Also CAB 129/45, CP (51) 127 of 8th May 1951, and CAB 128/19, CM (51), 35th Meeting, 10th May 1951.
25 FO 2418 to Washington of 10th May 1951, (DEFE 11/211, f 2249).
26 *Ibid.*
27 Demi-official letter of Foreign Secretary to Sir Gladwyn Jebb at the United Nations, 17th April 1951, (Copy in DEFE 11/212, f 2268A).
28 See, for example, Harris, Kenneth, *Attlee* (London, 1982) *op cit, p 472.*
29 New York 557 FO of 24th May 1951, (DEFE 11/212, f 2290).
30 Washington 472 to FO of 23rd May 1951, (DEFE 11/212, f 2287). Text of speech is in Congress Record, S.Res. 140, 82nd Congress, 1st Session, 17th May 1951.
31 Mao, *Manuscripts*, vol 2, pp 183–185.

32 Quoted, Hsü Yen, *op cit* pp 268–269.

33 See, for example, a Russian offer made through Sweden at this time, (USNARS, Washington, 695.001/6-151 and 795.00/6-1451).

34 Acheson, *op cit,* p 119.

35 For details including notes, see USNARS, Washington, 795.00/5-351.

36 Acheson, *op cit,* p 121.

37 See Mr Kennan's memorandum, with notes, in USNARS, Washington, 795.00/5-2551.

38 *Ibid.*

39 FO 2644 to Washington of 24th June 1951 (DEFE 11/213, f 2397).

40 Washington 1942 to FO of 24th June 1951, (DEFE 11/213, f 2398).

41 Washington 1953 to FO of 25th June 1951, (DEFE 11/213, f 2399).

42 Peking 1171 to FO of 25th June 1951 (DEFE 11/213, f2401).

43 See Admiral Kirk's telegram of 27th June 1951 to Washington, FRUS, *cit,* p 560.

44 See, for example, FO 2719 to Washington of 28th June 1951 (DEFE 11/213, f 2429A) and Washington 1998 to FO of 28th June 1951 (DEFE 11/213, f 2431).

45 See *Memorandum of Conversation, by the Director of the Office of North East Asian Affairs (Johnson)*, FRUS, *cit,* pp 566–569.

46 FO 2735 to Washington of 29th June 1951, (DEFE 11/213, f 2434).

CHAPTER 13

The opening of armistice negotations

When the news of armistice talks reached the War Office in London, a major in the Directorate of Military Operations remarked,

> 'Hurrah, it's true, the war is over!'

He did not believe this literally but mistakenly assumed that negotiation of a cease fire was simply a matter of formality.

It was far from that. Although both sides wished to bring fighting to an end for the same reason—recognition that the price of victory was higher than they cared to pay—each suspected that the other had entered negotiations to gain a military advantage.

This mistrust had some substance. Mao was never wholly convinced that his forces were incapable of defeating the United Nations forces. From time to time during the negotiations he re-examined the options for a renewal of offensive action. P'eng resisted the idea to the limits of his persuasion. On the other side, General Van Fleet never wholly accepted the necessity for a defensive strategy from mid-1951. But he lacked the means for a strategic offensive; these lay with the Commander-in-Chief who held fast to the policy of the Unified Command: to apply military pressure within but not beyond the standing resources in the theatre. In this, the United States and United Kingdom held together, though the former began to question its efficacy in time.

For all their suspicions, therefore, the Russians and the Chinese on one side of the table, the Americans representing their own interests and those of their allies in the war on the other, were negotiating with the same prime aim, an armistice to end the fighting and some form of ageement to ensure that it remained at an end.

The Koreans did not share this aim. Neither Kim Il-sung nor Syngman Rhee supported the idea of an armistice; each wished to continue the fight until the other was wholly defeated. Both were obliged by more powerful allies to take part in the negotiations. But unlike Kim, Syngman Rhee was not obliged to dissemble. The former, as Head of State and Supreme Commander of the NKPA, had to appear to be the leading authority and therefore to provide the major element of the Communist delegation, permitting the Chinese to preserve the fiction that they had no national forces in Korea*. The delegation which sat down to negotiate on 8th July thus comprised three North Koreans and two Chinese:

> Lieutenant-General Nam Il, NKPA—Chief Delegate†.
> Major-General Lee Sang-cho, NKPA.
> Major-General Chang Pyong-san, NKPA.
> Teng Hua, CCF—P'eng's Deputy
> Hsieh Fang, CCF—Peng's Chief of Staff‡

The United Nations delegation was composed of:

> Vice-Admiral C Turner Joy, USN¶—Chief Delegate.
> Major-General Henry I Hodes§, US Army.
> Major-General Laurence C Craigi**, USAF.
> Rear-Admiral Arleigh A Burke††, USN,
> Major-General Paik Sun-yup‡‡, ROK Army.

General Ridgway gave the delegation final words of advice before they set off by helicopter from Munsan-ni for Kaesong. 'Be dignified. Deal with them openly and honestly'.

General Paik has described their arrival and first encounter in a single storey Korean mansion, Naebongjang, once grand, now damaged by high explosive and shrapnel so that

> one could watch the clouds scurry across the sky through the holes in the ceiling of the main building. ... Admiral Joy sat in the middle of our delegation, facing Nam Il across the [rectangular] table. I sat at Admiral Joy's right, confronting Lee Sang-cho. The first meeting was frigid, with neither shaking hands or offering any form of verbal greeting. Ten people faced each other across the table, five from each delegation, but only the chief delegates spoke. The meeting proceeded with every statement interpreted by turns into Korean, English, and Chinese[1].

Admiral Joy opened by making it clear that he was under instructions to discuss only military matters relating to Korea, and that until an agreement to cease fire had been concluded hostilities would continue.

---

* To counter this, the State and Defense Departments directed that P'eng should be referred to by their delegation as 'Commanding General of the Chinese Communist Forces'. (See signal JCS 95438 of 2 Jul 51 to CinCUN, repeated in FRUS, 1951, vol vii, Part 1, pp 611–613; and in Hermes, Walter, G, *Truce Tent and Fighting Front*, Washington, 1966, pp 19–20).

† Nam Il, (1911–), a former schoolmate of Kim Il-sung, subsequently educated in the Soviet Union, in which he fought with the Red Army against Germany. In 1951, he was a vice-premier in Kim's government, and Chief of Staff of the North Korean People's Army. He spoke Russian, Chinese, and English.

‡ No rank is given for the Chinese; none were in use at that time in the People's Liberation Army.

¶ See Volume I, fn, p 43.

§ Deputy Chief of Staff, Eighth Army.

** Vice-Commander, Far East Air Forces.

†† Deputy Chief of Staff to Admiral Joy.

‡‡ Commander, ROK I Corps.

He proposed that they should at once agree an agenda to comprehend the control and separation of the two sides, the operation of an armistice commission to ensure compliance with the agreements reached, and early access through the Red Cross to prisoners of war together with arrangements for their repatriation.

Information about and access to prisoners of war was, indeed, the first item of business raised by Admiral Joy for the agenda. Its precedence was due to British influence[2] but the United States readily accepted this requirement. The United Nations Command had passed all details of the captives it held to the International Red Cross in Geneva. The North Koreans and Chinese had not reciprocated[*][3]. However, though raised with the best intentions, it was probably an error to reveal to the Communist side the importance of this matter to the United Nations. It suggested a means of securing concessions on other matters at a later stage. Now, General Nam Il indicated that the prisoners of war should wait until a cease fire and a demilitarised zone had been agreed. This latter zone, he proposed, should be centred on the 38th parallel[4].

The UN representatives did not agree with him. The Parallel ran arbitrarily across the peninsula, following much ground difficult to defend, as those who had laid out positions along it prior to the war had discovered. It seemed to General Ridgway only reasonable that the line adopted should be the battle line as it existed, a view supported in Washington. The North Koreans and Chinese had not hesitated to cross it when they had the opportunity.

Such a view overlooked the tendency of Communist negotiators to use or discard international conventions as it suited them[†]. In discussing beforehand transition to an armistice, the Soviet and Chinese hierarchy had expected that the United Nations alliance would also be thinking of this line[‡]. In the radio talk which publicly opened the door to negotiations, Malik had referred to 'a mutual withdrawal of forces from the 38th Parallel'. Reflecting on the vehemence of General Nam's insistence on its adoption, Dean Acheson commented,

> So it seems to me highly probable that the Russians and the Chinese, for whom they were acting, received a considerable shock when at the start of a negotiation to restore, as they thought, the *status quo ante*, they found us demanding a new line for our sphere of influence, not only more militarily significant but involving considerable loss of prestige for them. They would never imagine that what appeared to be trickery was wholly inadvertent on our part. ...[5]

---

* Fragmentary information had been released, principally through propaganda agencies.

† With regard to the parallel, see, for example, p 14 above.

‡ See, for example, p 174–175, above.

A further matter for disagreement was Nam's proposal that all foreign troops should be withdrawn from Korea, once the cease fire was implemented, on the basis that there would be no requirement for them thereafter. It was a longstanding Chinese precondition for an armistice, rejected by the United Nations because withdrawal of their forces was out of the question until the Republic of Korea's armed forces were fully able to defend themselves against renewed hostilities by the NKPA. It was impossible to say how long this would take. But Admiral Joy was ready for the proposal. It was a political matter, he responded, lying outside the scope of military armistice negotiations.

Both sides parted that afternoon. They had failed to agree an agenda but had laid out their basic positions. The United Nations team had also learned that their opponents intended to control the meeting area as it suited them—freedom of movement of the United Nations staff within it was severely restricted, for example, and the news correspondents in the United Nations press camp were refused admission, though numerous Communist press representatives—journalists and cameramen—were given facilities. Admiral Joy declared that these restrictions were wholly unacceptable to the United Nations Command.

Returning to their camp at Munsan-ni, the delegation discussed the day's proceedings. All agreed that they were in for a testing time. Between the news correspondents, the delegates, and their staff, bets were laid as to how many weeks it would take to obtain an agreement—some thought two weeks, more thought ten. On one point General Ridgway and Admiral Joy were certain: the constraints upon access and movement on passage to and inside the meeting area for his party must be removed. The facilities had to be the same for both sides.

Next day, after a repetition of arguments—in which Nam Il rejected proposals to open the prisoner of war camps to the International Red Cross as a 'humanitarian' and not a military matter—the admiral raised the matter of local conditions. Nam agreed to unrestricted movement of properly marked vehicles up and down the corridor through Panmunjom village provided that his liaison officers were previously informed. But he stood firm on denying access to correspondents from the UN base. Admiral Joy gave notice that the latter would accompany him next day, and if one was turned back, he and his team would go back.

Next morning, 12th July, the correspondents were refused entry with the main party at Panmunjom. The delegation returned to its camp. For the next two days, the Communist liaison officers warned that unless the UN delegation returned the negotiations would be jeopardised. On the 15th, the point was conceded; news correspondents accompanied the UN delegates to an afternoon plenary session, and Admiral Joy secured agreement that his vehicles should travel without warning or restriction up and down the corridor. Further, there should be no armed troops within five miles of Kaesong.

They seemed to be advancing. Agreement was reached that the first item of business should be the establishment of a demilitarised zone, General Nam noting that his proposal for the line of the 38th Parallel stood. It was further agreed that the next item should relate to 'concrete arrangements' for the establishment and functioning of an armistice commission, and that they should thereafter discuss arrangements concerning prisoners of war. This settled, Nam insisted that they should discuss the withdrawal of foreign troops. Neither side yielded on this point during the 18th and 19th July.

During the evening of the 19th, Admiral Joy told General Ridgway that they were deadlocked. Tired and vexed by hours of wrangling, he proposed recessing* until the Communist side had some fresh point to offer. The idea was judged in Washington to be premature and perhaps liable to embarrass the United Nations cause; after all, the United Nations alliance certainly intended to withdraw its troops when the time was ripe and would necessarily discuss the arrangements with their opponents[6]. It was a feature of National Security Council Policy 48/5. This response cooled passions. It was another reminder that they were in for a long haul.

As it happened next day the Imjin was in flood and impassable. The American Chinese interpreter, First-Lieutenant Kenneth Wu, carried his bicycle over the remains of the demolished road bridge to inform the Communist liaison team that his principals would not be attending. The meeting on the 21st achieved nothing, but the UN was surprised when General Nam finally proposed a four day recess to permit both sides to 'reconsider'. Little appeared to have changed on the 25th until the afternoon meeting. General Nam then introduced a new form of his original proposal: rather than themselves discussing the withdrawal of foreign troops, they should make recommendations to governments to discuss the matter. Admiral Joy decided to proceed cautiously:

> In order that we can make no mistakes about your proposal we should like to have in writing exactly what you said.
>
> NAM : That we can do.
>
> JOY : Can we have it now?
>
> [Meeting recessed at 14.27]

---

* The UN liaison staff had taken particular care during meetings concerning procedures to establish the difference between 'recessing' and 'breaking off' negotiations.

JOY: Do we understand your actual proposed item [for the agenda] to be, and I quote: 'Recommendations to the governments of the countries concerned on both sides' and I unquote. Correct?

NAM: Yes, that is the recommendation to the governments of the countries concerned on both sides.

JOY: We understand.

NAM: And I explained the contents of it.

JOY: You mean the rest, in other words, is just explanation?

NAM: Yes.

JOY: Is it intended that your new item 5 be discussed by our two delegations after an armistice agreement based on the four mutual[ly] agreed upon items is signed and in effect?

NAM: ...after having discussed the four items and reached an agreement on them, we will recommend to the governments concerned on both sides, and then we may discuss under this item the question of recommending to the governments...that within a definite time limit after the armistice becomes effective, a conference of their representatives of a higher level be convened to negotiate on the question of withdrawal by stages of all foreign armed forces from Korea.

JOY: In other words, you mean this is another agenda item which must be discussed before the agreement is signed?

NAM: To have the agreement on the armistice smoothly. See? So we present the first four items first and when we have discussed the armistice items. That is only a technical question. Before the signing or after. We want to have a 15 minute recess to consider that.

JOY: What I want to get clear is this—whether you mean if both delegations do not agree on the recommendation, you will not sign the agreement?

NAM: Your statement is duly noted[7].

After consultation in Washington on this development, the Joint Chiefs of Staff signalled General Ridgway that

> ... The UN would have no objection to having this question taken up along with other political questions involved in a settlement in Korea in some other manner after a military armistice has entered into effect and sufficient time elapsed to establish the fact that its provisions are being faithfully observed.
> ... Your proposal to agree to include in agenda of item 5 reading 'recommendations to the governments of the countries concerned on both sides' is approved. However, in agreeing you should have in mind that agreement to include item on agenda does not mean agreement to Communist statement accompanying their proposal. Further instructions will be sent as soon as possible on substantive position when item 5 is reached[8].

It had taken two weeks to agree on what to talk about. Item 1 was thus completed: Adoption of the agenda.

They prepared to negotiate in order:

Item 2: Establishment of a demilitarised zone.

Item 3: Concrete arrangements for a cease fire and armistice.

Item 4: Arrangements relating to prisoners of war.

Item 5: Recommendations to the governments of the countries concerned on both sides.

The JCS signals to General Ridgway indicated that 'the United Nations would have no objection...' An all American authority, the Joint Chiefs were nonetheless the agents of the United Nations. So, too, General Ridgway was the United Nations Commander-in-Chief. It would be umbrageous to object to free use of signal channels in communications with him, now using the international title of CinCUNC, now the national, CinCFE. But in discharging its responsibilities as the United Nations agent, the United States President, his cabinet officers and senior staffs were for the most part acting unilaterally.

This was accepted by their allies, the more readily by the United Kingdom because it was exclusively kept informed from day to day of events and developments, principally by informal meetings between Sir Oliver Franks and Dean Acheson or Dean Rusk, and the embassy in London and the Foreign Office, partly by Sir Gladwyn Jebb at the United Nations headquarters, occasionally through the military agency, the Joint Services Mission—the BJSM—in Washington, and Air Vice-Marshal Bouchier in Tokyo.

Sir Oliver was

> ...thankful that the Americans were left to run matters in this way so long as we knew what those matters were. It was difficult enough to run the negotiations within the apparatus of one government. It would have been disastrous if two had attempted it[9].

With this the British Government agreed. They respected Mr Acheson's good faith and trusted General Ridgway—all had completely recovered from MacArthuritis. Mr Morrison's only subscription of any importance to the armistice talks in 1951 was a review of options arising from a cease fire.

He endorsed the view of his own senior advisers that a cease fire—much as it was to be desired—would not end their problems. He was not

> ...hopeful that a general settlement can be brought about in Korea, and I think that after the armistice we must expect a prolonged stalemate lasting perhaps for several years, with a divided Korea.
> ... All this assumes an armistice. We must also consider the position that would arise in the event of the armistice negotiations breaking down. General Ridgway will of course be taking the necessary military precautions to guard against a resumption of the offensive. In the political field it is essential that the responsibility for any resumption of the fighting must not only lie with the Chinese and North Koreans, but must be publicly recognised as lying there beyond any doubt. Whilst I would not suggest any fettering of General Ridgway's freedom of action, I earnestly trust that the utmost care will be taken to guard against what might be considered provocative action on the part of the United Nations forces ...[10]

Mr Acheson responded on 19th July,

> ...In regard to 'a general settlement in Korea' I have given, and am giving, a great deal of thought to this matter. My present thoughts are only tentative ones but they accord with your own views that the prospects of bringing one about are not good. I think it is probable that we should regard an armistice as something with which we must live for a considerable time and that therefore it must be adapted to this end. ...two things stand out. One is that the purpose on the Communist side is to eliminate us and all western influence from Korea. The other is that, although they have not been able to do this, the military cost and the consequences of our attempting to unify Korea by force are greater than it is wise or possible to pay. Therefore it seems to me that the idea of unifying Korea through the UN by negotiation involved the attempt to get the Communists to give up their basic and publicly-stated policy and also to achieve a result which we are not able to achieve by force. I see no reason to believe that this can be done and that therefore to accept any sort of unification which the Communists would be willing to give would be to concede to them a Communist-dominated Korea.
> If this analysis is right and one turns to a general settlement based upon a divided Korea, one then encounters the grave probability that the South Koreans would not accept such a settlement and might be driven to actions which would either make an armistice impossible or lead to a renewal of conflict if an armistice had been entered into. ...[11]

These were days in which the United Nations side certainly, and the Communists probably, expected the armistice negotiations to be completed by the end of 1951. Mr Acheson's and Mr Morrison's words manifest a determination to pursue an armistice. There is as yet no indication that the Russians or Chinese considered abandonment of the talks or, for that matter, their continuation simply as a cover for some other strategem.

For Stalin, the object of the war—bringing the whole of Korea under Communist control—had not been attained. The American presence in the south made it unlikely that the opportunity would arise again.

However, there was no guarantee that the Americans might not continue the offensive back into the depths of North Korea. An armistice would preclude that; it might even persuade the United States to withdraw her forces at a later stage, reopening a chance to overcome the Republic of Korea. Still, Stalin was a deliberate man. With no reason to hurry the armistice negotiations, time and his opponents' natural impatience might provide an opportunity to tease concessions from them.

For China, the cost of maintaining forty divisions in active if diminished operations in Korea was enormous for an impoverished nation. The burden would have been acceptable to Mao if the policy had offered an important advantage in Korea or elsewhere in the Far East even distantly. But short of a military victory in the peninsula, it is difficult to descry what other dividend was in view. Mao already held the view that he was serving Russian interests as much as those of China in Korea; he stated it openly then among his associates as he was to state it publicly in later years,

> The leaders of the Communist Party of the Soviet Union...accuse us of hoping for a 'head-on' clash' between the Soviet Union and the United States and trying to push them into a nuclear war. Our answer is: no, friends. You had better cut out your sensation-mongering calumny. The Chinese Communist Party is firmly opposed to a 'head-on clash' between the Soviet Union and the United States, and not in words only. In deeds too it has worked hard to avert direct armed conflict between them. Examples of this are in the Korean war against United States aggression, in which we fought side by side with our Korean comrades... We ourselves preferred to shoulder the heavy sacrifices necessary and stood in the first line of defence for the socialist camp in order that the Soviet Union might stay in the second line[12].

What, then, explains the periodic withdrawals of the Communist delegations from the armistice negotiations if Russia and China wanted them to succeed? Frustration lay at the heart of the prolonged recessions or withdrawals by the United Nations representatives. On the other side the reasons were more complex.

As noted, they were probably surprised in the initial encounter at the rejection of the 38th Parallel as the line of demarcation; and perhaps also by the refusal to include the withdrawal of foreign forces in the agenda. Determination to get the best bargain available was an abiding factor. Whenever the United Nations team showed eagerness to attain a result, the other side exploited it. Suspicion also persisted; they were never wholly convinced, even to the last day, that the United States was ready to give up military force to gain its ends.

As a practical matter, the Communist delegates had even less authority to decide matters of policy than those of the United Nations. In reference back, their communications system was rudimentary. It took

Nam and his Chinese colleagues much longer to submit and receive the answer to policy points than the Americans, who had a secure direct link from Munsan-ni to Tokyo and Washington.

The human factor also militated in the truce tent and among the authorities which controlled its decisions. Like most ideologues, Communists cannot resist an opportunity for propaganda. But this may suggest the rigging of events for such purposes, and rigging there certainly was from time to time. The organisation included, however, scores of people who were given to righteous indignation. Their outbursts of protest, the vehemence of their anger, were often contrived but sometimes genuine. Their own inclinations and the tenets of Marxism/Leninism/Maoism combined to persuade them to extend their hatred of capitalism and the United States as its chief exponent to its representatives among the directors, staff, and members of the United Nations delegation. Equally, some of the latter, resentful of the evasions, trickery and abuse used by the Communist side, came to dislike many of its constituent members personally. They also developed bargaining skills.

Thus the UN team withdrew from the negotiations as a matter of both tactics and principle when a Chinese company carrying weapons marched past Naebongjang during the lunch interval on 4th August. They returned two days later on instructions from Washington and against General Ridgway's inclination.

Similarly, the Communist side withdrew on 22nd August on the basis of United Nations local security breaches which were contrived somewhat crudely by themselves, continuing their absence throughout September and much of October. In the latter period there were breaches by American aircraft which inadvertently killed and wounded several Chinese and local Koreans, errors freely admitted with regrets by the United States authorities. This long break was the more unfortunate because agreement had been reached to transfer, at General Ridgway's insistence, the meeting site from Kaesong, behind Communist lines, to Panmunjom, an intermediate point which *inter alia* was easier to identify from the air.

It was 25th October before negotiations were resumed. Seven weeks had passed since the teams had gathered at the table. The fighting front had been active during that time.

SOURCE NOTES: Chapter 13

1 Paik Sun-yup, General, *From Pusan to Panmunjom*, (New York and London, 1992), p 167.
2 It was first raised during the periodic briefing of diplomatic missions on the war, see FRUS *cit*, pp 533 and627, and in informal bilateral discussions immediately thereafter. Also FK 1551/21 (FO 371 92843).
3 See FK 1551/2, and series FK 1551/1, /5, /6, /7, 12/, 13/,/14, /16, /22, /24, /25 (FO 371 92843).
4 The full record of the meetings is contained in the 'Transcript of Proceedings, Meetings, Armistice Proposals'(G-3 091 Korea 348 series, USNARS, Suitland). For a description of accompanying events, see also Hermes, Walter G, *Truce Tent and Fighting Front*, (volume in the series, The United States Army in the Korean War), (Washington, 1966);Joy, Rear-Admiral C Turner,*How Communists Negotiate*, (New York, 1955), and Poates, Rutherford M, *Decision in Korea*, (New York, 1954).
5 Acheson, *op cit*, pp 124–125.
6 See CinCUNC HNC-115 of 19 Jul 51 to JCS, JCS 96802 of 19 Jul 51 to CinCUNC, CinCFE CX-67390 of 20 Jul 51 to JCS, JCS 96930 of 21 Jul 51 to CinCFE. These are contained in USNARS, Suitland, and may be seen to advantage with associated State/Defense Departments papers in FRUS *cit* pp 702–718. Note, signals to CinCUNC and CinCFE refer to General Ridgway commonly.
7 CinCFE CX-67670 of 25 Jul 51 to JCS, (USNARS, Suitland), also in FRUS *cit* pp 724–729.
8 JCS 97223 of 25 Jul 51 to CinCFE, (USNARS, Suitland), also FRUS, *cit*, p 730.
9 Conversation, author with Lord Franks.
10 FO 3377 to Washington of 11th July 1951 FK 1071/660 (FO 371 92788). See also in FRUS *cit* pp 675–678.
11 FRUS, 1955, *cit*, pp 698–701.
12 Mao Tse-tung, *Two different lines on the question of war and peace*, (article in The Peking Review, No 47, 1963).

CHAPTER 14

Adjustments to strategy

The news that the armistice negotiations had actually begun was received by the units of the United Nations Command in a variety of forms. Many ships' companies at sea and units ashore were first informed by radios tuned to the local forces' radio or the BBC World Service, but official statements followed in a matter of hours, percolating down through higher headquarters.

The event was something of an anti-climax. All ranks had been kept advised of the proposals between the respective Commanders-in-Chief and it did not occur to the majority of the officers and men in the United Nations Command that these might not come to fruition; it seemed a logical outcome to the weeks of successful operations. A few of the senior commanders would have withheld all details of the inceptory stages, even an inkling, to avoid the hopes of their subordinates being raised before the two sides actually met—there were apprehensions that the Communist side might be engaging solely in a short term propaganda exercise. But a free press was at work across the world. The subject of peace talks in Korea was prominent in newspaper and radio headlines. It was wisely decided in the Command Headquarters to maintain a flow of information coupled with the warning that talks would only succeed if the United Nations forces maintained offensive action. This was sound advice, but it was conveyed so extravagantly as to weary the recipients.

Admiral Scott-Moncrieff* reported to the Commander-in-Chief, Far East Station† on 15th July,

> From the inception of the direct approach by the Supreme Commander [CINCUNC] to the North Korean and Chinese Commanders, exhortations not to let up or in any way relax our vigilance have been issued with almost daily regularity from each level of the chain of command. Some examples...
>
> 'Let's hope for peace but let's make then quit' – '... At all times keep up our guard and never allow ourselves to be lulled into a false sense of security by possible glowing reports and desires for peace. We must continue on the

---

* Scott-Moncrieff, Rear-Admiral A K (later, Admiral Sir Alan) DSO (later, KCB, CBE) RN (1900–1980) replaced Vice-Admiral Sir William Andrewes as Flag Officer Second-in-Command, Far East Station and Commander Task Group 95.1 on 10th April 1951.

† Vice-Admiral (later, Admiral) the Hon. Sir Guy Herbrand Russell, KCB CBE DSO RN (1898–1977) replaced Admiral Sir Patrick Brind as Commander-in-Chief, Far East Station, on 7th February 1951.

attack until the bell actually rings. More important we must be alert to counter any conceivable act of treachery'.

The establishment of a safety corridor for the approach for the negotiators from the north, and the subsequent changes in the Free Area, also produced a maze of somewhat confusing instructions and situations...

It is interesting to note that not only is the Navy the most strongly represented Service among the delegates, but that the whole organisation of the peace camp, press relations, and communications is being run by the Navy. Almost all heads of Departments at COMNAVFE [Commander, Naval Forces, Far East], moreover, are now in Korea, which makes it virtually impossible to get anything from Tokyo.

[Our] delegates and the staff, live in a tented camp at Munsan-ni, at the southern end of the 'Kaesong Corridor'. The camp is well concealed and guarded, not so much from fear of enemy action as against the illegal infiltration of the Press correspondents. General Ridgway lives in a camp close by and pays frequent visits to the delegation. From the start, the Press took to itself the conduct of these Peace talks, and attempted to tell the Supreme Commander and the delegates what they should or should not do. Much speculation went on about the selected site, accommodation, access of reporters to the delegation and so on. A special ex-hospital train, being converted for the accommodation of [our] delegation, created a great stir. Every facility was laid on for the press. USS *Eldorado*, flagship of Commander, Task Force 90 (Vice-Admiral [I.N.] Kiland), with the APA [Assault Transport] USS *George Clymer* (the most 'luxoorious' transport in the United States Navy) were despatched with great secrecy—to Inch'on—so secretly that I have not been told officially, although it is in my parish and at one time I was ordered to have two destroyers immediately available at Pusan for a 'special escorting mission' to Inch'on, together with two destroyers and and a force of minesweepers. This turns out to have been laid on entirely for the press—*Clymer* for accommodation and *Eldorado* to handle communications. However, when the correspondents heard that they were to be at Inch'on, while the talks were at Kaesong, they created such an uproar with the Supreme Commander [*sic*] that Admiral Joy and the other delegates agreed to vacate the special train and move into the tented camp with the staffs, and the train, sited a good distance from the camp, now houses the correspondents[1].

This view of the opening rounds at Kaesong owed something to the nature of life at sea. Whatever was going on ashore, the warships had to cope round the clock with moving and navigating in all weathers, watchful and ready for natural hazards on a coast of perpetually shifting sand and mud banks, and man made hazards such as mines, air strikes, and coastal batteries. In that sense neither the admiral nor his officers and men needed much prompting to stay alert.

In the battle line across the peninsula, it was a different matter. While the United Nations Command would not be defeated at sea or in the air, given their resources, the weight of the Chinese People's

22. Major-General A J H Cassels, Commander, 1st British Commonwealth Division, with Brigadier T Brodie, Commander, 29th Infantry Brigade, August 1951. (Imperial War Museum)

23. Centurion tank of the 8th Hussars moving across captured enemy positions to support the advance of 3 RAR during Operation Commando, October 1951. (Imperial War Museum)

24. Crawl trench on Point 210 captured by 1 KSLI during Operation Commando, October 1951. (This picture, showing the view to the west, was taken in December). (Major P Duckworth)

25. 25-pounder detachment, having just crossed to the north side of the Imjin river, supporting Operation Commando, October 1951. (Imperial War Museum)

26. Kowang-san, Point 355. (King's Own Scottish Borderers)

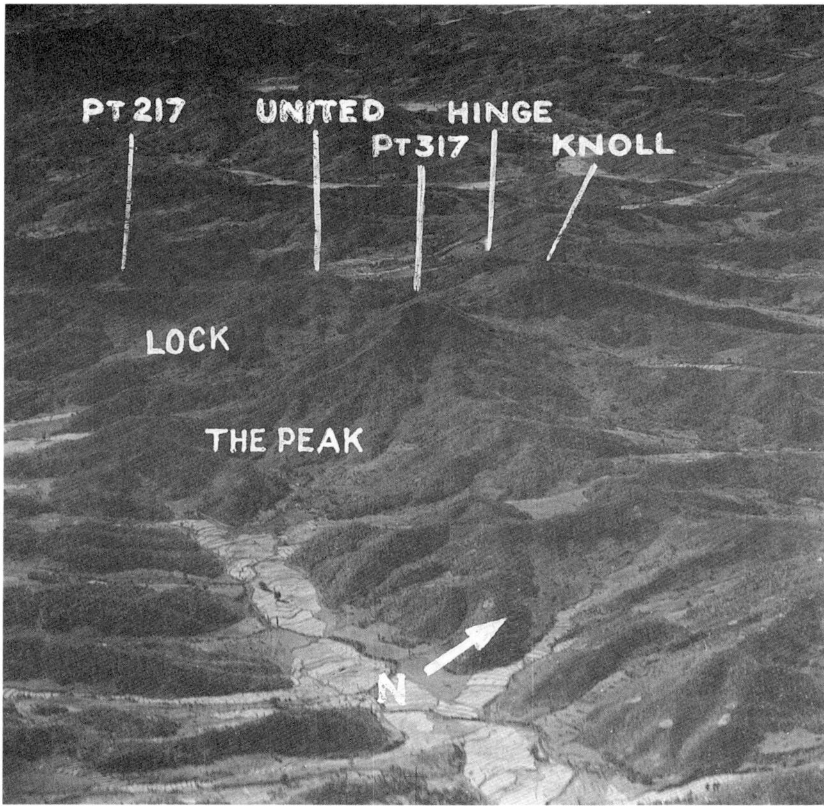

27. Maryang-san, Point 317. (King's Own Scottish Borderers)

28. The permanent bridge built by 28th Field Engineer Regiment at 'Teal', formerly 'Gloster Crossing'. The pontoon bridge is seen in use. The water level is at its lowest point. (5th Royal Inniskilling Dragoon Guards)

29. The Imjin in spate. (Major-General P Downward)

30. Teal bridge roadway is threatened by floods and remnants from Pintail, summer 1951.
(Royal School of Military Engineering)

31. The bridge at 'Pintail'. (Major-General A E Younger)

32. Bayton-Evans bridge. (Major-General A E Younger)

33. Combat Engineer of 28th Field Engineer Regiment clearing mines following Operation Commando. (Imperial War Museum)

Volunteers might yet, as an outside chance, throw the Eighth Army back to the Han River and the lower course of the Soyang. P'eng's Sixth Phase Offensive was half expected at the end of June[2]. Advice from Washington on the 24th that armistice negotiations might soon be opened—though how and where remained undetermined on that date—obliged General Ridgway to consider how such an event would effect his conduct of operations.

The possibility that they were about to be trumped, politically or militarily, by a Communist ruse diminished as meetings eventuated, and progressed at Kaesong. Welcome as it was, General Ridgway foresaw immediately a number of difficulties if the negotiations should be protracted. A long period of inactivity for the Eighth Army would raise problems of morale, particularly, he guessed, among his American forces. There would soon be newspaper campaigns to 'Bring the boys home'. These apprehensions occasioned the early reminders to all senior commanders in the United Nations Command, that they would assist the process of armistice negotiations by maintaining operational ascendancy[3]. The somewhat excessive response reflected their own recognition of the problem.

Reports from the Eighth Army units early in July, confirmed by a personal tour later in the month, reassured the Commander-in-Chief that the men in the field and on the Korean air bases had no false expectations of an early cease fire. Negotiations were welcomed by soldiers and airmen—no less, by those at sea—but in that period they were remote from their ambience if not from their locality. Coping with the enemy and the other pressures of operational life occupied the greater part of their daily life, particularly of the men whose morale was most at risk, those in or close to combat.

Interwoven with General Ridgway's anxieties was another. He recalled later that '...it seemed to me, with a cease fire faintly visible on the horizon, that I should do all I could to keep our losses at a justifiable minimum[4]. Accepting that he could continue to exercise varying degrees of pressure by maritime and air operations, the first requirement on land was to establish the conditions for a robust defence of the Eighth Army line. To this end,

> I immediately sent Lieutenant-Colonel A.D. Surles, Jr., of my staff to confer with Van Fleet, taking with him a map prepared by our planners that showed our present front-line positions: the Kansas line; a theoretical outpost line for Kansas; and a theoretical cease-fire line that would support the Kansas positions. I asked that Van Fleet tell me if he felt it practicable and desirable for the Eighth Army to seize the high ground between his front line positions and the theoretical cease fire line.

> In the light of later statements by Van Fleet to the effect that I had prevented him from driving on to total victory, it is interesting to recall his reply to this query. His views then were that he did not favour an advance by the Eighth Army to seize the ground at this time. An advance on the eastern front, he felt, would be costly in American lives and would gain real estate only. And, while an advance on the western portion of the front would be relatively easy, Van Fleet's view was that it could expose him unduly to offensive action by the enemy. He concluded that the cost in lives and the resulting vulnerability of the Eighth Army was too much to wager on the chance that there might be a cease fire. He also urged that the negotiations on the cease-fire, should any ensue, should take into account that portion of Korea west of the Yesong River and south of the 38th Parallel, which we had no desire to occupy, yet which might be traded at the bargaining table to gain the ground we desired in the eastern zone. ... I concurred in all these views and we decided to hold tight to see what the negotiations might bring[5].

Throughout June, the Eighth Army had been engaged in developing Kansas, the main defence line, and Wyoming, which bulged northwards from the Imjin river battle area to Ch'orwon and Kumwha, returning to Kansas on the Hwach'on reservor. Actually, the line of occupation generally exceeded these lines; UN reconnaissance forces were close to Kaesong in the west, and well to the north of Kansong in the east. This permitted the consolidation of outpost lines and, in some areas, of so-called 'patrol bases' two or three thousand yards ahead of them, though this was somewhat of a misonomer. From these advanced positions to the rear of the main lines, trenches were deepened and revetted, covered with timbers and earth, and masked by barbed wire and mines. Mortar and gun positions were protected in pits or by sandbagged walls. Three divisions of the Korean National Guard—internal security forces—were sent forward to assist in this work. Villages in the foremost areas were evacuated.

Among the forward defended localities and to the rear, the engineers built or improved roads and bridges. The railway capacity was increased. Reserve stocks were built up to 45 days of 'normal' consumption—the rate below the intensive demands of a major offensive or defensive action. Work on the expansion of air bases was pursued*.

The July rains severely tested this work. Bridges were swept away on the Imjin, for example, as the water level rose almost 20 feet overnight. Trenches were flooded. Some overhead cover and sandbag walls were washed away. Air photographs revealed that sections of the enemy defence works had been similarly damaged.

---

* In May, General Partridge had pressed for additional engineer aviation (airfield construction) units. Increments to those in the theatre were arriving in early July.

Those who had built best suffered least, and were able to remain reasonably dry underground. The Americans freely admitted that they were reluctant diggers of defences and a number of their infantry battalions now paid the penalty for work skimped. But in some cases, tactical requirements had disposed men on mountain sides on which, for days, stalwart GIs* clung to makeshift shelters on ledges.

When the first rainstorms passed, reconstruction began. In the United Nations line, Kansas had priority in resources, followed by Wyoming. Bridging was a more complex matter. Losses had not been due to poor workmanship but to the weight of water and debris which had exceeded the strength of the equipment available. The field engineers, American and British, had to consider ways and means of screening and reinforcing the anchorage of their pontoons in the battle zone and replacing them with more permanent structures†.

These activities, occupying the greater part of the Eighth Army, suited General Ridgway, holding 'tight to see what the negotiations might bring'. But he did not abandon all ideas of offensive action. General Van Fleet was still under remit to propose strategic operations within the capability of his forces as they stood. The Far East Air Force was engaged in extensive interdiction—Operation Strangle—of the enemy road network from the railheads, roughly from the line of the 39th Parallel to the battle zone. On 13th July, General Weyland, the air commander‡, was ordered to raise the level of air operations as a whole.

He was very ready to do so. Writing to General Vandenberg on 10th June General Weyland remarked that,

> Of the many opinions formulated during the course of current hostilities, few have had less foundation than that which envisages the current United Nations military position in Korea as being in the nature of a stalemate. To accept the theory...is to completely ignore the innumerable advantages of air power as a predominant weapon for destroying the enemy fighting machine and to acquiesce to the dangerous 'rule of thumb' whereby military success, regardless of cost, is measured solely in terms of geographical gain...[6]

General Weyland shared the view of many of his colleagues—inspired by events of the Second World War—that too much emphasis

---

* GI (from Government Issue), an enlisted member of the United States armed forces, principally Army, OED.

† There was particularly close cooperation between the American and British field engineers in the US I Corps, to the point that the former named their upper Imjin bridge after Captain B Bayton-Evans, Royal Engineers, killed on the river.

‡ General Stratemeyer had a severe heart attack on 20th May. Lieutenant-General Otto P Weyland, USAF (1902–84) succeeded him in late June as Commander. Far East Air Force. Lieutenant-General Partridge relinquished command of Fifth Air Force in June and was succeeded by Major-General Frank F Everest.

continued to be placed in modern warfare on the predominant ability of the ground forces to defeat the enemy. Korea was a theatre in which this concept persisted, he believed, and the time had come to prove that it was erroneous. Let the ground forces stand in their positions; the Far East Air Force would bring hostilities to an end by crushing the enemy's capability and will to fight.

An early measure was to extend Operation Strangle to the southern end of the North Korean railway system. Special interest was shown in P'yongyang as a target. Kim Il-sung's capital had been bombed many times during the first year of the war. It remained the seat of his government, contained an important railway junction and bridge across the Taedong, and enjoyed a high level of anti-aircraft protection. In this respect it was and remained a legitimate military target. But the aim in the third week of July was political as well as military: to remind the North Koreans that the United Nations could attack their centre of government at will and thus hasten armistice negotiations.

Though the notion that bombing P'yongyang would influence Stalin or Mao was misplaced, it was properly within the Commander-in-Chief's responsibilities. But General Ridgway had a good instinct for political sensitivities. He informed Washington of the intention to raid P'yongyang and adopted an idea earlier discarded by both British and American Chiefs, warning of raids by the dropping of leaflets*. General Bradley and his colleagues were against both the raid and the warning: 'to single out P'yongyang as the target for an all out strike during the time we are holding conferences might in the eyes of the world appear as an attempt to break off negotiations'[7].

The attitude demonstrates that the Joint Chiefs of Staff were as sensitive at their own level to outside opinion at this stage of events in the peace talks as their Commander-in-Chief in the Far East. But it was not only international opinion which refined their perception, or the views of the United States Government. Because the negotiations were being conducted by a military delegation, the Chiefs were personally determined to secure an armistice subject to certain conditions, and accepted that the run of negotiations would constrain operational enterprise.

This attitude was discovered by the British Embassy in Washington by chance a week or so before General Ridgway notified his intention to raid P'yongyang.

Picking up indications of heightened air activity from Air Vice-Marshal Bouchier's reports, the Foreign Office had expressed anxiety to Sir Oliver Franks on 11th July,

---

* See Volume I, pp 100–101, and p 121.

> ...from the political point of view it is important to ensure that during negotiations bombing is confined to targets which are military in the strictest definition. Please consult with the Joint Staff Mission and if you think appropriate put this point to the United States authorities in whatever way you think best[8].

During the following ten days Air Chief Marshal Elliot* made discreet enquiries among the Joint Chiefs of Staff including General Vandenberg, Chief of the Air Force Staff, and discovered their common resolve to encourage to the utmost the negotiations at Kaesong. In the course of these enquiries, further information from Air Vice-Marshal Bouchier indicated that air operations continued on the basis of battlefield as distinct from political requirements. There might come a time to advise greater restraint, Air Chief-Marshal Elliot guessed, but it had not yet arrived. Intervention in the current climate would simply reduce their credibility. Having just dealt with the exchange of views between Mr Morrison and Mr Acheson†, which nourished the open relations between the two governments, Sir Oliver Franks was in full agreement. He despatched the following polite rebuff on the 20th,

> Both Air Chief-Marshal Elliot and I felt that in view of...CAB 327 [Air Vice-Marshal Bouchier's most recent signal], it would be inappropriate for us to suggest this to the Americans unless some occasion were to arise when the point could be interjected without possibility of embarrassment. No such occasion has arisen[9].

They continued to hold this view when, after further representations by General Ridgway, the Joint Chiefs withdrew their objections to a large scale raid on P'yongyang providing that it was not singled out in press statements as an objective for massed attack[10]. Herein lay a nice point in public relations.

The rain clouds prevented the raid until 30th July, and even on that day conditions precluded the employment of bombers. Some 450 sorties were flown by fighters and fighter bombers against P'yongyang with indeterminate military results, and without apparent detriment to the peace negotiations. A second operation was launched on 14th August in clear weather. Sixty six B-29 medium bombers struck the target despite intense anti-aircraft fire‡. There was later debate in Washington that the raid might have occasioned the Communist withdrawal from negotiations on 22nd August[11], but this was simply speculation.

---

* Air Chief Marshal Elliot had succeeded Marshal of the Royal Air Force Lord Tedder as Head of the BJSM.

† Pp 190–191, above.

‡ Six of the escorting fighters were destroyed.

It did not persuade the Joint Chiefs to withhold permission for attacks on Rashin, in the extreme north east of Korea, an area hitherto forbidden to United Nations air operations because of its proximity to the Soviet border. There were manifest military targets in and around the port, which B-29s attacked without loss on 25th August under naval fighter escort. Yet this extension of the target area did not impress the senior officers of the Far East Air Force who believed that theatre air power was being constrained at the very time it should have been unleashed. Why had they sent out all those injunctions at the outset of the armistice talks, they asked one another, to keep fighing to make the enemy quit?

General Van Fleet also believed that he was unduly constrained, though his reasons for this outlook probably owed as much to emotion as to deliberate judgement. In July and over following months he submitted, in accordance with the Commander-in-Chief's instructions, a series of strategic plans, principally to carry the Eighth Army forward in the centre and eastern half of its frontage. Several of these involved amphibious landings on the east coast and all were withdrawn by the army commander, shortly after he submitted them, as being beyond his means.

Between these grander ideas, he applied his mind to operations that lay within his own authority. Halted on the edge of the enemy's principal defences, his line lay in some areas at a considerable disadvantage to that of his foe, the inevitable result of the arbitrary checks of battle. While debate continued in the armistice negotiations concerning the actual run of the respective defensive positions, he was anxious to discover the extent to which he was threatened or inhibited by enemy positions; and which of the enemy foremost localities were outposts, which their principal line.

These considerations coincided with his misgivings concerning the battleworthiness of his soldiers after weeks of relative inactivity. 'A sitdown army is subject to collapse at the first sight of an enemy effort, ... I couldn't allow my forces to become soft and dormant', he remarked in September 1951 of his reflections in July[12]. Such a statement is apt to excite the camps of pacifism and anarchy to a frenzy of contempt, but both the principle and the duty so expressed were valid. Evidence that the Communists intended to mount a summer offensive persisted—not surprisingly, P'eng was just then under orders to do so. There were also signs that the combat effectiveness of the Eighth Army was declining. Too much ammunition was being fired at shadows across the United Nations front. Among American formations, vigilance in observation posts was declining, patrols lacked enterprise. General Van Fleet would not have served his command by encouraging a drift to passivity among his fighting units.

He therefore set in hand numerous operations along Lines Kansas and Wyoming to seize the initiative and enhance local intelligence gathering. Two larger ventures were mounted, both of which had important consequences.

The first of these was in the X Corps area, now under command of General Almond's successor, Major-General Clovis E Byers*. On his eastern flank, among the Taebaek Mountains, the line ran along the southern edge of the Punchbowl, the bowl itself being the interior of a long extinct volcano enclosed within a characteristically sharp volcano rim. North Korean forces held the western, northern, and eastern segments of the rim, and three mountains to the west, the highest of which was Taeu-san, Hill 1179†.

These dispositions permitted the North Koreans to observe and shell at will the X Corps' forward supply routes, and offered a means of dividing X and I ROK Corps at the outset of an enemy offensive. General Van Fleet gave orders to drive the enemy off the high points concerned, and to capture ground which would enable him to shorten the line in the sector.

Taeu-san was captured in late July by the United States 2nd Infantry Division. All operations were then suspended by rainstorms, which continued intermittently into August. The ROK I Corps was then launched on to the south eastern rim of the Punchbowl but repeatedly failed. Its commander, Major-General Paik Sun-yup, was brought back from the armistice commission to direct operations and he at once pointed out that his soldiers lacked proper fire support; he had no guns above 105mm, and few of those. General Van Fleet provided a single 155-mm battery in direct support, and arranged naval air support. The corps took its objective at once[13].

Meantime, two ROK divisions and the United States 2nd became involved from 18th August in a dreadful struggle for the mountain heights west of Taeu-san; the ROKs first because General Van Fleet believed that it would develop their leadership. The North Korean positions were formidable, tactically well sited, deeply entrenched and strongly covered. The ROKs won their objectives a dozen times, but were too weak in numbers to hold them. After nine days, they broke back, carrying the supporting regiment of the 2nd Division with them.

The 2nd was drawn in, but then, and in following days, the tactical direction for the capture of what became known as 'Bloody Ridge', was

---

* From April 1951, General Ridgway had revised the rotation system for those serving in Korea. General and some other senior officers served for one year in Korea. Otherwise, officers and men in divisions were replaced after six months, those not in combat units one year. As noted, British Commonwealth forces served one year commonly in Korea.

† Heights are in metres.

flawed. Successive divisional commanders* applied their forces crudely and obstinately. Despite the lessons learned a year before on the Naktong, replacements for casualties were sent directly from the trucks which had brought them to companies in or entering the *mêlée*. They knew no one, could scarcely tell friend from foe. Some were young officers sent to lead a platoon they joined in darkness, among whom they fell as a stranger in the first clash of the following day.

The corps commander took a hand, extending the frontage of the offensive to include the Marine Division. With some luck, a late improvement in methodology, and more hard fighting, Bloody Ridge and a further segment of the Punchbowl was taken by 5th September.

Considerable casualties among the North Koreans, and their withdrawal locally, unfortunately encouraged General Van Fleet to order the capture of the next ridge to the north. Its heights posed no disadvantage of substance to the United Nations sector but they were fought for fiercely by the North Koreans into mid-October. What newspaper correspondents later called 'Heartbreak Ridge' was then taken by the United States 2nd Division and the French Battalion. The 2nd had lost its reputation at Kunu-ri in 1950†, and had striven since to regain it. Between 27th August and 15th October 1951 it lost 6,500 officers and men, to which the ROK and French losses must be added, and while casualties do not always betoken valour they did in this case. In the west and centre, General Van Fleet contemplated an advance to free the Ch'orwon—Kumhwa railway from aimed as distinct from random artillery fire, Operation Cudgel. In capturing this part of the Iron Triangle, the railway had been a prize for the United Nations Command, but through the summer it was too close to enemy positions to provide an assured line of supply. It was also under enemy observation at several points.

However, Cudgel was linked with another, more extensive enterprise, Wrangler—one of the several schemes involving an amphibious landing on the east coast. Daunted by the losses in X Corps, General Van Fleet withdrew it from the Commander-in-Chief's headquarters. In these circumstances, the United States I Corps commander, Major-General John W O'Daniel‡, proposed Operation Commando at the end of September.

At this stage, General O'Daniel was responsible for almost half the United Nations front, from the Kimpo Peninsula and mouth of the Imjin to Kumhwa. Two of the enemy's major approach routes thus ran into

---

* General Ruffner opened this operation but returned to the United States on 1st September. His deputy continued operations until Major-General Robert N Young arrived on 20th September.

† See Volume I, pp 332–334.

‡ Major-General (later, Lieutenant-General) John Wilson O'Daniel (1894–1975) succeeded Lieutenant-General Frank W Milburn in July 1951.

his lines. He had carried through a number of minor operations since July, some conceived by his very experienced and successful predecessor, others by his divisional commanders. The aim had been to increase security and to dominate the line of contact. But he was keen to do more. The injunctions of the Commander-in-Chief and Army Commander to maintain pressure on the enemy during the peace talks had fired him to enjoin an aggressive spirit upon all ranks, which was no more than was required of him. But his instructions bordered on the obsessive—'The signal for combat will be "sharpen your bayonets". This phrase will be used at every available opportunity[14].'

He had been advised of Cudgel and its linkage with Wrangler; securing the Ch'orwon—Kumhwa railway would ease his transportation burden. When Wrangler and thus Cudgel were cancelled, he proposed a modified form of the latter, which he titled Commando. It envisaged an advance of about six miles across the greater part of the corps front with five divisions. One of these was the newly formed 1st Commonwealth Division.

SOURCE NOTES: Chapter 14

1 FO 2FE/2960/11 of 15 Jul 51 in ADM 116/6228.

2 See Eighth Army G3 SS Report, June 1951 (USNARS, Suitland). Also Ch'i Te-hsueh, *op cit.*

3 The first of these was despatched to all commanders in the Commander-in-Chief's signal 65667 on 24th June 1951 (CINCUNC file, June, 1951, USNARS, Suitland). He continued to urge alertness during visits made over the following two weeks.

4 Ridgway, *op cit,* pp 182–183.

5 Ridgway, *op cit,* pp 181–182. See also statement of General Van Fleet in *Hearings Before the Committee of Armed Services: Ammunition Supplies in the Far East,* 83d Congress, 1st sess, 5th March 1953, pp 31–32.

6 Quoted Futrell, Robert Frank, *United States Air Force in Korea*, (1951), p 400.

7 Signal JCS 96938 of 21 Jul 51 to CINCFE, (USNARS, Suitland).

8 FO to Washington of 11th July 1951, FK 1015/191, (FO 371 92742).

9 FK 1015/191, (FO 371 92742).

10 CINCFE C-67474 of 21st July to JCS, JCS 96938 of 21st July to CINCFE, CINCFE C-675200 of 23rd July to JCS, and DA-IN 18440 of 25th July to JCS, JCS 97223 of 25th July 1951 to CINCFE, (USNARS, Suitland).

11 Conversation, author with Lord Franks.

12 Quoted, Hermes, *op cit,* p 81, fn 23.

13 There is a discrepancy between the description of this battle in Hermes, *op cit,* pp 83–84, and Paik, *op cit,* pp 176–177. The US X and ROK I Corps records support General Paik.

14 I Corps Letter of Instruction of 22nd July 1951 (USNARS, Suitland).

CHAPTER 15

1st Commonwealth Division is joined in battle.

Almost a year after the first proposal to expand the Commonwealth land force to divisional strength, Major-General A J H Cassels brought it into active operations on 28th July 1951[1].

From May onwards, he had been engaged in visiting the various commanders and headquarters in Japan and Korea with whom he would in one way or another be connected—including General Ridgway, Lieutenant-General Sir Horace Robertson, Lieutenant-General Van Fleet, Major-General Frank F Everest commanding the Fifth Air Force, and Lieutenant-General Milburn, commander, I Corps. All were anxious to hasten the formation of the division but he was able to explain that time on passage of the vehicle and stores ships alone precluded concentration of the additional men and equipment involved before mid-July. It was thus accepted that the target date for operational readiness should be 1st August.

General Cassels travelled on to tour all the British and Commonwealth formations in the forward areas. During June, the divisional staff gathered in Japan, where they lodged by General Robertson's invitation at his Headquarters, British Commonwealth Forces Korea (BCFK), at Kure, acquainting themselves with the base organisation from which their administrative support would flow and the personalities running it. In late June, the *HT Empire Orwell* delivered the British element of divisional headquarters and troops to Pusan. There they were joined by the Australian, Canadian, and New Zealand components of the staff*. The opening entry in the divisional war diary observed the difficulties of the Assistant Director of Medical Service—the chief medical officer—Colonel G Anderton, OBE, in eating the two lightly boiled eggs he had ordered for breakfast. Among the domestic stores missing—items had been looted during the loading of the stores ships in England—were teaspoons. Watched keenly by his brother officers and the mess staff, the colonel had to dispose of his eggs with a dessert spoon, which led to a series of mishaps. Several of the onlookers made

---

* Senior members, such as Lieutenant-Colonel E D Danby, Canadian Army, principal staff officer as General Staff Officer Grade 1 (GSO1), had joined in Kure. An Indian liaison officer and two South African Army officers joined at a later date.

the unkind observation that they were not going to submit to Colonel Anderton's surgery on the battlefield.

Later, as the headquarters exercised on the journey north to the line, the vehicle first aid kits were also found to have been looted. Punctures were mended with patches and adhesives borrowed on the road.

These minor vexations apart, staff procedures were practised, communications established and traffic passed among the various wireless stations, mobile and static, by day and night. Presently, the headquarters divided into its two operational components, Main—containing the central operating facilities—and Rear, from which administrative control was exercised. A small Tactical Headquarters, drawing on the resources of Main—was also put through its paces to permit General Cassels to control an operation from a distant vantage point for limited periods*.

While these activities continued under the direction of Lieutenant-Colonel Danby, the GSO1, General Cassels completed his arrangements for integration within the United States I Corps, and initial visits to units. In the latter respect, as he told the officers and soldiers he was shortly to command,

> ... I am fully aware that the great majority of the units in the division are now 'old stagers' in Korea and have earned themselves very high reputations. The deeds of the 25th Canadian Infantry Brigade, the 28th British Commonwealth Brigade and the 29th British Independent Brigade and their supporting arms and services will be remembered with admiration and respect wherever the Korean Campaign is discussed. It is now incumbent on us all to see that the reputation and deeds of the 1st Commonwealth Division earn the same high acclaim.
>
> I would ask you to remember that it is only by working as a team that this can be achieved. The old saying 'All for one and one for all' must be our motto...[2]

He was well aware that his first task was to draw together a force that was largely the sum of its former parts: the infantry would remain within the three brigades; divisional troops were to be formed principally by drawing in the armour† and the supporting arms—artillery, engineers, and signals‡—and services—supply and transport, medical, ordnance,

---

* This is not to be confused with the Commander's Rover Group—essentially General Cassels' jeep accompanied by a second containing his radios, and perhaps a third with a defence section—while he was 'roving' within the divisional area or visiting, for example, corps HQ. Frequent but erroneous reference is made in the war diaries of the period to brigade and battalion commanders' Tac HQs. These were actually rover groups; a tactical headquarters requires a range of resources beyond the capability of a battalion. A permanent tactical headquarters, from which the commander directs battles day by day is rarely required below corps, more frequently army, headquarters.

† The 8th Hussars and the Canadian C Squadron, Lord Strathcona's Horse, equipped with Sherman tanks.

‡ The greater part of each brigade's Royal Signals remained necessarily in place, though administered and supplied with technical equipment by a single squadron within the Divisional Signal Regiment.

electrical and mechanical engineers, provost, postal, pay, and education. Additional manpower provided for divisional headquarters and those units for which there had been no provision among the 'group' elements of the brigades. These included two British light fixed wing aircraft flights*, one for artillery observation, another for reconnaissance and liaison. But almost immediately there was an important loss; the Belgian battalion was removed, a consequence of developments not in Korea but in NATO†.

Yet the division was greater than the sum of its parts‡. As expected, brigades were shielded by the intromission of a major-general and his headquarters from the American practice of issuing impetuous, contradictory or fruitless orders to subordinates¶. It must be said that the Glosters would probably not have been lost if the April battle on the Imjin had been conducted under the Commonwealth Division headquarters.

However, this was by no means the only benefit from the reorganisation. The divisional field artillery, now numbering seventy two 25-pounder guns, continued for the most part to operate by batteries affiliated to infantry battalions, with the battery commanders forward according priority to fire as required of the infantry commanding officers. The artillery regimental commanding officers continued to coordinate fire at brigade level. But when divisional priorities required it, the guns could be switched rapidly to fire *en masse* on the instructions of the Commander, Royal Artillery, Brigadier W G H Pike§. The divisional fire control centre was run by the Brigade Major RA, Major P M Victory, MC. *Inter alia* it was his responsibility to ensure that the field regiments were located so as to be able to cover the entire divisional front and, within their more limited range, the 4.2-inch mortars of 170 Battery—raised initially to sixteen, subsequently twenty four, mortars by the formation of two additional batteries between September 1951 and February 1952**. The fire control centre was also able to switch the British

---

* General Cassels had asked for a detachment of helicopters but none were available either from the British or United States sources—see DEFE 4/45, COS (51) 119th Meeting. However, as the British Auster was too small for him to use with comfort, I Corps provided the larger L-19 Cessna as a personal aircraft.

† Within the NATO community, the Belgian forces were being re-equipped by the United States. It was decided that the battalion in Korea, which would be reinforced by those trained under the new arrangement, should serve with American formations.

‡ For the Divisional Order of Battle, see Appendix F.

¶ See pp 60–61.

§ Pike, Brigadier William Gregory Hudleston (later, Lieutenant-General Sir William) KCB CBE DSO (1905–1993).

** The additional batteries were formed in part from the light anti-aircraft battery. Due to manpower shortages, all batteries were maintained at two mortar troops, each of four barrels. The whole, three batteries numbering a total of twenty four barrels, were incorporated into 61st Light Regiment, Royal Artillery, in February 1952.

artillery to assist American or ROK divisions on its flanks; and to call upon these divisions, the American corps, and army artillery, for support from their guns and howitzers as occasion required.

Of course, the arrangements had obtained earlier when 16 New Zealand or 45 Field Regiments had been operating within independent brigades, but the divisional organisation was quicker in responding to calls for massed fire from within its own resources, and more effective in obtaining fire from American sources, because it had more to offer on a reciprocal basis[3]. From 17th December 1951, the divisional counter battery staff was reinforced and a locating battery added to the divisional artillery assets.

The field engineers were also considerably reinforced. Where there had been in 1950 one independent minor unit—55 Field Squadron—which had also assumed a fighting role in crisis—there were now three field squadrons and a field park squadron*, drawn together into a major unit, 28th Field Engineer Regiment, under Lieutenant-Colonel P N M Moore, DSO MC. Moreover, while Major Younger, commanding the independent 55 Squadron had been obliged to spend considerable time in engineer planning with one or another American corps' chief engineer, Colonel Moore was able to apply himself entirely to the direction of his engineer force. Planning, negotiating for additional labour from the Korean Service Corps†, or common engineer stores often in short supply—for example, timbers, barbed wire and sandbags—was undertaken in the division by a Commander, Royal Engineers[4], Colonel E W C Myers, CBE DSO. With greater resources, the British had more to offer their American allies for cooperative ventures and thus the close relationship established by Major Younger was widened.

Similarly, greater resources extended into the administrative field. The days when 27 Brigade's infantry had been obliged to offload their stores to pool trucks for troop movement were gone forever. Lieutenant-Colonel Crosbie‡ had over 500¶ trucks at his disposal. The chief medical officer had three field ambulances, and behind these the Norwegian Mobile Army Surgical Hospital. Later, the Canadian Field Dressing Stations provided 200 beds in the forward area. Provost—military police—postal, and pay services derived benefits from their greater numbers. The

---

* A field park squadron maintains stocks of engineer stores and a pool of plant and other specialised equipment. Previously, this work had been undertaken by a small element of 55 Squadron, whose capabilities were inevitably limited. The squadron was augmented by a detachment of the New Zealand Base Engineers.

† The field engineers were also provided with a contingent of 500 men from the Seoul Fire Service for road repairs. This was changed every ten days.

‡ Promoted from command of the 29 Brigade transport unit, 57 Company, Royal Army Service Corps.

¶ This total included an increment of 120 trucks for the numbers of pick up points for supplies, occasioned by drawing on British Commonwealth and United States sources.

chaplains were the exception; they had greater numbers of troops to serve. Generally, the infantry, armoured and artillery units with whom they lived had the majority of their time. The divisional troops were ministered to vicariously.

The only two branches persistently under strain in what was essentially a static battle zone were those providing ordnance services—the RAOC—and the electrical and mechanical engineers—the REME. The former had to supply weapons, vehicles, equipment including spare parts, and clothing derived from many sources for a division using items of British, United States, Australian, and Indian origin. The latter recovered and repaired items of these divers origins, swollen by increments provided to meet the special circumstances such as weather and the remoteness of some localities in Korea. In theory, the RAOC and REME should have broken under the load of their work. They did not partly due to rationalisation of their functions*, but as much because their officers and men often worked for twelve and more hours a day throughout the year of their service in Korea, during which they engaged themselves at all levels in remarkable feats of improvisation.

General Cassels was well suited to his Commonwealth command. His preceding appointment had been in Canberra as Head of the United Kingdom Services Liaison Staff, and thus he had been closely connected with the trials and triumphs of launching a Commonwealth force into Korea. He had also made friends with senior officers of the Australian forces. A Canadian meeting him in Tokyo in May described him as,

> ...a lean and erect six-foot four soldier. He has a high forehead, an aquiline nose, cold grey eyes and thin lips. Altogether, he looks much like some of the Roman generals that were pictured in our high school Latin readers[5].

If this description suggests an aloof character, it is at fault. General Cassels was shortly to demonstrate to his soldiers, as to the political and military establishments in Japan, an open and engaging manner combined with an ability to speak his mind firmly on matters of principle without giving offence. He brought with him considerable experience: a Seaforth Highlander since 1926, he had commanded in battle at successive levels to division in the Second World War—latterly involving collaboration with the Canadians—and an airborne division in Palestine immediately thereafter. He was then aged 44.

Due to dilatory arrangements in the British Ministry of Defence in opening the essential process of circulating a draft among the Commonwealth participants, he did not have a directive when he took up his new command. It was finally issued, three months late, in October,

---

* For details, see WO 308/27, Appx D, pp 6–8.

1951*. The text was principally concerned to cover him if he received orders contrary to allied aims or which threatened unduly his force. For whilst he was required,

> ...to carry out loyally any orders issued by [the Commander-in-Chief, United Nations Command] or by any American commander subordinate to him under whose command you have been placed [paragraph 3]

there were two stipulations.

> 5. If an order given by [CINCUNC], or by any American Commander subordinate to him under whose command you have been placed appears, in your opinion, not to accord with the object of the United Nations operations in Korea as declared in paragraph 1 above you will be at liberty to appeal to the Commander-in-Chief British Commonwealth Occupation Force who, before the order is executed, will represent the case to [CINCUNC], and report to the Australian Chiefs of Staff Committee and to the Canadian Chiefs of Staff through the Canadian Military Mission in Tokyo...

and

> 6. If an order...appears in your opinion to imperil the safety of the Commonwealth troops under your command, to a degree exceptional in war, you will inform [CINCUNC through the chain of command], that you will carry out the order but that you intend to report the circumstances and your reasons for your opinion to the Commander-in-Chief British Commonwealth Occupation Force for representation...[6]

This directive was not drafted on the basis of a deep mistrust of General Ridgway and his subordinate army and corps commanders but simply followed the tradition—and substantially the previous phraseology—of British governments placing their forces under foreign command; a tradition followed closely by the Canadians[7]. Yet although the provisions of paragraphs 5 and 6, were never employed, difficulties with I Corps commander and his staff brought General Cassels close on a number of occasions to invoking paragraph 6.

As previously noted, the American system of tactical command and control during 1950–51 had caused 27 and 29 Brigades unnecessary difficulties. Last to arrive, the Canadian 25th Infantry Brigade Group's inceptory encounter with IX Corps headquarters had been dispiriting. An attempt had been made by the latter to commit the force to battle on 19th May before its operational weapons, radios, vehicles and equipment were delivered forward[8]. Precisely because this order was related to a battlefield crisis—P'eng's second thrust of the Fifth Phase Offensive was then flowing across the Soyang—a force armed only with rifles would have achieved very little, while considerably at hazard. The commander, Brigadier J M Rockingham, pursued successfully what one

---

* See Appendix G.

of his officers described as 'dragging his heels while digging in his toes' until the requirement passed.

A month later, the brigadier was placed under command of the United States 1st Cavalry Division and ordered to relieve 28 ROK and 65 United States Infantry Regiments on Line Wyoming. He recalled that

> ... I was ordered to move the brigade at approximately 2300 hours, 17th June, but was unable to get a route on which to move the twenty five odd miles. Nor could I get I Corps or either of the divisions concerned to give me an assembly area into which to put my troops when I arrived at the other end. What actually happened was that I started, accompanied by my commanding officers, to reconnoitre the route and assembly area, without leaving any instructions with the main body of the brigade as to its move. As we reached each bridge or crossroad and found it was suitable, I would transmit orders to the brigade major over the wireless, giving him the route which the brigade was to follow. I had ordered them to move about two hours behind us and our relative positions were maintained until we reached the portion of the line in the 3rd Division area where we were to take over. ...[9]

This predicament was not brought about because the United States command and control doctrine made no provision for the arrangement of routes and assembly areas in movements directed but because the divisional staff offficers were unwilling to remedy on their own initiative errors or omissions in orders or to represent the requirement to their superiors until a crisis had developed. It was all one with the tendency observed among American staff officers—and often tactical commanders—to sit in headquarters playing military chess on maps rather than getting out to learn at first hand the ideas, operating circumstances, and problems of subordinate formations and units. As the inception of his command approached, General Cassels acquired first hand experience of these weaknesses.

On his initial visit to I Corps, he had mentioned to General Milburn the need to bring the Canadian brigade, then at some distance from 28 and 29 Brigades, into reserve behind his frontage of ten miles*. This was agreed but not honoured after Milburn's departure, as General Cassels discovered on 21st July when he returned to find that

> 25 Brigade had been moved, but instead of being put in reserve had been lent to 25 U.S. Inf Div (later relieved by 1 U.S. Cav Div) to protect their left flank, and that I was expected to take it over in that location. As this put all my brigades in the front line, and as the Canadians were separated from the others by two rivers, both of which were in flood, I protested strongly. After three days of argument and discussion it was agreed that 25 Brigade should move to a reserve area behind 28 and 29 Brigades[10].

---

* I Corps then held a front of sixty two miles, but some fourteen lay across the confluence of the Imjin and Han rivers and the Kimpo peninsula. The front with enemy forces in July was thus about fifty miles.

The compromise disposed 25 Brigade as corps rather than divisional reserve. Though this was undesirable during the period that the division entered operations as a body, it was justifiable. An enemy offensive still threatened. Brigadier Rockingham and his commanding officers reconnoitred a series of potential tasks to the rear of the corps zone, including counter-attacks on Chinese parachute landings round the Han bridges.

The Commonwealth division flag was formally hoisted on 28th July at a ceremony near Tokchong, the headquarters site. General Van Fleet* formally pronounced that the formation was a part of the United Nations Command. All radios to and from divisional headquarters to those under command or in support, on the flanks, and rearward to I Corps and the bases in Korea and Japan, were open but began from noon to function operationally.

As a result of considerable preparation the reorganisation was at once effective though, inevitably, over the next week or so, there were minor incidents of friction as those working under the old system of independent brigade groups adjusted to the new structure. The Canadian Official Historian quotes

> An example of the sort of situation which arose during the transition from brigade group to brigade status...involving the [Canadian] 57th Field [Engineer] Squadron. Brigadier Rockingham had ordered it to construct a tactical road into the position of one of the battalions, while the divisional commander of the Royal Engineers had arranged for the unit to level an air strip at Divisional Headquarters. Priority was ultimately given to the tactical road[11].

Brigadier Brodie discovered that the guns of 45 Field Regiment were 'no longer mine to dispose as I required'[12], even though they continued to be in direct support of 29 Brigade. These vexations soon passed amid the common burdens of operations.

During June and July, 29 and 28 Brigades, respectively left and right along the Imjin river, had been engaged on the same basis as the rest of the Eighth Army, strengthening and extending Line Kansas, and patrolling forward across the river. 1 Glosters, for example, returned to their former position now green with summer foliage on the Imjin, made two deep sorties across it during June. On the 29th, their War Diary noted that work on Line Kansas was progressing: 'overhead cover practically completed on all positions. Thickening of wire and improvement of camouflage [are] main tasks'.

---

* Among others present were Lieutenant-General Sir Horace Robertson, Major-General O'Daniel, Brigadiers Brodie, Rockingham and Taylor.

Operational enterprises thus absorbed all available manpower. However, whenever opportunity offered, all units engaged in training.

Units in active operations benefit from periodic training to remedy errors or deficiencies manifested in combat, and to develop methods and skills to cope with contingencies in view—for example, assaulting along narrow ridge lines. New junior leaders selected to replace those lost as casualties, and similarly new specialists, for example radio operators and crews for medium mortars and machine-guns, require instruction.

Most battalions in the Commonwealth Division were able to train during a period in reserve. 3 RAR had an extensive requirement; many of its number were due for repatriation during the summer. Though trained soldiers, their replacements were acquainted formally with the peculiarities of the Korean battlefield, time well spent. For whilst the principles of war are common to any theatre, their practice requires adaptation to local circumstances as between winter and tropical warfare, or fighting in mountains as distinct from plains.

Colonel Ferguson was also due for relief at this time—he had served in the theatre almost a year as second-in-command and commanding officer, a good deal longer in the battalion. His successor was Lieutenant-Colonel F G Hassett*. The change was not immediately welcomed by the veterans of 3 RAR as Professor O'Neill has observed.

> ... Ferguson's reposting [to command another battalion] was resented by many 3 RAR men. Although he was an undemonstrative man, he had led the battalion well in difficult operations, he was trusted and held in respect by all ranks and was held in particular esteem by the junior NCOs and privates[13].

In combat, a change of commanding officer invariably unsettles a unit. An incumbent of mediocre ability is often preferred to a prospective newcomer—'better the devil you know...' is the soldier's philosophy. A new commanding officer is invested with authority on appointment but he has to earn the respect of those he leads, and the quickest way for him to do that is to show competence in operations. An opportunity for Colonel Hassett to manifest his considerable talent in this field was fast approaching.

The breakdown of the peace talks in August coincided with the completion of General Cassels' inceptory tour, which included talks with many officers and men at battalion and company level. Though he was satisfied that all were active, he remarked that patrols beyond the Imjin, many far ranging, were rarely making contact with and identifying the

---

* Later, General Sir Francis Hassett KBE, AC, CB, DSO, MVO, Chief of the Australian Defence Force Staff, 1975–77.

main enemy line*. The frequent flooding of the river also threatened to isolate reconnaissance and fighting parties seeking to return before daylight to their own lines. He decided to draw closer to the Chinese by moving the greater part of the division across the Imjin. This would deny the Chinese space in no man's land from which to launch an offensive, and inhibit development of their defences. In notifying the corps commander of his intentions, it was agreed that the two brigades should advance to an extension of Line Wyoming from the east. This was Operation Minden.

The orders[14] overtook several brigade and battalion initiatives along the river line, and the tail end of operations in support of the United States 1st Cavalry Division, the Commonwealth Division's right hand neighbour. In essence, 1 KOSB secured the 'Teal' ford and ferry site close to the former Gloster Crossing. 'Pintail' crossing, just round the next northern loop upstream, was secured by 3 RAR and subsequently held by 1 KSLI. These movements took 28 Brigade effectively across the river by last light on 8th September, and the commanding officers of the latter two battalions, Lieutenant-Colonels Hassett and V W Barlow, unopposed, sought to push on but were restrained.

During the first week in September, Chinese patrol activity rose: on the 6th there were numerous minor clashes. General Cassels wished each phase of Minden to be undertaken deliberately, maintaining a firm hold on the crossing places.

The second task was the rapid construction of bridges at Widgeon, on the division's left flank with 1 ROK, Teal, and Pintail to replace ferries and pontoons, vulnerable to disruption when the river flooded. A large mixed force of American and British field engineers was employed to ensure speed of construction. They completed the work by 11th September[15].

Third, 29 and 25 Brigades crossed to assume the left and right forward defensive localities. By 14th September, the new positions were dug and covered at selected sites by a line of barbed wire and mines. 1 NF, 1 Glosters, and 1 RUR, all drawn into a wide line in that order in 29 Brigade, were augmented by individual rifle companies from 28 Brigade. In 25 Canadian Brigade, the three battalions, 2nd Royal Canadian Regiment (2 RCR), Princess Patricia's Canadian Light Infantry, and Royal 22eme Regiment (R22eR), were also holding a wide front, behind which they had support for a time from 1 KSLI. All patrolled and laid ambushes by night. C Squadron of the 8th Hussars and Lord

---

* An exception was a deep raid in mid-August by 2nd Battalion, The Royal Canadian Regiment, supported by a tank troop of Lord Strathcona's Horse, Operation Dirk, which penetrated the Chinese outpost line.

Strathcona's Horse on the respective frontages reconnoitred roads and tracks to the north west. Chinese tanks had been observed in these areas.

For their part, the Chinese struck back with a rising weight of fire, at first against any daylight movement, subsequently by day and night on outposts; in closing up, the foremost brigades were moving into the weight of the enemy supporting weapons including those with shorter ranges such as the Russian 76-mm gun, heavy and medium mortars. Air strikes augmented the Commonwealth counter-battery fire on artillery and mortar sites detected[16], but these were only partially successful; many Chinese batteries were drawn into deep bunkers between firing. Those that were obliged to remain in the open were obscured by excellent camouflage. In the second and third weeks of the month, enemy reconnaisance patrols were active and several of the Commonwealth positions were raided, though without success. These clashes were the valedictories of the 192nd Chinese Division, a formation of the Sixty Fourth Army, but its departure from the line into a reserve position was not then apparent. Their place was taken by the 191st during the last week of the month.

Minden completed, and the forward line thus conforming to Wyoming across the entire I Corps front, General Cassels prudently completed plans for a withdrawal back into Line Kansas[17], behind the Imjin, if an enemy offensive should oblige it. Meantime, preliminary instructions had been issued by General O'Daniel for the mounting of Operation Cudgel, shortly renamed and revised as Commando.

. . . . .

Speaking to the press on 30th September, General Van Fleet remarked that the basic mission of the Eighth Army was to seek out and destroy the enemy. To have been strictly truthful he would have added the rider 'within certain clear limits'. He was not engaged in a wholesale seeking out and destruction process because, all else apart, there were limits on the numbers of casualties he could accept in offensive ventures. It was this factor which militated chiefly when he set aside his grander plans in May and June, and weighed upon him when he saw the losses from the operations round the Punchbowl.

Talk of 'seeking out and destroying the enemy' was all part of maintaining pressure on the enemy; part also of preserving an offensive spirit within an army essentially on the defensive in strategic terms. Tactically, however, Operation Commando was launched for a sound reason. The ground held by the Chinese on I Corps front gave them direct observation from hilltops on some of the Imjin crossings and numerous stretches of the roads serving the Corps' defences. To capture these, the four divisions, 1 ROK, 1 Commonwealth, the United States 1st Cavalry and 3rd Infantry—knitting in with the United States 25th Division in IX Corps—would secure 'Jamestown', an advanced line* [18]. It was expected that the enemy would resist strongly; in addition to important observation posts, the new line contained portions of their main defences.

Within the corps' plan, the Commonwealth Division was to capture the remainder of the lower Sami-ch'on valley and its central tributary, an advance on average of two and a half miles to occupy a chain of hills in the southern sector, and two formidable mountains, Kowang-san—whose peak was Point 355—and Maryang-san—Point 317—in the north. The frontage of attack was considerable, eight miles held by an enemy division, and whilst many of the hills did not appear to be occupied, it was recognised that camouflage might be concealing a Chinese presence on any or all of them.

When planning such an infantry operation, a wise divisional commander allocates tasks to his brigades after looking two levels down. He considers the objectives on the basis of battalion capabilities and the fire support essential to accomplish them. He weighs the breadth and depth of the target area in which a brigade headquarters may readily maintain control of the operation. Enemy dispositions—at least six battalions in the line with three in reserve—frontage, ground features, approaches and distances, indicated to General Cassels that the operation should fall to two brigades, each reinforced by a battalion, with the weight of armoured support in the northern sector. To maximise his striking power, he decided to attack initially with one brigade at a time supported by the whole divisional artillery together with the batteries allocated from corps and army resources.

On this basis, Commando was to be carried through in three phases.

First, in the northern sector, 28th Commonwealth Brigade, reinforced by 1 NF and the 8th Hussars less one squadron, would capture Kowang-san and features immediately south west and north east on D-day.

Second, in the southern sector, 25th Canadian Brigade with 1 RUR would capture the line of hills overlooking the central tributary of the Sami-ch'on on D plus 1.

Third, both brigades would secure the remaining features to Line Jamestown on D plus 3, ready thereafter, if specifically ordered, to move on to Line Fargo.

---

* Plans were also made within Commando to exploit beyond Jamestown to 'Fargo', a mile and a half further on.

29 Brigade was in reserve*. D Day was 3rd October 1951.

Considerable preparations were required: reconnaissance; plans made and orders issued all the way down the scale to rifleman and light machine-gunner. Boundaries were adjusted with 1st ROK Division on the left and 1st Cavalry on the right. The remainder of 28 Brigade, the New Zealand and 45 Field Regiments moved across the Imjin. The telephone cable network was expanded. Considerable quantities of additional ammunition and other stocks were brought forward. The casualty collection and evacuation system was amplified.

Lieutenant-Colonel Moore's field engineers were crucial to this activity as his regimental war diary briefly discloses:

> 1 Oct. 12 Fd Sqn constructed a jeep track for 3 RAR... The first 200 yards were completed during night 1/2 Oct as that portion was under enemy observation.
>
> Heavy rain made newly constructed roads difficult to maintain, and 45 Fd Regt were unable to leave their positions...until 55 Fd Sqn had repaired the road leading to that position.
>
> 57 Cdn Fd Sqn continued work on road [to forward units]... Beyond that point no further work except blasting was permitted, as the alignment was then under enemy observation. ...[19]

Lashed by intermittent rain, forced at intervals to take cover from shellfire, the divisional engineers maintained and pushed forward the road network with dozers and graders and dumpers, with compression tools, picks and shovels. They kept open the bridges and ferries. Not infrequently, they were delayed by the discovery of mines, some laid many months before by one side or the other. In these conditions the roads and tracks for Operation Commando were prepared.

From 1st October, the divisional artillery fired on targets directly related to Commando but without departing so markedly from the established programmes of harassing fire as to raise enemy suspicions. At 0500 on 3rd October, however, the weight and frequency of fire steadily increased as American guns and howitzers† of the corps and army artillery joined the Commonwealth 25-pounders and 4.2-inch mortars.

On the left of the 28 Brigade attack, Lieutenant-Colonel Barlow deployed 1 KSLI under cover of night and the early morning mist on 3rd October. He was a very experienced officer, having commanded a

---

* Reduced to 1 GLOSTERS and one Centurion squadron. The major units of 29 Brigade were about to be replaced on completion of a year in Korea. The complement of minor units was relieved by individual replacements.

† C Battery, 17th Field Artillery Battalion (8-inch howitzers) C Battery, 204th Field Artillery Battalion (155-mm guns) A & C Batteries, 999th Field Artillery Battalion (155-mm self-propelled howitzers)

parachute battalion with outstanding success during the second world war. His task was to secure the ridge line between Points 210 and 227, placing the KSLI a mile west south west of the hill mass of Kowang-san, Hill 355. This involved an advance of almost 10,000 yards.

Colonel Barlow's plan involved the seizure of intermediate heights on his route by one company at a time supported by the Centurions of A Squadron, 8th Hussars. He recognised that broken ground and soft mud in paddy fields might hinder the tanks, and thus regarded their contribution as a bonus. His fire plan, which included support from the medium machine-guns of 2 PPCLI, took account of this factor.

This was just as well. D Company occupied Point 208 *en route* to 210 at 0600 on 3rd October without contest but the tanks were unable to keep up with them. Moving on, B and C Companies in parallel had to fight for their objectives a mile beyond D throughout the morning. Clearance of the enemy continued in the afternoon at a cost of 2 killed and twelve wounded. They had severely mauled a Chinese battalion in the process, capturing eight and killing about thirty of the two forward enemy companies. Colonel Barlow pressed forward to take advantage of this success but was halted by Brigadier Taylor because Kowang-san was still in enemy possession[20].

1 KOSB under Lieutenant-Colonel John MacDonald attacked at dawn on 3rd October. He aimed to capture two intermediate features with his C and B Companies, left and right, from which to cover the assault up the steep slopes of Kowang-san. From the outset,

> ... The rate of advance of both Companies was slow, due to the steep and densely wooded terrain and the difficulty of keeping direction and control.
>
> Shortly after crossing the start line, C Company came under heavy artillery and mortar fire and were further embarrassed by enemy snipers, who had laid low in the dense undergrowth and opened fire, after the leading platoons had passed them[21].

Despite these difficulties, the leading elements of C Company closed with the enemy on its objective but was too weak to capture the position; a considerable part of its fighting strength was dispersed along the approach route, clearing snipers. Colonel Macdonald drew the whole company back out of fire to prepare a second attack during the afternoon. B Company had completed its initial task and was digging in under fire. In mid-afternoon, the combination of A and C Companies broke the enemy on the spur running south east from Kowang-san, and A Company under Major G A Duncan rapidly exploited this achievement by capturing the south western spur.

By that time, it was evening. Defences had to be coordinated for the night; plans made for the following day. Wounded, accumulating in forward sheltered sites since the morning, had to be recovered, and prisoners brought back. Supplies were brought forward by the Korean and battalion porters. When these activities had been completed, 1 KOSB began to rest before resuming the struggle for Hill 355 on 4th October.

On the right flank of 28 Brigade, B Company of 3 RAR set off under Captain H W Nicholls through the gloom at 0300 to capture Point 199, a preliminary step to securing Maryang-san on 5th October. Trees amid high scrub, early morning mist, and the constant expectation of enemy entrapment imposed a slow pace. The journey of three miles took five hours, but there was no sign of the Chinese until they reached Hill 199 which was taken after a short bombardment and a brisk assault, killing or capturing the majority of the Chinese platoon in occupation. The Australians lost three wounded. Nicholls was soon joined by Captain J J Shelton's A Company and the two elements dug in against counter-attack[22].

For the remainder of 3rd October, 3 RAR supported the KOSB attack on Kowang-san, principally with a section of their medium machine-guns firing in enfilade. The 8th Hussars succeeded in moving three Centurions forward into the area of Point 199, from which, with the Australians, they engaged the Chinese in occupation of twin Points 220, respectively east and north east of Kowang-san. The first of these was scarcely within machine-gun range, but received many hits from the Centurions' 20-pounder guns. Across the 28 Brigade front, the divisional artillery fired 27,000 rounds during 3rd October.

Yet, for all the endeavours, the principal objective remained in enemy possession. 25 Canadian Brigade was due to advance some 3,000 yards to secure its Commando objectives on 4th October, Phase 2 of the operation, and expected to enjoy fire support from the whole divisional artillery in the process. But the tactical concept required Phase 1 to be completed first. Adjustments were necessary.

> During the evening the GOC [General Cassels] decided that H-hour [opening time] for the attack by 25 Cdn Infantry Brigade...would be delayed from 0600 hrs 4 Oct 51 to 1100 hrs 4 Oct 51. The divisional artillery would be available to 28 BRITCOM Infantry Brigade until 1100 hrs [after which] they would only have their direct support regiment [16 NZ Field Regiment] on call[23].

Under pressure of time to capture his initial objectives, Brigadier Taylor instructed 3 RAR to capture the twin Points 220 on 4th October as a means of assisting the KOSB ascending Kowang-san. It was not a task welcomed by Colonel Hassett; with Maryang-san in his sights for 5th October, he had hoped to limit the activities of his soldiers on the 4th. Still, as he reminded his O Group that evening, they did not want to find themselves moving on Maryang-san with Point 355 still occupied by Chinese artillery observers.

At 0500 on the 4th, then, Major Jack Gerke took his C Company in single file through darkness towards the northeasterly Point 220. The company left its base on a small feature above the Imjin and marched westwards along a rough track for 2 miles, passing initially through the deserted hamlets scattered round Chunggojan. Company Sergeant-Major A Stanley, checking the departure area, was vexed to discover that several of the heavily laden men had decided to discard their entrenching tools. At the first halt to close the company up he returned these with indignant whispers to the respective owners.

As the daylight grew, Major Gerke hastened. The morning was clear*. His plan was to form up briefly below the steepest face of the eastern feature believed, correctly, to be occupied by a Chinese platoon, and take it by surprise.

Following a short bombardment, one of many across the front at that hour, C Company launched itself at 9 o'clock and was inside the enemy position in a matter of minutes. Killing those in the trenches, the Australians had the best of the hand grenade and small arms exchanges with those in bunkers below. Private Jim Burnett led one group firing his Bren light machine-gun from the hip, thrusting through low scrub to the far side of the position. Pausing only to gather, two platoons pushed on westward to the second Point 220, held somewhat more strongly by the remainder of the local enemy company. Burnett's Bren was the first into a fire position to cover the assault, which rapidly quenched all opposition[24].

Meantime, Colonel Macdonald had launched his D Company under Captain R C Robertson-MacLeod together with the Battle Patrol under Lieutenant K Wilson up the south western spur of Kowang-san. Second-Lieutenant Barney Henderson, commanding a platoon in D Company, recorded,

> I can't remember if I slept that night [3rd/4th October] but all I do remember, as light came on 4 October, moving through the forward platoons of A Company to our start line and, while waiting there, seeing the top of 355 erupt as a massive artillery barrage blasted it to pieces. We were being supported by the whole weight of the divisional artillery—an awesome sight. How reassuring it was, as we struggled up the steep slopes towards our objective, to hear the crump of the shells. I saw my signaller drop his wireless set—so what—there was no time to stop. On we went in extended line, and still the guns supported us. As we started the final assault on the summit, the shellfire rolled northwards on to the final slope, leaving us to the destruction all around; there was not a tree or shrub standing. I swore at

* Contrary to some accounts, the majority of the records indicate a fine, clear day on 4th October 1951.

that moment I'd never be rude about Gunners again. By 1000 hours, D Company held the hill that had loomed over us for the past few days[25].

This assault had cleared the main mass of Kowang-san, but unknown to the KOSB Major Gerke's company was on the eastern slope, just below the high point, 355. Having taken the twin Points 220, like a good commander he had pushed on, clearing the remaining enemy from the eastern shoulder by 1215. D Company, 1 KOSB, reported its presence on the western side at 1130.

In after years, each battalion claimed the victory; neither recognised that the other had suffered opposition in their advance. In fact, partly by design, partly local initiative, the Chinese battalion on the 'great round hill', as it appeared to many, had succumbed to a pincer attack. Each battalion had received excellent supporting fire: Captain Robertson-MacLeod's force from his neighbour, B Company, and the mortarmen and machine-gunners of Support Company; Major Gerke's company from the RAR support weapons and the 8th Hussars tanks. Both benefitted greatly from the accurate and voluminous artillery fire directed by the New Zealand forward observation parties. The KOSB lost eight killed, one mortally, and 40 other wounded* over the two days of the action, 3 RAR ten wounded, one mortally on 4th October. Between them, on this second day, they had killed forty and captured twenty one† prisoners from the Chinese battalion, not counting the casualties carried off by the enemy.

Meantime, Colonel Barlow had pressed forward, taking advantage of the morning twilight. D Company under Major W J Cottle captured Point 210 at 1010, supported by 8th Hussar Centurions, capturing eleven prisoners and finding 41 Chinese dead with numerous abandoned weapons as they secured the position. They had lost one killed and seven wounded. As arranged, 2 PPCLI relieved them when 25 Brigade opened its own operation.

Promptly at 1100, Brigadier Rockingham advanced his brigade with three battalions in line: the Royal Ulster Rifles on the left, 2 RCR in the centre, 2 PPCLI on the right, spread thinly across unit frontages in excess of 2,000 yards. He was grateful for the loan of Major J Hardiman's company from 3 RAR to swell his force. Fortunately, as anticipated, the enemy defences were scattered, comprising a screen rather than a continous line of opposition. Even so, there was a fierce local battle before

---

* Because of disparities in the figures published to date, I have taken these details from the records notified by the battalion on AF. W3012C by name and number for the period 3rd and 4th October 1951. They include men attached from the Argylls.

† Seventeen initially, four more were discovered by the KOSB hiding in bunkers on 5th October, misreported by 1 KOSB as three and 28 Brigade headquarters War Diary as two.

Lieutenant C E S Curmi of D Company, 2 PPCLI, stormed Point 187 with his platoon. Believing the position to be held by a patrol, they found a Chinese company, killing twenty eight and capturing four.

By the end of the afternoon of Thursday, 4th October, from the Royal Ulster Rifles left flank on the paddy fields of the Samich'on to the right flank of 2PPCLI, all the objectives of the day had been secured, often under considerable long range but accurate fire, of which the RCR took the greatest volume. 1 KSLI had run to the limit of its Phase 3 tasks by capturing Hill 227. One major divisional objective remained to be taken: Maryang-san*.

Though smaller and marginally lower in height than Kowang-san, 'the great round hill', Maryang-san is more defensible. Its irregular spurs ascend through successive knolls to a crescent shaped ridge line on an arc of two miles. On some approaches the gradient is close to forty five degrees. Half a dozen ring contours rise above 300 metres on the ridge line. The spot height, Point 317, stands in the middle of the crescent's right horn.

As observed, 3 RAR had been ordered to capture Maryang-san, but the mass together with the probable numbers defending it was manifestly too great for a single battalion, notwithstanding the strong artillery support. General Cassels had accordingly provided a battalion of 29 Brigade to take a share. After consultation between Brigadier Taylor and Colonel Hassett, it was decided that the reinforcing unit, 1st Battalion, the Royal Northumberland Fusiliers, should capture Point 217 at the base of the crescent's left or western horn. 3 RAR would feint from the south east while attacking successively with two companies from the east. On this basis, the Chinese defending Maryang-san would be distracted.

The Northumberland Fusiliers had been allocated to 28 Brigade to support the first phase of the operation and remained for the third. Their difficulty in the latter was that they were advancing directly into the Chinese defences. A generous share of the 9,000 rounds of preliminary bombardment was thus allocated to their sector, and this was continuing as the battalion moved forward at 0600. But the enemy was sheltered by deep bunkers across the entire spread of Maryang-san. The attack slowed as the two leading companies, notably Z Company under Major R D Wilson, approaching from the south east, began to scale the steep approaches to Point 217. To the surprise of the British assailants, many Chinese came out of their trenches as the bombardment ended and were evidently unaware of their presence. Ten prisoners were taken by Z at this time but, in the process, the British encroachment was revealed. The

---

* Later, when this sector was taken over by the Americans, Maryang-san was nicknamed 'Baldy', Kowang-san, 'Little Gibraltar', but to the Commonwealth Division they were familiarly '317' and '355' after the principal heights on each feature.

response of the enemy standing to their fire positions in deep defences on a reverse slope was devastating.

Attempts to close were unsuccesful, despite considerable supporting fire which included, later in the morning, air strikes with napalm. The basic difficulty was that the only covered approach confined the advance to a single company. During a series of intense fire fights as the leading platoons, sometimes in rushes, more often by crawling, closed upon the enemy bunkers, Z lost thirty among the leading platoons including both platoon commanders and platoon sergeants[26]. Their situation was not improved when, by rare error between forward observation post and guns, a number of shells from the divisional artillery straddled Z Company. Anxious to discover any means of facilitating his battalion's progress, Colonel Speer enquired as to the progress of the Australians.

On the previous afternoon, 4th October, Colonel Hassett was much relieved to receive D Company back in his location from their Canadian attachment; for C Company was still absent on the slopes of Kowang-san. He thus had three rifle companies in hand for the ascent of Maryang-san. Early next morning, A Company with three Centurions moved forward from its positions to feint up the south eastern spur on which Chinese outposts had been identified. At 0445 Captain Nicholls moved with B Company towards the eastern flank of Maryang-san followed by D Company (Major Hardiman) at 0515.

The two assault companies marched silently in single file, each man laden with sixty to eighty pounds of battle necessities. At the outset, the assembly was assisted by moonlight but as dawn approached the mist began to rise across the paddy fields and creep up the hill slopes. Both B and D passed the eastern outskirts of Koyangdae village and ascended the scrub covered slopes behind it. The visibility grew worse. About 8 o'clock, the front end of D Company bumped into the rear of B, halted while Captain Nicholls sought to identify his position. Major Hardiman came up to him as he confessed to Colonel Hassett on his radio that he was lost. The commanding officer instructed him in plain terms to resolve this problem at once.

Aware that the operation depended on their judgement, the two company commanders conferred anxiously. When they parted, Major Hardiman believed that there was agreement to turn westward and was thus surprised when Nicholls set off north. Lieutenant J H A Young, commanding 12 Platoon recalled,

> We were resting on the wet grass on the fog-wrapped ridge when Major Hardiman came back to me and said he believed B Company had lost direction and gone off to the right. Since my platoon was just in the right direction to continue the advance towards [Point] 317, he handed me a map and compass. Not very happily we set off, with a map in one hand, a compass in the other, and trepidation over the rest of me. ...[27]

The rumble of the divisional and supporting American artillery bombardment could be heard distantly. Closer, on either hand though difficult to locate accurately, there were sounds of mortar and small arms fire. Major Hardiman was uncomfortably aware that the original plan, whereby B Company would clear the positions east of Point 317 whereafter D would take the peak and positions west of it, was unlikely to transpire. The entire task would now fall to D Company. The column trudged on and upward as the minutes spun past.

All this changed abruptly at 0915. Young's platoon was crossing a gully, the mist was thinning, when a machine-gun ahead opened fire. The leading Bren gunner was wounded. Hardiman, close behind, ordered Young to form a fire base while he brought up the remainder of the company.

The mist continued to screen the enemy defences as the other two platoons came into position. Hardiman kept them in place; assaulting on guesswork would have been foolhardy. But about 1030 it was possible to see the enemy on a ring contour some 70 yards ahead and above them. Attempts to gain artillery or battalion mortar support had foundered, principally because the company's location was uncertain. He decided to mass small arms and light mortar fire from two platoons and his medium machine-gun section while using Lieutenant Leary's 10 Platoon to close on the Chinese. Due to the latter's proximity this manoeuvre began by short rushes from one piece of cover to another. The Australian's one advantage, though this was not at once apparent, was that the enemy were as much concerned with the feint from the south as D Company's approach from the east. Breaking in, Lieutenant Leary was among the wounded but the battle continued under Lance-Corporal V J E Brown. Then Major Hardiman became a casualty. Lieutenant Young assumed command of the company. He sent 12 Platoon forward to reinforce Brown and those combing through the enemy bunkers.

Through these difficult hours, Colonel Hassett was located with his small battle headquarters on a ridge eight hundred yards to the south. C Company had returned from Kowang-san, providing him with a reserve, a particularly comforting asset as the principal thrust of his plan seemed to be astray.

From his wireless net, he knew that A Company was on course, engaging the enemy outposts, but B was fighting a battle in an unidentified location. D Company's radio was not responding—its aerial had been cut away by fire. The operator made emergency repairs and, to the colonel's considerable relief, Lieutenant Young was able to report their situation. Colonel Hassett believed he could see them—he ordered Young to display fluorescent aircraft recognition panels to indicate his position. At last this was fixed!

'Can you go on?', Colonel Hassett asked.

'Give me twenty minutes of heavy supporting fire and I'll have it,' Young responded[28].

The three Centurions adjacent to Colonel Hassett's command post began to supplement the fire of 16 New Zealand Field Regiment and the battalion's 3-inch mortars. As morning passed into afternoon, D Company worked its way through two more positions towards Point 317. At the same time, Colonel Hassett modified A Company's thrust line directly up the southern spur, drawing considerable Chinese fire. These tactics, combined with the Australians' dogged persistence, were successful.

Reports of further casualties in D Company persuaded Colonel Hassett that this small force should not be pressed to exhaustion. They might possibly capture Point 317 but would scarcely be strong enough to repel any substantial Chinese counter-attack. All his companies were under strength—a matter referred forcefully to Canberra by General Robertson on several occasions. A Company was engaged—as it seemed to Shelton, 'in a private war'. B Company, now located as holding a feature north east of Maryang-san, was well placed to reinforce D, but the colonel judged well that they, too, were approaching the limit of their strength. He had Major Gerke with him, following the events of the battle, and decided to commit C Company to the capture of the summit.

Time pressed. Gerke told Company Sergeant-Major Stanley on his radio to prepare for a quick move; orders would be issued as soon as he returned to his headquarters. Three hours later, after a forced march, preceded by air strikes, artillery, mortar, tank, and machine-gun fire, Gerke's company passed through D to storm the feature immediately east of Point 317, nicknamed 'Baldy'. The peak then lay one thousand yards beyond them across a saddle strewn with scrub. Even at that distance, it was clear that the topmost point rose steeply from its base.

Gerke decided not to delay on Baldy. The supporting air and ground fire switched to Point 317 and the features beyond. One platoon remained to search out bunkers, the other two swept on. On the far side of the saddle, they began to climb the final three hundred and fifty feet to the the summit, pressed close to the stony ground, expecting a rain of grenades from above. But there was no resistance. Point 317 finally fell at 1700, when the remainder of its garrison surrendered without contest. As Chinese retaliatory mortar and artillery fire began to fall among the Australians, the assault pioneers and a platoon of A Company arrived to reinforce them against counter-attack. Fighter and bomber aircraft returned to strike enemy infantry and gun positions identified behind Maryang-san by one of the division's aerial observers in an Auster of 1903 Flight. Unfortunately, the Australians' splendid persistence had not persuaded the Chinese to withdraw from their commanding positions on the south western spur.

By darkness on the 5th, the forward companies of the Northumberland Fusiliers had been withdrawn after a costly day. Z Company had been thrown back finally to its start line by counter-attack. Lieutenant-Colonel Speer cleared the remainder of his casualties, and reorganised within night defensive positions. Brigadier Taylor instructed him to take Point 217 next day, 6th October.

It has to be said that this was not a good idea. Although Colonel Speer adjusted the lines of approach for the 6th, the spur topped by 217 was too steep to be stalked from the west; from the south the ground was covered by numerous weapons firing from deep bunkers—hence Major Wilson's original selection of his approach line. Meantime, Brigadier Taylor had another idea. At 1930, he ordered 1 NF to pass a company through C Company, 3 RAR, and 'exploit' towards the head of the Point 217 spur from the north[29]. This would have involved a night march of some eight miles across the hills through trees and scrub followed by the ascent of Maryang-san, and passage down that part of the ridge still to be cleared. 3 RAR was instructed to patrol the area by way of assistance. The likelihood that the western half of the ridge would be heavily defended was discounted.

Colonel Speer objected that Z and Y companies which had been involved in the day's operations were still moving into their night defences, and were in any case too depleted for such an operation. W and X Companies were required for the attack on 6th October. The order was rescinded.

On Saturday, 6th October, the notion that the western end of the ridge was held by weak enemy forces was shown to be false. A platoon of 3 RAR snatched a wooded knoll about 500 yards west of Point 317, but was immediately counter-attacked. The Australians held fast under enemy artillery and mortar fire and further counter-attacks throughout the day. Colonel Hassett brought B Company up to reinforce the position and, arriving himself at 8 o'clock on the 7th, directed an attack upon the 'Hinge', a feature lying directly above Point 217. Assisted by almost every weapon within range, Nicholls' company took this at 0920, overcoming numbers superior to his own. In turn, the Chinese turned their own batteries upon the ridge repeatedly, firing on into the evening.

This hazard notwithstanding, Colonel Hassett continued to move porters up the hill with ammunition—the first requirement among other supplies—and down with casualties*. He had no doubt that a counter-attack would be launched against him, initially to recapture the Hinge; without it, the Chinese had no hope of recovering Maryang-san.

* Brigadier Taylor reinforced 3 RAR's Korean porters with those of 1 KSLI and 1 KOSB.

After a respite of thirty minutes on the evening of Sunday, the 7th, enemy fire intensified from 8 pm The adjutant recalled,

> At 8.30 pm the shelling eased and lifted, and the Chinese attacked.
>
> They attacked on three sides, expecting a dazed and battered enemy. Instead they found an enemy resolute and confident...a blazing perimeter of Australian rifles and machine-guns[30].

Then and twice more during the night, a Chinese battalion sought but failed to eject B Company from the Hinge. At the time, the Australians ascribed their survival largely to the swift and heavy responses of the divisional artillery*, which broke many of the approaching enemy waves but their success was due, fundamentally, to the determination of B Company to stand and fight. With this event, 3 RAR completed its task to capture and hold Maryang-san†.

On the previous day, the Northumberland Fusiliers' attack had again penetrated to Point 217, but again, though supported by air strikes from South African Mustangs as well as artillery, they were driven back by counter-attacks. In these operations, the battalion casualties were inevitably substantial. Over the two days, sixteen of their number had been killed or mortally wounded, ninety four wounded, and three missing, the total discounting a number of wounded who remained at duty. Their own persistence had not been futile. An important element of the enemy holding Maryang-san had been occupied continuously over two days.

At last, with the Australians in control of the ridge line, the Chinese surviving on the forward slopes drew off. Following a precautionary bombardment, the battalion intelligence officer and two sections of the assault pioneers walked into the Chinese positions on and around Point 217 on the afternoon of 8th October and found them abandoned, though full still of supplies. The Commonwealth Division had by then completed all its tasks in Operation Commando. It had defeated, for the time being, the 191st Division and thus the line quietened, though intermittent harassing fire continued across the divisional front, and two substantial attacks were made against 1 KSLI and 2 PPCLI on the 13th October. Counter-battery fire and air strikes had contained enemy supporting weapons but they were substantially intact in their bunkers. In the period of relief and reorganisation, the newly arrived 1st Battalion, The Royal

---

* The ground gained, and opened to movement by 28 Field Engineer Regiment, permitted an advance by elements of the divisional and supporting artillery, notably a New Zealand battery and C Battery, 17 US Field Artillery Battalion, extending range and facilitating engagement of the enemy gun positions.

† In the action, 3 RAR casualties were 20 killed, 104 wounded, of whom 15 remained at duty. They buried 283 Chinese dead, and captured 50 prisoners.

‡ The battalion, under command of Lieutenant-Colonel J H R Orlebar, replaced the Royal Ulster Rifles in 29 Brigade but was temporarily attached to 28 Brigade.

Norfolk Regiment‡ occupied Kowang-san, and the KOSB took over Maryang-san from the Australians. The 1st Battalion of the Royal Northumberland Fusiliers withdrew finally from the line, its tour in Korea completed.

To the south, 1st ROK Division had occupied its objectives after a short advance against light opposition. Immediately to the north, however, 1st Cavalry Division, committed to deep objectives across a mass of commanding features, had been obliged to fight for every height of consequence. As the Commonwealth Division settled on Jamestown, the 5th and 7th Cavalry were still struggling to complete their first phase. Extraordinary measures were taken to assist them: two self-propelled 155-mm guns, and one 8-inch, came forward to fire directly into enemy positions; B-26 medium bombers dropped 1,000 pound bombs on bunkers resisting all other fire. The 8th Cavalry were drawn in as fighting extended through a second week, finally ending on 19th October, when all objectives were secured. The division had been opposed initially by the Chinese 139th Division, reinforced subsequently by the 140th, and the men of the three cavalry regiments discovered that they had captured a portion of the enemy main defence line, comprehensively fortified and supplied, which had extended south across the Commonwealth front through Maryang-san and Kowang-san. Hence the discoveries commonly by men of both divisions of highly developed subterranean defences and extensive stocks of ammunition, equipment, food and water during the advance to Jamestown.

The 1st Cavalry Division knitted its left flank to the Commonwealth Division, its right on the United States 3rd. Both the latter and the 25th Division had had little difficulty during Commando; they had rapidly captured the sections of the Chinese outpost line marked as their objectives. However, the cost was not insignificant. The 1st Cavalry had lost almost 3,000 killed and wounded, the Commonwealth Division about 500, and the other three divisions 500 jointly, a total of 4,000. Due to helicopter evacuation of those most seriously wounded directly to surgery from the regimental aid posts, and a matured system of emergency aid and transportation available to the remainder, the recovery rate was high.

As the fighting decreased in I and X Corps—Heartbreak Ridge fell on 13th October—IX Corps launched spoiling operations on its front towards Kumsong, which was later raided successfully. These ended in the last week of the month.

General Cassels received a number of congratulations for the success of his force in Commando. Passing these on in an Order of the Day to all ranks, he remarked

> Our division has now completed its first attack and has gained all its objectives. I never had the slightest doubt that this would happen because

> I knew that I had well-trained and aggressive troops who could, and would, achieve anything that was reasonably demanded of them. The result has more than proved that my conviction was right.
>
> Any successful attack is the result of really good team-work and I am quite sure that this has been so in this case. The brunt of the actual fighting is borne by the infantry and the tanks but it must be clear to you all that, without the gunners and the sappers*, we could never have got to grips with the enemy and defeated him. At the same time, all these arms could not have even begun to function, or continued to operate without the endless work of all the services behind them. Ammunition, supplies, petrol, medical care, repair, recovery and traffic control were all vital to success.
>
> ... You have all had your share in the first real operation of this 1st Commonwealth Division and the speedy accomplishment of the task reflects the greatest credit on every individual ..

The division had begun Operation Commando as something of a mixed bag. There were the old hands who had been operating in Korea for up to a year. The newcomers included veterans of the Second World War and those who had never heard a shot fired in anger. At the end of the operation, they had a common experience of danger, endurance, dependence upon one another, and accomplishment. These bound them together as they entered the second winter of the war.

---

* 'Sappers' British nickname for military engineers.

SOURCE NOTES: Chapter 15

1 For the background to formation, see Volume 1, pp 93–109; also Grey, *op cit,* and F H Wood, *op cit,* Chapter VII. Details of assembly and preparation are in WO 308/27, 1 Commonwealth Division Periodic Report, 2 May–15 Oct 51.

2 Special Order of the Day, 28th July 1951. Issued to all formations and units. A copy is in most war diaries.

3 For a comprehensive description of the artillery organisation and capabilities, see Victory, Colonel P M, *The Royal Artillery in Korea,* MSS in the Royal Artillery Institution, Woolwich.

4 See, for example, HQRE War Diary entry, 9th October 1951.

5 Quoted, Wood, *op cit,* p 112.

6 CRO No 957 etc to UK High Commissioners of 12th October 1951 FK 1190/19, (FO 371 92831).

7 For an interesting discussion of Commonwealth attitudes to the directive, see Grey, *op cit.,* pp 106–108.

8 War Diary, Headquarters, 25th Canadian Infantry Brigade Group, 19th–20th May 1951.

9 See Brigadier Rockingham's account, quoted Wood, *op cit,* p 109. Also War Diary, 25th Infantry Brigade Group, 17th–19th June 1951.

10 WO 308/27—1 Comwel Div Periodic Report, 2 May–15 Oct 51, paragraph 4.

11 Wood, *op cit,* p 119, fn.

12 Conversation, author with Major-General Brodie.

13 O'Neill, *op cit,* vol ii, pp 172–173.

14 1 COMWEL War Diary, September, 1951, Div Operation Order—Op MINDEN. Brigade connected OOs are contained in respective war diaries.

15 See I Corps Engineers Journal, September 1951 (USNARS, Suitland) and 28 COMWEL Engr Regt War Diary for same period.

16 See, for example, 29 Brigade Operations/Intelligence Summary No 217, War Diary, September 1951.

17 Operation WATERLOO, see 1 COMWEL Div War Diary, September and October, 1951.

18 See Hq I US Corps Operation COMMANDO in G-3 file, and Corps Comd Report, October 1951 (Office of the Chief of Military History and USNARS, Suitland, respectively).

19 War Diary, 28 Field Regiment, October, 1951.

20 1 KSLI War Diary and conversation, author with Brigadier V W Barlow.

21 Macdonald, Major-General J F M, *The Borderers in Korea* (Regimental Publication, Berwick-on-Tweed), p 31.

22 3 RAR War Diary; also O'Neill *op cit,* p 186.

23 HQRA War Diary, 3rd October 1951.

24 War Diary, 3 RAR. See also O'Neill, *op cit,* volume ii, p 187; Daly, Colonel T, *Operation Commando, Korea, 2–8 October 1951,* (Australian Army Journal, March 1952); Bartlett, Norman, *op cit,* p 145.

25 Henderson, Colonel J B, *Kowang-san—Point 355,* (King's Own Scottish Borderers Chronicle, 1990), pp 59–60.

26 1 NF War Diary, October 1951, contains an account of the action with a useful sketch, made immediately after Commando, of the Chinese positions on Point 217.

27 Bartlett, *op cit,* p 146.

28 O'Neill, *op cit,* p 191; Bartlett, *op cit,* p 147.

29 28 Bde signal GO 13 of 051930 I (see War Diary, October 1951).

30 Keys, A G W, *Operation Commando* (Returned Services League magazine, *Reveille),* April, 1952, p 33.

CHAPTER 16

Marking the line

From the moment the armistice talks began in Korea, the war became a matter of secondary importance to the British government apparatus—politicians, officials, and Chiefs of Staff. It was not that they did not care about its outcome or their servicemen involved in it; simply, that, with rare exceptions, matters of abiding importance such as the economy, of rising consequence such as NATO and the rearmament of West Germany, Middle East oil, and the growth of Russian atomic power, were transcendent.

> For one thing [Field Marshal Slim later remarked] we were far less anxious about the day to day run of the battle. It looked as though we had the advantage, such as there was, and the presence of [General] Jim Cassels and a divisional organisation gave us greater confidence that our operations would be run on a better footing. Then, although we had to be prepared for the Chinese and North Koreans—or Russia—springing some tremendous surprise on us, we believed that there was going to be an armistice, even though it took much longer than we had initially expected...[1]

There had been a general expectation in London as in Washington that an armistice would be secured in a matter of days, certainly in a few weeks. Marshal of the Royal Air Force Sir John Slessor, Chief of the Air Staff, was inclined to believe that delays owed something to American handling.

> ...the Americans are conducting the command and direction of operations in Korea as though they were purely a US concern. I don't think it is good enough...we and the French have a tremendous interest in the Far East. ... HMG should adopt a role of something more than an interested spectator whom it is allowed to have such crumbs of comfort as drop from the United States table[2].

This view was not shared by the Foreign Office or the other Chiefs of Staff. At the 1st August meeting of the latter, the First Sea Lord said that in his view there were

> ...no sound grounds for our pressing to take part in the present armistice negotiations. The High Command in Korea was not an integrated Command; it was solely a United States Command. Therefore since the negotiations were purely of a military character being conducted by the High

Command, we had no claim to participate or even to send observers. The French, the Turks, the Indians and all other nations contributing forces in Korea were in exactly the same position as ourselves, and if we were to send observers, they would all have an equal claim to do so and would no doubt press their claim. Naturally, if there was likely to be a complete breakdown, we and the other nations participating would expect to be consulted.

SIR ESLER DENING [Foreign Office] said that the arrangements in Washington for keeping not only ourselves but also the other contributing nations informed of the progress of negotiations appeared to be perfectly satisfactory. There were bi-weekly briefing meetings in Washington to which all contributing nations sent representatives...In addition, there was a private arrangement whereby someone from the British Embassy in Washington was kept informed daily of all details of the situation and was shown General Ridgway's Reports.

DEAN RUSK had made it quite clear that the United States would welcome any ideas which we might have at any time as regards these negotiations. We must, naturally, maintain complete secrecy in this matter, or other contributing nations would wish to be treated on an equal footing with ourselves. ...

LIEUTENANT-GENERAL SIR NEVIL BROWNJOHN [Vice-Chief of the Imperial General Staff representing Field-Marshal Slim observed that]...it seemed from his reports that Air Vice-Marshal Bouchier was being kept well informed of the day-to-day progress of the armistice negotiations. Any ideas that we might have...should, naturally be fed in [sic] Washington rather in Korea. In these circumstances, he did not feel that we had any case to insist on observers being present at these negotiations. ...[3]

The special relationship continued, therefore. The door was open for the British to propose or comment on the run of policy. Occasionally, as earlier, this arrangement was taken to the point of imposition. For example, Air Chief Marshal Sir William Elliot in Washington, largely on the basis of Chinese protests, suggested that the Far East Air Force was preferentially attacking civilians in Korea, a charge which was hotly rejected by General Vandenberg, with good reason[4].

During the summer and autumn, due to developments at or associated with the armistice negotiations, the dialogue between the Foreign Office and State Department, and the respective Chiefs of Staff, continued intermittently, sometimes with American principals visiting London, mostly in Washington[5].

In these discussions, the United States led, the United Kingdom lagged. When the armistice talks began, British diplomacy concentrated on securing both a Korean and a Far East settlement. Because these implied concessions to China, the Americans resisted. Lacking in Herbert Morrison an informed and enterprising minister, the Foreign Office drifted. In an atmosphere of frustration exacerbated by evidence that the Americans were withholding important intelligence, fanciful ideas arose. Many officials agreed with a colleague's impression that 'we are going round and round, not in ever decreasing circles, but round the same ones'. A few suspected that the United States Government was not interested in an armistice, preferring a military solution. Another theory was that America, wishing to be shot of its onerous responsibilities in Korea would abandon the Republic following a a peace settlement. Sir Esler Dening pointed out that

> We must bear in mind the American political situation in all this... I believe that once the United Nations forces are withdrawn the country will become Communist dominated. But the administration cannot allow this to happen before the 1952 [presidential] elections[6].

Actually, the State and Defense Departments were not pursuing hidden policies but were certainly adamant that China should not benefit from its participation in the war. Mr Acheson and Sir Oliver Franks believed that the differences between the national positions would be reconciled, as they had in previous months[7]. The State Department was more immediately concerned as to what should be done if the armistice negotiations failed or, having succeeded, were used by the Communist side to cover renewed military action. Their initiative prompted further exchanges of ideas between the two capitals[8], latterly with a view to discussions. Mr Morrison, Mr Acheson and M. Schuman, the French Foreign Minister, were due to meet in Washington in the second week of September*. It was arranged that Mr Morrison and Mr Acheson should meet immediately beforehand and that their agenda should include the item 'Korea—next steps with or without armistice'.

At the end of August, amidst the distraction of a growing dispute concerning British oil interests in Iran, Mr Attlee drafted a memorandum to the Cabinet to focus his and their minds on the aim and scope of the Washington and Ottawa meetings.

> 4. The primary object of the talks with Mr Acheson will be for the two Ministers to assure themselves that United States and British policy are substantially in line on major issues; and where there are divergences to reconcile these if possible or find means of minimising their effect. The same applies generally to the tripartite talks also, for, although we do not admit the principle of Anglo-United States-French direction in global strategy (as opposed to purely Atlantic strategy), we must carry the French in most of the major political issues with which we are confronted....
>
> 8. Broadly speaking, I think the Foreign Secretary would be right in saying that His Majesty's Government consider events to have justified the policy

* A periodic tripartite meeting, prior to taking part in a North Atlantic Council in Ottawa. All three had been in San Francisco immediately beforehand as signatories to the Peace Treaty with Japan.

adopted by the West in this period. The policy of building up positions of strength and of offering firm resistance to any threat of aggression has been successful and the Soviet Union has suffered a series of setbacks. Apart from the successful armed resistance in Korea, we have provided the necessary deterrents to any move forward in Germany, Austria or Southern Europe and we have established without let or hindrance an Allied Supreme Command in Europe with additional American and British forces on the ground. We have instituted very substantial measures of rearmament designed to maintain the deterrent effect of the Atlantic alliance and we have refused to allow ourselves to be divided or turned from our purpose by Soviet propaganda or by the Peace Campaign or by the perils of the Four-Power talks. These experiences suggest that we should continue to resist encroachments and to build up our strength, but without provocation, and that above all we must remain united.

9. As our confidence and our strength revive, however, two concurrent dangers will have to be watched. The first is the risk that we might overlook or misjudge the reaction of the Soviet Union to some element in our policy which touches a sore spot in their security or around their perimeter. Unless the Western Powers make careful assessments of these risks and agree upon them there will always be a danger that the Soviet Union might be provoked to preventive war or at least to move over to a war economy, while the Western defence preparations are still at an elementary stage. This danger applies particularly to American policy in the Far East, but there are other matters, such as the establishment of air bases near the Soviet borders, which might be equally dangerous. There is, indeed, a risk that, owing to impulsiveness or under the pressure of excitable public opinion, United States policy might go to unreasonable lengths[9].

Ranging over the burden of defence expenditure, European integration, and the Middle East, the Prime Minister expressed his ideas concerning the 'Alignment of United States-United Kingdom Policies in the Far East'.

20. KOREA. The Foreign Secretary will wish to obtain assurances from Mr Acheson on the following lines:-

(a) That the policy of the United States Government is neither to withdraw prematurely nor to extend the war, and that they will continue to keep the South Korean Government firmly under control to prevent them frustrating United Nations policy.

(b) That the United States and United Kingdom Governments shall consult together on further references to the United Nations regarding Korea. We consider that if an armistice is secured the matter should go at a suitable stage initially to the Security Council and then be referred to the [General] Assembly. In the event of no armistice it will be difficult to avoid a general debate in the Assembly in the form of an inquest.

(c) If full-scale fighting breaks out again Korea, we would still hope that the United States Government would agree with us that the campaign should be confined to Korea and that a general offensive up to the Manchurian border should not be attempted. We should stand more or less on present lines, inflicting maximum loss on the enemy. Should, however, any Chinese offensive against the Kansas line be repulsed with heavy losses and general disorganisation, General Ridgway should have discretion to undertake tactical advances as is thought militarily desirable to follow up the retreating Chinese. Should he wish to make a major advance—such as to advance as far as the 'Northern Waist'—this would require the approval of Governments. If the new enemy offensive included large-scale air raids from points outside Korea, we should support a policy of retaliation. In that case we and the United States would have to reckon with the probability of general war with China, possibly extending to war with Russia.

(d) If all goes well in Korea and the way seems open to a gradual general improvement in the Far East situation, we hope that it will not be blocked by a rigid United States attitude towards the Chinese People's Government. If an armistice is arranged, we trust that the United States Government will agree in principle to sit round a table with representatives of Peking for the next round of talks which, in the first instances, should be confined to Korea. A meeting of representatives of some of the countries contributing aid to the United Nations in Korea, together with the Russians, Chinese, and possibly the North and South Koreans, might be a suitable forum. The ground for this meeting could be prepared by a specially appointed United Nations representative. If, in the view of the majority of the United Nations, a change-over in Chinese representation in the United Nations will contribute to a Far Eastern settlement we hope that the United States Government will accept the majority view. If we succeed in reaching a settlement in Korea we hope to pass on to wider discussions for a general settlement in the Far East. We do not, however, overlook the fact that even if an armistice is arranged we may have to face a prolonged political stalemate on the basis of a divided Korea.

CHINA, INCLUDING REPRESENTATION IN THE UNITED NATIONS

21. GENERAL POLICY. Whilst the United Kingdom and the United States Governments are both building up strength and will resist Chinese interference in the affairs of others, our joint aim should be stability and peace by avoiding interference in Chinese internal affairs, by keeping open the small windows to the West that are still in existence, and by consultation with like minded Governments including Asian Governments, and by the gradual relaxation of tension.

22. FORMOSA [TAIWAN]. The Foreign Secretary will seek an assurance from Mr Acheson that the assistance which the United States Government are giving to Chiang Kai-shek is solely for the purpose of the defence of Formosa and will not be misused for adventures elsewhere, including Burma. A policy of pin-pricking the Chinese is futile and dangerous.

23. CHINESE REPRESENTATION IN THE UNITED NATIONS. Unless there is some major change in the situation (e.g., an extension of the Korean war) we should continue our present flexible policy of voting to postpone the question of Peking's admission into United Nations organs (i.e., the moratorium). If, however, an armistice is secured in Korea, the absence of Peking from the United Nations may be a major stumbling-block in the subsequent

> political discussions. It is too early to decide whether it will be wiser to press for a change-over in Chinese representation in the United Nations before general political discussions, but the United States Government should be made aware that in our view Peking's representation in the United Nations will be an essential condition for a general settlement though we have at present an open mind on whether this change should take place before or after political discussions. It might, for example, be left until after general agreement on the terms of a settlement in Korea and be conditional on such agreement[10].

The memorandum continued on other matters, concluding with the reminder that Britain and France could only exceed their published defence expenditure by adopting a war economy—all else apart 'such a policy might well be to make the Russians follow suit...'

These ideas owed much to a comprehensive reading of the related Foreign Office telegrams and minutes, and of the views of the Chiefs of Staff. The reconciliation of different opinions and the enunciation of policy lines lay with Mr Attlee. It was noted with approval by the Cabinet on 4th September 1951[11]. With this in his private secretary's briefcase, Mr Morrison set off on his travels in North America.

The United States aim was 'To obtain British and French support for the U.S. position with respect to UN courses of action in Korea in case an armistice is successfully negotiated[12]'. The two nations and, as it transpired, France also, were close on objectives*. When he met Mr Morrison on 11th September, Mr Acheson wisely proposed to confine their talk 'to Korea and avoid discussing items such as Formosa and China'. As they proceeded it became evident that Mr Morrison's knowledge of the background was incomplete. He did not understand the composition of the Joint Chiefs of Staff, or know about the sensitivity of aerial targets in the extreme north of Korea. Although he had just come from the signing of the Japanese Peace Treaty, he was unaware that the United Kingdom had concurred in the formation of a Japanese paramilitary police force to supplement the defence of the Japanese islands†, weakened by the despatch of American occupation forces to Korea; and believed from Mr Acheson's remarks that he was proposing to prepare Japanese troops for Korea[13]. These deficiencies reflected adversely on those responsible for briefing the Foreign Secretary. They were in one instance offset by an erroneous statement on the American side[14].

The meeting raised military and political questions[15] which developed in the tripartite discussion—though not through M. Schuman's

---

* For a record of the discussion on Korea at the tripartite meeting, see Ottawa to Foreign Office No 26 of 18th September 1951 in FO 371/92811. This telegram was sent from Ottawa but the meeting had taken place in Washington. However, see Mr Acheson's reflections on this period in his *Korean War*, *cit*, p 127.

† The *Keisatsuyobitai* or National Police Reserve, established during General MacArthur's incumbency.

intervention—and in subsequent communications between Washington and London during the remainder of September and the first part of October.

The former were chiefly concerned with the extent of General Ridgway's authority. In the event that the armistice negotiations failed, there was agreement that he should not permit operations to fall away, leaving the enemy the opportunity to attack at leisure. Rather, he was to increase operational pressure. The Joint Chiefs proposed that he should have the discretion to advance as far as the northern waist, and to mount aerial attacks on the Yalu dams, from which the Chinese now took eighty per cent of the electric power generated, and one of which they used as a main crossing point into Korea. Aircraft engaged in this task would not be permitted to cross the border into the air space of North East China. However, in the event that enemy aircraft mounted air attacks on United Nations forces, especially air bases from airfields inside North East China, he should be permitted to retaliate against those airfields without prior consultation with the United States or any other government of the United Nations allies if he believed that his operational capability was at immediate risk.

Outside Korea, Mr Acheson again pressed the need for a maritime blockade of China by agreement among the allies that none of their ships would carry goods to Chinese ports.

These proposals occasioned considerable tooth-sucking among the British authorities. Gradually, however, they agreed to all but one of them, formally or informally. The Chiefs of Staff recognised on 19th September that, despite their preference for maintaining Kansas and Wyoming as the general defence line,

> should the Chinese for any reason become disorganised and demoralised it would be a pity to tie General Ridgway's hands to the point of preventing him from taking advantage of the situation; in these circumstances an advance by manoeuvre as far as the 'waist'—but definitely not beyond—might well be undertaken[16].

By 26th October, they had also changed their views on retaliatory bombing. In another forum, the Americans had agreed that if Egyptian aircraft should attack British positions in the Canal Zone, the Royal Air Force would retaliate without prior consultation between London and Washington. Thus, it seemed to General Brownjohn, 'neither reasonable nor prudent to continue to needle the Americans over what was really an almost analagous situation in Korea[17]'. This was generally agreed, in part an expression of their 'confidence in the discretion and wisdom of General Ridgway[18]'. However, on 25th October, Mr Attlee's Party lost the general election. Mr Churchill became Prime Minister on the evening of the 26th but immediately there were no ministers to approve the change of policy or otherwise. The Chiefs and Mr Scott at the Foreign Office decided that it would be better 'to shelve the matter for the moment'[19], and so it remained[20].

Ministers, Chiefs, and officials all agreed in September, however, that a maritime blockade beyond the restrictions as to goods was pointless. Short of complete physical interception of shipping, including Russian *bloc* merchantmen, which the United States did not propose, it was futile; a measure which would simply increase the economic dependency of China upon the Soviet Union. To soften the refusal, the Foreign Office, Admiralty, and Board of Trade agreed to review the possibilities of extending cargo restrictions among other nations.

Politically, measures discussed at the Washington meeting fell under two heads: action if armistice talks were successful; action to be taken if they were not.

If successful, it would be necessary to organise a United Nations body to conduct substantive peace talks with China, Russia, and the North Koreans. The composition of the United Nations representation would need careful consideration—the Security Council could not act in the circumstances, the General Assembly would be too large. Britain and France agreed with the United States that these talks should be confined to a Korean settlement involving a united democratic state in the peninsula, though all recognised the difficulties of reaching agreement with the Communists on this matter. Kim Il-sung and his regime had repeatedly shown that they were not willing to test their legitimacy by free and secret ballot.

If armistice terms were not agreed, a full report on the negotiations and the circumstances of failure should be made by General Ridgway to the United Nations, and this would be published. At the same time, the United States planned to enjoin their allies in Korea, and others who had not yet contributed armed forces to operations there, to reinforce the United Nations Command, which Britain and France were ready to support in principle. Both declared that their resources were exhausted. British agreement was also conditional on the fact that further contributions from allied states should not be made at the expense of NATO commitments.

The recruitment to four divisions—75,000 men—of the Japanese Police Reserve was discussed further in London. Suspicions that this was a means of boosting the United Nations forces in Korea fell away as various facts became known. First, they would have been completely unacceptable to the South Korean Government and people; their entry a magnificent propaganda issue for the Communist side. Second, the Japanese Government were opposed to the idea. From April 1952, when the Peace

Treaty restored sovereign power to Japan, the disposal of the force would be absolutely under national control, the only body answerable to the government for defence of the islands. Third, the United States' aim was to transfer progressively the responsibility for that defence from her own to Japanese forces.

Conspiracy theorists have sought to ignore these factors, attributing dark motives to America's enthusiasm for a potentially military Japanese force, but Washington had nothing to hide. If it was acceptable to raise German forces in Europe for NATO, as was then inevitable, it would have been acceptable to raise Japanese forces to serve the United Nations in the Far East. As it was, for the reasons manifested, the men concerned were never prepared for such a contingency. In September, those recruited were equipped with small arms and rocket launchers. A further six months training was required to prepare them for infantry capabilities, and no arrangements were in hand for the formation supporting arms[21]. The British government was content with the arrangement but hoped to obscure it 'to avoid any further provocation to Russia'. On hearing this at a Washington meeting, Dean Rusk remarked that 'almost everything we did these days was or could be regarded by Russia as provocation...Russia would not be prevented by the facts from claiming that she was menaced[22]'.

The substance of all these discussions was relayed to the Commonwealth participants in the Korean war by the Commonwealth Relations Office, though the Australians—and in part the Canadians—were informed of them directly by the State Department. The Canadians protested that they should be advised directly on all such matters. Nevertheless, all were in general agreement with the British policy lines[23]. Mr Casey* was uneasy about the arming of the Japanese Police Reserve but accepted it, apprehending that opposition might lead to increased pressure on Australia to reinforce its contingent in Korea[24].

These agreements formed the basis on which the new British government carried forward its part in the Korean war. However, just as it formed, the armistice negotiations began again—not at Kaesong but in Panmunjom, a village to the south west.

Having suspended the talks on 24th August on the complaint of security breaches in the neutral zone—some at least of which were certainly rigged—the Communist side proposed reactivation on 19th September† [25]. The Joint Chiefs of Staff were now ready to press General

---

* Rt Hon Richard Gardiner Casey (later, Lord Casey) (1890–1976), Australian diplomat and politician, had served as a member of the British War Cabinet, 1942–43, and as Governor of Bengal, 1944–46. In 1951 he became Minister for External Affairs in Mr Menzies' Government.

† The reason given was that the United Nations had admitted and regretted aerial attack in the Kaesong zone on 10th September 1951.

Ridgway's wish to remove the meeting site from Kaesong, proposing that this should be the first item for discussion when the talks resumed. But Ridgway believed that this would provide further opportunity to delay progress on the main issue, a cease fire, and insisted that the change should be negotiated between the liaison officers and endorsed by the respective Commanders-in-Chief prior to the return of the delegations. It was a wise and successful decision. The site transferred to Panmunjom, a small village south west of Kaesong, though the latter continued to be the Communist delegation's base. The greater part of the new, tented, conference centre was put in place by United States Army engineers on 24th October. The security of the United Nations representatives and freedom of movement to and from their base at Munsan-ni was thereby enhanced, their dependence on North Korean or Chinese facilities terminated. To reduce the danger of inadvertent attack by either side, American barrage balloons and searchlights physically marked the area.

The first subject of discussion on 25th October was Item 2 of the agenda: Establishment of a demilitarised zone as a basic condition for the cessation of hostilities. The essential task was to mark a median line. The sub-committee which had met previously to resolve Item 1, Major-Generals Lee Sang-cho and Hsieh Fang of the North Korean and Chinese armies, Major-General Hodes and Rear-Admiral Burke from the United States, discussed the matter.

Each side had similar requirements: militarily, to occupy ground of prime defensibility; politically, to accomplish its original objective. Yet the emphases differed. General Ridgway was primarily concerned with defensibility and used such latitude as he had to press for the best military option. The Joint Chiefs recognised the factor but were eager for a settlement to satisfy the political end; likewise the State Department. They misled themselves, perhaps, in believing that the outstanding three items on the agenda would be resolved in a matter of days.

On the Communist side, the political goal was paramount; territory was of importance only in so far as it contributed to that end. This was exemplified in the weeks of argument which followed, when the principal locality of contention was the city of Kaesong*, which had all but fallen to the United States I Corps immediately before the armistice talks were proposed. In this, as in all claims to territory, the authorities in Washington were inhibited by two apprehensions: that the Communists would revert to insistence on the 38th Parallel as the line of demarcation; and that the American public was growing impatient of delay due to bargaining for a few acres of ground.

---

* The possession of Kaesong offered depth to the defence of Seoul. To all Koreans it was of high importance as the ancient capital city. Prior to the war, it had lain inside the Republic of Korea and President Syngman Rhee had pressed his American ally for its return.

Ignorance of the details explains public attitudes but not those in positions enjoying access to full information. If the Communists had returned to arguing for the Parallel as the demarcation line, they would by implication have conceded Kaesong, and probably vexed American popular opinion. In the event, impatience in Washington, rather than public pressure, gave the city to North Korea in the interests of progress.

The principle finally adopted was that the line should be the line of contact, the central thread of a four kilometre zone separating the fighting units. But at what date? the UN Commander-in-Chief asked. If the present line was to be regarded as immovable, they would be imposing a *de facto* cease fire. At least, the Communists would be able to spin out the talks indefinitely. If so minded, they would be able to thin out their defensive line to concentrate numbers for a renewed offensive. General Ridgway and his representatives insisted that the line should be that held at the conclusion of the negotiations. This would offer General Ridgway the opportunity to exert military pressure for completion of the agenda.

Sitting in the conference tent day by day for long hours, the United Nations delegates spent each evening in exhaustive discussion before the evening signal reporting their account of the latest session and General Ridgway's own conclusions was sent to Washington. Briefing arrangements for the next session were completed on the following morning.

The State and Defense Departments' meeting on 12th November is revelatory in several aspects.

> GENERAL BRADLEY : ...on Korea. The position the Commies want to stick on is agreement to a line [as it is] now. We told Ridgway the other day to agree on the present line as a final line if we can get the rest of the points agreed to in a short time. I am damned if I understand why they refuse to put that forward on the basis of say ten days in which to settle the other points.
>
> MR MATTHEWS : We [State Department] agree that the situation is getting dangerous.
>
> GENERAL COLLINS : Why don't we send them a directive out there to do it?
>
> MR MATTHEWS : That would be fine from our point of view.
>
> GENERAL BRADLEY : Why can't we accept the present line of battle as the line as long as we get the rest of the points settled in a short space of time? We are not going anywhere on the ground.
>
> MR JOHNSON [STATE DEPARTMENT] : We agree.

ADMIRAL FECHTELER* : Let's tell him so.

GENERAL BRADLEY : I don't know why we were arguing about Kaesong. It didn't mean anything to us.

GENERAL COLLINS : Well, it was worth something in the form of security to Seoul.

GENERAL BRADLEY : It was certainly not worth taking a chance of a breakdown in the talks. It seems to me that someone ought go over all the telegrams and tell General Ridgway, or give him a directive to accept a line and agree it now if the rest of the points are settled in a reasonable length of time. If they are not, you will have to make adjustments in the line thereafter. The line the Commies are putting forward is better than the one we wanted in October in most respects.

MR NITZE [STATE DEPARTMENT] **:** It is really a question of time. How long should we set the time period for in which the other points must be agreed? If it is a month and then there are minor adjustments in the line that we could both agree to, that would be all right, but we won't be committed to a line after a month is up. You would want an adequate period of time in which to work out the other points.

GENERAL BRADLEY : I don't think a month is too long. What do you think, Joe?

GENERAL COLLINS : It is all right with me.

ADMIRAL FECHTELER : It's all right.

GENERAL COLLINS : I don't believe Ridgway ever did what we suggested.

MR JOHNSON : No, I don't think he did.

GENERAL BRADLEY : He said it would amount to a de facto cease fire.

MR MATTHEWS : It would not stop air action.

GENERAL COLLINS : He takes the point of view that if we agree to a line we could impose on ourselves a limitation of no attack, since we would not send our men out to get killed and then give up territory we had gained. ...Can't we have someone get on this thing right away with the State Department and get something cleared this afternoon?

GENERAL BRADLEY : Charlie [Lieutenant-General Charles H Bolté, Deputy Chief of Army Staff for Operations and Administration] you have the messages. Have you enough guidance? We all think this is as good for a period of time as the green line we [originally] proposed, or better.

---

* Admiral William M Fechteler, USN, succeeded Admiral Sherman as United States Chief of Naval Staff [Chief of Naval Operations] on the death of the latter in mid-summer.

GENERAL COLLINS : I think we should say the President directs him or desires to have it done.

GENERAL BOLTÉ : I'll have a draft down here before you leave this meeting.

GENERAL TWINNING [VICE-CHIEF OF THE AIR FORCE STAFF REPRESENTING GENERAL VANDENBERG] : If you agree on a line, your interdiction won't mean too much since little will be coming to the front.

GENERAL COLLINS : You will have artillery fire.

MR NITZE : Also, if you have a thirty day period they wouldn't know that you weren't going to start the fighting again.

GENERAL COLLINS : The thing to do is to send a directive. The question is whether you use the President's name.

ADMIRAL LALOR [SECRETARY TO THE JOINT CHIEFS] : We can clear it with the president by a despatch.

GENERAL COLLINS : OK.

MR MATTHEWS : We cleared the new date of January 3 for the Churchill meeting by that channel to the President.

GENERAL COLLINS : General Ridgway is a long way from home and carrying a great responsibility and I think we ought to say the President directs it....

GENERAL BRADLEY : If you put the President in you really suggest that the President has stepped in and the Joint Chiefs of Staff do not agree. He knows that every one of our directives is cleared with the President.

GENERAL COLLINS : I think we ought to be strong. We ought to accept some responsibility back here. That is what I am trying to do.

ADMIRAL FECHTELER : We can do that without dragging the President in....

GENERAL BRADLEY : Well, we will get that drafted[26].

Daily conferences no doubt followed each session on the Communist side, though all indications suggest that whatever was decided in Peking with or without advice from P'yongyang was obeyed without demur by the delegation at Panmunjom. It may be that General Hsieh grew personally abusive on instructions in mid-November[27] as the *impasse* persisted. However, on the 17th, after a brief delay in which they sought to resist any further modification of their position, General Hodes and Admiral Burke proposed to adopt the existing line for the term of thirty one days. If the negotiations were not concluded after a month, the line would follow any changes in positions, a proposal accepted with their opponents' rider that any final adjustments must be left until settlement of all other points in the agenda.

On 23rd November, the staff officers attached to the delegations began to trace the line, point by point. At the end of October, there had been some suspicions in Eighth Army headquarters that the enemy, anticipating agreement on Item 2, would attempt to regain those parts of its main line lost during the month[28]. Two limited but intense recovery operations were indeed fought in the period.

The first of these was on Maryang-san on 4th November. Two Chinese regiments launched a ferocious assault on the feature from approach trenches dug towards the Commonwealth line during the previous night. The Norfolks on Kowang-san, the KOSB* on Maryang-san, and the left flank company of 3 RAR on the right hand knoll of that feature, came under heavy shellfire during the afternoon. This intensified on the KOSB at 1600, when shells and mortar bombs were falling into the battalion area at the rate of 6,000 an hour. Company positions were lost to view in smoke and dust. At 1645, the first massed assault was launched. Swathes were cut through the enemy infantry by the divisional and corps artillery. The surviving enemy infantry were repelled by the small arms fire of the KOSB. Thirty minutes or so passed and then a second assault began, and similarly a third, and a fourth. As the action continued into the evening, the remnant of C Company defending the Hinge was withdrawn. The other positions hung on, often resisting their assailants hand to hand. When infantry action and artillery support drove the enemy masses back, Major P F King, the New Zealand supporting battery commander, with his signaller, Gunner Rixon, joined the vital work of carrying forward ammunition, though both had multiple wounds.

Still the Chinese attacks continued. B Company was forced off Point 217 but concentrated on the knoll above. Surrounded there, it forced a passage back about midnight. Private Bill Speakman, who had distinguished himself in the close fighting of the previous eight hours, held the final position with a few comrades before following the company†. Half of Major Robertson-Macleod's D Company held Point 317, from which they driven by overwhelming numbers. Isolated on another site, the other two platoons withdrew successfully some hours later. Led by Second-Lieutenant W Purves, they carried their wounded and all their weapons. By this time, 0300 on 5th November, the high points of Maryang-san had been lost, including the 3 RAR position despite an earlier successful counter-attack. The KOSB casualties were seven killed, eighty seven wounded, forty four missing. They had not relinquished the position

---

* Commanded by Lieutenant-Colonel D H Tadman, OBE. Lieutenant-Colonel Macdonald had taken command of 28th Commonwealth Brigade on the posting of Brigadier Taylor.

† For this action, he was awarded the Victoria Cross.

lightly. From enemy prisoners, air reconnaissance and patrol reports, it was plain that the Chinese losses exceeded 1,000.

Newly arrived in Korea, 1st Battalion, The Royal Leicestershire Regiment* was passed to 28 Brigade to recapture Point 217, the outlying strong point which had resisted the attacks of the Northumberland Fusiliers. The Leicesters were unable to penetrate its bunkers, reoccupied and reinforced by fire from the height above. On the other side of Point 317, Lieutenant B F Heckenberg led a diversionary attack from 3 RAR to recapture the Baldy feature yet again. Supported by continuous artillery and tank fire, his composite force some thirty strong destroyed the enemy platoon in occupation at a cost of six Australian wounded[29].

For the remainder of the month the Chinese shelled the Commonwealth Division's front for many hours a day, and made attempts to break into a number of sectors. Of these, the heaviest fell on the KSLI the 17th and 18th November. Isolated at times, their wire defences cut open and minefields breached, Colonel Barlow's forward company positions were lost, but quickly recaptured.

To the north east, Hill 395 in the 9th ROK Division sector was strongly contested between 5th and 17th November. The feature was lost and retaken many times. Yet two miles east of Kumsong, the 6th ROK Division succeeded in capturing the enemy outposts to a depth of two miles in the same period.

In sum, during November the Chinese attempted to recover not only ground they rated highly—such as Maryang-san and Hill 395—but also positions, such as those of the KSLI, whose defences appeared to be over-extended, a condition in much of the Commonwealth Division's frontage. Equally, while resisting to the limit of local resources, Chinese army commanders accepted the loss of outpost positions, declining to be drawn out of their main positions.

This is scarcely evidence to substantiate beyond doubt the theory that P'eng Te-huai's operations in November were linked with the bargaining at Panmunjom. Nonetheless, from the completion of demarcation at the end of the month, the enemy abandoned offensive action for the remainder of the winter, apart from the local engagements which arise between two opposing armed bodies *en vedette*.

---

* Commanded by Lieutenant-Colonel G E P Hutchins, DSO.

SOURCE NOTES: Chapter 16

1 Conversation, author with FM Lord Slim.

2 Letter to Lieutenant-General Sir Kenneth McLean, Chief Staff Officer to the Minister of Defence, 26th July 1951 (Slessor papers). See also in FK 1071/ (FO 371 92791) with minute by J H Shattock.

3 DEFE 4/45, COS (51) 124th Meeting.

4 Washington 2419 to FO of 7th August 1951, FK 1022/66 (FO 371 92758).

5 See, for example, DEFE 4/45, COS (51) 120th, item 9, and 124th Meeting, item 3B; also FRUS 1951, *cit*, p 768.

6 Minute of 28th July 1951, FK 1071/745 (FO 371 92791).

7 Conversation, author with Lord Franks.

8 See FRUS 1951, *cit*, pp 831–842, 859–864, 865–868, 877–893.

9 CAB 129/47, CP (51) 239 of 30th August 1951.

10 *Ibid.*

11 CAB 128/20, CM (51) 58, item 1.

12 FRUS 1951, *cit*, p 831.

13 FRUS 1951, *cit*, pp 895–898.

14 See FRUS 1951, *cit*, p 895, fn 7.

15 For the British record and associated discussions, see F1022/25/G, 28 and 29 (FO 371 92064).

16 DEFE 4/47, COS (51) 145th Meeting, item 1.

17 DEFE 4/48, COS (51) 171st Meeting, item 3.

18 See letter of Secretary to COS Committee to R H Scott, Foreign Office of 26th October 1951 in FK 1093/89G (FO 371 92811).

19 *Ibid*, following folios.

20 It was briefly reconsidered in December 1951 but was again shelved on the advice of the Chiefs of Staff F 1022/91G (FO 371 92065).

21 FJ 1022/29/G (FO 371 92529) and FK 1093/85 (FO 371 92811). See also series in FO 371 99473.

22 Washington 1006 to FO of 2nd October 1951 FK 1093/85 (FO 371 92811).

23 *Ibid*, also FK 1093/88—same series—and FK 1022/25G (FO 371 92756).

24 For a summary of Australian reactions in mid-September, 1951, see O'Neill, *op cit,* pp 262–263.

25 For the full text of the proposal, see FRUS 1951, *cit*, pp 923–4.

26 FRUS 1951, *cit*, pp 1122–1124.

27 See Hermes, *op cit*, p 118.

28 *Ibid*, p 119.

29 KOSB War Diary, 3 RAR War Diary, 1 R Leicesters War Diary, and 28 Brigade War Diary with battle report, November 1951. See also O'Neill, *op cit,* volume ii, pp 201–204, MacDonald, *op cit*, Chapter V.

CHAPTER 17

Old problems, new issues

Mr Churchill's return to power was attributed by his political foes to loss of confidence in Mr Attlee's government; specifically, its failure to sustain British interests abroad and to deliver the economic and social benefits at home promised in 1945. Yet, if it is true that elections are not so much won by opposition parties as lost by governments, the electorate cannot have been blind to the fact that the Conservative opposition was led by a man in his seventy-seventh year.

Mr Churchill's vigour and judgement were in question because his personality was a major factor for or against Conservative success. Widely respected abroad, his fund of popularity at home had grown, enriched perhaps, at a time when the Cold War was waxing, by his reputation as a doughty leader in crisis. At any rate, the floating element of the electorate decided in his favour.

With a clear, if modest majority*, Mr Churchill began at the end of October to recall members of his wartime staff—officials, and secretaries—to assist him in leadership of the British Government; one indeed of this circle, General Lord Ismay, becoming a member of his Cabinet as Secretary of State for Commonwealth Relations. Field-Marshal Lord Alexander† was to become Minister of Defence as soon as he could conveniently be withdrawn from office as Governor-General of Canada—Mr Churchill needed no urging to fill the post meantime. Among the Conservative Party in the Commons, Mr Eden‡ returned to his former post as Foreign Secretary.

Some of those who rejoiced at Mr Churchill's reappointment as Prime Minister believed, as the Archbishop of York put it, that he would 'do something to restore Great Britain to the place she once had among the nations'[1]. If this anticipated *inter alia* a more robust foreign policy underpinned by a concomitant increase in defence expenditure, the hope was vain. Mr Churchill had no such intention. He shared his predecessor's view that Stalin menaced western Europe with his enormous armed forces,

---

* In the new House of Commons, the Conservatives had 321 seats, Labour 295, and the Liberals 6.

† Alexander, Harold Rupert Leofric George, 1st Earl, of Tunis (1891–69), Field-Marshal, a commander-in-chief in the Second World War. He had been Governor-General of Canada since 1946.

‡ See Volume I, p 2, fn.

and thus supported Mr Attlee's promised contribution to NATO. Similarly, he believed it was essential to British interests to control the sea communications through the Mediterranean and the Middle East, and to deny victory to Communist arms in Malaya and Korea. Like Mr Attlee, he rued the cost of such policies but believed that they had to be met. If he was intent on adding elements to the armed forces, however, they would have to be paid for by savings elsewhere in the defence budget. The differences between the two prime ministers lay in style rather than policy.

For example, close alliance with the United States—the special relationship—was fundamental to their ideas concerning international security, but whereas Mr Attlee was exact in in his dealings with the American Government, Mr Churchill was indulgent, expecting if he had differences to move the President or his cabinet officers by references to the bonds of the past and their common reponsibilities to the world. Both approaches were effective. Visiting Mr Truman in the new year of 1952, he observed that

> British relations with China were a mere fiction; however, it would be difficult for the United Kingdom to withdraw their recognition now, particularly when armistice talks were going on in Korea[2].

The Korean war was not the focus of Mr Churchill's first speech on defence to the House of Commons in early December. Operations in the Suez Canal Zone and Malaya were of more immediate importance; collectively, they involved some 200,000 British servicemen and police and were solely the responsibility of the United Kingdom[3]. But this did not mean that he was remote from events in Korea. During November, he and Mr Eden were confronted with problems connected with the armistice negotiations, one new, one of longstanding.

Political procedure following an armistice, under discussion throughout the summer with the United States, Commonwealth members, France and other European allies, was still undetermined in the winter. Some body or group would have to represent the United Nations, or at least those members which supported the intervention against a Communist occupation of South Korea, to negotiate a peace settlement in the peninsula. Who should form it? Would its negotiations apply only to Korea? How might North Korea and, by association, Russia and China, be persuaded to agree to the unification of Korea on the basis of free elections?

In November, the Americans raised another aspect of the problem. Sir Oliver Franks sent the the following on 21st November 1951 to Mr Eden, then in Paris for a session of the United Nations General Assembly.

> ... Freeman Matthews and Nitze asked me to see them this afternoon... They said there was some urgency both because the truce negotiations might speed up and because after consulting us they would probably wish to consult certain other countries which had contributed forces in Korea.
>
> 2. ...a truce in Korea would probably be the prelude to a long period during which there would be no political settlement. ... It seemed to them necessary to take some action which would lessen the risk of a truce or armistice being broken by the North Koreans or Chinese during this period. The action they had in mind would also help to make the problems of inspection involved in a truce less difficult to negotiate.
>
> 3. They thought that, at some appropriate moment in connexion with a truce, if it came about, a public statement should be made which in suitable language would make it clear that the breaking of the truce in a major and deliberate way would be the occasion of military action going beyond Korea.
>
> 4. They were consulting us now about their plan to make such a statement at the proper time and they made it clear that the action they contemplated would be air action over the Yalu frontier coupled with a blockade of the China coast. They would hope to do this if it became necessary under the sanction of the United Nations but wished to be able to act with us and others even if a majority could not be got in the United Nations. They said it was not their intention in any public statement to indicate the specific nature of the actions that might be taken outside Korea.
>
> 5. They made it clear that frontier incidents and the like would not be the occasion of such action. What they had in mind and wished to warn against in advance was major action by the enemy in breaking a truce.
>
> 6. On the hypothesis that the truce would continue in being for a considerable time because of the difficulties of a political settlement they added that they thought some American troops perhaps two divisions would have to stay in Korea after a truce for several years. Although the South Korean troops were now much better and promising well they would not be adequate for a considerable period to defend Korea. The Americans very much hoped that we should be willing to leave troops in Korea after a truce and that our influence would be exerted in regard to Commonwealth forces also.
>
> 7. I asked whether the general assumption lying behind these suggestions was that if the truce was broken it would be North Korean and Chinese who would break it. Was it the case that they were not worried about the Russians? The Americans said they were not worrying about the Russians. They assumed that open intervention by the Russians in Korea would constitute a global rather than a regional issue[4].

As there was later to be within the Foreign Office an imputation of deceit by the United States in this proceeding—specifically, that by successive 'multiple bilateral consultations the Americans have succeeded in forcing their will on a reluctant majority[5]'—it would be as well to point out that the State and Defense Departments were following their practice of consulting first with the United Kingdom to sound out and develop their ideas. In particular, Mr Acheson intended initially that the declaration should be made only by the United States and United Kingdom, the principal contributors of forces to the Korean struggle. Thus there was no plan or attempt, as a member of the China and Korean Department alleged, to 'pick off other critics of the scheme one by one[6]'.

'It was becoming evident to the Americans by 16th November that any arrangements for inspection of entry ports after the armistice would be insufficient to prevent a build up of Communist forces by stealth. The Joint Chiefs signalled to General Ridgway on that date, 'State [Department] is exploring possibility of an announcement by participating nations of an Allied agreement which would serve as a deterrent to renewed aggression in Korea. ...[7]'.

The Foreign Office did not care for the idea. The Permanent Under Secretary, Sir William Strang, put this view to Mr Eden:

> ... 3. A public statement as proposed by the Americans some time after the conclusion of an armistice (exactly when is not clear) would have the worst possible effect on the prospects for a settlement. Our attitude at that stage should be conciliatory not threatening. Throughout the Korean war we have made it plain that we wish to limit hostilities to Korea. To threaten military action beyond Korea soon after hostilities are over would be misunderstood by world opinion; and would arouse resentment and suspicion among the Chinese and Russians too.
>
> ...we could however agree that mention might be made in the debates in the United Nations following the conclusion of a truce of the need for a free world to be on its guard to resist any further aggression of a similar kind[8].

When this telegram reached him in Paris, Mr Eden was on the point of travelling on to Rome for a meeting of the North Atlantic Council. Likewise Mr Acheson.

> Mr Acheson asked to see me this evening about Korea [Mr Eden informed the Prime Minister by telegram on 28th November]. The meeting on his side was attended by Lovett*, [General] Bradley and Pace [Army Secretary]. and I was accompanied by the Secretary of State for Air (Lord De L'Isle and Dudley], CAS, VCIGS, and [Air Marshal] Sir William Elliot.
>
> 2. Acheson said that since agreement has now been reached on Item 2 of the armistice negotiations, (the line for the cease fire), the negotiators now have to deal with Item 3, (the question of supervision). On this the American view had originally been that they should hold out for a very strict and complete system of inspection. They had now reached the conclusion that there was little prospect of persuading the Communists to agree to

* Robert A Lovett had succeeded General Marshall as Defense Secretary on 12th September 1951.

supervision strict enough to safeguard the security of the United Nations forces. It was not in the character of a Communist regime to accept inspection on the scale which would be necessary. The Americans therefore considered that it might be necessary to reduce our demands in this respect and the security of the United Nations forces would then demand some other form of safeguard. They had in mind to make a statement, if an armistice were agreed upon, to the effect that a breach of the armistice by the Communist forces would be a very serious matter and make impossible the localisation of the subsequent conflict. In Mr Acheson's words we should make it clear that if the Communists broke the armistice 'we should have to go after them'. In Berlin we were secured against attack not by the forces at our command [there] but by the knowledge that if our forces were attacked this would be regarded as an attack upon the North Atlantic Treaty allies. In Korea if an armistice were agreed upon we should want to reduce our troops there. But having regard to the ability of the Chinese to reinforce in Manchuria [North East China] and North Korea we could only do this if we could command an effective deterrent. If the arrangements for inspection were inadequate to guarantee us against a Communist build up in North Korea we could only be safeguarded by a knowledge on the part of the Communists that 'if they jump on us they will be for it'.

3. [General Bradley's assessment of varying levels of inspection was then set out, followed by these conclusions]

...Even with complete inspection facilities throughout North Korea our forces would not be safe for two reasons; first, because an air threat could be developed north of the Yalu river and second, because we could not demand that the rail communications in North Korea remain in the state of disruption to which our present air offensive had brought them. ...

4. ...Either we must insist on the fullest measure of inspection, (and even this as General Bradley had explained would not be 100 percent effective), or we must admit that the Communists would never agree to such methods—if so we must adopt a policy of taking their good intentions to a certain extent on trust and let it be known that if they should violate the armistice ' no holds would be barred'. By this he had in mind a blockade of China and the bombing of bases in Manchuria and China.

5. In reply to my questions Lovett and Bradley repeated that it could not be part of the armistice terms that the Communists must refrain from repairing the rail communications and airfields in North Korea.

6. Mr Acheson then said that General Ridgway should, of course, begin on Item 3 by trying to obtain the greatest possible measure of inspection. If he could get a degree of inspection which he regarded as adequate for the security of his forces well and good. If, however, he was obliged to retreat from that position, (which he would certainly do slowly), he would want to know whether there was any alternative assurance of security. ...

7. I asked whether it was suggested that these serious consequences would follow minor infringements of the armistice terms. Mr Acheson replied that this was certainly not his idea. The situation would arise only in case of a 'major attack on the forces of the United Nations'. General Bradley

confirmed this. Nor did he mean that any announcement of this kind should be made while the armistice negotiations were in progress; all that was necessary was that General Ridgway should know that he could accept a lesser degree of inspection than he would otherwise require because of the intention to issue (group undeciphered) warning which he had in mind.

8. In further discussion the Americans admitted that the need for a warning of this kind might continue for a very long time. On the other hand once an armistice was signed the likelihood would be that the danger of a violation would fade away. The longer the armistice was in force the more difficult politically would it be for the Communists to renew the war. General Bradley said that in his opinion the Communists would be unlikely to violate the armistice; they had suffered enough in the Korean war and he did not think they would want to begin fighting again at least until the disparity of the force in the area had become a very great temptation. Mr Acheson said that what was required was to make it clear to the Chinese that a renewal of fighting after the armistice this time would be far more serious than their incursion into the Korean war in 1950 and the fact that it could 'be the trigger'.

9. I asked what the Americans wanted us to do. ... They replied that this item would probably come up within the next two or three days and that there might be three or four more days sparring round the subject, after which the moment for decision would arrive. ...

10. ...[Mr Acheson] was doubtful, however, whether it would be possible to bring the United Nations into it.

Nor did he think that the statement should specify in any way what action would follow a breach of the armistice. ...

11. ...The Americans repeated in reply to my question that a blockade of China should be a part of the action. The number of ships entering Chinese ports had doubled in the past year and such a measure would undoubtedly hit the Chinese very hard. ...bombing attacks beyond the Yalu would also undoubtedly be necessary. ... No mention was made of atomic attacks[9].

The American account of this meeting is broadly similar but among points of difference reports that what Mr Acheson had in mind was 'a US-UK statement, or possibly a US declaration supported by the UK'.

Mr Lovett said that Mr Eden should realize that if there was a violation of the truce, our country would be swept with great indignation and the people would want to throw the book at the Communists. He did not think America would be alone in its rage. Mr Eden...was thinking of his own public opinion and wanted to be quite clear as to what it was we wanted to do[10].

This latter point was included in a complementary telegram from the Foreign Secretary to the Prime Minister despatched early on the 29th November[11]. Next day, the Prime Minister took the chair at a special meeting of the Chiefs of Staff committee to consider the British position.

The minutes of this meeting[12] contain several important errors of fact or comprehension. Either the participants had failed to grasp the points made by the Americans, or the secretary failed to make a true record of the proceedings*. Subsequent action indicates the latter. It is probable that the minute takers were overawed by the occasion and muddled by Mr Churchill's tendency to rambling statements, but no-one challenged them. Like as not, no one read them apart from the members of the China and Korea Department in the Foreign Office, who marked their copy with question marks and corrections[13].

Whatever was or was not said at the meeting, both the Foreign Office and the Chiefs of Staff had shifted from their instinctive rejection to acceptance in principle of the American idea. Mr Churchill agreed with them. He endorsed a memorandum handed to him at the Downing Street meeting by Field Marshal Slim proposing immediate discussion between the American and British Chiefs of Staff as to the nature of retaliatory measures, and subsequent consultation between the two governments prior to action 'in the event of Communist treachery'[14]. Australia, Canada, and New Zealand were to be advised of the American proposal.

Mr Eden conveyed the British view in a telegram to Rome on the evening of 30th November to be passed to Mr Acheson if possible before his departure or, 'failing him, Lovett and Bradley'.

> 3. ... We realise, however, that it may prove impossible to get any satisfactory arrangements and that, if the talks are not to be allowed to break down, Ridgway may have to proceed on the assumption that the Communists are acting in good faith. In that event, we agree that on conclusion of an armistice he should report back to the United Nations that it has not been possible to agree on what he considers adequate supervision arrangements, but that, in order to bring hostilities to an end, he has accepted arrangements, the effectiveness of which depend entirely on the *bona fides* of the other side.
>
> 4. We agree that in that event warning statements should be issued about the very serious consequences which would arise from a major breach of the armistice arrangements by the Communists. I do not consider that the warning should be made only by the United States and United Kingdom, nor do I think that a collective statement by the United Nations would be practicable. It seems to me that the statements should be made by...as many as possible of the countries contributing forces. These warnings should be in very general terms and, in our view, should if possible be identical...we might, for example, say that in the event of such a major breach, it might prove impossible to localise hostilities as hitherto. We should of course like to discuss the draft. ...

---

* For example, despite General Bradley's clear statement that 'the Communists would be unlikely to violate the armistice', the first minute remarked '(a). .We felt that the Communists would probably keep the Armistice; the Americans, on the other hand, were pessimistic'.

> 9. I know you will understand that we must inform Canada, Australia and New Zealand of these exchanges* [15].

Mr Acheson did not understand this last point. He and his colleagues had in mind an agreement with the British. Precisely how and when support would be gathered from other bodies or states—preferably those who had contributed armed forces to the United Nations command rather than the United Nations itself had not been considered, though it was expected that the British would, when the time came, settle matters with the Commonwealth countries in this category. Immediately, however, the State and Defense Departments were anxious to confine the discussions. For one thing, they feared that secrecy could not be assured in wider discussions. However, Canada was already in Mr Eden's confidence.

> Yesterday morning in Rome [Sir Pierson Dixon reported on 30th November] Mr Heeney, Secretary-General of the Canadian Ministry of External Affairs, spoke to me about the new American approach to the Korean armistice negotiations. ...he had derived the impression from the [British] Secretary of State that, in consulting us, the Americans assumed that we should be able to reply for Canada and the other Commonwealth countries concerned. Mr Heeney felt sure that the Canadian Government would expect to be directly consulted. ...[16]

By the beginning of December, Australia, Canada, New Zealand, and South Africa had been informed that the device of a post-armistice declaration had been agreed between the United States and Britain, and that a draft was being negotiated which would be discussed with them. Operating finely within the limits of international diplomacy, the Foreign Office did not inform the State Department that they had passed this news to Canberra, Ottawa, Pretoria, and Wellington, as they continued to discuss the principle of doing so over following weeks. Gradually, the Americans came to realise the true situation as Australian and Canadian representatives began to insist on direct consultation, and accepted it, *faute de mieux*[17].

Meantime, there were exchanges between London and Washington on details of the plan. Among military measures following breach of an armistice, the United States had again pressed for a maritime blockade of China. At last, the British produced figures to substantiate their argument that blockade was pointless. These were sent to General Bradley before he left Rome.

> 2. ... No figures are available for [international] shipping engaged in trade with China before February, 1951. At the end of February there were

---

* South Africa was added to this number.

158 ships of all nationalities excluding Soviet bloc engaged in China trade of which 64 were British and 56 Panamanian. At the end of November [1951] there were only 58 ships of which 26 were British and 17 Panamanian. In addition, there were 6 Polish ships engaged in this trade.

3. **TRADE**

United Kingdom exports to China by average monthly values in thousand pounds sterling were

1950	First Quarter	98
	Second "	182
	Third "	479
	Fourth "	436
1951	First Quarter	430
	Second "	250
	Third "	120

Hong Kong exports to China by average monthly values in thousand pounds sterling were:-

1950	First Quarter	5622
	Second "	4109
	Third "	6754
	Fourth "	10409
1951	First Quarter	13748
	Second "	10239
	Third "	5675

The figure for the third quarter of 1951 shows very clearly the effect of the United Nations embargo. These figures include exports by rail or sea to China.

Imports into Hong Kong from all sources during 1949 were at an average monthly rate of £14.3 million. During 1950 at £19.7 million and in September, 1951 at £20.7 million. Much of this increase can be attributed to the general rise in world prices. ...[18]

This data refuted the American belief that much British trade was slipping unchecked into China. They complemented the figures which both governments accepted relating to Soviet *bloc* trade with China, which further disclosed that a greater tonnage of goods travelled by rail from Russia to China than in ships' holds. In any case, it remained the British view that blockade operations attempting to turn back by force Russian merchantmen, possibly under naval escort, might occasion general war.

The blockade lobby in Washington drew off to reconsider its position[19]. Negotiations on the wording of the deterrent declaration continued. On 5th December, Mr Gifford, United States Ambassador in London, was instructed to discuss the following draft with Mr Eden.

We the nations participating in the Korean action support the decision of the Commander-in-Chief of the UN Command to conclude an armistice agreement. We hereby affirm our determination fully and faithfully to carry out the terms of the armistice. We expect that the other parties to the agreement will likewise scrupulously observe its terms.

The task ahead is not an easy one. We will support the efforts of the UN to bring about an equitable settlement in Korea based on the principles which have long been established by the UN, and which call for a united, independent and democratic Korea. We will support the UN in its efforts to assist the people of Korea in repairing the ravages of war.

We declare again our faith in the principles and purposes of the UN, our consciousness of our continuing responsibilities in Korea, our determination in good faith to seek a settlement of the Korean problem, and our resolution that aggression committed again in Korea will bring upon any country whose forces are involved the full retribution without geographic limitation it will in justice have earned[20].

In London, Mr Gifford came to the view that the wording was objectionable. Though two—almost three—paragraphs were of a general nature, the whole ended abruptly in an unmitigated threat. Not surprisingly; this was the authors' intention. A further instruction from Washington instructed the embassy to make it clear to the British that 'the final paragraph refers to China as well as North Korea...North Korea could not unaided, carry out an attack during the period immediately following the armistice[21].'

'This goes much further than the suggestion made by Ministers last week...[22]', Mr Shattock advised the Foreign Secretary on 7th December. He proposed a different conclusion:

We affirm our high resolve that if another act of aggression were to challenge again the principles of the United Nations we should again be united and prompt to resist. Should aggression be committed again in Korea the consequences would be so grave that it might prove impossible to confine hostilities to the peninsula of Korea.

'The US draft is too forthright and our own rather too weak,' Sir William Strang commented to Mr Eden.

This question is going to give us quite a bit of trouble, I fear [the Foreign Secretary responded on 8th December]. The US Ambassador told me last night that he regarded the American formula as too menacing. Hence his wish that our reply should go through him. ... I think we should be unwise to start with our own [text]. We can always move towards Americans; it would not be possible to draw back later[23].

But Sir William persuaded Mr Eden that if the British were to act as partners they must produce their own ideas. Mr Shattock's text—his last substantive contribution to this subject*—provided the basis of an agreement. Washington conceded this form of words for the final sentence:

> Should aggression be committed again in Korea the consequence would be so grave that it would, in all probability, not be possible to confine hostilities within the frontiers in Korea.
>
> In our view [the State Department added] foregoing revised language constitutes plain statement of fact without objectionable tone of ultimatum. To say anything less would in our opinion lack desired deterrent effect on Chinese[24].

As the Joint Chiefs of Staff told Air Chief Marshal Elliot, 'a truce violation must lead to an extension of the war against the China'[25].

The British Cabinet agreed to the revised formula[26]. Mr Eden advised Mr Acheson on 21st December that he would be consulting the four Commonwealth partners, an easier matter now as all had received the text directly from the State Department following acceptance of their association as such[27].

Australia and Canada had not thanked the British Government for keeping them informed about the deterrent declaration. It smacked of the abandoned system of imperial defence in which they were junior partners[28]. Anxious to show goodwill, Lord Ismay proposed an evenhanded policy: if any member of the Commonwealth should be discussing a subject directly with the United States, Britain would stand aside unless invited by either party to join in. Equally Britain, while keeping them informed, would expect her Commonwealth partners to do the same when she was discussing sensitive issues of mutual interest with America. But this was too much for Australia, anxious to strengthen its relationship with the United States. Mr Menzies preferred to deal with each contingency as it arose[29]. The Canadians suspected that such an arrangement would be open to manipulation by the British and American governments. This was a pity. It overlooked the fact that if the British had not told them, neither would have learned of it from the Americans, at any rate at so early a stage of the development. Shamefully, New Zealand's opinion was not sought; her Government was obliged to obtain a copy of Lord Ismay's proposal from Canberra. Disappointed, the Foreign Office agreed to inform the State Department whenever American information was passed to members of the Commonwealth[30].

There remained the problem of persuading India to support the decisions reached; India had a unit, albeit non-combatant, in the Commonwealth Division. Finally, there was the question as to how Pakistan and Ceylon† were to be informed.

---

* He was succeeded as Head of the China and Korea Department by Charles Johnston in December 1951.

† Later restyled Sri Lanka.

The State Department, meantime, decided to widen the range of consultation among its allies in Korea beyond the British Commonwealth group but was aware that, in so doing, secrecy might be jeopardised. Communications to Paris, Ankara, Athens, the Hague and Brussels were deemed to be secure. Those to the Philippines, Thailand, Colombia and Ethiopia were thought to be questionable. For similar reasons, Mr Acheson continued to be opposed to informing India, contributor of a medical unit to the United Nations Command.

It was thus embarrassing to the State Department when security was breached by its own officers. Reuters reported from New York on 12th January 1952 that

> American officials were quoted today as claiming that the United Nations allies in Korea had 'substantially agreed' to back up any Korean armistice with a warning they would take direct military action against China if the agreement were broken.
>
> If and when the warning was issued, and that would not be until an armistice was concluded, American officials were said to be confident it would be given with the backing of the United Nations allies fighting in Korea. This confidence was said to be based on responses so far received to the American proposal.

British and American news correspondents asked the Foreign Office to comment and received this statement, which was notified urgently to Mr Lamb in Peking.

> International consultations have of course been continuing for some time on the next steps to be taken after a Korean armistice. Various possible contingencies have been considered and a wide measure of agreement has been reached. Within this general context there has been discussion of the possibility of a major breach of an armistice agreement, but no commitments have been entered into on the action to be taken in that event[31].

As it happened, the effects of the revelation were minimal. The Soviet Union and China, supported by the international Communist Party press, were already engaged in a periodic campaign to attack United States conduct of the armistice negotiations—among a number of ploys, Mr Vyshinsky attacked United States policy in Korea but failed to attract international interest*. The newspaper disclosure was not taken up in this process. India, hastily informed of the declaration plan, was content to disagree amiably with the concept†. Only one parliamentary question was raised on the subject at Westminster, and that by a pacifist member[32]. Within the alliance, the Americans alone fretted, unnecessarily fearful,

* During the debate (Item 6) 'Measures to combat the threat of a new world war...'of the First Committee in the General Assembly, 12th January 1952., UN A/C.1./SR 487.

† Mr Fenner Brockway (Labour, Eton & Slough) on 29th January 1952.

as it transpired, that public acknowledgement would jeopardise 'whatever possibilities there are of obtaining an armistice agreement...[33]'.

The sensitivities in Washington to every matter that might bear upon a cease fire added to the burdens on General Ridgway and the negotiators at Panmunjom, the more unwelcome because they bore sensitivities of their own. Impatient to conclude the work, they were obliged to explore the possible consequences of every option for progress. At every turn, they apprehended the danger of offering or accepting some measure which, unwittingly would open fatally the agreement to exploitation by the Communist side at a later date. It was a wearisome business.

During December, the Americans' ability to bargain was made more difficult because both Items 3 [arrangements for the cease fire and armistice] and 4 [prisoners of war] were under discussion. There were thus multiple points for consideration, of which one, the inspection of armistice terms, had already prompted the State Department's initiative on the deterrent declaration with the United Kingdom. Even the exchange of data concerning prisoners of war required close scrutiny. Just at a time when the Communist delegation seemed to be ready to bargain on several points, General Ridgway and his team were left without instructions due to prolonged deliberations in Washington[34]. There were other distractions concerning Korea in the capital*. The Joint Chiefs felt it necessary to review in the National Security Council the administration's policy in North East Asia[35].

At the end of January 1952, another avenue was opened at Panmunjom. Sir Oliver Franks reported to London,

> Area of agreement so far reached has hitherto been embodied in sets of broadly worded principles. United Nations Command has recently been endeavouring to expedite preparation of actual text of armistice terms on points so far agreed in a form suitable for embodiment in final armistice agreement.
>
> 2. On Item 3 United Nations Command proposed on January 25th that a committee of staff officers [as distinct from delegates] be set up to resolve outstanding details and initiate joint drafting exercise. United Nations delegation suggested that airfields question could be either discussed concurrently or left on one side for the time being. Among detailed points not covered in general principles which will need to be worked out are lists of countries to provide inspection teams, location of teams, their exact rights and duties and arrangements for their logistic support etc.
>
> 3. On January 27th Communists agreed that staff officers should begin drafting and United Nations produced detailed suggested draft (text has not been received in Washington). ...

* For example, a United States maritime patrol aircraft was shot down by Soviet aircraft over international waters.

> 4. On Item 4 Communists have been pressing for full data regarding 44,000 prisoners not included in list recently handed over although they had been originally notified as captured through the International Red Cross. Of these, 38,000 were found to be former nationals of the Republic of Korea impressed into North Korean forces when most of South Korea was under Communist occupation. Of the remaining 6,000 majority are civilians who, although they were originally placed in prisoners of war camps, were subsequently found to have no military status. United Nations undertook on 72 hours notice to give supplementary data on everyone ever held by United Nations if Communists would provide similar data (e.g. regarding prisoners who died in camp, prisoners inducted into North Korean forces etc.). On January 28th United Nations introduced detailed text on prisoners of war in form suitable for embodying in final armstice agreement and proposed that this should be studied by staff officers. On January 29th Communists agreed to this proposal[36].

The details concerning prisoners indicated a new difficulty. The numbers the Communists admitted holding were far short of the totals they had earlier claimed to have taken. When challenged on this, they counter-challenged the United Nations figures. Determined on complete accuracy, General Ridgway ordered a comprehensive check of those held by the United States and ROK authorities. It was in this process that numbers of South Koreans impressed by the North were discovered, many of whom protested that they wanted to return to their homes in the south on release.

The question thus arose: was the United Nations alliance to send these men to the north forcibly? If not, repatriation would have to be on a voluntary basis. The Communist side agreed that civilians displaced and interned should be released to a region of their choice. Admiral Libby*, negotiating on Item 4, proposed that the origin of military prisoners of war should be judged on the basis of their place of residence, or that, at least, the individual prisoner should be given the option of returning to that place.

Mr Eden responded to Sir Oliver Franks on 2nd February.

> ... I hope that everything possible will now be done on our side to enable the negotiations to proceed smoothly to a finish without further delays or difficulties. With every day's delay at Panmunjom the risk of the general Far Eastern deterioration increases as other causes for tension are injected.
>
> 2. I am, however, concerned at the implication...that the United States Government are not at present ready to consider any compromise on the question of voluntary repatriation of prisoners of war. The difficulties are to some extent of the Americans' own making, e.g. by their action in including the names of South Koreans in the list of prisoners furnished to the

---

* Rear-Admiral Ruthven E Libby USN replaced Rear-Admiral Burke in the negotiating team on 11th December 1951.

International Red Cross. The difficulties which have arisen however must now be faced.

3. ...reclassification of South Koreans may go some way to solve the difficulty. The genuine humanitarian difficulties will however still remain and we are as anxious as the Americans to avoid, if possible, the necessity of sending back to Communist countries any Chinese or Koreans who might elect to remain in the free world. But there is another humanitarian argument much nearer home. The longer the United Nations Command and the Communists argue about the conditions of repatriation the longer United Nations prisoners of war in North Korea continue in detention. It occurs to us that a possible way out of the difficulty might be for the United Nations Command to suggest at Panmunjom that a neutral commission on the analogy of that already agreed for supervision [inspection] purposes under Item 3 might undertake the examination of prisoners of war on both sides to ensure as far as possible that there should be no forced repatriation in violation of humanitarian principles. (This is not necessarily ruled out by Communist rejection of suggestion for screening of prisoners of war by the International Red Cross. ... It is not yet clear however how far this proposal corresponds to one mentioned in press reports today as having been put to the Communists and rejected by them.

4. Above proposal is intended as a constructive attempt to solve what may prove the most difficult problem in the next stage of the armistice negotiations. We have tried to avoid making General Ridgway's task even more difficult and have therefore refrained from making suggestions except where we considered it important. I think however that the negotiations have now reached a stage where I would like to make clear to the United States authorities my sense of urgency[37].

On 8th February, Mr Acheson advised President Truman,

It now appears likely that the prisoners of war issue will shortly become the sole remaining fundamental issue in the Korean armistice negotiations.

This is a question of the utmost gravity...[38]

SOURCE NOTES: Chapter 17

1 Quoted by Gilbert, Martin, *Never Despair, Winston S. Churchill, 1945–1965* (London, 1988) p 649.
2 Prime Minister's visit to the President of the United States, 1952, Third Session, 8th January 1952, CAB 21/3058. For an even more forthright statement of Mr Churchill's view on the position of the Chinese Government, see the offical American account in CFM, lot M-88, box 160, D-5 series USNARS, Washington.
3 *Hansard*, 6th December 1951.
4 Washington 3688 to FO and Paris of 21st November 1951 FK 1022/74 (FO 371 92759). See also FRUS, 1951, *cit*, pp 1156–1158.
5 Minute by Mr Addis of 1st January 1952 on front cover FK 1022/96 (FO 371 92760).
6 *Ibid.*
7 FRUS, 1951, *cit*, pp 1142–1143.
8 FO 1736 to Paris of 22nd November 1951 FK 1022/74G (FO 371 92759).
9 Rome 653 to FO of 29th November 1951 FK 1022/76 (FO 371 92759).
10 FRUS 1951, *cit*, pp 1189–1193. This entry also includes a complete statement of those attending.
11 Rome 654 to FO of 29th November 1951 FK 1022/75 (FO 371 92759).
12 DEFE 4/39 COS (S) (51) 3rd Meeting.
13 See superscriptions on the copy of the minutes in FK 1022/76 (FO 371 92759).
14 The Chiefs had instructed the VCIGS to draft this advice on their behalf FK 1022/78G (FO 371 92759).
15 FO 1099 to Rome and Washington of 30th November 1951 FK 1022/76G (FO 371 92759).
16 Departmental minute of 30th November 1951 FK 1022/79G (FO 371 92759).
17 See series in FK 1022 in FO 371 92759 and 92760.
18 FO 1102 to Rome and Washington of 30th November 1951 FK 1022/76G (FO 371 92759).
19 See further ideas in BJSM ELL 229 of 20th December 1951 to Chiefs of Staff FK 1022/98G, (FO 317 92760); and FRUS 1951, *cit*, p 1352.
20 FRUS 1951, *cit*, pp 1249–1250.
21 Shattock to Tomlinson, 7th December 1951, FK 1022/81G (FO 371 92759 and 92760).
22 Departmental minute of 7th December 1951, FK 1022/85G, (FO 371 92759).
23 *Ibid.*
24 FO 6207 to Washington of 21st December 1951 FK 1022/85G, *ibid* and FO 371 92760.
25 FK 1022/98G, quoted as source note 19, above (FO 371 92760).
26 CAB 128/23 CC (51) 19 Conclusions; also FK 1022/98G, *ibid.*
27 For a modification of the arrangement in June 1952, see FK 1071/287 (FO 371 99575).
28 See, for example, 1071/7 in FO 371 99564, and series in FO 371/92760.
29 For an excellent summary of the Australian position, see O'Neill, *op cit*, Volume I, pp 272–274. Also, McGibbon, Ian, *New Zealand and the Korean War* (Auckland, 1992), Volume I, pp 258–259.
30 FK 1071/15G; also 1071/7, (FO 371 99564).
31 FO 36 to Peking of 12th January 1952 FK 1071/18 (FO 371 99564).
32 High Commission India 147 to CRO of 30th January 1952 FK 1071/39 (FO 371 99565).
33 For example, see FK 1071/36 and FK 1071/45 (FO 371 99565).
34 See, for example, Hermes, *op cit,* p 125–129, and FRUS, 1951, *cit*, pp 1290–1296.
35 NSC 118/1, see FRUS, 1951, *cit*, pp 1349–1352 and immediately following papers.
36 Washington 321 to FO of 29th January 1952 FK 1071/35 (FO 371 99565).
37 FO 669 to Washington of 2nd February 1952 FK 1071/35 (FO 371 99565).
38 FRUS, 1952–54, volume xv, Korea, Part I, p 44.

CHAPTER 18

Prisoners of War

At the end of June 1950, in the opening days of the Korean war, the North Korean People's Army captured substantial numbers of ROK soldiers as they struck across the 38th Parallel. Within a week they made prisoner all those members of the foreign community still in Seoul, including Captain Vyvyan Holt, the British Minister, Commissioner Herbert Lord of the Salvation Army, the Roman Catholic and Protestant bishops, priests and nuns[1]. Shortly afterwards, as the first American soldiers reached the battlefield, some of their number were taken prisoner, including Major John J (Joe) Dunn, Major-General William F Dean, commanding the 24th Division, together with a British journalist, Philip Deane. Thus, by the middle of July 1950 the Communist side had both Korean and American military, and a number of foreign civilians as captives[2].

The tally of captured American soldiers grew as formations of the United States Eighth Army reinforced piecemeal the battle front. These men, like the civilians who joined their columns, were inhumanly treated. Some were murdered within a few hours of being taken, contrary to the policy of the NKPA high command, though that was of little comfort to those being killed. Few of the wounded received medical treatment. Drinking water was often withheld from prisoners in this high summer season so that they drank from the rice paddy fertilised by human ordure. Dysentery and other enteric diseases spread as a consequence. They were rarely fed. The horrific marches to permanent camps continued through the autumn. The diplomatic representatives and Philip Deane joined Commissioner Lord and the others from the Christian missions in Seoul on the Yalu in October; their ages ranged from eighty two years to a nine month old baby. Troops from a variety of units under Major Dunn joined them, survivors of earlier marches. Now on the edge of winter, all wore summer clothing.

They marched for ten to twelve hours a day in chilling temperatures; the adults carried the infants; the stronger members carried or aided the weakest. Individuals who displeased the officer in charge were shot arbitrarily. Sick and wounded who did not die on the road were concentrated in unheated huts—were nailed up into a shanty on one occasion—to die in the frost. Almost one hundred perished—about half the column[3].

When fortunes turned in September 1950, small numbers of United Nations prisoners still distant from the Yalu river were recaptured as the battle swung to the north[4] while, in this manoeuvre, the Eighth Army and X Corps took considerable numbers of the North Korean People's Army*. Some of the latter were former South Korean residents, mostly adolescents but a number were former ROK Army soldiers, all pressed into service during the NKPA's occupation of the south. They did not at once declare their origin for fear of punishment by the ROK Government.

More American and ROK Army prisoners were taken when the Chinese entered operations, the greatest number in the fighting east and south of Kunu-ri[5]. British and Commonwealth prisoners were among those captured in the withdrawal south from Seoul. Almost all captured at this time were taken, to their advantage, by units of the Chinese People's Volunteers.

To their advantage... If a soldier or an aircrew member shot down and obliged to surrender had the choice, he would have been wise to pass into Chinese hands. For while both the CPV and the NKPA had similar official policies concerning the treatment of prisoners, the Chinese were better disciplined and, at the soldiers' level, more humane than the members of the North Korean People's Army†. They marched their prisoner of war columns unrelentingly but not brutally. Where there was severity, deception, and malevolence in their behaviour to prisoners it was used more commonly by political rather than military officers.

Neither the People's Republic of China nor the North Korean Government were signatories to the Geneva Convention. Each shared the view that military forces fighting against the Communist cause were, by definition, war criminals, political sinners. But they were sinners who should be given an opportunity to be brought to repentance by political education to join the struggle against imperialism and the capitalist camp.

The North Korean policy was enunciated to all political officers thus:

> 1. A PW is an enemy subject in our custody. ... Psychological retaliation is prohibited. He must be treated justly and humanely so that he may become convinced of his errors and, eventually, side with us on the common front.
>
> We must confidently carry out the task of demoralising the enemy in order to speed up national unification. At the same time, however, we must further increase our vigilance.
>
> ... If there are any [Korean] PsW who are desirous of serving in our Army, educate them under a special programme. ... Foreign PsW will be sent to PW camps[6].

---

* By 1st October 1951, these totalled approximately 30,000, see EUSAK War Diary, Provost Marshal Section, October 1950 (USNARS, Suitland).

† Private S A Mercer of the Glosters was wounded after surrender by a Chinese soldier but such incidents were exceptional.

The Chinese employed a system developed to turn Chiang Kai-shek's forces captured during the long years of civil war. It was called 'The Lenient Policy'.

> Every prisoner regardless of rank or nationality is to be treated in accordance with our policy of leniency to prisoners of war and escorted to the nearest local headquarters of the [North] Korean People's Army or the Chinese People's Volunteers. He is to be guaranteed:
>
> 1. Security of life.
> 2. Retention of all personal belongings.
> 3. Freedom from ill treatment or abuse.
> 4. Medical care if wounded or ill[7].

These provisions, the Chinese were often to say to their prisoners in Korea, were better than those of the Geneva Convention, but they were not. Pre-eminently, they precluded any intervention by the International Red Cross or a Protecting Power. The categorisation of the captive as a war criminal without exception opened other options to the captor, Chinese or North Korean, of a very different character.

For what would happen if the prisoner did not become a 'progressive', that is, a convert to the captor's political, economic, and social views following 'education'? What if he remained a 'reactionary', declining, as a part of this intransigence, to give military information, or information about his fellow prisoners? The commandant of No 1 Prisoner of War Camp on the Yalu gave a warning familiar to many prisoners of the CPV.

> After capture, prisoners must be friends and no longer adopt a hostile attitude; they must learn repentance and the meaning of peace. They are lucky to be alive after fighting for the capitalists and they should be grateful that they are prisoners of the Chinese and have the chance to study until they go home. ... The Lenient Policy is unchangeable but there must be no sabotage of study. A hostile attitude to study or any attempt to spoil other students' study will be punished. ... If you are friendly to us you will be treated as a friend, but the Lenient Policy has its limitations as regards our enemies* [8].

Punishment was at the discretion of, and to whatever degree was decided by, the captor as a means to coerce 'reactionaries', which included those attempting to escape. Lieutenants H C Cabral and G F B Temple were trussed for three months after recapture by the CPV so that their arm and shoulder joints were dislocated[9]. This was a case of deliberate,

* On 17th July 1952, *The Times* reported that Chou En-lai, Prime Minister and Foreign Minister of the People's Republic of China had made a public statement [on 13th July] that his government recognised the Geneva Convention with certain reservations. 'Prisoners of war who have been convicted as war criminals according to the principles established by the military tribunals of Nuremberg and Tokyo shall not be entitled to the benefits of the Convention.'

selective mistreatment. Whilst the North Korean Government forbade the murder of prisoners, torture to gain information was sanctioned and widely used, notwithstanding formal instructions to the contrary. Captain A H G Gibbon was among British prisoners taken to a North Korean interrogation centre just north of P'yongyang—known among prisoners as 'Pak's Palace', notorious for the brutality of its commandant. Among several forms of torture, bamboo slivers were thrust under Captain Gibbon's fingernails to elicit information about escape attempts in the camp[10]. The author was subjected to the 'water treatment'—a form of suffocation—by a North Korean political officer in P'yongyang a few months later for information concerning two other escapees[11]. At Kangdong camp, known as 'The Caves', prisoners were held in the summer of 1951 by the NKPA in darkness and partially flooded tunnels, in which the sick and wounded were denied treatment. Those who wished to be brought above ground and receive medical aid were required to engage in propaganda against the United States or their own country by making condemnatory broadcasts or written appeals. Lieutenant T E Waters gave instructions to a party of British soldiers to accept these terms, using such guile as they could to minimise their value. Though wounded, he did not feel able to do so himself as the only officer present, and he died in the Caves as a consequence*.

None of these were isolated or exceptional instances of misuse of or cruelty to prisoners of war by the Communist captors. However, the opening of the peace talks in the summer and the resumption of negotiations in the autumn of 1951 had a cumulative effect on the organisation and handling of prisoners. More than half the Americans captured had been killed or had died as prisoners, the greater number in North Korean hands. This was an embarrassment as the Chinese recognised that precise figures for exchange would have at some stage to be supplied. They had earlier boasted of capturing 65,000 prisoners but discovered that they held less than 12,000, of whom numbers were dying of sickness neglected. Towards the end of 1951, all prisoners of the United Nations Command other than Koreans were therefore concentrated in camps run by the CPV†. Within these, there was some degree of stability. Inhuman punishment, retained for a time for 'political' offenders, diminished, finally ceasing with one major exception, the subject of later comment.

---

* Reported to author by Sergeant P J Hoper (Glosters) and others. Lieutenant Waters was awarded the George Cross posthumously for his leadership during this period.

† The camps holding the civilian captives in the Manp'o area remained under North Korean administration until they were released.

The permanent camps gradually expanded under the *General Headquarters Prisoner of War Administration Command (KPA, CPV)*.

As each individual arrived at his allotted site he was required to complete an autobiography by answering questions under various headings, relating to family, including the address of parents or wife, financial status of the subject and his family, social relationships, political partiality, military career, ideas about the Korean War, and impressions of the CPV*. The demand did not surprise the prisoners. All had been ordered to give such details many times.

The penalty for failing to complete a form was immediate arrest and solitary confinement for an indefinite period. All prisoners believed this was too great a penalty to pay for refusal. Though most made false entries other than their names and Service numbers, one British soldier, went so far as to identify himself as:

> No. 1234567 Private Stalin, Joe. Red Army.
> Address: 1, Kremlin Terrace, Moscow.

This was not picked up at many points of movement along the prisoner of war chain because the Chinese lacked sufficient numbers trained in the English language to read all the forms completed at one time by large groups, such as the 29 Brigade columns following the battles of January and April 1951. Less obvious spoofs were even more difficult to detect in these circumstances; but once in a camp the shape and detail of false entries required cunning on the prisoner's part, and a good memory.

Inside the camps, the prisoners became aware that political expediency lay at the heart of everything required of them. They were not simply to obey the regulations because the captor power decreed them as in the German or Japanese camps of the second world war but because they were morally right. Disobedience of any sort, resistance of any sort was morally wrong. Escaping was iniquitous; it manifested a wish to break away from an environment of righteousness. Persuasion of others to disobey or resist or escape was heinous. Obedience was good, cooperation better, subscription to the system best of all.

In the summer of 1951, the majority of British and Commonwealth prisoners were concentrated in Camp 1 at Chongson† on the Yalu river‡. It was a dismal place. The American occupants included men who had been captured in 1950. Morale was low. Numbers had died of wounds or disease; deaths continued. Fusilier Derek Kinne of the

* For the complete questionnaire, see Appendix H. Copies of this were smuggled out by Lieutenant A F Blundell and Sergeant P J Hoper (Glosters).

† The Chinese name was Chiang Song.

‡ Originally titled Camp 3. Earlier groups of British prisoners had been sent to Camp 5 at Pyoktong.

Northumberland Fusiliers was looking out for the other occupants of the camp when,

> Round the corner of a house to my left I saw two men appear; two wretched, gaunt, bearded men, amazingly thin, who carried beween them, on a rough stretcher, a third...dead of starvation and neglect.
>
> They had barely passed me by when I heard a cry from some of our own men.
>
> "The Americans are going by."
>
> I sprang up and ran towards the road, eager to see I knew not what. ... The Americans were taking their daily 'exercise'. Four abreast, this body of men literally tottered along the road; gaunt, bearded men as I had just seen, equally wretched, equally ragged...
>
> I visited the 'hospital' in the old temple after a few days, Here their only comfort was a stoutly timbered floor. But the floor was already saturated with excrement from the many men sick with dysentery who had lain and died upon it; soaked, too, with pus that ran out from their wounds for which there were no proper dressings. The stench from these, the sickly faces of the 'patients', the rags that covered them gave rise to an atmosphere of decay. The Chinese doctor rarely visited them; gave them no medicine to speak of—aspirins for dysentery or beri-beri or anything else when he did. ...[12]

The various companies were separated from one another and forbidden to commingle except for periodic assemblies or special duties. The British took on the work of cleaning up the huts and burial of the dead. The medical officers, Captains Hickey and Patchett, were permitted to work for a time but without medical supplies, and were later dismissed, ostensibly because they were failing to improve the health of the captives*.

The main part of each day was occupied in 'education', that is, political indoctrination, conducted by readings from Communist works, discussions of readings, instruction in the aims and activities of American imperialism—with occasional references to British subservience to it—and the heroic resistance of the Communist powers. It was dull stuff, poorly delivered. The newly arrived British Commonwealth prisoners were even more unresponsive than the Americans.

At an early stage after arrival, attempts were made to enhance the process of education by reorganisation. The following orders issued at the time also disclose that the pupils had not taken their lessons entirely seriously:

---

* Captain (later, Major-General) A M Ferrie, RAMC, former medical officer of 1 RUR was permitted to work with an American medical officer at Pyoktong similarly for a brief time.

A. Disciplinary rules

1. All captured officers and men must correctly understand the Lenient Policy of our Army, observe the directions, and strictly adhere to the disciplinary rules.

2. All captured officers and men shall continue to abide by the study regulations, attend classes at the fixed times, and pay full attention to study. All squads should systematically read the issued reading materials.

3. These materials must be registered and kept in good form. It is absolutely forbidden to lose or damage any of them without justifiable reason.

B. Regulations

4. Every Sunday the squad should hold a daily life criticism meeting to review, in focal points, the carrying out of life and study disciplinary rules and regulations in the past week...

5. Except the serious sick men who have obtained the certificate of the doctor and permission from the platoon leader, (or the instructor), all the rest must attend classes. No pretext should be used for absence.

6. While attending classes everybody must be serious and in orderly manner; should line up to report the number of men present; pay full attention to lectures and taking notes; ask the permission from the instructor before leaving for latrine. The bad behaviours of disobedience, free action, making noises, joking and dozing are strictly forbidden.

7. After lectures the monitors must carefully organise the whole squad for discussion and keep a record of it for reporting to the authority after the meeting.

8. The discussion after lectures should be based upon the main ideas of each lecture. Everybody is allowed to voice his personal opinion frankly and straightforwardly, no matter how it differs from the others. The illegal acts of interrupting other speeches and disturbing the meetings are forbidden.

From the date of promulgation all captured officers and men must get themselves ideologically prepared to observe self consciously and enforce to the letter all provisions stipulated above.

Violators should be punished according to various cases[13].

These instructions made little improvement. Disciplinary action, at this stage principally confined to ordering offenders to engage in public self-criticism*, was failing; it was treated as a joke. The camp political staff were taken aback by their captives' behaviour, shocked to encounter open disinterest in indoctrination, and expectation of medical treatment, clothes, towels, toilet items, food, and shelter with other material benefits

* A procedure favoured in numerous Marxist circles, extensively in Communist Asia. An offender is required to 'confess' personal errors, give assurances that they will not be repeated, and, where appropriate, propose a penalty for the faulty conduct exposed.

and services, yet unready to submit wholly to their captor's requirements. The difficulty was that these officials were using methods successful in China during the victorious march of the People's Liberation Army, and the political hierarchy expected them to work in Korea. Neither headquarters nor camp staffs were able to comprehend that they were addressing men whose ideas concerning human rights were of a different order to those of the peasant population of China.

The interest of the United Nations negotiators at Panmunjom in prisoners of war made it apparent that, sooner or later, their conduct as captors would be scrutinised. In this context, as noted, they needed to keep alive as many of their charges as possible. Severe collective punishment was not therefore a suitable remedy for their problems at Camp No 1. Indeed, on this account, they were on the point of easing conditions in Camp 3, which then consisted mainly of 'reactionaries'.

Consideration of policy led to the view that the majority of the men at Chongson were being influenced secretly by the officers and warrant officers among them, and the British sergeants. If they were removed or dispersed, it was reasoned, the corporals and private soldiers would make progress. Arrangements were in hand during late September and early October 1951 to move the officers and warrant officers to a new location. On 13th October, the camp was bombed by American aircraft*, which may have hastened the process of segregation; part of the prisoners' accommodation was seriously damaged. At any rate, the new officers' camp†, designated No. 2, in the school at Pinch'ong-ni, was not completely ready when the officers from Chongson began to arrive from 18th October. Following their departure, the sergeants were split up among the American companies to inhibit their activities.

It was true that the British senior ranks had exerted influence in Camp 1 in resistance to indoctrination and propaganda stunts. When it was announced that the peace talks had begun, Colonel Carne circulated covertly instructions to suspend escape attempts for the time being‡. When attempts were made to gather signatures in support of a 'peace rally' organised by the Communist International, the officers made it known that they would not subscribe. The great majority of other prisoners also declined.

Segregation and dispersal made no immediate difference: the attitude to political education remained apathetic. Apart from a handful of individuals seeking their own interests and about twenty five bemused

---

* The village straddled the main east-west road running parallel with the Yalu river and was a regular supply route. The guard camp and defensive bunkers indicated military occupation in air photographs.

† Warrant officers were also confined in this camp, and American and Australian NCO aircrew.

‡ Due to the weight of his influence, Colonel Carne was separated from the remaining prisoners shortly after his arrival at Chongson.

by the persistent indoctrination, the great majority continued to resist efforts to use them as political tools. The collective sympathy of the camp may be judged from events on May Day, 1952.

The camp authorities announced that this day, International Labour Day, would be marked by special rations, football matches and other competitions, and a concert. On the experience of similar promises on previous occasions, the prisoners expected to be told the price they must pay for these benefactions. They were to march through the village carrying a number of Red Flags with hammer and sickle emblazoned. All companies declined. A compromise was reached with the abandonment of the flags—a Chinese 'colour party' was eventually placed well ahead of the column for the benefit of the official photographers. If the camp commandant judged this to indicate cooperation, he reckoned without the concert.

> The master of ceremonies chosen by popular accord was Sergeant 'Bill' Sykes of the Glosters ... a true Cockney, armed with a Cockney mother-wit. During the first part of the concert he was in great form, assisted by a 'stooge' in the audience—Keith Godwin, one of the foremost 'reactionaries' with a long jail sentence behind him and much still to come. They began on a note that held a special attraction for us: the use of phrases that marked the declarations of the Chinese and North Korean delegates at Panmunjom. ... Sergeant Sykes would apparently tire of attempting to humour this tedious heckler:
>
> 'We utterly and absolutely reject the unreasonable demands of your sides of the footlights,' he would reply. Or: 'This show is still running owing to the ceaseless efforts of our side and in the face of frivolous demands by your reactionary side'. And so on.
>
> But if this warmed and delighted the audience of prisoners it was too fast for the Chinese interpreters at the back to comprehend. Sitting with other Chinese 'officers' who spoke no English, they strove to catch what was being said in rapid fire dialogue between the two Englishmen. Inevitably, there came a time when they began to understand why some men were hysterical wuith laughter.
>
> 'Tell you what,' said Bill Sykes, 'They tell me Mao Tse-tung died the other day. When he got up to the gates of heaven, he met Saint Peter. "Who are you?" asked Saint Peter.
>
> > "I'm Mao Tse-tung.
> > "Who?"
> > "Mao Tse-tung.
> > "You can't come in here, then.
> > "Why not?
> > "We're not going to the trouble of cooking rice just for one" '
>
> ... As a great shout of laughter rose over this rather poor joke, I saw the interpreter nearest to me go very white and turn to the others translating

what had been said. Their faces became shocked in the instant that I watched them but I saw no more for Sergeant Sykes was continuing.

> 'Poem,' he announced.
> 'They seek him here, they seek him there,
> 'They seek for Mao everywhere.
> 'Should he be shot—or should he be hung?
> 'That demned, elusive Mao Tse-tung'[14].

As the audience expressed their appreciation, Sergeant Sykes was arrested, but the mass of prisoners rose up to support him. The guard company was turned out as they swarmed out into the village street surrounding the political and administrative officers seeking to remove him. Suddenly he was released. Watched by the gathering Chinese soldiers, the prisoners dispersed.

This surprising end may be accounted for by the fact that the Chinese and North Korean Governments were just then engaged in criticising the United Nations Command for shooting prisoners of war in their hands and did not want to find themselves accused of this on the Yalu. Whatever the reason, the sergeants were shortly sent away to form Camp 4.

Subtler methods were next employed in Camp 1 which had proved successful in the development of Camp 5 as a 'progressive' centre. Camp 'clubs' had been in process of forming with the stated aim of providing centres for 'recreational and cultural pursuits'. The latter comprehended the provision of propaganda in less blatant forms. Obligatory study was abandoned. Political officers selected individuals who seemed ripe for subversion—often recommended by 'progressive' prisoners for personal instruction. They would be called in for tutorials, encouraged by minor material benefits such as cigarettes and tea, access to the moderately improving medical facilities. Some were sent to Camp 5. Those cooperating with the captors' political programme thus grew in numbers and the groups they formed, though always in a minority, were more influential. Hard 'reactionaries' were marginalised, taken out of circulation into comfortless confinement or moved to Camp 3. As the months passed, the level of resistance diminished. Frustration, doubt, the tedium of life and apprehension of punishment eroded the prisoners' self-confidence and determination.

The Chinese published accounts of progress—or failure—in the peace talks belatedly in order to manipulate these to their advantage. Time was needed to decided upon the amount of fact to be disclosed, the order of presentation, the nature and form of editorial comment. Sometimes this was prepared locally to be presented by commandants or subordinate political officers to an assembly*, more often as part of the English language text within the run of international propaganda. The prisoners' hopes were raised as the armistice seemed to be in sight—due to the work of the Communist side—and were then dashed as negotiations stalled or were broken off—due it was said to the intransigence or machinations of 'the other side'. News released in this way was confirmed by periodic deliveries of Communist Party newspapers, the British *Daily Worker* among them. Some of the misrepresentation lodged among readers—the notion that 'If it's in the papers it must be true!'— militated in favour of the captors as, offering a glimpse of home, each edition was avidly read.

Frustration and doubt were thus encouraged. It seemed to some prisoners that their own people were taking an unconscionable time to agree a truce and, as settlement came to depend on the release arrangements for prisoners of war, they were disquieted to learn that the offer of a simple exchange had been refused by the United Nations negotiators. In the camps, the Chinese were quick to point out to the British Commonwealth prisoners that the United States—fat, capitalist, power mad America—was keeping them from going home because it did not suit her interests to end the war in Korea. More men came to mistrust their own national government on this account than any other.

These ideas were further fed by the visits of Communist journalists—Michael Shapiro, more effectively, Alan Winnington, of the *Daily Worker*, and an Australian, Wilfred Burchett, correspondent for the French left-wing newspapers *L'Humanité* and *Ce Soir*. The latter two were more influential in their chats to individuals rather than in their occasional talks to the assembled camps, and in accepting letters to families at home which they promised to mail under personal arrangements. They took photographs of individual prisoners to enclose in them. Mr Jack Gaster, a British lawyer and member of the Communist Party, visiting North Korea as a member of the International Association of Democratic Lawyers, was given access to Camps 1 and 5 in March 1952. The London *Daily Worker*† published an account of his observations, which included the following,

> They [the prisoners] get more meat, more fats, and more sugar to eat than anyone in Britain receives from a ration book. ... Their Chinese captors did not ply them with Marxist literature... they did one simple and effective thing. They gave the prisoners copies of the United Nations' Charter and advised them to read it and discuss what it meant. ... [Prisoners] administered their own discipline on a community basis. [If a prisoner was

* A tactic employed at local discretion in Camps 1, 3, and 5 during 1951 and early 1952 was a threat that 'reactionary' prisoners would not be repatriated at the end of the war. It was dropped when the Communists began to insist in truce negotiations on total repatriation of all prisoners without exception.

† Then the official newspaper of the British Communist Party. Its title was later changed to the *Morning Star*.

> brought back after escaping, the offence] was left to the company to deal with by way of extra sanitary duties or punishments of that sort.

Mrs Monica Felton, frequently described in the Communist press as 'an ordinary British housewife' was also chairman of the British National Assembly of Women, affiliated to the Communist front organisation, the Women's International Democratic Federation. Her first visit to North Korea was in May 1951 when she accepted evidence of alleged American and South Korean atrocities—massacre, rape, and torture. She brought back letters to the families of British prisoners of war. Awarded the Stalin Peace Prize in 1952, she journeyed to Moscow to accept it before travelling on to North Korea to visit the Prisoner of War General Headquarters and Camp 5 at Pyoktong. British prisoners were among the 'progressives' at this centre, as she made clear.

> ... I arrived at the prisoner of war camp and walked into the room where half-a-dozen young men were awaiting me.
>
> A tall, handsome young man stepped forward to shake my hand and said, 'My name's C......'
>
> I said, 'You've got your mother's eyes'. I know Mrs C......, a Liverpool woman who, with other mothers, recently asked Mr Churchill to do his best to end the war in Korea.
>
> The young man smiled. 'My mother has the right ideas.' There was a wonderful pride in his voice as he talked of the work his mother is doing in Britain to help bring peace to the world.
>
> Then Corporal S...... told me about his wife in Gloucester and how she organised a meeting in her house of 15 other wives and mothers of prisoners of war.
>
> I wished Mrs S...... could see his smile as he went on: 'I can't imagine my wife holding a meeting—but I suppose we've both changed an awful lot in the last two years. It's great, we've both changed the same way'.
>
> He had read, studied, discussed, and argued—and assured me that never once had the Chinese Volunteers tried to force any idea upon them. ...[15]

The passage of mail was another means of influencing prisoners. Until the latter part of 1951, mail collection and delivery was used as a rare means of marking some political event, more often as a means of disseminating political propaganda by 'progressives'—there was no limit to letters containing peace appeals. Thereafter, among the generality of camps, while incoming letters appeared in batches at random, most prisoners were permitted to send letters home more regularly, at first every two or three months, later at intervals of about a month. However, it became evident to all prisoners that some of their letters did not reach their destinations as, similarly, letters written to them failed to arrive. The Chinese blamed this on the United Nations, either on American bombing of the line of communication or the deliberate destruction of mail. Some men believed this. There was first hand evidence, however, that the Chinese deliberately destroyed some of their mail, outgoing and incoming. In Camp 2, for example, First-Lieutenant Charles [Chuck] Began came upon a pile of outgoing mail on a bonfire while taking a message to the staff offices outside the wire* [16].

Mrs Felton not only brought and collected mail during her visits, thereby adding to the warmth of her reception; she also established an organisation to contact relatives at home as a means to enhance Communist propaganda in the United Kingdom. It was not successful. The object of the ploy could not be concealed; it was betrayed by the political phraseology and methods of her associates. Ninety five per cent of those contacted rejected the contacts.

Still, her work contributed to subversion in the camps. So, too, did the work of a select group of prisoners. Among the British there were four men who had been active members of the Communist Party before the war. Declaring this on capture, they received special treatment, some at a 'peace fighters camp'—Camp 12—set up by the North Koreans in February 1951, in which selected Americans were engaged in political work. One of these men set about recruiting other British soldiers, principally from the 'Bean Camp', a transit camp containing numerous sick and wounded but lacking medical facilities, and the dreadful Camp 9, site of 'The Caves'. At Camp 12, prisoners were issued with fresh clothes, toiletries, cigarettes, reading materials, and books. They ate well three times a day. The medical centre contained drugs and dressings.

The British party with Sergeant Hoper was taken from 'The Caves' to Camp 12. When he queried the propaganda activities its occupants were engaged in, he was told by an American soldier,

> It's no game we're playing here, Sergeant. We don't care if you're Commies or not. We all want to stay alive and the way we're playing it now will keep us that way[17].

Herein lay another stimulus to accept the captor's requirements: survival. Most prisoners had witnessed deaths on the march, and deaths in the camps due to lack of basic necessities. Those who had survived on starvation rations came to recognise that the captor had the power at any time to cut, even to withhold altogether, food. All dreaded becoming sick because medical care was lacking everywhere except in special sites such as Camp 12 and, subsequently, Camp 5. Survival was the first instinct.

---

* On several occasions, mail for Chinese and NKPA prisoners was withheld by the United States PW Camp authorities as a punishment for rioting, but this was openly declared.

Later, from October 1951 when the Communist side reopened the negotiations at Panmunjom, rations improved. Tobacco was issued regularly. The staple diet of sorghum and cabbage was adequate though tasteless. When pork and rice, cigarettes and sugar, were offered as inducements to sign appeals to international peace committees, it needed a stubborn conscience to decline the option.

Fear also militated. While many were not gulled by the persistent attempts to indoctrinate them, they were unwilling to expose themselves to punishment, maintaining their self respect by minimal response to the requirements of the political officers. Even this took courage, for they saw the dreadful consequences meted out to that gallant band of junior NCOs and private soldiers who would not respond, continued to speak out against subversion, to show their contempt for those who had abandoned themselves to it, and to engage in escape attempts. Fusilier Kinne, Lance-Corporal Matthews, a REME gun fitter, and Corporal Godwin of the Glosters were among a group of British and American comrades in Camp 1 confined in 'The Kennels' for many weeks, unable to stand up or stretch out. There were others like them, a greater number still in Camp 3*. Sometimes 'reactionaries' were punished in the open, beaten by fists and staves, or made to stand for hours holding a rock above the head. Trussing up, accomplished with compressed handcuffs and wire, was also manifested. Often it also involved forcing the prisoner's head into a form of hangman's noose which was tightened by the victim's own movement. Throughout 1952, identification of trouble makers and potential escapees was also made easier for the captors by enlargement of the network of informers among the 'progressives'. These were augmented by a small criminal element, initially operating as black marketeers while prisoners still had money secreted upon them. When this option was exhausted, they formed a second, discrete element of the Chinese information network.

On arrival at Camp 2, the officers were rapidly reminded that the rules in force in the mixed ranks camps would continue to militate. Colonel Carne, accepted by officers among all the nationalities at Pinch'ong-ni as their leader, was removed after a rigged trial and kept in solitary confinement, in which he suffered periodic beatings for the remainder of the war. Several other officers, Major Harding and Major Weller of

* Camp 3 was originally a penal camp for 'reactionary' Americans, to which like-minded British Commonwealth prisoners were sent, some from Camp 5 when it was developed as a 'progressive' community, some from Camp 1. It was later filled out by new arrivals but retained a 'reactionary' reputation. British Commonwealth inmates were dispersed to Camps 1 and 5 in August 1952, the sergeants to Camp 4.

the Glosters among them, were similarly isolated though for shorter periods.

The British and American officers convicted at that time, and others later, of 'plotting' in one form or another, were held in makeshift cells in the village. These men, restless and bored, took what opportunities they could to communicate with one another*, by whispers if neighbours, by silent conversations to those next removed, most often on the daily release to a latrine when there were encounters coming and going. On such journeys, they glimpsed strange bearded faces through spyholes in doors or boarded up windows. Communication with them was possible only when guards paused to gossip at a distance as their charges passed. Gradually, it became apparent to the prisoners from the compound that there were others in the village who had never been into a camp.

Without exception these were pilots and other air crew members. Camp 2 was used for the prolonged interrogation of officers and NCOs believed to have specialist knowledge on matters of particular interest to the technical branches of the Chinese and North Korean air forces, and their Russian advisers†.

During the first half of 1952, such prisoners were also surveyed for use in a propaganda campaign. Its aim was to convince the outer world that the United Nations Command was conducting bacteriological operations—'germ warfare'—against the Chinese People's Volunteers, the North Korean People's Army nations.

Following a considerable incidence of typhus during the winter of 1950-51, the North Koreans accused the United States of deliberately spreading the disease. No evidence was presented. The accusation lapsed. On 18th February 1952, Moscow radio refloated the charge of germ warfare. This time, all the agencies had been primed. The diseases alleged to be transmitted had widened. The proposition was taken up at once and sustained not only by China and North Korea but by the Communist sponsored 'peace' organisations and Party agencies throughout the world. 'People's China', a national magazine with English among its many foreign language editions, carried an accusation on 16th March 1952 that American imperialism

> ... unscrupulously violates international conventions and becomes the enemy of human justice by committing the monstrous crime of waging large-scale bacteriological warfare.

---

* Colonel Carne was kept at a distance from all other prisoners and was thus incommunicado.

† Flight-Lieutenant Olaf Bergh, Royal Air Force, was among this number.

Initially, the accusation rested on the basis that the Americans were pursuing the experiments conducted by the Japanese in North East China during the Second World War, but now using Chinese and North Koreans captured during the Korean campaign for field tests*.

'... These are all well known facts,' the Peking People's Daily reported. Not well known enough apparently. Following allegations that anthrax, bubonic plague, and cholera were among the diseases being transmitted, evidence was asked for by governments and press outside the Communist *bloc*. None carrying conviction was provided. The Red Cross and the World Health Organisation proposed to investigate but were not invited. Instead, an 'International Scientific Commission' was asked to conduct an enquiry by the Chinese and North Korean Governments. Dr Joseph Needham FRS was the British member. He accepted the allegations before he left London for China[18]. Mr Jack Gaster, returned from investigating Anglo-American war atrocities with a commission from the International Association of Democratic Lawyers, confirmed the charges at a press conference in London on 23rd April 1952.

The investigators' impartiality was doubted. Moreover, as Professor A V Hill remarked, had the Americans wished to conduct trials of bacteriological warfare, they would not have '...made such fatuous experiments as those described in the [International Scientific Commission's] Report[19]'.

Those controlling the campaign decided that other forms of proof must be manifested. Prisoners of war would be produced to 'confess' to undertaking germ warfare operations. About twenty five pilots, navigators and other aircrew, officers and NCOs, were selected; most were unwilling or unsuitable for the requirement[20]. Attempts were made to 'persuade' Lieutenant-Commander R L Ettinger USN over many months, the first session of which lasted eighty two days[21]. He survived this and defied subsequent endeavours.

Five succumbed after similar pressures were applied to them. A few, temporarily 'brainwashed', may have believed for a time that they had indeed been the agents, witting or unwitting of germ warfare, but others simply gave way for the most obvious reason.

First-Lieutenant Kenneth L Enoch USAF confessed his guilt to international journalists, one of whom was Claude Roy from France.

* The data from these experiments by the Ishii Unit, together with a larger volume of material relating to other medical experiments carried out on human beings by the unit was annexed by the United States in 1945 on the same basis as bacteriological warfare and medical experimental data captured by the Soviet Union, the United States, and Britain from Germany were removed to their respective countries.

Carelessly, the Chinese political officers supervising the conference permitted Enoch to go to the urinal when Roy was there.

> I was in the toilet [Roy recalled] having a pee, and Enoch was next to me, and he said, 'Nothing was true in all that'.
>
> 'Why tell it then?' I asked him.
>
> 'I want to come back home.'
>
> I said, 'Yes, I can understand that; you are in a difficult situation. Listen, I am a journalist, I am a writer, I can re-tell the story you are telling me. Some good may come of it.'
>
> He said, 'Please don't do that!'[22].

The death of Stalin on 5th March 1953 was followed by further improvements in the living circumstances of the United Nations prisoners of war. It was not so much in material terms, though rice succeeded sorghum daily, cigarettes, sugar and toiletries were issued more frequently; rather, there were changes in the attitudes of the political officers, themselves sensitive to changes in the party line on any subject. Some of the persistent restrictions placed on the organisation of worship by Padre Davies, the Glosters' chaplain*, located in Camp 2, were removed by the pretence that they had never existed.

The central propaganda line concerning the prosecution of the war in Korea was further modified. In 1950 and 1951, the United Nations prisoners had been told that 'We are going to sweep you into the sea!' Then, as the line became stabilised, the declaration was modified: 'You will never defeat us!' Finally, in the spring of 1953 came the welcome phrase: 'No matter what you may do, we shall bring about peace in Korea!'

After a period of stalemate at Panmunjom, an exchange of sick and wounded prisoners was agreed, and the armistice talks were resumed. In the camps on the Yalu, limited numbers of inter-camp games were permitted, leading to a Prisoner of War Olympics staged at Pyoktong. Extra rations were provided for the latter. Official photographers and Communist *bloc* journalists and sympathisers were given almost unlimited scope to obtain material for publication. Prisoners were encouraged to write home about the events. Carried along on a wave of hope, few if any among them realised that they were being fittened and fattened for the return to their families and friends.

The authorities in Peking and P'yongyang regarded the United Nations and ROK captives as cannon fodder in the political struggle.

---

* The only other chaplain captured, Father Emil J Kapaun of the United States Army, died in 1950 due to want of medical treatment.

They took the same view of their own men held as prisoner of war in the south.

The Eighth Army had been overwhelmed by the volume of NKPA taken in August and September 1950 following the break out from the Pusan perimeter and the Inch'on landing*. Even so, adequate food, water, and medical facilities were quickly provided. Proper shelter, clothing, and canteen goods were supplied to them before the winter. By this time, also, the regular reporting of each prisoner's identity to the International Red Cross had been instituted and the camps opened to inspection by that body. The requirements of the Geneva Convention had thus been met. Political näiveté, flawed leadership and judgement among the American elements responsible subsequently marginalised these provisions, discredited the United States Government, and strained the United Nations alliance.

The prospect of withdrawal of the Eighth Army in January 1951 and the administrative inconvenience of prisoner of war stockades in the Pusan area led to a relocation plan. All those then held and subsequently taken were to be lodged on a large island, Koje-do, lying immediately south west of Pusan, apart from two groups. These were the sick and wounded in the prisoners' hospital, and those men who asserted that they were former members of the ROK Army.

The bulk of the Chinese prisoners were taken during the Eighth Army's advance to Line Kansas and in the defeat of P'eng's offensive in the late winter and spring of 1951. By the middle of the year, the population of Koje-do was as follows:

Prisoners:	NKPA	130,000
	CPV	20,000
		150,000
Civilians/refugees†		100,000
Native population		118,000

The original plan had provided for a camp—United Nations Command Prisoner of War Camp No 1‡—comprising four major stockades, contained by an inner and outer barbed wire fence. Each was subdivided into eight fenced compounds—thirty two in all. The maximum capacity of living huts, work and recreation centres, cookhouses, ablutions and latrines in a compound was 1,200, providing for a total of 38,400 prisoners. But the number of building sites was restricted. Administrative

* See Volume I, Chapter 7.

† These included North Korean administrators who followed the NKPA into South Korea in 1950, and suspected guerrillas and their families.

‡ To differentiate between the camps on the Yalu and Koje-do, the United Nations Camps are titled 'UNC 1' etc.

offices and living quarters for the camp commandant, staff, and guards, and accommodation for civilians and refugees filled the remaining sheltered ground.

Yet, secure facilities were still required for more than 100,000 prisoners. Extension to distant sites on the island would not only require considerable engineer effort but, no less importantly, would stretch the guard force beyond its capacity*. Further compounds were thus constructed between the four stockades to the point that UNC 1 became one huge complex of compounds continuously joined. Soon, even these were packed to excess[23].

In Pusan, the North Korean prisoners professing to be former members of the ROK Army had provided the leadership of the NKPA compounds. As remarked, they did not move to Koje-do. Leadership for internal administration on arrival there was organised on the basis of the Geneva Convention: the senior officer present represented the officers; other ranks elected their choice by secret ballot†. This was put into effect with the activation of each compound. It suited the prisoners well. Those compounds containing a majority of Koreans who wished to remain in in the south voted for leaders of the same mind. Those in which Communist Party discipline predominated chose a suitable leadership. Similarly, among the Chinese compounds, some contained a majority of men who did not wish to return to Communist rule‡; some were determined to go back. The attitude of the former was encouraged by the appointment of 'trusties' by the camp commandant, mostly former junior officers and military police in the Kuomintang. These men soon exercised 'discriminatory control over food, clothing, fuel and access to medical treatment'[24]. Devotion to the People's Republic of China was expressed as often as not in neighbouring compounds.

In October 1951 the United Nations Command discovered from captured documents and a dissident North Korean that selected men were being sent down from North Korea to become prisoners by surrendering or being captured as opportunity offered¶. Their task was to organise the captives to engage in 'strikes, disorders, and demonstrations'[25], a warning passed to the camp commandant with instructions to be vigilant. However, despite occasional surliness and minor acts of indiscipline—there was an ugly rock fight between compounds on 18th December 1951—the leadership appeared to be

---

* In North Korea, the UN prisoners were secured on the basis of two guards to one prisoner. On Koje-do, there were 48 prisoners to every one guard.

† Articles 79 and 80. The other rank elections were to be held every six months.

‡ The majority of these were men who had been captured by the People's Liberation Army from the Kuomintang forces, and had been converted *en masse* to service in the former. See Volume I, p 198.

¶ The greater number of these were North Koreans but included Chinese from February 1952.

functioning satisfactorily. Indeed, the camp staff believed that the greatest danger was the enmity between compounds of differing political favours. What was not realised was that the 'leaders' in the compounds under Communist control were simply the nominees of powerful but clandestine political committees, themselves part of an overall camp committee.

The importance of this operation to the Communist side is illustrated by the rank and authority of the North Korean sent to take overall control of the NKPA prisoners. Identifying himself as Private Cheon Moon-Il, Service Number 182117 on 'surrender', he was known in the camp as Roh Sun-saeng, but subsequently recognised as Pak Sang-hyon, one of the '43-man team' which had worked under the Russians in North Korea in 1945[26]. With his arrival, control by the North Korean Communist Party was made absolute over about half the NKPA captives.

A situation had thus developed that the minority view in pro- or anti-Communist compounds was suppressed by terror. Searching out of political opponents was a continuing process within the Communist majorities—Korean or Chinese. Those identified as being less than militant supporters were mostly murdered after arraignment before secret 'people's courts' sitting at night. The North Korean party writ extended into the the camp of the civil internees.

Among the interned civilians, Compound 62 refused to be screened in mid-February 1952 to discover whether they wished to return to North Korea after an armistice or remain in the south. It contained a hard core of Party members. They not only refused to submit to screening but attacked the security forces* [27] sent to enforce it with a variety of crude but effective weapons. Seventy seven internees civilians were killed among 200 casualties. The security force lost eighty four, including an American soldier killed. Suddenly, the United States Government realised that it was in danger of being pilloried in an enemy propaganda exercise.

Brigadier-General Francis T Dodd was appointed camp commandant in February 1952—the tenth commandant in fourteen months—to re-establish control in all compounds. The quality of his security force was poor, and short in numbers. *Inter alia*, the ROK Army guards among them were disgruntled because their own rations, supplied wholly by their own authorities, were inferior to those of the prisoners, who, grain apart, were supplied by the Americans. Some of the ROK guards were also violently anti-Communist. None were subject to the disciplinary authority of General Dodd. Prostitutes and publicans, licensed or otherwise, abounded. Men supposed to be on duty were

---

* These included a battalion of the United States 27th Infantry, sent as a temporary reinforcement.

frequently found to be with these women or in the bars, offences rarely punished effectively. Not surprisingly, there was a flow of money to subsidise both trades. It was fed in by the North Koreans. Among the women and traders were couriers for funds, messages, arms and equipment including radios, and lesser fry ready to act as agents to obtain information. The funds were channelled through guerrillas and Communist cells in the Republic of Korea. The manufacture of weapons was abetted unwittingly by the American authorities who provided metal working tools as part of a re-education programme for the prisoners, civil and military*. Punishment of prisoners known to be involved in torture and murder was not open to General Dodd. Whilst the United States accepted all the articles of the Geneva Convention in respect of prisoners of war, she had not ratified it. There was no provision in American law to permit the trial and punishment of enemy nationals held as prisoners. From the end of 1951, however, this was irrelevant; apprehending suspects and witnesses was not within the physical capability of the guard force. They lacked the strength to enter the compounds except for critical occasions, such as the rescue of American officers kidnapped on the perimeters, when they were obliged to open fire†.

Still, the general made some improvements, including warnings to anti-Communist Chinese trusties that they would lose their positions if internal oppression continued. From his investigation of a number of riots and the disorderly conduct of his ROK Army guards‡ [28], he also appears to have believed that by talking directly to the leaders in the Communist compounds he might earn their trust. This was the position at the beginning of April 1952.

By this time, at Panmunjom, the Communist side had agreed to consider the principle that some prisoners might refuse to be repatriated. Unwisely, the UN negotiators floated the notion that of 132,000 North Korean and Chinese military prisoners, about 116,000—a number guessed by the intelligence staff—would wish to return home. When screening was completed in all but seven compounds¶, it was discovered

---

* The re-education programme was part political—lectures were provided for those who wished to attend; there was no compulsion and none complained of—and part technical, for which the tools were supplied.

† For an independent description of conditions in the camp see the report by James Plimsoll on his visit with members of the UNCURK on 21st March 1952.

‡ General Ridgway asked the International Committee of the Red Cross to conduct their own investigation of the most serious of these on 18th February. In this case, the ICRC report did not attempt to adjudicate between the evidence of either captor or captives, but the allegations of the latter concerning forcible screening were more impressive by their detailed articulation than those of the camp commandant.

¶ Of seventeen Communist dominated compounds containing NKPA prisoners, seven refused to be screened. The latter were contiguous. General Ridgway obtained authority from Washington to discontinue attempts to screen them.

that only 70,000 of the total of 170,000 military and civil prisoners would accept repatriation*.

This lower figure surprised the camp staff, General Van Fleet, and General Ridgway, but none were more surprised than the Communist negotiators at Panmunjom or their governments. They denounced the entire exercise. Fortunately, the UN team was able to respond with a reminder that the Communists had repeatedly claimed to be holding 65,000 prisoners but could now produce only 11,599 names.

What none on the United Nations side realised, however, was the extent of control exercised over the Communist dominated compounds on Koje-do. Instructions were sent by radio that riots were to be fomented and plans for a mass break out resuscitated† [29]. These were to be conducted without regard for the loss of life among the prisoners involved.

On the afternoon of 7th May, Brigadier-General Dodd came to the sally port of Compound 76, under North Korean Communist control, in response to a request from it leaders to articulate grievances. In spite of the fact that members of the staff had been manhandled and a few kidnapped previously by prisoners, the general began talking to a group through the unlocked inner gate, though he declined their invitation to enter. When a work detail began to crowd in from the outside, he was seized and dragged in, a prisoner in his own camp.

While reinforcements were summoned, the acting commandant agreed to permit representatives from other compounds to join those in No 76 for a conference. As an example of the underestimation of his prisoners, he called Colonel Lee Hak-koo, a senior NKPA officer to attempt to mediate, and was surprised that he became the mutineers' spokesman as soon as he joined them. A people's court was convened to try General Dodd though, reasonably, Brigadier-General Colson, who had arrived to take charge‡, believed that General Dodd would be kept alive to maintain his value as a hostage.

Temporising while a battalion of the 9th Infantry was on passage to reinforce Koje-do, and the island was ringed by naval coastal craft, General Colson made ready to attack early on 10th May 1952¶. At dawn, the prisoners' committee sent out a list of demands, beginning with

---

* Those opting for repatriation were: 53,900 NKPA 5,100 CPV 3,100 former ROKA 7,200 civilians.

† The North Korean Government appears to have been a victim of its own propaganda in respect of guerrillas available to assist numbers of prisoners escaping to them. P'yongyang refused to believe that the once powerful guerrilla centres had been destroyed. Actually, whilst there were numerous guerrillas in South Korea in 1952, they were scattered survivors, passive except in their roles as couriers and intelligence gatherers.

‡ From his post as chief of staff, I (US) Corps.

¶ General Van Fleet visited Koje-do on the afternoon of 9th May. He had discussed forcible counter-action with General Ridgway and General Mark Clark, commander in-chief designate, both of whom accepted that forcible action might be necessary.

> Immediate ceasing...blood writing, threatening, confinement, mass murdering, gun and machine-gun shooting, using poison gas, germ weapons, experiment object of A-bomb, by your Command. ...

together with the abandonment of voluntary repatriation and screening. Formation of a representative group of NKPA and CPV prisoners was demanded as a preliminary to the interconnection of all compounds to the prisoners.

General Colson declined to accept the accusations of maltreatment and reminded the compound spokesmen that repatriation policy was under negotiation at Panmunjom. But he agreed to a cessation of screening and the representative group being formed after General Dodd's release. Haggling developed. A demand for desks, chairs, duplicating machines, and stationery for use by the representative group was met. Speaking on a telephone passed in to him, General Dodd persuaded General Colson to admit that there had been instances of bloodshed as a final concession to gain his release. On this basis, he was freed at 2130 that evening. His kidnappers had in their hands a signed statement from General Colson which included the words 'I can assure in the future that POW can expect humane treatment. ... I will do all within my power to eliminate further violence and bloodshed[30]'.

Denied access to Koje-do but informed of General Dodd's capture and release, journalists were anxious to discover and publish the circumstances. In Washington, the decision was made that the terms should be released but declared invalid as they were obtained under duress*.

It was now clear that discipline must be established. The anti-Communist compounds were to be moved to the mainland. The remainder would be split up, the Chinese being sent to Cheju-do, the NKPA and civilians to smaller camps, principally on Koje-do. But moving a mass of mutinous men was clearly likely to involve some degree of force. General Clark, the Commander-in-Chief†, and General Van Fleet were anxious that the International Red Cross should be given every chance to see what was being done both by way of the accommodation prepared and the measures adopted to persuade prisoners to move‡. Of the same

* Generals Colson and Dodd were reduced to colonel for their conduct on the recommendation of General Clark. With Brigadier-General Yount, their immediate superior, they were formally reprimanded for failing to see the import of the phrases conceded. See letter from Mr Frank Pace, jr, the United States Secretary to the Army to Senator Richard B Russell, Chairman, Senate Armed Forces Committee, 23rd May 1952, reported in the *New York Times*, 24th May 1952.

† General Ridgway had been selected to succeed General Eisenhower as Supreme Allied Commander, Europe. General Eisenhower was returning to the United States as the Republican presidential nominee. The post of SCAP had lapsed on implementation of the Japanese Peace Treaty but General Clark remained the UN and the United States Commander-in-Chief.

‡ A collection of ICRC prisoner of war camp inspection reports may be found in FK 1553/128 (FO 371 99641).

mind, the Joint Chiefs of Staff in Washington suggested to General Clark on 19th May 1952 another means of maintaining 'solid support of domestic and international opinion'.

> [2] C. Feasibility of 'internationalising' POW guard detachment on Koje by employing representative proportion of UN Forces along with United States in this capacity. Having forces from other UN countries share this responsibility has definite political advantages; however, we recognise that practical considerations in field may be overriding.
>
> 3. We note with approval your careful and thorough approach to this delicate problem. It would be helpful if you continue to keep us fully informed of progress of program[31].

The Netherlands Battalion was sent to Koje as a first step to 'internationalisation' of the disciplinary operation. One company from the Greek Battalion was ordered to join them with a further two companies from the Commonwealth Division. General Cassels received instructions from Lieutenant-General Bridgeford*—Lieutenant-General Robertson's successor—on 23rd May to this end.

On the basis of tactical availability, General Cassels ordered 1 KSLI and 1 RCR to provide the sub-units†. By chance, each commanding officer nominated his B Company. After rapid overnight arrangements, these two sub-units, entitled PETERFORCE collectively, entrained for Pusan on the morning of 24th May[32].

General Bridgeford gave this order without consulting beforehand the Commonwealth Governments; he saw it as an extension of operations in Korea. The selection of a British element did not disturb the British Government or Chiefs, but the inclusion of Canadians nettled Ottawa. Mr Steel warned London on 23rd May that the Canadian Ambassador in Washington, Mr Hume Wrong, had urged the State Department to rescind or suspend the deployment of the Canadian Battalion [sic][33].

By this date, the press had been informed of the international deployments to Koje-do. The Canadians accepted that withdrawal of their company in these circumstances would damage the allied cause at a time when the Soviet Union had joined China and North Korea in publicising and condemning American 'atrocities' on the island. For several weeks, they continued to complain. They relieved the Head of their Military Mission in Tokyo, Brigadier B A Connelly on the grounds that he had not instantly informed the Canadian Government of the deployment, and sought to censure and confine General Bridgeford. The Australian Government did not agree that there had been any breach of the

---

* Bridgeford, Lieutenant-General Sir William, KBE CB MC (1894–1971). After a distinguished career in three wars, he was Chief Executive (1953–1956) of the 1956 Olympic Games in Melbourne.

† 1 RCR had relieved the 2nd Battalion in the preceding month.

Commonwealth agreement on command and control, remarking that they would not have objected if an Australian contingent had been sent to Koje-do. Field-Marshal Slim told the Head of the Australian Defence Mission in London that he would support General Bridgeford '...to the hilt. He simply did what he was sent there to do'[34]. In a minute to the Prime Minister on 25th May, Sir William Strang took the same view adding

> 7. ... There is the further point that the employment of United Kingdom troops to restore order in the prison camps should strengthen our hand should we wish to approach the State Department about the administration of the camps[35].

Amour propre aside, the chief anxiety of the Canadian Government was the reaction of the electorate*. Still, Mr Saint Laurent† and his colleagues were not alone in being brought under pressure by those manipulating their prisoners on Koje-do. Mr Churchill's Government had been criticised by members of the Labour Party concerning events in the UN prisoner of war camps since March[36]. The Communist Party attempted to create a broad and abiding climate of hostility to United States policies in Korea using the Koje incidents as an example of American brutality. Its vehemence fired the ardour of its members and fellow travellers but warmed only briefly and moderately those in the citadels of social democracy and liberalism. Mr Attlee and his colleagues were not prepared to join the propaganda operations of the left wing of the Labour Party let alone the extreme left outside it on this issue. Their disquiet as to what had happened on Koje-do was closer to those of some Conservative members who considered that events would not have got out of hand if the British Army had been in charge. On that basis, they supported the employment of British troops. Drawing aside from the cut and thrust in the Commons on 26th May, Mr Attlee and Mr Chuter Ede sought out the Minister of State at the Foreign Office, Selwyn Lloyd,

> ...to render consternation at the report on the radio that British troops guarding the prisoners-of-war are not allowed to fire. They both pointed out that such a limitation would make it impossible to secure effective control. They both professed themselves as worried about the situation[37].

Meantime, Brigadier-General Haydon L Boatner had been transferred from the United States 2nd Division‡ to command on Koje-

---

* In the event, this was less vexed than politicians anticipated. See, for example, the *Montreal Star* and *Toronto Globe and Mail* of 29th May 1952.

† Saint Laurent, The Rt Hon Louis Stephen, (1882–1973), Prime Minister of Canada, 1948–57, and leader of the Liberal Party, 1948–58.

‡ Of which he was assistant commander.

do. He was a man of considerable moral courage, by no means a blinkered soldier unable to perceive the requirement for restraint of force in so far as this was possible.

Prior to his arrival, work had been set in hand to site and prepare the ground for new, smaller compounds, and the separation of factions. As the construction work was completed in one or another sector, the prisoners concerned were ordered to move. Those under Communist domination resisted but to a lesser extent than had been anticipated. During the waiting period, General Boatner had run several trial operations to enforce the removal of flags showing the hammer and sickle. Infantry detachments, each accompanied by two tanks, entered two compounds; others using tear gas broke into a third. All flags were removed and, incidentally, ninety five prisoners—ten found bound—who wished to remain in South Korea were brought out. There were no casualties on either side.

On 10th June, Colonel Lee Hak-koo was ordered to evacuate the prisoners in Compound 76 in groups of 150. When he refused, American airborne troops broke in, using tear gas, concussion grenades, bayonets and pick helves. After a struggle over two and a half hours, aided latterly by the use of flamethrowers and the appearance of six tanks, resistance was overcome. Thirty one of the NKPA had been killed—some by fellow prisoners pursuing revenge—139 wounded. A substantial armoury of weapons, including petrol bombs, was discovered. An American soldier was speared to death, and fourteen wounded from the 187th Airborne Regimental Combat Team. Seeing this result, Compounds 77 and 78 agreed to move as ordered. Sixteen murdered prisoners were found in Compound 77 after its evacuation.

B Company, 1st Battalion The King's Shropshire Light Infantry under Major D R Bancroft, landed on Koje-do on 25th May 1952 with their Canadian comrades. Their living conditions initially were poor—Koje-do was packed with reinforcing units—washing facilities were crude, recreational facilities non-existent, 'a crazy island of dust, dirt and evil smells'[38]. Self help, complemented by the British Army's capacity for scrounging and infiltrating the sources of whatever resources are to hand, made life tolerable. It was all part of the nomadic life of the soldier. What surprised the Commonwealth soldiers was the character of the permanent guard force, whose American component, living in relative comfort, complained about every facet of their life on the island. As one of the Shropshire Light Infantrymen recalled,

> ...they had no sense of anything but making money on the side or chasing the Korean whores. They hated one another and worst of all they hated the Koreans and the Chinese—the ROK guards just the same as the

> prisoners—they were all slit eyed, treacherous Oriental bastards. And one of the reasons was that they were afraid of them... The only reason they tolerated [the British and Canadians] and the other units from the line was because they knew that they could not handle the prisoners[39].

Ten days after their arrival, the Commonwealth companies were given their first commitment. On alternating days, they were responsible for guarding Compound 66, occupying seven guard towers and seven static posts outside the wire, and providing eight men to patrol between the outer rings of wire. But on the company commander's representations, backed by General Cassels when he visited Koje on 30th May, the British and Canadians also took over internal authority. The range of duties engaged one officer and ninety two other ranks throughout each twenty four hours, almost the entire company.

Internal authority was quickly established, though there was a difficult hour when two buildings, discovered by camp intelligence staff to conceal weapons and escape resources, including money, had to be demolished. Random attempts at disobedience were overcome by a show of force. There were minor disagreements with the camp administration, who were dissuaded from delivering petrol and timber containing ten inch nails for fires, but greater dissatisfaction with roving press correspondents, whose appearance here, as elsewhere, prompted demonstrations by prisoners[40].

On 13th June, compound security came to an end. The two companies were combined with an American battalion to move the 3,600 prisoners in batches to new sites. There was some doubt as to whether the inmates of Compound 66 would comply without force. But the breaking of resistance in Compound 76 on 10th June had persuaded those in 66, as in 77 and 78, to leave their weapons—a cache of knives, hatchets and spears—and obey instructions[41].

Field-Marshal Earl Alexander, the Minister of Defence, visiting the British and Canadians in the following week, found both companies 'in excellent form. It was a great pleasure to see them alert and cheerful in pretty grim surroundings[42].' Brigadier Bogert, the Canadian Brigade Commander, followed him on 7th July, when the anti-Communist compounds were holding a sports meeting*. He was presented with a garland of honour by a North Korean soldier[43]. In these peaceful circumstances, the Commonwealth companies began the journey back to their units in the battle zone next day.

---

* As this event was publicised by the United Nations Command it may have prompted the Chinese to organise the 'Pyoktong Olympic Games' for their own prison camps. Both Chinese and North Koreans followed closely, and frequently reacted to, news items concerning prisoners held in South Korea.

They were not to be replaced from the Commonwealth Division. The transfer of the anti-Communist prisoners to the mainland and the separation and reduction in size of the Communist compounds facilitated control of the latter, though the leadership continued to organise protests and minor riots to the end of the war. But in July, 1952, the end of the war was still a year away.

34. A late sortie by an aircraft of 17th Carrier Air Group, HMS *Theseus*, striking junks moving south with NKPA troops on the west coast, April 1951. (D House)

35. Lieutenant Leonard RN returns to *Theseus* after being shot down into the sea, 1951. (D House)

36. The United States Navy H03S-1 helicopter aboard *Theseus*, piloted by Chief Petty Officer Fridley USN. These aircraft were generously loaned to the British Commonwealth Naval Force by the United States until the Westland Dragonfly was brought into service. (D House)

37. Royal Naval and Royal Marine raiding party assembles to land at Choppeki Point, May 1951. (K Cox)

38. The party moves inshore—just prior to the opening of the action, May 1951. (K Cox)

39. Royal Naval landing party from HMS *Morecombe Bay* recovers a ROK raiding force from islands in the mouth of the Taedong, March 1952. (P D G Turk)

40. As above, the withdrawal. (P D G Turk)

41. *Ocean* (upper works seen top left) and *Bataan* refuelling at sea, June 1952, as Sub-Lieutenant Clapp RN is transferred to the oiler (tanker) by jackstay. Thirteen Royal Fleet Auxiliary tankers were employed in operational waters from 1950–53, together with five store and victualling ships, earning numerous official commendations for their devoted service. (G C David)

42. HMS *Crane* (frigate) negotiating ice between Cho-do and Sok-to, January 1953. (T W Cooper)

43. The anchorage at Cho-do in summer, 1952. (Lieutenant Colonel T Kitcat)

44. The same in winter. (Lieutenant-Colonel T Kitcat)

45. Beached fishing boat used for guerrilla raids and clandestine activities on Paengyong-do, Colonel Davenport's base for TE 95.15. (Lieutenant-Colonel T Kitcat)

46. Assault landing craft of 41 Royal Marine Commando during a raid in the Songjin area, north east Korea, 10th April 1951. (Royal Marines Museum)

47. The same—laying charges to cut the coastal railway. (Royal Marines Museum)

48. The same—the line is severed. (Royal Marines Museum)

SOURCE NOTES: Chapter 18

1 See Volume I, p 58.

2 See Appleman, *op cit,* Chapter VI. Also Deane, Philip, *Captive in Korea*, (London, 1953), Chapter 1, and Dean, William F, *General Dean's Story* (London. 1954), p 25 and following.

3 See, for example, Kenyon, Albert, *Valiant Dust*,(London, 1966), Chapters 9 and 10, and Deane, *op cit,* pp 99–112. Also conversation, author with Lieutenant-Colonel John J Dunn.

4 See, for example, Appleman, *op cit,* pp 64–65.

5 See Volume I, Chapter 12.

6 GHQ, FEC G-2 Sec Bulletin Enemy Documents Issue No 6 of 23rd June 1951 (USNARS, Suitland).

7 Chinese People's Committee for World Peace, *United Nations Prisoners of War in Korea*, (Peking, 1953), p 3.

8 Address to American, Australian, British, Filipino, French, and Turkish prisoners by Commandant, Camp No. 1, 17th August 1951, from notes taken on that occasion by a British prisoner, later passed to the Ministry of Defence.

9 Conversation, author with Major H J Pike. The author also saw the condition of these two officers a few weeks after they were unbound.

10 Conversation, author with Major A H G Gibbon and J B Smith, an American officer in the camp at that time.

11 See *The Edge of the Sword*, *cit*, Chapter 9.

12 Kinne, Derek, *The Wooden Boxes* (London, 1955), pp 64–65.

13 A copy of the orders smuggled out at the end of his captivity by Lieutenant A F Blundell.

14 Kinne, *op cit,* pp 106–7. Also reported to author by numerous former prisoners present, notably Mr R J Panting and Mr C Papworth.

15 Felton, Mrs M, article in *United Nations P.O.W.s in Korea*, (Peking, 1953), p 17; also *That's Why I Went*, (London, 1953).

16 *The Edge of the Sword*, *cit*, p 219. The author was present when First-Lieutenant Began reported this matter.

17 Conversation, author with Serjeant P J Hoper.

18 See *The Daily Worker* (London), 26th April and 8th May 1952. For a commentary on the campaign, see Clews, John, *The Communists' New Weapon—Germ Warfare*, (London, 1953).

19 Clews, *op cit*, Foreword.

20 See, for example, *The Edge of the Sword,cit*, pp 236–238.

21 See *The Korean War*, TV series, *cit*, Programme 5.

22 *Ibid.*

23 Headquarters, 2nd Logistical Command Report, May 1952 (USNARS, Suitland)

24 See FRUS 1952–1954, volume xv, Korea, pp 98–99.

25 For a comprehensive, documented account of this period of preparation, see *The Communist War in POW Camps*, Headquarters, United Nations and Far East Command (Military Intelligence Section, General Staff), 28 January 1953: G2 Section Report, January 1953 (USNARS, Suitland).

26 See Volume I, p 6, fn.

27 For an account of this event, see Hermes, *op cit,* pp 238–239.

28 See, for example, FK 1553/7G, and /11G, (FO 371 99638).

29 For example, see *The Communist War in POW Camps, op cit,* p 19.

30 Statement by Brigadier-General Charles F Colson to a Board of Officers, 12th May 1952. See release to UNCURK in UN A/AC.39/INF.71 of 21 May 1952.

31 FRUS 1952–54, *cit*, p 210.

32 War Diary, 1 COMWEL Div, May, 1952. See also Divisional GO 3 of 241515 I (May 52) in same file.

33 Washington 1033 to FO of 23rd May 1952, FK 1553/16G, (FO 371 99638).

34 For summaries of the different positions, see Grey, *op cit,* pp 153–156, O'Neill, *op cit,* pp 294–296, and Wood, *op cit,* pp 193–195.

35 FK 1553/24, (FO 371 99638).
36 For a selection, see FK 1553 series in FO 371 99638.
37 FK 1553/27, (FO 371 99638).
38 *History of the Corps of the King's Shropshire Light Infantry*, volume iii, (Regimental Publication, 1970), p 303.
39 EMB in conversation with author.
40 Report by the officer commanding the detachment of 1 KSLI, 15 Sep 52, FK 1553/86/G, (FO 371 99640).
41 UNC/FEC Command Report, June 1952 (USNARS, Suitland). Also summary report of operations on Koje-do by B Coy, 1 KSLI, attached to War Diary, and War Diary, B Coy, 1 RCR, May and June 1952.
42 In message relayed to Lieutenant-Colonel V W Barlow.
43 Wood, *op cit*, p 196.

CHAPTER 19

"Without the support of the indiscriminate bombing and bombardment by your air and naval forces your ground forces would have long ago been driven out of the Korean Peninsula..."*

Once the armistice negotiations were established, it became apparent to the flag and general officers in the United Nations Command that the land battle had come to a halt for the foreseeable future. All were reluctant to accept a draw as the likely outcome to the contest. It seemed then to the American air commanders that the war might yet be won by air power alone. Recognising that their carrier aircraft would complement those of the United States Air Force in Korea, and thus tend to follow rather than lead air strategy, the American admirals together with their British colleague, Rear-Admiral Scott-Moncrieff, sought means to increase pressure on the enemy from the sea.

Given air superiority over the whole peninsula, and air supremacy over the greater part of it together with the surrounding waters, and the absence of enemy submarines†, the naval forces were at liberty to go wherever weather and water depth permitted. They comprehended strong carrier, bombardment, patrol and escort elements, and an important amphibious capability. The quality of United Nations seamanship had been demonstrated outstandingly in the landings at Inch'on in September 1950, as in the evacuation of Wonsan and Chinnamp'o later in the year. Mines remained a hazard but counter-measures had contained their spread. Typhoons and winter ice had not halted maritime operations.

The men and the ships were therefore to hand to take on an enemy fleet, or to land a major ground force behind the Chinese and North

---

* Lieutenant-General Nam Il, senior North Korean delegate at Panmunjom, 14th August 1951.

† Although United Nations naval commanders were intermittently apprehensive of attack by Chinese or even Russian submarines, it is now apparent that the Soviet Union took pains to keep her naval units well clear of Korean waters—see Volume I, p 85, and Weathersby, *New Evidence from the Russian Archives*, pp 26–27, and Volkogonov, conversation with author. The North Koreans had no operational submarine capability at this time.

Korean lines. But no fleet threatened; and strategic operations ashore were in abeyance.

Still, three important functions remained to Admiral Joy and his command: threatening the enemy coasts; coastal blockade; and participation in land and air operations. Underlying these capabilities were complementary tasks, some arising necessarily in the course of prime duties—securing and policing the coastal supply lines, for example—and air sea rescue. Others overtook them, most unexpectedly the role of guardian and mentor to various clandestine operations.

While expecting that the naval forces would threaten the enemy coasts, Admiral Joy's land and air colleagues do not appear to have recognised for many months that this general responsibility would make an important contribution to the United Nations strategy. Yet it was successful beyond all expectations, and at very little cost.

From the summer of 1951, P'eng Te-huai maintained a strong force in north central Korea to counter United Nations landings, increasing the provisions to this end in the winter of 1952. The brilliant success of the Inch'on landings in September 1950 had impressed him deeply. To a greater or lesser extent he expected a repeat performance in the area of Chinnamp'o almost to the end of the war, though he was ready for an attempt on either coast. As observed earlier, he went so far as to maintain a mobile reserve to counter United Nations landings from the sea during the Fifth Phase Offensive. Thereafter, he relied upon his reserve armies to secure his coastal flanks, but was obliged to slant their deployment to meet the commitment. Otherwise, lacking any naval resources of his own, he remitted coastal enterprise and seaward defence to the North Korean People's Army.

Kim was delighted to undertake these independent roles; his influence in operations was otherwise marginal. The NKPA representatives in the joint headquarters at Shenyang made much of them, and reported the defeat of numerous United Nations landings during the latter half of 1951 and throughout 1952, claims which greatly exaggerated the reality* as the Chinese suspected. Even so, the accounts ensured that the senior partner did not lose sight of the United Nations sea power.

Then, at the end of November 1952, following a series of minor tactical but nonetheless bloody struggles with the Eighth Army in preceding weeks—the Shangamling campaign—the Central Military Commission in Peking discussed the outcome and drew what seemed to them an important conclusion. Many casualties on either side and the consumption of huge quantities of ammunition for a handful of mountain

* Several feint landings were made by American forces on the east coast, and a greater number on the west coast by the Royal Navy including ships' Royal Marine detachments during 1951–52.

tops demonstrated that the defence line was relatively immovable. Tu P'ing noted,

> ...the American [sic] forces on the frontal battlefield found themselves at an impasse, and had no tricks left worth playing. But the United States Government still would not face up to it and throw in the towel, and had fantasies of pulling off the miracle of another Inch'on landing. At this time Commander P'eng was in Peking in charge of day-to-day work. In a telegram which he sent to the leading comrades of the Volunteer Army on 23rd November 1952, he pointed out: we should immediately set about carrying out anti-landing preparation work to guard against enemy landings on our flanks next spring to tie in with a frontal offensive.
>
> In the first ten days of December, Chairman Mao, when he was having a meeting with the acting commander of the Volunteer Army, Teng Hua, was definite that the enemy would land on the western coast, and asked the Volunteer Army to draw up its own plan of action on the basis of this assessment.
>
> On 20th December [1952], the Party Central Committee sent instructions to the Volunteer Army to make ready all the necessary conditions for decisively crushing the enemy's venture of a landing operation and winning an even greater victory in the war[1].'

The West Coast Forces Combined Headquarters was to be reorganised and reinforced. Almost a quarter of a million troops were deployed in readiness to repel an amphibious operation which the United Nations had neither the inclination nor the means to mount. This was the achievement of occasional feints by allied warships; a strategic contribution of the first rank.

The enemy's perception of United Nations naval supremacy was dilated by the range and continuity of the other maritime operations.

Task Force 95 remained the standing authority for these activities, but from April 1951, the organisation was rationalized. Control of all naval operations fell to the flag of the American 7th Fleet. The chain of responsibility then ran as follows:

VICE-ADMIRAL H M MARTIN, USN [COMMANDER, 7TH FLEET, TASK FORCE 70]

- **TASK FORCE 77**
  - CARRIER DIVISION 3
  - ESCORT FORCES
- **TASK FORCE 92** — *Captain J M P Wright, USN*
  - SERVICE FORCE UNITS
- **TASK FORCE 95** — *Rear-Admiral A Smith, USN*
  - **TASK GROUP 95.1** — *Rear-Admiral A Scott-Moncrieff* RN [FO2IC]
    - WEST COAST
      - **TASK ELEMENT 95.10** — Task force base & administration
      - **TE 95.11** — Carrier
      - **TE 95.12** — Blockade
      - **TE 95.13** — Base: UK Frigates
  - **TG 95.2** *EastCoast*
  - **TG 95.5** *US Frigates*
  - **TG 95.6** *Minesweepers*
  - **TG 95.7** *ROK Navy*

To these were added *TG 95.14* a Bombardment Group, formed as required, and later *TG 95.15*, Islands Defence.

This arrangement had long been sought by Admiral Struble during his tenure as commander, Task Force 70. Within a few days of succeeding him on 28th March 1951, Vice-Admiral Martin was the beneficiary. Thereafter, as he attached or detached elements of the 7th Fleet to Korean operations, they remained under his command. His communications links with the other Korean Task Forces* and, no less importantly, with the Eighth Army and Fifth Air Force Headquarters, were simplified. In his absence in other waters†, his agent for Korean operations was Commander, Task Force 95.

On the west coast, Admiral Scott-Moncrieff continued his predecessor's practice of maintaining the blockade to the limit of his capabilities with a cruiser and a mixed force of Australian, British, Canadian, and New Zealand destroyers and frigates augmented by a Netherlands destroyer, Colombian and French frigates. These formed a Task Element [TE] under the senior officer on station, most frequently the cruiser commanding officer. The single light carrier of the Royal Navy disposed an air element in Admiral Scott-Moncrieff's Task Group 95.1, and occasionally assumed command of the blockade force as a matter of convenience.

Maintaining balanced forces in operations continued to require fine judgements in organisation and management; the numbers and types of units were barely sufficient to meet the demands. On average, each warship was at sea for twenty four days continuously—eighteen days on station, six days on passage to and from the base at Sasebo‡. Between times, ships were engaged for a total of twelve days in harbour in maintenance and reserve.

Finding a relief for the carrier, however, was beyond the resources of the Royal Navy in the Far East. Interim cover was provided by HMAS *Sydney* (Captain D H Harries CBE RA), and, successively, the United States Navy¶.

Maintaining watches, intermittently at action stations, often in heavy weather, periodically in sub-Arctic temperatures, made heavy demands on ships' companies. Time in harbour permitted a full rest each

---

* The amphibious group, submarine and anti-submarine forces remained directly under Admiral Joy.

† For example, the East and South China Seas, and the Taiwan Strait in which he was responsible to the United States naval commander-in-chief, Pacific Ocean [CINCPAC] at Pearl Harbour.

‡ Operations kept the Colombian frigate *Almirante Padilla* [Lieutenant-Commander J C Reyes Canal] at sea for 52 days during November and December 1951.

¶ The light carrier *Bataan* (Captain E Neale USN)—not to be confused with the Royal Australian destroyer of that name,and the escort carriers: *Sicily* (Captain J S Thach) USN, *Badoeng Strait* (Captain R L Johnson USN) *Rendova* (Captain E Fickling USN).

night and access by roster to local leave. Disciplinary cases were fractional. The numbers reporting sick were light.

During the first eight months of the war, attempts to run merchantmen to and from North Korean ports were negligible. The principal object of blockade, consequently, was the denial of sea infiltration routes to NKPA saboteurs and spies seeking to slip into the Republic of Korea. On the west coast this involved the regulation and inspection of numerous fishing fleets, and sampans involved in the transport of grain and livestock on which the local people in the spread of islands depended. Light patrol and amphibious craft of the ROK Navy were used by the blockade task group commander for much of this work.

However, the difficulty of communicating with fishermen, longshoremen and ROK naval crews persisted. A number of Korean officers and interpreters could read and write an elementary form of English, but few could engage in conversation. The ROKN liaison officer attached to HMS *Kenya* in April 1951 exemplifies the problem in a letter to her executive officer.

> Since I come to HMS Kenya I am sorry that always as I could not work fully.
> I am an imperfect English to speaking to hearing and to reading now, so hard to understand as everything.
>
> This morning a officer came to my room and he said me that perhaps you will go ashore today, you must wait always with you already.
>
> So I waited in my room with my all ready for a long time but nobody come to me for information.
>
> I didn't know that I must go to the ROK PF 62 and so I missed that ship.
>
> I think I am sorry.
>
> Would you kindly help for me? If you do help soon I shall become very well English and I shall can help to you more. I think so that.
>
> Goodbye.
>
> Yrs[2].

No doubt the author of this note was no less frustrated than his British allies. Rapid language courses were scarcely solving the problem. Attempts by the British to master Korean were even less successful. However, signs and experience in the usage of key words gradually developed a *lingua franca*, in which some members of the lower deck were particularly successful.

This same Korean naval officer may have been fortunate to have missed embarkation on *PF 62*. With a small landing party from *Kenya* and an officer from HMAS *Warramunga* (Captain O H Becher, DSO DSC

RAN), the ROK light frigate was steaming towards the island of Sinmi-do in the Yalu gulf on 11th April 1951, accompanied by three patrol craft. A report had been received that a Chinese or North Korean MiG 15 had crashed in the area and the aim was to find the pilot and any pieces of the aircraft.

Meantime, quite unknown to Captain Brock, officer in tactical command of the area in the *Kenya*, nineteen ROK soldiers under a senior private had parachuted on to Sinmi-do on the night 10th/11th April to discover whether it was occupied—there had been persistent rumours that a North Korean division was preparing to land there. They clashed with North Korean police and militia, capturing five before they withdrew over mud flats to an adjacent unoccupied island.

Over the next few days, under a recurrent threat of four North Korean Yak 9 fighters, Captain Brock's commitments multiplied. A rising wind and sea hindered the search of Sinmi-do and its environs for the reported MiG remains. Signs of distress from people on the neighbouring island—the parachutists—required investigation. An air-sea rescue facility was requested by the Fifth Air Force to cover a B-29 raid on the western Yalu bridges.

Amethyst (Commander P E Fanshawe RN), *Nootka* (Commander A B F Fraser-Harris DSC CD RCN), and *Warramunga* undertook the latter task. *Comus* (Lieutenant-Commander R A M Hennessy RN) joined *Kenya* as a reserve. A naval landing party searched Sinmi-do and the islands round about and found the ROK soldiers and their prisoners but nothing else. An American naval tug and a tank landing ship—grossly overladen with drums of aviation fuel on its upper deck due to signal muddles and delays—arrived with a helicopter to look for the MiG in surrounding waters. The ROK soldiers and their prisoners were evacuated.

All this occurred within three miles of the North Korean shore and within sixty miles of the Antung airfield complex. The Yaks made a pass over Sinmi-do on the 15th—'to our lasting mortification', Captain Brock reported, 'there was an electrical misfire [in the anti-aircraft system]. Lacking carrier support*, reliant on periodic air cover by the Fifth Air Force, he made arrangements to withdraw, instructing the LST meantime to ditch the fuel drums to limit her vulnerability to air attack.

When the helicopter completed its search—it discovered an aircraft fuel drop tank but nothing else in the shallows—the withdrawal began on 16th April. Four Yaks struck the ROK *PF62* superficially as she drew off, wounding five of her complement, but at the cost of one aircraft destroyed and another damaged in the encounter. During the evening of the 15th/16th, as a last contribution to the surprises of the expedition,

* The Seventh Fleet carrier force was screening Taiwan. *Theseus* and a single American carrier were required to maintain station in the Japan Sea in its absence.

a motor sampan appeared with guerrilla forces from Cho-do, unaware of any of the activities involved, including the interposition of the parachute force, and umbrageous at finding friendly forces in an area then in use by one of their raiding parties[3].

This tale of local enterprise reveals a number of flaws in the organisation and conduct of maritime operations. First, there was the continuing problem of excessive signal traffic among the higher headquarters, made worse by misuse of the precedence system*, delaying for long periods the passage of important messages correctly graded. This was exacerbated by the fact that United States senior commanders permitted—sometimes encouraged—their staffs to send detailed instructions to experienced subordinates, wasting signal transmission time, to say nothing of exasperating the subordinates concerned. Here, for example, is the signal sent from Commander, Task Force 95, to Admiral Scott-Moncrieff and Captain Brock initiating the operation in the Yalu Gulf.

> RECOVER MIG 12 SHOT DOWN 10 APL NEAR SINMI-DO... START ROK SHIPS TOWARD SINMI-DO IMMEDIATELY TO BEGIN SEARCHING... CONCEPT [*of operations*] CRUISER [*and*] DESTROYER ELEMENT OFFSHORE AS COMMUNICATION [*and*] LOGISTIC [*and*] COMMAND BASE WITH ROK CRAFT SEARCHING INSHORE. AVOID APPEARANCE AMPHIBIOUS LANDING. MAKE REQUEST JOC [*Joint Operations Centre*] ... TO PROVIDE SEARCH AND COVER PLANES. ESTABLISH COMMUNICATIONS DIRECT WITH JOC. USE EVERY EFFORT TO RECOVER PLANE AND PILOT. TAKE NEEDED PRECAUTIONS TO PREVENT SHIPS FROM GROUNDING. FURNISH ANY NEEDED LIAISON OR COMMUNICATION PERSONNEL TO ROK SHIPS. REPORT EVERY SIX HOURS NEGATIVE AND POSITIVE INFO[*rmation*] YOUR OPERATIONS AND SPECIAL INFO AT ONCE ...[4]

All else apart, Captain Brock did not need to be told to take precautions against grounding. Three months later, Captain W L M Brown OBE DSC RN in *Cardigan Bay* in company with *Glory* (Captain K S Colquhoun DSO RN) and the frigate *Hawea* (Lieutenant-Commander F L F Johnston, DSC RNZN) traced and recovered a MiG in shallow water by an admirable combination of air reconnaisance, seamanship, and improvisation. Discovering that Captain Brown, as Commander TE 95.12, had the matter well in hand, Admiral Scott-Moncrieff engaged himself principally in procuring a lifting facility from American resources at Inch'on. It was an admirable demonstration of exercising command with a light touch[5].

Whatever the imperfections of the command system in Task Force 95, they were exceeded by the confusion of clandestine intelligence

---

* 'Flash', the highest precedence intended for use in critical political or military circumstances, was used in two hundred and ten messages on one day, at random, from COMNAVFE and the 7th Fleet.

organisations working on the west coast, inspired and overseen by GHQ in Tokyo, and run through Eighth Army Headquarters in Korea. Just before handing over command, Vice-Admiral Andrewes advised the Commander-in-Chief in Singapore of problems arising from their lack of coordination.

> ...they range from intelligence missions to spontaneous 'vice raids'. They are mostly centred on the friendly islands off the coast, and in the performance of their missions they must in fact infringe the blockade. On occasions they work in cooperation with the ships of the ROK Navy, who thus get diverted from their primary duty. Sometimes they operate in unauthorised small craft where identification is well nigh impossible with the possible risk of an unfortunate accident. Nevertheless they can play a useful part in assisting the operations of Task Group 95.1 as well as pursuing their own aims, and warships and aircraft can support them in turn, if they are prepared to come a little more into the open. I have therefore felt it desirable to attempt some form of coordination of the maritime aspects of these activities...[6]

Two discrete organisations were involved: Leopard and Salamander. The first was run by the United States Army, primarily to engage coastal defences and to capture prisoners for its second function, obtaining intelligence. In the latter connexion, Leopard ran a network of agents but these never extended into the heart of North Korea. Salamander was operated by the Central Intelligence Agency for the Commander-in-Chief in Tokyo. It sought to insert and extract agents into and out of North Korea, but occasionally became involved in raiding operations to facilitate agent running. Communications between these organisations were scant.

Admiral Andrewes was successful in gaining the confidence of both groups, not simply because they came to recognise their dependence on him but no less because the advice he and his commanding officers offered invariably proved to be sound. Admiral Scott-Moncrieff stood in the same relationship after his assumption of command, making a point of seeing the Leopard and Salamander local representatives during his visits to the west coast, and the officers and NCOs of the United States Air Force signals and radar detachments among the islands[7]. He was thus able to form some judgement of their potential. Radio communications were established with the respective forward headquarters, and sometimes with raiding parties. But there were frequent changes of personality among the American officers running Leopard, few of whom seemed to have any experience of the work involved. Handover arrangements were cursory. There were several occasions when a departing Leopard controller or sub-controller did not wait to see his successor, who was thus obliged to learn his trade from scratch.

Salamander's greatest difficulty was finding high quality agents. As far as possible, North Korean natives were used who had some knowledge of the extraordinary restrictions imposed by the P'yongyang government on its people. Frequent changes of the North Korean local government pass systems* added to an agent's difficulties. Sometimes, an agent would land by parachute or from a small boat and lie up in the hills doing nothing other than devising a good story to tell on his return. Others, brave men and occasionally women, would penetrate to the target area. Many of these were caught, tortured, and eventually killed. Among the Koreans working for both Leopard and Salamander there were, from time top time, double agents.

By the summer of 1951, the 'Blockade' force had undertaken a number of minor landing initiatives of its own to obtain information as to targets for bombardment and seize prisoners. In the latter half of August, after riding out Typhoon 'Marge', the cruiser *Ceylon* (Captain G A Thring, DSO RN), destroyer *Charity* (Commander J A C Henley, RN), and frigate *Rotoiti* (Commander B E Turner, DCS, RNZN) landed a small force and successfully identified a North Korean strong point for bombardment. The Leopard chief controller accompanied the reconnaissance, as a result of which he requested Captain Thring to raid an area near to Mongumpo, just to the north of Choppeki point, to capture prisoners from an isolated detachment of the NKPA .

A company of two platoons from *Ceylon*'s Royal Marine detachment and a third from her stoker-mechanics was assembled under Captain H E Kelsey-Burge RM. The three warships ran in towards the beach in darkness, bombarded the target area for 12 minutes as soon as it was light and simultaneously launched the first platoon. The guns lifted to fire on deeper targets. Wading from their landing craft† on to a gently rising beach of mud and sand, the Royal Marines advanced to establish a covering position on a low ridge. The area was quiet and seemed deserted. But as they approached the ridge, mortar and small arms fire fell suddenly among them. Casualties quickly rose to seven. Responding with their own weapons and assisted by the ships' guns, the Royal Marines withdrew with their wounded.

Either Leopard's information had been faulty, or there had been a betrayal. The nature of the action suggested the latter. At all events, the numbers encountered merited further scrutiny. Returning later in the day, *Ceylon* observed troops in the open and bombarded the house into which they ran for cover. Next day, aircraft from *USS Sicily*, the carrier

* A North Korean citizen was not permitted to leave his village area without the knowledge of the local authority, or his district without a pass.

† The cruisers frequently carried a landing craft, vehicles and personnel [LVCP] for raiding.

on station, reconnoitred and struck covered positions inland, from which there were secondary explosions[8].

Another American element working amongst the islands was the west coast aircrew rescue detachment, manned by the United States Air Force. An excellent relationship developed between the air support and blockade Task Groups, 95.11 and 95.12, and this organisation. It received calls from aircraft in distress, and when they crash landed or their crews parachuted over land, directed helicopters to pick them up.

HMAS *Sydney*[*] was doubly a participant in the scheme in October 1951. The pilot and observer of an Australian Firefly crashed in open country close to Sariwon. The nearest helicopter was the carrier's own[†] but dusk was approaching and the friendly aircraft circling overhead, holding back the North Korean soldiers surrounding the stranded airmen, were running out of fuel. At last light, about 1815, when the overhead fighters were on the point of departing, the helicopter arrived to land precisely by the two Australians. As they were gathered its crewman, Callis Gooding, shot an approaching North Korean before leaping backing into his seat for a rapid and successful withdrawal under small arms fire[9].

In this period, several other aircraft from *Sydney*, hit by anti-aircraft fire, were rescued by flying boat or ship from the sea. A boat from the frigate HMAS *Murchison* (Lieutenant-Commander A N Dollard, DSC RAN) brought in a Sea Fury pilot who had got into his dinghy but was isolated in shallows. A boat from *Amethyst* rescued another in the Han exits on 26th October. The warship drills for launching a rescue boat were highly efficient. In the rough weather of August 1951, *Concord* (Lieutenant-Commander R A M Hennessy DSC RN) recovered a man overboard in nine minutes. Leaving Korean waters on 25th August after thirteen months in operations, *Kenya* had rescued ten aircrew.

Such incidents provided brief excitements during patrols. Much of the time at sea was spent in routine but no less demanding work such as chart validation and correction. The charts in use were based on Japanese hydrography. Many corrections had been made throughout 1950, but on the west coast of Korea, the immense tidal variation combined with the outflow of the major rivers to shift mud and sand continuously. Channel markers could never be wholly relied on. Inshore, the skills and instinct of navigating officers were frequently taxed to their limits.

---

* HMAS *Sydney* served in place of a Royal Navy carrier on the west coast from September 1951 to January 1952.

† A United States Navy helicopter detachment under Lieutenant J O'Mara USN had been embarked on *Sydney* when she joined Korean operations. The duty crew in this incident were Aviation Pilot A K Babbit and AAM(A) C C Gooding.

It was not easy for Admiral Scott-Moncrieff to meet the many demands upon his force during 1951 and 1952. He was responsible for the west coast, for a share of the frigates escorting troop transports and supply ships through Korean waters, and for the provision of relief warships on the east coast. He was therefore disturbed when the defence of the west coast islands threatened to tie down an inordinate number of his units.

When the Communist side believed that the armistice talks might be advancing to completion, and the possession of territory was of critical importance to the North Korean government*, a series of attacks was made to recover those islands held by the United Nations off the Ongjin pensinsula from the confluence of the Han, Imjin, and Yesong rivers northward across the 38th Parallel to the islands of the Yalu gulf just below the 40th.

The NKPA captured Sinmi-do on 9th October. Its neighbour, Taehwa-do†, fell to assault on 30th November 1951, despite the contribution of the battleship USS *New Jersey* to bombardment earlier in the month. These northernmost islands were then very sensibly abandoned. They were not worth the cost in ships, aircraft, and troops to regain and hold them.

Those further south were a different matter. Cho-do‡ and Sok-to, south west of the Taedong estuary, the Taechongs including Paengyong-do in the area of the 38th Parallel, and those scattered between Tungsan-got¶ and the Han confluence were of considerable value. Naval and air communications equipment had been installed on a number of them them beside the intelligence and aircrew rescue organisations. In late November, it was apparent that the North Koreans were reinforcing the shore batteries close to Sok-to, Cho-do and Paengyong-do.

With the loss of Taehwa-do on the 30th and six islets in Haeju Bay, there were repeated rumours that NKPA invasion forces were being assembled across the Ongjin peninsula. GHQ in Tokyo became alarmed. Instructions were issued on 2nd December that naval forces were to give priority above all other coastal activities to defence of the islands including Yongpyong-do, south of Haeju, and Tok Chok, off Inch'on, which contained important air force radio and radar sites.

Admiral Scott-Moncrieff at once put it to Admiral Martin that warships could not guarantee security of the islands; proper military

---

* The subject of the offshore islands was specifically discussed at Panmunjom on 27th November 1951.

† In the battle for Taehwa-do (also spelt Tae Wha-do), a British officer attached to the Leopard Group, Captain Leo Adams-Acton, was captured together with a public relations team of the Royal Navy, Sub-Lieutenant Denis Lankford RNVR and Naval Airman Penman.

‡ This is also referred to on some charts as Choda.

¶ Marked on the charts under the Japanese name, Fankochi Point.

garrisons under Army command were required. The west coast blockade and air groups would provide support. Admiral Martin agreed, and on this basis he opposed the drafting of ROK Marines, believing that their presence would simply strengthen the case for naval responsibility. However, he left negotiations to Rear-Admiral G C Dyer USN, who had succeeded Admiral Smith as Commander, Task Force 95. Admiral Scott-Moncrieff departed for Hong Kong in connection with his national responsibilities as commander of the British Far East Fleet at sea.

Admiral Dyer toured the islands concerned. In response to Admiral Scott-Moncrieff's suggestion, he obtained a number of additional amphibious craft from Task Force 90 for the evacuation of all civilian refugees among the fishing villages and brought in ROK Marines to strengthen the defences under the overall command of Colonel W K Davenport, United States Marine Corps. He then left for the east coast.

Just as he arrived at Wonsan, a signal informed Admiral Dyer that two unoccupied small islands between Sok-to and the mainland were falling to invasion. In haste, he returned to the west coast, assuming tactical command there. The cruiser USS *Manchester* (Captain Lewis S Parks, USN) as flagship, and destroyer *Comstock* (Captain E T Goyette, USN) joined *Ceylon* and the destroyers *Constance* (Commander P U Bayly, DSC RN) and *Sioux* (Commander P D Taylor, DSC RCN), with the frigate *Alacrity* (Commander H A L Luard, RN) in bombarding the enemy as ROK Marines and guerrillas struggled to eject the invaders. A battery in the coastal town of Amgak blew a hole in *Constance* above the water line but was then destroyed by *Ceylon*'s guns. Commander Taylor maintained close liaison with both Sok-to and the islet of Ung-do by putting small parties ashore from *Sioux* and embarking wounded on several occasions. On the night 16th/17th December, *Sioux* and *Constance* fired starshells as the North Koreans made a final attempt to recapture Ung-do. Under this illumination, the ROK light minesweeper *JML-301* sank a junk, while *Sioux* engaged two enemy mortar batteries. But despite these and subsequent actions by *Belfast* (Captain C A C Duckworth, DSO DSC RN) and *Cayuga* (Commander J Plomer, OBE DSC CD RCN) supporting guerilla operations, the two islets, connected by land to the mainland at low tide, were finally secured by the NKPA[10].

Admiral Scott-Moncrieff returned from Hong Kong in *Belfast* on 23rd December. He relieved Admiral Dyer as officer in tactical command immediately and then discovered that the latter believed there was a requirement for a flag officer to remain permanently in this post in order to oversee security of the islands. An added vexation was that there had been no air support for the battle in his absence because the carrier aircraft had been switched to other duties and air 'spotting' for naval bombardment had been passed to the Fifth Air Force. But the latter had no pilots trained in this work. He reported indignantly to Singapore in January 1952,

> The operations of the past three weeks bring out all the weaknesses in the American command system...the rigid command and lack of confidence in the man on the spot. The need to 'go on record' [in case of any subsequent enquiry as to errors]...
>
> A further weakness is the lack of intelligence available to me under present conditions when the local organisations who normally keep me supplied with operational intelligence are bottled up. Although there has been an improvement recently in passing on by Commander, Task Force 95, of certain TOP SECRET information, the source of reliability is never stated, and except in verbal discussions, no qualifying information is ever passed on...
>
> In the meantime...some sixteen (including ROK) ships of value well over £10,000,000 are tied up in yet another of these static tasks in a vulnerable position as a result of a threatened attack which may be launched by a few junks and a large number of small collapsible boats, and is only credible having regard to the characteristics of a resourceful and fanatical enemy. This loss of naval mobility, which has been such a feature of this war, is the price that has to be paid for the insufficiency of regular soldiers to carry out static garrison duties. More particularly, it is directly the result of failure to evaluate and agree the basic military requirements on a joint Service basis...[11]

Practical considerations necessitated a review of the organisation. Not least, Admiral Scott-Moncrieff could not be expected to remain at sea without relief, and the only flag officer available to provide it was Admiral Dyer himself. In the final arrangements, concessions were made to all. The inability of the United Nations Command to spare soldiers to garrison the islands was explained by General Ridgway in the New Year at an informal meeting, at which he confirmed his decision that they must be safeguarded by the navy 'to as great an extent as possible'. On 9th January 1952, at a conference aboard the USS *Wisconsin*, the West Coast Island Defense Element was formally established as TE 95.15 under Colonel Davenport on Paengyang-do. A second battalion of ROK Marines was posted to the force. The armed light craft, minesweepers, patrol craft, motor launches, and light assault boats were reinforced. The remainder of the refugees were to be evacuated, in all exceeding 20,000. But the requirement for warship pickets was reduced; Admiral Dyer accepted the compromise that ships would always be to hand to support any of the essential islands. It was mutually agreed on review that deployment of a warship in the Han estuary would depend on local circumstances. Most welcome to Admiral Scott- Moncrieff, Admiral Martin agreed that there was no requirement for a 'duty admiral' in tactical command on the west coast.

Still, given the responsibility to hold selected islands, Admiral Scott-Moncrieff applied himself to the task, visiting each of them several times. He had formed a special patrol, 'Swanny Force'* at the end of December 1951 to patrol the eastern approaches to Sok-to, and when others were able to take up this work he transferred it to the Haeju area. Here a new guerrilla organisation, Wolf Pack, under United States Army officers, had entered operations. He sent a frigate to support them.

Stretching his resources to the limit, he resumed patrols to the Yalu gulf and continued bombardments wherever targets were observed from the sea or air, not an easy task in the bitter and often stormy weather. Local enemy batteries, moving from one temporary positon to another were forced into prepared sites below ground. There was recurrent evidence of impending local invasions by the NKPA, several of which were launched in sensitive areas and repulsed. All inshore channels were swept of mines to assure clear passages. At the end of the month he embarked in *Murchison* to review the Han area and decided to withdraw the frigate on station due to the lack of facilities on the islands to correct gunfire. Returning down the Meioumu Channel in darkness, Admiral Scott-Moncrieff noted with approval the navigating skill of the captain, Lieutenant-Commander A A Dollard RAN, 'against a seven-knot current, using bearings of the tops of hills, most of which he had to memorise'[12].

As a result of his tours, the admiral reorganised and drafted fresh orders for his force. The Blockade group was to patrol four areas, Sok-to to Changsan Got†; Changsan Got south to Tungsan Got; the Haeju area; and the Han area. Subject to maintaining three destroyers or frigates‡ in the vicinity of Sok-to and Ch'o-do by night, and a destroyer with the landing ship carrying Swanny Force, all areas were to be regularly patrolled. The object was sevenfold.

a. To discourage offensive operations by the enemy by widespread activity.

b. To support the intelligence organisations and associated guerrillas (TE 95.15 under Colonel Davenport).

c. To prevent enemy minelaying.

d. To prevent movement of enemy junks in areas not covered by anti-invasion stations.

e. To control movements of friendly clandestine craft.

---

* Named after its first leader, Lieutenant G A Swanston, DSC RN, from *Ceylon*. He was later transferred as British Commonwealth Liaison Officer with the US Marine Corps commander, Colonel Davenport. Swanny Force was then run by a detachment from *Belfast*, later by the United States Navy.

† Marked on charts under the Japanese name, Choppeki Point.

‡ Together with an American ocean tug and landing ship mounting high explosive rockets, in association with ROKN patrol craft.

f. To control refugee movement and capture unauthorised craft.

g. The Han unit to provide a link with Wolfpack and to supply gunfire support if required[13].

Bombardment was to continue, but Admiral Scott-Moncrieff cautioned his captains to confine fire to as great an extent as possible to targets on which the fall of shot could be observed and corrected from the sea, from temporary observation posts ashore, or by air spotting*. He deprecated 'blind' shooting at targets identified inshore simply by a map reference and out of surface or aerial view.

Besides assistance in bombardment, the carrier task element [TE 95.11] was ordered to cover the Sok-to and Ch'o-do area with a pair of aircraft for as much of the day as possible against air attack or shore operations. Armed reconnaissance and strike sorties were to be operate within the entire coastal region from Chinnamp'o to the Han. Air cover was also to be maintained on a contingency basis for troop convoys approaching from the Yellow Sea[14].

These operations were carried forward, but not without difficulties. At times, one of the cruisers was needed on the east coast—*Belfast* or *Ceylon*—relieved in the summer in Korean waters by *Newcastle* (Captain W H C Rutherford, RN) and *Birmingham* (Captain J D Luce, DSO OBE RN). One or another of the frigate flotilla captains† then took her place in command of the Blockade group. Destroyers and frigates were similarly requested of Admiral Scott-Moncrieff, even his carrier from time to time. Whilst this was all in accordance with making best use of mobile forces, concentrating them temporarily for particular tasks, their absence from the west coast placed a strain on his resources.

Operations on the east coast were of a different character to those in the west. Tidal influence was negligible, likewise the incidence of legitimate fishing and trading craft. Five standing tasks had evolved during 1951 from the Bombline‡ to Chongjin, following the evacuation of north east Korea in the previous year. The southernmost task was performed by the Bombline element, required to give direct gunfire support to the ROK corps on the coast and northwards along the coastal railway. The Tail Light element patrolled to the edge of Wonsan harbour, connecting with the Engine Block patrol running inshore to Hungnam. The Windshield patrol covered the area from Wonsan to Songjin. The

* Day fighter/ground attack squadrons of the Fifth Air Force had by this time received instruction in air 'spotting' for naval bombardment.

† One or another of the commanders of 3rd or 4th Frigate Flotilla on the British Far East Station, each of whom was a captain, Royal Navy, was present for the greater part of Korean operations.

‡ The 'bombline' is drawn by the army for the air forces. Friendly aircraft are forbidden to attack behind it except for close air support. Targets in front of it may be attacked freely.

Northern patrol reached to Chongjin and protected at its southern limit the island of Yang-do. Here the guns of HMNZS *Taupo* (Lieutenant-Commander K A Craddock-Hartopp, MBE DSC RN), while in company with two American destroyers, sank fifteen North Korean motor junks attempting the capture of the island in February 1952.

Wonsan harbour was kept under siege by warships and garrisons on the majority of the surrounding islands*. 41 Royal Marine Commando was drafted to this area in June 1951 to enhance the local raiding capability. They were grossly misemployed. The local intelligence organisations were much more a law to themselves than on the west coast, at least until a costly accident prompted closer control of their movements[15], and did not want the commando as a rival. Admiral Dyer was unwilling to allow Colonel Drysdale or his successor, Lieutenant-Colonel F N Grant, to engage in enterprises without the most detailed scrutiny and control of his plans. As a consequence, these highly trained Royal Marines were restricted to a handful of small reconnaissance and minor raiding tasks, performed in an exemplary manner and at minimum cost, and occasional fire control ashore for the daily bombardment of targets in the Wonsan area[16]. Otherwise, they were stuck in garrison duty on the Wonsan harbour islands until December 1951, after which they returned home†. Admiral Scott-Moncrieff would have used them to better effect at Ch'o-do or in the Taechongs‡. As a consolation prize, he drew in the last of the Commando's reinforcement draft and attached its officers and men to his fleet Royal Marines¶.

The warships were better employed. They joined the Trainbusters Club with enthusiasm. HMCS *Crusader* (Lieutenant-Commander J H G Bovey, DSC CD RCN) topped the list with four trains destroyed[17]. Three of these were hit on the same day, 14th April 1953, between Iwon and Songjin. A fourth narrowly escaped her guns that evening.

Admiral Scott-Moncrieff's reorganisation was repeatedly tested throughout 1952. In the early months, the North Koreans quickly realised that there were gaps between provision of the tactical and reconnaissance combat air patrol (TARCAP) provided from the carrier. Between the

---

* These had been abandoned during the evacuation of X Corps in late 1950, but those of tactical importance had been recaptured.

† The most unhappy event of this part of their tour was the loss of QMS Day and four marines as prisoners. Their light assault craft broke down and they drifted ashore into enemy hands.

‡ By the intervention of the United States Marine Corps, 41 Royal Marine Commando was awarded the Presidential Citation in 1957 for its conduct in north east Korea in 1950. This delay was due to an omission to notify His Majesty's Government of the intention. Many months passed in the process of arranging formal proposal and acceptance.

¶ It was longstanding practice in the Royal Navy to use Royal Marines in a number of trades and duties on larger warships—for example, the manning of gun turrets in parallel with seamen gunners. A nucleus was thus disposed for shore operations.

departure of one pair of aircraft and arrival of the next, they engaged in concentrated shooting at islands and, more often, warships. The captain of *Bataan* (Commander W S Bracegirdle, DSC RAN) lost some of his clothing when a shell penetrated his cabin during a hot skirmish with the North Koreans[18]. In response, fire from sea and air was turned upon the batteries concerned, but the enemy guns damaged or destroyed were quickly replaced—Kim was determined to maintain his coastal artillery, albeit field and anti-aircraft equipments adapted for the role. The warships continued their attacks, however, wherever guns were identified, and the NKPA batteries regrouped to support attacks on islands from temporary positions.

Several small islands were lost; none of consequence were abandoned. A number of North Korean attacks were foiled: *Concord* (Commander C P Mills, DSC RN) drove back lines of NKPA marines advancing at low tide in the Haeju gulf in mid-March 1952. A minefield was later laid to hinder sorties by Communist forces on this route.

In midsummer, *Belfast* became involved in the most extensive of these actions. The report of Captain Duckworth, commanding officer—and concurrently commander TE 95.12—on 'The Battle of Changni-do' manifests their nature.

> Changni-do is a small island...in the vicinity of Paengyong-do, which has changed hands several times and is generally considered "neutral"... Leopard [intelligence director] values the island as a jumping-off place to the mainland for his agents. If Changni-do fell firmly into enemy hands, Kiron-do, Ohwah-do and Sunwi-do would inevitably follow suit and this would constitute a threat to the vital island of Paengyong-do.
>
> At 0915 on 15th July [1952], *Belfast* was en route from Yongp'yong-do to Taechong-do to fuel, when she received a 'Flash' report from Leopard that Changni-do had been invaded by 300 North Korean Army in rubber boats. Thereupon, *Belfast* closed Changni-do at best speed, arriving at 1000 and *Amethyst* joined me shortly after.
>
> The whole island was reputedly in enemy hands and CTE 95.11 was called upon to furnish air strikes (from *Ocean*, Captain C L G Evans DSO DSC RN) to hit anything in sight on the island or attempting to escape by sea.
>
> I ordered *Belfast* and *Amethyst* to provide one armed boat each to explore what was thought to be the invasion beach at the west end of the island, with instructions to collect any rubber boats left by the enemy. Many civilians could be seen sheltering in the caves along the beach and, in closing these to get information, the enemy, on overlooking cliffs, suddenly opened fire on our boats with machine-guns and mortars, forcing them to retire. One *Belfast* Royal Marine received a flesh wound in his leg—otherwise there were no casualties.
>
> *Amethyst*'s boat picked up a naked Korean on an off-lying islet... He had been landing some [agents] on Changni-do early that morning and, on

arrival, had found the island occupied... had been chased by the enemy and finally swam out to where he was picked up. It was from him that we learnt that the island had been invaded at about 150200 [July, local time]—that is, over seven hours before we received the news. He was unable to give any confirmation that the enemy had come by rubber boats. He, personally, had seen only one junk load.

Leopard reported to me that he would be unable to mount a counter-attack by his guerrillas before early the next next morning (Wednesday, 16th July), so the remainder of the day was spent in gunning opportunity targets and ensuring that none of the enemy escaped.

Ar 1645, when the TARCAP (Tactical Reconnaissance and Combat Air Patrol) was absent, *Amethyst* was engaged by a battery of guns, estimated to be 76 mm calibre... on the mainland and beat a hurried retreat until she outranged them at 12,000 yards, after some 30 to 40 rounds had been fired at her, the nearest falling some 20 yards off. Amethyst replied with 78 rounds of 4- inch. A secondary explosion was observed and one gun ceased to fire. The battery was masked from *Belfast* by the island at this time but, with *Amethyst* spotting, we engaged the target with 26 rounds of 6- inch until all the guns were silenced.

At 1945, *Belfast* was taken under fire by another mainland battery. About 20 rounds were observed, the nearest 200 yards short. The battery was quickly silenced with 12 rounds of 6-inch and 3 rounds of 4- inch.

None of these shore batteries have been known to fire in the past and this strong reaction seemed to indicate that the enemy wished us to keep our distance while he evacuated his forces from the island during the night. Although *Amethyst* and *Belfast* could cover escape to the north and south, shoal water prevented cover of the narrow channel between Changni-do and the mainland, so I ordered *PC 702* [Commander Min ROKN] to join me from the Haeju approaches at best speed. On her arrival, I placed a liaison team on board and, in company with my armed LCP(L) [light personnel landing craft], these two craft patrolled the channel all night.

At about 1900, Lieutenant McBride US Army arrived from Paengyong-do in a motor junk firing on one and a half cylinders. He, and Sergeant Denny US Army, had been sent by Leopard (Major Dye) to organise the guerrilla counter-attack, which was to be mounted from Ohwa-do. After a brief conference, in which H hour and the landing beaches were decided upon, he went on his way, already a tired man and to be a much wearier one before the next day's fighting was over.

He asked me for assistance with towing the guerrilla junks, as he had only this broken down craft to tow twelve junks and sampans. However, I could not afford to relinquish *PC 702* from her patrol until daylight and I told him he must do the best he could on his one and a half cylinders.

In the event, he was so delayed in mustering his 200 guerrillas and persuading them to a concerted course of action, that his tow was only half way across from Ohwa-do when dawn was already breaking. I had to order the channel patrol to withdraw at this time as they were right under the guns which had fired at *Belfast* the previous evening. I therefore ordered *PC 702* to take the guerrilla craft in tow and to make haste—as they were already an hour late on H hour and it would shortly be broad daylight.

As things turned out, this was a most unfortunate decision. It was found that *PC 702* was unable to steam slow enough and first one rotten tow rope parted and then another. After three attempts I told McBride to carry on towing with his junk—at whose snail's pace the guerrilla tow ropes could just stand the strain.

The counter invasion finally landed three and a half hours late, but, fortunately, by that time the first TARCAP had arrived and they met with no opposition from the beach. Fanning out in two companies, one under Lieutenant McBride, the other under Sergeant Denny, they made good progress at first along the high ground on the north and south sides of the island. They were supported by fire of all ships—*PC 702* doing some very accurate shooting on his own initiative and the bombing and strafing of USS *Bataan*'s planes. All went well, until about 1000, when the advance was held up on both sides of the island by the most bitter resistance put up by a few brave [men of the] North Korean Army in well defended positions on a hill which commanded the whole island. Neither bombs nor naval gunfire could dislodge them and I formed the opinion that our guerrillas would sit where they were all day and let us do the job for them, unless I drastically curtailed the support they had been receiving. I therefore told CTE 95.11 [Captain Neale USN—aircraft carrier commanding officer] to discontinue further strikes, McBride to seal off the enemy's retreat across the island channel, and, at 1200, sailed *Belfast* to Taechong-do to carry out her delayed refuelling.

These tactics seem to have had the desired effect, for the guerrillas, reinforced by a further 50 from Kirin-do, then really got down to fighting and, by the time I returned to Changni-do at 1800, the island was in our hands, except for one small area of resistance. It was about this time that *PC 702* distinguished herself by capturing one NKA officer and five other ranks swimming to the mainland. The NKA officer, reported to be an ardent Communist turned out to be an old school chum of the First Lieutenant of *PC 702*. These prisoners, and others sent off from the island, were despatched to Paengyong-do in *LST 898* [tank landing ship].

Belfast received 11 Korean casualties on board, including one female, and my medical staff did admirable work dealing with some very seriously wounded... *Amethyst*'s medical staff did equally good work with the wounded sent to her and were assisted by an American Doctor flown off by CTE 95.15's helicopter [islands defence group]... Sergeant Denny, who had been wounded in the neck and hand...was otherwise a walking case... Lieutenant McBride reported on board *Belfast* at 1930 that evening. After some 36 hours without sleep and little food and drink, he was very exhausted, but was well looked after and quickly revived. His report was disappointing. After all this effort over the past 48 hours he reckoned that only 70 NKA had been killed or captured... I felt fairly confident that no enemy had escaped once our blockading force had arrived; so, either the initial report of 300 NKA had been greatly exaggerated, or the bulk of the invaders left the island after the seizure about 150200 and before the arrival of my blockading force at

> 151000, [July, local time] which was only half an hour after Leopard's first report of the capture of the island.
>
> In fact, as POW interrogation and other intelligence finally elicited on Saturday, 19th July, only 156 NKA invaded Changni-do coming in two sail junks and four "folding" boats. The final count of enemy losses was 80 Killed in Action, 42 prisoners of war, 30 drowned and 4 unaccounted for. This was more satisfying. Among the POW was the Battalion Commander who was found hiding in a cave on Saturday, 19th July.
>
> I am still a bit sceptical about the 30 drowned...[19]

Minesweeping continued as the summer advanced, and chart correction. On the night 25th/26th September 1952, HMCS *Nootka* (Commander R M Steele DSC CD RCN) played cat and mouse with a junk laying mines south of Ch'o-do. Propelled by oars, this craft, cut down to within eighteen inches of the waterline to reduce her radar profile, had already laid four mines in a swept channel to the south. The crew took to rafts as the Canadian destroyer closed in the darkness and despatched a recovery party in a motor cutter. One North Korean officer opened fire and was killed as the cutter approached. Commander Steele suspended further action until daylight, when the five surviving members of the minelayer were picked up from the water and the junk was taken under tow[20]. This appears to have been the last attempt by the North Koreans to lay mines directly in swept channels, though others were floated at random through the Taedong estuary. Most drifted back into coastal shallows, but several found their way into the patrol channels, from which they were swept by the devoted minesweepers of the United States Navy. Mines apart, inshore operations were as ever at risk due to the hazards of the mudbanks continually shifting under tidal influence, exacerbated from time to time by the outflow of rain floods. Chart correction and the resiting of channel markers was an endless task. Despite the time given to this work, warships touched these hazards periodically, occasionally grounding temporarily, as they were drawn into support for the guerrillas and intelligence gathering organisations.

HMS *Ocean* (Captain C L G Evans, DSO DSC RN), relieved *Glory* in May 1952. Her aircraft squadrons took part on 11th July in an immense raid on the P'yongyang area by land based and maritime aircraft, in which their targets were railway marshalling yards[21].

The aircrew of the United States Air Force in the Far East respected their colleagues of the naval air arm, and no wonder: taking off and landing on a speck tossing in the sea was an accomplishment in itself. But there was much more to their credit than this. The naval and marine corps pilots were highly skilled operators of their day and night fighters, reconnaissance, and day fighter/ground attack aircraft. Their turn round on the deck was swift: refuelling and rearming, debriefing and rebriefing, recovery and repair were all accomplished with the minimum of delay.

However, the primary role of the aircraft—seeking and destroying surface ships or, in the case of the marines, supporting their forces ashore—combined with a determination to maintain their independence of the United States Air Force, caused them to operate systems alien to the latter. A naval liaison officer was installed at the Fifth Air Force Joint Operations Centre in November 1950 but integration, with full communications facilities, was not effected until 12th July 1953.

One of the reasons why completion of this important joint capability took so long to establish was that the Air Force esteemed the naval air forces but regarded their contribution as of minor importance compared to the range and weight of their own capabilities. On the basis of being the principal in air operations, with no other function or distraction, the Air Force naturally assumed an absolute right to shape and control air strategy, and to direct tactical sorties.

Moreover, the successive commanders of the Far East Air Force and the Fifth Air Force took the view that, given the opportunity, they could win the war in Korea solely by application of the air power in their hands. Quite simply, they would crush the enemy's ability and hence will to continue the fight.

Given the opportunity... This meant that they should have the authority to destroy the enemy air forces and bases including those in North East China, the classic first move in winning the air battle. With air superiority assured, they would turn their attention to demolishing enemy manufacturing and supply capacity, while cutting off the flow of supplies to the front line, the process known as interdiction of the battlefield. Finally, their whole force would be concentrated to destroy the enemy land forces in their defences: headquarters and communications, artillery, and infantry would be crushed.

These ideas were unrealisable. The United States Government and their British partners together with most if not all of the other allies within the United Nations Command were unwilling to sanction sorties into North East China for sound political reasons—excepting the case in which the Soviet Union entered the struggle in Korea, raising the level of combat to general war, or another, in which the Chinese and North Korean air forces became so powerful that they threatened to destroy the United Nations ability to maintain an air defence. Of these two cases, the first came to be seen as highly improbable. The second appeared in the first part of 1951 to be a possibility. MiG 15s were being launched from the Antung group of airfields in increasing numbers and piloted with growing skill. General Partridge warned the Fifth Air Force in March 1951,

> Present world tension indicates that all possible action be taken in preparation for air attack without warning[22].

Whilst he was doubtless right to prepare against such a contingency, we know now that his apprehension was misplaced. Stalin had no intention of joining the Korean war. China wished to win control of North Korean air space but knew that it lacked the means to overcome the United States air resources. Kim Il-sung alone nurtured hopes of a comprehensive air victory but he was the junior partner in every sense, a poor relation whose views were listened to politely but carried no weight in policy making.

In any case, China was not going to be knocked out of the war by the loss of its north eastern airfields. Its essential manufacturing capacity lay far beyond the reach of American aircraft. Its forces on the battlefield were not going to be cut off by interdiction. The United Nations air forces had the means to reduce severely the number of railways operating, the bridges standing, and the road transport motoring to the front line, but the Chinese and North Koreans together had the means to supplement their transport by using men, mules and ponies travelling over country tracks, crossing rivers at night in small boats. Moreover, they became very skilled in the repair of railway tracks and bridges, and in the concealment of the facilities they had restored.

In the defence line, in the support and administrative zones behind, Chinese and Koreans alike dug deep shelters progressively from May 1951 to protect themselves and their workplaces. As month by month the United Nations aircraft roved across North Korea numbers of the urban populace were occupied in underground factories—small arms, vehicle spares, radio and telecommunications industries were developed among these.

On 30th April 1951, just after the air forces had played a major part in defeating the opening stage of P'eng's fifth campaign, General Ridgway directed General Stratemeyer to maintain air superiority throughout the theatre, including Japan, and to provide

> ...general air support for United Nations forces in Korea, to include:
>
> (A) Close air support of surface forces.
>
> (B) Interdiction, including isolation of the battle area.
>
> (C) Air transport, troop carrier, and air evacuation.
>
> (D) Special missions, including electronic countermeasures, psychological, and clandestine [warfare][23].

General Stratemeyer was disappointed by what he regarded as the limitations imposed on him by these instructions, but he had plenty to occupy him just then; there were many calls on his resources. P'eng's follow-on forces had to be defeated, and the MiG-15 squadrons in North East China were making it difficult to penetrate the north western corner of Korea between the Ch'ongch'on and Yalu rivers. While these struggles continued, he was succeeded by General Weyland.

The new FEAF commander also felt constrained by his directive; it supported an implication perceived and resented in his headquarters that the air forces were an adjunct to the Eighth Army[24]. With the extraordinary circumstance in the summer in which sea and air elements were able to manoeuvre while the ground remained stabilised, General Weyland and Lieutenant-General Frank F Everest—who succeeded General Partridge in command of the Fifth Air Force in June 1951—believed that a door of opportunity had opened to them.

Operation Strangle, the concept of their predecessors, would be exploited to the limit, gathering weight as the forward airfields in Korea were resuscitated and extended. They were confident of meeting and overcoming any sustained challenge from the MiG-15s in the north west, and of containing any attempt to bring airfields in North Korea—even Sinuiju, tucked in beneath the MiG umbrella—into operational use.

Through the summer, autumn, and early winter of 1951 the air offensive continued with bombs, napalm, rockets, and cannon. The Communists' attempts to develop airfields southwards towards the Taedong river, defeated in the run up to the Fifth Phase Offensive, were again frustrated. The clearance by the North Koreans of a section of P'yongyang to create an airstrip on a main road within the city was pointless; the Superfortress B-29s of the 19th and 30th Groups cratered the area even as Strangle began. Sinuiju was progressively ruined.

The railways and roads were repeatedly struck, and with them locomotives, rolling stock, motor vehicles of all kinds. Headquarters and communications centres, supply dumps, and troop concentrations were hit by day and night.

Low level reconnaissance and attack on small or narrow targets was costly in aircrew and aircraft. The aircraft were vulnerable to light weapons on the ground—cannon, even machine-guns often damaged vital points*. Tactical adjustments were made to minimise losses but the enemy also adjusted the deployment of anti-aircraft weapons, enhancing at the same time deception schemes. For example, rows of lights placed alongside hillsides in parallel to roads to suggest truck columns at night

---

* The Korean war demonstrated that the complexity of modern aircraft made them more vulnerable to basic anti-aircraft weapons within their optimum range.

were extremely successful decoys. Huge numbers of dummy positions indicating supply dumps and communications were built among the villages or surrounding areas. Canvas strips, painted to manifest rail cuts, were laid over newly repaired sections of the line. Labour gangs became so skilled that, during the winter months, they could repair considerable lengths of the permanent way cut between dusk and midnight—as was the Fifth Air Force operating practice—opening it to traffic from midnight to sunrise. As noted, greater care was taken in the concealment of true targets. The FEAF intelligence staff was surprised to learn from prisoner of war interrogation that soldiers had marched from the Yalu to the 38th Parallel without once being attacked from the air*.

It should not be thought, however, that Operation Strangle was a failure. If it did not force the Communist side to conclude an armistice at Panmunjom, as some of its proponents had hoped, it certainly constrained military enterprise in North Korea. For whilst it did not stop supply—Communist artillery equipments and ammunition stocks conveyed to the forward areas actually rose during the later half of 1951—the free run of United Nations aircraft across P'eng's lines of communication made it plain that any movement of his forces out into the open, a prerequisite for offensive action, would be doomed.

In all these operations, the British Commonwealth air elements took a full part. The 2nd South African Air Force Squadron, flying F-51s—Mustangs—was employed in the ground attack role†. By September 1951, its pilots had flown almost 5,000 sorties, the majority within Operation Strangle. 77 Squadron of the Royal Australian Air Force returned to operations in July after an absence for conversion from the propellor driven Mustang to the British Meteor 8 jet, changing in the process to the fighter-interceptor role‡. However, clashes with MiG-15s close to the Yalu in the late summer showed that the Meteors' speed, and climbing and turning capability at high altitude, were inferior; the Meteor was an aircraft of the preceding generation[25]. In September the squadron was drawn back to escort and interceptor operations south of the Ch'ongch'on river though, even there, MiGs and Meteors sometimes met, and when the encounters took place at lower levels the 77 Squadron pilots gave a good account of themselves.

---

* The author moved extensively up and down the western sector of North Korea between June and December 1951 while escaping and being recaptured and was only once in an area subjected to air attack by day or night.

† The squadron was re-equipped with the F-86F from December 1952.

‡ The squadron did not welcome adoption of the Meteor. Its performance was inferior to that of the MiG-15, and there was no commonality of spares in the theatre. The aircrew wished almost unanimously for conversion to the American F-86 Sabre, superior in performance, and for which there was an assured supply line in Korea.

From the west coast, the carrier on station contributed to Operation Strangle on the basis of priorities. First call on her sorties was to cover the task group against air attack. The direction of bombardment was frequently the next requirement; thereafter, the aircraft were available for close air support of units in the defence line or interdiction. Particular tasks were agreed daily between Task Force 77 and the Joint Operations Centre in Seoul. At times, three carriers were operating, at others only the west coast station offered a flight deck to Commander TF 77. In the latter case, sortie rates might drop but flying hours increased as the Fireflies and Sea Furies were despatched to distant targets.

By March 1952, it was apparent to many in the Far East Air Force that they were not winning the war by air operations. Their resources were finite and they were spread too thinly. A study group suggested that, accepting the need to maintain air superiority, which would of itself include a measure of interdiction, all other resources should be concentrated on destroying selectively targets deemed to be particularly damaging to the enemy[26]. This formed the basis of an 'air pressure strategy'.

A number of targets suggested themselves: the Fifth Air Force had identified over a period of time several supply areas, a light ammunition plant among other factories engaged in war production, and repair shops. At FEAF headquarters, General Weyland had earlier revived the proposition that they should attack the hydro-electric power plants on the Yalu river and the major reservoirs in North Korea, but he made the error of submitting this to the Joint Chiefs of Staff directly through General Vandenberg's office. Inevitably consulted, General Ridgway did not care for the attempt to bypass his authority, and took his time in considering the proposal. No decision had been reached when he handed over command to General Clark on 12th May 1952.

As soon as he had acquainted himself with the lineaments of his command, General Clark put this question to his principal commanders:

> What can I do militarily and otherwise to make the Communists realize that the price of peace is not as cheap as they are trying to make it?[27]

It was a very welcome query to General Weyland. He explained that he had sanctioned intensive bombing of the factories and dumps identified by the Fifth Air Force, which was then in hand under the direction of its third commander, Lieutenant-General Glenn O Barcus. At the same time, he recommended destruction of the hydroelectric installations.

The Koje island prisoner of war riots distracted General Clark for some days thereafter but the matter was discussed again on 6th June, and a complete plan was submitted on the 11th. This offered two options.

The six generating complexes, each of which contained several plants, were as follows:

Sui-ho, 25 miles upstream from the mouth of the Yalu.

Funei on the reservoir of the name in the far north east.

Chosin and Fusen on the reservoirs of those names.

Kyosen east of Fusen.

Kongosan, south of Wonsan*.

All these were within General Clark's discretion as targets except for Sui-ho which lay just astride the Korean frontier with China but supplied power to both countries.

The first option set aside Sui-ho, and the two smallest plants, Funei and Kongosan. The second proposed the inclusion of Sui-ho with Funei, Chosin, and Kyosen. It was recognised that the authority of President Truman would have to be sought for an attack on Sui-ho. General Weyland remarked that he would need also the assistance of carrier aircraft in order to complete the raid swiftly. Speed was important to reduce the development of an enemy aerial counter-attack. As it was, the aircraft attacking Sui-ho would be running through 'MiG Alley' in the north west.

The second option was submitted to Washington. Detailed plans were meantime completed in Tokyo. Vice-Admiral Robert P Briscoe, USN, who had succeded Admiral Joy as COMNAVFE, was ordered to assist General Weyland, the 'coordinating agent' for the operation.

Presidential authority was granted on 19th June[28]. Heavy cloud delayed the attack early on the morning of 23rd June but drifted favourably before noon. The strike was ordered for 1600 hours. Successive attacks were in readiness for the 24th, concluding with night bombing.

Under cover of F-86 Sabre interceptors, seventy naval aircraft† appeared over the Yalu at 1600, half to strike anti-aircraft sites, the remainder to bomb. They were followed 10 minutes later by one hundred and thirty four USAF F-80 Shooting Stars and F-84 Thunderjets. Clouds of dust and smoke rose from the target, obscuring the river for several miles. But the area was empty and clear at 1900 when two reconnaisance aircraft were escorted back by Sabres. The photographs they brought back confirmed destruction of the generating plants.

Chosin, Fusen and Kyosen were also struck at 1600 hours by a combination of carrier and Air Force aircraft‡. These areas were attacked

---

* Some of these, as shown on the USAF charts at the time, are Japanese names. For example, Chosin and Fusen, should properly be, in Korean, Changjin and Pujon.

† From the USS *Boxer*, *Philippine Sea*, and *Princeton*.

‡ The carrier *Bon Homme Richard* also contributed to this attack.

again by day and night next day. Over 1,500 sorties were involved. Two naval aircraft were the only losses, but their pilots were recovered.

These casualties were due to anti-aircraft fire, not air attack. The Chinese and North Korean air defence centre at Antung, warned by radar of an approaching air fleet, believed that the airfields in the locality were about to be attacked. One hundred and sixty MiGs withdrew to distant air bases. The remainder did not leave their dispersal sites.

The consequential loss of power to North Korean military installations and factories was extensive. Although repairs and auxiliary plant gradually supplied essential services, repeated raids ensured that the full hydroelectric generating capability was not restored during the war. Indeed, the damage was of such magnitude that recovery was not effected for some years after the armistice.

There was, however, a minor political price to pay. America'a allies, and particularly the United Kingdom, were vexed that they had not been warned beforehand about the attack on Sui-ho[29]. On this point, and in view of the proximity of Sui-ho to North East China, Members of Parliament in London questioned again the command and control arrangements in Korea. Ministers were advised that British views should contribute to policy making in Tokyo and at Panmunjom[30]. Vexation was the greater because Field-Marshal Lord Alexander, Minister of Defence, had been in Tokyo and Washington as the operation was prepared and launched[31]. Challenged, the American Chiefs of Staff enjoyed a brief 'perverse satisfaction at having escaped for once the burden of consultation with their British partners'[32].

In London, the Cabinet considered their situation on 24th June, though not as a matter of first importance. Mr Churchill was chiefly concerned to make it clear to the House of Commons that the air attacks had nothing to do with Field-Marshal Alexander's coincidental presence in Tokyo and Washington[33]. The item was taken again on the following day, when Mr Eden, Foreign Secretary, remarked that he was going to raise the lack of consultation with Mr Acheson. Mr Churchill agreed but did not wish to occasion any 'divergence of view...between the Governments of the United Kingdom and the United States'[34].

By chance, Mr Acheson happened to be in London at this time and had been invited previously to speak to a group of members of all parties from both Houses. *Inter alia*, he addressed the matter of consultation.

> If I may digress for a moment, I shall make some remarks about a matter which is one of controversy and which I would not speak about in England were it not for the fact that this is off the record. I shall restrict my remarks to what I think it is my duty to say to you at this time. This is about the matter that you have been debating in the last 2 or 3 days.

> ... One question you would ask [about the bombing] is: shouldn't the British Government have been consulted about this? To that, my answer would be 'yes'. It should have been; indeed, it was our intention to do so. It is only the result of what is known in the United States as a 'snafu' that you were not consulted about it.
>
> ... If you ask me whether you had an absolute right to be consulted, I should say 'no' but I don't want to argue about absolute right.
>
> What I wanted to say is that you are a partner of ours in this operation, and we wanted to consult you; we should have, and we recognise an error. ...[35]

Unfortunately, political differences did not permit the Labour Party to drop the subject. Mr Attlee and his former government colleagues may have wished to return to the attack having been bested in a censure debate on the Korean war on 26th February. At any rate, they wished to make the point that they had been stricter in the terms of Anglo-American partnership than the Conservatives. The United States now showed signs of throwing off restraint in the war, risking an extension of operations into China. The Prime Minister seemed ready to accommodate this shift.

Mr Churchill reminded the House of Commons on 1st July,

> ...do not let us blind ourselves to the terrible cost that is being paid for their patience by the people of the United States. I think we ought to admire them for the restraint they have practised, instead of trying to find fault with them on every occasion...
>
> I was, I think, the first in this House to suggest, in November 1949, recognition of the Chinese Communists. I thought at that time that the Americans had disinterested themselves in what had happened in China, and as we had great interests there and also on general grounds, I thought that it would be a good thing to have diplomatic representation. ... But there is one thing which usually severs diplomatic relations, and that is the shedding of blood on a large scale by warlike action.
>
> It is remarkable that in spite of the fact that the Chinese have in no way responded to our diplomatic gesture and have, on the contrary, treated us with scorn and have shed the blood of our own soldiers and that of our allies, we should not only continue—our Government has continued the policy of the previous [Labour] Government—to accord them diplomatic recognition; but if we followed the advice of the party opposite, we would make it a major effort of policy to persuade the United States with their twenty thousand dead, to do the same thing while the fighting was still going on.

Still, though he was ready to defend the United States, the Prime Minister decided to increase British representation in the Korean theatre. It was plain that the United States were not prepared to yield a seat at Panmunjom but were prepared to appoint a British deputy chief of staff to General Clark, an offer agreed to by Australia, Canada, and New Zealand[36]. The Prime Minister explained to his colleagues in Cabinet that same morning,

> ... This officer would be under the orders of the Supreme Commander [commander-in-chief] and would owe allegiance and loyalty to him. He could not, therefore, act as a direct link with the British Chiefs of Staff and the United Kingdom Government. On the other hand, the Supreme Commander was anxious to make this appointment*...and would undoubtedly tend to seek his advice on matters on which the United Kingdom Government might be expected to hold strong views...[37]

Air Vice-Marshal Bouchier was to continue as before. Major-General S N Shoosmith was shortly appointed to the new post†. He took it up at a time when General Clark was reorganising his command, principally to placate the wish of the Air Force to be put on an even footing with the Army in standing. An 'army command, Far East,' was set up, and as it related to the theatre as a whole, the options for incumbency excluded General Van Fleet. Either a new personality and staff was required or the Commander-in-Chief and his headquarters complement had to double. General Clark wisely chose the latter. There was thus no change in substance. Another measure, more reassuring to the Air Force and Navy was the creation of a joint staff within the Far East and United Nations Headquarters overwhelmingly manned previously by the United States Army. In turn this led to yet another organisational scan to find manpower savings which could be passed to the Fifth Air Force in Korea. There, Army and Air Force continued to be underposted.

It was on this account that General Weyland had accepted experienced pilots from the Royal Air Force, following an informal arrangement between MRAF Sir John Slessor and General Stratemeyer. The idea was to attach instructors from the Central Fighter Establishment, and potential instructors, to F-86 fighter-interceptor wings in operations‡.

Flight-Lieutenant S W Daniel was the first to arrive. Flying an F-86A in 4th Fighter Interceptor Wing, he was awarded the Air Medal and

---

* The idea had come to General Clark as a result of the Koje island incident, and had been supported by the United States Government, but with some reservations by the Joint Chiefs.

† General Clark knew this officer from common service in the Italian campaign. He later claimed that he had suggested his selection—see Mark W Clark Papers Section 3, 110–111, USAMHI, and Grey, *op. cit*, pp 126–129 for a consideration of this subject. General Shoosmith's Directive is at Appendix K.

‡ In 1950, General Stratemeyer had invited Wing Commander P Wykeham Barnes (later Air Marshal Sir Peter Wykeham, KCB DSO OBE DFC AFC RAF) to Korea to advise on night intruder operations under a similar informal arrangement. See AIR 20/7796. He was followed by Wing-Commander J E Johnson (later, Air Vice-Marshal CB CBE DSO DFC RAF DL). Both officers flew extensively on operational missions and reported comprehensively on the conduct and organisation of ground attack by night.

United States Distinguished Flying Cross during completion of one hundrd sorties into North Korea during the autumn and winter of 1951–52. His success led to a request for a widening of the scheme. A group of four pilots followed, led by Wing-Commander John Baldwin DSO DFC AFC RAF. All had previous experience in flying Sabres during attachments to the United States Air Force. Arriving in Korea on 13th February 1952, they separated in pairs, Wing-Commander Baldwin and Flight-Lieutenant R Knight to the 51st Fighter-Interceptor Wing at the K-13 air base located at Suwon. Squadron-Leader W Harbison and Flight-Lieutenant B J Spragg joined the 4th Wing at Kimpo—K14. They were soon active in North Korean air space with their American colleagues, and contributing to the general fund of operational ideas[38]. Unfortunately, this high success was marred on 15th March.

Nine days after being awarded the American Distinguished Flying Cross, Wing-Commander Baldwin's aircraft disappeared. Flying on weather reconnaissance above the Chinnamp'o area, the other members of his flight climbed out of cloud at 7,500 feet. To their surprise, on reaching a clear sky 'Wing-Commander Baldwin was not in sight, and no radio transmissions were received from him'. They were unable to see him or any other single aircraft in the area and returned home. An air search was mounted later that morning but found no sign of the missing aircraft and made no radio or other contact with the wing commander. As he was never brought into a prisoner of war camp, his instant death was assumed[39]. The loss of this exceptionally skilled and experienced fighter pilot was a reminder to them all that the margin of survival on every sortie was narrow.

Four more officers followed, but they required a conversion course, conducted over six weeks at Nellis Air Force Base near Las Vegas, Nevada. Arriving in Korea on 19th June 1952, they were posted to the wings at K-13 and 14, where the leader, Squadron-Leader J R H Merrifield was delighted to progress from the A model to the uprated F86-E, 'a delightful aeroplane to fly. ... It has no vices and very few flying limitations', though he conceded its climb limitations—'30 minutes to 40,000 feet with full tanks'[40]. By the end of the war, twenty one RAF pilots had served with the 4th and 51st Fighter Interceptor Wings.

Each tour was approximately four months. As one group went home another was in training at Nellis. Sixteen officers in all completed active operations. All of them damaged one or more MiG-15s during combat, several were credited with 'kills':

Squadron-Leader G S Hulse shot down two—though, sadly, was later killed in combat himself—Flight Lieutenants J H Granville-White, J H

J Lovell and J M Nicholls*, and Flying Officer R T D Dickinson, one apiece†.

For a time the MiG-15 squadrons were able to challenge United Nations aircraft advancing up 'MiG Alley' to Sinuiju. As the Chinese and North Korean pilots were gaining experience, they were led by Soviet *bloc* pilots whose voices could be heard speaking Russian frequently‡. Russians, Poles, and East German pilots were not allowed to fly south of the Ch'ongch'on, however, to ensure that accident or injury would not lead to a drift southward to the political embarrassment of capture. Gradually, from the end of 1952, squadrons evolved which were manned only by Chinese or North Koreans. At the same time, Russian anti-aircraft batteries which had long covered the north west end of 'MiG Alley' were withdrawn. Chinese troops manned this sector as North Koreans took over from Russian batteries at Manp'o-jin.

Yet even before this change was completed, the high spirit and skill of the United Nations fighter pilots had outmatched the MiGs with their F-86 E models. By the spring of 1953, they had assured air superiority for the remaining months of the war.

It was a considerable achievement. The combined air forces of the Chinese and North Koreans exceeded 2,000 aircraft in the latter half of 1952. The United Nations in Korea, Japan and Okinawa operated about 1,500, including those in maritime air squadrons. On balance, the Communist fighter and bomber complements were more modern after this date¶. Communist ground controlled interception radars [GCI] were in operation from June 1952, when four more airfields were constructed within the Antung complex§. Searchlights were also brought into use in cooperation with the Russian M-39 85mm anti-aircraft guns and associated radars.

United Nations fighter-bombers and bombers continued to cut supply lines to the limit of their capabilities, and to pursue targets of particular value to the enemy. The problem was that there had never been very many in the latter category and by 1953 they were hard to find. The chief success of the experienced target intelligence section in

---

* Later, Air Marshal Sir John Nicholls, KCB CBE DFC AFC RAF. He was subsequently credited with forcing a second into a ground crash, following evasive action.

† Pilots of the Royal Australian and Royal Canadian Air Forces were also credited with official 'kills' of MiG 15s. Flying Officer E A Glover, RCAF, topped the list with three. Lieutenant P Carmichael, RN, *Ocean*, was the first pilot in Korea to destroy a MiG with a piston engine aircraft.

‡ This was the language of instruction in both the Chinese and North Korean national squadrons. See Smorchkov, *op cit*, and Lobov, G, *Blank Spots of History: in the skies of North Korea*, Aviatsiya Kosmonavitka No 10 (Moscow, October 1990).

¶ These details exclude the Soviet Air Force but include all aircraft within those of the Chinese and North Koreans.

§ These were in order of operation: Antung, Ta ku-shan, Ta tung-kou, Feng Cheng, Kuan tien, Ta pao, and Kachiapa.

Tokyo was the discovery of factories reopened or redeployed. Naval intelligence identified others of longstanding in the extreme north east. However, the latter were either within five miles of North East China or about ten from the Soviet Union. While authorising the attacks, the American Government '... agreed that General Clark would inform the appropriate British military officers in his headquarters and that the Department of State would inform the British in Washington' in sufficient time to protest if they saw fit[41].

From 1952, it was the practice to drop leaflets warning civilians that air raids would be made on railways and roads carrying military traffic, and on towns and villages in the vicinity. But this did not help North Korean citizens whose movements were restricted closely by the P'yongyang government. Their dwelling and work places were ordained. Notification that they were to be bombed was not considered a justification for leaving them, even on a temporary basis.

P'yongyang continued to be a target throughout the war and was largely reduced to rubble, under which Kim Il-sung and his associates enjoyed luxurious and sheltered working and living accommodation[42]. Those not in posts attracting special protection had to rely on shelter of lesser quality and availability. In the capital and along the main routes, large numbers of civilians were killed*. But so, too, were considerable numbers of troops. The Communist propaganda which depicted most casualties from air raids as being elderly, infirm, or infants was far from the truth.

It is similarly untrue that every building in Korea north of the Bombline was reduced to rubble, every road ruined. Many country roads were unaffected; villages and small towns scattered along them were untouched, though many concealed troops during the winter months. Remote areas were attacked when it was known that they contained economic targets, such as mines, or because photographic reconnaissance had picked up evidence of military presence.

In all these operations, the sea and air forces exercised their options to manoeuvre, separately and collectively from the summer of 1951 into the spring of 1953, while the armistice negotiations at Panmunjom advanced slowly, halted, and crept ahead briefly before coming to an apparent *impasse*. Throughout, the naval forces had the harder life; at sea, the ships were frequently 'nearer Heaven than land', as Hakluyt observed. In the land bases, the air wings enjoyed a more sheltered and

* Seeing napalm in use in newsreel of a raid on P'yongyang, Mr Churchill was greatly disquieted, and conveyed this to General Bradley and Field-Marshal Alexander on 22nd August 1952. '...No one ever thought of splashing [napalm] about all over the civilian population. I will take no responsibility for it.'

stable life except for the aircrew. Like mediaeval knights, they were mounted and launched by their supporters, who watched for their return.

An F-86E pilot described in a letter to his brother in the winter of 1952 the process of early rising, breakfast, and briefing before dawn, take off and climb to height as the winter sun gradually lit the peninsula.

> '...and then we look from 40,000 feet for the River Yalu below us because this is the line beyond which we can't go, even though it shelters the enemy air force. We cannot see the people below, but I dare say they can see us on these bright sunny days, or anyway see the 'con' trails, and shake a fist at us...[43]

Not all those seeing the F-86s in the Yalu region shook their fists. The United Nations prisoners walking the exercise yards and camp byways often saw them come and go. One, at least, took comfort from the appearance of these shining specks, sometimes engaged in dog fights with MiG-15s, sometimes unchallenged. The prisoner could reflect, as they turned for home, that within minutes the pilots would have landed in the south, debriefed, collected their mail, and walked to the mess for a beer. It was a glimpse of friends; an assurance that the world he knew and longed to return to was waiting. He wished them a safe journey back to the Han river[44].

SOURCE NOTES: Chapter 19

1 Tu P'ing, *In the Headquarters of the Volunteer Army* (Peking, 1989), Chapter 14, Part 3.
2 *Kenya*, Report of Proceedings, 4th–17th April 1951, Appendix V, (ADM 116/6218).
3 *Ibid*; also comment by FO2IC.
4 *Ibid*, Appendix III.
5 *Cardigan Bay*, Report of Proceedings, 23rd July 1951; also Periodic Report of Proceedings No 39 by FO2IC, 19th August 1951 (ADM 116/6212 and ADM 116/6228, respectively, and ADM 116/6229).
6 FO2IC comment of 5th April on *Belfast*'s Report 12th–21st March 1951 (ADM 116/6211).
7 See, for example, 41st RoP, FO2IC for 10th to 29th September 1951, paragraph 17, (ADM 116/6228), and *Belfast*, same period, paragraph 4 (ADM 116/6211).
8 Report of Proceedings, 15th–31st August 1951, *Ceylon* (ADM 116/6213).
9 Report of Proceedings, HMAS *Sydney*, 3rd October 1951–26th January 1952 (ADM 116/6223).
10 See FEC-G3 files, December 1951, USNARS, Suitland; Naval FE Command Historical Reports, December 1951–January 1952 (copy in Naval Academy Library, Annapolis, Md.); Field, James A., jr., *op cit*, 423–425; British Naval Staff History, *cit*, pp 200–205; Thorgrimmsen & Russell, *op cit*, pp 80–84; Reports of Proceedings of RN, RAN, RCN, RNZN warships involved, December 1951 in series ADM 116/6211, 6212, 6214, 6216.
11 Report of Proceedings, FO2IC, December 1951, pp 28–29 (ADM 116/6229).
12 Report of Proceedings, January 1952, FO2IC, p 14, *ibid.*
13 For the precise form of these paraphrased instructions, see Commander Task Group 95.1 signal of 260015Z [Jan 52]. See Report of Proceedings, FO2IC, January 1952, Appx I (ADM 116/6229).
14 See FO2IC Report of Proceedings, February 1952, Appendix I, *ibid.*
15 See Report of Proceedings, FO2IC, 9th January–4th February 1952, paragraph 17, *ibid.*
16 See Report of Proceedings, 41 RM Commando, July–December 1951 (ADM 116/6227), with comment of FO2IC, 31st March 1952.
17 Cagle, W, & Manson, Frank A, *The Sea War in Korea* (USNI, Annapolis, 1957), p 360.
18 Report of Proceedings, *Bataan*, February 1952 (ADM 116/6210).
19 *Belfast* Report of Proceedings, 2nd to 21st July 1952, Appendix I (ADM 116/6211).
20 A full account of this incident, based on interviews with Commander Steele and his ship's company, is in Cagle and Manson, *op cit*, pp 204–208.
21 See Report of Proceedings, *Ocean* (ADM 116/6221); also Lansdown, John R O, *With the Carriers in Korea* [Worcester, 1992], pp 240–241.
22 Futrell, *op cit*, p 275.
23 CINCFE Directive to Commanding General, Far East Air Force, 30th April 1951, GHQ FE G-3 files [USNARS, Suitland], also CINCFE signal C-61367 to JCS (same date).
24 For a summary of these views, see Futrell, *op cit*, pp 440–441.
25 See the Official Papers of Marshal of the Royal Air Force Sir John Slessor, Folder IIIE, (AC 75/28/23), f 53, para 6. However, see also MOD London Chiefs of Staff signal TOK 69 of 121954A (September 1951) to Bouchier, TOKS and CABS]; and AVM Bouchier signal TOKYO TRAIN 34 of 191205A [September 1951] to MOD LONDON [Chiefs of Staff]. Also Futrell, *op cit*, p 608.
26 Futrell, *op cit*, pp 442–445.
27 Clark, General Mark W, *From the Danube to the Yalu*, (New York, 1954), pp 69–74.
28 JCS signal 911683 of 19th June 1952 to CINCFE. For associated documents, se Futrell, *op cit*, pp 449–50, fn 35.
29 See FK 1091, (FO 371/99599).
30 FK 1194/25 and /28, (FO 371 99614).
31 FK 1091/15, (FO 371 99598).
32 Recalled by Lord Franks in conversation with author. See also FRUS, 1952–54, volume xv, *cit*, pp 356–357.
33 C.C. (52), 62nd Conclusions, CAB 128/25.

34 C.C. (52), 63rd Conclusions, CAB 128/25.
35 Acheson, *op cit*, p 136. See also Tokyo 1082 to FO of 27th June 1952 in FK 1194/36, (FO 371 99614), and Washington 1218 to FO of 24th June 1952 in 1091/16, (FO 371 99598).
36 See FO 842 to Tokyo of 16th June 1952 in FK 1194/25, and Tokyo 1020 to FO of 17th June in FK1 194/30, (FO 371 99614).
37 C.C. (52), 64th Conclusions, CAB 128/25.
38 See Squadron Leader W Harbison's Report in AIR 8/1709, para 34.
39 RAF P4 (Cas) Folder 439166/52.
40 Report by Squadron Leader J R H Merrifield, 24th February 1953, AIR 20/8929.
41 FRUS, 1952–54, volume xv, *cit*, pp 458–459.
42 See Thames Television programme *cit*, final, evidence of Tibor Meray.
43 Letter of 21st December 1952 shown to author by Lieutenant-Colonel T Harrison USAF.
44 Author's reflections at this time.

CHAPTER 20

Maintaining a principle

The latter end of April 1952 was one of those periods when the United Nations prisoners of war believed that the armistice was imminent; and as all the information reaching them was selected by their captors, it may be that the Chinese and North Koreans thought so too. As noted, their delegates at Panmunjom had shown some readiness to accept voluntary repatriation but expected that the minimum number returning to them would be 110,000. The suggestion that the number was only 70,000—the figures based on partial screening—was unacceptable. Notwithstanding agreement on all other points for an the armistice, the disagreement on repatriation of prisoners prevented a conclusion.

In May 1952, after almost a year at the negotiating table, Admiral Joy was succeeded as senior delegate by Lieutenant-General William K Harrison, one of several changes in the United Nations team*. With no sign of any opening for progress, General Clark instructed General Harrison to meet the Communists as rarely as possible while rescreening continued in the new, dispersed camps. It was already apparent by the end of May that the number willing to return voluntarily to the north would exceed 80,000, but he wisely decided to obtain as accurate a figure as possible before making any announcement; some prisoners continued to resist screening of any sort. In any case, there was agreement between the Tokyo and Washington headquarters that as the new greater figure still fell far short of 110,000, publication would suggest a form of bargaining which might lead to false hopes of settlement.

In May, General Clark also began to consider the unilateral release of Korean civilians, accepted as such by the Communists, from internment. Political circumstances in the Republic persuaded him to pause, however, and distracted him in the business of negotiating. President Rhee declared martial law in the area of Pusan—the temporary capital—on 25th May as a means of coercing his opponents in the National Assembly. The United Nations alliance was reminded that democracy in the Republic of Korea, in so far as it applied, was continually at risk.

---

* Admiral Joy had passed beyond his tour of duty in the Far East. General Harrison was deputy commander, Eighth Army.

Britain sent a strong protest to President Rhee. Australia's condemnation was the more influential because it was delivered by Mr James Plimsoll, who effectively held the UNCURK together by his presence*. Even the United States, to whom resolution of the problem inevitably fell, had difficulty in bringing President Rhee under control. Mr Muccio, patient and experienced after a long and turbulent relationship as America's ambassador to the Republic of Korea, opened his report to Washington on 12th June with these words,

> I have just spent the most futile hour with Pres. Rhee that I have ever spent with him[1].

One problem was that General Van Fleet tended to favour presidential autocracy in the Republic of Korea. Syngman Rhee knew it. He also knew well that his allies would not abandon his people to Communist rule, and were unlikely to depose him; corrupted as he was by power he stood above financial corruption, and there were few if any less corrupt and better fitted in government and standing to direct the country's affairs.

Still, General Van Fleet was ordered to prepare a military plan to protect the Assembly membership and if necessary to arrest the president—Operation Everready[*sic*], a good title; as long as he was in office, it might be required at any time. Early in July, strong advice from Mr Muccio and Mr Plimsoll, combined with the adaptability of Korean political life, produced a rough compromise between the South Korean political factions.

During this crisis, Mr Panikkar, Indian Ambassador to China, an occasional channel of important information directly from Peking†, had been summoned by Chou En-lai on 15th June 1952. During a conversation over two hours, two possible lines for settlement of the prisoner of war dispute had been advanced. The first was based on a direct settlement involving 90,000 North Koreans and 20,000 Chinese—virtually, the entire number of the latter—perhaps even 100,000 provided that this included all the Chinese. The alternative assumed that all prisoners desired repatriation but on arrival at Panmunjom and, separated from all forms of United Nations 'military escort', could be interviewed by the four neutral supervisory nations agreed previously‡ and Red Cross

---

* Attempts by the Australian Government to withdraw him from UNCURK to another post were cancelled because Mr Acheson pleaded for his retention in Korea. For an account of this, see O'Neill, *op cit*, vol. i, p 307, also FK 1071/658, FO 371 99590.

† See, for example, Volume I, p 216.

‡ The negotiators had agreed to request Sweden, Switzerland, Poland and Czechoslovakia to form the armistice supervisory commission.

representatives. These details were passed to the Foreign Office by the Indian High Commissioner in London[2].

Passing them on to the State Department, Mr Greenhill, First Secretary of the British Embassy in Washington, concluded that 'The Foreign Ofice is somewhat sceptical about this proposal…[3]'

Sir Christopher Steel, British Minister at the Embassy, and Mr Greenhill met State Department officials again on 19th June. Mr Hickerson, American Assistant Secretary of State for UN Affairs, noted that further study of Panikkar's account stipulated a 'neutral' site for interviews rather than 'Panmunjom', that 'recommendations' were to be made for disposal rather than a determination, and that there had been no mention of the Red Cross. He continued,

> I told Sir Christopher that it was our impression that the Chinese Communists have not put anything in writing and that we have only reports based on Panikkar's recollection. Sir Christopher agreed that that was his impresssion. … Dismissing alternative 'a', I stated that alternative 'b' has interesting possibilities. If the Communists really want an armistice this might be a reasonable basis for achieving it and offers a face-saving device. …
>
> I then suggested that in our view the kind of message which the Indians should send to Peiping [Peking] would read as follows:
>
> The alternative 'b' which Chou En-lai is reported to have offered as a possibility for breaking the deadlock in the armistice negotiations, is interesting and would seem to offer possibilities for progress. There are, however, a number of points in regard to this proposal which require clarification and elaboration. It would be desirable to know what channel or machinery would, in Chou En-lai's view, be appropriate for such clarification and elaboration.
>
> We would hope that the Indians would use this language, without indicating US authorship, but describing this as the US reaction in which the UK concurred. Sir Christopher agreed with this approach and suggested that it might be even better if this message were represented as the UK reaction in which the US concurred. I indicated we would have no objection and that we would leave the matter to the UK Foreign Office.
>
> I then informed Sir Christopher of some of the points in the message which, in our preliminary reaction, seemed to require elaboration or clarification. For example, is it intended that this interviewing of PWs by a neutral commission should take place before or after an armistice? Would the steps outlined be written into the armistice agreement? How could resisting PWs be brought to Panmunjom except under a 'military escort'? (Mr U Alexis Johnson pointed out that we may have trouble getting them there even under military escort, since these are persons who would resist repatriation and who would not have full faith in the outcome of the proceeding). We also wished to know whether persons not resisting repatriation would be exchanged before this procedure begins since we are, of course, anxious to

> obtain the return of our own PWs. Also, what if there is a disagreement among the neutrals as what the true wishes of a PW are? ...
>
> I told Sir Christopher that we have not told either our people in New Delhi, or at US [delegation to the] UN of these latest developments and that we considered it important that as few as possible know about them. In about a week, however, when Ambassador [Chester R.] Bowles returns to New Delhi, we intend to inform him fully, and we hope that the UK Foreign Office would instruct its High Commissioner at New Delhi to work closely with Ambassador Bowles. I expressed the hope also, since Sir Christopher indicated that Sir Gladwyn Jebb and the Commonwealth countries have already been informed, that these would be urged to exercise the greatest discretion...* [4]

While the Indian Government pressed the Chinese for further proposals, the hydroelectric plants were bombed—Nehru believed that this action might vex the Peking Government; but equally, various statements by two Russians at the UN headquarters, a member of the United Nations staff and a delegate†, seemed to encourage hopes that a means of settling the prisoner question might be impending. On 14th July, however, the British High Commissioner in New Delhi reported,

> Pillai‡ informed [us] today that Indian Embassy in Peking has now received a note from Chinese Government... Full text has not been telegraphed but from summary it was clear that upshot was that Chinese Government were no longer willing to negotiate on basis of alternative [b].... They were now only prepared to discuss solution on basis of alternative [a]. ...[5]

Details following confirmed that this was exactly the case. Mr Nehru did not know what to make of it; he was half persuaded that the bombing of the power stations was not the cause of the change—certainly, the Chinese press and radio made no special reference to it. Discussions between the Foreign Office and Mr Gifford, American Ambassador in London, led to no conclusion. Mr Gifford reported,

> 2. Tentative thinking in FonOff is cannot allow negots rest on this note. It will be necessary request further clarification from [Government of India]. Perhaps Kaul¶ cld reopen question with [Chinese Government] pointing out unacceptability of alternative 'a' which wld be not only degrading to UN

---

* As often before, security in Washington was wanting. Reuter's published a story on 23rd June, based on 'authoritative sources', that the US, UK, and India were discussing a new plan to resolve the deadlock on repatriation. On this occasion, however, the British appear to have been the culprits [See FK 1071/325, (FO 37 99577) cover minute.]

† Respectively, Constantin Zinchenko, Assistant Secretary General, and A P Morozov, Soviet representative on the Legal Committee of the United Nations. See, for example, Washington 1271 of 30th June 1952 to FO and other contacts in FO 371 99576 and 99577.

‡ N R Pillai, Permanent Secretary, Indian Foreign Office.

¶ Mr Panikkar had vacated his post. Mr T N Kaul was in charge of the Indian embassy in Peking pending the arrival of his replacement.

but also damaging to [Chinese Government] as their refusal to accept rescreening would have to be publicised[6].

This logic was not pressed upon Chou En-lai or his colleagues, who appear to have been working for a further concession; probably, as already suspected by General Harrison and his colleagues at Panmunjom, an agreement to return all Chinese prisoners, while leaving a residue of North Koreans to be screened.

Mr Churchill, reviewing the repatriation question, was briefed on 3rd July that General Harrison was looking for an arrangement which would permit the Chinese access to those opposing exchange. Sir William Strang, Permanent Under Secretary at the Foreign Office, suggested that

> ...we should not try to persuade the Communists to participate in an interrogation process but...try to get them in practice to accept the results, whilst leaving them a way of retreat to explain to their own public why fewer men have come back than they had lost, and for this purpose to put the blame on the United Nations.
>
> 9. I should add [Sir William concluded] that when we in the Foreign Office first heard of this proposal (which has not yet been submitted formally to Washington by General Harrison) the Foreign Secretary commented that he thought this would in effect be an agreement to disagree, and would leave unresolved the serious doubts and misgivings which had divided public opinion here. The Foreign Secretary thought moreover that there were obvious disadvantages in deliberately courting a charge of 'illegal and forcible detention'.

The Prime Minister minuted these papers,

> I do not like it at all. I agree with Mr Eden. We must not grovel, but they may stew. The bombing (inside Korea) may be salutory[7].

On 12th July, reacting to suggestions by Mr Addis in the China and Korea Department that accommodation of the Chinese might be necessary after all, Mr Churchill made his view clear beyond question.

> SIR WILLIAM STRANG
>
> MR EDEN TO SEE
>
> In my view there can be no question of forcing any Chinese prisoners-of-war to go back to Communist China against their will. These are the ones, above all others, who carry with them the moral significance, as the ones who had opted for us would certainly be put to death or otherwise maltreated.
>
> W.S.C.

Undaunted, Mr Addis responded on 22nd July,

> Our view in the Dept. has been that North Koreans forcibly repatriated

would be more likely to be victimised than the Chinese and secondly that it is not certain that Chinese forcibly repatriated would be 'put to death or otherwise maltreated'.

There seems however no point in sending a reply to [the Prime Minister's] minute at this stage.

On this, his superior, Mr C H Johnston, commented,

I shd. hate to be a forcibly repatriated Chinaman, all the same[8].

Mr Eden resumed the enquiries. Thanking Mr Nehru for his government's efforts, he suggested that every effort should be made to discover why the second option 'b' had been withdrawn. Ambassador Bowles presented the same message from the United States[9]. There were late suspicions that some of the details had sprung from Mr Panikkar's imagination[10], but this may have been unworthy. In any case, the option was void. Made desperate by frustration, ministers, senior officials and military officers in Canberra, London, and Washington cast about for fresh ideas. A few of those devised were absurd, others inept, none fruitful. The American and British authorities now came to the view individually and collectively that their next step should be to rally the United Nations General Assembly to challenge the Communist position. In agreement with the American delegation at the United Nations, Sir Gladwyn Jebb recommended that they should produce policies to meet two possible situations:

(a) that an armistice is concluded before October 14th [before the Assembly gathered],

(b) that there is no armistice when the Assembly opens and that the position in the truce talks is essentially the same as it is today[11].

In the first case, they would have to resuscitate their ideas for a political conference to conclude a peace treaty and the unification of Korea. In the more likely second case, they should plan to obtain an Assembly vote approving the efforts in combat and at the negotiating table of the United Nations Command, and calling upon the Communists to accept the principle of voluntary repatriation of prisoners. Assuming a negative response from Peking and P'yongyang, the Americans proposed to return to their earlier proposal. The Assembly should instruct the Additional Measures Committee to consider the consequences. Mr Hickerson proposed this as an 'affirmative' policy, to Sir Gladwyn Jebb.

...the whole history of the Korean war had shown that the only way to get results was to exert the maximum pressure on the Chinese. I [Jebb] disputed this thesis and argued that, while pressure must no doubt be kept up, our major aim must be to devise some means by which the Chinese could accept our point of view on the prisoner of war question without undue loss of face. ... There was no indication of what precise 'additional measures' [the Americans] would suggest; but I imagine these would include withdrawal of diplomatic representatives and a tightening of the blockade[12].

Sir Gladwyn was right. Such a package, which included the severing of all diplomatic relations with China, was put to the British embassy in Washington on 14th August[13]. Transmitting the details*, Sir Oliver Franks reported that

... 4. When Hickerson asked whether we had any immediate reaction to the State Department's proposals we said that...we would confine ourselves for the time being to one observation. ...it was of no small importance that Hong Kong should remain a part of the free world. ... The colony could hardly survive indefinitely if all trade with the Chinese mainland were cut off. Hickerson at once replied that it was certainly not part of the intention of the American proposals to create a risk that Hong Kong might be lost. ...

5. On the asumption that you will find these United States proposals quite unacceptable the sooner we are instructed to say so the better[14].

They were back on the blockade tack. The previous British objections to it remained valid; and were underpinned by the high level of economic security controls maintained by the United Kingdom. Thanking the State Department for early consultation, the Foreign Office confirmed Sir Oliver's expectations on 6th September, adding,

Severance of diplomatic relations would not harm or frighten the Communists, but...would lose us our embassy in Peking, which still has value as an observation post[15].

In following his own inclinations, Mr Eden had first to convince the Prime Minister, who believed the Foreign Office was taking 'too stiff a line' with the American ally. 'Proceed as you please,' Mr Churchill conceded, 'but don't let us fall out with US for the sake of Communist China'[16]. Private guidance was sent to Washington on 6th September, which was copied to Australia, Canada, New Zealand, and South Africa.

2. The American proposals raise the whole question of the objectives of the United Nations Command in Korea. Our first objective has been to oppose and hold in check the act of aggression committed first by North Korea and afterwards by China. This has been substantially achieved by the stabilisation of the fighting front on the general line of the 38th Parallel. Our next objective has been to bring the fighting to an end and secure an armistice on terms satisfactory to the United Nations Command. If an

* Contained in a discussion paper which had not then been seen by Mr Acheson.

armistice can be achieved, our objective would be to reach by negotiation a political settlement of the Korea problem. Our final aim has been to work for a settlement with the Chinese of other outstanding problems such as Formosa [Taiwan].

3. The criterion which possible further Assembly resolutions or actions against China should be judged is, we think, the extent to which they would be likely to contribute towards these aims. ...[17]

Although the Prime Minister had enjoined that Britain should 'not be at the forefront of opposition to the Americans', the United Kingdom was inescapably in that position. Australia, Canada, New Zealand, and South Africa were the subsequent points of consultation. All considered Mr Hickerson's ideas excessive or 'too extreme' as New Zealand put it[18]. South Africa, previously reluctant to contribute to policy concerning the war, offered a full appreciation.

...United States Government...proposals for using General Assembly and Additional Measures Committee to proclaim total economic embargo of China and North Korea. If these proposals were presented to General Assembly, communists could build powerful case to show that at United States' instigation the United Nations Command had deliberately stalled in armistice negotiations in order to induce United Nations, as instrument of United States policy, to apply full economic sanctions against China. This might have sufficient ring of truth to impress Asian opinion.

(b) Nor do stalling tactics serve any useful purpose. If speculation about Chou En-lai's recent visit to Moscow is correct, that Chinese are seeking more material support than Russians are ready to give, and that Russians would like to see early truce as war is having effect of building China into important and potentially rival military power*, there is much to be gained by pressing on with negotiations.

(c) As regards prisoners of war, Union Department of External Affairs believe that public opinion in most Western countries would be deeply shocked if any concession were made which would endanger or delay safe return of our own prisoners in communist hands. Communists have strong card here, and will continue to play completely without scruple. Consequently any formula providing for separate settlement of prisoners of war issue after armistice would have most disturbing effect on public opinion and would strengthen communists' bargaining position...[19]

Sir Gladwyn Jebb discussed Mr Hickerson's paper in confidence with his French colleague in New York, and the French Government supported the British reaction†. Meantime, the State and Defense Departments had

---

* This was one of several rumours then circulating. But see conversation between Mr Gross and Mr Malik reported by former from New York on 26th September 1952, (USNARS, Washington, 795.00/9-2652).

† France was thereafter consulted directly by the United States.

conceived modifications to the arrangements for dealing with recalcitrant prisoners. These would be put to the Communist side in an effort to bring about a cease fire before the General Assembly met.

General Harrison thus addressed the meeting at its morning session on 28th September.

> For many weeks the prisoner of war issue has blocked the achievement of an Armistice in Korea. On 1 July we suggested to you that a solution to the problem must be one that to a reasonable degree meets the requirements of both sides. You have admitted the soundness of that proposition.
>
> It must now be clear to you that one of the requirements of our side which cannot be compromised is that of no forced repatriation...

Reviewing the previous offers for the interviewing of prisoners either in their camps or in the demilitarised zone, employing one or a combination of the International Red Cross, teams from neutral nations, joint teams of military observers, or Red Cross representatives from each side, he now put three options to General Nam Il and his colleagues.

First, to bring all prisoners to an exchange point in the demilitarised zone which would be established on a cease fire. There each man would be checked by name and number in the presence of International or national Red Cross representatives or joint military teams, or a combination of these bodies. Each individual would then be free to rejoin his own side or return to those who had been his captors.

Second, prisoners who wished to return to their own side would at once be exchanged. Those who opposed repatriation would thereafter be brought in small groups to the exchange point and there freed. Following interview by representatives from mutually agreed countries not participating in the war, and in the presence of Red Cross and/or joint military teams, they would be free to go to the side of their choice.

The third option embraced elements of the first two. Prisoners wishing to be repatriated would be exchanged immediately after the armistice. Those opposing it would be be freed in the demilitarised zone where, without questioning, interview, or screening, they would make a choice of either side. If desired, this also would be under the observation of Red Cross representatives.

General Harrison then proposed that the delegations should recess until 8th October to permit the Communist side to consider the proposals, but Nam Il said that they wished to meet again at 2 o'clock.

When they returned to the conference table in the afternoon, Nam rejected all the options offered, affirming the requirement that all prisoners should be exchanged without exception. He took fifteen minutes to make this point, after which the delegations recessed until 8th October[20].

In the week before this meeting, the Joint Chiefs of Staff had been considering what military options they might take if General Harrison's proposals were rejected. Excepting operations against the Soviet Union, or the employment of nuclear or chemical weapons, they reviewed five forms:

a. amphibious, airborne, or ground offensives to increase pressure on enemy and possibly secure the waist or other areas of Korea.

b. air attacks on airdrome complexes.

c. blockade of China proper with coordinated air attacks on transportation centers using augmented forces.

d. air attacks on communications centers in north and central China and in Manchuria [North East China].

e. combinations or variations of actions outlined above[21].

General Clark was instructed to consider, in consultation with the Commander-in-Chief of the United States Navy in the Pacific, which of these options he favoured given the following resources:

Case I Forces now available to CINCFE for use in Korea.

Case II All forces presently under CINCFE Command [effectively, two divisions in Japan].

Case III Same as Case II augmented (not before Spring 1953)*.

General Clark replied on 29th September. A land offensive with his resources in Korea and Japan would not secure the results required, or justify his own losses in the process. An extension of the air war into North East China was within his capability but appeared unlikely to force the enemy to an armistice agreement, though it might do so in cooperation with deeper air attacks and a naval blockade.

Options with the reinforcements specified were another matter: they would offer a means of putting two marine divisions ashore in combination with an airborne force. With the relief of two UN divisions from the line by ROK formations and the employment of the two divisions in Japan, a manoeuvre force of seven divisions could be created for operations with strengthened sea and air forces. When he and his staff had had time to review options for their use he would make his recommendations[22].

---

* 82nd Airborne Division and a second Marine Division (with ground and air components) plus two ROK divisions and six regiments. two medium bomber wings and three fighter-bomber wings, with additional troop carrier aircraft, two carriers, a battleship, five cruisers, forty one destroyers, and amphibious shipping for 1/3 of a division.

In the State Department, Mr Hickerson was busy with preparations for the General Assembly. In so far as the Korean item was concerned, there was some doubt as to timing; many in the Department believed that the debate on the war should not take place at the United Nations until after the presidential election on 4th November. This was also the view of the Democratic Party, which hoped—vainly—that the war would not be an issue in that contest. Then, Mr Hickerson was aware at the beginning of October that Sir Oliver Franks had warned Mr Acheson of opposition to the additional measures he had floated, some of which he had not discussed with the Secretary of State. On 2nd October he sent the latter a memorandum reviewing the situation.

> ... There is a difference of opinion within the Department on the desirability of pursuing our 'second stage' [additional measures] proposals in the face of strong opposition from some of our best friends in the United Nations. The seriousness of the economic or psychological effect of an embargo upon Communist China, even if faithfully applied by the free world, is open to dispute. It will take a major effort on our part to push such proposals through the Assembly; Members are loathe to assume additional commitments of this type, and their resentment over our pressure tactics will be reflected in their action on other important problems.
>
> On the other hand, the United Nations will not be exerting the utmost pressure for an armistice unless additional measures are adopted. ...[23]

He suggested a lesser range of sanctions, chiefly applied to maritime trade against China and North Korea—Admiral Fechteler continued to report that merchantmen under the British flag were engaged extensively along the Chinese coast*. In the event, consideration of additional measures, which many had expected to be the major issue within the alliance, hung fire. It was overtaken by the an unexpected division on the exchange of prisoners. Mr Eden made it clear in a telegram to Washington on 10th October that they could not simply let the matter drop following the rejection on 28th September, which Nam Il repeated on 8th October. But this left open the matter of what should be done to avoid the drop. Having no new ideas, he allowed himself to be tempted by a departmental lobby proposing the revival of an earlier and discredited option as a British initiative. This was, he reminded the Cabinet on 30th September,

> ...broadly, that both sides should carry out all the articles of the armistice agreement already agreed between them and that the disposal of prisoners

* He was misinformed on two accounts. Local trade with Hong Kong was included. British registered ships chartered by foreign companies were almost invariably judged to be covering British cargoes. In any case, none of these were carrying prohibited goods. Maritime trade with China continued to decline during 1952–53.

> whose status remained in dispute after the cease fire should be the subject of later negotiations. He would be grateful if his colleagues would keep this proposal in mind, as he might have to seek their authority to press it upon the United States Government at a later stage[24].

He was wasting their time. Sir Oliver Franks, as much by implication as pronouncement, advised against it on 10th October, and the idea was put into and remained in reserve* [25].

The Seventh Session of the General Assembly opened in New York† in the third week of October. Mr Eden decided not to attend personally until the results of the United States presidential election were known, likewise M Schuman, the French Foreign Minister. Selwyn Lloyd‡, Minister of State, led the British delegation *ad interim*. Mr Acheson, conscious that his standing would diminish if his party lost the election, attended almost continuously for a fundamental reason he was later to recall.

> My own purpose was to support armistice terms that our Government, carrying the main responsibility for conducting the war, believed would end the fighting with the greatest hope of keeping it ended and of stability thereafter. To do this required holding the British steadily on course with us, keeping the support of the Latin American and European states, a group that could defeat any harmful proposal and was essential to any useful one, and, finally, guarding against proposals of two adroit operators, Krishna Menon of India, [accepted as] leader of the Arab-Asian states, and Lester B. Pearson of Canada, President of the Assembly. These would give the appearance, without having the effect, of achieving our purpose, thus gaining support among delegates from 'uncommitted' nations[26].

The first task he set himself was to secure the endorsement of the policy to date of the United Nations Command as carried forward by its executive agent, the United States. To this end, the support of twenty one nations was expected: fourteen of the fifteen nations with armed forces in Korean operations, two of the three supplying medical support, and four others¶. The exceptions were South Africa, which was anticipating withdrawal under attack for its racial policies, and India, which had a field ambulance in Korea but was not prepared to support the United States initiative, believing it to be unrelenting.

---

* The Chiefs of Staff were also alarmed that Mr Eden's suggestion might react against British prisoners of war. See COS (52), 145th Meeting (DEFE4/57) Tuesday, 14th October, and 151st Meeting, 3rd November 1952.

† In new premises at Turtle Bay.

‡ Lloyd, Rt Hon Selwyn Brooke, (later Baron Selwyn-Lloyd) (1904–1978).

¶ Australia, Belgium, Canada, Colombia, Ethiopia, France, Greece, Luxembourg, the Netherlands, New Zealand, the Philippines, Thailand, Turkey, the United Kingdom, and the United States, with Denmark and Norway (medical support), Honduras, Iceland, Nicaragua, and Uruguay.

The opening item to be taken in the First Committee was the Korea situation. Mr Acheson made an opening speech widely admired for its lucidity, moderation, and force. Over two and threequarter hours*, he traced the history of the Korean conflict to the final outstanding point in the armistice negotiations, winning over a number of delegates. All seemed to be moving forward satisfactorily. By majority vote, the Republic of Korea had been invited to participate, the North Koreans had been excluded. But within the Commonwealth Group, which met at Assembly gatherings, an idea was being mooted which threatened divisions within the twenty one nations.

> At a meeting of the Commonwealth delegations today [Selwyn Lloyd informed the Foreign Office on 28th October] Mr Krishna Menon stated that the Indian delegation would not vote in favour of the joint resolution. He stated that ...the Indian Government did not approve of all the United Nations negotiators had done, did not feel that an armistice would be brought nearer by the passage of a resolution sponsored *inter alia* by the United States and opposed by the Soviet *bloc*. He felt that any such resolution would inevitably be regarded by the Chinese Government as in the nature of an ultimatum. He thought that the action most likely to be helpful would be the passage of a resolution, if necessary by only a small majority, in regard to which both groups of Great Powers might perhaps abstain.
>
> 2. It was not at all clear how Mr Menon expected such a result to come about. The line on which his mind was working was, however, the following. He clearly doubted the strength of the legal premise on which the legal case for refusing forcible repatriation is based and evidently felt that under the Geneva Convention the Chinese have a better case than the United Nations negotiators are prepared to admit. He therefore thought that the United Nation negotiators should be prepared to go further than they have hitherto done in accepting and applying the principle that all prisoners of war should be repatriated. The kind of solution which he appeared to contemplate was that both sides should hand over their prisoners of war to what he termed a protecting Power, which might well be the Neutral Nations Supervisory Commission provided for under Article 37 of the Draft Armistice Agreement. ...once the prisoners of war had been handed over to the protecting authority, the latter would be free to use all means other than force to persuade the prisoners of war to return to their respective countries of origin. There would be no time limit during which prisoners of war, who were in the early stages unwilling to return home, should be maintained under the control of the protecting authority. ...
>
> 3. ... I should be glad to know whether you consider that the Indian delegation should be encouraged to pursue discussions on these lines[27].

Mr Eden was ready to encourage pursuit, as were a number of his officials, but urged caution. They were aware that frustration was a poor servant of judgement.

* In his book quoted, Mr Acheson claims he spoke for two hours. The UN record is quoted here.

Few in the American or British delegations cared for Krishna Menon. He was regarded as vauntingly ambitious, ever ready to exploit his authority to the limit to serve his image as an international statesman. He encouraged the idea that he had exceptional contacts with the Soviet Government and understood the mind of the Peking government. But a new key was needed to unlock the negotiating door. Although Mr Menon's ideas were vague, they seemed to contain the germ of a new idea. By chance or design, word came just then of further meetings between the new Indian Ambassador in Peking and Chou En-lai which suggested the use of a neutral intermediary[28]; a deliberate encouragement, perhaps, to accept Mr Menon's concept. Whether this was true or not, Mr Eden continued to urge caution, not least because considerable practical difficulties were seen in implementing it[29]. He was also anxious to accommodate United States views.

Unfortunately, Mr Acheson did not see the development in this way[30]. His party lost the election on 4th November and from that moment, as he had apprehended, he was seen as the Secretary of State of a government that would be out of office on 20th January 1995. His Korean war policies had been attacked by the Republican Party for more than two years. They had wounded him, not least in making those policies an issue in the election. It was his aim to deliver to the new government, when it assumed office under General Eisenhower at the end of January, the endorsement of his work and that of his colleagues by the General Assembly, and that would include a resolution affirming the principle of voluntary repatriation.

Mr Menon's scheme seemed to him to threaten that; to offer to those supporting it a means of slipping out of the obligation the United Nations Command had assumed in this matter because it was inconvenient. The vagueness of Mr Menon's scheme—he changed tack from day to day when pressed for details—aroused his suspicions; and the core of it appeared to be no more than a rehash of ideas considered and discarded, the latest of which had been fielded by the Mexican President*.

A Canadian idea also distracted Mr Acheson—and not only Mr Acheson.

> My dear Anthony [Selwyn Lloyd wrote to Mr Eden on 3rd November], I think you should know that [Lester] Pearson is in a somewhat volatile frame of mind. The present resolution sponsored by the United States, the United Kingdom etc., provides for the President of the Assembly transmitting it to the Chinese Communists. He has some idea of suggesting, possibly publicly, that there should be a cease fire whilst the Communists were

---

* Indonesia and Peru also made proposals to solve the dispute.

> considering the resolution. He thinks once the shooting stops, it will not begin again...[31]

By this time, Mr Acheson had come to see himself as endangered by an external plot, but continued to negotiate towards a plan which could be contained within the proposal to be put before the Assembly[32]. Mr Eden conveyed some of his colleague's difficulties to London following a lunch meeting on Sunday, 9th November 1952.

> ... 3. Mr Acheson added that he hoped very shortly to have the views of the Pentagon on the type of proposal which the Indians had in mind. He explained that he was in a very delicate position. If the Pentagon saw strong objection to any proposed solution it would not necessarily help if President Truman approved it; the view of the Pentagon would become known and General Eisenhower [president elect] would be likely to support it. If, on the other hand, the Pentagon were persuaded, this would help with General Eisenhower. ...
>
> After lunch Mr Acheson and I were joined by M. Schumann. We agreed to meet again after Mr Vyshinsky's speech in the first committee tomorrow morning and my speech in the plenary [session] on Tuesday morning to consider the situation with the object of encouraging one good resolution on Korea which might be forwarded by a representative of the neutral bloc[33].

One good resolution... All the twenty one powers were agreed on this aim. Mr Acheson wished it to exclude Mr Menon's ideas. He foresaw a situation in which prisoners would be delivered to the demilitarised zone where, due to a compromise in the wording of the armistice agreement, they would be snatched away by North Korean and Chinese forces, or condemned to remain in some intermediate camp, rotting in limbo. His suspicions were aggravated by a resumption of discussions in Peking between the new Indian Ambassador, Dr N Raghavan, and Chou En-lai, once more suggesting the possibility of Chinese concessions[34].

Nevertheless, in the course of many conversations, the notion of establishing a commission to supervise the exchange of the prisoners of war gained some American interest, and that this body might be the 'neutral' commission agreed upon to supervise the implementation of the armistice agreement overall. The word 'neutral' occasioned some discussion. The Americans did not regard Czechoslovakia or Poland as neutral, and wished for representation by India with Sweden and Switzerland, but it was accepted that the Chinese and North Koreans regarded all three as partial to the United Nations Command. Indeed, the Communist group regarded no state as 'neutral'; all were committed more or less to one side or the other.

To strengthen his hand, Mr Acheson obtained a statement from President Truman that the view he expressed was not simply a matter of ministerial enterprise but represented the opinion of the United States Government. This failed to inhibit the development of the Menon plan, even though its provisions began to assume a form that its originator did not entirely support. By 15th November, Mr Eden was able to report to London

> 3. Though there are admittedly drafting imperfections, this [latest draft] resolution does contain our essential needs. It would clearly be immensely valuable if whole Assembly except Russians and satellites would endorse one resolution. ...[35]

Unhappily for Mr Acheson, he did not know that Mr Churchill was continuing to peruse the Foreign Office telegrams and would certainly not have agreed to a split with the United States Government or abandonment of the voluntary repatriation principle*. His anxiety thus persisted: on the morning of 20th November, he warned President Truman and General Eisenhower that any divisions between Britain, Canada, France, and the United States

> 'would not be confined to Korea but would also have implications in NATO ...[36]

He wrote later in the day to the President:

> ... I think we have reached a situation in this debate [in New York] in which it is no longer a question whether the draft resolution we and the 20 other states sponsored is to pass or the compromise resolution introduced by Krishna Menon of India will pass. Our resolution, you will remember, was a straightforward endorsement of the UNC position in the armistice negotiations. The Indian resolution includes complex procedural arrangements for carrying out the disposition of POWs and was drafted by him in such a way as to make it as easy as possible, in his opinion, for the Communists to accept it. We have now reached a point at which the only question is whether we can lead the 20 powers to amend Menon along the lines worked out with the Joint Chiefs of Staff.
> Menon made an emotional speech today in the political committee. It was fuzzy but nevertheless seemed to exert a powerful appeal to a large number of wavering delegations.
>
> As I mentioned to you, our basic problem has not been with Menon but with the British, Canadians and French, who feel strongly we should accept Menon's resolution even though it waters down considerably the principles on which we have taken our stand at Panmunjom. The British, Canadians and French think such a resolution might produce an armistice. They have grave apprehensions about what the new administration may do regarding Korea, and therefore show a desperate anxiety to exhaust all possibilities

---

* The British Chiefs of Staff were equally resolute on the essential principles, including 'no forcible detention'. See COS (52), 151st Meeting, Minute 4 (DEFE 4/57), and FK 1071/663 (FO 371 99590).

for an armistice now, however remote. They argue that even if an armistice were not to result, Menon's resolution would still attract solid Asiatic support. They are very soft on our principles, particularly our insistence that all POWs who do not wish to return home be freed within a short space of time.

Following your instructions, I laid it on the line with Eden today. I said we wanted to know whether he was with us or against us. He assured me that he wanted to be with us. I told him we could not accept an arrangement for the prisoners which left them no alternative except repatriation or continuing to rot in a POW camp, as is now provided in Menon's resolution. He agreed they they could not either, but he stressed the importance of not changing Menon's resolution so much that Menon might be unable to vote for it himself. I told Eden that he might have to choose between our vote or the Indian vote, and he said that in that case he wanted ours.

I think we may be able to work this out. ... The British seem to be moving in our direction, but have not yet come far enough. ...[37]

This was not how the British saw the situation. The American anxieties were recognised; the British aim was to keep pressing for modification of the resolution, embracing the State Department's requirements while simultaneously carrying the Indian vote[38]. They believed it could be done.

Mr Acheson's report to President Truman on 21st November was more optimistic.

Dear Mr President, I am able to report to you some brightening of the prospects here in the UN debate on Korea...

For one thing the British have prepared the way for agreement with us on modifications that must be made in the Menon resolution. We were pleased to note that Eden in his speech before the Political Committee today indicated a considerable measure of agreement with the considerations we had been arguing with some force. While endorsing the Menon resolution, Eden indicated support for major modification to provide for making the Repatriation Commission effective by strengthening the position of the umpire, and for the release of prisoners not repatriated to UNKRA or some other UN agency to care for and resettle them.

The other major hopeful development is that Spender of Australia* is taking a strong initiative behind the scenes to solidify support among the 21 powers for a series of modifications of the Menon resolution. During the day Friday [21st November 1952], Spender plans to put before a subcommittee of the 21 sponsors proposals to meet our main points. If there is general agreement on these propositions, he will then endeavour to get agreement on language for amendments. ...[39]

Mr Edens reported on that day to the Prime Minister,

---

* Sir Percy Spender was then Australian Ambassador to the United States.

My speech before the First Committee yesterday has been generally well received here and the United States delegation commented favourably on it to the Press. ... So far, the Communist delegations have given no hint of their attitude to the resolution, though the Czechoslovak representative today said that he had referred it to his Government and must reserve his position meanwhile.

4. [At the 21 Powers meeting] Gross (United States) urged that decision must be taken by [them] today [21st November] which must be incorporated in the Indian draft before the 21 Powers could vote, to give it priority over their own resolution. Gross said that failing such agreement the United States Government would vote in favour of priority for the 21 Power resolution. He explained that Mr Acheson wished to speak in the First Committee on Monday afternoon, when the general debate on the Korean question is due to close, and that agreement among the 21 Powers was urgently required in order that he could prepare his speech. Gross argued that matter was urgent also because, as time passed, there was risk of the 21 Power front breaking up. ...

5. After the Minister of State [Lloyd] had pointed out that, so far from being a concession by us, an Indian resolution incorporating our views about the use of force represented an important victory, I suggested that it would be impracticable for the 21 Powers to make a decision today. ...we should retain flexibility in negotiations and should use the next forty-eight hours to try, by private discussions, to get Krishna Menon to accept voluntarily those of the amendments to which we attach importance. ...[40]

The Americans were hustling their allies and their bluff was called. Eden's suggestion was adopted. But the British then had their own anxieties that forty eight hours would be insufficient to cover their own negotiations and references back to New Delhi.

After further conversations with Mr Menon and Mr Pearson today [22nd November, Mr Eden reported on that day], Mr Menon undertook to submit to his Government by telegraph amended texts of the two essential paragraphs...

2. These are designed to meet the points which I raised in my speech on Thursday, and certainly go a long way to do so. This is also the Canadian view, and will, no doubt, be that of a large number of other delegations, sone of whom did not even want to amend the Indian text at all.

3. I am, however, by no means sanguine that the Americans, in their present mood, will agree to these texts when they see them. Acheson is away in Canada, and at his request I have seen Gross. Gross hinted that the main objection comes from Pentagon [Defense Department] but Acheson himself could not have been more rigid, legalistic and difficult. While Gross was with me Associated Press put out a report. I showed this to him, pointing out that there had never been any argument about no forcible repatriation, on which we were all agreed. He was much embarrassed at such a reference to what was supposed to be a private meeting and hinted that this was indicative of the pressure upon him. ...

> 5. If the Americans persist in demanding that the committee take binding decisions tomorrow night, there will be acute embarrassment, and very likely a clear division of view. Naturally we should not want this to be public, but though no press are present, a committee of this size can never be confidential. I have done my best to dissuade the Americans from holding the meeting until Monday. We hope, however, that by tomorrow night Menon's amendments will have been made public. ...[41]

The Indian Government accepted the greater part of the proposals put to them, inspiring recognition at last from Mr Acheson of the 'great value of an Indian resolution embodying our principle... ' so that he 'would not wish to lose Indian support.' Even so, he sought further concessions. Accepting residual imperfections, Mr Lloyd reckoned that as the text stood it was acceptable 'to go forward as a basis for an armistice agreement'[42].

With the consequences of these differing views undecided, the Russian chief delegate, Mr Vyshinsky, made his own contribution. Addressing the First Committee on the afternoon of 24th November, he scorned the Indian resolution[43]. It was wholly unacceptable in his view; and since he never uttered publicly—and rarely privately—any view that did not have the approval of Marshal Stalin, he was making it plain that the Communist side would not accept any arrangement for voluntary repatriation of prisoners. Next to speak, Mr Acheson commended 'the Indian initiative warmly'[44]; rather more warmly than he had intended before Mr Vyshinsky unexpectedly intervened. American support was further assured when China ignored—and later rejected—the resolution*. Meantime, Mr Eden had been setting the record straight with the New York press with good results on the Monday morning.

> ...Today's editorials show a steadier tone [he informed Mr Churchill that evening].
>
> 2. The *New York Times* says the various differences among the free nations on the truce resolutions pertain to questions of approach and method and not of principle. There is no disagreement on the one really vital issue. The free nations want a truce to come as quickly as possible, but it must come honourably and honour demands that there be no yielding involving the disposition of lives of prisoners against their will. In this specific case India has made the issue plain. Britain has reaffirmed her support and America is not at variance. ...
>
> 3. Anne O'Hare McCormick in her *New York Times* column says that the Indian attitude points significantly to the fact that the free nations of Asia, desperately anxious as they are for a cease-fire that would presumably

* This was formally announced by Chou En-lai on 29th November—see UN Press Release PM/2456. However, a negative reaction was anticipated when selected elements of the Chinese press gave prominence to Mr Vyshinsky's speech on 24th November 1952. See, for example, Shanghai *Ta Kung Pao* of the 24th November 1952.

prevent the Korean war from spreading, would not welcome even that relief at the cost of a serious rift between the United Kingdom and the United States.

4. The *Herald Tribune*'s obvious reference to the confusion created by the mismanagement of American publicity at the week end accuses the United States delegation of acting with unnecessary haste and harshness. 'First, it turned down the proposals before they had been formally set forth by the Indian representatives. Second, it announced with a rather shattering finality a split with British representatives. This hardly seems the conduct of a great and self-confident power but rather of men who have grown tired and nervous in their jobs. The Indian proposals have certain obvious drawbacks. Yet there remains the overriding consideration that genuine gains could be derived by the agreement of all friendly countries upon a plan set forth with much care and thought by the principal Asian government. If the struggle must go on it will do so in a better light if the burden of turning down the proposals were to fall upon the Communists'. ...[45]

On 1st December, after a further round of negotiations between the United States and India, mostly conducted by Anthony Eden or Selwyn Lloyd, and Lester Pearson, a resolution was agreed and put to the First Committee of the General Assembly. It finally overtook the original 21 Power draft calling on the Chinese and North Koreans to concede the outstanding point; a draft from which Mr Acheson had been progressively prised by argument. The Menon resolution *Noted with approval* 'the considerable progress towards an armistice made by negotiation at Panmunjom... *Noting further* that disagreement between the parties on one remaining issue, alone, prevents the conclusion of an armistice, ...' requested the President of the General Assembly to convey to China and North Korea proposals for solution of the *impasse*. Essentially, it provided for those refusing repatriation to be safeguarded by a Repatriation Commission which would explaining their rights to return to their country of origin or not as they desired and to protect them from any form of coercion.

The Commission—drawn from Czechoslovakia, Poland, Sweden and Switzerland—'shall at its first meeting and prior to an armistice proceed to agree upon and appoint the umpire who shall at all times be available to the Commission and shall act as its Chairman unless otherwise agreed. ...' Finally, any prisoners remaining for disposal after 120 days following the cease-fire would be passed to the United Nations for disposition 'in accordance with international law'[46]. The resolution was passed by a majority of 53 to 5 [the Soviet *bloc*]. Nationalist China [Taiwan] abstained.

Next day, the 2nd, a Russian proposal rejecting the principle of voluntary repatriation for prisoners of war, and proposing a cease fire while the entire question of exchange was put to an international commission was rejected by 41 votes to 5 [the Soviet *bloc*], with 12 abstentions*. On 3rd December, the General Assembly passed the Indian resolution subject to a minor amendment, while rejecting an amended version of the Russian proposal[47].

In retrospect, the British Foreign Office judged well the potential of Mr Menon's initiative. It was not that he had hit upon a novel solution—much of what he proposed had been discussed many times in one form or another. The value of it lay in his nationality: he was an Indian and thus an Asian as distinct from a North American or western European advancing a resolution to break the cease-fire deadlock. With the Canadians, notably Lester Pearson as President of the General Assembly, the British delegation advanced and moulded it.

This process was resisted by the United States initially because Mr Acheson was wedded to an entirely different concept—a 'simple' condemnatory General Assembly resolution which would lead to the Additional Measures Committee; and partly because he was accustomed to leading in consultation with the British and found this process suddenly reversed, just at a time when his governmental responsibilities, faithfully—sometimes brilliantly—conducted were coming to an end. Yet the outcome was by no means harmful to his reputation; rather the opposite. It is a pity that he recalled it with bitterness more than a decade later.

Krishna Menon lost more than he gained in esteem. From a torrent of words, principally a mish mash of legal and political theories and assumptions, he offered the core of an idea which he made lustrous by reminding the 21 Power delegations that it would be supported by the Arab-Asian group and, no less, by the Soviet Union, a claim publicly dishonoured by Mr Vishinsky. His rejection might have been attributed to the many amendments to the draft, but this did not serve as an excuse. The Russians objected to the Menon plan because it embodied from the outset the principle of voluntary repatriation.

Mr Vyshinsky also disillusioned British politicians, among them the leader of the Liberal Party, Mr Clement Davies, who had pressed the government not to dismiss Mr Vishinsky's speech at the opening of the General Assembly proceedings but to pursue any options for progress it might contain.

These issues are a reminder that, at the end of 1952, the allies in the United Nations Command had no firm idea as to Communist intentions in Korea except an instinctive feeling that, in a situation of stalemate in the land defences and mounting costs upon their economies,

---

* Those abstaining were: Afghanistan, Argentina, Burma, Egypt, India, Indonesia, Iran, Iraq, Lebanon, Pakistan, Saudi Arabia, Syria.

it was more likely than not that they would come to a settlement. As a matter of fact, Mr Menon's resolution had brought them closer to it than the allies realised.

SOURCE NOTES: Chapter 20

1 FRUS, 1952–54, volume xv, Korea, Part I, pp 324–326.
2 FO 2412 AND 2413 of to Washington 17th June 1952 to Washington, FK1071/304, (FO371 99575).
3 FRUS, 1952–54, *cit* pp 340–341.
4 *Ibid*, pp 344–346. See also Washington 1179 to FO of 19th June 1952, FK 1071/308, and UKHC New Delhi 777 to CRO of 17th June 1952, FK 1071/309, (FO 371 99576).
5 UKHC New Delhi 887 to CRO of 14th July 1952, FK 1071/399, (FO 371 99580).
6 FRUS, 1952–54, *cit* p 407.
7 Foreign Office Minute PM/WS/52/65 of 3rd July 1952, annotated by Prime Minister, FK 1071/370, (FO 371 99578)
8 FK 1071/409, (FO 371 99581), and conversation, author with Sir Charles Johnston.
9 FRUS, 1952–54, *cit*, pp 407–408.
10 See, for example, FRUS, 1952–54, *cit*, pp 447–448.
11 New York 213 to FO of 18th July 1952, FK 1071/444 (FO 371 99583).
12 *Ibid.*
13 FRUS, 1952–54, *cit* p 453.
14 Washington 864 to FO of 14th August, FK 1071/438, (FO 371 99582). See also FRUS, 1952–54, *cit* pp 453–456.
15 FO 3697 to Washington of 6th September 1952 FK/1071/438, (FO 371 99582).
16 FK 1071/482, (FO 371 99584).
17 FO 3698 of 6th September 1952 to Washington, *ibid.*
18 See UKHC New Zealand 527 of 5th September 1952 to CRO, FK 1071/476, *ibid.* Also McGibbon, *op cit*, volume i, p 280.
19 UKHC South Africa 247 to CRO of 29th August 1952, FK 1071/466, (FO 371 99583). See also FK 1071/ 524, (FO 371 99585).
20 For the record of the meeting, see FRUS, 1952–54, *cit* pp 545–548. Also FK 1071/528, (FO 371 99585).
21 JCS 919187 of 1701, 23rd September 1952 to CINCFE (USNARS, Suitland), and FRUS, 1952–54, *cit*, pp 527 528.
22 *Ibid*, pp 548–550.
23 FRUS, 1952–54, *cit*, pp 551–552. See also Washington 1814 of to FO of 23rd September 1952, FK 1071/508; and New York 298 (FO 371 99585) of 26th September 1952 to FO, FK 1071/519.
24 C.C. (52) 82nd Conclusions, Minute No 1, CAB 128/25.
25 FO 4291 to Washington of 10th October 1952, FK 1071/560, Washington 1918 to FO (same date), FK 1071/551, (FO 371 99586). FO 4089 to Washington of 11th October 1952, FK 1071/564, (FO 371 99587).
26 Acheson, *op cit*, p 138.
27 New York 712 to FO of 28th October 1952, FK 1071/583 and 584, (FO 371 99587).
28 UKHC New Delhi 1334 to CRO of 28th October 1952, FK 1071/586, (FO 371 99587) and 1360 Of 5th November, FK 1071/620, FO 371 99589.
29 See, for example, FO 882 amd 883 to New York of 5th November 1952 repeated to the Commonwealth in Y 412 of 6th November 1952 in FK 1071/622, (FO 371 99589).
30 See FRUS, 1952–54, *cit*, pp 566–568.
31 FK 1071/626 (FO 371 99589).
32 FRUS, 1952–54, *cit*, pp 586–589.
33 New York 759 to FO of 9th November 1952 , FK 1071/627, (FO 371 99589).
34 FRUS, 1952–54, *cit*, pp 589–590.
35 New York 808 to FO of 15th November 1952, FK 1071/644, (FO 371 99589).
36 Truman, *op cit*, pp 548–549.
37 FRUS, 1952–54, *cit*, pp 662–663.
38 See FK 1071/661, (FO 371 99590).

39 FRUS, 1952–54, *cit*, pp 663–664.
40 New York 858 to FO of 21st November 1952, FK 1071/664, (FO 371 99590).
41 New York 866 to FO of 22nd November 1952, FK 1071/665. See also FK 1071/667—both in FO 371 99590.
42 New York 876 amd 877 to FO of 24th November 1952, FK 1071/673 and 672, (FO 371 99590).
43 For the text of his speech, see UN document A/C.1/SR. 529
44 New York 884 to FO of 25th November 1952, FK 1071/674, (FO 371 99590).
45 New York 885 to FO of 24th November 1952 , FK 1071/675, (FO 371 99590).
46 See UN document A/2278 of 2nd December 1952.
47 UN document A/PV.399.

CHAPTER 21

Fighting for a principle

General Van Fleet did not find it easier to live with the political constraint of operations in 1952 than 1951. Characteristically, he wanted to be up and doing things, defeating the enemy array. In the spring of 1952, in the second year of his command, he found some outlet for his energy in the enhancement of his defences.

The Chinese, manning the western and central front, and the North Koreans holding the mountainous eastern sector, had both been heavily reinforced with artillery and mortars. There was a requirement to resite a number of the United Nations forward positions on the slopes lying behind crest lines—the 'reverse' slopes—a change in turn necessitating the relocation of numerous machine-guns posts. In any case, many of the latter had been positioned hastily in former enemy trenches or bunkers following struggles for territory. It had been difficult to adjust these in the frozen ground of the winter months. Thus too many embraced frontal arcs, too few were sited in enfilade to fire across the approaches to neighbouring friendly positions. Barbed wire fences were similarly in need of realignment. Not least, the summer would bring rainstorms. While the ground softened, but before it turned to mud, there was much to do, including the development of drainage systems. He gave instructions to his corps commanders accordingly[1].

The Marine Corps excepted, the American soldiers were reluctant trench diggers. The requirement was now so evident, however, that they responded energetically. The ROK formations had long been enthusiastic in field works and had acquired expertise by 1952 in the technicalities of fortification and the art of siting. Their chief problem lay in a scarcity of basic materials: tools, timber, angle irons and wire. A talent for improvisation, highly developed among the peasant farmers and artisans in their ranks, provided some compensation for these deficiencies.

The Commonwealth Division dug deep and, on the whole, organised its defences well with arcs of fire linking the front in width and depth. But events during the winter of 1951–52, following Operation Commando, necessitated reorganisation and renovation of their positions. There had been several sharp battalion battles in November 1951—attempts were made to occupy the foremost heights held by 1 KSLI and the Leicesters;

and attacks were launched on the PPCLI and 2nd Royal 22e*. Although ground lost was wholly recovered, the positions regained had been smashed by artillery fire. Considerable work was required to reinstate them.

Then, from 20th November, General Cassels' request for a reduction in his frontage of 19,000 metres, due to shortage of manpower, was granted; but it involved a limited shuffle sideways. For the advantage of a front reduced to 15,000 metres held by two brigades†, the division passed Kowang-san and all its territory to the east to the American 3rd Division, but assumed about two miles of the defence line west of the Samich'on. This change alone necessitated considerable resiting as well as refurbishment of the defence works on a temporary basis during the winter and more extensively in the spring.

General Cassels was concerned throughout the winter that his soldiers should be kept warm and fit in the defensive line, prerequisites of alertness and morale in the sub-arctic temperatures‡. As a result of this policy, enemy attempts to penetrate his line were frustrated. Active operations within the division were confined to 'patrolling, harassing and the odd minor raid'; he had resisted an extraordinary scheme for an armoured raid on a target seven miles behind the enemy line[2]. But he was apprehensive that with the warmer weather Generals Van Fleet and O'Daniel would be seeking a return to ill-considered projects. Eighth Army's Operation Snare implemented between 10th–16th February 1952 encouraged this expectation.

> ... Briefly, it entailed stopping all artillery, tank and mortar fire and all patrolling for the period... The aim was to make the enemy so curious that they would come in some strength to see what was happening and we would kill them in large numbers and capture some prisoners.
>
> My own view [General Cassels reported] was that the operation would give the enemy exactly the opportunity he wanted to improve his defences on the forward slopes and to work his way forward with impunity. As we had spent the previous month using every possible means to force the enemy back and off the forward slopes and had destroyed many of his bunkers, I protested strongly against this operation. ...
>
> I regret to say that the result has been exactly as I and all my commanders anticipated. ...[3]

---

* These Chinese attacks were launched while the line of demarcation was being finalised at Panmunjom.

† Previously, the divisional share on the consolidated Line Kansas-Wyoming had required seven battalions forward, thus preventing the disposal of a complete brigade in reserve.

‡ The *Sunday Despatch* on 6th January 1952 attacked War Office arrangements for failure to supply adequate winter clothing, stoves and ancillary items. The reports were exaggerated, but the Quartermaster-General's staff had showed some want of urgency in pressing procurement from the previous summer, and were negligent in supplying the sizes required. (See WO 216/492, and the divisional Periodic Report, 15th October 1951, 15th February 1952, Appendix D, paragraph 2.)

Just as he had apprehended, also, as the weather warmed and the refurbishment of defence works was completed, various offensive enterprises were set in hand across the United Nations front. These varied in scope from substantial tactical battles for ground of advantage to the capture of prisoners. All were designed to keep the fighting soldiers 'sharp', the American term which sometimes meant 'alert', but was more often meant to convey 'offensively minded'.

It is, of course, very easy to deride the senior commanders in Korea at this time for their pursuit of an offensive spirit, but they would have been in breach of their duty if they had allowed a wholly passive mood to develop among those required to defend the United Nations line. As observed earlier, the Chinese and North Koreans maintained to the limit of commanders' and political officers' abilities an offensive outlook. If the opportunity had presented itself to revert to an offensive strategy, Mao and, even more, Kim Il-sung, would have done so up to the final stage of armistice negotiations.

Adoption of a purely defensive attitude among the United Nations divisions would have encouraged Communist aggression and weakened the means to resist it. Soldiers occupying positions from which they never make a sortie rapidly develop an acute sense of self-preservation. If the enemy in contradistinction dominates no-man's land, raids freely to take prisoners or seize local points of vantage, the image of his invincibility grows. The idea is nurtured that when a defensive position is pressed it cannot be held, so it is abandoned. And it is abandoned more readily by those who have been in position for a number of months and are thus looking forward to being sent home at the end of a set term of operations. Similarly, when there seems to be a strong chance that an armistice will be concluded shortly, even those who have recently come into the line think twice about holding a piece of ground tenaciously. Survival becomes the first aim of the soldier.

General Cassels observed in his periodic report for the winter of 1951–1952,

> ... If the peace talks break down and we have to start operations again I feel there is likely to be a drop in morale and it will take a little time and considerable effort on the part of all leaders to get things going.
>
> In this connection it is very noticeable that, after about nine months in Korea, the 'hard core' of a unit (company commanders, warrant officers etc) lose a lot of their 'sparkle'. This of course applies mainly to infantry units[4].

Thus the pursuit of active operations had a sound basis. Mastering no-man's land by laying ambushes, reconnoitring the enemy's positions, occasionally raiding by fighting patrols or larger forces to take prisoners or knock out particularly vexatious enemy observation posts were doubly advantageous. These limited enterprises checked enemy aggression and heightened the morale of those undertaking them. But their use required a sense of proportion. The advantages would be dissipated if they led to unwonted casualties.

Thus, it was reasonable in June for the American 45th Division* to engage in the progressive seizure of enemy observation posts looking deep into its positions west of Ch'orwon for the loss of fourteen killed and one hundred wounded. The enemy's ability to shell and mortar its defence line was appreciably limited as a consequence. But it was not reasonable to raid repeatedly for prisoners at a high cost in casualties when the results were nugatory due to the strength of the enemy's line. Between 20th and 24th June, 1 PPCLI, 1st Battalion, The Royal Canadian Regiment (Lieutenant-Colonel P R Bingham), 1st Battalion, The Welch Regiment (Lieutenant-Colonel H H Deane) and the 1st Battalion, 22e Regiment (Lieutenant-Colonel L F Trudeau) lost fourteen killed among seventy six casualties—the greater part of a company—without bringing back a single live prisoner. As in the UN positions, the enemy were fighting from deep bunkers.

> During the last month [General Cassels reported in June 1952] we have been ordered to produce one prisoner every three days and have been authorised to use up to a battalion to achieve this. In fact, we have put in a series of company raids ... they have been comparatively costly. As a result I have ordered that they should be suspended and we are trying some other methods. ... As we know quite well what enemy divisions are in front of us I cannot see the point of this and have said so and have asked if there is any special reason behind the request. I have made it clear that I will do all in my power to get as many prisoners as possible, but that I consider a series of battalion or company raids a most unprofitable way of doing it, unless the need is considerably greater than I think it is. At present this has been agreed, but I do not know how long it will last. ... The Commander of 1st US Marine Division on my left† visited me on 29th June and raised this very point. He is in complete agreement with my views[5].

When General Cassels referred to 'other methods', he had ambushes principally in mind: seeking to capture prisoners from one or another of the many enemy parties venturing at night into no-man's land. North Korean prisoners had been taken in this way during the winter. However, as he remarked, they knew well the details of the formations directly to their front and were by no means dependent on prisoners for information about enemy activities. Another important source was the

* The 45th was one of two National Guard divisions mobilised and deployed to Japan to replace regular formations sent to Korea. It relieved 1st Cavalry Division, which returned to Japan in November/December 1951. The 40th Division similarly relieved the 24th in December/January 1952.

† Major-General John T Selden USMC. The division, numbering more than 30,000, came into the sector immediately west of the Commonwealth Division in March 1952, relieving the latter's forces west of the Samich'on.

monitoring of enemy clear language radio traffic*, employing an American specialist detachment, with auxiliary stations provided by the Commonwealth Signals Regiment. The specialists included Chinese, Korean, and Russian linguists—the latter language was heard infrequently, and was used in connexion with artillery and anti-aircraft operations[6].

Raids and ambushes took place in darkness. The division also mounted daylight operations, including sorties to draw out fire from suspected weapon sites. Several of these were undertaken by the 5th Royal Iniskilling Dragoon Guards.

The regiment under Lieutenant-Colonel A Carr OBE†, had arrived in December to relieve the 8th Hussars, bringing only their personal and regimental baggage‡; otherwise, they took over everything from the latter. The 8th had worked hard and succesfully to bring their mobility and fire power to the support of the infantry of 29th Brigade and, later, the Commonwealth Division for almost a year despite the problems of narrow roads, steep hills and, for half the year, soft paddy. The formation of a static line changed the requirement. As the division completed resettlement on its reduced frontage, the 5th Dragoon Guards—5 DG—assisted in the struggle for forward observation sites but then settled the majority of its tanks in selected localities amongst the entrenched infantry posts, including one considered previously unapproachable by armour just between Kowang-san and Point 227, for which the KSLI had fought valiantly on several occasions.

Direct fire from the tank 20-pounder guns and machine-guns was frequently called for by patrolling infantry or engineers working in no-man's land, and added weight to local defence. Each troop had a series of targets on to which it could switch fire at short notice by day or night. Troop officers accompanied infantry patrols from time to time to acquire experience of the customer's requirements on the ground. Two of the three 'sabre'—tank—squadrons were deployed forward with 28th and 29th Brigades¶ as each took its turn in the line. The third remained in reserve for mobile operations.

In mid-February, however, the whole regiment made a grand sortie

---

* As previously noted, the Chinese and North Koreans listened similarly to the United Nations traffic. The Commander, Royal Signals, 1st Commonwealth Division, also monitored divisional radio communications to ensure that radio 'discipline'—that is, correct use of security procedures—was maintained to deny information to the enemy. Where possible, telephone lines were in use to minimise the use of radio, but these were often destroyed by bombardments, when it was necessary to revert to speech by 'wireless'.

† He was succeeded in command in April 1952 by Lieutenant-Colonel R de C Vigors DSO.

‡ They also brought numerous Phillips' razors. Before leaving England, an enterprising corporal from the Regiment wrote to the Dutch electric company to ask for a razor for his tank crew. The company sent enough for all crews.

¶ The Canadian brigade continued to be supported directly by its own armoured squadron from Lord Strathcona's Horse.

to draw out the enemy artillery positions. Two squadrons on the west with 28 Brigade engaged in Operation Liverpool, Major T M H R Tomkin's B Squadron on the right with 1 Royal Leicesters of 29 Brigade, Operation Ascot. Troubled initially by friendly as well as enemy mines, Liverpool began slowly, but the leading troops of Major H C Walker's C Squadron brought the broken crest of Hill 227, recaptured by the Chinese, under fire. Ascot began better but the Centurion tracks failed to grip the frostbound slopes. One of their number, seeking to traverse a hillside, turned over.

As the venture closed during an overcast afternoon, the enemy guns responded obligingly, raking the Centurions' armour with shrapnel. Numerous fresh sites were disclosed to the divisional counter-battery staff. A greater immediate threat to 5 DG was the intervention of Chinese anti-tank guns, one of which holed a C Squadron turret, while solid shot, probably fired by Chinese field artillery, rang across the front of several other tanks. Enemy radio conversations in the late stages of the battle suggested that they were apprehensive of armoured thrusts from the United Nations forces.

From this and following sorties, 5 DG came to appreciate the limits of their potential. They exercised to improve their ability to move quickly into no-man's-land to assist the recovery of ground lost. There was an abiding obstacle to quick reaction: mines.

On 17th June, General Cassels launched a reinforced squadron* of 5 DG, supported by the divisional artillery to raid the enemy line in daylight. This was Operation Jehu, one of a number of operations employed by the divisional commander as an option to night raiding into the deep fortifications of the enemy line. The engineers had opened gaps in their own minefields. Lieutenant Charles Taylor's troop led the advance westward at 0500, skirting the flooded paddy fields to pass below Point 227. To avoid using the track in the approach valley, which was almost certainly mined, and staying well clear of the flooded paddy fields in which they would have rapidly become bogged, the tanks travelled on the intervening bunds. But their weight was too much for these mudbanks. They cracked and broke. The water flooded out, along the track and shoulders creating a quagmire for those following. Taylor's troop continued alone, penetrating to the reverse slopes of the Chinese outposts, whose occupants were taken by surprise. They belonged to the Chinese 119th Division. A mountain gun began to fire to provide assistance but this was quickly knocked out by a Centurion's gun. Sergeant [later, Major] E Bertrand, observed from his turret that his tank was

* The four troops of A Squadron reinforced by one from B, and another from Lord Strathcona's Horse. Just prior to the operation, all crew commanders of one troop became casualties in a mine burst as they made a reconnaissance of the ground on foot.

> ...running up a fairly narrow spur with a long enemy communication trench dangerously near the tank track, and to cap it all, the danger of a bunker collapsing under the weight of a 50-ton Centurion...[7]

By this time the troop was under considerable artillery fire. Taylor's tank caught fire—he climbed out to extinguish it.

Meantime, the remainder of Major G W R Monckton's reinforced A Squadron was seeking a way forward, providing intermittent covering fire to Lieutenant Taylor's troop while receiving bursts of 122-mm shellfire from the artillery of the Chinese Fortieth Army. A Squadron sergeant-major's tank was hit ten times. The force was extended to its limit. Colonel Vigors ordered it to withdraw over the only optional route, a southern loop up and down a series of steep spurs, on which the rearguard lost an officer killed and two wounded—one a New Zealand artillery officer. Three tanks remained bogged on the edge of a protective minefield, and in attempts at recovery, two armoured recovery vehicles joined them. Captain P K Cuthbert one of the regiment's EMEs* was wounded. The 5 DG teams persevered, despite further casualties, to free three of the five on the 17th June, but the onset of heavy rain hindered recovery of the remaining two. General Cassels instructed Colonel Vigors to leave them until conditions improved.

In daylight also, A Company of 1st Battalion, The Royal Australian Regiment—1 RAR—raided Hill 227 on 2nd July to seize a prisoner, a baptism of fire—the battalion had only recently arrived under Lieutenant-Colonel I Hutchison DSO MC. This was Operation Blaze. At a glance, the operation appeared foolhardy, a reversion to the blinkered perceptions and muddles of the western front in 1914-18. The company was to attack directly across ground broken by the shellfire of both sides. The enemy was located below ground in deep bunkers connected by open communication trenches. Exceptionally, there was insufficient divisional or corps artillery to open the fortifications. Air strikes arranged for the evening of 1st July and again early on the morning of the 2nd were cancelled due to low clouds.

Yet Brigadier T J Daly†, commanding 28th Brigade, a sound and experienced commander, persisted in the plan. The night raids in June which had all failed to capture a prisoner had been expensive in casualties due in part to the difficulty of finding entry points within the enemy defences in darkness. They might do better in daylight. The Chinese positions lacked barbed wire here. The target area was a series of outposts five hundred yards from the attacking company's positions, and the

---

* Electrical and Mechanical Engineers.

† Later, Lieutenant-General Sir Thomas [James] Daly, (1913–), Chief of the General Staff, Australian Army. He had succeeded Brigadier Macdonald in command of the brigade, which then comprised two Australian and two British battalions.

locality, Point 227, could be supported by 1 RAR's own machine-guns and mortars immediately to the south in addition to those of 1 Welch on Kowang-san to the north*.

Shortly after 0830 on the morning of 2nd July, Major D S Thomson's A Company ran on to the objective. Some jumped into the communication trenches and attempted to penetrate bunker entrances using grenades and flame throwers. Several bunkers had been hit by the truncated heavy artillery; some were unoccupied; two spewed small arms fire. The Australians began to dig into these from above, despite the onset of Chinese artillery and mortar fire. One bunker collapsed on its occupants, blazing petroleum was poured into the other.

These events had taken an hour and a half. Although Major Thomson's own radio and that of his artillery officer had been destroyed, sets were taken from the nearest platoons. He reported the situation. It was clear to Colonel Hutchison that there were no enemy alive to be captured and his soldiers, though successful in destroying the Chinese outposts, were falling to enemy fire to no purpose. He called them back[8].

Operation Blaze cost 1 RAR three killed and thirty four wounded. A night raid was tried on 13th/14th July by 3 RAR at a cost of sixteen casualties. General Cassels sent full details to Major-General Paul W Kendall, who had succeeded General O'Daniel in command of I United States Corps, remarking that, on the evidence of these two and numerous other raids, he intended to discontinue this activity for a time[9]. The declaration fortunately coincided with an intervention by General Clark, but nonetheless considerably displeased General Kendall.

The American and Korean divisions continued raiding on a substantial scale in the first half of July. General Clark permitted this for a time, possibly because he had rejected a proposal of greater magnitude by General Van Fleet to advance to the north of P'yonggang, and did not wish to hold the army commander on too tight a rein. But he was becoming disturbed by the lack of success and high casualties† in the sorties for prisoners. On 19th July he declined a proposal from General Van Fleet to mount a major raid from the Commonwealth Division[10].

The summer monsoon inhibited operations widely during the second half of July 1952. Lieutenant-Colonel Moore, commanding officer of 28th Field Engineer Regiment, was continually aware that a sudden rise in the level of the Imjin after rainstorms could sweep away bridges

---

* The divisional boundaries were again adjusted, but not substantially extended, with the arrival of the Marine Division on the western flank and the 1st ROK Division to the east. During the summer and early winter, the left flank was on the Samich'on, the right included the whole of Kowang-san.

† A reinforced battalion of the 11th ROK Division lost thirty three killed and one hundred and ninety three wounded and missing during a raid on 8th July 1952 without capturing a single prisoner.

and ferries, leaving only cableways to supply the division on the north bank. He took some comfort from the rainfall figures during the first three weeks of the month but knew that storms might yet develop. His squadrons were ready to switch to flood control at short notice*, but meantime had plenty to do. Tracing and marking the many hastily laid mines on Line Kansas remained an urgent task—a Korean labourer displaced a boulder on 14th July which set off a mine, killing him and wounding two members of 64 Field Park Squadron drawn into this work. The field squadrons were busy with road maintenance and the extension of jeep tracks. Others were employed in cutting timber for infantry defences and the tanks emplaced among them. A new bridge, capable of carrying Centurions, was completed at the Pintail site.

On the night 26th/27th July, there was heavy rainfall. The river rose eighteen and a half feet at Pintail. Smaller bridges upstream were swept away, adding to a mass of debris floating westward at nine feet a second. Tank and anti-tank fire was used to break it up. But the flood passed without serious consequences.

From the 29th, the rain returned, continuing throughout the day into the 30th. On that day, the Engineers' Regimental War Diary noted:

> 0725 hrs 2 of the massive steel shearwaters at TEAL washed over by the force of the water, and leaning on the bridge. They were clear of debris. ...
>
> 0835 hrs Two further shearwaters collapsed. 12 Squadron is managing to keep bridge clear of debris.
>
> 0900 hrs 4 assault boats sent to KOSB, who are cut off on PINK 1, to supply them. Rubber attack boats also sent to [Divisional Provost Company] RMP [marooned] and to carry 20-pounder ammunition for tanks above PINTAIL which are also marooned ...
>
> 1000 hrs River still rising. Now 36 ft from [above] winter level at PINTAIL. ...
>
> 1200 hrs TEAL bridge out...[11]

The engineers were obliged to abandon all other work to re-establish communications. Fortunately, their Korean labour force had acquired many skills and were thus able to make an important contribution to clearance and repair. Of 6.5 inches of rain in July, 5.5 had fallen in five days. Defences were flooded across the front.

1 Royal Norfolk had attempted without success to capture a prisoner on 30th July by lying up in the area of Hill 118 on the extreme right flank of the division. The plan was to place a platoon forward to inspire

* The engineer counter flood plan, NOAH's ARK, provided specified tasks at all critical points and embraced a company of 1 PPCLI and the divisional searchlights.

enemy reconnaissance. When the Chinese arrived in their location, the remaining two platoons of Captain C E Eberhardie's B Company would rush forward to capture as many as possible. To distract the approaching enemy, battle simulation panels had been made up by a Royal Engineers detachment accompanying B Company. A variety of artillery and mortar target areas had been registered in the vicinity and were on call to Captain Eberhardie. An Auster of 1903 Air Observation Post flew over the area on the evening of 2nd August to report any signs of enemy activity. There were none.

The plan succeeded somewhat extravagantly. Rather than despatching a reconnaissance patrol to investigate the area of Hill 118, the local Chinese regimental commander sent the best part of a company. The lone platoon in ambush was overrun on first encounter. Some of the survivors fell back on Captain Eberhardie's position to tell the story. He had already called for defensive fire, called for more, and carried on with the plan. In the ensuing *mêlée*, four Chinese were captured, all wounded. Painstakingly, the company made its way back, carrying its own wounded but shedding three of the prisoners who had died *en route*. At 00.55, they entered the battalion area. Colonel Orlebar ordered C Company to patrol to Hill 118 to pick up any wounded including those of the enemy. But although five Chinese were discovered all were dead. The patrol brought back one dead and two wounded of B Company*. Unhappily, the wounded prisoner brought in died on evacuation to the casualty collecting post of 26th Field Ambulance[12].

This local operation, no trifling matter to Colonel Orlebar's battalion, but small in relation to the divisional front, should not give the impression that the Commonwealth soldiers became casualties principally because they were engaged in such initiatives. Almost continuously, one or another point of the front was engaged either by enemy artillery or mortars, or by enemy parties. For example, on the night the Royal Norfolk ambush was laid, a Chinese company attacked an outpost of 1 Welch on the north west spur of Kowang-san, seeking prisoners as like as not. The Welch platoon commander managed to pull back after hand to hand fighting. Four of his men were killed and six wounded in an action lasting a matter of minutes.

Thankfully, war is not a process of unremitting battle for fighting formations. There were many quiet days in the sultry summer of 1952, when the chief irritants were mosquitoes breeding copiously in the stagnant water of the abandoned paddy fields. Those in the forward brigades, dug in amongst scrub and thin copses behind crest lines, were in position for about four months, during which battalions were rotated

* 1 R Norfolk War Diary states that they lost three killed and 21 wounded overall in the operation. However, this was later corrected to 18 wounded, the majority of whom remained at duty. A total of fourteen Chinese bodies were subsequently found on the battle site.

in and out of brigade reserve. In this rearward location, there would be opportunities to shower and see a cinema show*. Each brigade would itself move into divisional reserve at the end of that term for six to eight weeks to engage in training. In the line, the requirements for observation, extension and maintenance of defences, and security duties—single sentries by day, double sentries by night—were not onerous. What taxed men was the instinctive awareness that their position might be brought under enemy fire at any moment or, at night, that it might be subjected to attack. This was the familiar challenge of being *en vedette* all day and every day they were in the battle zone. For the infantry, there was the further demand of outpost duty, and of reconnoitring, ambushing, or raiding across no-man's land. Some part of this fell also to the tank crews in the line, artillery forward observers, and a good deal to the field engineers. The latter continued to bear the seasonal burden of coping with the floods. The Imjin rose again in August by forty one feet in three hours.

To be out of the line in divisional reserve permitted the officers and men of the brigades an uninterrupted night's sleep, a boon enjoyed by the majority of the remainder in the divisional area except for periodic night duties on watch and, amongst the divisional artillery, frequent work in night firing. But security was required everywhere, and alertness. Chinese medium and heavy artillery periodically shelled as much of the divisional area as it could reach even though much of the working area was out of view behind hill crests†. Reconnaissance and terrorist groups were persistently infiltrated through the front lines, and several of the latter attacked single RASC supply vehicles south of the Imjin. The great majority were caught because all Arms reported or investigated questionable movement. To provide a complete relief from this environment, the standing arrangement first instituted for the independent 27th and 29th Brigades continued for the division: all ranks were given local leave in Japan during their tour in Korea‡ on the basis of five full days excluding travelling time. In addition, a divisional rest camp, run by the British Women's Voluntary Services, had been established in a village on the seashore close to Inch'on. Its chief clients were members of the brigade in reserve. Periodically, variety artists toured the divisional area, sometimes giving three shows a day¶.

---

* Each major unit had its own film projector with a trained operator. A circulation library of films was maintained by divisional headquarters.

† For example, following an intense shelling of enemy infantry, guns, and mortars from 14th–17th August 1952, by the Commonwealth artillery, the Chinese responded on 13th/14th September, though less discriminately.

‡ Manpower difficulties had necessitated an extension of the original tour of one year in Korea to eighteen months from the end of 1951, but this was to include only one winter.

¶ An account by Carole Carr of one of these is at Appendix K.

These reliefs, combined with regular deliveries and collection of mail, ample food, tobacco, and a ration of alcohol, contributed to continuance of a remarkably high level of morale as the war entered its third year, and a second year of peace negotiations at Panmunjom. They contributed; but the root of that morale lay in the ability of the men to accept the abiding dangers and discomforts of the battlefield so distant from their families for a variety of reasons unique to each individual, ranging for most among such factors as comradeship, a spirit of adventure, and some sort of belief in the cause. Medical records illuminate this hardihood in the very low numbers of men reporting sick. Typically, from January to May inclusive in 1952, daily rates of attendance at sick parade were 9.2 per 1,000 men. Battle casualties involving evacuation numbered 267 among some 8.000 within the range of enemy weapons during these months, but those with 'battle exhaustion' totalled only 9.

Indeed, of much greater concern to the commanders was the incidence of venereal disease. 2,451 men were treated during this five month period, roughly half infected by Korean prostitutes, half by prostitutes in Japan. Fortunately, the majority of infections were 'non specific' and the men concerned were returned to duty within twenty four hours. Even so, the incidence was about 24 per thousand men in the division, despite widespread education and the availability of prophylactics. Counter-measures were more successful in the prevention of malaria* and haemorrhagic fever[13].

On 7th September, General Cassels completed his term as divisional commander and departed to command the British corps in Germany. Sometimes the departure of general officers goes unnoticed among the junior members of their force; they may not even know his name. Occasionally they know his name and are heartily glad that he is going. Few, if any, members of the 1st Commonwealth Division were unaware of General Cassels' name and personality; he visited them frequently in and out of the line. None welcomed his departure. By common agreement among their commanders, his leadership had persuaded all elements to unite unreservedly in their duties, and inspired their confidence in his direction of their operations†.

---

* Paludrine was used to immunise individuals against malaria. It was generally effective, but did not counter one form of the disease spread by a Vivax strain. The late [non-medical] Dr Peter Farrar was the first to draw the attention of the British Army medical services to the fact that malaria revived in a number of men after their return from Korea, of whom he was one, following his service there with the Royal Fusiliers. For an explanation and details see the *Journal of the Royal Army Medical Corps*, volume 116, No 1., January 1970—letter of A P Hanaway, Australian Army Medical Services.

† Five South African officers had joined his command by this date. In all, ten served during the campaign: four on the divisional staff, two with the armoured units, three with the artillery, and one with an infantry battalion.

His successor was Major-General M M Alston-Roberts-West*, formerly of the 43rd and 52nd Light Infantry. He had commanded an infantry battalion and two brigades in the Second World War. Field-Marshal Slim chose him because he 'had a good record as an infantry soldier and knew how get on with all sorts of people'[14]. By the time he reached the divisional area, the new commander realised that some arrangements had to be made about his name.

'It was plain to me,' he remarked later, 'that the Americans could take a double-barrelled name—Bedell Smith, for example—but not a triple. Of course, I'd had this problem throughout my life so when I went to see General Kendall at I Corps I made it plain that I expected to be plain Mike West'.

He was aware that there had been what General Cassels considered to be occasional difficulties with General Kendall but gave not the slightest sign of this when he called at I Corps Headquarters. By what he regarded as a stroke of luck, among several Australian and Canadian patrol actions during September, 1 RAR captured a prisoner in a chance encounter—'Lance-Corporal McCarthy seized him by the throat', his patrol commander reported—and 1 RCR completed a brilliant small scale operation.

The latter followed a successful reconnaissance led by Lieutenant H R Gardner. The patrol hid for two days in disused defences behind the enemy outposts, from which they were able to observe the comings and goings of the enemy locally, including their use of a kitchen. Returning after an absence of sixty hours, Gardner's party had much valuable information, and gave rise also to a return visit on 24th September. With Corporal K E Fowler, who had accompanied him previously, he led a fighting patrol to the kitchen area, attracted a linesman by breaking a signal cable, and carried him off as a prisoner. These results stilled muted complaints by some of the I Corps staff that the Commonwealth Division was insufficiently aggressive.

The division's chief problem, as General Cassels explained to his successor, was inadequate numbers. None of the national components was manned to the establishments agreed. In September 1952, the 1st Royal 22e in the Canadian Brigade was almost three hundred officers and men under strength. Among others, replacements were often short or late[15]. They lacked any cushion of numbers among units to compensate for the absence of men on leave, the maintenance of which was considered imperative, and battle casualties.

On this account, General West decided to reduce brigade tours in the line to eight weeks with four in reserve. He did so as there were signs

* [Later, Lieutenant-General Sir] Michael Alston-Roberts-West, KCB, DSO [1905–1978].

that the Chinese People's Volunteers were raising the tempo and pressure of operations. The Shangamling campaign was moving towards a climax.

P'eng Te-huai was in Peking at this time, said to be sick, certainly working there in the Central Military Commission. Teng Hua held the command in his place[16]. It is evident that the Chinese high command believed that General Van Fleet's extension of outposts was part of a strategic plan to break open their front. From midsummer, they deployed additional artillery—the final *tranche* of the military equipment package supplied by the Soviet Union[17]—both to cover the front and to support tactical offensives in selected areas. Those pressed hardest were the ROK formations, in particular 9th ROK Division, north west of Ch'orwon in the first half of October. Major-General Kim Jong-oh's force demonstrated skill and a resilience which surprised the Chinese and delighted the American high command. It validated General Clark's policy of expanding the ROK Army to bear an increasing share of the line[18].

In the latter part of the month, the weight of attacks fell upon the I Corps area, engaging the 1st Marine Division, the Commonwealth and 1st ROK Divisions. 1 RCR, holding Kowang-san, had received intimations at the beginning of October that the Chinese were planning to capture this important feature. Certain defence works were heavily shelled from time to time, collapsing a number. Bursts of shellfire continued on 17th and 21st October. On the 23rd, 4,000 shells fell in the battalion positions, mostly on the company holding the north western heights, until 1900, when an assault captured the heights. The divisional artillery at once turned its entire power on to the ground seized, the enemy approaches to Hill 355 as a whole and fire support locations. The speed of response was due to use of a fire plan long in the mind of Lieutenant-Colonel E M D Leslie, commanding 1st Royal Canadian Horse Artillery. Some 12,000 shells and mortar bombs fell upon the enemy engaged. Major F Klenavic, acting as commanding officer of 1 RCR, thereafter recovered the ground during the early hours of 24th October by playing military checkers with deliberate skill. Hill 355 was once more wholly in Commonwealth territory at dawn, but until its possession was absolutely assured, the 1st Battalion, Royal Fusiliers (commanded by Lieutenant-Colonel G R Stevens OBE), which had recently arrived in Korea, and 1 PPCLI each provided a company to reinforce Major Klenavic's strength.

The line quietened for some days, which suited the division well as various organisational rearrangements were due. The first of these was the relief of 1 Welch, leaving Korea at the end of its tour. As a temporary move, General West detached 3 RAR from 28 Brigade to take their place in 29 Brigade, an arrangement which somewhat surprisingly disturbed Lieutenant-General Bridgeford, the Australian commander-in-chief. He did not approve. As he had no authority in operational matters, and no breach of agreement was involved, his displeasure fell upon Brigadier Daly. The brigadier had good reasons of his own for welcoming the deployment; 3 RAR were then low in numbers and had been selected by him because 1 Welch were at that time in a quiet sector on the Samich'on, the divisional left flank.

By chance, just after they took over, the neighbouring United States Marines were fiercely engaged on their side of the boundary. The 133rd Chinese Division of Forty Sixth Army were renewing attempts in previous weeks to capture a number of low hills giving observation directly to the north, up the course of the Samich'on. Principal among them was a curving feature named the 'Hook' by the Commonwealth Division during previous responsibility for the area. Thrown back briefly, the Marines recaptured the ground, during which they were assisted by considerable fire from 29 Brigade, including 3 RAR's medium machine-guns.

More generally, boundaries within the I Corps line were being readjusted under plan SOVEREIGN. The Commonwealth Division passed 2,000 yards of its line between the Imjin and Kowang-san to 1st ROK Division on its eastern flank. 28th Commonwealth Brigade came into the line in this right sector of the line and the Canadian 25th moved into reserve.

In the left sector, 29th Brigade assumed responsibility westwards across the Samich'on for the Hook area. Brigadier Ricketts, the brigade commander, ordered 1st Battalion, The Black Watch—1 BW—(commanded by Lieutenant-Colonel D McN C Rose DSO) to occupy this position by first light on 4th November 1952[19]. Because of the size and importance of the position, a fifth rifle company, a company of 2 R 22e was placed under Colonel Rose's command*. The United States Marines continued to be the division's and thus also the battalion's neighbour to the west.

Standing to arms at sunrise, 0701 on 4th November, Colonel Rose's force saw their positions for the first time. The last of the Marines had withdrawn. The land looked lifeless. Tumbled and broken by the heavy fire during recent fighting, the defences were in a poor state. Apart from keeping a sharp look out, there were two priorities on the Hook that chilly morning: reestablishing covered firing positions and making ready for the occupation of night outposts. Brigade Headquarters passed an

* The position had been held by 1st Battalion and an element of 3rd Battalion, 7th Marine Regiment. Although an American Marine or Army battalion had only three rifle companies, these each numbered over 200. Due to manpower shortages, the strength of a British Commonwealth rifle company was then about about 100. However, 1 BW had not been heavily engaged since its arrival in July and had 884 all ranks against an establishment of 869. Each of its rifle companies had 5 officers and at least 130 other ranks.

intelligence report during the forenoon that the 7th Marines were to be attacked that night. It was assumed in 1 BW's command post that if this had any validity it applied to them.

Again, as a part of the routine activity in the line, all ranks stood to arms towards dusk at 1734. About an hour later, A Company, centre right, picked up an enemy message in English:

> This is Chinese People's Army. You have until midnight to get off hills.

It was probably a deceptive measure; a company of the enemy 399 Regiment was at that moment on its way to attack the left hand outpost of the Black Watch, 'Ronson', which Second-Lieutenant J G M MacGuigan had just relieved with the greater part of his platoon. The assault ran silently up to the post but as they arrived enemy shellfire fell on to its parent, B Company, destroying the telephone line and radios to the rear.

Learning that some of those in his front position were wounded, Second-Lieutenant MacGuigan went forward to arrange for their evacuation, exchanged fire with several Chinese intruders and was killed as he pressed on. Shells were falling on Ronson. Confusion mounted. Several soldiers took wounded back to B Company. Some of the wounded crawled back. Corporal J S R Reekie organised a withdrawal of those still active but was killed by shrapnel before he could follow them. Private McKinley was knocked over by a mortar blast and found himself pinned to the ground by a dead Chinese soldier. Other enemy combing the area came upon him. They removed the contents of his pockets and ammunition pouches but assumed he was dead.

An hour later, Black Watch patrols searched Ronson and the surrounding area. The enemy had gone. Trip flares were laid and their own dead recovered—five in addition to Second-Lieutenant MacGuigan and Corporal Reekie. Four had been wounded. One was missing. While the search continued, the divisional and Marines' radio monitors picked up the following Chinese conversation:

> Did you occupy Bear? Is there any Pig there?
>
> I will find out. Wait. There are no Pig... We have captured one Boar[20].

During the next fortnight, the Hook positions were repeatedly shelled and mortared, and sniped by small arms fire. The Black Watch radios picked up broadcasts in English advising them that their presence was known and that they would all be killed*. Below the foremost outpost, 'Warsaw', the Chinese dug a number of caves, sufficient to shelter several

* The intercept detachment picked up more definite information that the Hook area was to be attacked on the night of the 18th, but in error it was not passed to the battalion (see DO/21 of 26th November 1952 from Commander 29 Brigade to Divisional HQ in 29 Brigade and 1 BW War Diaries for November).

hundred men, presumably shelters for gathering assault parties. These were demolished by the engineers. 3 PPCLI (Lieutenant-Colonel H F Wood*) was concentrated behind 1 BW, at notice to provide counter-attack forces for Colonel Rose if necessary.

On the 18th November, one or more of 1 BW's positions were fired on intermittently throughout the day, continuing after last light. Night outpost parties and patrols set out on their various tasks. Ronson was occupied without incident, but the party *en route* to Warsaw met a large number of enemy. Shortly afterwards, Major A D H Irwin, commanding A Company, reported from the Hook feature, left centre in the line, that he was being attacked by a Chinese company running in from three directions.

What followed was a classic example of Chinese methodology in this late phase of the campaign. The days of Chinese infantry hordes swarming into the assault under light supporting fire were past. In those circumstances, they had enjoyed a superiority of about five or six to one, an advantage offset by the power of United Nations supporting fire. To minimise the effect of this, they attacked by night whenever possible, infiltrating and surprising the UN infantry to destabilise them.

On the Hook in November 1952 an enemy battalion numbering about 500 was attacking another some 850 strong, though only 500 of the latter were manning the company positions on the objective. The defence had the advantage of strong, varied and and flexible fire support, and the protection of trenches and bunkers from which fire could be directed to support neighbours, though intermediate crests made it difficult to cover every approach. Those attacking had the benefit of darkness to conceal their final approach and the damage done to the Black Watch obstacles and firing posts by their artillery. They were also able to concentrate their numbers initially at selected points just outside their own supporting shellfire.

These methods, adapted to the static line, were frequently practised by the Chinese infantry during periods in reserve. Bold action continued to characterise their assaults to confuse and dismay the defending commander. If they were resisted at one site, they would switch to another, seeking always weak points to maintain the initiative. Such tactics, based on venerable principles, were well suited to the Chinese soldiers. They were not readily daunted by casualties. The leaders in platoons and sections had been carefully selected and developed by young ardent political officers; initiative in action was widely encouraged and rewarded. Continuous propaganda persuaded the majority of men that capture would carry them into a regime of oppression and torture. The battalion

* First brigade major of 25th Canadian Brigade in Korea, and subsequently the Canadian Official Historian for the campaign.

which attacked 1 BW on the night of 18th November manifested the hardihood, courage, and sound training of P'eng Te-huai's infantry.

Countering such a body required a steadfast force and determined leadership. Major Klenavic had shown this in re-establishing 1 RCR's authority in the sector lost on Hill 355. Shortly after 2100 hours on the night 18th/19th, Colonel Rose had to show whether he and his battalion had the heart and skill to throw back their assailants.

Warsaw was lost pre-emptively. Ronson was taken. The whole of A Company was invested, and it was thought—erroneously—that Second-Lieutenant Black's platoon had been effectively destroyed. A considerable part of the battalion from front to rear was under enemy shell or mortar fire by 2130.

As ever, on such occasions, the enemy seemed to be everywhere and rampant. The shock of their first appearance followed by a second and third wave alarmed those surrounded. First reports reflected this. Apprehensions were raised by information brought into one or another company by wounded stragglers from ambushed patrols. But the level of excitement and apprehension quickly diminished. Gradually Colonel Rose and his officers in the command post were able to identify a number of precise areas held in the area of attack, and a number occupied—the daytime artillery observation bunker in the centre of the Hook feature was one of these. It also became apparent that detachments of Chinese were roaming about, feeling out the edge of platoon positions. With Major R Pont RA, his supporting battery commander*, Colonel Rose called for fire wherever enemy were known to be in the open, and by conjecture over the approaches to the Hook from the west and north. Major Pont's battery, which had responded initially with the battalion's 3-inch mortars, was quickly reinforced by the whole of 14 Field Regiment (Lieutenant-Colonel P H Carey RA), and the rocket battery of the 11th Marines. There was much more to come.

The growing fire response and the fact that A Company had held firm despite the loss of some of its entrenchments checked the Chinese momentum. Colonel Rose decided to to clear the Hook feature as quickly as possible. Somewhat inadvisedly at 0059, he ordered his resident 5DG troop commander, Lieutenant M J C Anstice, to send a tank up to straddle the Hook ridge 'to make the men feel there was some support going in with them'[21]. Tanks are particularly vulnerable in close actions at night: almost inevitably, the Centurion was tank was holed by an anti-tank rocket as it reached its destination and set on fire, the driver wounded. Anstice and his remaining crew coped with these problems, drew off and returned to the night tank area from which they could provide a better service.

* Commanding Q Battery, 14th Field Regiment, Royal Artillery.

Meantime, Brigadier Ricketts had moved two companies of 3 PPCLI to reinforce the Black Watch. He had also been assured that the entire divisional artillery, including the 4.2 mortars of 61st Light Regiment, would fire as required by the battalion together with the 105-mm guns of the 11th Marines*,which had joined their rocket battery already in action, and a 155-mm battalion of I Corps' artillery.

Interception details from the enemy radios continued to come via brigade headquarters, though these diminished after midnight. As a later message was to indicate, the assault battalion was running short of men.

Still, the fighting was far from over. Colonel Rose continued to reinforce A Company with elements from his B and D Companies, the assault pioneers and medium machine-guns. The Pipes and Drums were already in the action. Major C M Moir, commanding D Company, joined Major Irwin to take command of the various platoons counter-attacking from the A Company area. The artillery support flowed. Variable time fuses were employed to burst shells in the air above the enemy in open ground.

There were several lulls, when it seemed that the main body of the Chinese force had withdrawn. But between 5 and 6 o'clock on the morning of the 19th several pockets of resistance were encountered among the entrenchments: Major A D Rowan-Hamilton commanding B Company was among those wounded at that time. Major Irwin called for additional men.

> Have you any reserve left? [Colonel Rose asked Major Irwin].
> No.
> Stick it out[22].

Colonel Rose was confident that the enemy potential was waning. He continued to search out possible hiding places on the forward slopes of his line while calling forward C Company of 3 PPCLI†. As this body closed on the Hook area at dawn, it was found to be clear of the enemy. Colonel Rose went forward.

The battle was over. Collection of the dead and remaining wounded began.

The battalion had lost 107 all ranks—sixteen killed‡ or mortally wounded, seventy six wounded, and fifteen missing—in numbers a rifle company. An account of enemy dead exceeded 100, but some had been removed with all their wounded by the survivors as they withdrew to their

---

* The 11th Marine Regiment was the artillery formation of the division. Its 2nd and 3rd Battalions fired 2,200 rounds for 1 BW during the Hook battle.

† The other company, B, was occupying the Black Watch B Company's position, vacated when the latter moved to reinforce A Company.

‡ Including Second Lieutenant J P K Doig, initially listed as missing.

lines. Relative to the numbers involved, it had been a costly struggle. The Black Watch had triumphed because its officers and men had fought to the finish. The deep refuge tunnels had saved a number in areas overrun, from which occupants had re-emerged to continue the struggle. Those caught in the open initially or shelled out of posts such as Ronson had found their way to other sub-units which they had reinforced. The artillery and 3-inch mortars had applied their fire with devastating effect. Above all, Colonel Rose had controlled the operation steadily, gathering reserves and committing them at key points.

Shortly after the Hook battle, General West decided that he was going to put all three of his brigades in the line as a means of easing their frontages and providing them with the means to effect relief of battalions in exposed areas as often as they considered appropriate. A risk was involved: the arrangement left him without any reserve of substance in the event of a renewed enemy offensive, but he thought this unlikely. He was also well aware that the Commonwealth Division would be relieved from the line completely for some weeks in February. If he needed to revert to the longstanding form of deployment, he could do so when they returned to the forward positions in the spring of 1953.

By 2nd December, therefore, his line was manned as follows:

Left: 25th Canadian Brigade [Brigadier M P Bogert CBE DSO ED]
3 PPCLI
2 R 22e
1 RCR } in
1 BW } reserve

Centre: 29th British Brigade [Brigadier D A Kendrew CB DSO *vice* Brigadier Ricketts]
1 King's [Lieutenant-Colonel A J Snodgrass OBE]
1 DWR [Lieutenant-Colonel F R StP Bunbury DSO]
1 BW detached to 25 Brigade

Right: 28th (Commonwealth) Brigade [Brigadier T J Daly DSO OBE]
1 RF
1 RAR
3 RAR } in reserve

Divisional Reserve 1 DLI [Lieutenant-Colonel P J Jeffreys reserve DSO, OBE] - detached from 28 Brigade.
Brigade 1 R Tks
1st Battalion, The Royal Tank Regiment, [Lieutenant-Colonel G C Hopkinson] *vice* 5 DG.

B Squadron [*vice* C Squadron],
Lord Strathcona's Horse (Royal Canadians),
Major J S Roxborough.

The divisional artillery continued to be deployed to cover the front but regimental* and battery affiliation continued within the brigades. Brigadier G P Gregson DSO MC succeeded Brigadier Pike as Commander, Royal Artillery.

As they settled into their new locations, General Eisenhower visited the division. The president-elect had come to Korea to see the operating conditions for himself and to hear the views of commanders as to their circumstances. The Communist press described his journey as 'secret', which it certainly was not; but though they had been informed officially of the event, the international press were not permitted, by his decision, to accompany him. The Commonwealth commanders found him 'anxious to learn... He was ready to listen and gave the impression that he was determined not to let the war drag on[23]'.

Action and counter-action fell away during the months of deep winter, though there were several sharp clashes in January. The greater number of patrols were confined to reconnaissance. All units were able to enjoy Christmas and New Year festivities, though men in the foremost battalions were obliged to stagger their indulgence. In the early part of 1953, General West sensed from remarks made to him by General Kendall that there would be a reversion to raiding for prisoners to meet weekly targets. He hit upon an idea to dissuade his superior.

Though British Commonwealth doctrine already stated that patrols should be mounted only to satisfy a specific objective, he decided to set this out—ostensibly for his subordinates, actually for his corps commander. He wrote a memorandum entitled *Patrol Policy*, which began as follows:

> 1. The overall object of patrolling is to dominate NO-MAN'S LAND, but each patrol muct have its own specific object.
>
> [Examples followed]
>
> 4. ... On no account will commanders send out patrols for patrolling sake, nor will they order sub-units to provide so many patrols per so many days. Any form of routine patrolling is dangerous because it invites enemy ambush, it kills initiative, it wearies the men both mentally and physically, and it achieves little. ...[24]

This stratagem worked. Five days after copies had reached corps headquarters, the staff issued instructions to all divisions that patrols would be undertaken only on the basis of a particular local requirement.

* 14 Field Regiment was relieved by 20 Field on 25th December 1952.

This prompting did not endear General West to General Kendall, however; he became more overt in his criticism of the Commonwealth Division and its commander.

His chief complaint was that the British expected special treatment, but to the extent that this was true it related only to the facts that the establishment of a British or Commonwealth infantry division was considerably lower than its American counterpart, and the manning fell consistently short of establishment by up to twelve per cent.

In this connection, a form of relief was in train. On the suggestion of General Clark to General Bridgeford and after discussion by him with with General Cassels, the Commonwealth governments concerned had agreed to make use of the United States system of KATUSA—Korean Augmentation to the United States Army.

Herein lay admirable examples of American enterprise and drive. The ROK Army training programme had improved rapidly in quality and quantity, a change stemming from the close relationship General Van Fleet had struck personally with President Rhee and his senior military officers. When agreement was given in Washington to General Clark's proposal to increase the number of ROK divisions, the supply of recruits exceeded the requirement. It was thus proposed that Korean soldiers should reinforce United States divisions, themselves intermittently manned below establishment.

The British Commonwealth governments moved more slowly, chiefly due to queries concerning organisation by those who had nothing to do with the matter[25]. The advantages were clear, however. By the end of 1952, it was accepted that these men would not be counted against establishment, would serve as soldiers as distinct from domestics or porters, and be under the operational control of their Commonwealth commanders. This idea, begun in July 1952, finally took effect from the end of March 1953[26]. One hundred Korean soldiers, each of whom had completed advanced recruit training, were posted to each battalion in the division. They were known as KATCOMS.

All among the infantry, British soldiers were to be seen demonstrating the confidence, not entirely unfounded, of an ability to being able to commuicate with foreigners of whose languages they have, at best, scant knowledge. In many cases, their efforts were unnecessary; almost half the newcomers spoke basic English, which rapidly improved. All picked up a working knowledge within a matter of weeks. Although the commanding officers of the RCR and R22eR had some reservations, the Koreans were wholly accepted and made a valuable contribution to the final run of operations.

The final run...indeed it suddenly seemed that the war might be drawing to an end in this British coronation year. From 30th January to 8th April 1953 the Commonwealth Division was relieved in the line by 2nd United States Infantry Division[27]. During this time, a succession of events appeared to be revitalising the political and military environment of the Korean war. In February, President Eisenhower withdrew the 7th Fleet as a barrier to operations between Taiwan and the mainland of China. To General Clark's relief, agreement was given in principle to the trial of prisoners of war attacking United Nations guards or other prisoners—a minor matter in itself but a sign of changing policies in Washington. At about this same time, it was agreed by the new government that General Clark should suggest to P'eng and Kim Il-sung an exchange of sick and wounded prisoners.

Coincidentally, Stalin died on 5th March 1953. The Communist world went into mourning; but there were shortly signs in Moscow that Stalin's successors might show some willingness to resolve differences, or at least to be less intransigent in discussing them. In so far as the Korean war was concerned, the Russian Government agreed to intervene with the North Koreans to release the diplomats, missionaries and others held captive on the Yalu river since 1950. On 28th March, Kim and P'eng agreed to exchange sick and wounded prisoners, adding,

> At the same time, we consider that the reasonable settlement of the question of exchanging sick and injured prisoners of both sides during the period of hostilities should be made to lead to the smooth settlement of the entire question of prisoners of war, thereby achieving an armistice in Korea for which people throughout the world are longing. Therefore our side proposes that the delegates for armistice negotiations of both sides immediately resume the negotiations at Panmunjom. ...[28]

Arrangements were at once set in hand to conduct the exchange, but there was some reluctance to resume the suspended peace talks until there was evidence that they might make substantive progress. The United States Government was equally determined that the resumption of talks should not be a condition of exchanging the sick and wounded.

These events had passed, and the prospects for peace seemed to be improving as the Commonwealth Division went back into the line. Lieutenant-General Bruce C Clarke had now replaced General Kendall as corps commander. The antipathy of the latter to the Commonwealth Division had extended to open criticism of General West and his force at a meeting of divisional commanders, a matter which General West had felt obliged to report to Lieutenant-General H Wells CBE DSO, who had just succeeded General Bridgeford as Commander-in-Chief, British Commonwealth Forces in Korea. This incident, following a number of adverse comments in his reports, was probably the cause of General Kendall's removal[29].

As March passed, General West apprehended that his soldiers would find the enemy more aggressive on their return to the line. After two difficult years in command, General Van Fleet was succeeded on 11th February by Lieutenant-General Maxwell D Taylor*, an intellectual who had excelled as a battlefield commander and staff officer in the Second World War and following years. He shared General West's patrolling and raiding philosophy but, as a consequence of the policy changes he introduced in tactics and training, divisional and corps commanders swung to an excessive interest in the detail of arrangements by their subordinates to safeguard life and limb of those making sorties[30]. Commanding officers were called to account for any mishap which might have been avoided. Understandably, they took exceptional measures to avoid clashes with the enemy to as great an extent as possible. The 2nd United States Infantry Division was no exception. When the Commonwealth Division took its place, returning to the Samich'on and the Imjin, to Point 225 and Kowang-san, the Chinese, as Brigadier Kendrew remarked, 'had got distinctly above themselves[31].

The division was fully ready to cope with this. The period out of the line had been well spent in training. Unit and formation commanders had reviewed errors and omissions which the run of recent operations had disclosed. It was properly left to commanding officers to decide how much of the time available should be allocated to refreshing and developing individual skills, how much to team activities—say, the rifle section or the 3-inch mortar detachment—and, working up the scale, through patrolling and raiding to the battalion in counter-attack. Brigade headquarters held study days for officers, and conducted at least one exercise for each battalion. Divisional headquarters exercised each brigade as a whole.

A number of the younger cavalry and infantry officers were astonished that they should be occupied in training having just come out of a successful run of operations. Their seniors responded by pointing out that the numbers of their casualties demanded that none should rest on his laurels. They should be aiming to reduce casualties in the future by drawing on the lessons battle had taught them.

Appropriately, the greatest discretion had been left to the commanding officers. In the matter of individual training, Lieutenant-

---

* Taylor, Maxwell Davenport, (1901–94), later General, Chief of Staff, United States Army, Chairman, Joint Chiefs of Staff of the United States. On retirement, he held several diplomatic posts.

Colonel Jeffreys, for example, was not satisfied that his Durham Light Infantrymen were responding as accurately with their weapons in the sudden encounter battle as he required. In minor collective training, Lieutenant-Colonels Bunbury and Stevens, respectively commanding the 1st Battalions of The Duke of Wellington's Regiment and the Royal Fusiliers, exercised their headquarters and each rifle company in the planning, mounting, and conduct of patrols. Signalling and other specialist cadres were held. There were cadres for junior non-commisioned officers. The employment of the 3.5-inch rocket launcher against firing ports in bunkers was widely practised. All units engaged in field range practices, and used live ammunition in small scale tactical exercises, sometimes with greater attention to battle simulation than safety. Brigadier J G N Wilton DSO OBE, who succeeded Brigadier Daly as commander of 28th Commonwealth Brigade in March, was compelled to take cover briefly from shots whistling overhead as he approached the site of one such exercise.

Military training was interspersed with physical exercise—'pokey drills'*, hill running, games of all kinds. The hours and days spent in these and the many other activities were invaluable in the return to the battle line.

After consultation with his brigade commanders, General West confirmed the deployment of all three brigades to the line, though grouped somewhat differently, largely due to the layout adopted by the 2nd Division

Left: 29th British Brigade (Brigadier D A Kendrew)

- 1 BW – in the Hook area
- 1 Kings – east of the Samich'on
- 1 DWR – behind 1 BW
- 1 RCR – behind 1 Kings
- C Squadron 1 R Tks between 1 DWR and 1 RCR but with troops detached forward

Centre: 25th Canadian Brigade (Brigadier J V Allard CBE DSO ED)

- 1 R22eR – on the spurs of Songgok and Hamurhan
- 3 PPCLI – area of Sanjom-ni
- 2 RAR – reserve
- B Squadron, Lord Strathcona's Horse, on the rear left flank of the brigade with troops forward

* This term related to strengthening the muscles required for shooting by individual exercises—holding the rifle in extensions from the body upwards and in arcs from the shoulder. It was a development from service in India in the late 19th century.

Right: 28th Commonwealth Brigade (Brigadier J G N Wilton)
1 RF – area of Hill 159
1 DLI – Kowang-san, Hill 355
3 RAR – reserve on divisional right boundary with 1 ROK Division
B Squadron, 1 R Tks, behind the two forward battalions but with troops forward

The divisional artillery had not enjoyed a full rest; its batteries had reinforced the 2nd United States Division's guns. Among these now was a welcome addition, 74th (Battleaxe Company) Medium Battery (Major A J Batten DCM RA)*, equipped with 5.5-inch guns, had joined in the second week in March. This was an important reinforcement which would enable Brigadier Gregson's counter-battery staff to reach out to enemy artillery positions well beyond the 25-pounders of the field regiments†.

Brigade and battalion commanders at once entered a patrol programme to reconnoitre no-man's-land and the enemy front. The Black Watch captured a prisoner on the night 23rd/24th April, during which 3 PPCLI had two patrols in action. These were the overture to a series of fighting patrols and raids. 1 Royal Fusiliers, 1 DLI, and 3 RCR were principally involved, the latter two in ambushes. The Chinese struck back, raiding into 3 RCR's positions‡, from which they were ejected, and those of the Royal Fusiliers, which they failed to penetrate due to the rapid response from the divisional artillery. There was a flurry of patrol action by both sides around the Hook, from which 1 BW brought in three wounded prisoners[32].

At some date in April, Chan Ts'ai-fang, commander of the Chinese 46th Army, decided to make a third attempt to capture the ground immediately west of the Samich'on in order to force back the United Nations line in this sector. Such a move was expected by General West; the loss of either the Hook or the adjacent features in the Marines' sector, including Detroit, Vegas, and Elko—the Nevada compex—would oblige I Corps to cede a depth of 4,000 yards in the vicinity.

In May, the United States 25th Division relieved the Marines. The Turkish Brigade under command was placed on the right flank, next to the British 29th. Considerable transport was seen moving into the enemy line in the middle of the month some 7,000 yards to the north of the area which was engaged by the corps artillery. It was taken to indicate an impending attack.

However, there were other signs to indicate this. Enemy tactical radio traffic increased considerably in the third week of May. A deserter

---

* Detached from 32 Medium Regiment RA in Hong Kong.

† For the background to the provision of this battery, see Cabinet Office AL 1200/107(B), CAB 157/19.

‡ 3 RCR had taken over from 1 R22eR on completion of their tour of duty in Korea.

came into 1 DWR's positions stating that his unit* was practising an assault on the Hook for an attack which would take place within eight weeks of 12th May[33]. Colonel Bunbury, whose battalion had taken over the Hook area on the 13th, considered that it would be sooner rather than later. The Duke's pressed on with an extensive programme of defence works.

Yet the first thrust was made into the Nevada complex in the early morning of 15th May. An intense but relatively limited battle took place, as both sides exchanged considerable fire. 1 DWR gave strong support from the common flank. The Commonwealth artillery fired in unison with the guns of the 25th Division. The Turks held their ground.

The accrual of further intelligence, including probing attacks against 1 DWR, made it likely that this was not the end but the beginning of the operation. From all later evidence, the enemy aim on 15th May had been to take selected outposts, and to identify main positions. In readiness for whatever was to follow, the corps artillery allocated:

four batteries of 155-mm howitzers

two batteries of 155-mm guns

one battery of 8-inch howitzers

one battery of 240-mm howitzers

one rocket battery.

Brigadier Kendrew reinforced the Duke's with two companies of the Black Watch from 22nd May. General West moved 1 RF from 28 to 29 Brigade as a second reserve. The level of radio interception persuaded these two commanders to move a complete battalion to occupy the right half of the Hook sector. 1 King's moved across the Samich'on into the position†. The Black Watch took their place.

The Chinese plan was to put four battalions into the Nevada complex from the 120th Division, three on to the Hook from the 133rd Division. Extraordinary quantities of artillery and mortar ammunition were available for preliminary shooting to reduce enemy defence works, the bombardment preceding—and in certain areas accompanying—the assault, and in supporting fire on call or on direction after the assault force had closed with the British and Turkish foes. Routes across no-man's-land, forming up places, daylight observation posts, advanced dumping sites for small arms and medium mortar ammunition replenishment, were reconnoitred extensively by night from 20th May. To as great an

* 2nd Battalion, 399 Regiment, 133rd Division.

† Initially, the 1 BW occupied the left hand sector because it had two companies there but was relieved by 1 Kings on the 27th May, after the latter had concluded a diversionary raid.

extent as possible, the remainder of the line on either side fell quiet, though a single retaliatory raid was made by the Chinese into 28 Brigade lines in the last week of May after 2 and 3 RAR had harrassed them severely over a number of days.

On the Hook, Colonel Bunbury drove his companies hard in the enhancement of their basic defences. None were worked harder than the assault pioneer platoon, which had been sent forward both to hold a linking position between Hill 121 and the Hook and to work through much of the night wiring, mining, improving firing bays and shelter tunnels in the foremost areas. Second-Lieutenant John Stacpoole decided to tell his commanding officer on 26th May that his soldiers were in need of a night's rest, but while making his way back was hit by shrapnel from the rising shellfire. Though he protested in the regimental aid post that he was only scratched, his bluff was called when he lost consciousness and was thus evacuated as the battle began on the following day, 29th May 1953.

For more than a week, about 500 shells and 500 mortar bombs had fallen daily on to 1 DWR and, latterly, 1 Kings. The Turks received no less. On the 29th, the rate increased as 122-mm shells worked over the Duke's protective wire, bunkers and communication trenches, particularly those of D Company holding the Hook feature with the assault pioneers. Towards evening, the company headquarters, observation post and the greater part of the right forward platoon's positions were wholly reduced. The communication trench facing Warsaw was blocked. In the King's area, the principal feature, Hill 146, also became a target for the 122-mm shells.

Overhead, the artillery air observation post pilots conducted counter-battery shoots almost continuously, assisted by the the aircrew of the light liaison flight. They were obliged to move their circuits frequently to elude Chinese light anti-aircraft fire.

In the last half hour of daylight on the 28th, the numbers of incoming shells exceeded 1,000 an hour. Immediately after sunset at 1947, the assault began. The outer wire was in tatters, at best a partial obstacle to the Chinese infantry, though a few intermediate fences remained intact and separated assault parties. Two companies of the leading Chinese battalion penetrated rapidly to the Hook itself. The close garrison of the principal height—a rifle platoon of D Company—was assailed by enemy entering their broken bunkers through the communication trenches to throw grenades while others stuffed satchel charges* through embrasures. Leaving a number of dead, the defenders withdrew back into the shelter tunnels.

---

* Guncotton or other made up explosive charges carried in cotton satchels. These were less effective than grenades but capable of stunning a number of men in a confined space.

Two battles developed over the next four hours. Most persistent was the pressure to break all resistance in D Company's localities; the other involved attempts to pass round its flanks, initially on the western side, later on the eastern towards Hill 146 in 1 King's sector. These moves drew in two other Chinese battalions. For something over four hours, the Duke's position was widely invaded by the enemy, some moving in groups, some regrouping, many small parties engaged in close quarter fighting.

The United Nations supporting fire was meantime falling widely[34]. Concentrations fell upon those seen from bunkers or by more distant observers against the divisional and tank searchlights providing illumination. The 4.2-inch mortars searched out re-entrants and reverse slopes likely to be used by the enemy. From time to time a dreadful blanket of shrapnel would descend from air burst shells upon all above ground. The forward tanks of C Squadron, 1 R Tks, sniped with their 20-pounders and poured volumes of small arms fire from their machine-guns.

With his companies holding firm, Colonel Bunbury's aim was to clear the D Company area while his own and supporting fire destroyed or drove out the enemy. Passing the defence of Pt 121 to a rifle company of 1 Kings, he gathered his own A and B Companies. Occasionally he received news of a similar battle taking place in the Turkish Brigade area but as these gave no indication of his flank being opened he wisely left Brigadier Kendrew and General West to watch events in the Nevada complex*.

Some time after 0030 on the 29th, the enemy ability to sustain offensive action fell away. The radio monitors intercepted calls to those in reserve to come forward to carry off wounded. The reserves responded that they were scarcely able to cope with their own heavy losses from United Nations fire. The Duke's counter-attack—A Company with parts of B and C had joined the remnant of D—began to work through the Hook position at about 0130 on 29th May. The feature was clear at 0430, but a number of tunnels blown in during shelling or by those fighting within them, had to be searched for friend or foe. Considerable numbers of enemy drawing back to the north were shelled at 0500. Their losses had been very high indeed, scarcely less than a thousand considering the dead remaining and the numbers known to have been evacuated. The Duke's had lost twenty killed and one hundred and six wounded among a total of 148 including their artillery observation parties from 45 (Q) Field and 121 Light Batteries, and the King's[35].

In the Turkish Brigade area the battle continued into the afternoon, when General Bruce Clarke, I Corps commander, decided against the

---

* 29 Brigade Headquarters had a liaison officer with the Turkish Brigade.

recovery of several outposts in enemy hands. The Turks and 1st Battalion, United States 14th Infantry had fought doughtily to hold the entire area at a cost of 395 casualties, of whom a substantial number, 150, had been killed[36].

The Royal Fusiliers relieved the Duke's on the Hook. They were not left in peace; mortars continued to fire daily on the area as Royal Engineers and infantry began the huge task of repairing the damaged defences, many of which had been levelled.

More enjoyably, the division celebrated the Queen's Coronation on 2nd June. Red, white, and blue smoke was fired by the field guns just before 1000 that morning (Korean time). Just after the hour, the tanks in the forward positions each fired a single 20-pounder shot, the signal for three cheers by groups of men, wherever they were, for Her Majesty. At noon, a ceremonial parade was held, while South African Sabres, and Sea Furies of the Royal Navy from *Ocean* flew past but did not overshadow the Austers of 1903 and the Light Liaison Flight offering a similar courtesy some 500 feet below them.

Although they did not then know it, the members of 1st Commonwealth Division had fought their last battle in the war. For whilst there were still many patrol actions to come and occasional local actions against the Chinese, P'eng chose to attack elsewhere in the remaining weeks.

Bringing a fresh army into the line, the 68th, he made a series of thrusts without apparent regard for casualties against the ROK divisions in central Korea, drawing in also the United States 7th. Across some 40,000 yards, positions were lost to a depth of 3,000, but only after considerable fighting. Heartbreak Ridge was lost. Another feature on whose slopes both sides had lost many men, Porkchop, was surrendered on 11th July. General Taylor had to decide whether the retention of this strip of territory was worth yet more great losses. He took the view that it was not[37].

Perhaps the last full action engaging British Commonwealth Forces involved the RAR on the Hook, on the edge of a late enemy attempt to push the Marines out of the Nevada complex. On 26th July, Lieutenant-Colonel Jeffreys had prepared on orders a counter-attack by 1 DLI to recover a company area in the vicinity. The auguries were not good; reconnaissance showed that a preliminary bombardment had not cleared the main body of the enemy from the bunkers they held. More artillery was called for, after which the decision to assault or not would be made.

'I leave it to you, Peter,' said Brigadier Wilton, departing from the DLI command post.

Colonel Jeffreys looked at the objective again after the smoke of further shellfire had cleared. Like General Taylor, he wondered whether the little hill lost to the brigade was worth a life when everything suggested that the war was about to end. He, too, decided it was not and stood the waiting soldiers down[38].

Three days later, the armistice agreement was concluded at Panmunjom. The Eighth Army ceased firing at 2200 hours.

SOURCE NOTES: Chapter 21

1 Signal CG EUSAK GX 5831 of 11 May 52 to all corps, Army Command Report, May 1952 (USNARS, Suitland).
2 Periodic Report, 1st Commonwealth Division, (hereafter 'Periodic Report') 15th October 1951–15th February 1952, paragraphs 1 and 4 [WO 308/27].
3 *Ibid*, paragraph 6.
4 *Ibid*, paragraph 7.
5 *Ibid*, 15th February–30th June 1952, paragraph 11. See also Meid, Lieutenant-Colonel Pat, and Yingling, Major James M, USMC, *US Marine Operations in Korea, volume v*, (1972), p 93.
6 See, for example, Periodic Report, October 1951–February 1952, Appendix B, paragraph 20.
7 War Diaries, Divisional HQ, and 5DG, June 1952. See also Sergeant Bertrand quoted in Blacker, General Sir Cecil and Woods, Major-General H G, *Change and Challenge* (1978), pp 106–107.
8 See War Diaries, 1 RAR and 28th Commonwealth Brigade, July 1952. Also O'Neill, *op cit*, volume ii, pp 243–247.
9 Letter Comd 247 of 15th July 1952 to Corps Commander, I Corps Command Report, G-03 Sect, July 1952, (USNARS, Suitland).
10 See Hermes, *op cit*, pp 292–293.
11 War Diary, 28 Field Engineer Regiment. See also War Diary of 1 PPCLI relating counter flood work by one of its companies.
12 War Diary, 1 R Norfolk and 29th Infantry Brigade.
13 See Periodic Report for 15th February to 30th June 1952, Appendix C, pp 4 and 5. Also, War Office Brief for the Minister of Defence (Lord Alexander) of 5th June 1952, MO1 Collection, Annex G.
14 Conversation, author with Field-Marshal Lord Slim.
15 See Wood, *op cit*, p 203, and General West to the Adjutant-General, War office, of 29th October 1952 (only in the Australian Archives, CRS A2107. K1.05.). Also, Periodic Reports, October 1951–February 1952 and February 1952–June 1953.
16 For details of numerous appointments and replacements, see *The war to resist America and aid Korea*, cit, Chapter XI, Section 3, *op cit*.
17 Hsü, Yan *op cit*, p 32.
18 Hermes, *op cit*, pp 340–345.
19 War Diary, 29th Infantry Brigade.
20 War Diary, Commonwealth Division intelligence supplement, 5th November 1952, and 1 BW—Report on Ronson, night 4th/5th November 1952.
21 War Diary, 1 BW, November 1952, Outline of Events, 18th/19th November.
22 *Ibid*.
23 Observation of a divisional staff officer in a private letter to his brother.
24 Periodic Report, 1 November 1952–1 April 1953, Appendix A.
25 See FK 1194/124–5 and 129–137, (FO 371/99618).
26 See MO1 Collection, folios marked severally as 575, 292, 193, 28A/172, attaching also EUSAK Circular 117 of 19th August 1852.
27 For details of the reliefs, see Divisional Operation Orders No 11 and 14 in Divisional Headquarters War Diaries for January and April 1953 respectively.
28 For the complete statement, see FRUS, 1952–1953, cit, pp 818–819
29 See, for example, I Corps Command Reports of 14th and 28th January, and 23rd February 1953 (USNARS Suitland). See, also, Grey, *op cit*, p 142.
30 Periodic Report, 1 November–1 April 1953, parapgraph 19.
31 Conversation, author with Major-General D A Kendrew.

32 War Diaries, Divisional Headquarters, brigade headquarters and units concerned. Also Periodic Report 1 April to 1 August 1953, Annexure 1 to Appendix B. See also O'Neill, *op cit*, volume ii, pp 266–274, and Wood, *op cit*, pp 223–236; and personal accounts in the various British Regimental Headquarters.

33 Periodic Report, 1 April to 1 August 1953, Appendices A and B; and Annex C to 29 Brigade Opps/Int Summary No 138 of 20 May 1953..

34 See War Diary, Headquarters Royal Artillery, 1st Commonwealth Division, May 1953, for the initial fire plan and subsequent responses.

35 Periodic Report, 1 April 50 to 1 August 1953. See also War Diaries of the formations and units concerned for May and June 1953, and personal accounts in Regimental Headquarters of 1 DWR and 1 Kings.

36 Comd Report, I US Corps, May 1953. Also 25th US Division and 14th Inf Regt Comd Reports, May 1953 (USNARS Suitland).

37 Comd Report IX Corps, and KMAG Comd Report, June 1953 [USNARS]. Also Hermes, *op cit*, pp 465–476, (USNARS Suitland).

38 Conversation, author with Brigadier P J Jeffreys.

CHAPTER 22

Peace without victory

On the United Nations side, political policy during the final six months of the war was, more than at any other period in the negotiations, devised, controlled, and finalised by the United States.

During the final weeks of President Truman's administration, British intervention had been crucial in reshaping and finally gaining American support for the Indian resolution in the General Assembly. Thereafter, somewhat to Mr Eden's vexation, the influence of Mr Churchill's Government was minimal. It was due as much as anything to the broad aims of the two heads of the governments concerned.

Mr Churchill was implacably anti-Communist and thus supported the denial of Communist aggression in the Far East; but his principal aim in overseas and defence policy was to reduce the danger of war in Europe. He believed as strongly in his ability to persuade Stalin to come to some sort of *modus vivendi* as he had in 1945[1], if not alone, then in partnership with his old friend General Eisenhower, as he told his Principal Private Secretary, John Colville, in June 1952,

> ... if Eisenhower were elected President, he [Churchill] would have another shot at making peace by means of a meeting of the Big Three. For that alone it would perhaps be worth remaining in office. ... [and later] Winston has several times revealed to me his hopes of a joint approach to Stalin, proceeding perhaps to a congress in Vienna where the Potsdam Conference would be reopened and concluded[2].

These notions may be dismissed as the dreams of a grand old man hankering for a return to the heights of his career. Even so, he was again the Prime Minister, and there was a requirement not only to reduce the threat of a potentially devastating war but also to reduce the expenditure on armaments which, with the requirements of NATO added to Korea, problems with Egypt, and a succession of colonial campaigns, was becoming insupportable[3]. He was thus content to leave the direction of armistice negotiations in Korea to President Eisenhower.

The President had promised during his election campaign that he would bring the war in Korea 'to an early and honorable end'[4]. It was one of a number of promises he had made at the hustings, of which the reduction of public expenditure was of first importance. In this he had widespread support among his Republican Party sponsors. Contrarily, a *coterie* within the Party favoured a renewed military effort, disregarding cost, sufficiently powerful to persuade China and North Korea to sue for peace. John Foster Dulles, President Eisenhower's Secretary of State, had some sympathy for this view.

The first indication of a change from Democrat policies came on 2nd February 1953, when the newly elected President made his State of the Union speech. Reviewing the neutralisation of the Taiwan Strait by the United States Navy, he remarked that there was

> ... no longer any logic or sense in a condition that required the United States Navy to assume defensive responsibilities on behalf of the Chinese Communists, thus permitting those Communists, with greater impunity, to kill our soldiers and those of our United Nations allies in Korea. ... The 7th Fleet would therefore be withdrawn at once.

The announcement was not well received by his allies, particularly the United Kingdom, which had not been consulted about, had not even been informed of, the change of policy, as much as anything because the new British Ambassador, Sir Roger Makins*, was not on the same close terms with Mr Dulles as his predecessor had been with Mr Acheson†. Mr Eden told the House of Commons that the change 'might have very serious repercussions without compensating military advantages'.

This was a response of umbrage rather than logic. It was unlikely that Chiang Kai-shek would attack the mainland, but if he did it would simply add to China's military burdens. Those burdens made it even more unlikely that China would attack Taiwan. It was a cheap and safe way to signal to the Chinese that American strategy concerning Korea was changing.

Anglo-American relations were not helped by unwillingness in London to become involved in a scheme for the trial by international courts martial of persistently violent and murderous Communist prisoners of war[5], though British criticism had earlier been directed at the United States for their failure to discipline effectively those engaged in this behaviour. The Foreign Office and Chiefs of Staff were apprehensive that a formal measure of this kind might be used as an excuse to coerce British prisoners.

However, Mr Eden initiated in February the approach which led to the exchange of sick and wounded prisoners, following a meeting with M. Paul Ruegger, President of the International Committee of the Red Cross. During a visit to Peking at the end of 1952, M. Ruegger had

---

* Makins, Sir Roger Mellor KCMG, later 1st Baron Sherfield GCB GCMG (1904–).

† Early in January, in the preparations for the transfer of power, officials in the State Department had informed the British and Australian embassies informally that withdrawal of the 7th Fleet from the Taiwan Strait was an option under consideration by the incoming administration.

suggested to Chou En-lai the possibility that the Red Cross might be given official access to the prisoners held by the Communists. Chou declined to discuss the proposal, but agreed that arrangements might be made to place sick and wounded prisoners in safety zones[6]. This slight concession encouraged Mr Eden to suggest to Mr Dulles that they should make a formal proposal to exchange sick and wounded prisoners of war.

The State Department was not at first enthusiastic; in Geneva during December 1952 the Executive Committee of the International Red Cross had considered an Indian resolution to make such an exchange. It was carried by 15 votes to 2—Russia and China being the dissenters. Officials suggested that if the Communist side wished to proceed on these lines, they had there an excellent chance to indicate it, but had chosen the opposite course.

The British idea was to make the proposal at the next General Assembly Meeting on 24th February. Mr Eden suggested that the allies should eschew any further political initiatives at this meeting and simply take note that the Communist side had rejected the Indian proposal for a settlement. To this should now be joined an appeal for an immediate exchange of the sick and wounded prisoners.

The Americans agreed with this in principle at a meeting in Washington with Mr Tomlinson, counsellor at the British Embassy. They had, in fact, warmed to the possibility of exchanging the sick and wounded but wanted to venture it through the armistice team at Panmunjom: a signal had been sent to General Clark that afternoon with the proposal[7].

Fron this initiative came the agreement from Kim and P'eng to the limited exchange, what came to be known as 'Little Switch'. As the necessary administrative arrangements to effect it were considered, Chou En-lai made a public statement on 30th March, shortly after returning from Stalin's funeral in Moscow. It proposed in the name of China and North Korea

> ... that both parties should undertake to repatriate immediately after the cessation of hostilities all those prisoners of war in their custody who insist upon repatriation and to hand over the remaining prisoners-of-war to a neutral state so as to ensure a just solution to the question of their repatriation.[8] ...

Captain Holt with the interned diplomats and missionaries crossed into North East China on 9th April to return to their homes. Little Switch took place on 20th April*.

* The United Nations exchanged 6,670 sick and wounded prisoners (5,640 Koreans including 446 civilians; 1,030 Chinese) for 684 held by the Communists. The selection of individuals for inclusion among the latter (471 ROK, 149 US, 32 British, 5 Australians, 2 Canadians, 1 South African plus 24 others) was partly motivated by political bias. Some 375 UN sick and wounded were kept back by the Communists.

On 26th April, the negotiations for a final settlement resumed after the months of suspension. During this period, contact had been maintained by liaison officers. Principals among the delegations had changed and thus some were meeting for the first time, though Generals Harrison and Nam Il remained as chairmen of their respective groups.

Those forming the United Nations Command hoped that they were approaching a settlement; the Communists had conceded the major point of non-forcible repatriation. Three questions had next to be agreed. How and by whom would prisoners be held while their own side sought to persuade them to return home; and for how long should this process extend? The Communists wished all such prisoners to be transported to a neutral country distant from Korea, and the time for persuasion to be six months. The United Nations Command believed that transportation was unnecessary, and that three months would prove adequate for persuasion—their own preference was thirty days. There had also, in their expressed view, to be a clear agreement that prisoners unpersuaded should be released immediately at the end of the term adopted.

These questions were to occupy three months of thrust and parry in slow motion. It is difficult to know why the Communists prolonged the talks after the prime concession. There are grounds for believing that the decision to agree armistice terms were set in hand before Stalin's death[9]. Suggestions have been made that they wished to recover important territory in the static defence line; but the greater gains were made after the final points were settled. Beating the enemy off hilltops in May and June may have been a means of soothing political pride wounded by the necessity to yield on the repatriation principle.

While the United Nations Command held back during the summer from seeking to gain, or persisting in the recovery of, tactical features lost, President Eisenhower continued to plan for a reversion to full scale military operations if the Communist side should show a clear disinclination to negotiate, or to resume an offensive strategy. In this he expected the support in principle of his British ally[†] [10]. With extraordinary skill, he let it be known that he was gathering a force sufficient to advance to the narrow waist of the Korean peninsula, and that he would use atomic weapons if they should be expedient. The strength of his position stemmed from two considerations: he had the means to raise hugely the tempo of the war; and he was not bluffing. He encouraged the Joint Chiefs in military planning and restrained the hawkishness of John Foster Dulles. His former war time chief of staff,

---

† For Commonwealth discussion of this problem, see 'Commonwealth Prime Ministers' Meetings Nos. 1 and 2' of 3rd and 4th June 1953, CAB 133135.

General Walter Bedell Smith*, now in the State Department, assisted the process of measured firmness in the application of this policy.

Step by step, the negotiations advanced. The Communists agreed that the prisoners declining repatriation should be interviewed in Korea, and that they should be protected and administered by a force from India. A Neutral Nations Repatriation Commission was to be formed by representatives from Czechoslovakia, Poland, Sweden and Switzerland with India. The term for interviews with prisoners was set at sixty days. The first four nations would also provide members of a Neutral Nations (Armistice) Supervisory Commission. But as these vital details were agreed upon, President Rhee intervened on his own behalf.

During April and May, the President had come increasingly to believe that the interests of the Korean people were being marginalised at Panmunjom. Passionately opposed to the settlement proposed, his aim was the unification of Korea and he saw all too clearly that unification would be made more not less difficult by a military armistice. He had also intermittent anxieties that the Republic of Korea might be left to its own devices once the war was over. Although the ROK armed forces had grown in strength—they were then rising towards twenty divisions—he would need quantities of American military equipment and supplies to defend his territory, and very much more to overcome the NKPA and Chinese 'volunteers'. In either case, he would also depend essentially on American air power.

A series of meetings with Generals Taylor and Clark, and Ellis O Briggs—Mr Muccio's successor as United States ambassador—obtained, as they thought, all reasonable assurances for the future security of the Republic of Korea militarily and economically. If President Rhee had been simply concerned with political power, they might have sufficed. But he was not. He had been struggling all his life for the liberation of Korea as an entity and he was ready to wreck the negotiations on this issue. Early in the morning of 18th June, he contrived the 'escape' of 25,000 militant anti-Communist members of the North Korean People's Army. At least these men would not be subjected to the consultation process by his North Korean and Chinese enemies.

There was consternation in the United Nations alliance, scarcely reduced by the knowledge that some 1,000 of those freed had been caught by United States forces, and that 8–9,000 prisoners of the same mind were still safely in custody under American guards. It was widely believed that, as a consequence of this arbitrary act, China and North Korea would

---

* Smith, General Walter Bedell (1895–1961), after leaving the United States Army in 1950 he was appointed Director of the Central Intelligence Agency by President Truman. In 1953, he joined President Eisenhower's Government as Under Secretary of State, that is, next in seniority to Mr Dulles.

cancel, or at any rate stand back from, the agreements reached. There were also expectations of enmity between the populace in South Korea and the United Nations military forces in their midst.

Much of this was a reaction of panic. Mr J A Graham, British Minister to the Republic of Korea, reported on 24th June,

> ... Popular enthusiasm for release of prisoners (which is quite genuine) is to considerable extent independent of desire to wreck the armistice. People are simply pleased at release of compatriots and relatives. Support for any further sabotage of the armistice would be certainly less widespread.
>
> 3. I would therefore suggest that before going so far as asking Rhee to accept the United Nations resolution [armistice settlement] (public rejection of which would practically force our hand) United Nations Command should try by patient and private argument (mixed with thinly veiled threats) to make Rhee see reason. We should persevere even if first results are negative. I think there is a faint hope that when the first glamour of his defiant gesture has worn off Rhee may become more sensible. ...[11]

Mr Graham might have underestimated the nature and extent of popular feeling; Mr Walter S Robertson—Assistant Secretary of State and Mr Dulles' envoy—was mobbed on his arrival in Seoul, and whilst some of the demonstrations were rigged, there were many spontaneous gatherings. The far left apart, political ranks had been closed. From 25th June to 12th July, Robertson and Briggs listened daily to President Rhee's bill of complaints, some of which contradicted others. But Mr Graham was right in predicting that the 'glamour' of defiance would wear off. Rhee argued himself into recognition that too obstinate a stand might destroy him and the Republic of Korea.

The price for his agreement to the armistice terms was not cheap. He obtained a mutual security pact in which the ROK Army expansion to twenty divisions should be underwritten by the United States taxpayer; an economic aid programme of which the first payment should be 200 million dollars; and high level consultation on the the forthcoming permanent peace treaty.

These negotiations took twenty four days—18th June to 12th July 1953—an interval which provided one minor but important advantage to the United Nations Command, particularly to Rear-Admiral E G A Clifford CB RN, FO2IC of the British Far East Fleet and Commander of the Commonwealth and Allied Forces, West Coast*.

Admiral Clifford had succeeded Admiral Scott-Moncrieff on 23rd September 1952—slightly in advance of the date intended due to the

---

* From January 1953, the West Coast naval and island elements had been retitled Task Units, as follows: Commander West Coast—CTU 95.1; Carrier Force —CTU 95.1.1; Inshore cruiser—CTU 95.1.2; Ch'o-do naval force—CTU 95.1.4; Paengyong-do—CTU 95.1.5; Haeju area naval force—CTU 95.1.6; Islands defence command—CTU 95.1.3.

latter falling ill in the final weeks of his term of command. This occasioned no difficulty. The organisation of the force was attuned to its tasks. Working relationships among its international components and externally with the Seventh Fleet were excellent. Admiral Gingrich, Commander of Task Force 95, his immediate superior, assured him that he had no intention of intruding upon the direction of west coast operations, a policy he followed throughout the remainder of his incumbency*. In this respect, Admiral Clifford was better placed than General West, who assumed command of the Commonwealth Division at approximately the same time.

In broad terms, however, the two senior British officers were involved similarly in circumstances of strategic and, to no mean extent, tactical stalemate: holding the enemy in check while maintaining a potential for offensive options if the Chinese and North Koreans should suddenly abandon the armistice talks. But this did not mean that operations had become torpid or prescriptive. In the late summer months, *Ocean*'s Fireflies and Sea Furies had twice been attacked by MiGs, the first such encounters for the west coast carriers. Whilst the naval pilots survived these in part by evasion, in part by successful counter-attack, the incidents were a reminder that the enemy fighter force maintained some capacity for enterprise†. And even in such predictable features of naval action such as mine laying, the North Korean were continually trying new methods. *Nootka*'s detection of the minelaying junk‡ occurred just after Admiral Clifford's arrival. Though this venture was foiled, others were attempted. At the least, a number of mines were floated out of the Taedong estuary every day until 1st May 1953.

By September 1952, a command had been established to comprehend the raiding and intelligence gathering forces on both coasts, described as Covert, Clandestine and Related Activities, Korea—generally referred to by its American Marine and Army members as 'C-crack', from the abbreviation CCRAK. The Korean partisans had been organised into 'regiments' under their leadership, a title which suggested a greater regularity than these warrior bands possessed. A tendency to exclusivity persisted among those recently arrived as members of the directing staffs but, like their predecessors, those concerned came to recognise within a month or two their dependence on naval support, not least when ice bridges began to form in mid-winter between the CCRAK islands and the mainland, raising their vulnerability to the superior numbers of the North Korean forces ashore*. Still, in comparative terms,

---

* Admiral C E Olsen USN succeeded him on 12th February 1953.

† These particular interventions also exposed inadequacies in the flow of radar information between the Fifth Air Force and Seventh Fleet.

‡ Page 314.

liaison between those on the islands and those at sea improved year by year.

In the spring of 1953, as observed, the armistice negotiations reopened after a recess exceeding six months. In London before departure, Admiral Clifford had been briefed on the United Nations objectives, the progress made and the problems outstanding, but during the greater part of his command the talks had been in abeyance. With their resumption on 26th April, he studied the implications of a settlement to his own forces. He thus became acquainted with Operation 'Pandora'.

In late April, Pandora was an outline plan for the separation of the two sides in the waters of the west coast. Some twenty islands, principally Ch'o-do and Sok-to, the most northerly of those in continuous occupation, were to be evacuated within five days of the armistice coming into force. Five other groups, namely, Paengyong-do, Taechong-do, Soch'ong-do, Yonp'yong-do, and U-do, were to be retained and reinforced. Civilians in the former category were to be given the option of withdrawing to the Republic of Korea. The military elements—intelligence gathering and early warning agencies, the air-sea rescue organisation, and the necessary defence forces, partisan or otherwise—would be required until the cease fire was implemented. This latter consideration meant that whatever remained on the northern islands could not exceed the capability to evacuate them within five days.

Between the time Pandora was first drafted early in 1952 and the reopening of negotiations in late April 1953, the equipment deployed on Ch'o-do and Sok-to had grown in range and volume. Equally, the resources of the Islands Defence Group had been expanded; for example, in artillery†. A check of the civil population in 1953 disclosed that it was considerably greater than the estimate made in 1952.

It was thus apparent to Admiral Clifford that the plan for separation required recasting and completion as a matter of urgency. The first step was to discover precisely what had to be moved and then to ensure that he had the resources to hand to complete the evacuation in the stipulated period.

Enquiries were pressed with the agencies and detachments in the islands, Commander Task Force 95 (by then, Admiral Olsen), the Eighth Army including the CCRAK organisation, and the Fifth Air Force. The movement bill comprised 45,000 civilians in the islands to pass to the DPRK who wished to become citizens of the Republic of Korea, and 2,300

---

* For the most part, the warships managed to break the ice before it stabilised.

† When General Maxwell D Taylor visited Ch'o-do and Sok to in April 1953, Admiral Clifford persuaded him that the garrison needed field artillery to 'retaliate on the batteries which frequently fired on them from the mainland'. The Army Commander sent him two 90mm guns and crews. (Report of Proceedings FO2IC No 61, ADM 116/6229).

tons of heavy weapons and technical equipment.

Admiral Clifford was determined not to use fighting ships as transports; they would be required to control and assure the security of the coastal waters during the operation. Admiral Olsen agreed to provide a minimum of five United States and two ROK tank landing ships for the duration of Pandora.

As to his own facilities, Admiral Clifford had acquired a means of taking his headquarters to sea; HMS *Tyne* [Captain A J F Milne-Home] arrived at Sasebo on 7th April 1953 to replace *Ladybird*. Although she was a destroyer depot ship, manned by a reduced complement, she had a capacity to maintain station at sea, the necessary communications, and sufficient armament to protect herself in the environment of the west coast. Her accession was therefore timely.

Yet just how timely was not then apparent. Little Switch was imminent. Rotation continued. For instance, *Glory** [Captain E D G Lewin RN], approaching the end of her long tour in Korean operations, including two winters, was on the point of her first encounter with MiGs and a final round of sorties embracing the battle lines and heartland of the enemy. Those arriving in the theatre expected to serve there through the winter of 1953.

Still, preparations for Pandora advanced as the American negotiators attempted to settle the prisoner of war issue at Panmunjom. The talks were in recess on Coronation Day, 2nd June, an occasion marked by all of Her Majesty's Commonwealth ships whether on or off station, the Dutch frigate H Neth MS *Johan Maurits van Nassau* [Commander N W Sluijter R Neth N], and various ships, great and small, of the United States Navy. On the 8th June, agreement was reached between the warring parties on the exchange of prisoners. On the 16th, after attempts to win further territory on land, the Communists were ready to agree on the final line of demarcation. By this time, Pandora was in operation.

It was in operation because the Commander-in-Chief had spelled out to those on the coastal flanks that from the moment the armistice was signed, civilians who had been under the jurisdiction of the North Korean state on 25th June 1950 would be prohibited from moving to that of the Republic of Korea. Any resident of, for example, Ch'o-do, who wished to escape from it would be unable to do so following the cease fire. The evacuation of these civilians was thus to be set in hand at once, an arrangement welcomed by Admiral Clifford as it offered an opportunity to clear non-combatants in advance of the military withdrawal. Admiral Olsen despatched the additional tank landing ships

* Captain T A K Maunsell RN had succeeded Captain Colquhoun as commanding officer on 23rd April 1952 but fell ill on 28th November and, after a brief interregnum under Commander D E Bromley-Martin RN, Captain Lewin assumed command on 14th December.

he had promised, adding the assault transport USS *Lenawee* [Captain D M McCrae USN] to the commitment*.

For reasons difficult to understand, the commander of the CCRAK failed to inform Task Force 95 when he ordered the partisan infantry regiments to begin evacuation of selected west coast islands on 9th June. Admiral Clifford learned from *Birmingham* (Captain C W Greening DSC RN), who had been approached by local commanders on the 10th, and received official confirmation on the 11th. By that time he had decided to sail in *Tyne* to the operational area. This required a considerable effort in finding sufficient hands to bring the ship's company to strength; all ships in harbour at the time contributed. Escorted by the frigate *Morecambe Bay* (Commander J J E Farnol DSC RN), *Tyne* left Sasebo at 1900 on the 12th. A signal had been received from the Commander-in-Chief in Tokyo to all senior commanders that an armistice was imminent.

Admiral Clifford's chief of staff, Captain R F Leonard RN, had been responsible for the completion of Pandora. Unhappily, in both the personal and professional sense, he fell ill just as it was implemented and died on 24th June. Its provisions were, however, comprehensive. When the admiral arrived at Paengyong-do on the 14th to assume command, he discovered that Captain Greening had made considerable progress in evacuation and redeployment assisted by the respective commanders on station, Commander R D Ritchie MVO RN, Commander Task Unit 95.1.4 at Ch'o-do in *Modeste*, Commander G R Davis Goff DSC RNZN, Commander Task Unit 95.1.5 at Paengyong-do in *Hawea*, and Commander H D Ellis RN, Commander Task Unit 95.1.6 in the Haeju area—principally in the shallow waters round Yongp'yong-do—in *Sparrow*. Order had been brought to the embarkation process by naval detachments in ships' boats, or aboard the ROK light naval craft. The weather remained generally fair.

Even so, expecting notification at any moment of an armistice, it was far from certain that all the island residents concerned would be evacuated in time, for the great majority opted to remove themselves from Kim Il-sung's administration. Random night bombing by North Korean Yak-18s, intermittent shelling by shore batteries, and the sighting of junks filled with troops confirmed that the enemy were aware of the evacuation programme and meant to hinder it. *Ocean* began to examine ways and means of dealing with the slow flying night air intruders. The Commonwealth warships and the *Johan Maurits van Nassau* suppressed all attempts at interference at sea or from the shore. The arrival of *Lenawee* on the 15th considerably accelerated the transportation of civilians. The arbitrary release of prisoners of war by President Rhee disposed ample time for their delivery.

---

* In addition to a capacious hold, the *Lenawee* carried also twenty four landing craft.

Admiral Clifford's plan envisaged the staging of the latter together with a proportion of the partisan infantry regiments—some of whom were accompanied by dependents—on Paengyong-do, Taech'ong-do, and Yongp'yong-do. This worked well, initially, but problems grew as the days passed. This was due principally to two causes. First, a number of the partisans began to move back on to the islands they had abandoned; they had received information that the ROK government was unwilling to recognise the armistice agreement. Then, a considerable proportion of the civilians in transit took the view that the locations in which they would be settled within the Republic of Korea would not permit them to continue their livelihood, fishing or farming.

To these difficulties was added a third. As a result of President Rhee's arbitrary action on 18th June, there was a danger that some of the islands containing or covering those on which United Nations radar and signals equipment were sited would fall to the enemy. It seemed likely on 16th June that a clandestine enemy detachment was already in position on Ch'o-do[12].

By 20th June, however, security was assured and it was possible to revive the rotation or replacement of ships—Sparrow, for example, had reached the end of her tour; it was desirable to relieve one cruiser, Newcastle [Captain W H C Rutherford RN] remained in place of Birmingham. Admiral Clifford decided that he could not himself depart without an attempt to settle the overcrowding on Yongp'yong-do. On the morning of 22nd June, he landed there, primarily to discuss the refugee position.

> A formal welcome had been prepared for me. A Korean Marine Corps Guard awaited my inspection, banners of greeting were held aloft, and the road through the village was lined with war veterans, YWCA girls, prominent villagers, the Bible class, and an enormous number of schoolchildren. After listening to the children sing I was driven to the principal school, where, on the playground, yet more children in large numbers were being inoculated and vaccinated by the Medical Officer of HMAS Culgoa (Commander D A H Clarke RAN) with Korean assistance. Although the disposal of Korean civilians cannot be held to come within the assigned task of CTG 95.1 it was plain that a decision on the refugee question was needed and that it would not be forthcoming from anyone else[13].

There were 14,000 Koreans on the island, of whom only 7,800 were genuine residents. Of the remainder, some had drifted there during the war; the greater number were refugees in transit from islands evacuated. Admiral Clifford gave his judgement. There would be no physical coercion to move the latter but the supplies of rice would be reduced to feed the original populace, some 7,800. This did not immediately persuade the balance to leave but it created a climate for movement. During the remainder of the month, the majority accepted transportation to the resettlement sites awaiting them, while those who owned junks struck a bargain with the United Nations civil affairs authorities to be permitted to enter the Inch'on area[14]. Admiral Clifford returned to Sasebo, satisfied that the final phase of Pandora could be completed within the terms of the armistice. He reckoned without his air force colleagues. The Tactical Air Direction Centre on Ch'o-do was dismantled following the cease fire at the end of July. Most of the equipment had been loaded into a tank landing ship

> ...when information was received that the 5th Air Force required it to resume operations. At that stage it was not practicable to re-erect the gear in the time allowed and, after much argument, the 5th Air Force agreed to the evacuation proceeding. Some of the TADC personnel were embarked in Birmingham however, and...provided radar cover up to the Yalu River required by the 5th Air Force.

By 1st August, [Admiral Clifford] was able to report that the evacuation of the West Coast Islands was complete[15].

To the relief of the United Nations alliance, the Communist side reacted moderately to President Rhee's disruptive tactics on 18th June. Mr A Price reported from Peking,

> ... The papers appeared several hours late today and contained no editorial comments [on the release of the prisoners]. A study of all today's Press suggests, however, special care has been taken to avoid giving articles on this subject first place. ...[16]

The Chinese were set on completion of the armistice. Chinese and Korean newspapers, no less those of the Soviet *bloc*, subsequently ran a short, scathing criticism of the deceitful nature of the United Nations 'camp', but did not contend that the release of the prisoners cancelled the agreements reached. Quite the contrary, as the UN prisoners were told at this time, 'No matter what attempts your side makes to wreck the prospects for peace, we shall force them to meet their obligations[17]'.

Still, Mao and his associates intended to impose their own penalties. Shortly, P'eng resumed heavy attacks on the Americans and ROK forces in the central sector. He lost considerable numbers of his own men in the struggle, perhaps 30,000 killed and wounded by ground and air fire, but he inflicted a further 14,000 casualties on the United Nations Command, principally by quantities of shellfire. If Syngman Rhee and his senior military officers needed a demonstration of Communist military power in Korea, this provided it.

Meeting at Panmunjom on 19th July, General Harrison told Nam Il that the United Nations forces would maintain the armistice, once signed, even if the ROK Army broke it, though they would not themselves attempt to restrain them by force. Thus Syngman Rhee had weakened the strong position of his allies. American policy had secured all the concessions necessary for a truce but had lost the moral advantage which flowed from the accomplishment. The Republic of Korea had also lost in July more ground of tactical importance in central Korea.

In these circumstances, the armistice agreement was signed at 1012 am on 27th July 1953*. For a further twelve hours, fire continued to be exchanged, but thereafter all hostile action ceased. Three years, one month, and two days after Kim Il-sung had invaded the Republic of Korea, the war was over.

---

* For the text, see Appendix L.

SOURCE NOTES: Chapter 22

1 See, for example, Prime Minister's personal telegram T.675/5 No. 2255 of 29th April 1945 to Stalin. PREM 3/356/6.

2 Colville, Sir John, *The Fringes of Power: Downing Street Diaries, 1939–55* (1985), pp 650–651, and 653–4.

3 See, for example, Cabinet Conclusions No. 71 of 23rd July 1952 (CAB 128/25), and Mr Churchill's speech of 5th March 1953 to the House of Commons.

4 For the development of this pledge, see Hughes, E J, *The Ordeal of Power: a Political Memoir of the Eisenhower Years*, (1963), pp 32–35.

5 FRUS, 1952–54, *cit*, pp 804–805.

6 For Mr Eden's account of this, see *Full Circle* (London, 1960), pp 24–25.

7 FRUS, 1952–1954, *cit*, pp 785–790.

8 *Jen Min Piao*, 30th March 1953.

9 For example, the statement by General Dmitri Volkogonov to the Yonhap News Agency, Republic of Korea, 22nd June 1953.

10 See, for example, Memo by Robert Cutler to the Secretary of Defense, 21st March 1953, FRUS 1952–1954, *cit*, p 815.

11 Korea 208 to FO of 24th June 1953, FK1071/533, (FO 371 105504).

12 Reports of Proceedings, FO2IC No. 62 and Report on Evacuation of Islands on the West Coast, June–July 1953 (ADM 116/6229) and *Birmingham* (ADM 116/6210), *Hawea* (ADM 116/6218), *Modeste* and *Morecambe Bay* (ADM 116/6219), and *Sparrow* (ADM 116/6222).

13 Special Report of Proceedings FO2IC *cit*, 22nd June 1953 (ADM 116/6229).

14 *Ibid.*

15 Report of Proceedings FO2IC, *ibid.*

16 Peking 377 to FO of 19th June 1953, FK 1071/480, (FO 371 105502).

17 Comment made to author among many prisoners at the time.

CHAPTER 23

Conclusions and reflections

So, from 10 pm on 27th July 1953, the zone of combat along the coasts of Korea, along the line of demarcation, and in the air above land and sea, became a zone of armed vigilance. As mutually agreed, both sides withdrew at least two kilometres from the line of demarcation within seventy two hours; and within ten days all the naval and military forces, supplies and equipment of the United Nations Command were drawn back from the coastal waters and islands of the other side.

The Military Armistice Commission with its observer teams, the Neutral Nations Supervisory Commission, and the Indian Custodian Force[1] opened for business. The prisoner of war exchange began: 'Big Switch' succeeded the limited repatriation of 'Little Switch' in the preceding April*. Shortly, there were attempts to develop a peace treaty and to unify Korea, what Mr Churchill was later to describe to the House of Commons as 'stubborn and tangled discussions'[2]. They bore no fruit either at Panmunjom or, in 1954, at Geneva. The suspension of hostilities thus hung on the truce agreement alone.

One arrangement among the United Nations alliance occasioned second thoughts. During the late stages of the Truman administration they had agreed that the Communists should be warned formally, following an armistice, of the consequences—the 'Greater Sanctions'—if there should be any renewal of operations. Circumstances had changed since December 1951, Sir Winston Churchill† reminded his national and international colleagues in April 1953: Stalin was dead; the Cold War was declining. An open challenge to the integrity of China's signature would be difficult to justify. To this consideration another was added. A bold statement that the United Nations participants would be ready to resume the war might encourage President Syngman Rhee to find some means of wrecking the armistice. After considerable discussion[3], it was decided to make a Joint Policy Declaration, but without ostentation, slipping it in as a supporting document to General Clark's report of 7th August 1953 to the Secretary-General of the United Nations‡. It read:

* For details of the exchange, see Appendix M.

† The Order of the Garter was conferred on Mr Churchill in that month, hence the change in title.

‡ General Clark's report on the conclusion of the armistice negotiations was submitted to Hr. Dag Hjalmar Agne Carl Hammarskjöld (1905–61), who had succeeded Hr. Trygve Lie.

> We, the United Nations members whose military forces are participating in the Korean action, support the decision of the Commander-in-Chief of the United Nations Command to conclude an armistice agreement. We hereby affirm our determination fully and faithfully to carry out the terms of that armistice. We expect that the other parties will likewise scrupulously observe its terms.
>
> The task ahead is not an easy one. We will support the efforts of the United Nations to bring about an equitable settlement in Korea based on the principles which have long been established by the United Nations, and which call for a united, independent and democratic Korea in repairing the ravages of war.
>
> We declare again our faith in the principles and purposes of the United Nations, our consciousness of our continuing responsibilities in Korea, and our determination on good faith to seek a settlement of the Korean problem. We affirm, in the interests of world peace, that if there is a renewal of the armed attack, challenging again the principles of the United Nations, we should again be united and prompt to resist. The consequences of such a breach of the armistice would be so grave that, in all probability, it would not be possible to confine hostilities within the frontiers of Korea.
>
> Finally, we are of the opinion that the armistice must not result in jeopardising the restoration or the safeguarding of peace in any other part of Asia* [4].

There was some further discussion of the Greater Sanctions at Bermuda in December 1953 during a conference between the American, British, and French heads of government†. While Sir Winston and President Eisenhower were lunching alone on the 4th, the latter remarked that the United States 'would expect to strike back with atomic weapons at military targets...areas that were supporting the aggression' if there was any deliberate breach of the Korean armistice by the Communists. Although the record of this meeting[5] indicates agreement by the British Prime Minister to the idea, President Eisenhower was later to disclose that, when the matter had been discussed more fully, various qualifications had been raised by his ally.

During a meeting of the National Security Council on 10th December, a review of the Bermuda Conference included the following.

> Secretary Dulles stated that...he would confine his remarks this morning to matters of special concern to the National Security Council. The first of these matters was the attitude of the British and French to normalising the use of atomic weapons. Secretary Dulles said that both the British and

* This final paragraph had been introduced by France to cover Indo-China.

† A meeting with President Eisenhower and M J Laniel, the French Prime Minister had been arranged for April, but had first been postponed due to French political difficulties and again because Sir Winston had a stroke in June. Mr Dulles, Mr Eden, and M. Georges Bidault, the French Foreign Minister took part.

French exhibited a very stubborn resistance to any idea of the automatic use of atomic weapons, even in the case of a Communist renewal of hostilities in Korea.

The President interrupted to say that he had explained our proposed intentions and courses of action in the event that the Communists broke the truce in Korea, along the lines which he and the Secretary of State had indicated at the last NSC Meeting*. Sir Winston, however, had opposed the use of atomic weapons even in Korea and adjacent areas, unless a course of action were agreed by our UN allies in advance.

Secretary Dulles pointed out Sir Winston's conviction that if the United States took the initiative in the use of such weapons there would be a world wide revulsion which to Secretary Dulles indicated that our thinking on the atomic weapon was several years in advance of the rest of the free world. Sir Winston also indicated the very great anxiety of the British people lest, on account of their exposed position, they would suffer if the Soviets retaliated against our use of atomic weapons by attacking the population centres of the British Isles. Secretary Dulles emphasized that no final conclusions had been reached in his discussions on the subject with Churchill and Bidault, but he pointed out that the United States had not renounced its right to use atomic weapons if war were forced upon us by the Soviet Union.

The President then stated that there was a short sequel to the conversations on the subject which Secretary Dulles had just described. In his last talk with the President, Sir Winston had indicated greater concern that no announcement should be made, rather than great concern over their actual use by the United States. Sir Winston had related this concern about an announcement of our intention to the President's forthcoming speech to the UN†, which he felt would appear incompatible with any announced intention to use atomic weapons. The gist of Sir Winston's view, said the President, was let us plan to use these weapons if necessity arose, but let us not talk about these plans. In the circumstances, therefore, the President stated that the best follow-up of the Bermuda discussions of atomic weapons would be discussions between the US and the British Chiefs of Staff. The President also admitted that Sir Winston seemed to have a point as to the psychological disadvantages of a contrast between the President's UN speech and an announcement of intention by the United States to resort to the use of these weapons...[6]

The United Kingdom was no more ready to acquiesce in the use of atomic weapons in Korea without consultation than in Europe, however much Mr Churchill sought in private conversation with the President to soften the hard edge of objection by references to his political position. It is a moot point whether, if China and North Korea had reopened the war in the peninsula, the United States would have used atomic weapons without reference to or in spite of objections by her allies; an immense

* 173rd Meeting.

† On 8th December 1953, immediately following the Bermuda conference.

fund of goodwill would have been forfeited in Europe and Asia in either case. The fact was that, so long as the Eisenhower administration remained apprehensive of a renewal of hostilities in Korea, the British position remained a reference point in the planning of responses, sometimes to the vexation of the Joint Chiefs of Staff and their supporters.

Except when it suited them, the American military hierarchy tended to overlook the fact that the special relationship was not simply fostered by Britain alone. Notwithstanding the shifts of power post-1945, the United States assumed that Britain remained her best friend; at any rate, for the anglophobes in her midst, an inextricable partner in the circumstances of the times. Thus, setting aside the brief period of Mr Byrne's follies, America had pressed a reluctant Britain to be her partner in the pursuit of Korean reunification, though that activity was marginalised by the expansion of Russian power in Europe. Perhaps Mr Bevin alone saw in 1949 that the two matters were interrelated. The frustration of Stalin by the formation of the Atlantic Alliance may well have persuaded him to sanction and support Kim's proposed subjugation of South Korea.

Of course, having different standpoints, the Anglo-American partners did not always agree on priorities or options, as in the Middle East, which was then of lesser importance to the United States. The failure of the Truman/Marshall post-war policy in China convinced the American Government that they could not do business with Mao Tse-tung. Mr Attlee and Mr Bevin believed that the Chinese leadership would tire of Russian exploitation and take up economic opportunities outside the Soviet *bloc*. To that end, the western powers had to give full recognition to the People's Republic. Whatever the disagreements between London and Washington, few were irreconcilable, and none weakened the common resolve of Mr Acheson and Mr Bevin to check the spread of Communist power.

The reasons for entering the Korean war were similar in both capitals but not identical. The Americans did so because they saw Kim's invasion of the south simply as Soviet expansion by proxy. Mr Attlee and Mr Bevin responded because they believed primarily that, whatever the extent of Soviet involvement, it would be fundamentally wrong to allow armed aggression to flourish as it had done in the 1930s. On further reflection, both Prime Minister and Foreign Secretary took the view that they could not, in any case, seek American assistance in countering Communist expansion in Europe but excuse themselves from this duty in the Far East. Besides, there was always the expectation that if Mao should attack Hong Kong, the United States would come to their assistance.

Yet this does not explain another aspect of Britain's special value as an ally to America at this time: the size of the forces she sent to Korea.

49. The Samich'on river, summer, 1952. (Major J A Foulis, RAPC)

50. The reverse slope of Point 159, an advanced infantry and tank outpost south west of Kowang-san. (5th Royal Iniskilling Dragoon Guards)

51. Bunker built by the Royal Engineers to protect the Centurion tank of 5DG on Point 187, August 1952. (5th Royal Iniskilling Dragoon Guards)

52. Tank entering the bunker. (5th Royal Iniskilling Dragoon Guards)

53. The same, taken from the front of the bunker. On 5th September, by a million to one chance, an HE shell entered the turret when the tank had drawn back essentially for maintenance, killing the crew, Sergeant Wykes, Lance Corporal Metcalfe, Troopers Cahill and McFadyen, *Change and Challenge* History of 5th Royal Iniskilling Dragoon Guards 1928–1978 by General Sir Cecil Blacker and Major General H G Woods, p 110 (Colchester, 1978).

54. 14th Field Regiment, Royal Artillery positions in the Commonwealth area, summer 1952. (Imperial War Museum)

55. 'The Hook' position: the feature is top right, 'Green Finger' is in the left foreground, with 'Warsaw' behind. The 'Ronson' standing patrol 'Knob' site is right centre. (Imperial War Museum)

56. Repairing defences on the reverse slope of the Hook area, summer 1952. (Imperial War Museum)

57. 5DG tanks in harbour, summer 1952. (Major F W Garnett)

58. 'Hoochies'—dugouts—on the reverse slope of 1 DWR positions, with a deep communication trench in rear, winter, 1952. (Major W F C Robertson, The Duke of Wellington's Regiment)

59. 1 DWR 3-inch mortar firing posts, same period. With the immediately preceding picture, the development of defences is apparent. (Company Sergeant-Major W Norman, The Duke of Wellington's Regiment)

60. Members of a fighting patrol of 1 DWR immediately after returning to their to their own lines, November 1952. They are wearing the winter uniform which had progressively entered service from the winter of 1951/52. (The Duke of Wellington's Regiment)

61. 'The Flying Fox'—funicular supply system rigged by the Royal Engineers and 1 DLI to A Company's position on Kowang-san, Point 355, summer 1953. (The Durham Light Infantry)

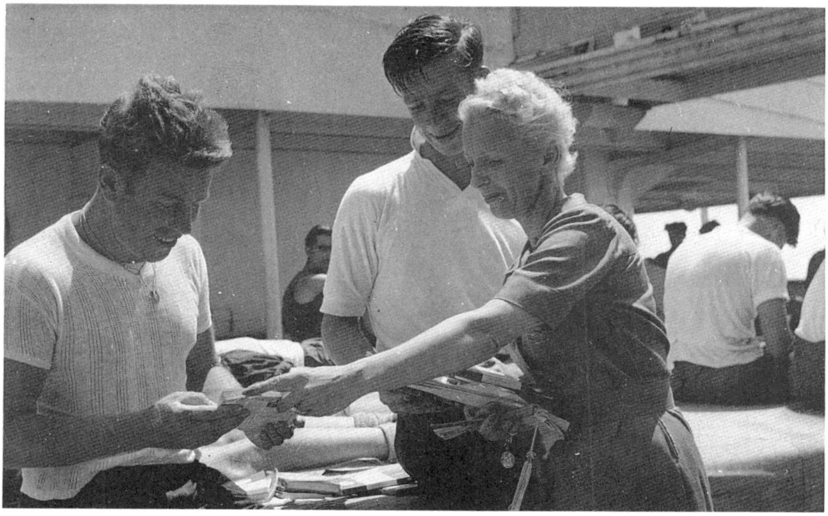

62. Going home—distribution of games and other gifts aboard the troopship from a representative of the Women's Voluntary Services. The WVS made an important contribution to the welfare services of the Commonwealth Division from 1951, including considerable assistance with Red Cross representatives to the reception and support of returning prisoners-of-war. (Mrs Peggie Mordern, WVS)

63. Home at last—Trooper Richardson arrives at Southampton, September 1953. (Hulton)

The naval squadron contributed to the United Nations Command in July 1950 was considerable in numbers and range of warships, and the Royal Navy was sufficiently strong to maintain them on station. If it had been the only British contingent, as the Chiefs of Staff in London intended at that time, it would still have been greater in aggregate than that of any other nation except the United States. But in the crisis on the Naktong in 1950, Britain responded to American appeals for troops by despatching the reinforced 29th Brigade, their only true reserve—preceding this by fielding the 27th Brigade from Hong Kong despite their conviction that the Hong Kong garrison was already inadequate to deter a Chinese incursion. From these beginnings, maritime operations on the west coast of Korea were undertaken largely by the Commonwealth naval forces, and two brigades were maintained in Korea until the Commonwealth division further strengthened the contribution.

Unlike the subscription of those nations which contributed on a token basis, the Commonwealth contribution was indispensable to the commander-in-chief. The British bore the main burden in this provision.

Without it, America would have been obliged to provide these forces herself; the numbers and fighting power were essential to operational resilience. There was no other nation able or willing to contribute on such a scale. West Germany and Japan were still under occupation, forbidden to raise military forces. In Asia, Pakistan and India had the numbers to contribute formations of divisional size but for differing reasons declined to do so. In western Europe, France alone with Britain had the strength to send substantial forces to Korea but her economy was overburdened, her political establishment in turmoil while she struggled to maintain the security of overseas territories, particularly Indo-China, and resuscitate her conscript forces to meet the needs of home defence and NATO. Thus she sent only a single warship for a tour and a battalion to Korea.

Finding additional forces would have placed the United States in difficulties—her military manpower was stretched almost to exhaustion. The military manpower of the United Kingdom, and no less her economy, was equally stretched with rising commitments to NATO, in the Middle East and Malaya. But, as on other occasions before and since, she chose to extend her resources beyond her means. The choice was supported by parliament and nation.

The collective Commonwealth military response may have obscured the scale of the British dimension. Australian, Canadian, and New Zealand naval and ground contingents integrated so rapidly within the British formations that it was difficult to tell one from another—nor did it matter to the Americans what came from where to join the United Nations Command in 1950.

Perhaps it was partly due to this collective success that President Truman and, more surprisingly, Mr Acheson, lost sight of the political nature of the Commonwealth in the first year of the war, assuming that the United Kingdom was still an imperial matriarch whose offspring would follow her unquestioningly. Mr Eden had to correct this view in the second half of 1951. But it took some time for the State Department to understand the subtle and productive nature of Britain's relationship with her former dominions, particularly Australia and Canada. The connections between London and New Delhi were similarly difficult to understand. It did not help Mr Acheson to know that India taxed his and Mr Attlee's patience alike. It was no less difficult for him to accept later that Mr Eden's championship of the Menon proposals contributed to the final settlement of the war.

In all these relationships, personal inclinations swayed results. Mr Attlee and Mr Truman, plain men in personality and politics, respected one another. Very different in character, Mr Acheson and Mr Bevin held one another in high regard. But the standard bearer of the alliance from 1948 to the end of 1952 in his close friendship with Mr Acheson, in his extraordinary capacity for judging the American political and popular moods, and in the brilliance of his diplomacy over the whole range of Anglo-American relations, was Sir Oliver Franks. It is a matter of judgement whether he should or could have been persuaded to remain in Washington for the remainder of the war. He might have been as successful with Mr Dulles as his predecessor, the change of interface involved was within his capacity, but he felt it was time to leave and his wishes were respected[7].

With the entry of the Conservative Government, continuity of the relationship was assured because Mr Churchill was emotionally as well as politically dedicated to their preservation; but its character was modified. For one thing, the Korean war was on an entirely different footing: the line had stabilised; armistice talks were in train. Mr Churchill was concerned with the wider world scene, anxious to make his final contribution to international politics by some settlement of differences with Stalin and, on the latter's death, to exploit any possibility of better relations with his successors, as he explained to the House of Commons,

> ... Studying our own strength and that of America under the massive American shield, I do not consider it unreasonable or dangerous to conclude that internal prosperity rather than external conquest is not only the deep desire of the Russian peoples, but also the long-term interest of their rulers[8].

His difficulty in this aspiration was President Eisenhower, who did not believe that the character of the Russian leadership had changed. The two men were able to argue the point without acrimony; they were friends. This was not true of Mr Eden in his relationship with Dean Acheson or John Foster Dulles.

Occasional differences apart, relations between the British and American Chiefs of Staff were amiable in the wide range of common interests they dealt with during the period 1950-53, though, with Lord Tedder's departure from Washington, there was less access to the Chairman (Bradley) and the single-Service chiefs. They shared anxieties as General MacArthur's strategy overran itself at the end of 1950, but the British chiefs suffered the consequences more acutely because they were consultants, not executives in the higher direction of the war. Field Marshal Sir William Slim recalled that,

> ...we greatly wanted to have that capability—that is, to have MacArthur reporting directly both to the Americans and to ourselves—but we knew in our hearts that it simply would not have worked. No commander can be answerable to more than one headquarters. And the Americans could not have worked on the basis of day to day long range consultation with us on the direction of MacArthur[9].

Actually, General Eisenhower had answered to Washington and London both from the Mediterranean and northwest Europe during 1942-45, but the political and military circumstances of those years are scarcely comparable with those in Korea in 1950 and 1951. Neither the Congress nor the American people would have understood such an arrangement in Korea. The frustration of the British chiefs peaked when it became apparent that their American colleagues had lost control of MacArthur as he resumed his advance to the Yalu. Reassured by General Ridgway's conduct as army commander, they welcomed with the Prime Minister and Foreign Office his appointment in General MacArthur's place, as later the accession of General Clark. From April, 1951, they fretted only when the Communist prisoners were able to seize the initiative temporarily on Koje-do and, intermittently, during the truce talks when the American negotiators seemed to be splitting hairs.

If the British chiefs had had a choice of post to fill in the higher direction of events from the middle of 1951, they would have opted for a place among the armistice negotiators[10]. They were not convinced that a British presence at the table would have upset American public opinion or the other allies but failed to convince the Foreign Office. But it was not a matter that fired Mr Morrison. Political misfortunes discouraged Mr Attlee from taking up contentious enterprises. When the idea was officially mooted it was too late; the opportunity had passed.

In retrospect, it is just possible that Sir Oliver Franks' standing in Washington might have persuaded President Truman and Mr Acheson to admit him to their discussions of the bargaining process at Panmunjom.

If Sir Esler Dening had arrived in Tokyo earlier—rather than in August 1951—he might have been acceptable as an adviser at the commander-in-chief's level. Given American agreement in either case, the other governments contributing to the United Nations Command would probably have accepted such participation by the United Kingdom without demanding a place for themselves; the magnitude of British arms in operations would have been persuasive.

The British were perhaps too diffident in exploiting the sum of their naval and military contribution not only in quantity but also in quality. Within a few weeks of their arrival in the Korean theatre, their seamen and soldiers had won a high reputation among senior American commanders. Comparisons are invidious. The international press reports of the time tended to suggest that the Americans divisions in the Eighth Army broke in any serious encounter with the enemy to the point that the impression persists. It is false. United States infantry and armour were involved in several spectacular failures but fought doughtily on many more occasions which were at best briefly credited, more often ignored by the foreign press, and rarely known among other national contingents in the theatre. The American gunnery was first rate. But in several aspects of operations it is fair to say that the British—and Commonwealth—forces were superior to their comrades in the United States Army.

First among these was the performance as leaders by the non-commissioned officers and a unique body of warrant officers—sergeant-majors and the like—which optimised the process of command and control of men, weapons and equipment to the lowest level. All military forces necessarily dispose non-commissioned officers but the British system of selection and training, and the special standing accorded them were unique to the Commonwealth at the time of the Korean war.

The capabilities of these men in leadership extended the practice of delegation. As observed, captains of warships of whatever size were expected to take on all manner of contingencies without requiring close instructions from above; likewise battalion and, to a considerable extent, squadron, battery, and company commanders. As a part of this philosophy, the more senior ranks were based forward, the headquarters behind being manned by officers relatively junior in rank. Curiously, this arrangement encouraged the assumption of greater responsibility by junior staff officers which sometimes irked American higher headquarters as, similarly, they were annoyed by the readiness of the British to question orders at times.

These complaints were well founded but arose because British officers were encouraged to express dissenting ideas about plans and operational proceedings to their seniors, either as staff officers or subordinate commanders, when operational occasion seemed to warrant it. Of course they were required to obey orders at once when the senior concerned returned a different view; but the process obliged the latter to take a second look, however briefly, at a plan or its development. As a practice it was incidental in part a product of personality, but it was not exceptional. If it produced occasions when persistently argumentative officers had to be pointed firmly in a given direction, it worked against such dangerous customs as the reinforcement of failure to which several American divisional commanders were prone. Not least, the philosophy of maximum delegation preserved the standing chain of command to its limits. General Almond's practice of interposing units or groups within one commander's area answerable to a commander elsewhere was eschewed.

These arrangements were enhanced within the Commonwealth army component by the regimental system. A soldier will readily fight for his country when the struggle lies within or on the approaches to his homeland. He may fight no less ardently for a great cause but this type of motivation is difficult to maintain through a long and harsh campaign in a remote land. What keeps most men fighting in war is comradeship, giving to and drawing from the group with whom hardships and dangers, comforts and passing pleasures are shared. A regiment of long standing provides an environment in which this simple but powerful function of the spirit flourishes, embracing even those who have come from other such bodies. It carries forward a sufficiency of familiars when numbers have fallen as casualties, and provides a family to which those restored to fitness may return. This system worked very well in Korea, irrespective of the balance between regulars and national service men, and the element of recalled reservists which swelled for a time and then fell away among them. It was to this end that the armoured regiments and infantry battalions arrived as a body and departed as such after a tour despite the advantages, from a purely organisational view, of 'trickle posting' in and out, which had to be applied among the majority of units in other Arms.

The numbers of Americans fighting in Korea were such that many scarcely knew that the British were in the field, but those who fought closely alongside them valued their company, foremost the United States Marine Division. This same consideration was as true for the prison camps as the battlefield.

From the British forces, 1,060 officers and men were taken as prisoners of war, the majority from the Army*. As observed, their treatment by Communist captors was dire, involving prolonged attempts at political subversion. By the end of 1951, it had become apparent to

* Of the total, 82 died in captivity. For further details, see Appendix N.

the Service Ministries in London that a fraction of this number, some forty for reasons then unknown, were engaging in enemy propaganda. Prisoners' letters published in newspapers such as the *Daily Worker** suggested that they had adopted Communist ideology. With similar evidence to hand, there were apprehensions in Washington that a majority of American prisoners including officers were becoming disaffected. On this basis, the Defense Department was unwilling to develop a 'ratline'—an escape line—for captives on the grounds that it might quickly be betrayed by prisoners working for the enemy. The British thought this unlikely but were unable to proceed without their ally.

The sick and wounded in the camps returned under Little Switch in April 1953, provided some direct evidence as to circumstances in the camps and the political outlook of prisoners, but it was difficult to determine what proportion had been repatriated because they espoused the Communist cause. It was known within the United Nations Command that a number of sick, wounded, and disabled remained in North Korea after the exchange ended but this was not acknowledged at Panmunjom by the responsible Chinese and North Korean officers. In all probability they lacked this information. It seems likely that the choice of non-Korean sick and wounded for exchange was delayed by the Chinese for one reason or another.

On 9th April, Captain R P Hickey, captured as medical officer of the Glosters on the Imjin, was taken to Pyoktong, Camp 5 and also headquarters of the Chinese Prisoner of War Command, and saw there a number 'who were clearly very ill indeed'[11] but there was then no indication as to how many would be repatriated. Indeed, in the second week of April there was considerable uncertainty among the prisoners as to whether there would be an exchange at all; expectations were based on rumour. No reason was given for moving Captain Hickey to Pyoktong; he was not required to express an opinion on medical cases, or warned that he would be tending those in special need during their journey. His only instruction was to attend anti-American lectures with invalids and others. When it was announced on the 13th at Pyoktong that an exchange agreement had been concluded, there was still no indication as to who would benefit.

At last, as trucks arrived to carry sick and wounded south, the first names were called, continuing piecemeal until the last vehicle had departed. Captain Hickey and a disabled officer with him were then sent back to their camp. More than a thousand had been earmarked for exchange†: 684—Koreans and other nationalities—were chosen, leaving some 400 at one or another site who were manifestly ill or who qualified

* Then the official newspaper of the British Communist Party. Its title was later changed to the *Morning Star*.

† There were no South Koreans at Pyoktong.

on account of substantial disablement. They had been left behind because they were not political 'progressives'. This is not to say that all 684 exchanged were in that category—far from it; but among that number some were in markedly better health than individuals left behind, men judged likely to proclaim the Communist view of the war to the outer world. A proportion reverted to 'reactionary' status as soon as they were restored to their own lines. The remainder justified their captors' confidence, readily expressing views from arrival at the exchange point that the United States had instructed South Korea to initiate the war in order to enrich her own commerce, and had perpetrated a range of atrocities during the conflict including bacteriological operations, 'germ warfare'. The handful of British men in this group were more reticent, but gave similar opinions when asked, adding that the British Government was guilty of belonging to 'a reactionary clique'.

The British, the other Commonwealth governments concerned, and the United States were thus alerted to the possibility that some of those returning under Big Switch would be similarly disaffected.

In the event, their apprehensions proved to be greatly exaggerated. The mass of men released betwen 5th August and 6th September 1953 were manifestly delighted to be returning home to an environment they saw as infinitely superior to anything the Communists had to offer, and contemptuous of their captors' philosophy and practices. These were not simply the minority of active 'reactionaries', or the men captured after compulsory study was abandoned. The greater proportion who had attended study without disruption or demur, who had signed a peace petition occasionally to keep out of trouble, and even those who had come to question over the years of truce negotiations the wish of their respective governments to end the war were of the same mind. For a short time, forty or fifty reserved their position. On their return home, they abandoned any final doubts as to the motives of the United Nations alliance in the war. It is notable that, from among this latter group, there were several men who still had terms of active duty to complete in the Services. Following their leave, they made no effort to withdraw from it and, more importantly, seven extended their engagements. One British prisoner chose not to be repatriated*.

On exchange, the United Nations prisoners were issued with uniforms and comforts in Korea and rapidly evacuated to Japan. All ranks were debriefed individually at Kure. On the basis of the information obtained, less than a dozen men were identified as having been actively

---

* One of 22, chiefly Americans, who elected to stay with the Chinese, he had a good reputation among his fellow prisoners. His genuine interest in Communism had never persuaded him to betray others—indeed, he had often helped sick and wounded comrades. After some years in China, he returned home without any penalty.

engaged in enemy propaganda. A few among them were notorious for betrayal of their comrades' escape attempts or disruption of political programmes.

The Government came to the view that none of this number should be charged or disciplined. They were all due for release from the Services and in any case free to hold what political views they wished. At a court martial it would be necessary to prove that their acts had been of significant advantage to the enemy. Charges of treachery would be difficult to establish because some vital points probably depended on hearsay (that is, reports of what Chinese officials had said) which was inadmissible. The numbers involved on both counts were 0.07 per cent of the total number of prisoners. Contrary to a report made by the United States Consul in Southampton to Washington on 18th Septmber 1953, none of the prisoners considered to have been subverted were placed under observation by the security services following their return home[12]. The only penalty for those converted to the Communist cause was the derision of their peers, exercised briefly. These former errors seemed unimportant as men adjusted joyfully to a familiar life, the pleasures of Japan, and the knowledge that they would soon be sailing home.

Those identified as informers in the camps alone continued to be challenged at random during the general celebrations abroad and welcoming ceremonies at home. Between times, on the returning troopships, they were endangered, at risk to revenge*.

British servicemen had never before been held as prisoners of war by a Communist power. They were entirely unprepared for the environment of subversion in which they were immersed. When all the evidence had been examined the Ministry of Defence remarked,

> ... Viewed in the light of the resources at their disposal the success of the Chinese may be considered comparatively small. In reality it may be less than is at first apparent, for there were many reasons which had nothing to do with political convictions that made a prisoner appear 'progressive'.
>
> In the winter of 1950-51 material conditions in the prison camps were such that many prisoners gave politically 'correct answers' so that they might enjoy, if not better conditions, at least a sporting chance of staying alive. ...[13]

On the basis that others might have similar experiences in some future conflict, an inter-Service advisory panel was assembled under Major-General C E A Firth to consider what, if any, changes should be

---

* During the voyage home, the author was called to the stern of the troopship one night by a warrant officer to prevent several of these men being cast into the sea. They were placed in protective custody for the remainder of the journey.

made to the rules concerning responses to interrogation, and the scope of training to resist coercion. The following conclusions were recorded.

> 7. A prisoner of war interrogated and not being subjected to duress is to confine his answers to name, rank, number and date of birth only.
>
> 8. A prisoner of war interrogated under duress, and no longer capable of confining himself to name, rank, number and date of birth, is to govern his behaviour by four rules, viz:-
>
> (a) never volunteer any information;
>
> (b) never give away military information;
>
> (c) never give information about fellow prisoners of war which leads to their selection as valuable subjects for interrogation;
>
> (d) keep fighting and hoping[14].

A new syllabus of training for those likely to be made prisoners was introduced. Similar measures were adopted for the United States forces* following an enquiry†.

Subsequently, studies were made by psychiatrists, psychologists, and others, principally Americans, into the behaviour of one or another group of United Nations prisoners during the Korean war. Many were misled by the pursuit of false notions: for example, that numbers in Korea were unique in giving some form of military information following capture. Captives in shock from the action in which they have been captured, in fear of or put to torture, or threatened with murder have been a fruitful source of military information through the history of warfare. Much information has flowed indeed from prisoners who have not been subjected to any duress. Hence the persistent attempts by the Eighth Army in 1952-53 to take prisoners. Similarly, the very low number who attempted escape after capture‡ was judged to be illustrative of a lack of spirit among the United Nations prisoners. *Pro rata*, about the same number attempted to escape in Korea as from the Japanese camps, 1941-45, but few were successful in either case primarily bacause of physical appearance. It was not easy for a white or black man, possessed of nothing but determination and his wits, to pass unnoticed through an oriental nation closely policed. The establishment of a 'rat line' in Korea to assist prisoners to escape, providing maps, food, and a rendezvous with a naval landing party or helicopter would have greatly increased the chances and the numbers of those making the attempt. As it was, all the United Nations

---

* The British enquiry exchanged views with the United States.

† By the Defense Advisory Committee on Prisoners of War.

‡ This does not comprehend aircrew rescued before capture, or indeed any others cut off who managed to return to their own lines.

prisoners of war who escaped from the Yalu camps—and indeed most from elsewhere—were recaptured.

General comparisons of circumstances within the Japanese and German prison camps for British—or American—prisoners in the Second World War and those in Korea are mostly unrewarding[15]. The Japanese camps were characterised by deprivation of physical necessities, and extremes of brutality relating to disobedience or non-compliance on a narrow band of issues, principally the provision of labour and military courtesies. Setting aside the murder of selected prisoners by the SS in 1944-45, the German camps were conducted on the basis of the Geneva convention, admitting for most of their existence Red Cross food parcels, and a regular exchange of mail including the admission of textbooks from the homeland for study. Not unimportantly, the German authorities accepted occasional visits to camps by representatives of a neutral protecting power. Political considerations were at most minimal in the Japanese and German systems of administration.

In Korea there were extremes of physical brutality and deprivation for many months which tapered off as soon as truce talks prompted the Chinese to realise that they needed to keep as many prisoners alive as possible for exchange. It was for this reason that they withdrew all non-Korean captives from the North Koreans late in 1951, in whose custody considerable numbers were dying.

Once their potential for information was exhausted, the prisoners in German and Japanese hands were a tiresome burden. For the Chinese the extraction of military intelligence was, with certain exceptions, of secondary importance. Foremost, prisoners could be used in the propaganda industry and some at least turned against the 'bourgeois capitalist structures' of their respective nations. To this end, they had drawn on and modified the systems originally conceived for use against Nationalist China, and by the Russians in the coercion of other Soviet peoples. Prisoners were confined in small compounds, for example, not so much to facilitate physical control as to create communities which progressively learned to police themselves as political education advanced, encouraged by punishment or reward.

In the Korean camps, the Chinese also carried forward their expertise in 'brainwashing'—confused by some of the subsequent studies with political indoctrination[16]. They persuaded a few aircrew that they had dropped germ weapons after being brought by months of isolation, moral and physical pressure, to a state of confusion. All recovered as soon as they returned to contact with the outer world. Others survived this process. As a general principle, all but a handful declined to confess to something they knew to be untrue.

This was equally true of the resistance in the camps—largely passive but nonetheless deeply rooted—to political indoctrination. Fusilier Kinne spoke for them when he rejected Chinese attempts to purvey falsehoods[17]. The manipulation of facts to suit revolutionary ends was unacceptable to them; they did not appreciate Lenin's ideas concerning 'socialist morality'. More fundamentally, the problem for the instructors was that they were attempting to sell notions of liberty and economic regulation which were inferior to those within the experience of their students.

The control and administration of the North Korean and Chinese captives by the United Nations Command manifests misunderstandings on a similar scale but of another kind coupled with ineptitude and oppression. Administrative corruption was rife from the outset: South Korean guards on short rations were notorious for stealing the food destined for North Korean prisoners during the early period of captivity. But the long running and gross mistreatment of prisoners later manifested was not inflicted by the United States camp authorities or their auxiliaries but by Communist prisoners upon those who were anti-Communist and *vice versa*. These struggles, and the brutalities involved, were conceived and conducted by direction from China and North Korea. The anti-Communist prisoners were respondents. The men murdered or maimed were pawns in a propaganda exercise.

The Americans were blameworthy only in so far as they organised the prison camps on false assumptions, the product of inexperience in coping with Communist foes. Their greater error was a failure to recognise, subsequently to cope with, the early growth of insubordination.

. . . .

At the end of any war a number of questions are commonly asked. Who won? Was it worth the struggle and loss? What were the consequences? What conclusions may be drawn from the event?

Neither of the contending sides won an outright victory; the war ended in a stalemate. But this may be said: the North Koreans opened the war with the intention of seizing the Republic of Korea. In this they failed, ending with somewhat less of the peninsula than they had at the beginning. The Chinese entered to evict the United Nations forces and complete for the North Koreans what they had failed to do for themselves. In this they, too, failed. Both nations were obliged to accept finally what they long denied: some 14,000 Chinese prisoners of 20,000, 36,000 North Koreans of 112,000 chose not to return home.

Kim Il-sung used his military rebuff in 1950 as a means of ridding himself of those senior military officers less than devoted to his person or suited to the role of scapegoat—or both. He used the final necessity of an armistice to dispose of political rivals. A party purge was set in hand just before the truce document was signed. Pak Hon-yong was the principal victim[18]. It was easily accomplished; the war had enabled Kim to consolidate his control of the entire security apparatus. Yet, contrary to the claims of his courtiers, he was less competent in directing the rebuilding of an economy smashed by the war he had initiated. One million civilians had been killed and about 100,000 members of the NKPA. The survivors included many gravely wounded and disabled. Electric power, transportation, fuel, manufacturing and other machinery and plant, fertilisers, and seeds were widely lacking.

The plans adopted for the restoration of industry and agriculture following a soviet-model produced poor returns. Ten years after the war Kim was accusing 'passive elements and conservatives' of failing the nation[19]. He was about to identify new scapegoats. Under his absolute rule, North Korea has remained one of the poorest nations in the world.

China lost from wounds and sickness close to 1,000,000 of her troops and spent huge sums in operations. The Chinese people paid doubly by direct taxation—part in 'voluntary' contributions raised by public subscription—and in the loss of plant and materials to war manufactures and supply. Some also paid with their lives, for the campaigns against 'bandits, reactionaries and other traitors' during 1951-52 were as much due to the central government's frustration with the drift in the war as the associated economic stagnation and malaise among party workers at home. Whilst criminals, Kuomintang agents, and dissenters were certainly run down in this period, involving 800,000 or more arrests, it also embraced individuals punished, even killed, simply because they were believed to lack commitment to the regime[20].

From an external point of view, Mao's decision to succeed where the the North Koreans had failed is widely thought to have enhanced the status of the People's Republic of China, due chiefly to the spectacular early victories of the Chinese People's Volunteers over the United States component of the United Nations Command, and later in denying a renewed advance beyond the area of the 38th Parallel. Chinese propaganda agencies certainly fostered such a notion; the well used phrase 'China stands up' was resuscitated at the end of the war. Chou En-lai's influence at the Bandoeng Conference in 1955 is sometimes attributed to these military accomplishments. A number of Asian nations were readier to support the admission of the Peking Government to the United Nations when the war concluded.

Within the great bureaucracy he directed, however, Mao paid a personal price for his participation. The Chinese People's Volunteers entering Korea were commanded by general officers who were his loyal comrades and accompanied by a band of young political officers dedicated to Mao and his ideas. While the former no doubt accepted the general principle that the revolutionary spirit counted for more than military technology, the latter believed it implicitly. Many of these company and battalion political officers perished as heroes in the great battles of 1950-51. Those that survived became progressively disenchanted; likewise numbers of commanders at various levels. Their experience in Korea led them to support P'eng Te-huai's drive for reorganisation of the People's Liberation Army on a professional basis, re-equipped with modern weapons from the Soviet armoury. These ideas, pressed at a time of his own growing opposition to Mao's Great Leap Forward, contributed to P'eng's downfall, when the much admired soldier was ultimately led in chains to be humiliated in the Peking football stadium before 40,000 members of the PLA. Twelve senior officials and general officers were caught up with him among many others[21]. The depth and persistence of the outrage at his treatment may be judged by the fact that repeated attempts were made to rehabilitate him while he was imprisoned, and after his death from the injuries he suffered in captivity. They continued through the remainder of Mao's lifetime, a manifestation of the disenchantment of Army veterans, until he was rehabilitated in memory by Teng Hsiao-p'ing in December 1978[22].

Before the Korean war, the People's Liberation Army was Mao's servant, the guarantor of his power. After it, the loyalty of its officers and men was never wholly assured. Even Lin Piao, ordered to restore party discipline within its ranks[23], failed at the height of his zeal to eradicate dissension and discontent[24].In the direct sense, the United Nations Command was victorious in the war. It was formed to maintain the Republic of Korea, and in that it succeeded. But in the course of operations the aim shifted. Following the defeat of the North Korean People's Army in the autumn of 1950, the opportunity seemed to offer and was exploited to reunite the Korean people, long an objective of the United Nations. Anxious to have the whole cake rather than two thirds, the respective governments—not least the British Government—failed to heed China's warning to stand off.

Of course, Mao might have entered the war even if the United Nations had remained behind the 38th Parallel; there are indications that he had this in mind*. But having authorised the advance to the north, the United Nations, specifically, the United States, lost control of its commander-in-chief and, consequently, all options other than a general advance to the Yalu. Among these was the opportunity to seize and fortify the narrow waist of North Korea, much to the vexation of the British Chiefs of Staff.

---

* See, for example, Volume I, p 271.

The United Nations victory was thus qualified. In the United States, the entire intervention came to be regarded as a failure, if not a defeat; political and public opinion expected the nation to win wars without qualification. Forty years were to pass before a monument was raised with governmental encouragement to the 33,629 members of the American armed forces who had lost their lives in Korea. But from the end of 1953 the event rapidly passed out of popular view. The Cold War in Europe and nuclear deterrence became the prime interest of overseas and defence policy for the United States until the war in Viet Nam progressively distracted the Johnson administration. The United States aims there were broadly similar to those in Korea, and equally rooted in idealism, but the task was labyrinthine, beyond her political stamina and military capacity. American suggestions that Britain should join the struggle were put to and refused by two British prime ministers, Harold Macmillan and Harold Wilson, in part due to the Korean war experience.

In the 1960s, Britain was still a considerable power in Europe, the Middle and Far East, her standing exalted by her statecraft and military capability, apparently recovered from the *débâcle* of the Suez expedition. But successive governments were already moving towards withdrawal from as many overseas territories and security commitments as possible. In the Far East, the defence of Hong Kong remained an obligation, as did the security of the newly established state of Malaysia. Though SEATO was moribund by 1965 and the Communist rebellion in the Malay peninsula defunct, the security of the newly established Malaysian state had to be underwritten. Units of all three Services and the Commonwealth units were then defending the former British Borneo territories against seizure by President Sukarno's regime in Indonesia.

As a matter of politics, the environment in Indo China was ominous to all parties in the British parliament—and unworthy to some in the Labour Party—considerations which had applied to Korea in 1950. But in 1950 the British had not experienced the denial of a right to strategic policy making as they entered military operations with the United States. The political as distinct from the strategic influence the United Kingdom enjoyed to one degree or another in the war by 1953 had emphasised rather than eased the frustration of senior officials in the Foreign Office and the Chiefs of Staff, an impression which remained with their successors[25].

In their turn, briefing ministers on the consequences of cooperation in Viet Nam, they cited the Korean war experience: the presence of British forces in the American command would not secure a British vote or even a voice in the direction of operational policy in the theatre.

This was a weighting factor in the political arguments against participation. It was misleading, however, to couple this with a statement that Korean war costs had crippled the British economy. For one thing, operations in Viet Nam were of an entirely different character and the scale of intervention undetermined. For another, the assertion was untrue.

Some myths die hard, however. Even ten years later, a senior official reminded an inter-departmental meeting that participation in the Korean war had extinguished the British post-war recovery programme. No doubt this additional item of expenditure contributed to the steady rise in public expenditure during and after the war years, but the sum was a mite compared to the volume of British rearmament for NATO during the same period.

Manning costs in Korea were negligible, involving the emoluments of recalled reservists for about one year, those on short-service engagements, and a fraction of those extended in National Service. The greater number of all others involved would have been employed and thus paid in other theatres if not in Korea.

Clothing, equipment, vehicles, arms and, nominally, the greatest expense of all, ammunition, were drawn from the huge residual Second World War stocks. If not used in Korea, all would have eventually have been sold at knock down prices later, having become obsolete, unserviceable or, in the case of the ammunition, destroyed having reached the end of shelf life. For the stocks far exceeded usage in Korea or any other theatre. The only charge on this account to the taxpayer arose from reductions in sales' receipts. Even so, the public accounts system charged the greater proportion of items to the original manufacturing or purchasing costs plus departmental expenses.

Significant expenditure directly attributable to the war falls under three heads. The first is transportation, the troopships and merchantmen, civil and military aircraft, which carried men and operating requirements to and from the war. The second is consumables of various sorts.

Sailors, soldiers, and airmen would have been fed whether they were in Korea or elsewhere, so the consumption of rations may be assessed on the same basis as emoluments. But additional rations were required for the winter months, and expensive forms were required on a greater scale, principally individual ration packs for various periods. The expenditure of surgical and medical stocks was exceptional. Petrol, oil and lubricants were consumed at war rates and drawn from American sources. The same was true of engineering items such as barbed wire. These and certain of the transportation charges involved a currency reconciliation within the Korean Operations Pool Account run by the Australian authorities on behalf of themselves, the United Kingdom and New Zealand*.

---

* See Appendix P.

It should also be observed that it would have been cost-effective to send a division to Korea rather than two brigades in the late summer of 1950. The support slice for an independent brigade, such as that despatched to Japan and Korea, is expensive in men and equipment relative to the numbers engaged in combat. A bold decision to form the Commonwealth division at the outset would have not have cost more over the term of the war. The presence of a major-general in command, three brigades, full divisional supporting arms and services would have precluded the intermittent misdirection of the 27th and 29th Brigades.

Still, assessment of cash costs takes second place to the cost of a war in lives. Among a standing commitment of some 27,000, and a total contribution of 81,084 from all three Services, the British lost 1,087 killed, dead of wounds, to the sea, by battle accident or by sickness*. To what end?

Initially there was the assertion of a principle: aggression should be opposed. Mr Attlee's remark that 'the fire in Korea may burn our house down' explained the object of British intervention. But judgements should comprehend the event, first to last.

If the United Nations Command failed to unite Korea, it preserved an opportunity for the Republic of Korea to prosper in peace and democracy. The intervention was made on behalf of a state still recovering from prolonged Japanese occupation, possessing crude ideas about and no experience of democracy. Its first president and his party governed on fascist lines. Corruption and oppression were widespread. The economy was precarious.

None of these considerations justified the forcible substitution of Syngman Rhee by Kim Il-sung. Indeed, many North Koreans demonstrated before and during the war a preference for living in the southern Republic, despite all they been told about it in state propaganda. Whenever the opportunity to march south offered, hundreds of thousands took to the road in all weathers to enter President Rhee's fief at risk to their lives. They hugely outnumbered those who passed in the other direction as the shifts in population over the years indicate.

Twenty five years after the war ended, the work and skill of those in South Korea—in the Republic of Korea—were rewarded by a booming economy. Food and clothing were cheap and available. Villages had running water and electricity. Bicycles abounded. The rebuilt cities and towns were beginning to experience the disadvantages of expanding motor traffic. By 1993, the Republic was established as a dynamic economy in Asia, widely engaged in trade with Japan, China, and Russia among other neighbours, in America and Europe, and in Australasia. These were

---

* For details, see Appendix Q.

the material benefits of being rescued from the embrace of Kim Il-sung. When this self-styled 'Great Leader' died in 1994, the Democratic People's Republic of Korea was wholly undemocratic, hugely in debt, unable to reverse a declining economy. The mass of the populace lived at subsistence level.

During most of the forty years from 1953-1993, the people of the Republic of Korea were themselves subject to authoritarian governments, led overwhelmingly by military senior officers. Political opposition was repressed. This was due in great measure to the fact that the underground Communist Party, directed and financed from North Korea, menaced the security and accomplishments of the south through much of this time. But often the process of defeating Communism was extended to the eradication of any party, the imprisonment of any individual, critical of government policies.

Even so, the Republic of Korea was not simply an unrelenting police state through these years which happened, incidentally, to be unusually efficient in the development of its economy. Education flourished within it. The sea and air borders were increasingly opened. Communications, including radio and television, multiplied. Encouraged by a host of international friends led by the United States, democratic practice advanced. Opposition parties became tolerated. Multi-party elections followed. Forty years after the Korean war ended, a civilian, a former political refugee and prisoner, became head of state. It took the peoples of Europe somewhat longer to develop and consolidate democratic usage.

The Koreans in the south did all this for themselves. They have discharged thereby any debt owed to the United Nations forces whose struggles won them an opportunity to build a new state. Among these, the British may draw satisfaction from their part in a distant obligation, honourably discharged.

SOURCE NOTES: Conclusions and reflections

1 For an account of the operations of this force, see Prasad, S N, *History of the Custodian Force (India) in Korea 1953–54*, (Government of India, 1976).
2 *Hansard*, 3rd November 1953.
3 For summaries of these, see O'Neill, *op cit*, Volume I, pp 363–367; also McGibbon, *op cit*, Volume I, pp 334–337.
4 FRUS, 1952–54, *cit*, pp 1170–1176.
5 Eisenhower Papers—Memorandum of Conversation, President Eisenhower, Prime Minister Churchill, December 1953.
6 FRUS, 1952–1954, *cit*, pp 1654–1655. See also Memoranda of Conversations and Plenary Session Minutes 5–7 December 1953, Eisenhower Papers; and PREM 11/418.
7 For an explanation, see Danchev, Alex, *Oliver Franks: Founding Father*, (London, 1993), pp 135 and 139.
8 *Hansard*, 3rd November 1953.
9 Conversation, author with FM Lord Slim.
10 *Ibid.*
11 Conversation, author with Captain R P Hickey.
12 State Department Records 695A.0024/9-1853, DS (USNARS, Washington).
13 *Treatment of British Prisoners of War in Korea*, Ministry of Defence publication (London, HMSO), 1955, p 35.
14 *Report of the Advisory Panel on Prisoner-of-War conduct after capture*, attached to the Principal Personnel Officers' Committee paper P.P.O./P.(55)7, 2nd September 1955 (DEFE 10/127).
15 See, for example, the address of the Major W E Mayer US Army, to the Conference of Professors of Air Sciences, November 1956, Misc. Conferences [United States Air Force Historical Records, Langley Air Force Base].
16 Professor William Sargant in *Battle for the Mind* (London, 1957) illustrates the distinction in a comprehensive study.
17 For example, Kinne, op cit, pp 92 and 96.
18 See, for example, Scalapino and Lee, *op cit*, Part I, pp 436–452.
19 *On the People's Economic Plan for 1968*, speech by Kim Il-sung, see Foreign Broadcast Information Service [of the United States], Supplement, 3rd May 1968, taken from P'yongyang broadcast, 23rd April 1968.
20 See, for example, Chesneaux, Jean, *China, The People's Republic, 1949–1976*, (Hassocks, Sussex, 1979), pp 40–41, and Schram, Stuart, *Mao Tse-tung*, (London, 1967), pp 246–248.
21 See MacFarquhar, Roderick, *The origins of the Cultural Revolution*, (London, 1983), vol 2, pp 242–243.
22 For an account of this process, see Dömes, *Jurgen, Peng Te-huai, the man and the image* (London, 1985), Chapter 5.
23 *Ibid*, pp 246–247.
24 See, for example, Joffe, Ellis, *Party and Army: Professionalism and Political Control in the Chinese Officer Corps, 1949–1964* (Cambridge, Mass, 1965), pp 142–143.
25 Conversation, author with FM Sir Richard Hull [former Chief of the General Staff].

APPENDIX A

United Nations General Assembly Resolution 498(v) of 1st February 1951

THE GENERAL ASSEMBLY

1. *Noting* that the Security Council because of lack of unanimity of the permanent members has failed to exercise its primary responsibility for the maintenance of international peace and security in regard to Chinese Communist intervention in Korea;

2. *Noting* that the Central People's Government of the People's Republic of China has not accepted United Nations proposals to being about a cessation of hostilities in Korea with a view to peaceful settlement and that its armed forces continue their invasion of Korea and their large-scale attacks upon United Nations forces there;

3. *Finds* that the Central People's Government of the People's Republic of China by giving direct aid and assistance to those who were already committing aggression in Korea and by engaging in hostilities against United Nations forces there has itself engaged in aggression in Korea;

4. *Calls* upon the Central People's Government of the People's Republic of China to cause its forces and nationals in Korea to cease hostilities against the United Nations forces and to withdraw from Korea;

5. *Affirms* the determination of the United Nations to continue its action in Korea to meet the aggression;

6. *Calls* upon all States and authorities to continue to lend every assistance to the United Nations action in Korea;

7. *Calls* upon all States and authorities to refrain from giving any assistance to the aggressors in Korea;

8. *Requests* a committee composed of the members of the Collective Measures Committee as a matter of urgency to consider additional measures to be employed to meet this aggression and to report thereon

to the General Assembly; it being understood that the Committee is authorised to defer its report if the Good Offices Committee referred to in the following paragraph, reports satisfactory progress in its efforts;

9. *Affirms* that it continues to be the policy of the United Nations to bring about a cessation of hostilities in Korea and the achievement of United Nations objectives in Korea by peaceful means and requests the President of the General Assembly to designate forthwith two persons who would meet with him at any suitable opportunity to use their good offices to this end.

APPENDIX B

Organisation of the 27th British Commonwealth Brigade and the 29th British Independent Infantry Brigade Group, January/February 1951

27 BRIGADE

Commander
BRIGADER A B COAD

Headquarters staff

Brigade Major
(MAJ J D STEWART)

GSO 3
Intelligence Officer

DAA & QMG
(MAJ A HUNTER)
Staff Captain 'A'
Staff Captain 'Q'
Transport Officer
Brigade Ordnance Officer
Brigade Electrical & Mechanical Engineer

Provost
Bde section

Camp staff including Defence & Employment Platoon

29 BRIGADE

Commander
BRIGADIER T BRODIE

Headquarters staff

Brigade Major
(MAJ K R S TREVOR)

GSO 3 (Operations)
GSO 3 (Staff Duties)
GSO 3 (Liaison)
GSO 3 (Intelligence)
Intelligence Officer & specialist sections

DAA & QMG
(MAJ B J EASTWOOD)
Staff Captain 'A'
Staff Captain 'Q'
Brigade RASC Officer
Brigade Ordnance Officer
Brigade Electrical & Mechanical Engineer
Pay, Chaplains, Postal services etc.,

Provost
Bde (GHQ) Company(f)

Camp staff including Transport Officer and Defence & Employment Platoon

27 BRIGADE	**29 BRIGADE**
Brigade Signals Signal Troop, Royal Signals	*Brigade Signals* Signal Squadron, Royal Signals
ARMOUR	*ARMOUR* 8th The King's Royal Hussars (8H)
	Commanding Officer **LT COL SIR WM LOWTHER bt**
	Regimental Headquarters including: Reconnaissance and Signals Troops
	Three sabre squadrons, each 20 Centurion tanks
	Troop, Royal Signals LAD, REME
	C Squadron, 7th Royal Tank Regiment (C Sqn, 7 RTR) *Officer Commanding* **MAJOR A J D PETTINGELL**
	Four troops, each 4 Churchill tanks (c)
INFANTRY (b) *1st Battalions:* The Middlesex Regiment (1 MX)	*INFANTRY (b)* *1st Battalions:* The Royal Nothumberland Fusiliers (1 NF)
Commanding Officer **LT COL A N MAN**	*Commanding Officer* **LT COL K O N FOSTER**
The Argyll & Sutherland Highlanders (1 A&SH) **LT COL G L NEILSON**	The Gloucestershire Regiment (1 GLOSTERS) **LT COL J P CARNE**
3rd Battalion, The Royal Australian Regiment (3 RAR) **LT COL I B FERGUSON**	Royal Ulster Rifles (1 RUR) **LT COL R J H CARSON**

each, with Headquarters Company, Support [Weapons] Company and four rifle companies (periodically reduced to three in 27 Brigade)

27 BRIGADE	**29 BRIGADE**
ARTILLERY 16th Field Regiment, Royal New Zealand Artillery (16 Fd Regt) *Commanding Officer* **LT COL J W MOODIE**	*ARTILLERY* 45th Field Regiment, Royal Artillery (45 Fd Regt) *Commanding Officer* **LT COL M T YOUNG**

each with three batteries of 8 x 25-pounder field guns, total 24 guns, and a light aid detachment, ROME and RNZEME

	Troop, Royal Signals
	11th (Sphinx) Light Anti- Aircraft Battery (11 LAA Bty) *Officer Commanding* **MAJ L V F FAWKES**
	170 Mortar Battery (170 Mor Bty) *Officer Commanding* **MAJ T Y FISCHER-HOCH**
	Counter-mortar Radar Troop *Officer Commanding* **CAPTAIN C S R DAIN**
	ENGINEERS 55 Independent Field Squadron, RE (55 Indep Fd Sqn) *Officer Commanding* **MAJ A E YOUNGER**
SUPPLY AND TRANSPORT Artillery Ammunition Platoon, RNZASC	*SUPPLY AND TRANSPORT* 57 Company, Royal Army Service Corps, (57 Coy) (d) and Workshop Platoon, REME *Officer Commanding* **MAJ M G M CROSBY**
MEDICAL 60th Parachute Field Ambulance, IAMS (60 Para Fd Amb) *Commanding Officer* **LT COL A G RANGARAJA**	*MEDICAL* 26th Field Ambulance, RAMC (26 Fd Amb) *Commanding Officer* **LT COL A MCLENNAN** with: 22 Field Surgical and 9 Field Transfusion Teams, 223 and 224 Mobile Dental Teams

27 BRIGADE	29 BRIGADE
ORDNANCE (e) 27 Brigade Ordnance Field Park (OFP) Royal Army Ordnance Corps *Officer Commanding* **MAJ J MOCKFORD**	*ORDNANCE* (e) 29 Brigade Ordnance Field Park, (OFP) *Officer Commanding* **CAPT H W B HATCHER**
ELECTRICAL & *MECHANICAL ENGINEERS* 11 Infantry Workshops (11 Inf Wksps)	*ELECTRICAL &* *MECHANICAL ENGINEERS* 10 Infantry Workshops (10 Inf Wksps)
Royal Electrical & Mechanical Engineers	
Officers Commanding **MAJ J R MATTHEWS**	*Officers Commanding* **MAJ J C SMITH**
	29 Brigade and Support Troops Light Aid Detachment (LAD)
PAY 27 Brigade Field Cash Office (FCO) Royal Army Pay Corps	*PAY* 208 Field Cash Office, (FCO)

Notes—see variously in text, (b) to (f).

a) As will be apparent, 29 Brigade was more than twice the strength of 27 Brigade and backed by a Field Maintenance Area and supporting organisation of the British Commonwealth Korean Base (see Volume I, Appendix R). Fortunately, this was of sufficient magnitude to support 27 Brigade progressively from December 1950, when its withdrawal to Hong Kong was suspended, without extra resources.

b) *Infantry*—The British battalions in 27 Brigade were manned nominally at 650 all ranks, effectively about 560 present in operations. Those in 29 Brigade were established at 983 to which were added first reinforcements of 185, maintaining 880 in operations.

c) *Armour*—The Churchills were originally disposed as 'Crocodiles' - flamethrowing tanks towing a trailer with flame fuel - but were more frequently employed solely with their 75mm gun as the main armament.

d) *Transport*—57 Company RASC had 90 x 3-ton trucks for the supply and transport of brigade units, in addition to those employed for its own domestic purposes. These were periodically shared with 27 and, later, 28 Brigades, but the distance between the operational areas often meant that the latter were obliged to rely on United States resources to lift troops. As difficulties in obtaining American trucks persisted, the New Zealand transport platoon, deployed to supply 16 Field Regiment with gun ammunition became a maid of all work, while giving first call on its services to artillery ammunition requirements.

e) *Ordnance*—Each REME workshop was supported by a stores section, RAOC additional to the units shown.

f) *Provost*—To provide 29 Brigade with a military police unit of sufficient strength, 249 GHQ Provost Company, Royal Military Police, had been deployed to it numbering 4 officers and 86 other ranks—disposing four strong operating sections. The 27 Brigade section numbered 16 all ranks.

g) See also Volume I, Appendices H, K, and N.

APPENDIX C

Despatch arrangements for 28th Brigade

[Graded in 1951 as] TOP SECRET

0185/737/(SD2)

Minutes of a meeting held in Room 220, The War Office, 16 March 1951, to examine the best method of relieving 27 Infantry Brigade in KOREA.

1. There were present :

		Copy No
Brigadier W.H. Lambert	DDSD(A) Chairman	1
Major-General H. Bainbridge	DMP	2
Colonel D.S. Gordon	GSO 1 Inf	3
Colonel I.H. Good	AAG AG Coord	4
Colonel B.J. Leech	AAG AG2	5
Lieut Colonel A.M. Field	GSO 1 MO2	6
Lieut Colonel P.H.W. Brind	GSO 1 SD2	7
Lieut Colonel C.J. Deedes	GSO 1 SD4	8
Lieut Colonel R.C. Dyke	AAG MP1	9
Major M.E.M. MacWilliam	DAQMG Q(Ops)1(c)	10
Major J.H. Gibbon	GSO II SD2 (Secretary)	11

2. *The Chairman* explained that the object of the meeting was to examine how best to relieve 27 Infantry Brigade in KOREA.

He said that a signal had been sent to General MacArthur asking whether he was prepared to release 27 Inf Bde but that so far no reply had been received.

If a negative reply was received, the CIGS is to most anxious to relieve 27 Inf Bde as soon as possible.

3. The problem can be divided into three parts:–

(a) relief of 1 Mx and 1 A & SH.

(b) relief of HQ 27 Inf Bde.

(c) relief of the rest of the brigade.

4. The two primary factors to be taken into consideration were:-

(a) that the two battalions should go to HONG-KONG in the first place to collect their families, regimental silver etc, and then come back to the UK.

(b) the relieving battalions should be at a strength of 600. There can be no question of bringing them up to the strength of 29 Inf Bde.

5. *DMP* explained that there were three fundamentals to be considered in selecting the relieving battalions:-

(a) it is easy to maintain the relieving battalions if they are chosen from the same groups as 1 Mx and 1 A & SH.

(b) against (a) the groups concerned have had a heavy drain on them in the way of casualties and the other battalions in their groups have been milked. It might, therefore, be better to change groups.

The DPA favours changing groups because of the officer problem.

(c) These reliefs should be completed with the minimum of disturbance to other battalions.

6. If these reliefs are to be carried out quickly they should be carried out as far away from the UK as possible.

7. *DMP* stated that as a result of considerable examination he felt that there were three possible solutions:-

(a) 1 A & SH relieved by 1 KOSB from HONG-KONG. This involves a change of group but as the Lowland Brigade Group is the shadow group for the Highland Brigade Group the reinforcement problem is already in hand. It would be necessary to switch some National Service intakes from the Highland Brigade Group to the Lowland Brigade Group.

(b) 1 Mx relieved by 1 RWK now on their way out to FARELF. There would in this case not be a greater number of men to sort out, but the battalion is composed mostly of young soldiers and the unit has recently been re-activated from an ABTU role.

(c) 1 Mx relieved by 1 KSLI from HONG-KONG. They belong to a different group and are at present due to take over from 1 KOYLI in MALAYA. This course helps from the personnel point of view because 1 KSLI could take over the surplus of 1 KOYLI which would avoid milking the rest of the Light Infantry Brigade too much.

8. *AG2* suggested that 1 Wilts, now in HONG-KONG, should relieve 1 KOYLI in MALAYA and be in turn relieved by 1 Manch in HONG-KONG. It was agreed that this was a matter for GHQ FARELF.

9. Of the other battalions considered, it was decided, after discussion, that 1 R Leicesters were too weak in strength and had too many ineligibles to be of value for this immediate purpose. It would take the whole reinforcement pool to make them up to a strength of 600.

10. It was suggested that a battalion of the East Anglian Brigade might be taken for the purpose but it was decided that 1 Suffolk, now in MALAYA, were due back next year and should not be employed.

11. *Inf* said that there are only three battalions available in the Light Infantry Brigade to support 1 KSLI and that of these 1 DCLI was well below strength. These battalions would have to be milked until September when the present plan for training reinforcements really comes into its own.

It was decided, after discussion, that 1 KSLI had approximately 500 personnel eligible for KOREA and would not therefore require very much reinforcing.

12. It was agreed that any reliefs from the UK would take four months and that this was not acceptable because, if 27 Inf Bde has to be relieved, the reliefs would have to be carried out in about four weeks from the date the decision was taken, and completed in six weeks.

13. It was also agreed that that the reliefs could be carried out more quickly than this but the urgency might not now be as great as it was when 27 Inf Bde originally went to KOREA. In the latter case, units left HONG-KONG within 10 days.

14. *MO2* raised the question of the gap that would be left in HONG-KONG if relief took place in KOREA. It was agreed that unless the relieving battalions came from the UK/BAOR there was bound to be a hiatus in HONG-KONG, MO2 would inform the other ministries concerned.

15. Among other points discussed were:-

(a) 1 RWK would need a big sort-out if they were used.

(b) 1 Wilts cannot be used as they are in the same group as 1 Glosters, already in KOREA.

(c) Use of MELF Bns would gain nothing as re-sorting would have to take place from the UK.

16. *DMP* stated that there would be a requirement to fly out some personnel to make up 1 KSLI because they were unlikely to be able to take over the KOYLI's surplus till June.

17. It was decided to recommend:-

(a) that 1 KOSB should relieve 1 A & SH.

(b) that 1 KSLI should relieve 1 Mx.

(c) that HQ 28 Inf Bde should relieve HQ 28 Inf Bde. (This includes Sig Tp, LAD, and Def and Emp Pl)

18. The question whether these battalions should take their own vehicles or take over those already in KOREA was discussed but no firm decision was arrived at. It was thought best to leave the decision to FARELF.

19. It was decided that, if it was essential to relieve the administrative units at present within 27 Inf Bde, this could be done as follows:–

(a) 11 Inf Wksps and Stores Sec could be relieved by 16 Inf Wksps and Stores Sec at present in HONG-KONG.

(b) 27 Inf Bde Ord Fd Park was raised from SINGAPORE and could be relieved by an exchange of personnel between SINGAPORE and KOREA over a period of four/five months.

(c) the remaining units in the bde should stay but their personnel be changed over.

20. In any event an extra Inf Wksp is required in HONG KONG to replace the one in KOREA.

21. *DMP* raised the question of what personnel should return to the UK with 1 Mx and 1 A & SH.

After discussion it was decided that it should be recommend that:-

(a) all returned sick or wounded in reinforcement groups should come back with their units.

(b) men who have served for less than one month with these battalions should join the relieving battalions.

22. It was agreed that the further relief of 27 Inf Bde after it had staged in HONG KONG should be the subject of a further examination.

J.H. Gibbon,
Major GS, (Secretary),
SD 2,
17 Mar 51.

Distribution:–

To those present, notably,

DDSD (A)	[one of the two deputies to the Director of Staff Duties]
DMP	[Director of Manpower Planning—the equivalent to DSD on the Adjutant-General's staff]

and

DMO	[Director of Military Operations]
MO 1	[coordination branch, Military Operations]
MO 2	[Far East branch]
MI 2	[Far East branch, Military Intelligence]
DMT	[Director of Military Training]
MT 1	[coordination branch]
MT 9	[branch with training aspects involved]
DCIGS Coord	[coordination branch, Deputy Chief's office]
DWD	[Director of Weapons Development]
GS(W)1	[coordination branch, DWD]
DSD	[Director of Staff Duties]
SD 1	[coordination branch]
SD 4	[UK/BAOR branch]
SD 7	[Arms Plot branch]
RA 1	[coordination branch, Director, Royal Artillery]
Sigs 5	[unit dispositions, Director, Royal Signals]
Sigs 7	[equipment dispositions]
D Inf	[Director of Infantry]
Inf (a) and (b)	[branches responsible for infantry dispositions and manpower]
VAG	[Vice Adjutant-General]
AG Coord	[coordination branch, Adjutant-General's office]
MP 1	[coordination branch, Director of Manpower Planning]
AG 1	[coordination branch for provision of personnel]
AG 2	[branch responsible for allocations of personnel to the Infantry]

Q (Ops) 1	[coordination branch for Vice Quartermaster-General]
Q (AE)	[control and disposition of army weapons and equipment]
D Mov	[Director of Movements]
Q (M) 2 & 8	[branches responsible for movements arising]
DF (a) and (c)	[deputies concerned, Director of Finance]
F1	[coordination branch]
QMGF	[finance section, Quartermaster-General]

[Curiously, no copy was sent to the DPA [Director of Personnel Administration], though provision was made for two his branches, AG1 and AG 2.]

Notes

1. This document illustrates further (see also volume 1, Appendix G), War Office methodology in the disposition of forces to operations; and manifests some of the problems of finding the manpower to meet requirements when the Army was committed across the world and largely dependent on men available successively for eighteen months of National Service to fill its junior commissioned and non-commissioned ranks.

2. As apparent from the text of Chapter 3, the requirement for a second British brigade in Korea was confirmed and 27 Infantry Brigade was relieved by 28 Brigade on the basis of the proposals made at the meeting on 17th March 1951. These were sufficiently comprehensive to obviate the need for any further general meeting as soon as the CIGS had approved the principal proposals. The General Staff executive branches then issued the orders for these to be effected. Decisions left to General Sir John Harding, Commander-in-Chief Far East Land Forces, were carried forward under his arrangements.

3. Mention is made of 'Brigade Groups', for example the 'Highland Brigade Group'. These were not fighting formations but groups of regiments associated on the basis of geographical or other regimental commonality as a means of reinforcing from one battalion to another as the commitment of each changed. Thus 1 RWK (1st Battalion, The Royal West Kent Regiment), employed as an ABTU ((Infantry) Arm Basic Training Unit) for a term of three years, was posted with sufficient officers, warrant and non-commissioned officers and soldiers for instructional and domestic purposes only. At the end of this period, when it was committed to active operations, its strength had to be doubled and specialists provided among them. These were found by a preferential allocation of officers and men from National Service drafts and an element of cross-posting—'milking'—from other battalions in the Home Counties Group.

4. Where a 'group' was unable to find sufficient manpower, the War office drew the necessary numbers from its 'shadow' or affiliated group. The Lowland and Highland Scottish Groups were clearly well suited to shadow one another. This system accounts for the numbers of casualties badged to Highland regiments being discovered among the casualtiesof 1 KOSB (1st Battalion, The King's Own Scottish Borderers).

5. A copy of the minutes of the Meeting on 27 Infantry Brigade replacement is in the MO1 Collection, with connected papers in WO 216/342.

4. The numbers established for field forces units of all Arms depended on their task, inevitably. Because Korea was a general war, 29 Brigade was despatched at 'higher' establishment; its battalions exceeded 1,000 all ranks. However, it was impossible to maintain this strength. Thus the British battalions of 27 and 28 Brigades were posted to about 600, and those in 29 Brigade eventually fell to about 700. See also Volume 1, p 128 and footnotes thereto.

APPENDIX D

Order of Battle, 22nd April 1951

The Chinese People's Volunteers (CPV)
The North Korean People's Army (NKPA)

CPV Commander and concurrent Political Commander
P'ENG TE-HUAI*

Deputy Commander/Political Commander
TENG HUA

Commander: Front Headquarters NKPA
LT GEN KIM UNG†

Deputy Commanders
HAN HSIEN-CH'U
(Operations)

HSUEH-CHI
(Logistics)

P'IAO YI-YU‡
(Political)

Chief of Staff
HSIEH FANG

NKPA	**NKPA**	**NKPA**
I Corps	*III Corps*	*V Corps*
LI KWON-MU	**YU KYONG-SAN**	**PANG HO**
8 Division	15 Division	6 Division
47 Division	45 Division	12 Division

CHINESE		**CHINESE**		**CHINESE**	**CHINESE**
19 Army Group[¶]		*3 Army Group*[¶]		*9 Army Group*	*13 Army Group*
YANG TE-CHIH		**CHEN K'ENG**[§]		**SUNG SHIH-LUN**	**LI T'IEN-YU**
Sixty Fifth Army		*Fifteenth Army*	*Twelfth Army*	*Twenty Seventh Army*	*Fortieth Army*
193 Division		29 Division	34 Division	79 Division	118 Division
194 Division		30 Division	35 Division	80 Division	119 Division
195 Division		31 Division	40 Division	81 Division	120 Division
Sixty Fourth & Sixty Third Army		*Sixtieth Army*		*Twentieth Army*	*Thirty Ninth Army*
190 Division	187 Division	179 Division		58 Division	115 Division
191 Division	188 Division	180 Division		59 Division	116 Division
192 Division	189 Division	181 Division		60 Division	117 Division

Reserve: *20 Army Group*

Support Forces: (in addition to those organic within armies)

Armour
- Four tank regiments
- One motorised infantry regiment

Engineers
- Eleven regiments

Signals
- Seven regiments

Artillery
- Eight gun/howitzer divisions
- Four anti-aircraft divisions

Transport & Supply
- Four railway troop divisions
- Ten truck regiments

Notes

Forces are set out from west to east as viewed by the United Nations Command.

* Although Chinese and North Korean command was formally maintained through a joint headquarters in Shenyang, North East China, executive command of both national forces in Korea was exercised by P'eng Te-huai. Orders to the NKPA were issued through the Korean element on his staff to the NKPA Front Headquarters. See also note ‡, below.

† P'iao Yi-yu was a Korean serving in the People's Liberation Army.

‡ Kim maintained an oversight of Korean operations, principally to note performance, and was responsible for reinforcement and supply of his troops.

¶ In the absence of Chen K'eng, who was ill, the army group was commanded by Wang Chin-shan, his deputy, during the offensive.

§ All divisions in 19 and 3 Army Groups had been reinforced to at least 10,000 men.

1. Maps not printed.
2. Maps not printed.
3. Maps not printed.
4. Maps not printed.
5. Map not printed.

APPENDIX E

1st Commonwealth Division Order of Battle, 1st August 1951

Commander
MAJOR-GENERAL A J H CASSELS

Headquarters and Principal staff officers

GSO 1
LT COL E D DANBY (CAN)
AA & QMG
LT COL A W N L VICKERS

ARTILLERY INFANTRY BRIGADES

Commander
BRIGADIER W G H PIKE
Brigade Major
MAJ P M VICTORY

2nd Regiment, Royal Canadian Horse Artillery
Commanding Officer
LT COL A J B BAILEY

16th Field Regiment, Royal New Zealand Artillery
Commanding Officer
LT COL J W MOODIE

45th Field Regiment, Royal Artillery
Commanding Officer
LT COL M T YOUNG

11th (Sphinx) Battery, Royal Artillery
Officer Commanding
MAJ L V F FAWKES

170th Light Battery, Royal Brigade
Officer Commanding
MAJ T V FISCHER-HOCH

ENGINEERS

Commander
COLONEL E C W MYERS

28th Field Engineer Regiment, Royal Engineers
Commanding Officer
LT COL P W M MOORE

57th Independent Field Squadron Royal Canadian Engineers
Commanding Officer
MAJOR D H ROCHESTER

64th Field Park Squadron, Royal Engineers
Officer Commanding
MAJ J A KEER

SIGNALS

Commander, Divisional Royal Signals and Signal Regiment
LT COL A L ATKINSON

SUPPLY & TRANSPORT

Commander, Royal Army Service Corps
LT COL M G M CROSBY

10 Company RNZASC
54 Company RCASC
57 Company RASC

MEDICAL

Assistant Director of Medical Services
COLONEL G ANDERTON

25th Canadian Field Ambulance, Royal Canadian Army Medical Corps
Commanding Officer
LT COL B L P BROSSEAU

26th Field Ambulance, Royal Army Medical Corps
Commanding Officer
LT COL A MCLENNAN

60th Indian Parachute Field Ambulance
Commanding Officer
LT COL A G RANGARAJ

ORDNANCE

Commander, Royal Army Ordnance Corps
LT COL M F MACLEAN
1st Commonwealth Division Ordnance Field Park
1st Commonwealth Division Stores Distribution Unit

ELECTRICAL & MECHANICAL ENGINEERS

Commander, Royal Electrical & Mechanical Engineers
LT COL H G GOOD.

10 Infantry Workshops, REME
16 Infantry Workshops, REME
191 Canadian Infantry Workshops, RCEME

ARMOUR

8th Hussars
Commanding Officer
LT COL SIR WM LOWTHER bt
C Sqn, Lord Strathcona's Horse
Officer Commanding
MAJ J W QUINN

INFANTRY BRIGADES

25th Canadian Infantry Brigade
Commander
BRIGADIER J M ROCKINGHAM

2nd Battalion, The Royal Canadian Regiment
Commanding Officer
LT COL R A KEANE

2nd Battalion, Princess Patricia's Canadian Light Infantry
Commanding Officer
LT COL J R STONE

2nd Battalion, Royal 22e Regiment
Commanding Officer
LT COL J A DEXTRAZE

28th British Commonwealth Brigade
Commander
BRIGADIER G TAYLOR

1st Battalion, The King's Own Scottish Borderers
Commanding Officer
LT COL J F M MACDONALD

1st Battalion, The King's Own Shropshire Light Infantry
Commanding Officer
LT COL V W BARLOW

3rd Battalion, The Royal Australian Regiment
Commanding Officer
LT COL F G HASSETT

29th British Infantry Brigade

Commander
BRIGADIER T BRODIE

1st Battalion, The Royal Northumberland Fusiliers Divisional Royal
Commanding Officer
LT COL M C SPEER

1st Battalion, The Gloucestershire Regiment
Commanding Officer
LT COL D B A GRIST

1st Battalion, The Royal Ulster Rifles
Commanding Officer
LT COL R J H CARSON

AVIATION

1903 Independent Air Observation Post Flight, Royal Artillery
Officer Commanding
MAJ R N L GOWER

1913 Light Liaison Flight
Officer Commanding
CAPTAIN P DOWNWARD

Notes

a) As will be independent from several unit titles, the divisional troops were formed from the Arms and Services, other than infantry, with the three originally independent brigades. Some integrated—not least the Divisional Provost Unit—with considerable success.

b) Some minor units are omitted due to size, which were nonetheless of considerable importance, such as the Royal Engineers Postal elements, and the Intelligence Corps units. The Pay and Dental units were 'blistered' on to larger units for economy of domestic manpower. The REME organisation subsumes the vital Recovery detachments. Chaplains, though established principally at brigade headquarters, were for the most part permanently attached to major units, from which they also toured allotted minor units.

c) The Air OP Flight was under command of the Commander, Royal Artillery, though it was located at and shared the air strip facilities with the Light Liaison Flight. the Field Security organisation.

APPENDIX F

Directive to Major-General A J H Cassels

1. The role of the force under your command, is, as an integral part of the United Nations forces, to act in operations in Korea, designed to restore international peace and security in the area.

2. This force is composed of contingents contributed by the Governments of the United Kingdom, Canada, Australia, New Zealand and India. Contingents may be contributed by other Commonwealth countries in the future.

3. It has been agreed by the Governments who support the United Nations action in Korea that unified direction is essential for co-ordination and control of forces contributed by them. To this end, the force under your command has been placed under the supreme command of the Head of the United Nations Unified Command, Korea. You will carry out loyally any orders issued by him or by any American Commander subordinate to him under whose command you have been placed.

4. Commander-in-Chief, British Commonwealth Occupation Force, will act as Theatre Commander for the purpose of non-operational control and general administration of the United Kingdom, Australian, and New Zealand Army and Air Force and Canadian and Indian Army Forces which have been or may be made available to the United Nations for operations in Korea. He will exercise this control through Administrative Headquarters, British Commonwealth Forces Korea.

5. If an order given by the Head of the United Nations Unified Command Korea, or by any American Commander subordinate to him under whose command you have been placed, appears, in your opinion, not to accord with the object of the United Nations operations in Korea as declared in paragraph 1 above you will be at liberty to appeal to the Commander-in-Chief British Commonwealth Occupation Force who, before the order is executed, will represent the case to the Head of the United Nations Unified Command, Korea, and report to the Australian Chiefs of Staff Committee and to the Canadian Chiefs of Staff through the Canadian Military Mission Tokyo. You will, however, first inform the Head of the United Nations Unified Command, Korea, through any

American Commander subordinate to him, under whose Command you have been placed, that you intend to appeal, and you will give your reasons therefore.

6. If an order given by the Head of the United Nations Unified Command, Korea, or by any American Commander subordinate to him under whose command you have been placed appears, in your opinion, to imperil the safety of the Commonwealth troops under your Command, to a degree exceptional in war, you will inform the Head of the United Nations Unified Command, Korea, through any American Commander under whose command you have been placed, that you will carry out the order but that you intend to report the circumstances and your reasons for your opinion to the Commander-in-Chief British Commonwealth Occupation Force for representation to the Head of the United Nations Unified Command Korea, and report to the Australian Chiefs of Staff Committee and to the Canadian Chiefs of Staff through the Canadian Military Mission Tokyo.

7. A report, which may be later classified as "A despatch to be published", covering the operations of all Commonwealth forces under your command, will be prepared by you for submission to the Australian Chiefs of Staff Committee and the Canadian Chiefs of Staff (through the Canadian Military Mission Tokyo) through the Commander-in-Chief British Commonwealth Occupation Force and the Head of the United Nations Unified Command, Korea. Your attention is drawn to Army Order 404 of 1920, a copy of which is attached to this Directive*.

8. You will forward periodically to the War Office situation reports on operations in which your forces are engaged. Copies of these reports will also be sent to the Commander-in-Chief British Commonwealth Occupation Force for distribution to Australia, Canada, New Zealand and India.

---

* Not attached. This order gives guidance to two matters to be included and the form of presentation.

APPENDIX G

Prisoners of War Questionnaire

(used by the 'Chinese People's Volunteers' in the Korean War)

1. "AN OUTLINE OF AUTOBIOGRAPHY"
[First form of requirement]

I. Brief description of yourself.

1. Names, serial number, rank, age, outfit and duty.
2. Nationality, race and origin, native town, present address.
3. Education.
4. Specialties.
5. Hobbies.

II. Family (both yourself and parents) financial condition.

1. Members of family (name and occupation, political affiliation and religious beliefs).
2. Stock and property.
3. The principal resource of family income, monthly income, expenditure and savings.
4. Financial tie between you and your parents or wife.
5. Attachments with your parents while you were in the armed forces.
6. Parents' address.

III. Social relationships.

1. Names and present address of your closest relatives and friends (colleagues, superiors, teachers, schoolmates, etc.).
2. Their occupation, religious beliefs and political affiliations.
3. Give degree of relationship between you and them.

IV. History in detail.

A. *Life prior to joining the armed forces*

1. Birthday and birthplace.
2. School life, the schools you attended, when and where.
3. Professional life (both during and after schooldays) your jobs and pay.
4. Your political activities and party affiliations both during and after schooldays.

B. Military career

1. When, where, why and how did you enter the armed forces?
2. Assignments (time, places, units, rank, duties and principal functions).
3. Your intimate colleagues (officers and men) in the past various assignments.
4. What kind of military training have you received (when, where and in which units?) The main courses and subjects studied?
5. How many times have you entered the armed forces?
6. Have you ever been discharged? If so list your civilian jobs and pay (time and place).
7. Did you fight in World War II? If so where and what duties?
8. Were you wounded or captured during World War II? If captured when, where and how did you get out?
9. How many campaigns have you participated in, when and where?

V. Social activities and political affiliations.

1. What party social bodies and religious groups have you joined (time and place) when?
2. When did you work for them, what were your functions and activities in the organizations?
3. The training and eduction you received from the organizations which you joined.
4. What is the nature and purpose of the organization you have joined?
5. When were the organization founded and who were the leaders?
6. Have you kept contact with the organization (prior to and after capture)?
7. What are the activities of the parties, organizations and religion (which you belonged to) in the armed forces? Are these activities legal or not?
8. What is your impression towards various political parties and social bodies in your country?

VI. Prior to and since capture.

1. Your sentiments and feelings at being sent to Korea, after getting into combat and since capture?
2. Impressions of the Chinese People's Volunteers.
3. Time and place of capture[1].

2. "AN OUTLINE OF YOUR AUTOBIOGRAPHY."
[Alternative and fuller form of requirement]

(A) Name, Age. Nationality. Address. Education. Languages you can speak. Amy Rank. Duty. Length of service. Religious and political belief. Hobbies. Specialities. Mention characters. Time of capture.

(B) Economic situation of yourself and your parents. How did you arrange your income and expenditure? Describe the hardship you had before and how you overcome them? When was your prosperous time? Why?

(C) All your relatives situation (include your parents brothers and sisters) — Name. Age. Occupation. Address. Religious and political belief. Brief economic situation. Familiarity with you. How did they influence your thought and action?

(D) Your friends situation — The same as item (C).

(E) Do you like to travel? Give the name of the places you have visited and resided before (both in civilian and military life) which place you like best? Why? Have you acquaintances at those places? What's your impression of those places?

(F) Occupations you have done before (prior joined the army)? What were your favourite jobs? Why? What did you learn from each job?

(G) Life prior joined the armed forces:
School life; Names of school attended. When and where? Your favourite subjects. Did you study hard? Why?
Thoughts and ambitions in different periods. What influenced you?
Events on hardships. Love. Hatred and miserable this in different periods. Social activities.
When where and how you got married?

(H) *Military career:*
When where and how joined the armed forces.
Assignments in sequence (time place unit rank duty).

Training received (when where what).
Campaigns participated (when where wound or not).
Decorations in each campaign. Why?
Promotion in each assignment. Why?
Demotion in each assignment. Why?
Have you been captured in last war?
Have you ever been discharged? Why?
Your feeling toward army life.
When where and how you got captured in Korea? How many places have you stayed since capture? What have you done and seen at those places?

(I) Your point of view towards U.S. imperialist government. Labour Party. Conservative Party. Communist Party. Foreign and domestic policy of Labour government. Relationship between U.S. and Great Britain. Soviet Union and People's China prior capture.

(J) Your feeling at being sent to Korea and after getting into combat. What was your opinion of this Korean war at that time?

(K) A brief and complete description of your change of thought after capture (describe every factor which influenced to change your thought; cite concrete examples like books? lectures? and persons).

(L) Your point of view towards U.S. imperialist government. Labour Party. Conservative Party. Communist Party. Foreign and domestic policy of your present government. Relationship between U.S. and Great Britain. At present time. What makes you changed?

(M) Your point of view towards C.P.V., U.S.S.R. and People's China at present time. What makes you changed? Your point of view toward peace and world peace movement.
How shall you plan to joint this movement and seek peace in future?

(N) Plan of your future after release and backing home.

(O) Do you think that the Labour Party can establish Socialism in Great Britain?

(P) What do you plan to do in this camp before release? Do you have any suggestions to improve our study and daily life conditions in this camp?[2]

3. "OUTLINE OF SELF-ANALYSIS"

[Form to be completed by those in camps in early 1951, having already completed at least one 'autobiography'. This was also presented to prisoners arriving at a camp from February 1951 to complement an 'autobiography' to be demanded on arrival]

I. Degree of family influence

1. a) Number of persons in your family.
   b) Occupation of family members
   c) Family living standards (including married members).
   d) Influence created by family environment (prior to entering socially yourself......state period).

2. What knowledge and understanding did you gain from your parents, grandparents, etc.? What part of this family teaching created the deepest impression?

II. Degree of school influence

a) What were your favourite subjects?
b) Most preferred outside activities?
c) What were your future plans, ambitions whilst at school?

III. Between leaving school joining army what influence had society upon you.

1. a) Name various jobs you had.
   b) Explain jobs and how long you worked in each of them.
   c) How did you secure these jobs?
   d) What interest did you take in these jobs?

2. a) Were you satisfied or happy with these various jobs? Why?
   b) In the case of dissatisfaction with the jobs what did you plan at the time?

IV. What influence or impressions did the Army life have upon you?

1. a) What were reasons for joining the army?
   b) What ideas were in your mind at the time of joining the army?

2. a) What were feeling and ideological attitude towards army life, e/g/ salary, ranks. discipline, etc.?

3. a) What schooling, training, education did you receive in the army?
   b) What occurrences, happenings or information on same influenced you most whilst in the army, e.g. lectures, speeches, discussions, etc.?

V. What were feelings and views towards participating in the Korean War?

1. a) What lectures on the Korean war did you receive from your superior officers just prior entering the war?
   b) How did you feel about certain points or problems raised in these lectures, etc.?

2. What do you think about U.S. participating in the Korean war before you were captured?

3. What do you think about the K.P.A and C.P.V. and the U.S.S.R. before your capture?

APPENDIX H

Directive for Deputy Chief of Staff, Korea

You have been appointed to the Staff of Commander-in-Chief, United Nations Command, in the capacity of Deputy Chief of Staff. You will carry out all the duties associated with such an appointment and you will be responsible to the Commander-in-Chief, United Nations Command.

You are not the channel for passing the views of the United Kingdom Chiefs of Staff to the United Nations Commander. This will continue to be done in Washington.

You will not pass on any information which you may receive from the Commander-in-Chief, United Nations Command, or his staff, without the authority of the Commander-in-Chief.

These instructions have been agreed with the Chiefs of Staff of Canada, Australia, New Zealand and South Africa.

Notes

1. Papers relating to this instruction are contained in the MO 1 Collection and FO 317/99616. The latter contains a Brief to General Shoosmith issued by the British Chiefs of Staff Committee (FK 1194/99), together with a note by Mr R H Scott (FK 1194/90).

2. In this same file, FK 1194/86, the Minister of Defence (Field Marshal the Earl Alexander of Tunis) sets out in a minute to the Prime Minister changes to be made in the Commonwealth Liaison Arrangements in Tokyo, and a new Directive for the C-in-C, British Comonwealth Forces in Korea.

APPENDIX J

Carole Carr in Korea

In 1952, I was appearing in the B.B.C. variety show 'Calling All Forces'. In it, I sang songs requested by servicemen and women serving overseas, and received so much mail, that I offered to go and thank the boys and girls personally. I was invited by the War Office to tour (through C.S.E.) Korea, Hong Kong, Japan and Malaya.

I arrived in Seoul on September 9th. '52, with a pianist and a comedian. For most of the three weeks we spent in Korea, we lived in converted ambulances, and until we arrived, I had not given a thought to 'ablutions'. I was the only female there apart from the nurses at the Norwegian M.A.S.H., but I need not have worried. Everywhere I went, there would be a newly dug path to a little shack with LADIES painted on the door! Showers were more of a problem, but often a group of damp and grumbling officers would be called out of their bath house, so I could shower in solitary splendour while the C.O. stood guard outside!

We did two or three concerts a day, and always impromptu shows in the evening. I remember doing a show for the Black Watch, and being piped through the gate, a wonderful hospitality from everyone, especially from Major Dolan and other Canadians at 25th. Bde. But one of my most vivid memories, is the show we did for the Welch Regt. in a rain storm. They were getting soaked, so I asked them if they wanted me to carry on. The yelled YES, but they had the last laugh. Suddenly the canvas roof over the stage caved in, and I was drenched...to a wave of cheers and whistles. Afterwards, the C.O. said my stock had gone up 100%, whether because I had 'carried on singing' or because my dress had clung in a most revealing way, your guess is as good as mine!

I did not go in for glamour in Korea. I had to wear uniform all the time, except on stage, and then I wore quite ordinary day dresses. The boys wanted a link with home, and I tried to be as natural as possible. Once, during a show for the Innsk. Dragoon Guards, when I asked for song requests, a voice called out, 'Don't sing, just stand there'! As you can imagine, our shows were pretty informal!

I remember having tea with General West, who was very charming and complimentary about our shows, and discussing the excellent quality of food in all the camps I visited. I felt that some of the British troops were getting spoilt, as one day, we stopped to chat to a group who were having a meal by the roadside. Their mess tins were full of great chunks of turkey with all the trimmings. When I asked one of them how he was enjoying the meal he replied with disgust, 'Cor! It's b———g TURKEY AGAIN'!

Being the only girl in the party, I was always treated with great respect. However, a sergeant in the R.M.P's. gave me a huge service torch with which to deal with 'anyone who got fresh'. I felt rather alarmed, especially as later that night, I woke to feel the caravan lurch as someone sat on the step. I grabbed the torch and waited, but finally fell asleep. The next morning at breakfast, the R.S.M. said he hoped I had slept well, as he had put a guard on my caravan all night! I felt rather foolish, and NEVER had to use that torch as a defense weapon!

We had an exciting visit to Blazer Battery, a couple of miles from the front. I was asked if I would like to fire a twenty-five pounder at the Chinese, but I hastily declined. This was a correct decision, as another artiste who went there several weeks latter, *did* fire a gun, and there was a lot of trouble at home about it. However, I was presented with two still-hot shell cases, which stand in my fireplace to this day.

We did one show for the Americans at I Corps. I was apprehensive as none of them had ever heard of me, but they turned out to be a great audience. Afterwards, I was told it was because we were all young… I was just twenty-four…and they were sick of being entertained by 'stateside rejects' who were 'doing the boys a favour' by going out there. Rather cruel, but they, like our boys, wanted to see young artistes.

Visits to hospitals were always emotional and very draining. After doing a show, I was always asked to go round the wards to meet the very sick men. Once in the B.C.G.H. at Kure, I me a young, badly injured Canadian soldier who had just had a leg amputated. He had been married just before leaving for Korea, and he was worried that his wife, Laura, would not be able to love 'such a wreck'. He asked me to sing the song, 'Laura' just for him, which I did, very quietly, and tearfully. It was the hardest thing I did out there. I never heard the outcome, but I like to think Laura stood by him.

One of my proudest possessions is a copy of 'Ocean Saga'. the story of the Commission of the Light Fleet Aircraft Carrier, H.M.S. Ocean. In Sept. '52, while 'Ocean' was re-ammunitioning in Kure, I was taken on board by helicopter to meet the ship's company, and have breakfast with the Captain. The visit had a flattering write-up in the 'Saga', but there is one piece I found missing.

'During the months on patrol, Carole received more song requests from the men of 'Ocean' than any other ship or unit, and seldom did she let her programme end without some reference to the ship, which

Carole came to look upon as her own special care. One English newspaper remarked that should the Admiralty ever lose trace of 'Ocean', a phone call to Carole Carr would supply all the necessary information! Unquote.

Of all those on active service I came across in Korea, none were braver than the army reconnaissance pilots. I remember watching an Auster flying at tree top level towards the enemy lines, then all hell seemed to break loose. He came back safely, however, and seemed to think nothing of it!

I very soon ran out of signed photographs, and I gave the last one to an Australian, who seemed very grateful. 'You still got rationing in England?' he asked. 'Afraid so' I replied. Several weeks later, a huge parcel arrived at my home. It was a splendid fruit cake baked by a kind Australian lady, and with it was a note which read, 'Thank you for cheering up my boy...he thinks you're a beauty!'

Another time, an officer was so worried that I might be cold at night, that he gave me his parka, which was a great sacrifice on his part.

Everyone showed me kindness and great hospitality, and I felt deeply privileged to have been allowed to go to Korea.

Carole Carr

13.10.87.

APPENDIX K

Armistice Agreement

AGREEMENT BETWEEN THE COMMANDER-IN-CHIEF, UNITED NATIONS COMMAND, ON THE ONE HAND, AND THE SUPREME COMMANDER OF THE KOREAN PEOPLE'S ARMY AND THE COMMANDER OF THE CHINESE PEOPLE'S VOLUNTEERS ON THE OTHER HAND, CONCERNING A MILITARY ARMISTACE IN KOREA

Panmunjom, July 27, 1953

PREAMBLE

The undersigned, the Commander-in-Chief, United Nations Command, on the one hand, and the Supreme Commander of the Korean People's Army and the Commander of the Chinese People's Volunteers, on the other hand, in the interest of stopping the Korean Conflict, with its great toll of suffering and bloodshed on both sides, and with the objective of establishing an armistice which will insure a complete cessation of hostilities and of all acts of armed force in Korea until a final peace settlement is achieved, do individually, collectively, and mutually agree to accept and to be bound and governed by the conditions and terms of armistice set forth in the following Articles and Paragraphs, which said conditions and terms are intended to be purely military in character and to pertain solely to the belligerents in Korea.

ARTICLE I

MILITARY DEMARCATION LINE AND DEMILITARISED ZONE

1. A Military Demarcation Line shall be fixed and both sides shall withdraw two (2) kilometres from this line so as to established a Demilitarized Zone between the opposing forces. A Demilitarized Zone shall be established as a buffer zone to prevent the occurrence of incidents which might lead to a resumption of hostilities.

2. The Military Demarcation Line is located as indicated on the attached map*.

3. The Demilitarized Zone is defined by a northern and southern boundary as indicated on the attached map*.

4. The Military Demarcation Line shall be plainly marked as directed by the Military Armistice Commission hereinafter established. The Commanders of the opposing sides shall have suitable markers erected along the boundary between the Demilitarised Zone and their respective areas. The Military Armistice Commission shall supervise the erection of all markers placed along the Military Demarcation Line and along the boundaries of the Demilitarised Zone.

5. The waters of the Han River Estuary shall be open to civil shipping of both sides wherever one bank is controlled by one side and the other bank is controlled by the other side. The Military Armistice Commission shall prescribe rules for the shipping in that part of the Han River Estuary indicated on the attached map*. Civil shipping of each side shall have unrestricted access to the land under the military control of that side.

6. Neither side shall execute any hostile act within, from, or against the Demilitarised Zone.

7. No person, military or civilian, shall be permitted to cross the Military Demarcation Line unless specifically authorised to do so by the Military Armistice Commission.

8. No person, military or civilian, in the Demilitarised Zone shall be permitted to enter the territory under the military control of either side unless specifically authorised to do so by the Commander into whose territory entry is sought.

9. No person, military or civilian, shall be permitted to enter the Demilitarised Zone except persons concerned with the conduct of civil administration and relief of persons specifically authorised to enter by the Military Armistice Commission.

10. Civil administration and relief in that part of the Demilitarised Zone which is south of the Military Demarcation Line shall be the responsibility of the Commander-in-Chief, United Nations Command; and civil administration and relief in that part of the Demilitarised Zone which

---

* Map not displayed

is north of the Military Demarcation Line shall be the joint responsibility of the Supreme Commander of the Korean People's Army and the Commander of the Chinese People's Volunteers. The number of persons, military or civilian, from each side who are permitted to enter the Demilitarised Zone for the conduct of civil administration and relief shall be a determined by the respective Commanders, but in no case shall the total number authorised by either side exceed on thousand (1,000) persons at any one time. The number of civil police and the arms to be carried by them shall be as prescribed by the Military Armistice Commission. Other personnel shall not carry arms unless specifically authorised to do so by the Military Armistice Commission.

11. Nothing contained in this Article shall be construed to prevent the complete freedom of movement to, from, and within the Demilitarised Zone by the Military Armistice Commission, its assistants, its Joint Observer Teams with their assistants, the Neutral Nations Supervisory Commission hereinafter established, its assistants, its Neutral Persons Inspection Teams with their assistants, and of any other persons, materials and equipment specifically authorised to enter the Demilitarised Zone by the Military Armistice Commission. Convenience of movement shall be permitted through the territory under the military control of either side over any route necessary to move between points within the Demilitarised Zone where such points are not connected by roads lying completely with the Demilitarised Zone.

ARTICLES II

CONCRETE ARRANGEMENTS FOR CEASE-FIRE AND ARMISTICE

A. GENERAL

12. The Commanders of the opposing sides shall order and enforce a complete cessation of all hostilities in Korea, by all armed forces under their control, including all units and personnel of the ground, naval, and air forces, effective twelve (12) hours after this Armistice Agreement is sided. (See paragraph 63 for effective date and hour of the remaining provisions of this Armistice Agreement.)

13. In order to ensure the stability of the Military Armistice so as to facilitate the attainment of a peaceful settlement through the holding by both sides of a political conference of a high level, the Commanders of the opposing sides shall

(a) Within seventy-two (72) hours after this Armistice Agreement becomes effective, withdraw all of their military forces, supplies, and equipment from the Demilitarised Zone except as otherwise provided herein. All demolitions, minefields, wire entanglements and other hazards to the safe movement of personnel of the Military Armistice Commission or its Joint Observer Teams, known to exist within the Demilitarised Zone after the withdrawal of military forces therefrom, together with lanes known to be free of all such hazards, shall be reported to the Military Armistice Commission by the Commander of the side who forces emplaced such hazards. Subsequently, additional safe lanes shall be cleared; and eventually, with forty-five (45) days after the termination of the seventy-two (72) hour period, all such hazards shall be removed from the Demilitarised Zone as directed by and under the supervision of the Military Armistice Commission. At the termination of the seventy-two (72) hours period, except for unarmed troops authorised a forty-five (45) day period to complete salvage operations under Military Armistice Commission supervision, such units of a police nature as may be specifically requested by the Military Armistice Commission and agreed to by the Commanders of the opposing sides, the personnel authorised under paragraphs 10 and 11 hereof, no personnel of either side shall by permitted to enter the Demilitarised Zone.

(b) Within ten (10) days after this Armistice Agreement becomes effective, withdraw all of their military forces, supplies and equipment from the rear and the coastal islands and waters of Korea of the other side. If such military forces are not withdrawn within the stated time limit, and there is no mutually agreed and valid reason for the delay, the other side shall be the right to take any action which it deems necessary for the maintenance of security and order. The term 'coastal islands', as used above, refers to those islands which, though occupied by one side at the time when this Armistice Agreement becomes effective, were controlled by the other side on June 24, 1950; provided, however that all the islands lying to the north and west of the provincial boundary line between Hwanghae-Do and Kyonggi-Do shall be under the military control of the Supreme Commander of the Korean People's Army and the Commander of the Chinese People's Volunteers, except the island groups of Paengyong-Do (37°58' N, 124° 40' E), Taechong-Do (37° 50' N, 124° 42' E), Sochong-Do (37° 46' N, 124° 46' E), Yonpyong-Do (37° 38' N, 125° 40' E), and U-Do (37° 36' N, 125° 58' E), which shall remain under the military control of the Commander-in-Chief, United Nations Command. All the islands on the west coast of Korea lying south of the above-mentioned boundary line shall remain under the military control of the Commander-in-Chief, United Nations Command. (See Map 3.)[3]

(c) Cease the introduction into Korea of reinforcing military personnel; provided, however, that the rotation of units and personnel, the arrival in Korea of personnel on a temporary duty basis, and the return to Korea of personnel after short periods of leave or temporary duty outside of Korea shall be permitted with the scope prescribed below. 'Rotation' is defined as the replacement of units or personnel by other units or personnel who are commencing a tour of duty in Korea. Rotation personnel shall be introduced into and evacuated from Korea only through the ports of entry enumerated in paragraph 43 hereof. Rotation shall be conducted on a man-for-man basis; provided, however, that no more than thirty-five thousand (35,000) persons in the military service shall be admitted into Korea by either side in any calendar month under the rotation policy. No military personnel of either side shall be introduced into Korea if the introduction of such personnel will cause the aggregate of the military personnel of that side admitted into Korea since the effective date of this Armistice Agreement to exceed the cumulative total of the military personnel of that side who have departed from Korea since that date. Reports concerning arrivals in and departures from Korea of military personnel shall be made daily to the Military Armistice Commission and the Neutral Nations Supervisory Commission, through its Neutral Nations Inspection Teams, shall conduct supervision and inspection of the rotation of units and personnel authorised above, at the ports of entry enumerated in paragraph 43 hereof.

(d) Cease the introduction into Korea of reinforcing combat aircraft, armoured vehicles, weapons and ammunition; provided, however, that combat aircraft, armoured vehicles weapons, and ammunition which are destroyed, damaged, worn-out, or used up during the period of the armistice may be replaced on the basis of piece-for-piece of the same effectiveness and the same type. Such combat aircraft, armoured vehicles, weapons and ammunition shall be introduced into Korea only through the ports of entry enumerated in paragraph 43 hereof. In order to justify the requirement for combat aircraft, armoured vehicles, weapons, and ammunition to be introduced into Korea for replacement purposes, reports concerning every incoming shipment of these items shall be made to the Military Armistice Commission and the Neutral Nations Supervisory Commission; such reports shall include statements regarding the disposition of the items being replaced. Items to be replaced which are removed from Korea shall be removed only through the ports of entry enumeration in paragraph 43 hereof. The Neutral Nations Supervisory Commission, through its Neutral Nations Inspection Teams, shall conduct supervision and inspection of the replacement of combat aircraft, armoured vehicles, weapons, and ammunition authorised above, at the ports of entry enumerated in paragraph 43 hereof.

(e) Ensure that personnel of their respective commands who violate any of the provisions of this Armistice Agreement are adequately punished.

(f) In those cases where places of burial are a matter of record and graves are actually found to exist. permit graves registration personnel of the other side to enter, within a definite time limit after this Armistice Agreement becomes effective, the territory of Korea under their military control, for the purpose of proceeding to such graves to recover and evacuate the bodies of the deceased military personnel of that side, including deceased prisoners of war. The specific procedures and the time limit for the performance of the above task shall be determined by the Military Armistice Commission. The Commanders of the opposing sides shall furnish to the other side all available information pertaining to the places of burial of the deceased military personnel of the other side.

(g) Afford full protection and all possible assistance and co-operation to the Military Armistice Commission, its Joint Observer Teams, the Neutral Nations Supervisory Commission, and its Neutral Inspection Teams, in the carrying out of their functions and responsibilities hereinafter assigned; and accord to the Neutral Nations Supervisory Commission, and to its Neutral Nation Inspection Teams, full convenience of movement between the headquarters of the Neutral Nations Supervisory Commission and the ports of entry enumerated in paragraph 43 hereof over main lines of communication agreed upon by both sides (See Map 4),[4] and between the headquarters of the Neutral Nations Supervisory Commission and the places where violations of this Armistice Agreement have been reported to have occurred. In order to prevent unnecessary delays, the use of alternative routes and means of transportation will be permitted whenever the main lines of communication are closed or impassable.

(h) Provide such logistic support, including communications and transportation facilities, as may be required by the Military Armistice Commission and the Neutral Nations Supervisory Commission and their Teams.

(i) Each construct, operate, and maintain a suitable airfield in their respective ports of the Demilitarised Zone in the vicinity of the headquarters of the Military Armistice Commission for such uses as the Commission may determine.

(j) Ensure that all members and other personnel of the Neutral Nation Supervisory Commission and of the Neutral Nations Repatriation Commission hereinafter established shall enjoy the freedom and facilities necessary for the proper exercise of their functions, including privileges, treatment, and immunities equivalent to those ordinarily enjoyed by accredited diplomatic personnel under international usage.

14. This Armistice Agreement shall apply to all opposing ground forces under the military control of either side, which ground forces shall respect the Demilitarised Zone and the area of Korea under the military control of the opposing side.

15. This Armistice Agreement shall apply to all opposing naval forces, which naval forces shall respect the waters contiguous to the Demilitarised Zone and to the land area of Korea under the military control of the opposing side, and shall not engage in blockade of any kind of Korea.

16. This Armistice Agreement shall apply to all opposing air forces, which air forces shall respect the air space over the Demilitarised Zone and over the area of Korea under the military control of the opposing side, and over the waters contiguous to both.

17. Responsibility for compliance with and enforcement of the terms of provisions of this Armistice Agreement is that of the signatories hereto and their successors in command. The Commanders of the opposing sides

shall establish within their respective commands all measures and procedures necessary to ensure complete compliance with all of the provisions hereof by all elements of their commands. They shall actively co-operate with one another and with the Military Armistice Commission and the Neutral Nations Supervisory Commission in requiring observance of both the letter and the spirit of all the provisions of this Armistice Agreement.

18. The costs of the operations of the Military Armistice Commission and the Neutral Nations Supervisory Commission and of their Teams shall be shared equally by the two opposing sides.

B. MILITARY ARMISTICE COMMISSION

1. COMPOSITION

19. A Military Armistice Commission is hereby established.

20. The Military Armistice Commission shall be composed of ten (10) senior officers, five (5) of whom whall be appointed by the Commander-in-Chief, United Nations Command, and five (5) of whom shall be appointed jointly by the Supreme Commander of the Korean People's Army and the Commander of the Chinese People's Volunteers. On of the ten (10) members, three (3) from each side shall be of general or flag rank. The two (2) remaining members on each side shall be major-generals, brigadier-generals, colonels, or the equivalents.

21. Members of the Military Armistice Commission shall be permitted to use staff assistants as required.

22. The Military Armistice Commission shall be provided with the necessary administrative personnel to establish a Secretariat charged with assisting the Commission by performing record-keeping, secretarial, interpreting, and such other functions as the Commission may assign to it. Each side shall appoint to the Secretariat a Secretary and an Assistant Secretary and such clerical and specialised personnel as required by the Secretariat. Records shall be kept in English, Korean, and Chinese, all of which shall be equally authentic.

23. (a) The Military Armistice Commission shall be initially provided with and assisted by ten (10) Joint Observer Teams, which number may be reducted by agreement of the senior members of both sides of the Military Armistice Commission.

(b) Each Joint Observer Team shall be composed of not less than four (4) nor more than six (6) officers of field grade, half of whom shall be appointed by Commander-in-Chief, United Nations Commander, and half of whom shall be appointed jointly by the Supreme Commander of the Korean People's Army and the Commander of the Chinese People's Volunteers. Additional personnel such as drivers, clerks, and interpreters shall be furnished by each side as required for the functioning of the Joint Observer Teams.

2. FUNCTIONS AND AUTHORITY

24. The general mission of the Military Armistice Commission shall be to supervise the implementation of this Armistice Agreement and to settle through negotiations any violation of this Armistice Agreement.

25. The Military Armistic Commission shall:-

(a) Locate its headquarters in the vicinity of Panmungom (37° 57' 29" N., 12° 40' 00" E.). The Military Armistice Commission may relocate it headquarters at another point within the Demilitarised Zone by agreement of the senior members of both sides on the Commission.

(b) Operate as a joint organisation with a chairman.

(c) Adopt such rules of procedure as it may, from time to time, deem necessary.

(d) Supervise the carrying out of the provisions of this Armistice Agreement pertaining to the Demilitarised Zone and to the Han River Estuary.

(e) Direct the operations of the Joint Observers Teams.

(f) Settle through negotiations any violation of this Armistice Agreement.

(g) Transmit immediately to the Commanders of the opposing sides all reports of investigations of violations of this Armistice Agreement and all other reports and records of proceedings received from the Neutral Nations Supervisory Commission.

(h) Give general supervision and direction to the activities of the Committee for Repatriation of Prisoners of War and the Committee for Assisting the Return of Displaced Civilians, hereinafter established.

(i) Act as an intermediary in transmitting communciations between the Commanders of the opposing sides; provided, however, that the foregoing shall not be construed to preclude the Commanders of both sides from communicating with each other by any means which they desire to employ.

(j) Provide credentials and distinctive insignia for its staff and its Joint Observer Teams, and a distinctive marking for all vehicles, aircraft, and vessels, used in the performance of its mission.

26. The mission of the Joint Observer Teams shall be to assist the Military Armistice Commission in supervising the carrying out of the provisions of this Armistice Agreement pertaining to the Demilitarised Zone and to the Han River Estuary.

27. The Military Armistice Commission, or the senior member of either side thereof, is authorised to despatach Joint Observer Teams to investigate violation of this Armistice Agreement reported to have occurred in the Demilitarised Zone or in the Han River Estuary; provided, however, that not more than one half of the Joint Observer Teams which have not been despatched by the Military Armistice Commission may be despatached at any one time by the senior member of either side on the Commission.

28. The Military Armistice Commission, or the senior member of either side thereof, is authorised to request the Neutral Nations Supervisory Commission to conduct special observations and inspections at places outside the Demilitarised Zone where violations of this Armistice Agreeement have been reported to have occurred.

29. When the Military Armistice Commission determines that a violation of this Armistice Agreement has occurred, it shall immediately report such violation to the Commanders of the opposing sides.

30. When the Military Armistice Commission determines that a violation of this Armistice Agreement has been corrected to its satisfaction, it shall so report to the Commanders of the opposing sides.

3. GENERAL

31. The Military Armistice Commission shall meet daily Recesses of not to exceed seven (7) days may be agreed upon by the senior members of both sides; provided, that such recesses may be terminated on twenty-four (24) hour notice by the senior member of either side.

32. Copies of the record of the proceedings of all meetings of the Military Armistice Commission shall be forwarded to the Commanders of the opposing sides as soon as possible after each meeting.

33. The Joint Observer Teams shall make periodic report to the Military Armistice Commission as required by the Commission and, in addition, shall make such special report as may be deemed necessary by them, or as may be required by the Commission.

34. The Military Armistice Commission shall maintain files of the reports and records of proceedings required by this Armistice Agreement. The Commission is authorised to maintain duplicate files of such other reports, records, & c., as may be necessary in the conduct of its business. Upon eventual dissolution of the Commission, one set of theabove files shall be turned over to each side.

35. The Military Armistice Commission may make recommendations to the Commanders of the opposing sides with respect to amendments or additions to this Armistice Agreement. Such recommeded changes should generally be those designed to ensure a more effective armistice.

C. NEUTRAL NATIONS SUPERVISORY COMMISSION

1. COMPOSITION

36. A Neutral Nations Supervisory Commission is hereby established.

37. The Neutral Nations Supervisory Commission shall be composed of four (4) senior officers, two (2) of whom shall be appointed by neural nations nominated by the Commander-in-Chief, United Nations Commander, namely, Sweden and Switzerland, and two (2) of whom shall be appointed by neutral nations nominated jointly by the Supreme Commander of the Korean People's Army and the Commander of the Chinese People's Volunteers, namely, Poland and Czechoslovakia. The terms 'neutral nations' as herein used is defined as those nations whose combatant forces have not participated in the hostilities in Korea. Members appointed to the Commission may be from the armed forces of the appointing nations. Each member shall designate an alternative member to attend those meetings which for any reason the principal member is unable to attend. Such alternate members shall be of the same nationality as their principals. The Neutral Nations Supervisory Commission may take action whenever the number of members present from the neutral nations nominated by one side is equal to the number of members present from the neutral nations nominated by the other side.

38. Members of the Neutral Nations Supervisory Commission shall be permitted to use staff assistants furnished by the neutral nations as

required. These staff assistants may be appointed as alternate members of the Commission.

39. The neutral nations shall be requested to furnish the Neutral Nations Supervisory Commission with the necessary administrative personnel to establish a Secretariat charged with assisting the Commission by performing necessary record-keeping, secretarial, interpreting, and such other functions as the Commission may assign to it.

40. (a) The Neutral Nations Supervisory Commission shall be initially provided with, and assisted by, twenty (20) Neutral Nations Inspection Teams, which number may be reduced by agreement of the senior members of both sides on the Military Armistice Commission. The Neutral Inspection Teams shall be responsible to, shall report to, and shall be subject to the direction of, the Neutral Nations Supervisory Commission only.

(b) Each Neutral Nations Inspection Team shall be composed of not less than four (4) officers, preferably of field grade, half of whom shall be from the neutral nations nominated by the Commander-in-Chief, United Nations Command, and half of whom shall be from the neutral nations nominated jointly by the Supreme Commander of the Korean People's Army and the Commander of the Chinese People's Volunteers. Members appointed to the Neutral Nations Inspection Teams may be from the armed forces of the appointing nations. In order to facilitate the functioning of the Teams, sub-teams composed of not less than two (2) members, one of whom shall be from a neutral nation nominated by the Commander-in-Chief, United Nations Command, and one of whom shall be from a neutral nation nominated jointly by the Supreme Commander of the Korean People's Army and the Commander of the Chinese People's Volunteers, may be formed as circumstances require. Additional personnel, and such drivers, clerks, interpreters, and communications personnel, and such equipment as may be required by the Teams to perform their missions, shall be furnished by the Commander of each side, as required, in the Demilitarised Zone and in the territory under his military control. The Neutral Nations Supervisory Commission may provide itself and the Neutral Nations Inspection Teams with such of the above personnel and equipment of its own as it may desire; provided, however, that such personnel shall be personnel of the same neutral nations of which the Neutral Nations Supervisory Commission is composed.

2. FUNCTIONS AND AUTHORITY

41. The mission of the Neutral Nations Supervisory Commission shall be to carry out the functions of supervision, observation, inspection, and investigation, as stipulated in sub-paragraphs 13(c) and 13(d) and paragraph 28 hereof, and to report the results of such supervision, observation, inspection and investigation to the Military Armistice Commission.

42. The Neutral Nations Supervisory Commission shall:-

(a) Locate its headquarters in proximity to the headquarters of the Military Armistice Commission.

(b) Adopt such rules of procedure as it may, from time to time, deem necessary.

(c) Conduct, through its members and its Neutral Nations Inspection Teams, the supervision and inspection provided for in sub-paragraph 13(c) and 13(d) of this Armistice Agreement at the ports of entry enumerated in paragraph 43 hereof, and the special observations and inspections provided for in paragraph 28 hereof at those places where violations of this Armistice Agreement have been reported to have occurred. The inspection of combat aircraft, armoured vehicles, weapons, and ammunition by the Neutral Nations Inspection Teams shall be such as to enable them to properly ensure than reinforcing combat aircraft, armoured vehicles, weapons, and ammunition are not being introduced into Korea; but this shall not be construed as authorising inspections or examinations of any secret designs or characteristics of any combat aircraft, armoured vehicle, weapon, or ammunition.

(d) Direct and supervise the operations of the Neutral Nations Inspection Teams.

(e) Station five (5) Neutral Nations Inspection Teams at the ports of entry enumerated in paragraph 43 hereof located in the territory under the military control of the Commander-in-Chief, United Nations Command; and five (5) Neutral Nations Inspection Teams at the ports of entry enumerated in paragraph 43 hereof located in the territory under the military control of the Supreme Commander of the Korean People's Army and the Commander of the Chinese People's Volunteers; and establish initially ten (10) mobile Neutral Nations Inspection Teams in reserve, stationed in the general vicinity of the headquarters of the Neutral Nations Supervisory Commission, which number may be reduced by agreement of the senior members of both sides on the Military Armistice Commission. Not more than half of the mobile Neutral Nations Inspection Teams shall be despatched at any one time in accordance with requests of the senior member of either side of the Military Armistice Commission.

(f) Subject to the provisions of the preceding sub-paragraph, conduct with delay investigations of reported violations of this Armistice Agreement, including such investigations of reported violations of this Armistice Agreement as may be requested by the Military Armistice Commission or by the senior member of either side on the Commission.

(g) Provided credentials and distinctive insignia for its staff and its Neutral Nations Inspection Teams, and a distinctive marking for all vehicles, aircraft, and vessels, used in the performance of its mission.its mission.

43. Neutral Nations Inspection Teams shall be stationed at the following ports of entry:-

Territory under the military control of the United Nations Command

Inchon	(37° 28' N, 126° 38' E)
Taegu	(35° 52' N, 128° 36' E)
Pusan	(35° 06' N, 129° 02' E)
Kangnung	(37° 45' N, 128° 54' E)
Kunsan	(35° 59' N, 126° 43' E)

Territory under the military control of the Korean People's Army and the Chinese People's Volunteers

Sinuigu	(40° 06' N, 124° 24' E)
Chongjin	(41° 46' N, 129° 49' E)
Hungnam	(39° 50' N, 127° 37' E)
Manpo	(41° 09' N, 126° 18' E)
Sinanju	(39° 36' N, 125° 36' E)

These Neutral Nations Inspection Teams shall be accorded full convenience of movement within the areas and over the routes of communication set forth on the attached map (Map 5).[5]

3. GENERAL

44. The Neutral Nations Supervisory Commission shall meet daily. Recesses of not to exceed seven (7) days must be agreed upon by the members of the Neutral Nations Supervisory Commission; provided, that such recesses may be terminated on twenty-four (24) hour notice by any member.

45. Copies of the record of the proceedings of all meetings of the Neutral Nations Supervisory Commission shall be forwarded to the Military Armistice Commission as soon as possible after each meeting. Records shall be kept in English, Korean, and Chinese.

46. The Neutral Nations Inspection Teams shall make periodic reports concerning the results of their supervision, observations, inspections and investigations to the Neutral Nations Supervisory Commission as required by the Commission and, in addition, shall make such special reports as may be deemed necessary by them, or as may be required by the Commission. Reports shall be submitted by one or more individual members thereof shall be considered as informational only.

47. Copies of the reports made by the Neutral Nations Inspection Teams shall be forwarded to the Military Armistice Commission by the Neutral Nations Supervisory Commission without delay and in the language in which received. They shall not be delayed by the process of translation or evaluation. The Neutral Nations Supervisory Commission shall evaluate such reports at the earliest practicable time and shall forward their findings to the Military Armistice Commission as a matter of priority. The Military Armistice Commission shall not take final action with regard to any such report until the evaluation thereof has been received from the Neutral Nations Supervisory Commission. Members of the Neutral Nations Supervisory Commission and of its Teams shall be subject to appearance before the Military Armistice Commission, at the request of the senior member of either side on the Military Armistice Commission, for clarification of any report submitted.

48. The Neutral Nations Supervisory Commission shall maintain duplicate files of the reports and records of proceedings required by this Armistice Agreement. The Commission is authorised to maintain duplicate files of such other reports, records &c., as may be necessary in the conduct of its business. Upon eventual dissolution of the Commission, one set of the above files shall be turned over to each side.

49. The Neutral Nations Supervisory Commission may make recommendations to the Military Armistice Commission with respect to amendments or additions to this Armistice Agreement. Such recommended changes should generally be those designed to ensure a more effective armistice.

50. The Neutral Nations Supervisory Commission, or any member thereof, shall be authorised to communicate with any member of the Military Armistice Commission.

ARTICLE III

ARRANGEMENTS RELATING TO PRISONERS OF WAR

51. The release and repatriation of all prisoners of war held in the custody of each side at the time this Armistice Agreement becomes effective shall be effected in conformity with the following provisions agreed upon by both sides prior to the signing of this Armistice Agreement.

(a) Within sixty (60) days after this Armistice Agreement becomes effective, each side shall, without offering any hindrance, directly repatriate and hand over in groups all those prisoners of war in its custody who insist on repatriation to the side to which they belong at the time of capture. Repatriation shall be accomplished in accordance with the related provisions of this Article. In order to expedite the repatriation process of such personnel, each side shall, prior to the signing of the Armistice Agreement, exchange the total numbers, by nationalities, of personnel to be directly repatriated. Each group of prisoners of war delivered to the other side shall be accompanied by rosters, prepared by nationality, to include name, rank (if any) and internment or military serial number.

(b) Each side shall release all those remaining prisoners of war, who are not directly repatriated, from its military control and from its custody and hand them over to the Neutral Nations Repatriation Commission for disposition in accordance with the provisions in the Annex hereto: 'Terms of Reference for Neutral Nations Repatriation Commission.'

(c) So that there may be no misunderstanding owing to the equal use of three languages, the act of deliver of a prisoner of war by one side to the other side shall, for the purpose of this Armistice, be called 'repatriation' in English, '遣 返' (song hwan) in Korean, and '송 환' (ch'ien fan) in Chinese, notwithstanding the nationality or place of residence of such prisoner of war.

52. Each side ensures that it will not employ in acts of war in the Korean conflict any prisoner of war released and repatriated incident to the coming into effect of this Armistice Agreement.

53. All the sick and injured prisoners of war who insist upon repatriation shall be repatriated with priority. In so far as possible, there shall be captured medical personnel repatriated concurrently with the sick and injured prisoners of war, so as to provide medical care and attendance *en route*.

54. The repatriation of all the prisoners of war required by sub-paragraph 51(A) hereof shall be completed within a time limit of sixth (60) days after this Armistice Agreement becomes effective. Within this time limit each side undertakes to complete the repatriation of the above-mentioned prisoners of war in its custody at the earliest practicable time.

55. Panmunjom is designated as the place where prisoners of war will be delivered and received by both sides. Additional place(s) of delivery and reception of prisoners of war in the Demilitarised Zone may be designated, if necessary, by the Committee for Repatriation of Prisoners of War.

56. (a) A Committee for Repatriation of Prisoners of War is hereby established. It shall be composed of six(6) officers of field grade, three (3) of whom shall be appointed by the Commander-in-Chief, United Nations Command, and three (3) of whom shall be appointed jointly by the Supreme Commander of the Korean People's Army and the Commander of the Chinese People's Volunteers. This Committee shall, under the general supervision and direction of the Military Armistice Commission, be responsible for co-ordinating the specific plans of both sides for the repatriation of prisoners of war and for supervising the execution by both sides of all the provisions of this Armistice Agreement relating to the repatriation of prisoners of war. It shall be the duty of this Committee to co-ordinate the timing of the arrival of prisoners of war at the place(s) of delivery and reception of prisoners of war from the prisoner of war camps of both sides; to make, when necessary, such special arrangements as may be required with regard to he transportation and welfare of sick and injured prisoners of war; to co-ordinate the work of the joint Red Cross teams, established in paragraph 57 hereof, in assisting in the repatriation of prisoners of war; to supervise the implementation of the arrangements for the actual repatriation of prisoners of war stipulated in paragraphs 53 and 54 hereof; to select, when necessary, additional place(s) of delivery and reception of prisoners of war; to arrange for security at the place(s) of delivery and reception of prisoners of war; and to carry out such other related functions as are required for the repatriation of prisoners of war.

(b) When unable to reach agreement on any matter relating to its responsibilities, the Committee for Repatriation of Prisoners of War shall immediately refer such matter to the Military Armistice Commission for decision. The Committee for Repatriation of Prisoners of War shall maintain its headquarters in proximity to the headquarters of the Military Armistice Commission.

(c) The Committee for Repatriation of Prisoners of War shall be dissolved by the Military Armistice Commission upon completion of the programme of repatriation of prisoners of war.

57. (a) Immediately after this Armistice Agreement becomes effective, joint Red Cross teams composed of representatives of the national Red Cross Societies of the countries contributing forces to the United Nations Command on the one hand, and representatives of the Red Cross Society of the Democratic People's Republic of Korea and representatives of the Red Cross Society of the People's Republic of Chins on the other hand, shall be established. The joint Red Cross teams shall assist in the execution of both sides of those provisions of this Armistice Agreement relating to the repatriation of all the prisoners of war specified in sub-paragraph 51(a) hereof, who insist upon repatriation, by the performance of such humanitarian services as are necessary and desirable for the welfare of the prisoners of war. To accomplish this task, the joint Red Cross teams shall provide assistance in the delivering and receiving of prisoners of war by both sides at the place(s) of deliver and reception of prisoners of war, and shall visit the prisoner of war camps of both sides to comfort the prisoners of war and to bring in and distribute gift articles for the comfort and welfare of the prisoners of war. The joint Red Cross teams may provide services to prisoners of war while *en route* from prisoner of war camps to the place(s) of deliver and reception of prisoners of war.

(b) The joint Red Cross shall be organised as set forth below:-

(1) One team shall be composed of twenty (20) members, namely, ten (10) representatives from the national Red Cross Societies of each side, to assist in the delivering and receiving of prisoners of war by both sides at the place(s) of delivery and reception of prisoners of war. The chairmanship of this team shall alternate daily between representatives from the Red Cross Societies of the two sides. The work and services of this team shall be co-ordinated by the Committee for Repatriation of Prisoners of War.

(2) One team shall be composed of sixty (60) members, namely, thirty (30) representatives from the national Red Cross Societies of each side, to visit the prisoner of war camps under the administration of the Korean People's Army and the Chinese People's Volunteers. This team may provide services to prisoners of war while *en route* from the prisoner of war camps to the place(s) of delivery and reception of prisoners of war. A representative of the Red Cross Society of the Democratic People's Republic of Korea or of the Red Cross Society of the People's Republic of China shall serve as chairman of this team.

(3) One team shall be composed of sixty (60) members, namely, thirty (30 representatives from the national Red Cross Societies of each side, to

visit the prisoner of war camps under the administration of the United Nations Command. This team may provide services to prisoners of war while *en route* from the prisoner of war camps to the place(s) of delivery and reception of prisoners of war. A representative of a Red Cross Society of a nation contributing forces to the United Nations Command shall serve as chairman of this team.

(4) In order to facilitate the functioning of each joint Red Cross team, sub-teams composed of not less than two (2) members from the team, with an equal number of representatives from each side, may be formed as circumstances require.

(5) Additional personnel such as drivers, clerks, and interpreters, and such equipment as may be required by the joint Red Cross teams to perform their missions, shall be furnished by the Commander of each side to the team operating in the territory under his military control.

(6) Whenever jointly agreed upon by the representatives of both sides on any joint Red Cross team, the size team may be increased or decreased, subject to confirmation by the Committee for Repatriation of Prisoners of War.

(c) The Commander of each side shall co-operate fully with the joint Red Cross teams in the performance of their functions, and undertakes to ensure the security of the personnel of the joint Red Cross team in the area under his military control. The Commander of each side shall provide such logistic, administrative and communications facilities as may be required by the team operating in the territory under his military control.

(d) The joint Red Cross teams shall be dissolved upon completion of the programme of repatriation of all the prisoners of war specified in sub-paragraph 51(a) hereof, who insist upon repatriation.

58. (a) The Commander of each side shall furnish to the Commander of the other side as soon as practicable, but not later than ten (10) days after this Armistice Agreement becomes effective, the following information concerning prisoners of war:-

(1) Complete data pertaining to the prisoners of war who escaped since the effective date of the data last exchanged.

(2) In so far as practicable, information regarding name, nationality, rank, and other identification data, date and cause of death, and place of burial, of those prisoners of war who died while in his custody.

(b) If any prisoners of war escape or die after the effective date of the supplementary information specified above, the detaining side shall furnish to the other side, through the Committee for Repatriation of Prisoners of War, the data pertaining thereto in accordance with the provisions of sub-paragraph 58(a) hereof. Such data shall be furnished at ten-day intervals until the completion of the programme of delivery and reception of prisoners of war.

(c) Any escaped prisoner of war who returns to the custody of the detaining side after the completion of the programme of delivery and reception of prisoners of war shall be delivered to the Military Armistice Commission for disposition.

59. (a) All civilians who, at the time this Armistice Agreement becomes effective, are in territory under the military control of the Commander-in-Chief, United Nations Command, and who, on June 24, 1950, resided north of the Military Demarcation Line established in this Armistice Agreement shall, if they desire to return home, be permitted and assisted by the Commander-in-Chief, United Nations Command, to return to the area north of the Military Demarcation Line; and all civilians who, at the time this Armistice Agreement becomes effective, are in territory under the military control of the Supreme Commander of the Korean People's Army and the Commander of the Chinese People's Volunteers, and who, on June 24, 1950, resided south of the Military Demarcation Line established in this Armistice Agreement shall, if they desire to return home, be permitted and assisted by the Supreme Commander of the Korean People's Army and the Commander of the Chinese People's Volunteers to return to the area south of the Military Demarcation Line. The Commander of each side shall be responsible for publicising widely throughout the territory under his military control the contents of the provisions of this sub-paragraph, and for calling upon the appropriate civil authorities to give necessary guidance and assistance to all such civilians who desire to return home.

(b) All civilians of foreign nationality who, at the time of Armistice Agreement becomes effective, are in territory under the military control of the Supreme Commander of the Korean People's Army and the Commander of the Chinese People's Army and the Commander of the Chinese People's Volunteers shall, if they desire to proceed to territory under the military control of the Commander-in-Chief, United Nations Command, be permitted and assisted to do so; all civilians of foreign nationality who, at the time this Armistice Agreement becomes effective, are in territory under the military control of the Commander-in-Chief, United Nations Command, shall, if they desire to proceed to territory under the military control of the Supreme Commander of the Korean People's Army and the Commander of the Chinese People's Volunteers, be permitted and assisted to do so. The Commander of each side shall be responsible for publicising widely throughout the territory under his military control the contents of the provisions of this sub-paragraph, and for calling upon the appropriate civil authorities to give necessary guidance and assistance to all such civilians of foreign nationality who desire to proceed to territory under the military control of the Commander of the other side.

(c) Measures to assist in the return of civilians provided for in sub-paragraph 59(a) hereof and the movement of civilians provided for in sub-paragraph 59(b) hereof shall be commenced by both sides as soon as possible after this Armistice Agreement becomes effective.

(d)

(1) A Committee for Assisting the Return of Displaced Civilians is hereby established. It shall be composed of four (4) officers of field grade, two (2) of whom shall be appointed by the Commander-in-Chief, United Nations Command, and two (2) of whom shall be appointed jointly by the Supreme Commander of the Korean People's Army and the Commander of the Chinese People's Volunteers. This Committee shall, under the general supervision and direction of the Military Armistice Commission, be responsible for co-ordinating the specific plans of both sides for assistance to the return of the above-mentioned civilians, and for supervising the execution by both sides of all the provisions of this Armistice Agreement relating to the return of the above-mentioned civilians. It shall be the duty of this Commission to make necessary arrangements, including those of transportation, for expediting and co-ordinating the movement of the above mentioned civilians; to select the crossing point(s) through which the above-mentioned civilians will cross the Military Demarcation Line; to arrange for security at the crossing point(s); and to carry such other functions as are required to accomplish the return of the above-mentioned civilians.

(2) When unable to reach agreement on any matter relating to its responsibilities, the Committee for Assisting the Return of Displaced Civilians shall immediately refer such matter to the Military Armistice Commission for decision. The Committee for Assisting the Return of Displaced Civilians shall maintain its headquarters in proximity to the headquarters of the Military Armistice Commission.

(3) The Committee for Assisting the Return of Displaced Civilians shall be dissolved by the Military Armistice Commission upon fulfilment of its mission.

ARTICLE IV

RECOMMENDATION TO THE GOVERNMENTS CONCERNED ON BOTH SIDES

60. In order to ensure the peaceful settlement of the Korean question, the military Commanders of both sides hereby recommend to the Governments of the countries concerned on both sides that, within three (3) months after the Armistice Agreement is signed and becomes effective, a political conference of a higher level of both sides be held by representatives appointed respectively to settle through negotiation the questions of the withdrawal of all foreign forces from Korea, the peaceful settlement of the Korean question, &c.

ARTICLE V

MISCELLANEOUS

61. Amendments and additions to this Armistice Agreement must be mutually agreed to by the Commanders of the opposing sides.

62. The Articles and Paragraphs of this Armistice Agreement shall remain in effect until expressly superseded either by mutually acceptable amendments and additions or by provision in an appropriate agreement for a peaceful settlement at a political level between both sides.

63. All of the provisions of this Armistice Agreement, other than paragraphs 12, shall become effective at 2200 hours on July 27 1953.

Done at Panmunjom, Korea, at 1000 hours on the 27th day of July, 1953, in English, Korean, and Chinese, all texts being equally authentic.

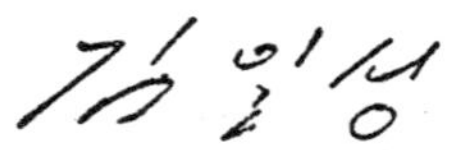

KIM IL SUNG

Marshal, Democratic People's Republic of Korea.
Supreme Commander Korean People's Army.

PENG TEH-HUAI

Commander,Chinese People's Volunteers.

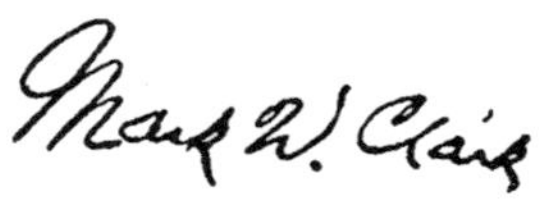

MARK W. CLARK

General, United States Army.
Commander-in-Chief, United Nations Command.

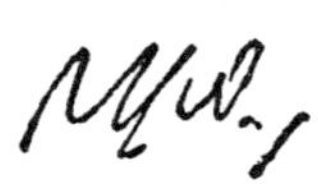

NAM IL

General, Korean People's Army.
Senior Delegate, Delegation of the Korean
People's Army and the Chinese People's Volunteers.

WILLIAM K. HARRISON, JR.

Lieutenant-General, United States Army.
Senior Delegate, United Nations Command Delegation.

ANNEX

TERMS OF REFERENCE FOR NEUTRAL NATIONS REPATRIATIONS

COMMISSION (SEE SUB-PARAGRAPH 51 (B))

I. GENERAL

1. In order to ensure that all prisoners of war have the opportunity to exercise their rights to be repatriated following an armistice, Sweden, Switzerland, Poland, Czechoslovakia and India shall each be requested by both sides to appoint a member of a Neutral Nations Repatriation Commission which shall be established to take custody in Korea of those prisoners of war who, while in the custody of the detaining Powers, have not exercised their right to be repatriated. The Neutral Nations Repatriation Commission shall establish its headquarters within the Demilitarised Zone in the vicinity of Panmunjom, and shall station subordinate bodies of the same composition as the Neutral Nations Repatriation Commission at those locations at which the Repatriation Commission assumes custody of prisoners of war. Representatives of both sides shall be permitted to observe the operations of the Repatriation Commission at those locations at which the Repatriation Commission assumes custody of prisoners of war. Representatives of both sides shall be permitted to observe the operations of the Repatriation Commission and its subordinate bodies to include explanations and interviews.

2. Sufficient armed forces and any other operating personnel required to assist the Neutral Nations Repatriation Commission in carrying out its functions and responsibilities shall be provided exclusively by India, whose representative shall be the umpire in accordance with the provisions of Article 132 of the Geneva Convention, and shall also be chairman and executive agent of the Neutral Nations Repatriation Commission. Representatives from each of the other four Powers shall be allowed staff assistants in equal number not to exceed fifty (50) each. When any of the representative of the neutral nations is absent for some reason, that representative shall designate an alternate representative of his own nationality to exercise his functions and authority. The aims of all personnel provided for in this paragraph shall be limited to military police type small arms.

3. No force or threat of force shall be used against the prisoners of war specified in paragraph 1 above to present or effect their repatriation, and no violence to their persons or affront to their dignity or self-respect shall be permitted in nay manner for any purpose whatsoever (but see

paragraph 7 below). This duty is enjoined on and entrusted to the Neutral Nations Repatriation Commission. This Commission shall ensure that prisoners of war shall at all times be treated humanely in accordance with the specific provisions of the Geneva Convention, and with the general spirit of that Convention.

II. CUSTODY OF PRISONERS OF WAR

4. All prisoners of war who have not exercised their right of repatriation following the effective date of the Armistice Agreement shall be released from the military control and from the custody of the detaining side as soon as practicable, and, in all cases, within sixty (60) days subsequent to the effective date of the Armistice Agreement to the Neutral Repatriation Commission at locations in Korea to be designated by the detaining side.

5. At the time the Neutral Nations Repatriation Commission assumes control of the prisoner-of-war installations, the military forces of the detaining side shall be withdrawn therefrom, so that the locations specified in the proceding paragraph shall be taken over completely by the armed forces of India.

6. Notwithstanding the provisions of paragraph 5 above, the detaining side shall be the responsibility for maintaining and ensuring security and order in the areas around the locations where the prisoners of war are in custody and for preventing and restraining any armed forces (including irregular armed forces) in the area under its control from any acts of disturbance and intrusion against the locations where the prisoners of war are in custody.

7. Notwithstanding the provisions of paragraph 3 above, nothing in this agreement shall be construed as derogating from the authority of the Neutral Nations Repatriation Commission to exercise its legitimate functions and responsibilities for the control of the prisoners of war under its temporary jurisdiction.

III. EXPLANATION

8. The Neutral Nations Repatriation Commission, after having received and taken into custody all those prisoners of war who have not exercised their right to be repatriated, shall immediately make arrangements so that, within ninety (90) days after the Neutral Nations Repatriation Commission takes over the custody, the nations to which the prisoners of war belong shall have freedom and facilities to send

representatives to the locations where such prisoners of war are in custody to explain to all the prisoners of war depending upon these nations their rights and to inform them of any matters relating to their return to their homelands, particularly of their full freedom to return home to lead a peaceful life, under the following provisions:-

(a) The number of such explaining representatives shall not exceed seven (7) per thousand prisoners of war held in custody by the Neutral Nations Repatriation Commission; and the minimum authorised shall not be less than a total of five (5);

(b) The hours during which the explaining representatives shall have access to the prisoners shall be a determined by the Neutral Nations Repatriation Commission, and generally in accord with Article 53 of the Geneva Convention Relative to the Treatment of Prisoners of War;

(c) All explanations and interviews shall be conducted in the presence of a representative of each member nation of the Neutral Nations Repatriation Commission and a representative from the detaining side;

(d) Additional provisions governing the explanation work shall be prescribed by the Neutral Nations Repatriation Commission, and will be designed to employ the principles enumerated in paragraph 3 above and in this paragraph;

(e) The explaining representatives, while engaging in their work, shall be allowed to bring with them necessary facilities and personnel for wireless communications. The number of communications personnel shall be limited to one team per location at which explaining representatives are in residence, except in the event all prisoners of war are concentrated in one location, in which case, two (2) teams shall be permitted. Each team shall consist of not more than six (6) communications personnel.

9. Prisoners of war in its custody shall have freedom and facilities to make representation and communications to the Neutral Nations Repatriation Commission and to representatives and subordinate bodies of the Neutral Nations Repatriation Commission and to inform them of their desires on any matters concerning the prisoners of war themselves, in accordance with arrangements made for the purpose by the Neutral Nations Repatriation Commission.

IV. DISPOSITION OF PRISONERS OF WAR

10. Any prisoner of war who, while in the custody of the Neutral Nations Repatriation Commission, decides to exercise the right of repatriation, shall make an application requesting repatriation to a body consisting of a representative of each member nation of the Neutral Nations Repatriation Commission. Once such an application is made, it shall be considered immediately by the Neutral Nations Repatriation Commission or one of its subordinate bodies so as to determine immediately by majority vote the validity of such application. Once such an application is made to and validated by the Commission or one of its subordinate bodies, the prisoner of war concerned shall immediately be transferred to and accommodated in the tents set up for those who are ready to be repatriated. Thereafter, he shall, while still in the custody of the Neutral Nations Repatriation Commission, be delivered forthwith to the prisoner of war exchange point at Panmunjom for repatriation under the procedure prescribed in the Armistice Agreement.

11. At the expiration of ninety (90) days after the transfer of custody of the prisoners of war to the Neutral Nations Repatriation Commission, access of representatives to captured personnel as provided for in paragraph 8 above, shall terminate, and the question of disposition of the prisoners of war who have not exercised their right to be repatriated shall be submitted to the Political Conference recommended to be convened in paragraph 60, Draft Armistice Agreement, which shall endeavour to settle this question within thirty (30) days, during which period the Neutral Nations Repatriation Commission shall continue to retain custody of those prisoners of war. The Neutral Nations Repatriation Commission shall declare the relief from the prisoner of war status to civilian status of any prisoners of war who have not exercised their right to be repatriated and from whom no other disposition has been agreed to by the Political Conference with one hundred and twenty (120) days after the Neutral Nations Repatriation Commission has assumed their custody. Thereafter, according to the application of each individual, those who choose to go to neutral nations shall be assisted by the Neutral Nations Repatriation Commission and the Red Cross Society of India. This operation shall be completed within thirty (30) days, and upon its completion, the Neutral Nations Repatriation Commission shall immediately cease its functions and declare its dissolution. After the dissolution of the Neutral Nations Repatriation Commission, whenever and wherever any of those above-mentioned civilians who have been

relieved from the prisoner of war status desire to return to their fatherlands, the authorities of the localities where they are shall be responsible for assisting them in returning to their fatherlands.

V. RED CROSS VISITATION

12. Essential Red Cross service for prisoners of war in custody of the Neutral Nations Repatriation Commission shall be provided by India in accordance with regulations issued by the Neutral Nations Repatriation Commission.

VI. PRESS COVERAGE

13. The Neutral Nations Repatriation Commission shall ensure freedom of the press and other news media in observing the entire operation as enumerated herein, in accordance with procedures to be established by the Neutral Nations Repatriation Commission.

VII. LOGISTICAL SUPPORT FOR PRISONERS OF WAR

14. Each side shall provide logistical support for the prisoners of war in the area under its military control, delivering required support to the Neutral Nations Repatriation Commission at an agreed deliver point in the vicinity of each prisoner of war installation.
15. The cost of repatriating prisoners of war to the exchange point at Panmunjom shall be borne by the detaining side and the cost from the exchange point by the side on which said prisoners depend, in accordance with Article 118 of the Geneva Convention.

16. The Red Cross Society of India shall be responsible for providing such general service personnel in the prisoner of war installations as required by the Neutral Nations Repatriation Commission.

17. The Neutral Nations Repatriation Commission shall provide medical support for the prisoners of war as may be practicable. The detaining side shall provide medical support as practicable upon the request of the Neutral Nations Repatriation Commission and specifically for those cases requiring extensive treatment or hospitalisation. The Neutral Nations Repatriation Commission shall maintain custody of prisoners of war during such hospitalisation. The detaining side shall facilitate such custody. Upon completion of treatment, prisoners of war shall be returned to a prisoner of war installation as specified in paragraph 4 above.

18. The Neutral Nations Repatriation Commission is entitled to obtain from both sides such legitimate assistance as it may require in carrying out its duties and tasks, but both sides shall not under any name and in any form interfere or exert influence.

VIII. LOGISTIC SUPPORT FOR THE NEUTRAL NATIONS REPATRIATION COMMISSION

19. Each side shall be responsible for providing logistical support for the personnel of the Neutral Nations Repatriation Commission stationed in the area under its military control, and both sides shall contribute on an equal basis to such support within the Demilitarised Zone. The precise arrangements shall be subject to determination between the Neutral Nations Repatriation Commission and the detaining side in each case.

20. Each of the detaining sides shall be responsible for protecting the explaining representatives from the other side while in transit over lines of communication within its area, as set forth in paragraph 23 for the Neutral Nations Repatriation Commission, to a place of residence and while in residence in the vicinity of, but not within each of, the locations where the prisoners of war are in custody. The Neutral Nations Repatriation Commission shall be responsible for the security of such representatives within the actual limits of the locations where the prisoners of war are in custody.

21. Each of the detaining sides shall provide transportation, housing, communication, and other agreed logistical support to the explaining representatives of the other side while they are in the area under its military control. Such services shall be provided on a reimbursable basis.

IX. PUBLICATION

22. After the Armistice Agreement becomes effective, the terms of this agreement shall be made known to all prisoners of war who, while in the custody of the detaining side, have not exercised their right to be repatriated.

X. MOVEMENT

23. The movement of the personnel of the Neutral Nations Repatriation Commission and repatriated prisoners of war shall be over lines of communication as determined by the command(s) of the opposing side

and the Neutral Nations Repatriation Commission. A map showing these lines of communication shall be furnished by the command of the opposing side and the Neutral Nations Repatriation Commission. Movement of such personnel, except within locations as designated in paragraph 4 above, shall be under the control of, and escorted by, personnel of the side in whose area the travel is being undertaken; however, such movement shall be subject to any obstruction and coercion.

XI. PROCEDURAL MATTERS

24. The interpretation of this agreement shall rest with the Neutral Nations Repatriation Commission. The Neutral Nations Repatriation Commission, and/or any subordinate bodies to which functions are delegated or assigned by the Neutral Nations Repatriation Commission, shall operate on the basis of majority vote.

25. The Neutral Nations Repatriation Commission shall submit a weekly report to the opposing Commanders on the status of prisoners of war in its custody, indicating the numbers repatriated and remaining at the end of each week.

26. When this agreement has been acceded to by both sides and by the five Powers named herein, it shall become effective upon the date the Armistice becomes effective.

NAM IL
General, Korean People's Army.
Senior Delegate, Delegation of the Korean People's Army and the Chinese People's Volunteers.

WILLIAM K. HARRISON, Jr.
Lieutenant-General, United States Army.
Senior Delegate, United Nations Command Delegation.

TEMPORARY AGREEMENT SUPPLEMENTARY TO THE ARMISTICE AGREEMENT

In order to meet the requirements of the disposition of the prisoners of war not for direct repatriation in accordance with the provisions of the Terms of Reference for Neutral Nations Repatriation Commission, the Commander-in-Chief, United Nations Command, on the one hand,

and the Supreme Commander of the Korean People's Army and the Commander of the Chinese People's Volunteers on the other hand, in pursuance of the provisions in paragraph 61, Article V, of the Agreement concerning a military armistice in Korea, agree to conclude the following Temporary Agreement supplementary to the Armistice Agreement:-

1. Under the provisions of paragraph 4 and 5, Article II of the Terms of Reference for Neutral Nations Repatriation Commission, the United Nations Command has the right to designate the area between the Military Demarcation Line and the eastern and southern boundaries of the Demilitarised Zone between the Imjin River on the south and the road leading south from Okum-ni on the north-east (the main road leading south-east from Panmunjom not included), as the area within which the United Nations Command will turn over the prisoners of war, who are not directly repatriated and whom the above-mentioned areas of custody designated respectively by a certain number of armed forces of the detaining sides to the above-mentioned areas of custody designated respectively by both sides to be turned over to the Neutral Nations Repatriation Commission and the armed forces of India for custody. After the prisoners of war have been taken over, the armed forces of the detaining sides shall be withdrawn immediately from the areas of custody to the areas under the control of their own side.

(c) The personnel of the Neutral Nations Repatriation Commission and its subordinate bodies, the armed forces of India, the Red Cross Society of India, the explaining representatives and observation representative of both sides, as well as the required material and equipment, for exercising the functions provided for the Terms of Reference for Neutral Nations Repatriation Commission shall be specifically authorised by the Military Armistice Commission to have the complete freedom of movement to, from, and within the above-mentioned areas designated respectively by both sides for the custody of prisoners of war.

4. The provisions of sub-paragraph 3 (c) of this agreement shall not be construed as derogating from the privileges enjoyed by those personnel mentioned above under paragraph 11, Article I, of the Armistice Agreement.

5. This Agreement shall be abrogated upon the completion of the mission provided for in the Terms of Reference for Neutral Nations Repatriation Commission.

Done at Panmunjom, Korea, at 1000 hours
on the 27th day of July, 1953,
in English, Korean and Chinese, all texts
being equally authentic.

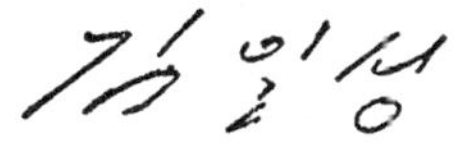

KIM IL SUNG
Marshal, Democratic People's Republic of Korea.
Supreme Commander Korean People's Army.

PENG TEH-HUAI
Commander, Chinese People's Volunteers.

MARK W. CLARK
General, United States Army.
Commander-in-Chief, United Nations Command.

NAM IL
General, Korean People's Army.
Senior Delegate, Delegation of the Korean
People's Army and the Chinese People's Volunteers.

WILLIAM K. HARRISON, JR.
Lieutenant-General, United States Army.
Senior Delegate, United Nations Command Delegation.

APPENDIX L

Prisoners of War Exchange, Little Switch and Big Switch

National Origin	LITTLE SWITCH	BIG SWITCH	TOTAL
United States	149	3,597	3,746
Republic of Korea	471	7,862	8,321
British Commonwealth :			
Australia	5	21	26
Canada	2	30	32
New Zealand	-	1	1
South Africa	1	8	9
United Kingdom	32	946	978
Belgium	-	1	1
Colombia	6	22	28
France	-	12	12
Greece	1	2	3
Netherlands	1	2	3
Philippines	1	40	41
Turkey	15	229	244
Total UNITED NATIONS FORCES :	**684**	**12,773**	**13,457**
North Korea	5,640	70,183	75,823
China	1,030	5,640	6,670
Total COMMUNIST FORCES :	**6,670**	**75,823**	**82,493**

Notes

1. North Korean totals include 9,350 civilians interned including 23 children. Of the remaining prisoners of war, 491 were women.

2. Chinese prisoners included one woman.

3. The Canadian figures do not include Sqn-Ldr A R McKenzie RCAF, who was held in China until 5th December 1954, when he was released through Hong Kong.

4. 22,604 North Korean and Chinese prisoners held by the United Nations opted initially not to be repatriated. Of these, 188 North Koreans and 440 Chinese decided to return to their own side, 15 and 23 respectively died while still under Indian custodial control, 12 and 74 elected to settle in India. Finally:

7,604 North Koreans } elected to return to UN control,
14,235 Chinese } the Koreans ultimately passing to the Republic of Korea, the Chinese to the Kuomintang in Taiwan.

5. Among the UN prisoners in the Communist Camps, 359 held by the Communists declined repatriation (335 ROK, 23 US, 1 UK). After discussions within the custodial system, 325 Koreans, 21 Americans, and 1 Briton elected to stay with the Communist side, though the latter elected later to leave China of his own accord to return home. Of the balance, 2 Koreans elected to go to India, 8 Koreans and 2 Americans returned to the United Nations side.

APPENDIX M

British Prisoners of War in Korea

	RN	RM	ARMY	RAF	TOTAL
Repatriated	4	18*	955	1	978
Known to have died as a PW	-	9†	62	-	71
Presumed to have died as a PW	-	1	9	-	11
TOTAL IDENTIFED AS HAVING BEEN TAKEN PRISONER:					**1,060**

* This figure excludes the Royal Marine who opted to remain with the Communist side.
† Includes members of the Royal Navy—for example, sick berth attendants—serving with the Royal Marines.

Notes

1. Those 'Known to have died as prisoners' were identified as such by prisoners repatriated.

2. Those 'Presumed to have died...' were identified as having been alive when captured but who were neither declared thereafter by the Communist side nor known of by other UN prisoners of war.

APPENDIX N

The Korean Operations Pool Account (KOPA)

When the Korean War broke out in 1950, the residual element of the original British Commonwealth Occupation Force (BCOF) in Japan was provided by Australia. As remarked in Volume I, this included a small military and air base on which the British Government proposed to rely as soon as it agreed to contribute land forces to the United Nations Command in Korea. This concept was acceptable to the Australian authorities, but it was made apparent that such an arrangement would require to be put on a proper financial footing: in addition to providing substantial increments to the base facilities, the United Kingdom would be billed for its consumption of Australian resources. While discussions were proceeding as to a mutually acceptable accounting system, the Australian Commander-in-Chief, BCOF, proposed a simple system whereby each nation should pay on the basis of the number of its *land* forces involved on a daily basis. The arrangement was accepted by Australia, Britain and, as Kayforce was committed, by New Zealand equally. The Korean Operations Pool Account was opened accordingly.

Payment was to be made in sterling, the three nations being members of the sterling area. However, it rapidly became clear that the United States would be providing essentially certain items to the KOPA members for payment in dollars, of which all were short, none more so than the United Kingdom, responsible for sterling balances throughout the world. It was agreed that KOPA should run a special dollar account to be funded on the same basis of paying its share consonant with its numbers on a man/day basis; payment to be effected at some future date.

The arrangements overall were notified throughout British Commonwealth Forces in Korea (which included the base in Japan) in General Routine Orders Serial 27 on 5th June 1951, as follows:

188. KOREAN OPERATIONS POOL ACCOUNT
(a) The following is circulated for general information.
Instructions for any action necessary within the Theatre in connection with the Pool Account have been or will be issued separately.

(b) The UK, Australian and New Zealand Gcvernment have agreed that the cost of maintenance of their contingents cf BCFK will be pooled and split between them in prportion to the size of the contingents. The commencing date for this arrangement has not yet been fixed but a date in 1950 is probable and in dealing with current matters it should be assumed that the Pool is already in force.

(c) The Canadian and Indian Governments are believed to be considering the matter but have not yet agreed to join the Pool. For Pool accounting purposes, therefore, transactions with Canadian and Indian contingents must continue to be reorded in the same manner as transactions with other UN Forces. BCOF are outside the Pool. (GRO 172 dated 22 May 51 refers.)

(d) Brief particulars of the Pol are as follows:-

Pay and Allowances
(i) Each of the Govts concerned will be directly responsible for the pay and allowances of its own forces.

Amenities
(ii) Cash grants from public funds for the maintenance or supplementation of amenities provided in kind will be the direct responsibility of the Govt concerned.

Transport of Troops
(iii) The cost of transport of all troops including reinforcements to and from the Theatre is to be a direct responsibility of the parent Govt concerned.

Cost of Initial Equipment
(iv) Each of the Govts concerned is to bear the direct cost of the initial personal and unit equipment of its contingent up to scales laid down in its war equipment tables and cost of transport thereof to and from the Theatre.

Stores etc for Maitenance
(v) The value of all stores and supplies, other than those detailed in the last preceding paragraph, which are sent to the Theatre, or otherwise obtained for the maintenance of the Force and the cost of the transport thereof, is to be charged to the Pool Account.

Barrack Stores etc
(vi) All barrack stores and all mess furniture and equipment other than that included in unit equipment are to be treated as maintenance stores and charged to the Pool Account.

Local Procurement
(vii) Expenditure incurred locally on works services, local purchase of stores, and services generally, will be charged to the Pool Account.

Local Civilian Labour
(viii) The cost of local civilian labour will be charged to the Pool Account.

> *Accounting*
> (ix) The Pool Account is to be compiled by the Australian Treasury, but a certain amount of information will be required from the Theatre to support entries in the Account. It is envisaged that the cost of stores, supplies etc will be sent to the Theatre and costs of transport thereof will be reported direct by the Govts concerned to the Australian Treasury. This includes stores etc of Australian origin supplied by BCOF. Local expenditure will be reported directly through Chief Paymaster BCOF to MELBOURNE. Stores, supplies and services received from US or other UN Forces will eventually become a charge against the Pool. Stores, supplies and services supplied for other UN Frces will eventually become a credit to the Pool. Payments for services rendered to NAAFI or other non-entitled bodies or for payment issues to officers and OR, and other similar items will become a credit to the Pool. The value of stores sent out of the Theatre will become a credit to the Pool. Some check on the equipment holdings of units arriving in or leaving the Theatre will be necessary.
>
> *Sharing of Pool Account Costs*
> (x) The total of the Pool Account is to be apportioned between the participating Govts on a percentage basis. The percentages are to be calculated by comparing the total of the establishments authorised for units, formations etc, for which each Govt has assumed responsibility, with the total establishment of the Force. The percentages are to be adjusted on each major alteration to the constitution of the Force. In the case of the UK contingent it is anticipated that the necessary calculations will be made by the War Office.

Canada joined KOPA on 29th July 1951. Being a member of the dollar area, she was less reluctant to settle dollar debts than her Commonwealth associates, and indeed urged prompt settlements, which they considered unwise; for all wished to postpone for as long as possible settlement of dollar debts.

These had been mounting principally in the supply of petrol, oil and lubricants, rations (intermittently), engineer stores, and air transportation services. All the Commonwealth contingents drew on the United States for the 3.5-inch rocket launcher. The Canadian Government incurred charges widely for weapons spares and ammunition due to their use of American equipment.

Some compromise on settlement was agreed in that sterling balances were cleared on a regular basis. Canada settled her dollar debts directly with Washington, Otherwise, the United States was content to stand her account over until the war had concluded. By 1955, the three Commonwealth partners were anxious to settle. A huge bill was then presented by the financial offices in the Pentagon and Fort MacNair which exceeded all expectations. It was soon discovered that it related to Commowealth naval and air units in addition to the land forces embraced by KOPA. There were, moreover, claims of a very general nature, notably in the supply of petrol, oil and lubricants, and a special agreement concerning charges in this particular had been overlooked by the United States. Capitation charges had been made on the false assumption that Commonwealth units were of the same size as its American counterpart. Items already charged to and paid for by the Canadian contingent were again being charged. The three KOPA members had also to admit among themselves that, in seeking to rebut many of the claims, the bills and other vouchers had long been destroyed, and their accounting procedures had not provided for the system of supply and demand, 'open house' as one of the senior American delegates to the later conferences described it.

Negotiations continued into 1958 into what the Comptroller of the United States Army Budget described as 'a can of worms'.

Finally, settlement figures were agreed upon which involved a reduction for the Army claims from US$ 81.68 million to 68.40 million. This was later adjusted to 62.77 million.

If nothing else, KOPA had operated to the benefit of its members in the matter of sterling payments. It had also provided sufficient material to enable its representatives negotiating the dollar settlements to bargain successfully.

Sources
Australia: See KOPA papers in CA46, A2111, and CA 68, A649 (Mitchell, ACT).
New Zealand: Some notes on the Korean Operations Pool Account by Brigadier E A Pope and Lieutenant Colonel W J Crosby.

APPENDIX P

British Casualties in the Korean Theatre of War

	RN		RM		ARMY		RAF	
	Offrs	OR	Offrs	OR	Offrs	OR	Offrs	OR
Killed/died	26	18	2	28	98	879	12	15
TOTAL DEATHS : 1,078								
Wounded	5	14	3	63	185	2,404	-*	-*
TOTAL WOUNDED : 2,674								

Notes

1. The figures of those killed/died include deaths of those 'Missing presumed killed', 'Missing presumed died as a prisoner of war', those who died of wounds or from battle accidents.

2. Those who died of wounds in the Royal Navy include one Chinese locally employed.

3. Items marked * for the Royal Air Force indicate that no figures are available for wounds.

KOREA SOURCE DOCUMENT

Source Documents and Bibliography

Source Documents

United Kingdom

In the United Kingdom, the author has had unrestricted access to the files of all Departments of State and ministries involved directly or indirectly in the events of the Korean War. In so far as this volume is concerned, these were:

Cabinet Office
Lord Chancellor
Foreign Office
Colonial Office, Commonwealth Relations Office, and Dominions Office
Treasury
Ministry of Defence
Admiralty } subordinated to the Ministry of
War Office } Defence but still operating as
Air Ministry } individual departments of state.
Ministry of Supply
Board of Trade
Ministry of Transport
Attorney-General

Legislation now permits me to mention that I have also had full access to the material held by:

SIS
Security Service
GCHQ

The process of selecting records to be permanently preserved which is carried out in all Government Departments has, in respect of the records relating to the United Kingdom's participation in the war, inevitably left some gaps. Rationalisation of working papers, for example, has resulted in the reduction of the Chiefs of Staff working papers after Volume 21 to the minutes of the Chiefs' meetings in bound volumes. However, as these indicate, once the armistice talks began and the battle line became stabilised from June 1951, meetings devoted to or principally occupied by national or international aspects of the war were no longer required.

Prior to that, the volumes, originally under the series reference G/Kor/volume number, contain a continuous picture of the Chiefs' interest and involvement in, and responses to, the running of the war, and include connected 'diptels', the Foreign and Commonwealth Relations Offices telegrams. In order to obviate the need for the researcher in the Public Record Office to call initially at least for numbers of departmental documents concurrently, many of the early source notes in this volume locate associated telegrams and occasionally other items with the minutes of the Chiefs' meetings in the appropriate volume of the G/Kor/ series.

However, for any detailed study of British policy during the period it will be necessary to consult bound volumes of the telegrams contained in the Foreign and Commonwealth Relations Offices' records and associated papers in, for example, the files of the Far Eastern Department. These carry forward also the essentials of the Defence Department picture for the period following Volume 21 of the Chiefs of Staff working papers. The run of these telegrams, minutes and other papers, relating to overseas policy connected with Korea, have been fully preserved and are contained in the Public Record Office under the series references following. The only exceptions are the selected overseas and defence policy documents witheld from public view. I have had full access to and taken account of this class.

Minutes of Cabinet and Cabinet Committee meetings, including preparatory papers for agenda items, have all been preserved and the series in which they are to be found are shown below. The same applies to records of standing inter-departmental committees or those formed to deal with business arising from the war.

Service unit and command diaries have been preserved intact with minor exceptions. For example, there is no war diary for 1st Battalion, The Gloucestershire Regiment, during the month of April 1951. It had not been finalised by me, as the adjutant, when the battalion was broken up in the Imjin battle of 22nd–25th April. Another unit's diary was lost by fire. Another one, at least, was lost in the postal system. It may be helpful to point out that war diaries are not hour to hour records. A naval Report of Proceedings or the war diary of an Army unit in the field is sometimes made up daily, more often once a week or month. Both forms are based on the unit's operations log complemented by notes, copies of signals, annotated charts or maps, together with copies of administrative returns rendered to higher headquarters—for example, the names of officers and the numbers by trade and duty of other ranks on strength or temporarily absent, are attached to all Army war diaries when they are rendered monthly.

Copies of Reports of Proceedings for all Commonwealth warships, and the war diaries of all Commonwealth land force units, are held in the United Kingdom Public Record Office, though these do not include all attached papers for Australian, Canadian, and New Zealand units. On this account, some of the references to these records relate to the originals in the national archives of the Commonwealth country concerned.

Series References

Prime Minister's Office	PREM 3 PREM 8 PREM 11
Cabinet Office	CAB 21 CAB 65 CAB 66 CAB 69 CAB 79 CAB 80 CAB 84 CAB 99 CAB 120 CAB 124 CAB 126 CAB 128 CAB 129 CAB 130 CAB 131 CAB 133 CAB 134 CAB 139
Foreign Office Commonwealth Relations Office	FO 371 [Far Eastern Department 1950–1953] FO 800
Dominions Office	DO 35
Colonial Office	CO 537
Defence departments	DEFE 4 DEFE 5 DEFE 7 DEFE 10 DEFE 11 DEFE 33
	ADM 1 ADM 116 ADM 167

Defence departments *(Continued)*	WO 32 WO 36 WO 163 WO 193 WO 203 WO 208 WO 216 WO 242 WO 259 WO 281 WP 308
	AIR 8 AIR 19 AIR 20 AIR 27 AIR 28
Treasury	T171/397–402
Board of Trade	BT 11

Commonwealth

Thanks to the generosity of the Australian and Canadian Governments, I have had access to their archives containing ministerial, external affairs, and defence documents. I exclude New Zealand because I have had access to their documents by correspondence; and latterly have had the benefit of the work presented by the New Zealand historian for the period, Mr Ian McGibbon. Principal series references to Australia and Canada are shown below.

Australia

Mitchell, ACT (Political, External Affairs, Defence, and Treasury)	CA 12 CA 18 CA 46 CA 68 A2111
Australian War Memorial, Canberra, (War diaries, BCOF, Defence Committee, Naval History, Professor O'Neill's papers)	ACT AWM 85 AWM 89 AWM 114 AWM 123 AWM 124
Defence Archives and Historical Section, Russell, ACT (Joint Administrative Plans)	JAPC agenda and reports, 1951–53

Canada

Public Archives, Ottawa –	
Political and External Affairs	RG 2
War diaries	RG 24 (17)
Naval History series	1480
	1650
	1926
Naval Reports of Proceedings	

NB. During the writing of both volumes of this history, many Canadian state papers relating to the Korean War were still held in the records of the Departments of National Defence and External Affairs, eg DofEA 8254, 1941–51.

United States of America

I have enjoyed extensive access to United States archives.

The complete range of documents quoted selectively in the State Departments's official publications under the general title, *Foreign Affairs of the United States*, is available in the National Archive on Pennsylvania Avenue, Washington, DC. The National Security Council papers are in the same location in the series RG 273.

The Joint Chiefs of Staff files (at Suitland, Maryland, during the period of my research), are contained in a series of case files under the prefix 'CCS' (Combined Chiefs of Staff), with which are associated notes and memoranda by the Chairman and members, and copies of documents relating to action on matters such as Presidential or National Security Council decisions.

The Army records at the same site overlap between the extensive sets of series. They are not therefore listed. The researcher would be advised to decide to seek first a *resumé* of a particular item or period of interest in the form of the army or corps 'journal' or the monthly summary of events, or to ask directly for the formation or unit war diary concerned, with which will be connected orders and message files. These are not always continuous as lower levels for the same reasons that apply to British war diaries. Intelligence information ranges from immediate contact or observation reports to the specialist productions of the Allied Translator and Interpreter Section following, for example, prisoner-of-war interrogations. At the high levels—GHQ in Tokyo and in Headquarters Eighth Army—journals, chiefs of staff memoranda etc, supplement the picture of policy making, reaction to events, and the day to day working of the commander and his staff.

Further information is available in personal papers (and some official papers retained by senior commanders) at the following sites:

US Army Military History, Fort Carlise, Pennsylvania.
Lieutenant-General Edward M. Almond—papers and oral history.
General Matthew B Ridgway—personal papers.
Brigadier-General Haydon L. Boatner—personal papers.
General Mark W. Clark—personal papers.
Major-General Bruce C. Clarke—personal papers.
Brigadier-General S L A Marshall—papers on the Korean War.
Lieutenant-General John W. O'Daniel—personal papers
General Maxwell D. Taylor—personal papers.

Douglas MacArthur Memorial Library, Norfolk, Virginia.
This contains the MacArthur Memorial Bureau Archives, including both the General's extensive official, demi-official, and personal papers, and those of his personal staff. Of note are:

SCAP Records, 1947–51	RG 5
GHQ, Far East Command records, 1947–51	RG 6
Signals collection, 1945–51,	RG 9
Personal letters, 1932–64	RG 10

Dwight D. Eisenhower Presidential Library, Abilene, Kansas

Eisenhower papers

The full range of United States Navy Records was made available to me in the Navy Yard, Washington, DC; and likewise those of the United States Marine Corps, through the Historical Division of the Corps Headquarters. A comprehensive range of subject lists provides the researcher with an immediate choice of opening. Considerable additional naval material, including oral histories, is held at the United Naval Institute, Annapolis, Maryland.

A range of valuable material on the Korean War, supplementary to that in the Army archive, is held similarly by the Office of the Chief of Military History in Washington, DC.

The records of the United States Air Force are located at Bolling Air Force Base and, as with the other Services, offers entry by subjects, notably units, policies, operations, manpower, logistics, and tehnology. It contains a range of personal papers including those of Generals O P Weyland and George E. Stratemeyer, and Hoyt Vandenberg.

Official Publications

UNITED KINGDOM

Farrar-Hockley, Anthony, *The British Part in the Korean War, Volume I: A Distant Obligation* (HMSO, 1990)

Yasamee, H.J. and K.A. Hamilton with Isabel Warner and Ann Lane, *Documents on British Policy Overseas, Series II, Volume IV, Korea, 1950–1951* (HMSO, 1991)

Naval Staff History, *British Commonwealth Naval Operations, Korea, 1950–53* (Ministry of Defence, 1967)

Defence Programme, Statement by the Prime Minister in the House of Commons on Monday, 29th January, 1951 (Cmd. 8146) (HMSO, 1951)

Further Summary of Events relating to Korea, October 1950 to May 1951, (Cmd 8366) (HMSO, 1951)

Report on the Proceedings of ther Sixth Session of the General Assembly of the United Nations held at Paris, 5th November 1951–4th February 1952 [with Annexes] (Cmd 8547] (HMSO, 1952)

Documents relating to the Discussion of Korea and Indo-China at the Geneva Conference, 27 April–15 June 1954. Miscellaneous No 16 (HMSO, London, 1954)

Linklater, Eric, *Our Men in Korea* (HMSO, 1952)

Treatment of British Prisoners of War in Korea (HMSO, 1955)

To All Returning Prisoners of War from Korea British Army, (The War Office D.P.S., June 1953)

AUSTRALIA

O'Neill, Robert, *Australia in the Korean War* (Australian War Memorial, Canberra)

Volume I : *Strategy and Diplomacy* (1981)

Volume II: *Combat Operations* (1985)

CANADA

Thorgrimsson, Thor and E.C. Russell, *Canadian Naval Operations in Korean Waters, 1950–55* (Department of National Defence, Ottawa, 1965)

Wood, Lieutenant-Colonel Herbert Fairlie Wood, *Strange Battleground, Operations in Korea and their effects on the Defence Policy of Canada* (Department of National Defence, Ottawa, 1966)

DEMOCRATIC PEOPLE'S REPUBLIC OF KOREA

Documents and Materials Exposing the Instigators of the Civil War *in Korea* (Ministry of Foreign Affairs, P'yongyang, 1950)

INDIA

Prasad, S N, ed. B Chakravorty, *History of the Custodian Force (India) in Korea 1953–54* (New Delhi, 1976)

NEW ZEALAND

Ian McGibbon, *New Zealand and the Korean War, Volume I: Policy and Diplomacy* (OUP, Melbourne, 1991)

REPUBLIC OF KOREA

The History of the United Nations Forces in the Korean War, six volumes (Ministry of National Defence, Seoul, 1973)

UNITED STATES OF AMERICA

Schnabel, James F and Robert Watson, *The Joint Chief of Staff and National Policy* (1979), volume 3 in the series, *The History of the Joint Chiefs of Staff* (Wilmington)

United States Naval History Division

Field, James A, *History of the United States Naval Operations, Korea* (Washington, DC, 1962)

Headquarters, United States Marine Corps, Historical Division

Meid, Lieutenant-Colonel Pat and Major James M Yingling USMC, *Operations in West Korea*, volume V in series (Washington, DC, 1972)

Office of the Chief of Military History

The United States Army in the Korean War series (Washington DC):

1. Schnabel, James F, *Policy and Direction, The First Year* (1972)
2. Appleman, Roy E, *South to the Naktong, North to the Yalu* (1961)
3. Mossman, Billy C, *Ebb and Flow* (1990)
4. Hermes, Walter G, *Truce Tent and Fighting Front* (1966)

Cowdrey, Albert E, *The Medics War* (1987)
Gough, Terence J, *US Army mobilisation in the Korean War* (1987)
Gugeler, Captain Russell A, *Combat Actions in Korea* (1954)
Sawyer, Major Robert K, *Military Advisors in Korea: KMAG in Peace and War* (1962)
Westover, John G, *Combat Support in Korea* (1987)

United States Air Force Historical Branch

Futrell, Robert F, *The United States Air Force Operations in Korea, 1950–1953* (New York, 1961) and *Far East Air Force Report on the Korean War* two volumes (Washington, DC-released as an unclassified document 19th October 1977)

Department of State

Foreign Relation of the United States (Washington, DC) series:

volume VII, Korea, 1950 (1976)
volume VII, Korea and China, 1951 (in two parts), (1983)
volume XV, Korea, 1952–1954 (in two parts) (1984)

POW, Report by the Secretary of Defense's Advisory Committee on Prisoners of War (Washington, DC, 1955)

Books
(Chinese names are shown as noted in national and international catalogues over the period)

Acheson, Dean, *Present at the Creation* (London, 1969)
Adams, Sherman, *Firsthand Report: the story of the Eisenhower Administration* (New York, 1961)
Barclay, Brigadier C N, *The First Commonwealth Division: the story of the British Commonwealth Land Force in Korea*
Barclay, Roderick, *Ernest Bevin and the Foreign Office, 1932–69* (London, 1975)
Bartlett, Norman, ed., *With the Australians in Korea* (Canberra, 1954
Baylis, John, *Anglo-American Defence Relations 1939–84* (London, 1984)
Blacker, General Sir Cecil and Major-General H G Woods, *Change and Challenge: 5th Royal Iniskilling Dragoon Guards, 1928–57*, (Colchester, 1978)
Bullock, Alan, *Ernest Bevin, Foreign Secretary* (London, 1983)
Cagle, Malcolm W and Manson, Frank A, *The Sea War in Korea* (USNI, Annapolis, 1957)
Chai Cheng-wen and Zhou Yong-tian, *A record of actual events of The War to Resist America and Aid Korea* (Peking, 1987) and *Negotiations at Panmunjom* (Peking, 1989)
Chesneaux, Jean, *China, The People's Republic, 1949–1976* (Sussex, 1979)
Chou En-lai (see Zhou En-lai)
Clark, General Mark, *From the Danube to the Yalu* (London, 1954)
Collins, General Lawton J, *War in peacetime: The History and Lessons of Korea* (Boston, 1969)
Colville, John, *The Fringes of Power: Downing Street Diaries, 1939–55* (London, 1985)

Cotton, James and Neary, Ian, eds, *The Korean War in History*, (Manchester, 1989)
Cummings, Bruce, *Child of Conflict, The Korean-American Relationship, 1943–53* (Seattle, 1983)
Cunningham-Boothe, Ashley, ed, *Marks of Courage* (Record of British honours and awards, in Korea, 1950–1953) (Bristol, 1991)
Danchev, Alex, *Oliver Franks: Founding Father* (London, 1993)
Davies, Revd S J, *In Spite of Dungeons* (London, 1954, repub, currently, 1993)
Dean, Major-General William F, *General Dean's Story* (London, 1953)
Deane, Philip, *Captive in Korea* (London, 1953)
Dömes, Jurgen, *Peng Te-huai, The Man and the Image* (London, 1985)
Du Ping (also Tu P'ing), *In the headquarters of the CPV* (Peking, 1989)
Eden, Anthony, *Full Circle* (London, 1960)
Farrar-Hockley, Anthony, *The Edge of the Sword* (London, 1954, repub, currently, 1993)
Fehrenbach, T R, *This kind of War* (New York, 1963)
Foot, Rosemary, *The Wrong War: American policy and the dimensions of the Korean War conflict, 1950–53* (Ithaca, 1985)
Foster, D F—see Pickersgill, J W
George, Alexander L, *The Chinese Communist Army in Action* (London, 1967)
Gilbert, Martin, *Winston S Churchill* official biography, Volume VIII, *Never Despair, 1945–65* (London, 1988)
Goodrich, Leland M, *Korea, a Study of US Policy in the United Nations* (New York, 1956)
Goodwin, Geoffrey L, *Britain and the United Nations* (London, 1957)
Gowing, Margaret, *Independence and Deterrence, Britain and Atomic Energy, 1945–52* (London, 1974)
Grey, Jeffrey, *The Commonwealth in the Korean War* (Manchester, 1988)
Griffith, Brigadier-General Samuel B, III, *The Chinese People's Liberation Army* (London and New York, 1967)
Grist, Lieutenant-Colonel Digby, *Remembered with Advantage* (Gloucester, 1976)
Harding, Colonel E D, *The Imjin Roll* (Gloucester, 1976)
Harris, Kenneth, *Attlee* (London, 1982)
Hastings, Max, *The Korean War* (London, 1987)
Hayes, Richard, F, *The Awesome Power* (Baton Rouge, 1974)
Henderson, Gregory, *Korea, the Politics of the Vortex* (Massachusetts, 1968)
Higgins, Marguerite, *War in Korea* (New York, 1951)
Higgins, Trumbull, *Korea and the fall of MacArthur* (Oxford, 1960)
Hinton, Harold C, *China's Turbulent Quest: an analysis of China's foreign relations since 1949* (Bloomington and London, 1972)

Hiscocks, Richard, *The Security Council, a study in adolesence* London, 1973)
Hong Xuezhi, *Memoirs of the War to Resist the United States of America and Resist Korea* (Peking, 1990)
Hsü Yen (see Xu Yan)
Huang Chen-hsia, *Chung-kung chun-jen chi* (Hong Kong, 1968), see also Whitson, William
Inglis, A I, see under Munro, J
Jackson, Robert, *Air War over Korea* (London, 1973)
Jane's Fighting Ships 1950–1953 (London and New York, 1951–54)
Jang Xiangze, *The United States and China* (Chicago, 1988)
Joffe, Ellis, *Party and Army: Professionalism and Political Control in the Chinese Officers Corps, 1949–64* (Cambridge Mass, 1965)
Jones, Francis S, *No Rice for Rebels* (London, 1956)
Joy, Admiral C Turner, *How Communists negotiate* (New York, 1955)
Karig, Walter, *Battle Report* (New York, 1952)
Kaufman, Burton I, *The Korean War: Challenges in Crisis, Credibility, and Command* (New York, 1986)
Kennan, George F, *Memoirs, 1952–63*, two volumes (Boston, 1967 and 1972)
Kenyon, Albert, *Valiant Dust* (Savlation Army, London, 1966)
Khruschev, Nikita, *Khruschev Remembers* (London, 1971)
Kim Ch'angsun, *Puk Han siponyon-sa* (Seoul, 1961)
Kim Chun-kon, *The Korean War* (Seoul, 1973)
Kim Hak-joon, *The unification policy of South and North Korea* (Seoul, 1977)
Kinkead, Eugene, *Why they collaborated* (London, 1960)
Kinne, Derek, *The Wooden Boxes* (London, 1955)
Kolko, Joyce and Gabriel, *The Limits of Power. The World and US Foreign Policy 1945–54* (New York, 1972)
Korean War, The Ground Battle History Institution of Japan (Tokyo, 1969)
Ladd, J D, *The Royal Marines* (London, 1980)
Lansdown, John R P, *With the Carriers in Korea, 1950–53* (Worcester, 1992)
Leckie, Robert, *The Korean War* (London and New York, 1962)
Lee Chong-sik, *The Politics of Korean Nationalism* (Berkeley and Los Angeles, 1965), and with Scalapino, Robert A, *Communism in Korea*, two volumes (Los Angeles, 1972)
Lie, Trygve, *In the Cause of Peace* (New York, 1954)
Long, Gavin, *MacArthur as Military Commander* (London, 1969)
Lowe, Peter, *The Origins of the Korean War* (London, 1986)
Luard, Evan, *Britain and China* (London, 1962)
MacDonald, Callum, *Korea: the war before Vietnam* (London, 1986)
MacDonald, Major-General J F M, *The Borderers in Korea* (Berwick upon-Tweed, 1954)
MacFarquhar, Roderick, *The Origins of the Cultural Revolution*, two volumes (London, 1974 and 1983)

McClellan, David S, *Dean Acheson, The State Department Years* (New York, 1976)
McCormack, Gavan, *Cold War, Hot War* (Sydney, 1983)
Manchester, William, *American Caesar, Douglas MacArthur* (London, 1979)
Manson, Frank A—see Cagle, Malcolm W
Mao Zedong (also Mao Tse-tung), *Selected Works* four volumes (1956), *Manuscripts since the establishment of the People's Republic of China* two volumes, September 1949 to December 1950 and January to December 1951 (Peking, 1987 and 1988)
Military History Research Section of the Military Science
Academy of China, *History of the War to Resist America and Aid Korea* (Peking, 1988)
Mosley, Leonard, *Dulles* (New York, 1978)
Munro, J A and Inglis A I (eds), *Lester Pearson Memoirs, 1948–57* (London, 1974)
Neary, Ian, see Cotton, James.
Nie Rongzhen (also Nieh Jung-chen), *Memoirs* (Peking, 1984)
Odgers, George, *Across the Parallel: the Australian 77th Squadron with the United States Air Force in the Korean War* (Melbourne, 1952 and London, 1953)
Oliver, Robert T, *Syngman Rhee. The Man behind the Myth* (New York, 1954)
Paik Sun-yup, General, *From Pusan to Panmunjom* (London and New York, 1992)
Panikkar. K M, *In Two Chinas* (London, 1955)
Pedersen, Lorenz Ulrik, *Norge i Korea* (Oslo, 1991)
Peng Dehuai (also Peng Te-huai), *Autobiographical notes* (Peking, 1981), *Selected writings on Chinese military affairs* (Peking, 1988)
Poates, Rutherford M, *Decision in Korea* (New York, 1954)
Rees, David, *Korea: The Limited War* (London, 1964)
Ridgway, General Matthew B, *The Korean War* (New York, 1956) *The Royal Ulster Rifles in Korea* (Belfast, 1953)
Scalapino, Robert A and Chong Sik-lee, *Communism in Korea* two volumes with separate index, (Los Angeles, 1972)
Schram, Stuart, *Mao Tse-tung* (London, 1967)
Shipster, Colonel J N, *The Diehards in Korea* (Middlesex Regiment, 1979)
Simmons, Robert R, *The Strained Alliance, Peking, P'yongyang, Moscow and the Politics of the Korean War* (New York, 1975)
Smith, Gaddis, *Dean Acheson*, volume XVI in Robert E. Ferrell (ed), *The American Secretaries of State and their Diplomacy* (New York, 1972)
Stairs, Denis, *The Diplomacy of Constraint, Canada, the Korean War and the US* (Toronto, 1975)
Stone, I F, *The Hidden History of the Korean War* (London, 1952)
Suh Dae-sook, *The Korean Communist Movement* two volumes (Princeton NJ, 1967 and 1970)
Truman, Harry S, *Memoirs* two volumes (New York, 1955 and 1956)

Tu P'ing (see Du Ping)
Vatcher, William H, *Panmunjom: The story of the Korean Armistice Negotiations* (New York, 1958)
Williams, Francis (with Lord Attlee), *A Prime Minister Remembers* (London, 1961)
Williams, Philip M, (ed), *Hugh Gaitskell* (Diary) (London, 1983)
Whitson, William W, and Huang Chen-hsia, *The Chinese High Command, a History of Communist Military Politics*, 1927–71 *(London, 1973)*
Woods, Major-General H G, see Blacker
Xu Yan (also Hsü Yen), *The First Trial of Strength. A review and reappraisal of the History of the War to Resist the United States and Aid Korea* (Peking, 1990) Ye Yumeng, *Black Snow, the first account of the CPV's fighting in Korea* (Peking, 1989) and *Blood along the Seoul River: the second reportage of the CPV's fighting in Korea* (Peking, 1990)
Zhou Enlai (also Chou En-lai), *Selected Works* two volumes (1983 and 1984)

Academic Theses

Macdonald, James Angus, jr, *The problem of US Marine Corps Prisoners in Korea* (History and Museums Division, US Marine Corps) (Washington DC, 1988)
Tsui David Chak Wing, *China's Decision to enter the Korean War: motivations and objectives*

Newspapers and news agencies, magazines and journals

Age (Australia)
American Mercury (USA)
Army (USA)
Army Quarterly (UK)
Asian Survey (US)
Associated Press (UK)
Auckland Star (New Zealand)
Australian Defence Journal
British Army Journal
Bulletin (State Department, USA)
China Quarterly (UK)
Colliers (USA)
Crowsnest (Royal Canadian Navy Journal)
Daily Express (UK)
Daily Worker (UK
International Security (USA)

Economist (UK)
English Historical Review (UK)
Foreign Affairs (USA)
Jen Min Pao (People's Daily) (China)
Life (USA)
Manchester Guardian (UK)
Montreal Star (Canada)
Newsweek (USA)
New York Herald Tribune (USA)
New York Times (USA)
Observer (UK)
Ogonyok (Russia)
Ottawa Citizen (Canada)
Pacific Historical Review (USA)
Political Quarterly (USA)
Pravda (Russia)
Reuters
RIIA publications (Chatham House) (UK)
RUSI Journal (UK)
Saturday Evening Post (USA)
Sydney Morning Herald (Australia)
(Shanghai) Ta Kung Pao (China)
Times (UK)
Times of India
Time Magazine (USA)
Toronto Daily Star (Canada)
Toronto Globe & Mail (Canada)
Twentieth Century (UK)
US News and World Report (USA)
Washington Post (USA)
Yonhap (Republic of Korea)

Cinema and Television—news and international affairs

Gaumont British News (UK)
Pathe Gazette (UK)

The Korean War, produced by Philip Whitehead for Thames TV/(6 parts) Channel 4/WGBH Boston/Australian Broadcasting Commission

INDEX

B

O

Q

R

Z

ACK

FROM : HQ 29 BRIT Inf Bde

T O : 1 RS 1 KINGS 1 DWR A
29 BRIT Inf Bde LAD

INFO : Comd
A/Q

Security Classification

UNCLAS

CEASE FIRE (.) all fire
time synchronisation will be
and 2150 hrs (.) operative o
at 2200 hrs (.) ACK

Degree of Precedence

PRIORITY

O. C.
ADTT.
2 i/c
PRI
Q. M.
CRQMS